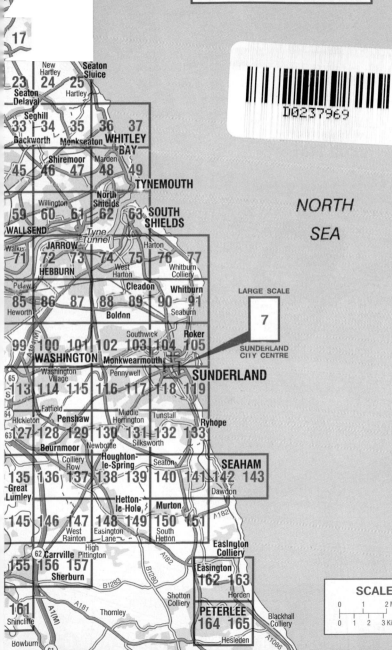

NORTH

SEA

17

23 Seaton Delaval | New Hartley **24** | **25** Seaton Sluice / Hartley

Seghill **33** | **34** | **35** | **36** | **37**
Backworth | Monkseaton | **WHITLEY BAY**

45 | Shiremoor **46** | **47** | Marden **48** | **49**

TYNEMOUTH

59 | Willington **60** | North Shields **61** | **62** | **63** SOUTH SHIELDS

WALLSEND

Walker | **JARROW** **71** | **72** | **73** | **74** | Harton **75** | **76** | **77**
HEBBURN | West Harton | Whitburn Colliery

Pelaw | Cleadon | Whitburn
Heworth **85** | **86** | **87** | **88** | **89** | **90** | **91**
Boldon | Seaburn

Southwick | Roker
99 | **100** | **101** | **102** | **103** | **104** | **105**
WASHINGTON | Monkwearmouth

LARGE SCALE
7
SUNDERLAND CITY CENTRE

Washington Village | Pennywell | **SUNDERLAND**
65 S **113** | **114** | **115** | **116** | **117** | **118** | **119**

Fatfield | Middle Herrington | Tunstall
Rickleton | Penshaw | Ryhope
64 **63** **127** | **128** | **129** | **130** | **131** | **132** | **133**
Bournmoor | Newbottle | Silksworth

Colliery Row | Roughton-le-Spring | Seaton | **SEAHAM**
135 | **136** | **137** | **138** | **139** | **140** | **141** | **142** | **143**
Great Lumley | | | | | | | Dawdon

| Hetton-le-Hole | Murton
145 | **146** | **147** | **148** | **149** | **150** | **151**
West Rainton | Easington Lane | South Hetton | A182

High Pittington | Easington Colliery
62 Carville **156** | **157** | | Easington **162** | **163**
155 | Sherburn | | Horden
B1280 | A182 | B1280
161 | | Shotton Colliery | **PETERLEE**
Shincliffe | A181 | Thornley | **164** | **165** | Blackhall Colliery
Bowburn **61** | | | Hesleden | A1086

SCALE
0   1   2 Miles
0   1   2   3 Kilometres

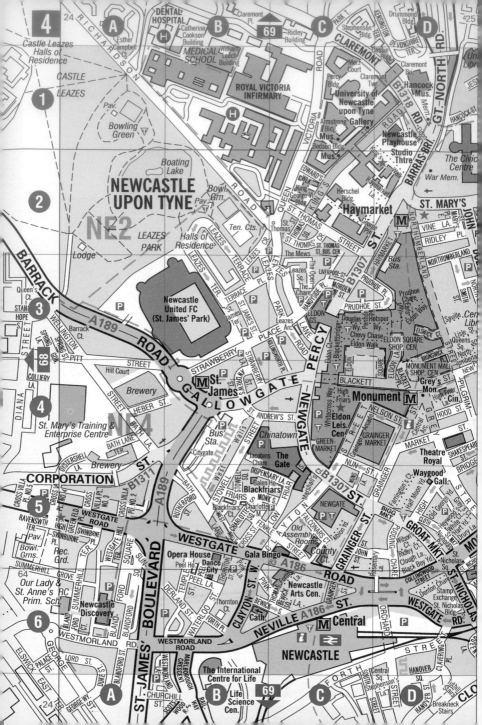

CONTENTS

Key to Map Pages	2-3	Index to Streets, Towns, Villages and selected Places of Interest	166-286
Large Scale City Centres	4-7		
Map Pages	8-165	Index to Hospitals, Health Centres and Hospices	287-288

REFERENCE

Motorway	**A1(M)**	Car Park Selected	🅿
A Road	A1	Church or Chapel	†
Proposed		City Wall	⋂⋂⋂⋂⋂
B Road	B1288	Cycleway	🚲
Dual Carriageway		Fire Station	■
Tunnel	A19	Hospital	🅗
One-way Street		House Numbers Selected Roads	13 8 4
Traffic flow on A Roads is also indicated by a heavy line on the driver's left.		Information Centre	🅘
Restricted Access		National Grid Reference	420
Pedestrianized Road		Park & Ride	Kingston Park P+🚍
Track		Police Station	▲
Footpath		Post Office	★
Residential Walkway		Toilet	▽
Railway	Level Crossing · Heritage Sta. · Station	with facilities for the Disabled	▽
Metro Line	Tunnel **M**	Viewpoint	🕱 ☀
Local Authority Boundary		Educational Establishment	🞓
Posttown Boundary		Hospital or Health Centre	🞓
Postcode Boundary within Posttowns		Industrial Building	🞓
		Leisure or Recreational Facility	🞓
Built-up Area	MILL ST.	Place of Interest	🞓
		Public Building	🞓
Map Continuation	54 Large Scale City Centre 4	Shopping Centre or Market	🞓
		Other Selected Buildings	🞓

Copyright of Geographers' A-Z Map Company Ltd.

Head Office:
Fairfield Road, Borough Green, Sevenoaks, Kent TN15 8PP
Telephone 01732 781000

www.a-zmaps.co.uk

Copyright © Geographers' A-Z Map Co. Ltd. 2004

Ordnance Survey® This product includes mapping data licensed from Ordnance Survey® with the permission of the Controller of Her Majesty's Stationery Office.
© Crown Copyright 2004. Licence number 100017302
Edition 6 2004

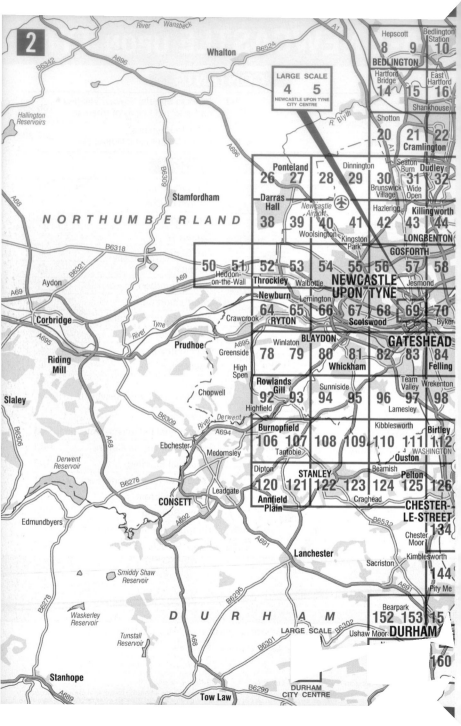

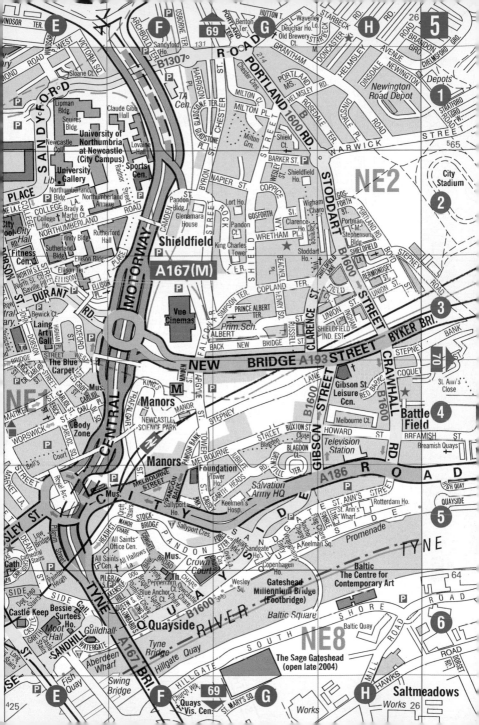

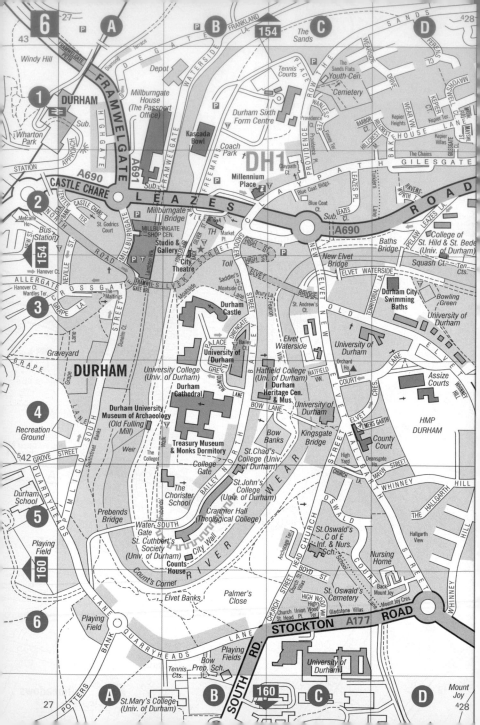

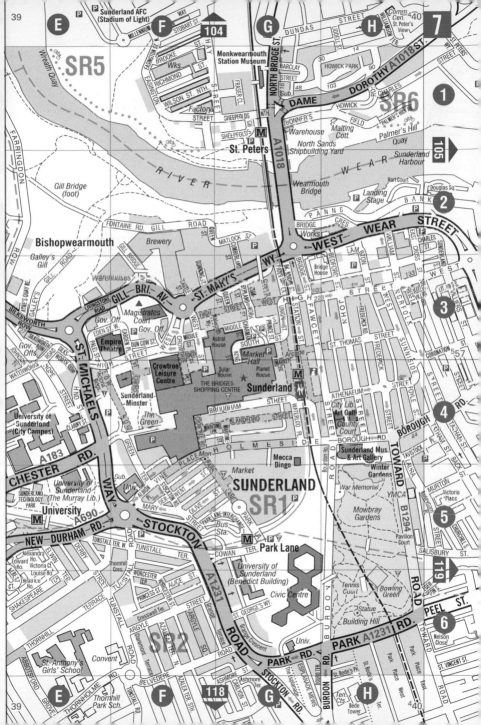

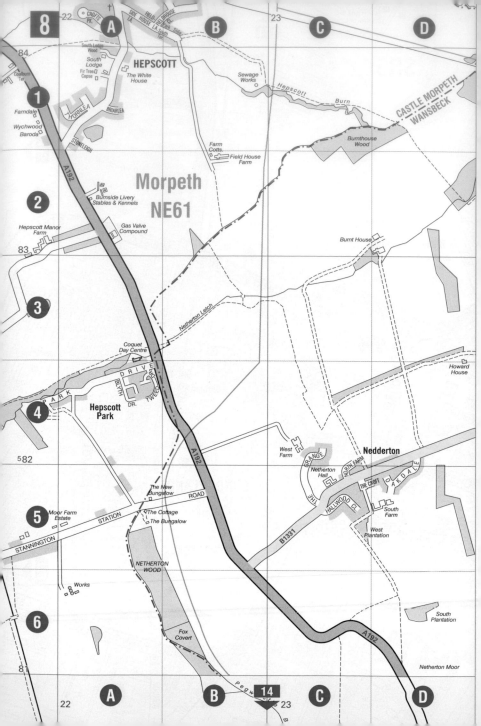

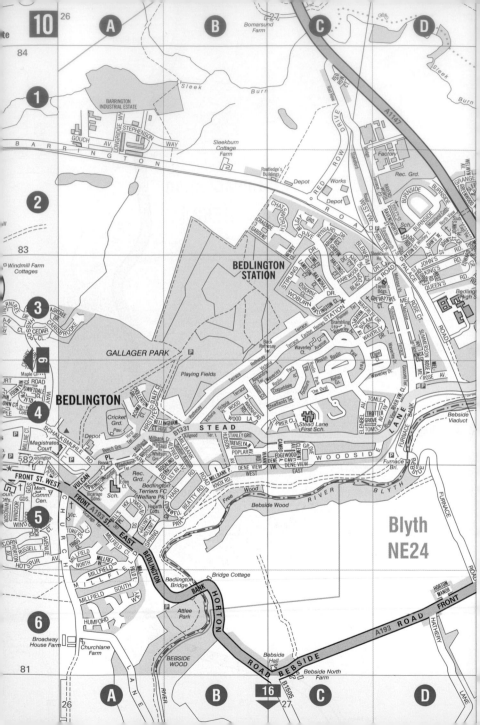

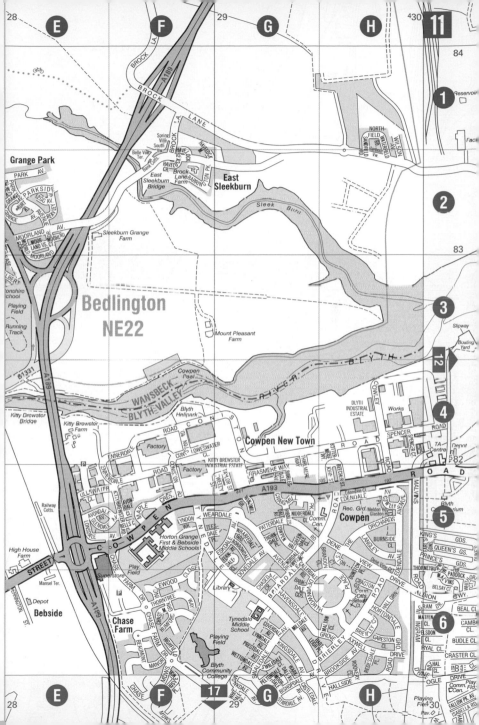

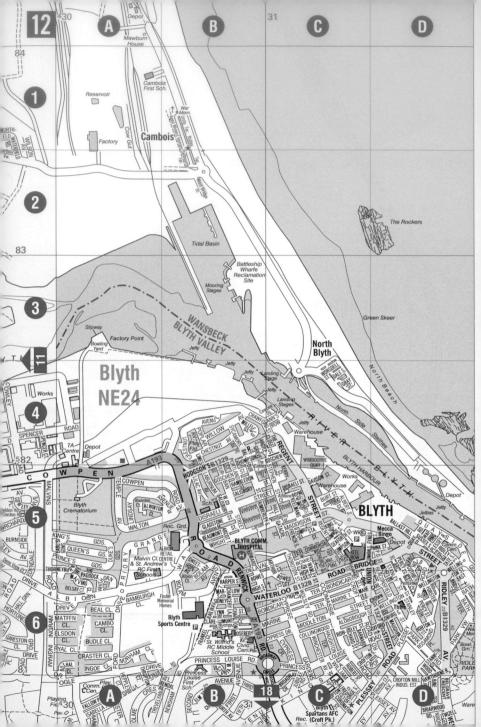

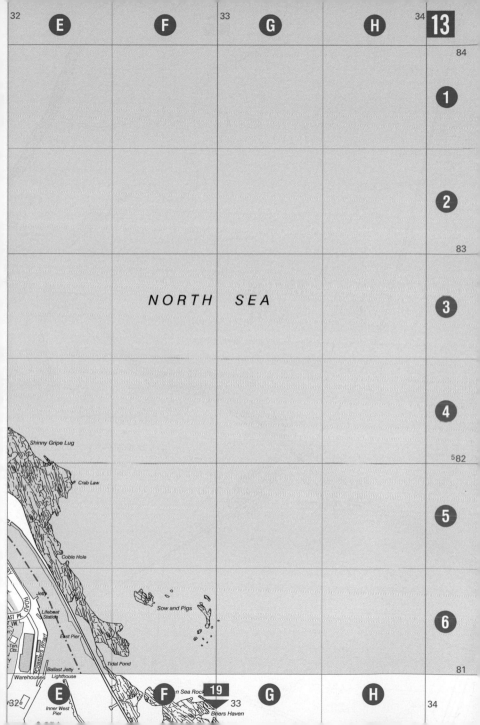

84

1

2

83

NORTH SEA

3

4

⁵82

Shinny Gripe Lug

Crab Law

5

Coble Hole

Jetty

Lifeboat
Station

Sow and Pigs

East Pier

6

Ballast Jetty

Warehouses   Lighthouse

81

Tidal Pond

n Sea Rock

Inner West
Pier

33

Briers Haven

ROAD

AST PV

EAST PW.

-Ten.
Cts.

Ten
Cts.

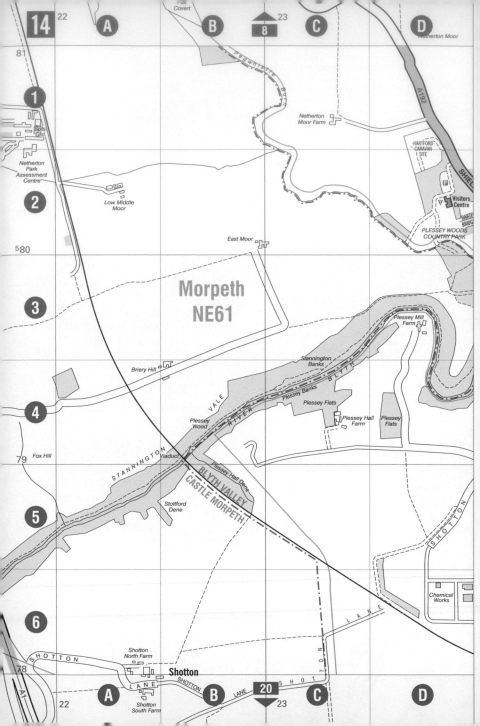

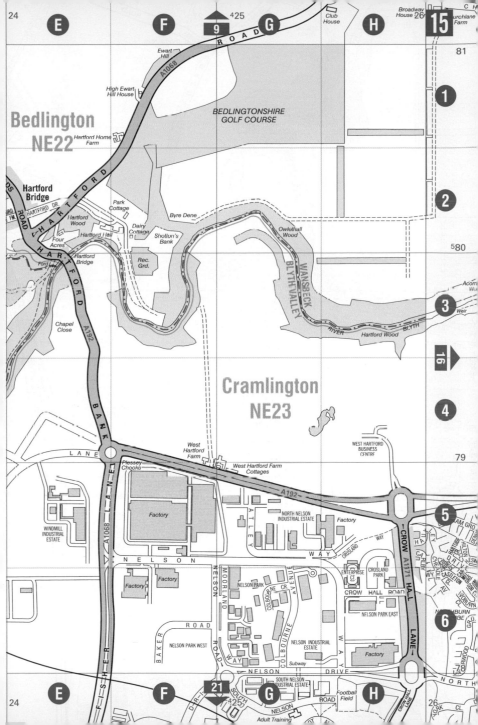

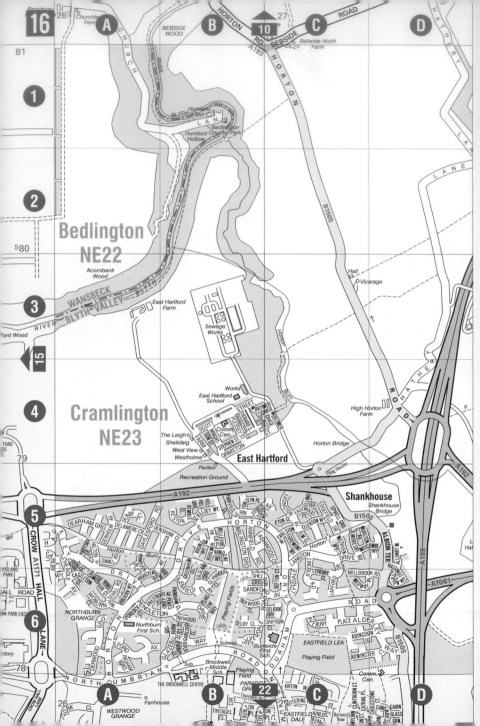

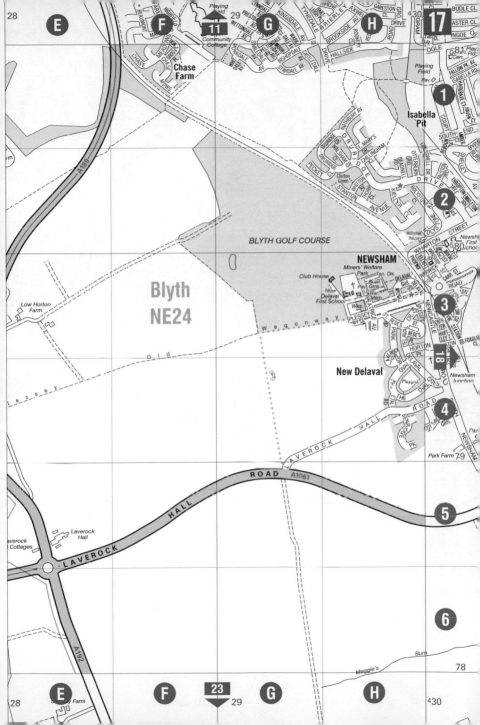

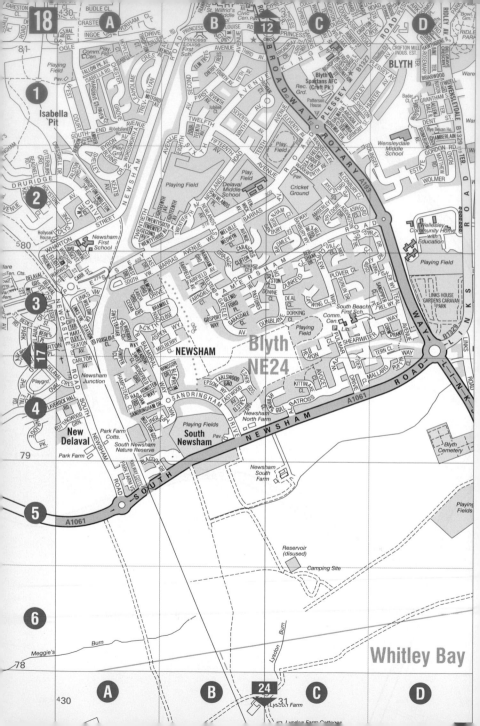

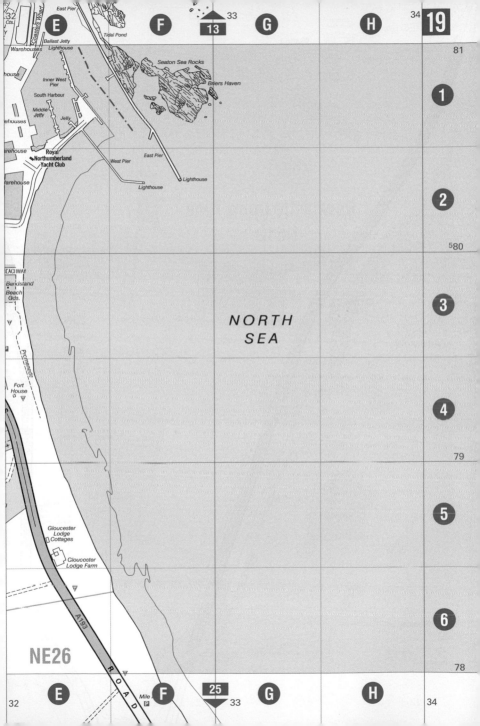

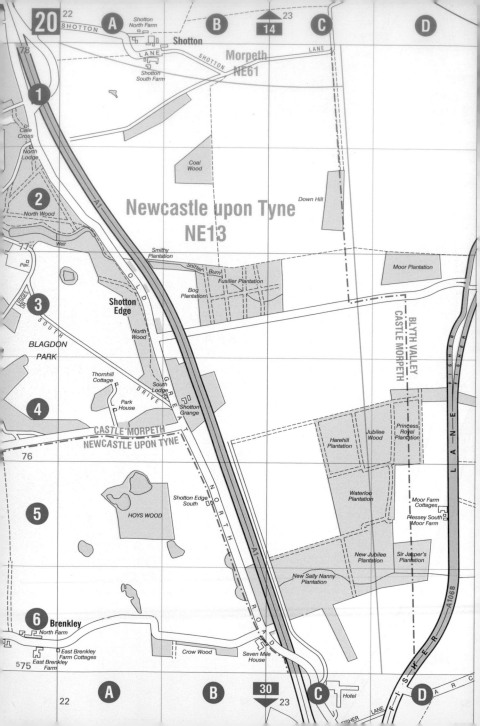

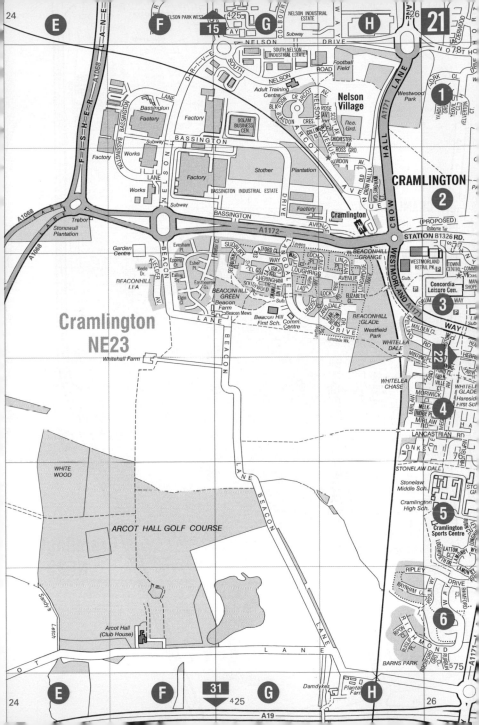

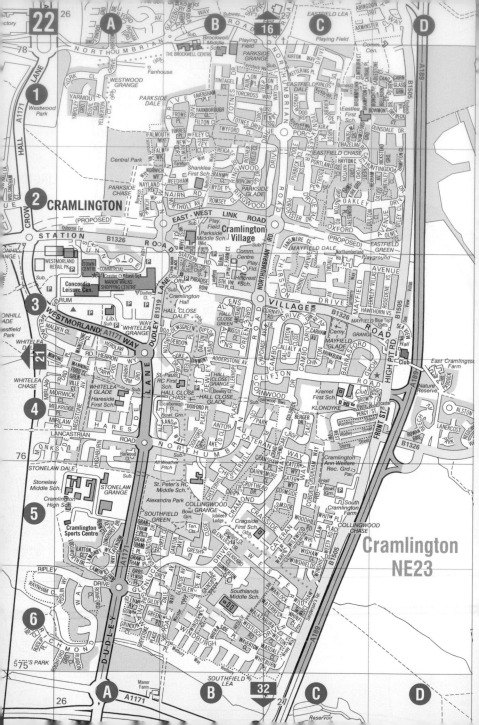

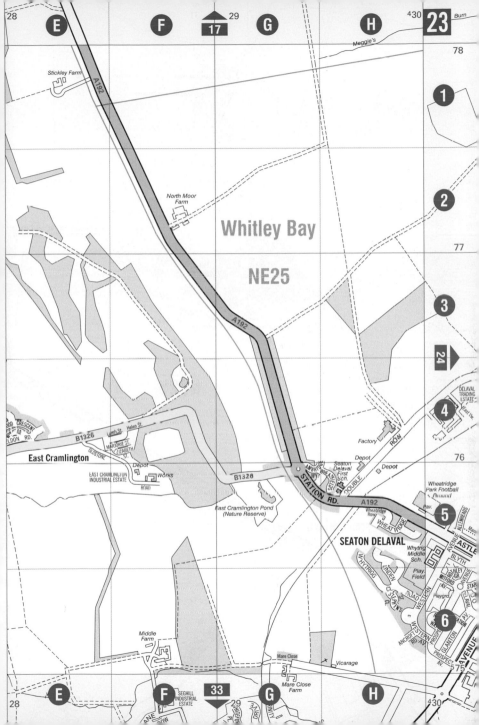

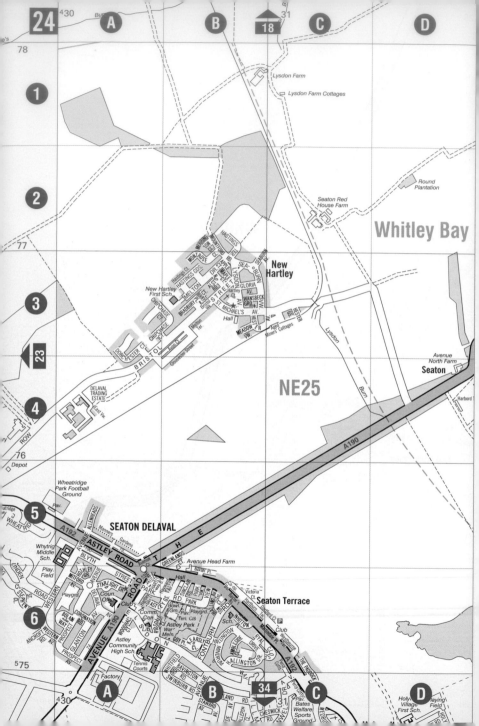

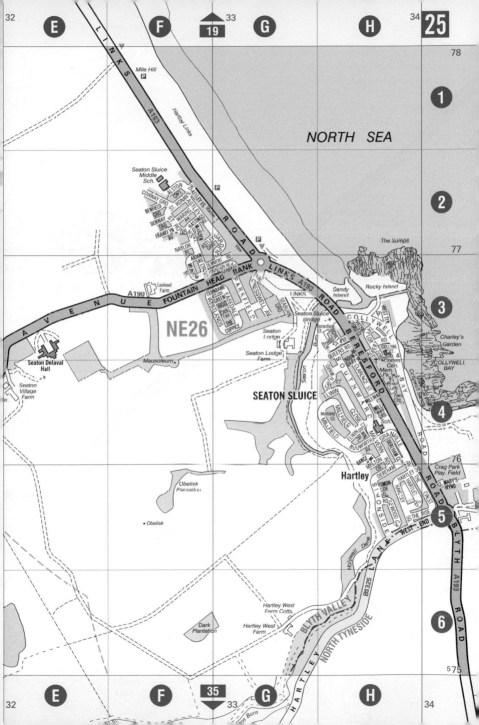

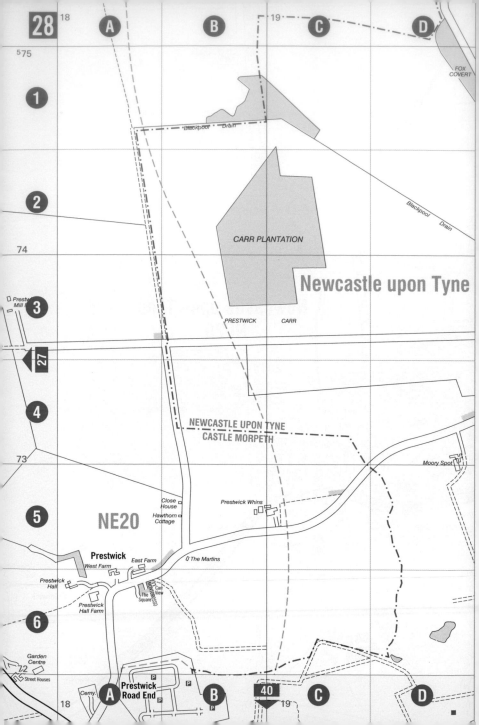

575

1

2

74

3

Prestwick Mill

27

4

73

5

NE20

6

72

18

Blackpool Drain

CARR PLANTATION

Newcastle upon Tyne

PRESTWICK CARR

NEWCASTLE UPON TYNE
CASTLE MORPETH

Blackpool Drain

FOX COVERT

Moory Spot

Close House

Hawthorn Cottage

Prestwick Whins

Prestwick

East Farm

West Farm

The Martins

Prestwick Hall

Prestwick Hall Farm

Morpeth Rd

Rose View

The Square

Garden Centre

Street Houses

Cemy.

Prestwick Road End

A B 19 C D

A B 40 19 C D

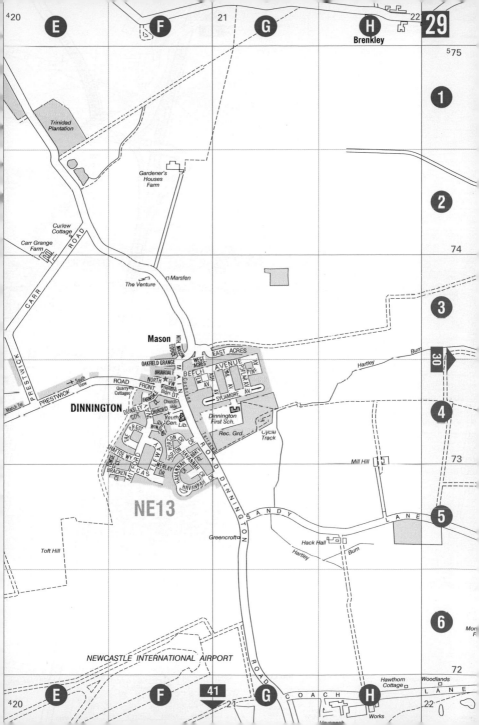

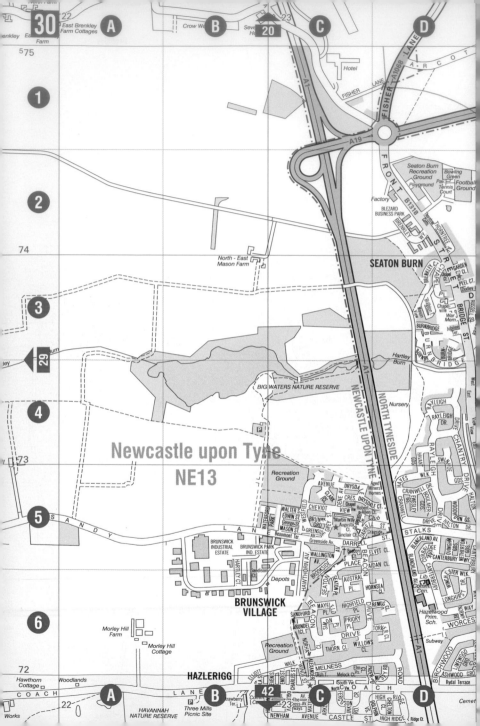

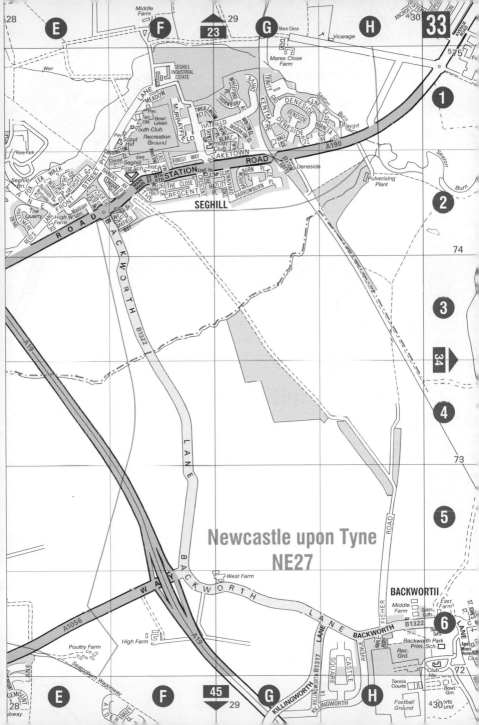

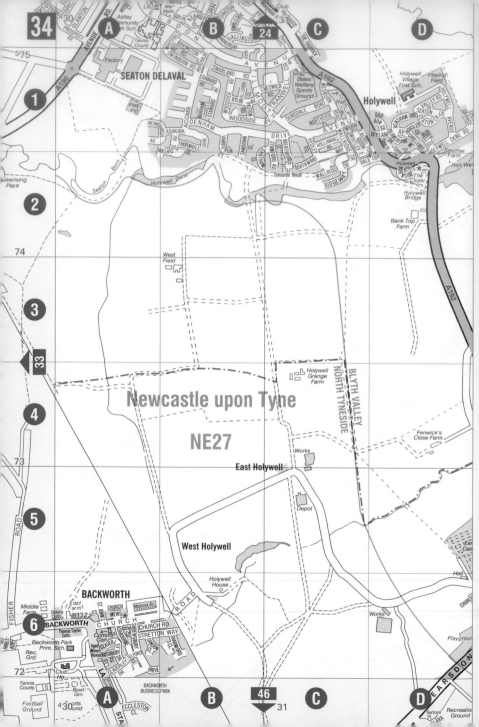

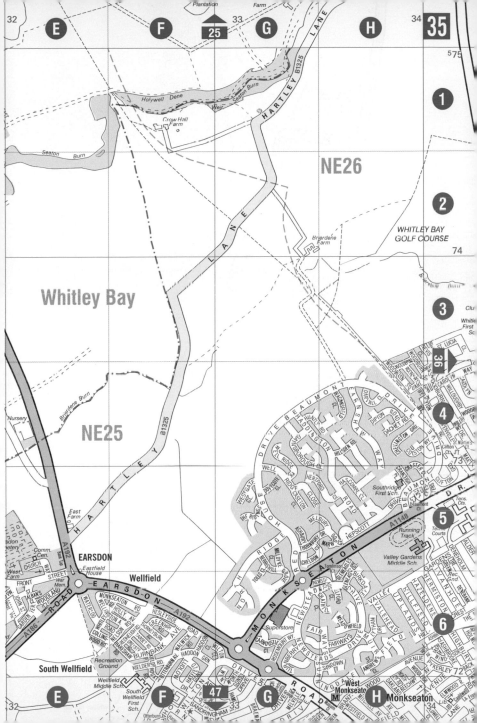

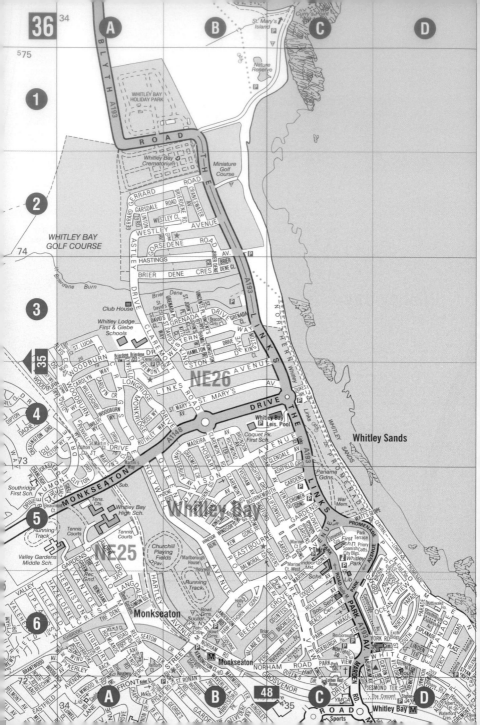

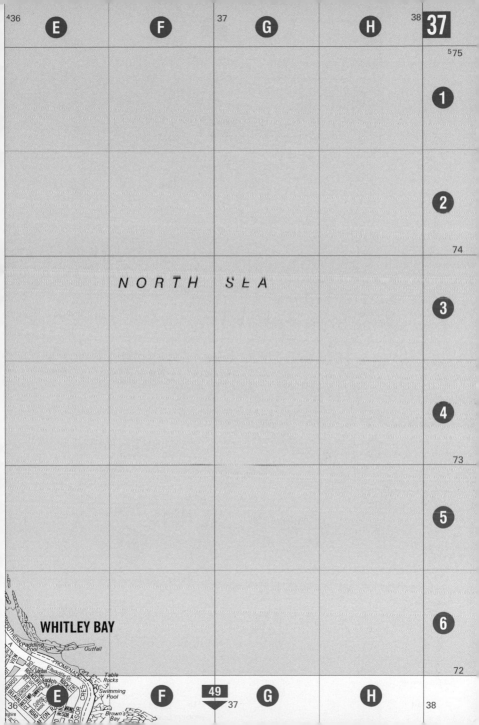

NORTH SEA

WHITLEY BAY

Paddling Pool

Outfall

PROMENADE

Table Rocks

Swimming Pool

Brown's Bay

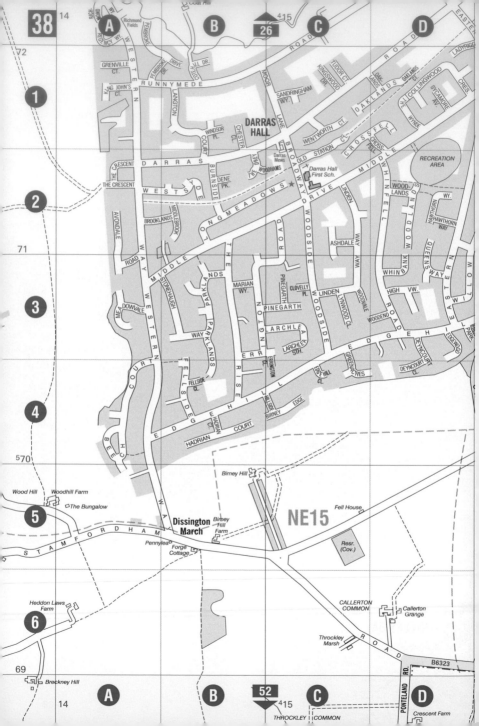

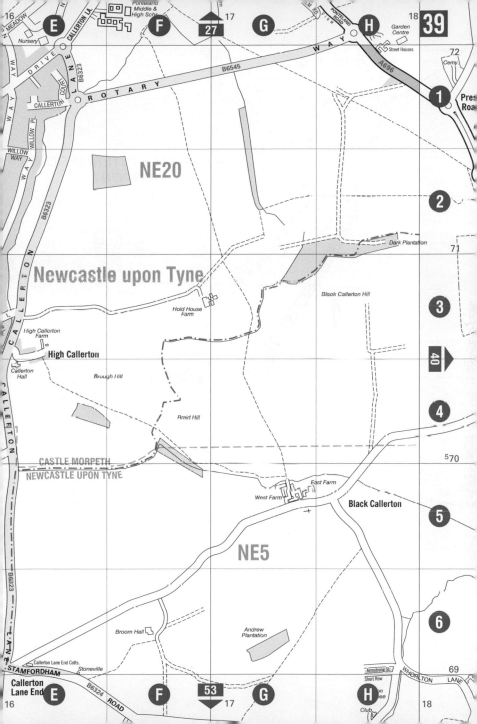

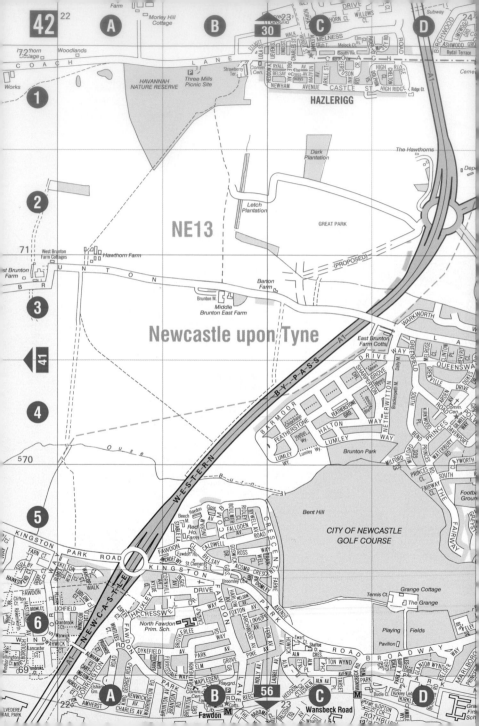

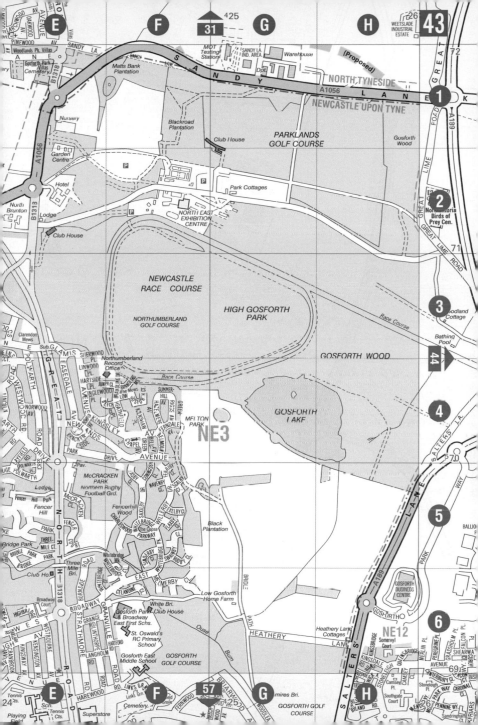

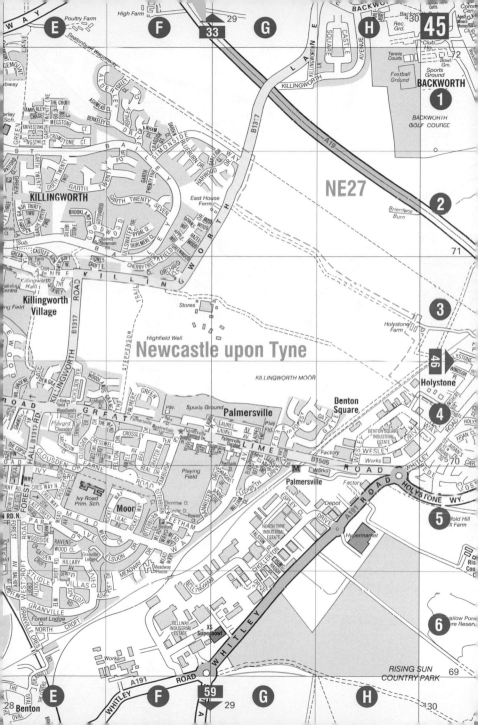

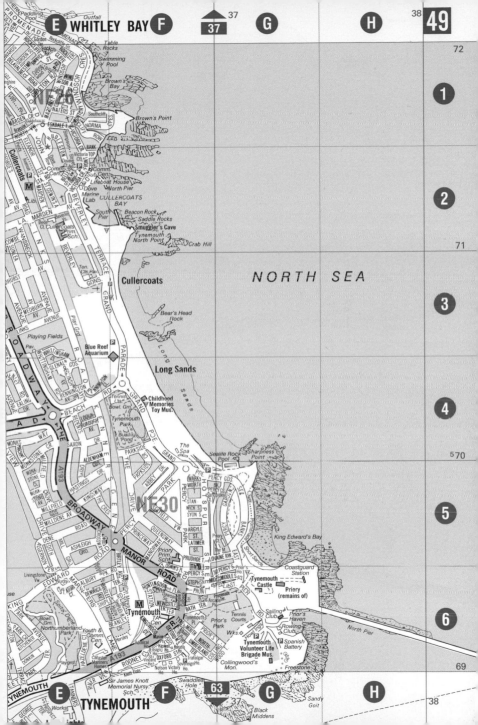

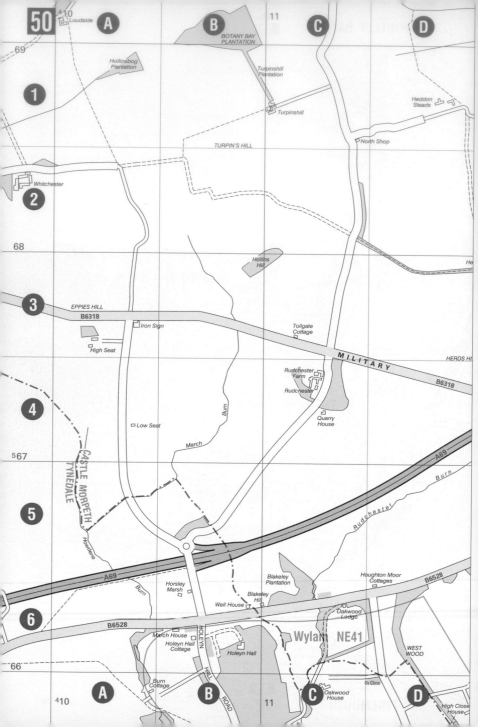

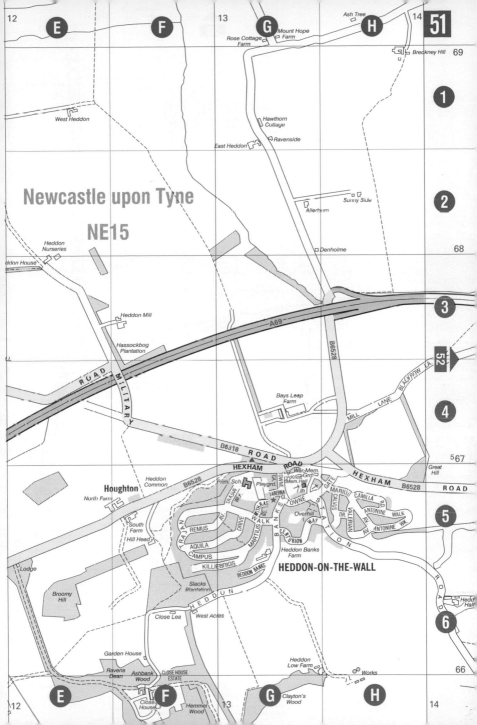

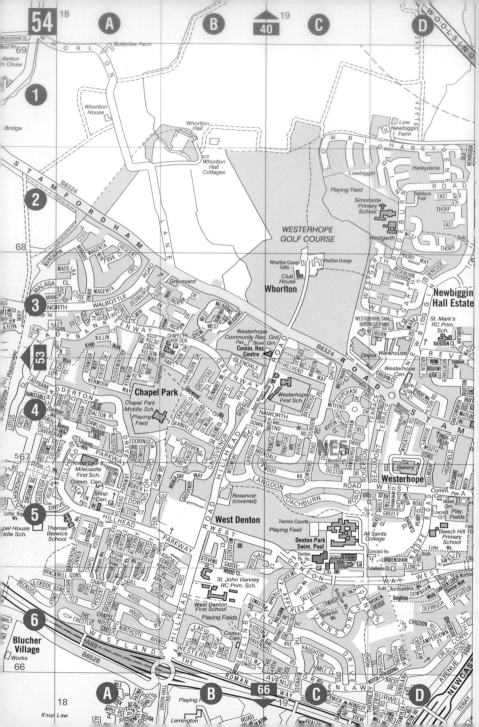

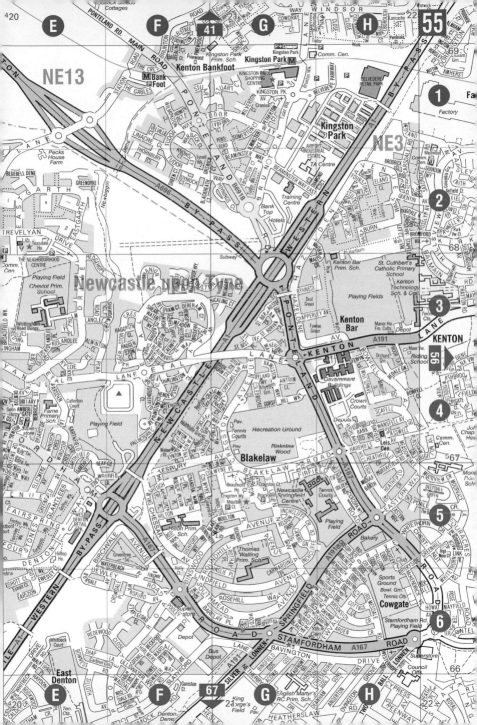

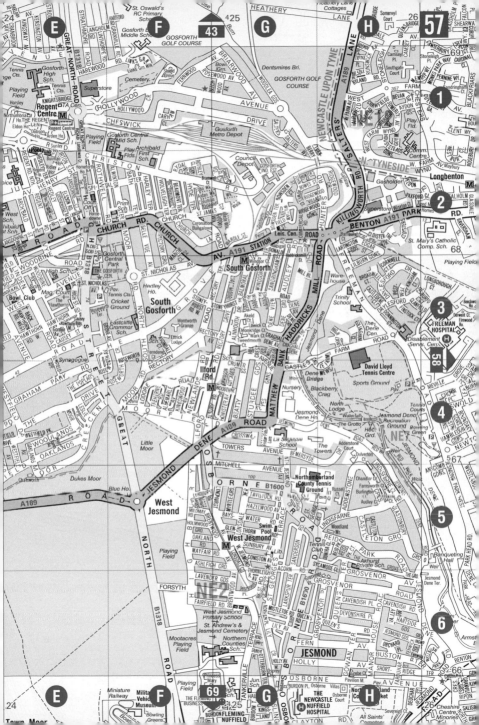

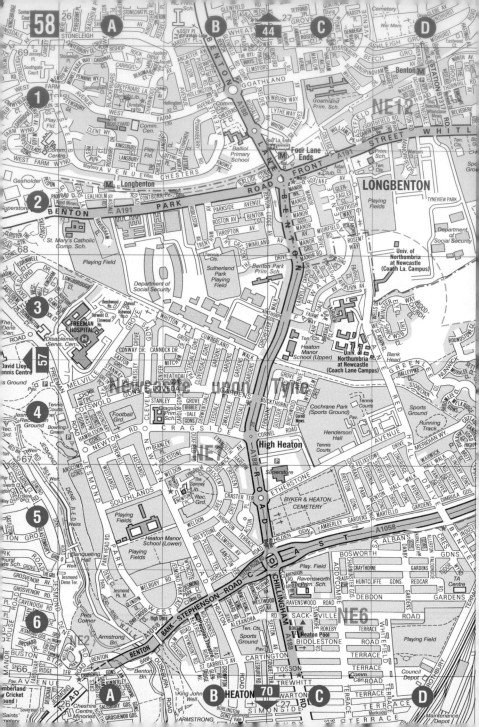

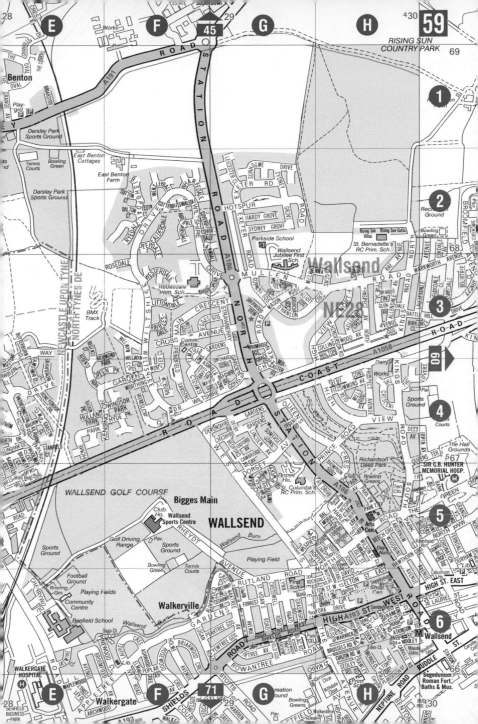

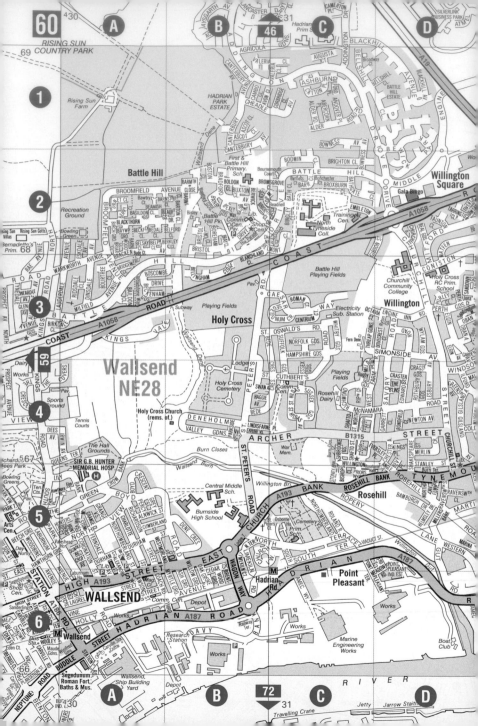

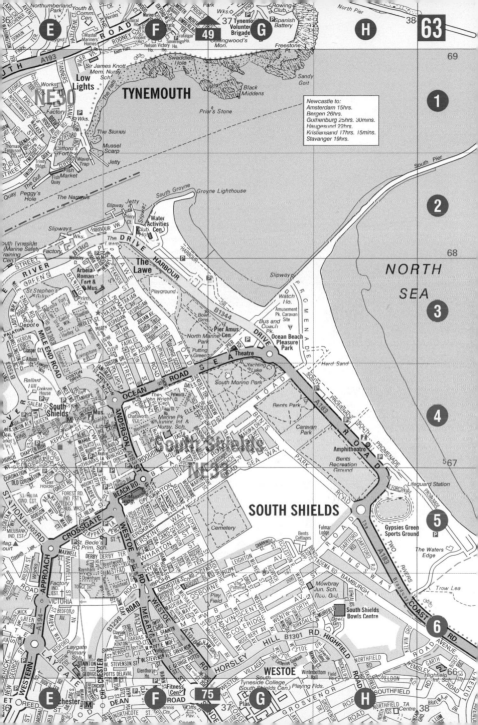

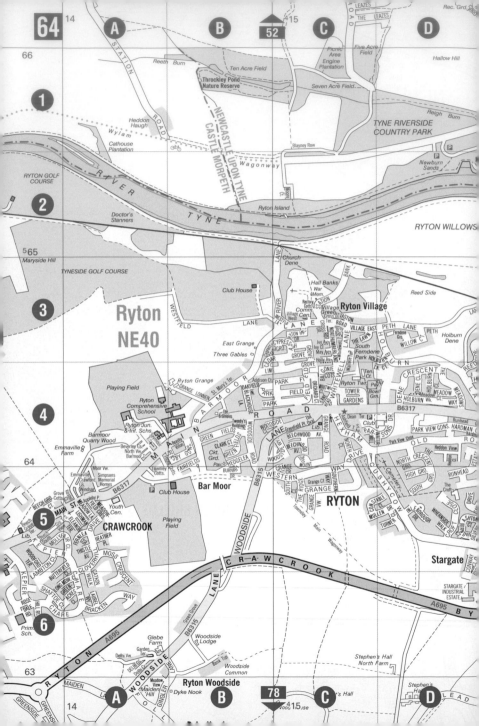

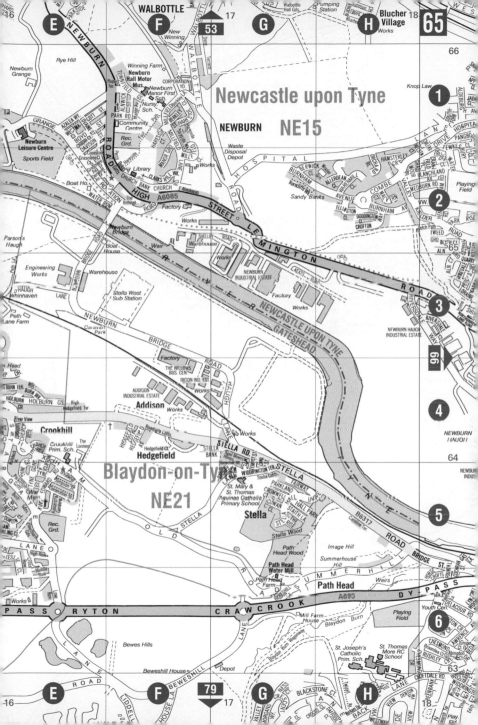

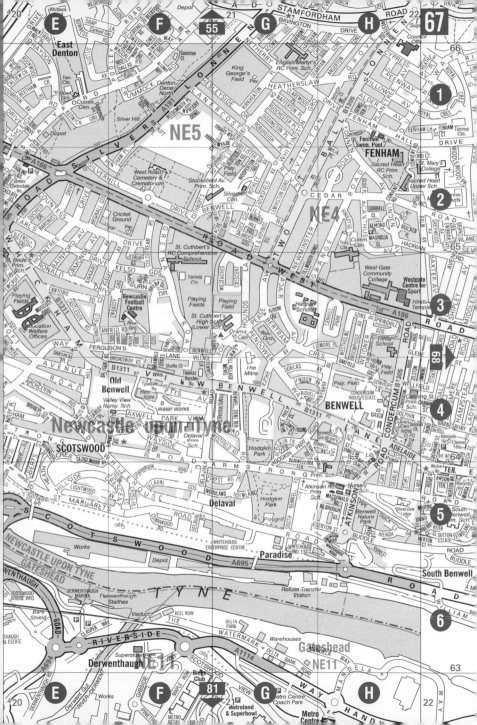

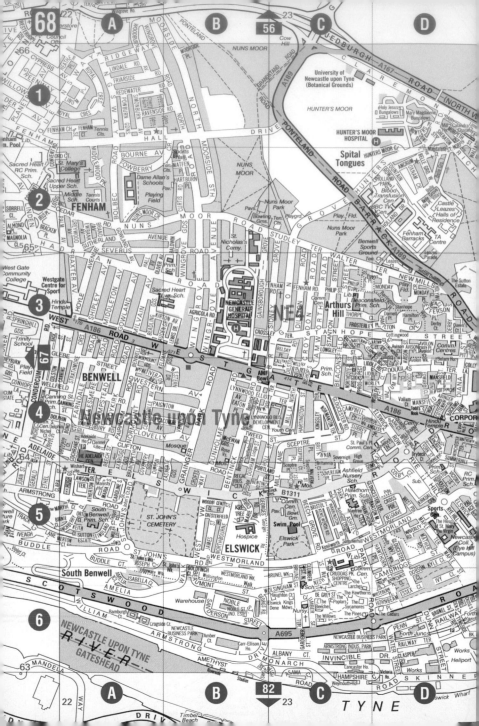

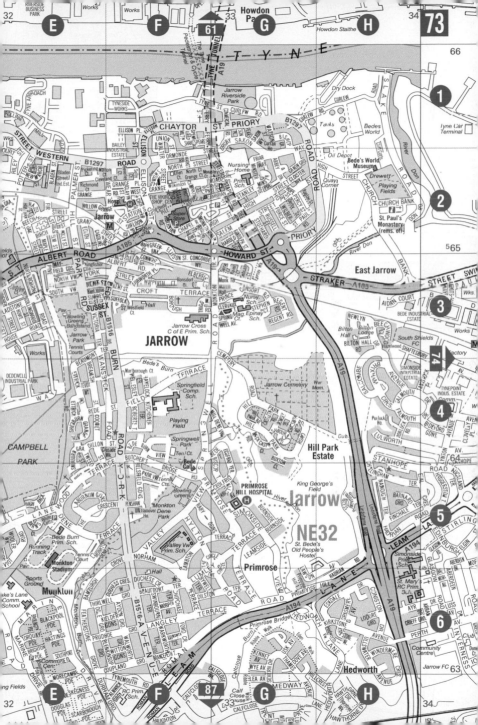

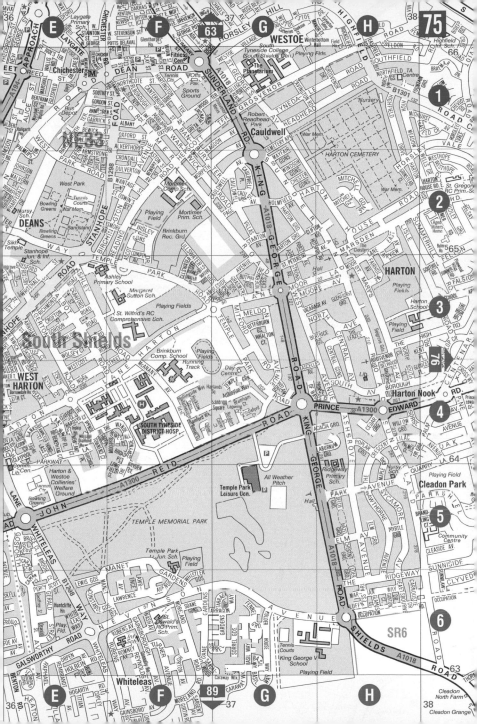

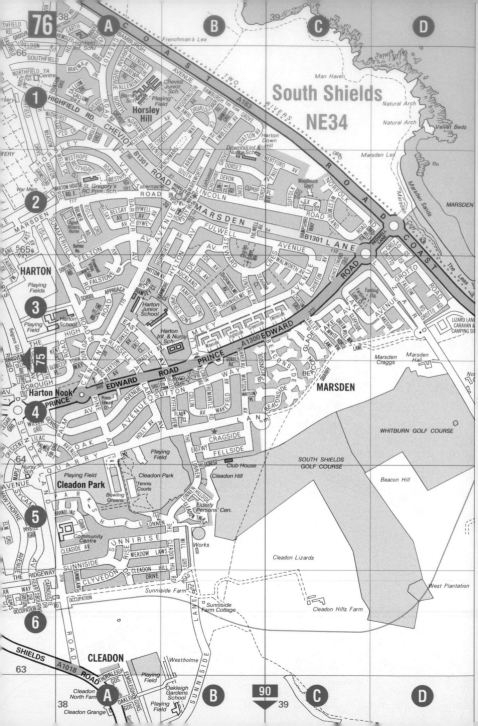

BAY

Natural Arch

Marsden Rock

Smugglers' Cave

NORTH SEA

Hob & Joan Orchard

North Lizard Riding School

Reservoirs

Lizard Cottages

Club House

Lett House

Marsden Quarries

A183

Souter Point Lighthouse

Lizard Point

Lighthouse View

Byar's Hole

TWO RIVERS ROAD

SOUTH WAY KITCHENER RD.

Sunderland

A183

Potter's Hole

Lizards Farm

SR6

WHITE SHEARWAY ROCKS GROVE

Arthur Ter.

South

Marsden Primary Sch.

Playing Field

Marsden Ter.

LIZARD LANE

CRESCENT

LILAC VIEW

RISE

MARSDEN AVENUE

Play grd.

FARRIER

WHEATALL DR.

WHEATALL VIEW

SOUTER

HINDON Sq.

Whitburn Colliery

91

AVENUE

41

WHEATALL

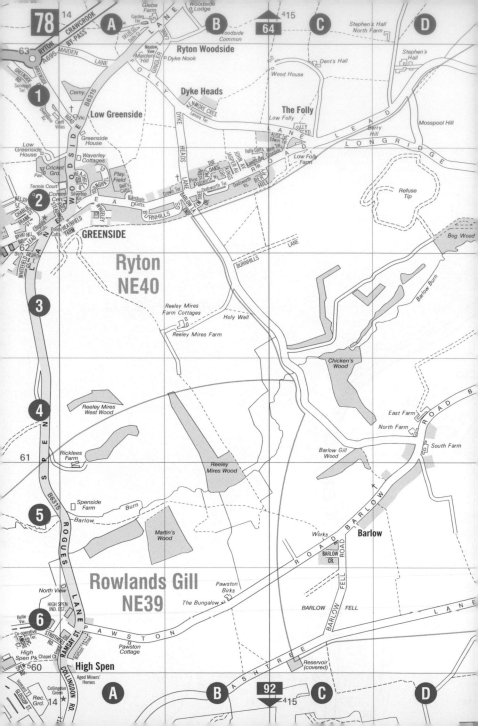

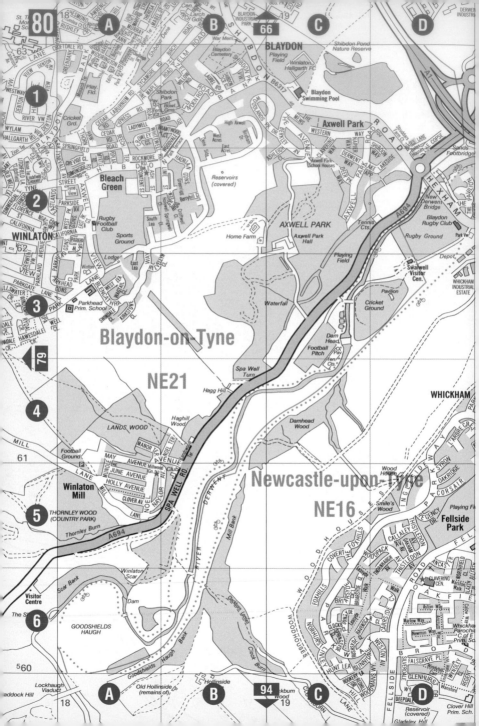

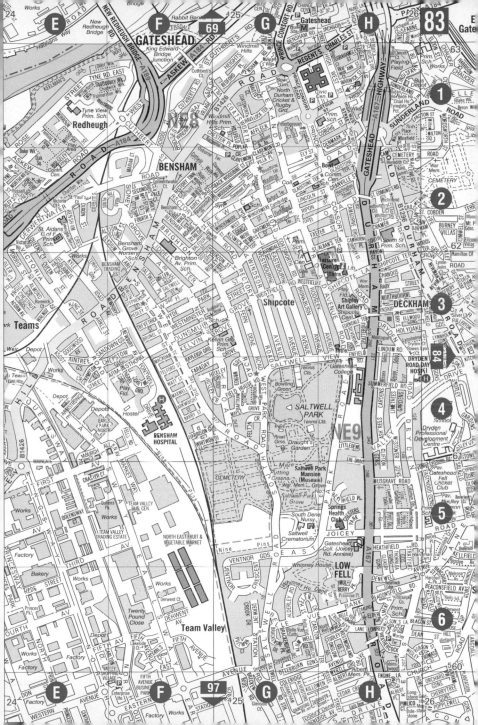

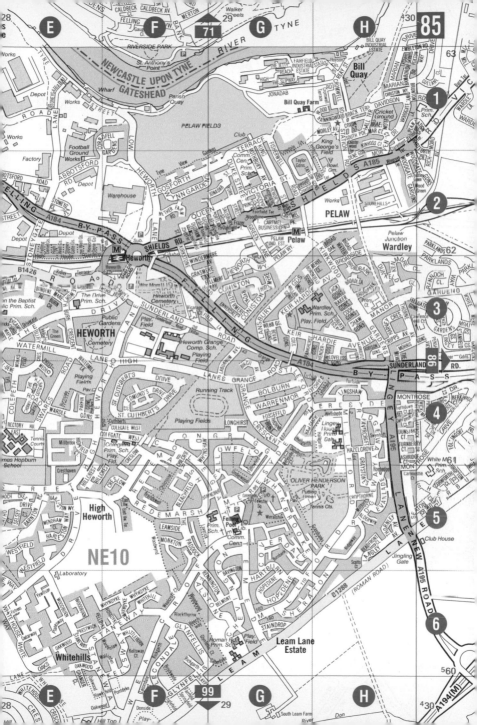

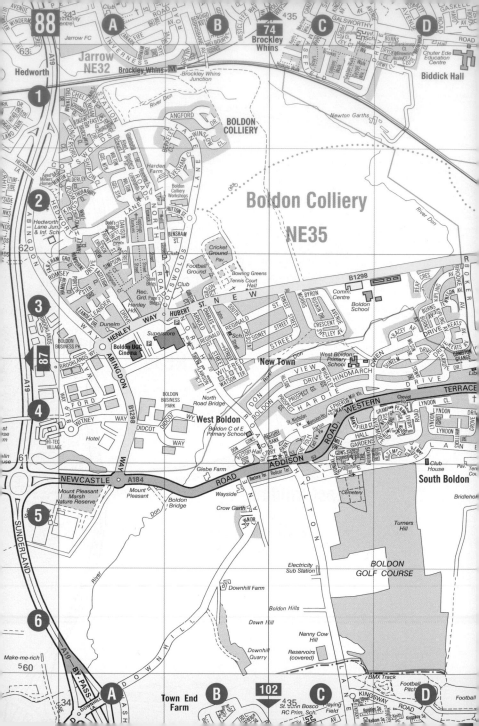

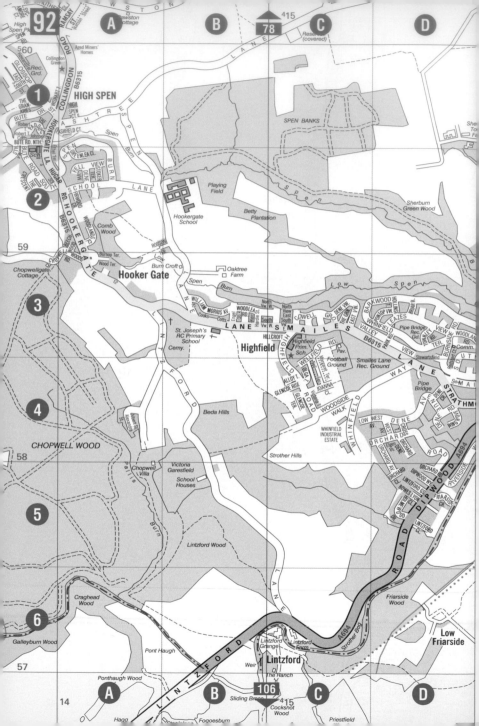

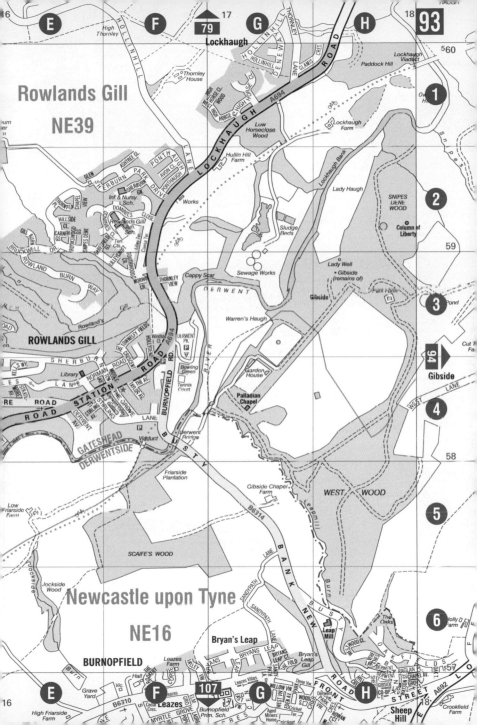

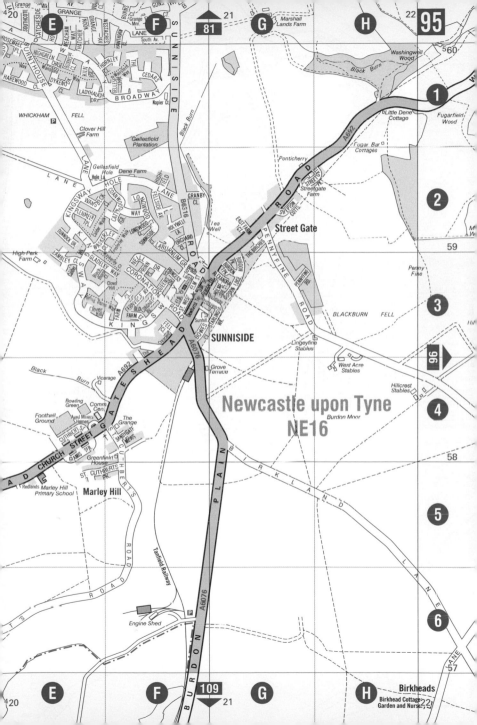

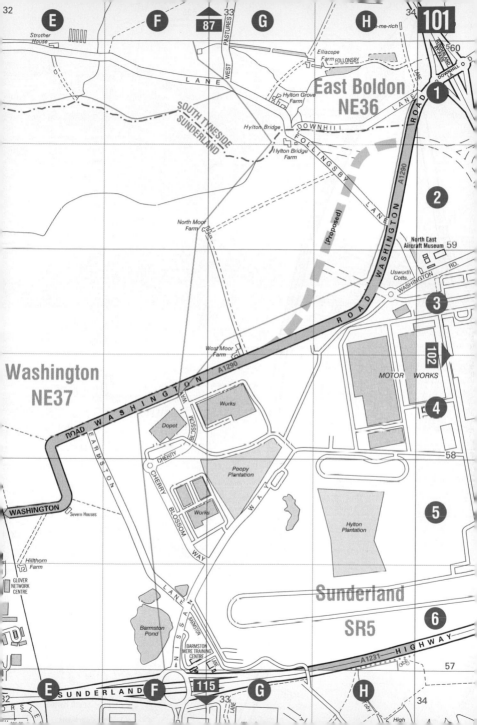

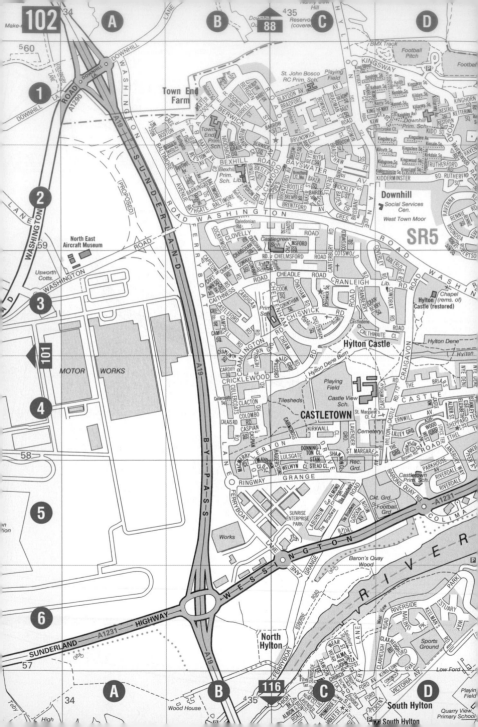

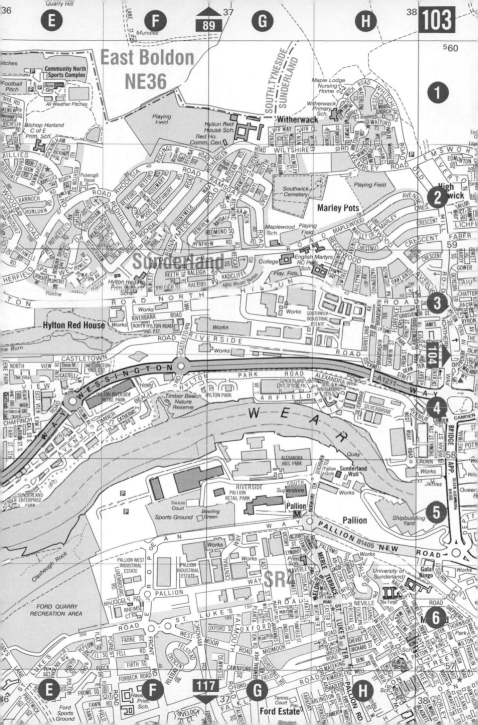

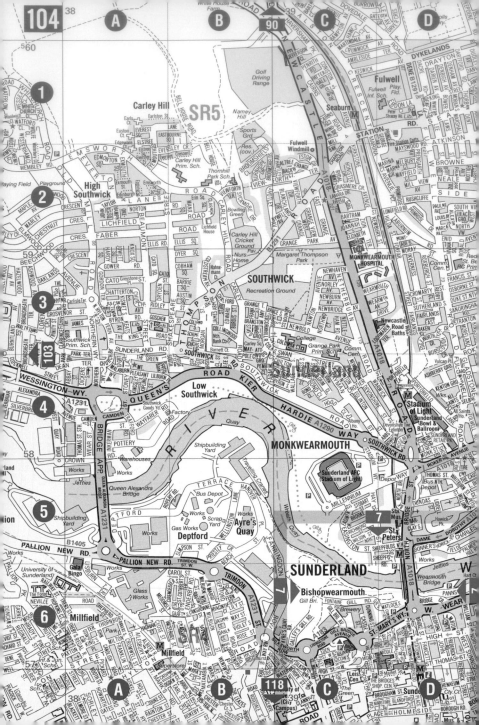

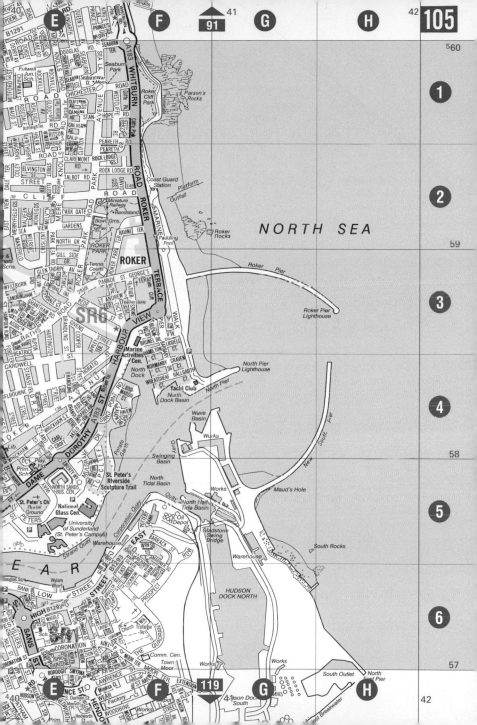

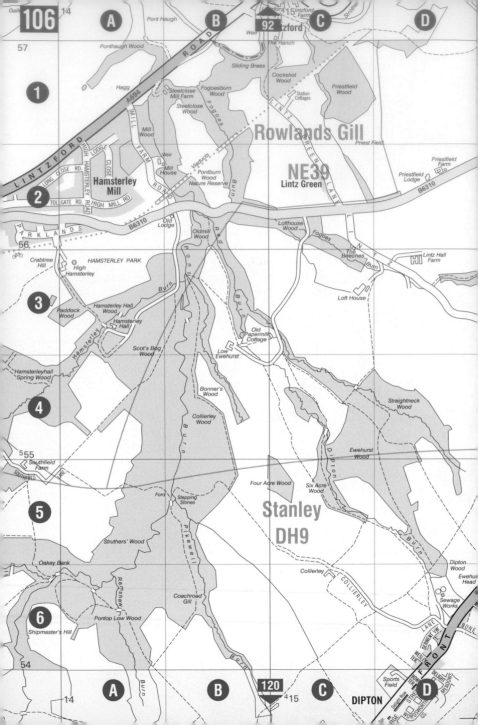

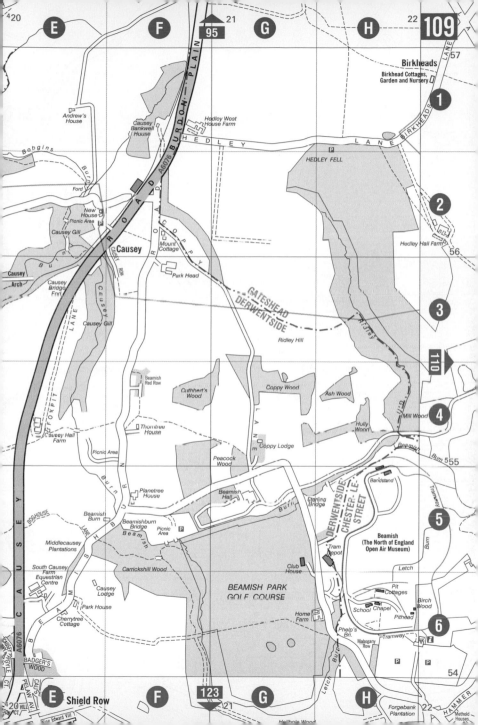

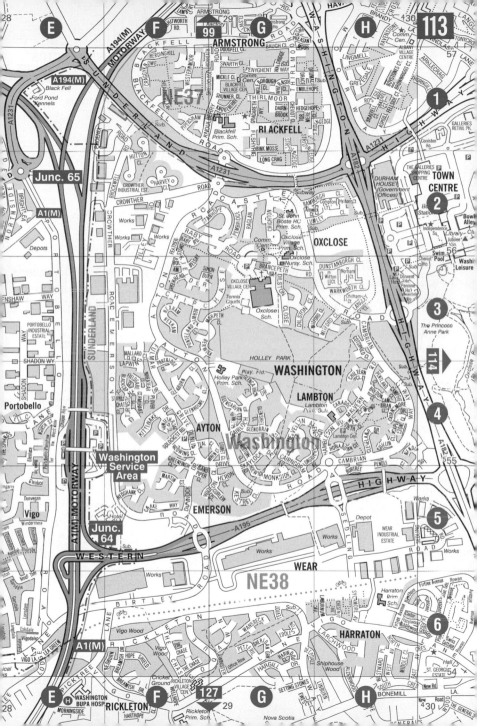

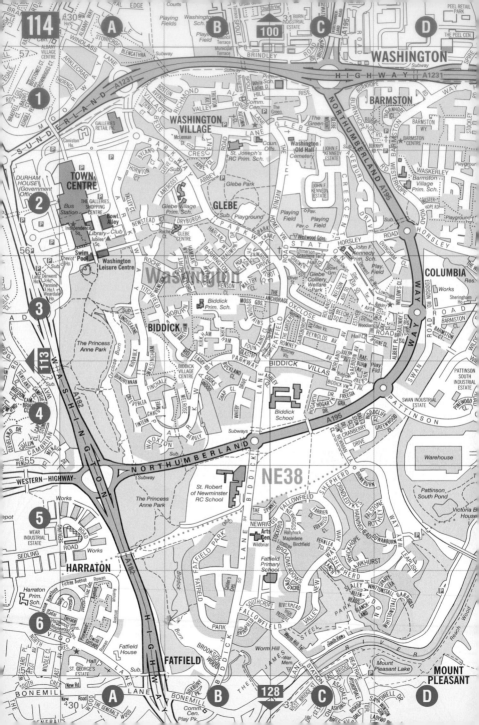

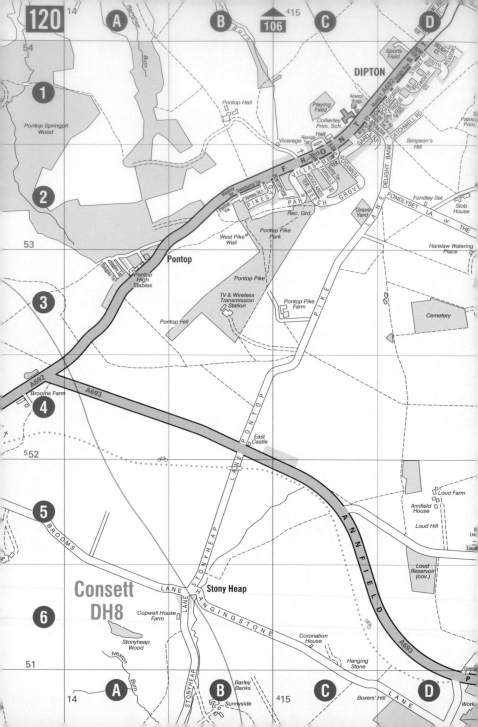

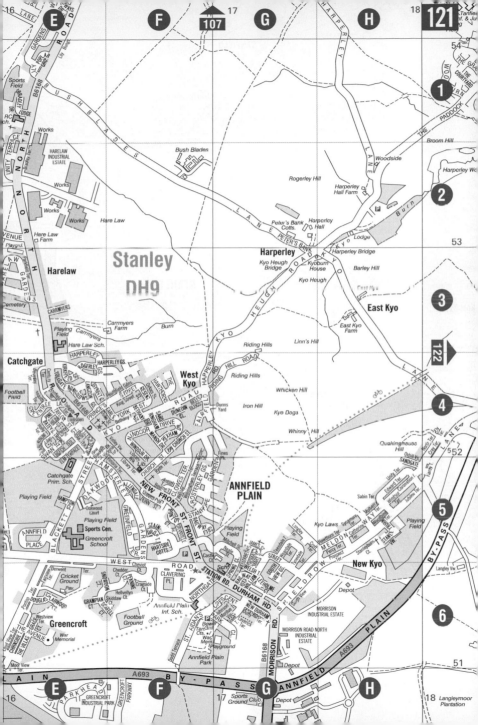

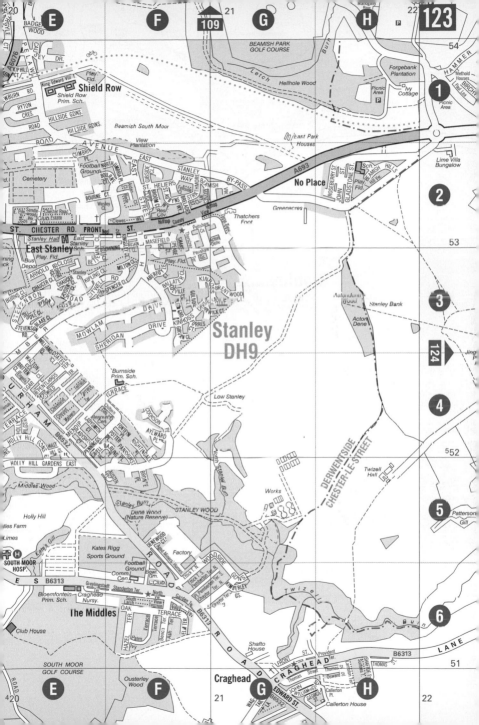

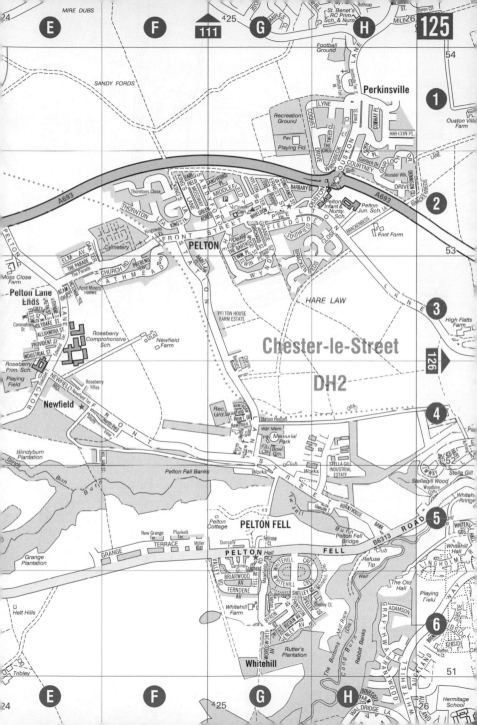

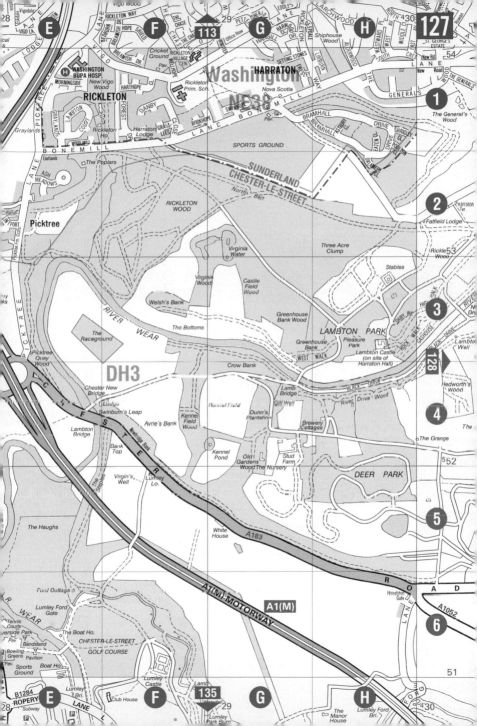

Washington NE38

HARRATON

RICKLETON

Picktree

DH3

SUNDERLAND
CHESTER-LE-STREET

RICKLETON
WOOD

Virginia
Water

Virginia
Wood

Castle
Field
Wood

Welsh's Bank

Tho Bottome

Greenhouse
Bank Wood

LAMBTON PARK

Three Acre
Clump

Stables

Pleasure
Park

Lambton Castle
(on site of
Harraton Hall)

The
Raceground

Greenhouse
Bank

WEST WALK

Crow Bank

BLACK DRIVE

Chester New
Bridge

Swinburn's Leap

Avrie's Bank

Kennel
Field
Wood

Kennel Field

Dunn's
Plantation

Lamb
Bridge

Gill Well

River Drive Wood

Lambton
Bridge

Bank
Top

Virgin's
Well

Lumley
Lo.

Kennel
Pond

Old
Gardens
Wood The Nursery

Stud
Farm

Brewery
Cottage

DEER PARK

The Haughs

White
House

A183

A1(M)

A1(M) MOTORWAY

Ford Cottage

Lumley Ford
Gate

The Boat Ho.

CHESTER-LE-STREET

GOLF COURSE

Tennis
Courts
Riverside Park
Pav.

Bandstand

Bowling
Greens
Pavilion

Sports
Ground

Boat Ho.

Lumley
Castle

Lamb
Bridge

B1284
ROPERY LANE

Subway

Lumley
Bri.

Club House

Lumley
Park Burn

A1052

The Grange

The

Hedworth's
Wood

Lambton
Well

Hawthorn
Gate

Lumley Ford
Bri.

The Manor
House

128

135

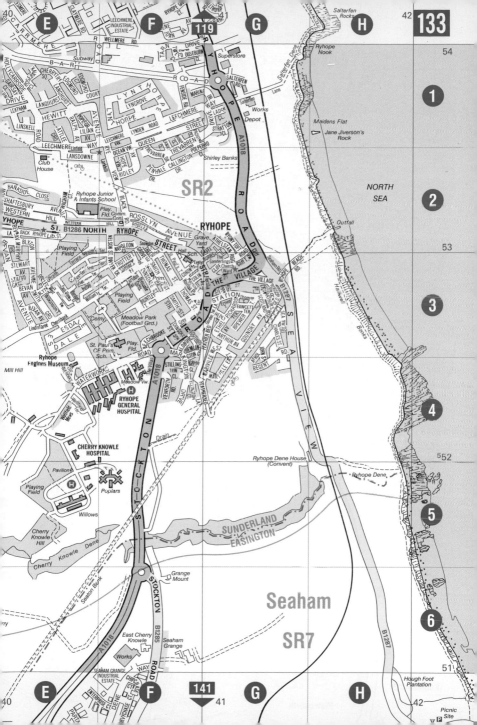

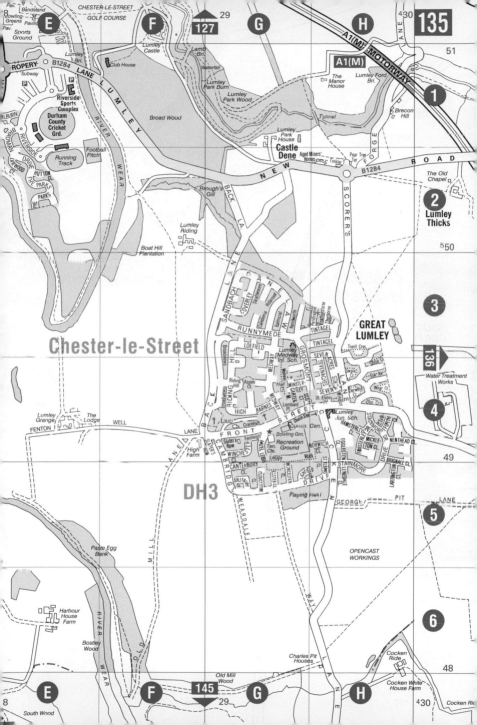

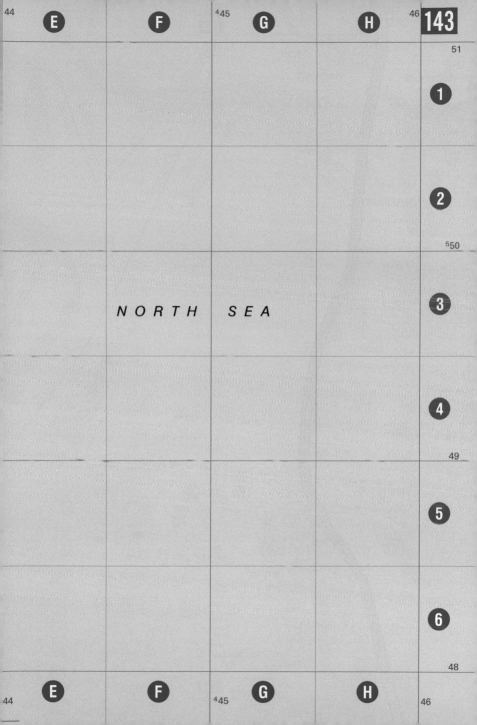

N O R T H   S E A

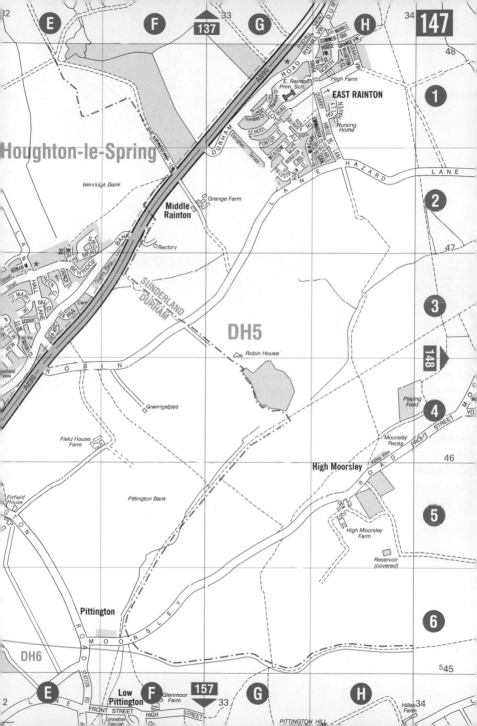

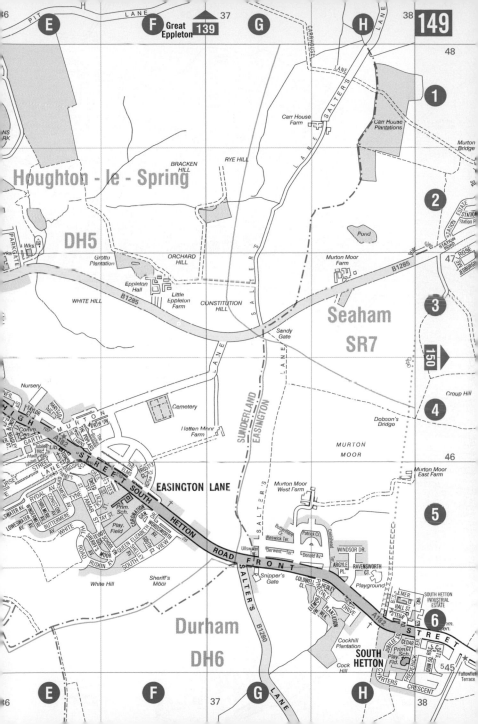

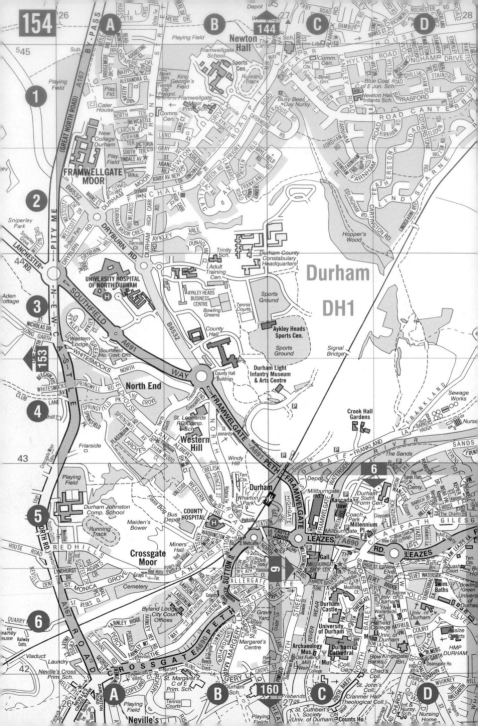

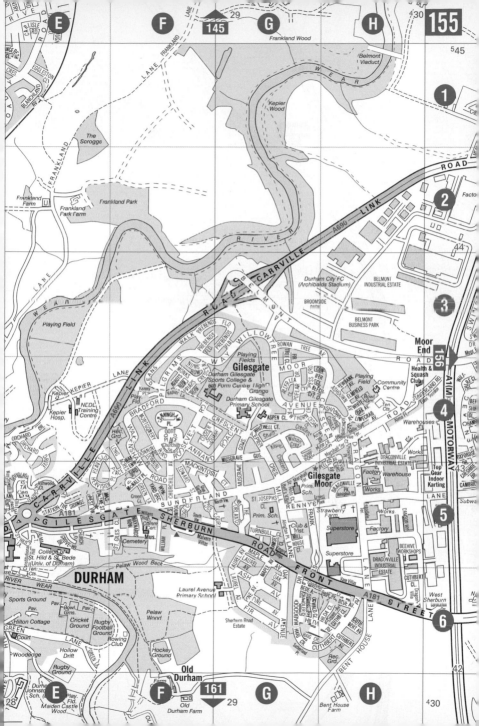

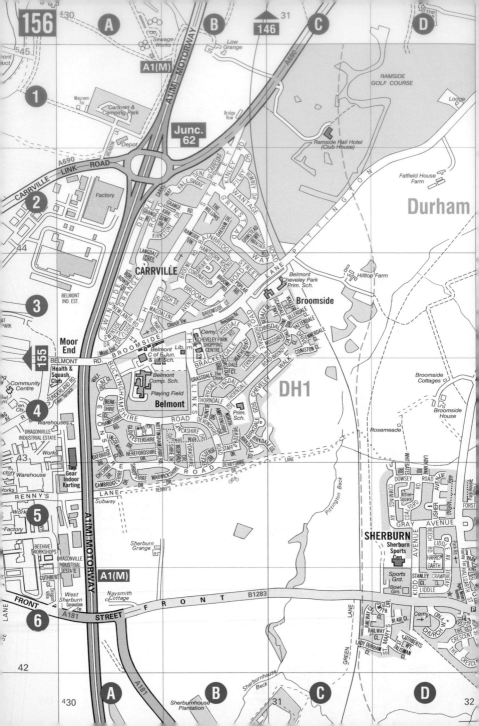

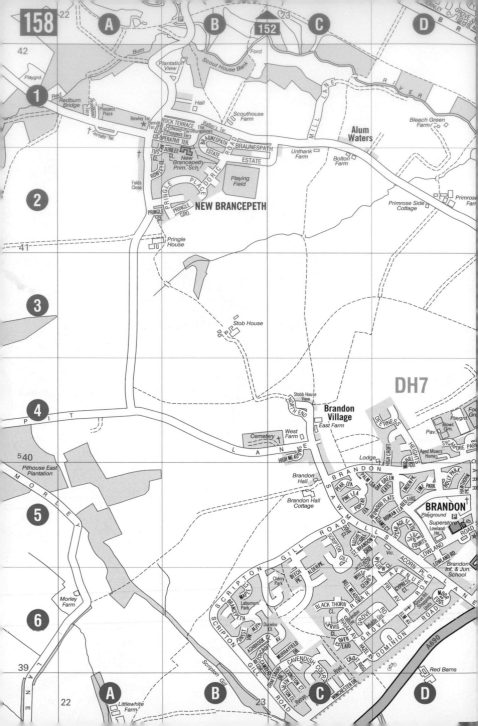

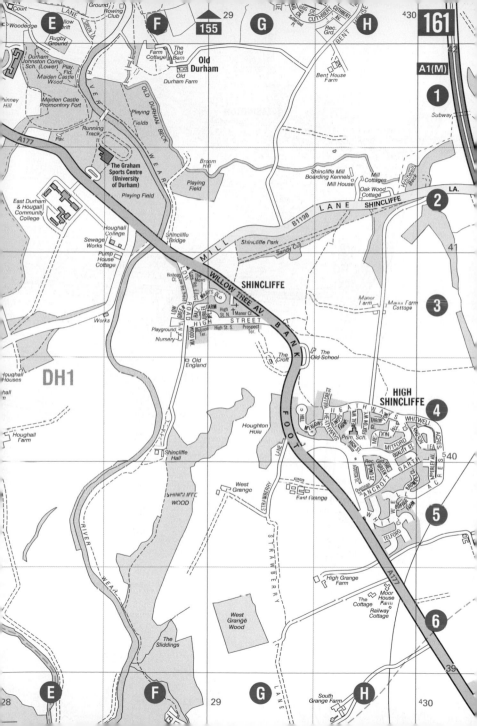

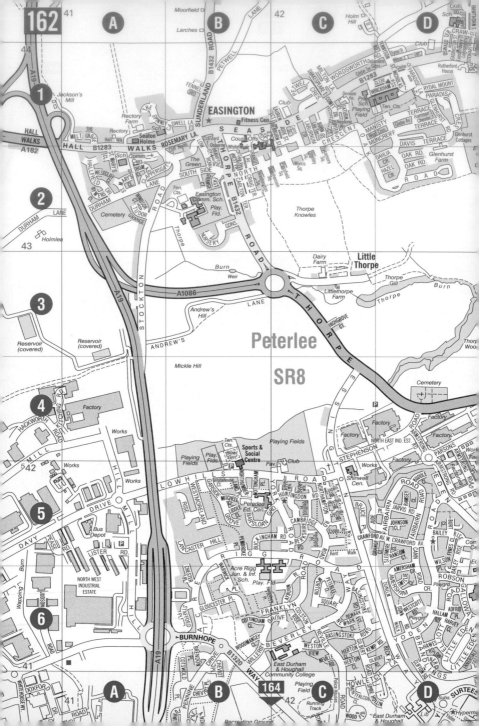

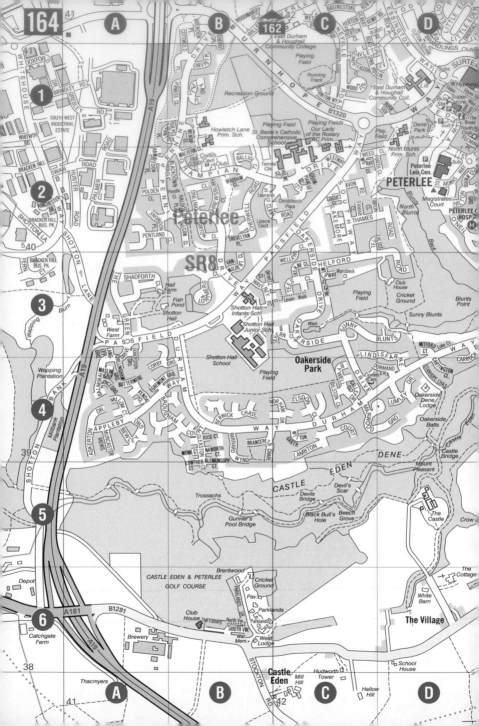

INDEX

Including Streets, Places & Areas, Industrial Estates, Selected Flats & Walkways,
Stations and Selected Places of Interest.

HOW TO USE THIS INDEX

1. Each street name is followed by its Postcode District and then by its Locality abbreviation(s) and then by its map reference;
   e.g. **Abbey Dr.** DH4: Hou S . . . 1F **137** is in the DH4 Postcode District and the Houghton-le-Spring Locality and is to be found
   in square 1F on page **137**. The page number is shown in bold type.

2. A strict alphabetical order is followed in which Av., Rd., St., etc. (though abbreviated) are read in full and as part of the street
   name; e.g. **Annville Cres.** appears after **Ann St.** but before **Ann Wlk.**

3. Streets and a selection of flats and walkways too small to be shown on the maps, appear in the index with the thoroughfare to
   which it is connected shown in brackets; e.g. **Aged Miners Homes** SR2: Ryh . . . .2E **133** (off Cheviot La.)

4. Addresses that are in more than one part are referred to as not continuous.

5. Places and areas are shown in the index in **BLUE TYPE** and the map reference is to the actual map square in which the town
   centre or area is located and not to the place name shown on the map; e.g. **ANNFIELD PLAIN 6F 121**

6. An example of a selected place of interest is **Arbeia Roman Fort & Mus. . . . 3E 63**

7. An example of a station is **Airport Station (Metro). . . .2B 40.** Included are Rail **(Rail)** and Metro **(Metro)**.

8. Map references shown in brackets; e.g **Abbotsford Gro.** SR2: Sund . . . 2C **118** (6E **7**) refer to entries that also appear on the
   large scale pages **4-7**.

GENERAL ABBREVIATIONS

App. : Approach	**Fld.** : Field	**No.** : Number
Arc. : Arcade	**Flds.** : Fields	**Pde.** : Parade
Av. : Avenue	**Gdn.** : Garden	**Pk.** : Park
Bk. : Back	**Gdns.** : Gardens	**Pas.** : Passage
Blvd. : Boulevard	**Gth.** : Garth	**Pl.** : Place
Bri. : Bridge	**Ga.** : Gate	**Pct.** : Precinct
Bldg. : Building	**Gt.** : Great	**Prom.** : Promenade
Bldgs. : Buildings	**Grn.** : Green	**Ri.** : Rise
Bungs. : Bungalows	**Gro.** : Grove	**Rd.** : Road
Bus. : Business	**Hgts.** : Heights	**Shop.** : Shopping
Cvn. : Caravan	**Ho.** : House	**Sth.** : South
Cen. : Centre	**Ho's** : Houses	**Sq.** : Square
Chu. : Church	**Ind.** : Industrial	**Sta.** : Station
Chyd. : Church Yard	**Info.** : Information	**St.** : Street
Circ. : Circle	**Intl.** : International	**Ter.** : Terrace
Cl. : Close	**La.** : Lane	**Twr.** : Tower
Coll. : College	**Lit.** : Little	**Trad.** : Trading
Cnr. : Corner	**Lwr.** : Lower	**Up.** : Upper
Cott. : Cottage	**Mnr.** : Manor	**Va.** : Vale
Cotts. : Cottages	**Mans.** : Mansions	**Vw.** : View
Ct. : Court	**Mkt.** : Market	**Vs.** : Villas
Cres. : Crescent	**Mdw.** : Meadow	**Vis.** : Visitors
Cft. : Croft	**Mdws.** : Meadows	**Wlk.** : Walk
Dr. : Drive	**M.** : Mews	**W.** : West
E. : East	**Mt.** : Mount	**Yd.** : Yard
Ent. : Enterprise	**Mus.** : Museum	
Est. : Estate	**Nth.** : North	

LOCALITY ABBREVIATIONS

Ann P : **Annfield Plain**	Burn : **Burnopfield**	Cow : **Cowpen**
Back : **Backworth**	Cal : **Callerton**	Cra : **Cramlington**
Beam : **Beamish**	Camb : **Cambois**	Din : **Dinnington**
Bed : **Bedlington**	Carr : **Carrville**	Dip : **Dipton**
Bir : **Birtley**	Cas E : **Castle Eden**	Dud : **Dudley**
B Col : **Blackhall Colliery**	C'twn : **Castletown**	Dun : **Dunston**
Bla T : **Blaydon-on-Tyne**	Cha P : **Chapel Park**	Dur : **Durham**
Bly : **Blyth**	Ches S : **Chester-le-Street**	Eas : **Easington**
Bol C : **Boldon Colliery**	C'wl : **Chopwell**	Eas L : **Easington Lane**
B'don : **Brandon**	Cle : **Cleadon**	E Bol : **East Boldon**
Bras : **Brasside**	C Dene : **Clough Dene**	E Cram : **East Cramlington**
Bru V : **Brunswick Village**	Con : **Consett**	E Har : **East Hartford**

E Her : **East Herrington**
E Sle : **East Sleekburn**
Edm : **Edmondsley**
Gate : **Gateshead**
Gos : **Gosforth**
Gt Lum : **Great Lumley**
G'sde : **Greenside**
Ham C : **Hamsterley Colliery**
Ham M : **Hamsterley Mill**
H Brl : **Hartford Bridge**
Has : **Haswell**
Heb : **Hebburn**
Hed W : **Heddon-on-the-Wall**
Hep : **Hepscott**
Hes : **Hesleden**
Hett H : **Hetton-le-Hole**
H Pitt : **High Pittington**
H Shin : **High Shincliffe**
H Spen : **High Spen**
H'wll : **Holywell**
Hou S : **Houghton-le-Spring**
Jar : **Jarrow**
Ken : **Kenton**
Kib : **Kibblesworth**
Kil : **Killingworth**
Lam P : **Lambton Park**
Lead : **Leadgate**
Leam : **Leamside**

Lem : **Lemington**
Longb : **Longbenton**
Monk : **Monkwearmouth**
Mur : **Murton**
Nel V : **Nelson Village**
New B : **New Brancepeth**
Newc T : **Newcastle upon Tyne**
News : **Newsham**
New S : **New Silksworth**
N Shi : **North Shields**
Ouc : **Ouston**
Pelt : **Pelton**
Pen : **Penshaw**
Pet : **Peterlee**
Plaw : **Plawsworth**
Pon : **Ponteland**
Row G : **Rowlands Gill**
Ryh : **Ryhope**
Ryton : **Ryton**
Sco G : **Scotland Gate**
S'hm : **Seaham**
Sea : **Seaton**
Sea B : **Seaton Burn**
Sea D : **Seaton Delaval**
Sea S : **Seaton Sluice**
Seg : **Seghill**
Shad : **Shadforth**
Sher : **Sherburn**

Shir : **Shiremoor**
S Het : **South Hetton**
S Shi : **South Shields**
S'wck : **Southwick**
Spri : **Springwell**
Stly : **Stanley**
Sund : **Sunderland**
Sun : **Sunniside**
Swa : **Swalwell**
Tan L : **Tanfield Lea**
Thro : **Throckley**
Ush M : **Ushaw Moor**
Usw : **Usworth**
Walk : **Walker**
W'snd : **Wallsend**
Wash : **Washington**
Well : **Wellfield**
W Bol : **West Boldon**
W Rai : **West Rainton**
W Sle : **West Sleekburn**
Whi : **Whickham**
Whit : **Whitburn**
Whit B : **Whitley Bay**
Wide O : **Wide Open**
Wool : **Woolsington**
Wylam : **Wylam**

A

Abbay St. SR5: S'wck 4A **104**
Abbey Cl. NE25: Whit B 1H **47**
  NE38: Wash 2B **114**
Abbey Ct. NE8: Gate 2H **83**
Abbey Dr. DH4: Hou S 1F **137**
  NE5: Cha P 4H **53**
  NE30: N Shi 5F **49**
  NE32: Jar 2G **73**
Abbeyfield Cl. NE8: Gate 2D **82**
Abbey Leisure Cen. 5C **144**
Abbey Rd. DH1: Dur 5D **144**
  NE30: Wash 2B **114**
Abbey Rd. Bus. Pk. DH1: Dur . . .5B **144**
Abbey Rd. Ind. Est.
  DH1: Dur 5B **144**
Abbey Ter. NE27: Shir 2C **46**
Abbeyvale Dr. NE6: Walk 2H **71**
Abbeywoods DH1: Dur 5C **144**
Abbeywoods Bus. Pk.
  DH1: Dur 5B **144**
Abbot Ct. NE8: Gate 6H **69**
Abbotsfield Cl. SR3: New S 4H **131**
Abbotsford Gro.
  SR2: Sund 2C **118** (6E **7**)
Abbotsford Ho. NE24: Bly 1A **18**
Abbotsford Pk. NE25: Whit B 1B **48**
Abbotsford Rd. NE10: Gate 2D **84**
Abbotsford Ter. NE2: Newc T 1F **69**
Abbotside Cl. DH9: Ous 5F **111**
Abbotside Pl. NE5: Cha P 6B **54**
Abbotsmeade Cl. NE5: Newc T . . .1F **67**
Abbots Row DH1: Dur 4F **155**
Abbotside Pl. NE5: Cha P 6B **54**
Abbot St. SR8: Eas 1F **163**
Abbots Wlk. DH9: Beam 1B **124**
Abbots Way NE16: Whi 4F **81**
  NE29: N Shi 4H **47**
Abbotsway NE32: Jar 3A **74**
Abbs St. SR5: S'wck 4D **104**
Abercorn Pl. NE28: W'snd 1C **60**

Abercorn Rd. NE15: Newc T 4E **67**
  SR3: E Her 1F **131**
Abercrombie Pl. NE5: Newc T 5F **55**
Aberdare Rd. SR3: E Her 2G **131**
Aberdeen DH2: Ous 6H **111**
Aberdeen Ct. NE3: Ken 5H **41**
Aberdeen Dr. NE32: Jar 5A **74**
Aberdeen Twr. SR3: E Her 1G **131**
Aberford Cl. NE5: Cha P 3H **53**
Aberfoyle DH2: Ous 6H **111**
Aberfoyle Ct. DH9: Stly 3F **123**
Abernethy DH2: Ous 5H **111**
Aberwick Dr. DH2: Ches S 3A **134**
Abigail Ct. NE3: Gos 2G **57**
Abingdon Ct. NE3: Ken 6H **41**
  NE21: Bla T 6A **66**
Abingdon Rd. NE6: Walk 2H **71**
Abingdon Sq. NE23: Cra 6C **16**
Abingdon St. SR4: Sund 2H **117**
Abingdon Way NE35: Bol C 2H **07**
Aboyne Av. NE4: Newc T 4D **68**
Aboyne Sq. SR3: E Her 6F **117**
Acacia Av. DH4: Hou S 2E **137**
  SR8: Pet 1H **165**
Acacia Gro. NE31: Heb 5C **72**
  NE34: S Shi 4H **75**
Acacia Rd. NE10: Gate 1B **84**
Acanthus Av. NE4: Newc T 2H **67**
Acer Ct. SR2: Sund 3D **118**
Acklam Av. SR2: Sund 6G **119**
Acomb Av. NE25: Sea D 3A **34**
  NE28: W'snd 6B **46**
Acomb Ct. NE9: Gate 3B **98**
  NE12: Kil 2D **44**
  NE22: Bed 4A **10**
  SR2: Sund 6F **119**
Acomb Cres. NE3: Ken 5B **42**
Acomb Gdns. NE5: Newc T 1G **55**
Acorn Av. NE8: Gate 3E **83**
  NE22: Bed 5H **9**
Acorn Cl. NE9: Gate 2D **98**

Acorn Pl. DH1: Dur 6A **144**
  DH7: B'don 5D **158**
Acorn Rd. NE2: Newc T 5G **57**
Acorn St. DH2: Beam 2D **124**
Acre Rigg Rd. SR8: Pet 6B **162**
Acton Dene DH9: Stly 2G **123**
Acton Dr. NE29: N Shi 5H **47**
Acton Pl. NE7: Newc T 5B **58**
Acton Rd. NE5: Newc T 1D **66**
Adair Av. NE15: Newc T 3G **67**
Adair Way NE31: Heb 4D **72**
Adams Bldgs. DH9: Dip 1C **120**
  NE15: Newc T 5D **66**
Adamsez Ind. Est.
  NE15: Newc T 5D **66**
Adamson St. DH2: Ches S 6H **125**
Adam St. SR8: Pet 1H **165**
Ada St. NE6: Walk 3F **71**
  NE33: S Shi 6F **63**
Ada St. E. SR7: Mur 3D **150**
Ada St. W. SR7: Mur 3D **150**
Adderstone Av. NE23: Cra 4B **22**
Adderstone Ct. NE2: Newc T 4H **57**
Adderstone Cres. NE2: Newc T . . .5H **57**
Adderstone Gdns. NE29: N Shi . . .4F **47**
Addington Cres. NE29: N Shi 1A **62**
Addington Dr. NE24: News 2C **18**
  NE28: W'snd 6B **46**
ADDISON 4F **65**
Addison Cl. NE6: Newc T 3B **70**
Addison Ct. NE28: W'snd 6F **61**
  NE40: Ryton 1B **64**
Addison Gdns. NE10: Gate 3H **85**
Addison Ind. Est. NE21: Bla T 4F **65**
Addison Rd. NE6: Newc T 3B **70**
  NE15: Lem 2B **66**
  NE36: W Bol 4C **88**
Addison St. NE29: N Shi 3C **62**
  SR2: Sund 1F **119**
Addison Wlk. NE34: S Shi 1C **88**
Addycombe Ter. NE6: Newc T 5C **58**

Adelaide Cen., The
NE4: Newc T 4A **68**
Adelaide Cl. SR1: Sund 6F **105**
Adelaide Ct. NE8: Gate 6G **69**
Adelaide Ho. NE4: Newc T 4A **68**
Adelaide Pl. SR1: Sund 6F **105**
Adelaide Row SR7: S'hm 4B **142**
Adelaide St. DH3: Ches S 1C **134**
Adelaide Ter. NE4: Newc T 4H **67**
Adeline Gdns. NE3: Ken 5C **56**
Adelphi Cl. NE29: N Shi 5G **47**
Adelphi Pl. NE6: Walk 4E **71**
Aden Ct. DH7: Ush M 3C **152**
Aden Twr. SR3: E Her 1G **131**
Adfrid Pl. SR8: Pet 6D **162**
Admiral Ho. NE30: N Shi 6F **49**
Admiral Way SR3: E Her 4E **131**
Adolphus Pl. DH1: Dur 5H **155**
SR7: S'hm 4C **142**
Adolphus St. SR6: Whit 2F **91**
Adolphus St. W. SR7: S'hm 4B **142**
Adrian Pl. SR8: Pet 2E **165**
Adventure La. DH4: W Rai 2D **146**
Affleck St. NE8: Gate 1G **83**
Afton Ct. NE34: S Shi 4E **75**
Afton Way NE3: Ken 1A **56**
Agar Rd. SR3: E Her 1F **131**
Aged Miners' Cotts.
NE25: Sea D 3C **24**
NE27: Shir 4B **46**
Aged Miners' Home
NE16: Burn 1G **107**
NE34: S Shi 2A **76**
Aged Miners Homes
DH2: Ches S 5C **126**
(Pelaw Bank)
DH2: Ches S 4B **134**
(Union La.)
DH2: Pelt 3E **125**
DH2: Plaw 1A **144**
DH3: Gt Lum 2H **135**
DH4: Hou S 3G **137**
(Dairy La.)
DH4: Hou S *3F 129*
(off Chester Rd.)
DH5: Hett H 3C **148**
DH5: Hou S 3B **138**
DH6: Sher 6D **156**
(Hallgarth St.)
DH6: Sher 6G **157**
(Local Av.)
DH7: B'don 6E **159**
(Burnigill)
DH7: B'don 4D **158**
(Deerness Hgts.)
DH7: Ush M 4C **152**
DH9: Stly 5F **123**
NE5: Newc T 4B **54**
NE7: Longb 2A **58**
NE11: Kib 1E **111**
NE12: Dud 5A **32**
NE13: Bru V 5C **30**
NE16: Sun 4E **95**
NE21: Bla T 4G **65**
NE24: Camb 1B **12**
NE25: Sea D *6B 24*
(off Ryal Cl.)
NE27: Back 6A **34**
NE27: Shir 2D **46**
NE35: Bol C 2H **87**
NE39: H Spen 1A **92**
NE40: Ryton *5E 65*
(off Stargate La.)

Aged Miners Homes SR2: Ryh . . .2E **133**
(off Cheviot La.)
SR3: New S 6A **118**
SR5: C'twn 3G **103**
SR7: Mur 2B **150**
SR7: S'hm 2F **141**
(Lord Byrons Wlk.)
SR7: S'hm 6B **142**
(Shrewsbury St.)
SR8: Pet 6F **163**
Aged Mineworkers' Homes
NE15: Thro 5B **52**
Agincourt NE12: Kil 1D **44**
NE31: Heb 2B **72**
Agnes Maria St. NE3: Gos 2C **56**
Agnes St. DH9: Stly 2D **122**
Agricola Ct. NE33: S Shi 3E **63**
Agricola Gdns. NE28: W'snd 1B **60**
Agricola Rd. NE4: Newc T 3B **68**
Aidan Av. NE26: Sea S 3F **25**
Aidan Cl. DH9: Stly 2F **123**
NE13: Wide O 5D **30**
NE27: Longb 4A **46**
Aidan Ct. NE7: Newc T 2C **58**
NE32: Jar 3H **73**
Aidan Ho. NE8: Gate 1H **83**
Aidan Wlk. NE3: Gos 2F **57**
Aidan Way DH5: Hett H 6C **138**
Ailesbury St. SR4: Sund 6A **104**
Ainderby Rd. NE15: Thro 5B **52**
Ainsdale Gdns. NE5: Cha P 5A **54**
Ainsley St. DH1: Dur 5B **154**
Ainslie Pl. NE5: Newc T 6G **55**
Ainsworth Av. NE34: S Shi 6C **74**
Ainthorpe Cl. SR3: New S 2B **132**
Ainthorpe Gdns. NE7: Newc T 3B **58**
NE9: Gate 6H **83**
Aintree Cl. NE37: Wash 6B **100**
Aintree Gdns. NE8: Gate 4E **83**
Aintree Rd. SR3: E Her 1F **131**
Airedale NE28: W'snd 2F **59**
Airedale Gdns. DH5: Hett H 3B **148**
Aireys Cl. DH4: Hou S 3G **137**
Airey Ter. NE6: Walk 4G **71**
NE8: Gate 2F **83**
Airport Freightway
NE13: Wool 3C **40**
Airport Ind. Est. NE3: Ken 1G **55**
Airport Station (Metro) 2B **40**
Airville Mt. SR3: New S 5A **132**
Aisgill Cl. NE23: Cra 3B **22**
Aisgill Dr. NE5: Cha P 6A **54**
Aiskell St. SR4: Sund 1A **118**
A J Cooks Cotts. NE39: Row G . . .3B **92**
Akeld Cl. NE23: Cra 4B **22**
Akeld Ct. NE3: Gos 3G **57**
Akeld M. SR6: Monk 4E **105**
Akenside Hill
NE1: Newc T 5G **69** (6F **5**)
Akenside Ter. NE2: Newc T 1H **69**
Alanbrooke Row NE31: Heb 6A **72**
Alansway Gdns. NE33: S Shi 1F **75**
ALBANY 6A **100**
Albany Av. NE12: Longb 6D **44**
Albany Ct. NE4: Newc T 6C **68**
Albany Gdns. NE26: Whit B 1D **48**
Albany Ho. NE3/: Wash 6A **100**
SR5: S'wck 4C **104**
Albany M. NE3: Ken 5C **56**
Albany Rd. NE8: Gate 6A **70**
Albany St. E. NE33: S Shi 1F **75**
Albany St. W. NE33: S Shi 1F **75**
Albany Ter. NE32: Jar 5D **72**

Albany Village Cen.
NE37: Wash 1H **113**
Albany Way NE37: Wash 6A **100**
Albatross Way NE24: News 4C **18**
Albemarle Av. NE2: Gos 4F **57**
Albemarle St. NE33: S Shi 4E **63**
Albert Av. NE28: W'snd 5H **59**
Albert Cl. SR2: Sund 2C **118** (6E **7**)
Albert Dr. NE9: Gate 1H **97**
Albert Edward Ter. NE35: Bol C . . .1A **88**
Albert Pl. NE9: Gate 1H **97**
NE38: Wash 3D **114**
Albert Rd. NE22: Bed 3E **11**
NE26: Sea S 3H **25**
NE32: Jar 2F **73**
(Chapel Rd.)
NE32: Jar 3E **73**
(Park Rd., not continuous)
SR4: Sund 6A **104**
Albert St. DH1: Dur 4B **154**
DH2: Pelt 4C **124**
DH3: Ches S 6C **126**
DH9: Stly 3C **122**
NE2: Newc T 3H **69** (3G **5**)
NE24: Bly 5C **12**
NE31: Heb 2B **72**
NE39: C'wl 4A **92**
SR7: S'hm 5C **142**
Albert Ter. NE12: Longb 4C **44**
NE26: Whit B 1D **48**
NE33: S Shi 5E **63**
Albion Ct. NE6: Newc T 4B **70**
NE24: Cow 6B **12**
NE33: S Shi 3E **63**
Albion Gdns. NE16: Burn 2F **107**
Albion Pl. SR1: Sund 1C **118** (5F **7**)
Albion Retail Cen. NE24: Cow 5B **12**
Albion Rd. NE29: N Shi 1C **62**
NE30: N Shi 1C **62**
Albion Rd. W. NE29: N Shi 2C **62**
Albion Row NE6: Newc T 4A **70**
(not continuous)
Albion St. NE10: Gate 5C **84**
SR4: Sund 1C **116**
Albion Ter. NE9: Spri 4F **99**
NE23: Cra 5D **16**
NE29: N Shi 1C **62**
Albion Way NE23: Cra 6D **16**
NE24: Bly, Cow 6A **12**
Albion Yd. NE1: Newc T . . .4F **69** (5C **4**)
Albury Pk. Rd. NE30: N Shi 6E **49**
Albury Pl. NE16: Whi 6E **81**
Albury Rd. NE2: Gos 4F **57**
Albyn Gdns. SR3: Sund 4A **118**
Alconbury Cl. NE24: News 2C **18**
Alcroft Cl. NE5: Cha P 4H **53**
Aldborough Cl. NE24: Bly 6C **12**
Aldbrough Cl. SR2: Ryh 3F **133**
Aldbrough St. NE34: S Shi 4C **74**
Aldeburgh Av. NE15: Lem 1A **66**
Aldenham Gdns. NE30: N Shi 4E **49**
Aldenham Rd. SR3: E Her 1G **131**
Aldenham Twr. SR3: E Her 1G **131**
Alder Av. NE4: Newc T 1H **67**
Alder Cl. DH5: Hett H 2B **148**
Alder Ct. NE25: Whit B 1A **48**
Alder Cres. DH9: Tan L 6F **107**
Alderdene Cl. DH7: Ush M 6E **153**
Alder Gro. NE25: Whit B 5A **36**
Alderlea Cl. DH1: Dur 4G **155**
Alderley Cl. NE35: Bol C 2A **88**
SR2: Sund 5F **119**
Alderley Dr. NE12: Kil 1E **45**

Alderley Rd. NE9: Gate 6G 83
Alderley Way NE23: Cra 6C 16
Alderman Wood Rd.
　　DH9: Tan L 1C 122
Alderney Gdns. NE5: Cha P 5A 54
Alder Pk. DH7: B'don 6C 158
Alder Rd. NE28: W'snd 1C 60
　　NE29: N Shi 6E 47
　　SR8: Pet 1H 165
Aldershot Rd. SR3: E Her 2F 131
Aldershot Sq. SR3: E Her 2F 131
Alder St. SR5: C'twn 4D 102
Alder Way NE12: Kil 1C 44
Alderwood NE8: Gate 2F 83
　　NE38: Wash 1H 127
Alderwood Cres. NE6: Walk 6F 59
Alderwyk NE10: Gate 5H 85
Aldhome Ct. DH1: Dur 1A 154
Aldin Grange Hall
　　DH7: Ush M 5F 153
Aldin Grange Ter. DH7: Ush M . .4E 153
Aldin Ri. DH7: Ush M 5E 153
Aldridge Ct. DH7: Ush M 5C 152
Aldsworth Cl. NE9: Spri 4F 99
Aldwick Rd. NE15: Newc T 3D 66
Aldwych Dr. NE29: N Shi 6F 47
Aldwych Rd. SR3: E Her 2F 131
Aldwych Sq. SR3: E Her 2F 131
Aldwych St. NE33: S Shi 5G 63
Alexander Dr. DH5: Hett H 2B 148
Alexander Ter. NE13: Bru V 6C 30
　　SR6: Monk 2D 104
Alexandra Av. SR5: Sund 4H 103
Alexandra Bus. Pk.
　　SR4: Sund 5G 103
Alexandra Cl. DH1: Dur 1A 154
Alexandra Dr. NE16: Swa 3G 81
Alexandra Gdns. NE29: N Shi 1A 62
　　NE40: Ryton 5E 65
Alexandra Ho. SR2: Sund 5E 7
Alexandra Pk. SR3: Sund 3B 118
Alexandra Rd. NE6: Newc T 6B 58
　　NE8: Gate 1G 83
Alexandra St. DH2: Pelt 3E 125
　　NE28: W'snd 5A 60
　　NE39: C'wl 4A 92
Alexandra Ter. DH4: Pen 1F 129
　　NE5: Newc T 4D 54
　　NE9: Spri 4F 99
　　NE16: Sun 3G 95
　　NE22: Bed 4B 10
　　NE26: Whit B 1D 48
Alexandra Way NE23: Cra 4A 22
Alexandria Cres. DH1: Dur 6B 154
Alexandrina St. SR7: S'hm 4B 142
Alford DH2: Ous 5H 111
Alford Grn. NE12: Longb 6C 44
Alfred Av. NE22: Bed 4B 10
Alfred St. NE6: Walk 3E 71
　　NE24: Bly 1C 18
　　NE31: Heb 4B 72
　　SR7: C'hm 5C 142
　　SR8: Eas 1E 163
Alfred St. E. SR7: S'hm 5C 142
Alfreton Cl. DH7: B'don 6C 158
Algernon NE12: Kil 6D 32
Algernon Cl. NE6: Newc T 2C 70
Algernon Ct. NE6: Newc T 2C 70
　　　　　　　　(off Algernon Rd.)
Algernon Ind. Est. NE27: Shir 4D 46
Algernon Pl. NE26: Whit B 1D 48
Algernon Rd. NE6: Newc T 2C 70
　　NE15: Lem 3A 66

Algernon Ter. NE30: N Shi 5E 49
Algiers Rd. SR3: E Her 2E 131
Alice St. NE21: Bla T 2H 79
　　NE33: S Shi 1E 75
　　SR2: Sund 2C 118 (6F 7)
Alice Well Vs. SR4: Pen 4F 115
Aline St. SR3: New S 2B 132
　　SR7: S'hm 4C 142
Alington Pl. DH1: Dur 5G 155
Alison Dr NE36: E Bol 4F 89
Alison Ho. NE6: Newc T 2B 70
　　　　　　　　(off Heaton Rd.)
Allandale Av. NE12: Longb 6D 44
Allanville NE12: Kil 6B 32
All Church NE15: Newc T 3F 67
Allen Av. NE11: Gate 4E 83
Allendale Av. NE28: W'snd 3H 59
Allendale Cres.
　　DH4: Pen 1E 129
　　NE27: Shir 2E 47
Allendale Dr. NE34: S Shi 1A 76
Allendale Pl. NE30: N Shi 6F 49
Allendale Rd. DH7: B'don 5E 159
　　NE6: Newc T 4D 70
　　NE24: Bly 1D 18
　　SR3: E Her 2F 131
Allendale Sq. SR3: E Her 6G 117
Allendale St. DH5: Hett H 3C 148
Allendale Ter. DH9: Ann P 5F 121
　　NE6: Walk 4F 71
Allenheads NE5: Newc T 6C 54
　　NE25: Sea D 5A 24
　　NE38: Wash 6C 114
Allens Grn. NE23: Cra 3B 22
Allen St. DH3: Ches S 1C 134
　　SR8: Eas 1F 163
Allerdean Cl. NE15: Lem 2H 65
　　NE25: Sea D 1B 34
ALLERDENE 4A 98
Allerdene Wlk. NE16: Whi 5E 81
Allergate DH1: Dur 6B 154 (3A 6)
Allergate Ter. DH1: Dur 6D 154
　　　　　　　　(off Allergate)
Allerhope NE23: Cra 4B 22
Allerton Gdns. NE6: Newc T 5D 58
Allerton Pl. NE16: Whi 6D 80
Allerwash NE5: Newc T 6C 54
Allgood Ter. NE22: Bed 4B 10
All Hallows La.
　　NE1: Newc T 4G 69 (5F 5)
Allhusen Ter. NE8: Gate 2B 84
Alliance Pl. SR4: Sund 6B 104
Alliance St. SR4: Sund 6B 104
Allingham Ct. NE7: Newc T 4E 59
Allison Ct. NE11: Dun 2F 81
Alloa Rd. SR3: E Her 1F 131
Allonby M. NE23: Cra 5D 16
Allonby Way NE5: Newc T 1F 67
ALLOTMENT, THE 4D 46
Alloy Ter. NE39: Row G 4C 92
All Saints Cen. NE1: Newc T 5E 5
All Saints Ct. NE29: N Shi 1H 61
　　SR6: Monk 4D 104
All Saints Dr. DH5: Hett H 6C 138
All Saints Ho. SR6: Monk 4D 104
All Saints Office Cen.
　　NE1: Newc T 5F 5
Allwork Ter. NE16: Whi 4F 81
Alma Pl. DH1: Dur 4H 155
　　DH4: Hou S 4G 129
　　NE26: Whit B 1D 48
　　NE29: N Shi 1C 62
Alma St. SR4: Sund 6C 102

Alma Ter. DH1: Dur 5E 155
　　　　　　　　(Gilesgate)
　　DH1: Dur 1A 160
　　　　　　　(off Neville's Cross Bank)
　　NE40: G'sde 1C 78
Almond Cres. NE8: Gate 3E 83
Almond Dr. SR5: C'twn 5C 102
Almond Gro. NE24: News 3A 18
Almond Pl. NE4: Newc T 2H 67
Almond Ter. SR8: Pet 6H 163
Almoners Barn DH1: Dur 2A 160
Almshouses NE15: Thro 2F 65
Aln Av. NE3: Ken 6C 42
Aln Ct. NE15: Lem 3A 66
Aln Cres. NE3: Ken 6C 42
Aln Gro. NE15: Lem 2A 66
Alnham Ct. NE3: Ken 6A 42
Alnham Grn. NE5: Cha P 5A 54
Alnmouth Av. NE29: N Shi 3H 61
Alnmouth Dr. NE3: Gos 3G 57
Aln St. NE31: Heb 3B 72
　　　　　　　　(not continuous)
Aln Wlk. NE3: Ken 1C 56
Alnwick Av. NE26: Whit B 6C 36
　　NE29: N Shi 3H 61
Alnwick Cl. DH2: Ches S 2A 134
　　NE16: Whi 4E 81
Alnwick Ct. NE38: Wash 2H 113
Alnwick Dr. NE22: Bed 4F 9
Alnwick Gro. NE32: Jar 1F 87
Alnwick Rd. DH1: Dur 6C 144
　　NE34: S Shi 3E 75
　　SR3: E Her 1G 131
Alnwick Sq. SR3: E Her 1G 131
Alnwick St. NE15: Thro 1F 65
　　NE28: W'snd 5A 60
　　SR8: Eas 1E 163
　　SR8: Pet 4F 163
Alnwick Ter. NE13: Wide O 4E 31
Alpine Cl. DH4: Hou S 4D 128
Alpine Ct. DH2: Ches S 6C 126
Alpine Grn. NE36: W Bol 4D 88
Alpine Way SR3: Sund 4A 118
Alresford NE12: Kil 1D 44
Alston Av. NE6: Walk 3E 71
　　NE23: E Cram 4D 22
Alston Cl. NE28: W'snd 3E 61
　　NE29: N Shi 6G 47
Alston Cres. SR6: Monk 6C 90
Alston Gdns. NE15: Thro 5D 52
Alston Gro. NE26: Sea D 2F 25
Alston Rd. NE25: Sea D 3B 24
　　NE38: Wash 1F 115
Alston St. NE8: Gate 2E 83
Alston Wlk. DH6: Sher 6E 157
　　SR8: Pet 6E 163
Alston Way DH7: B'don 5E 159
Altan Pl. NE12: Longb 6B 44
Altree Grange SR5: S'wck 2C 104
Altrincham Twr. SR3: E Her 1G 131
ALUM WATERS 1C 158
Alum Well NE9: Gate 6H 83
Alum Well Rd. NE9: Gate 6G 83
　　　　　　　　(Carlton Ter.)
　　NE9: Gate 6H 83
　　　　　　　　(Cross Keys La.)
Alverston Cl. NE15: Lem 1A 66
Alverstone Av. NE9: Gate 1G 97
Alverstone Rd. SR3: E Her 2F 131
Alverthorpe St. NE33: S Shi 1F 75
Alwin NE38: Wash 6G 113
Alwin Grange NE31: Heb 2D 72
Alwinton Av. NE29: N Shi 5H 47

Alwinton Cl. NE5: Newc T 3E 55
NE24: Cow 5A 12
Alwinton Ct. NE24: Cow 5A 12
Alwinton Dr. DH2: Ches S 2A 134
Alwinton Gdns. NE11: Gate 6C 82
Alwinton Rd. NE27: Shir 2E 47
Alwinton Ter. NE3: Gos 2F 57
Alwyn Cl. DH4: Hou S 6C 128
Amalfi Twr. SR3: E Her 1G 131
Amara Sq. SR3: E Her 1G 131
Ambassadors Way
        NE29: N Shi 5F 47
Amber Ct. NE4: Newc T 6B 68
        NE24: Bly 1A 18
Ambergate Cl. NE5: Newc T 4E 55
Amberley Chase NE12: Kil 1E 45
Amberley Cl. NE28: W'snd 3E 61
Amberley Gdns. NE7: Newc T 5C 58
Amberley Gro. NE16: Whi 6E 81
Amberley St. NE8: Gate 2D 82
        SR2: Sund 2E 119
Amberley St. Sth.
        SR2: Sund 2E 119
Amberley Wlk. NE16: Whi 6F 81
Amberley Way NE24: News 2C 18
Amble Av. NE25: Whit B 1D 48
        NE34: S Shi 1B 76
Amble Cl. NE24: Bly 2A 18
        NE29: N Shi 3H 61
Amble Gro. NE2: Newc T 2A 70
Amble Pl. NE12: Longb 4F 45
Ambleside NE15: Thro 5D 52
Ambleside Av. NE34: S Shi 3G 75
        SR7: S'hm 3E 141
Ambleside Cl. NE25: Sea D 6B 24
        SR8: Pet 6E 163
Ambleside Gdns. NE9: Gate 1A 98
Ambleside Grn. NE5: Newc T 1F 67
Ambleside Ter. SR6: Monk 1C 104
Amble Twr. SR3: E Her 1G 131
Amble Way NE3: Gos 1D 56
Ambridge Way NE3: Ken 2B 56
        NE25: Sea D 5G 23
Ambrose Ct. NE21: Bla T 2H 79
Ambrose Pl. NE6: Walk 3H 71
Ambrose Rd. SR3: E Her 1F 131
Amec Dr. NE28: W'snd 6D 60
Amec Way NE28: W'snd 6C 60
Amelia Cl. NE4: Newc T 6A 68
Amelia Gdns. SR3: E Her 2E 131
Amelia Wlk. NE4: Newc T 6A 68
        (not continuous)
Amen Cnr. NE1: Newc T 5G 69 (6E 5)
Amersham Cres. SR8: Pet 6D 162
Amersham Pl. NE5: Newc T 5F 55
Amersham Rd. NE24: News 3B 18
Amesbury Cl. NE5: Cha P 4H 53
Amethyst Rd. NE4: Newc T 6B 68
Amethyst St. SR4: Sund 6H 103
AMF Bowling
        Newcastle 4B 68
        Washington 2A 114
Amherst Rd. NE3: Ken 1A 56
Amos Ayre Pl. NE34: S Shi 4B 74
Amphitheatre 4H 63
Amsterdam Rd. SR3: E Her 1G 131
Amusement Pk. Cvn. Site
        NE33: S Shi 3G 63
Amy St. SR5: S'wck 3B 104
Ancaster Av. NE12: Longb 1B 58
Ancaster Rd. NE16: Whi 5D 80
Anchorage Ter.
        DH1: Dur 1D 160 (5C 6)

Anchorage, The DH3: Ches S . . .6D 126
        DH4: Hou S 3F 129
        NE38: Wash 3C 114
Anchor Chare NE1: Newc T 5G 5
Ancona St. SR4: Sund 5H 103
Ancroft Av. NE29: N Shi 6B 48
Ancroft Pl. NE5: Newc T 1F 67
Ancroft Rd. NE25: Sea D 6H 23
Ancroft Way NE3: Ken 5B 42
Ancrum St. NE2: Newc T 2D 68
Ancrum Way NE16: Whi 6D 80
Anderson St. NE33: S Shi 4F 63
Anderson St. Nth.
        NE33: S Shi 4E 63
Andover Pl. NE28: W'snd 1C 60
Andrew Cl. NE6: Walk 3G 71
Andrew Rd. SR3: E Her 2E 131
Andrew's La. SR8: Eas 3A 162
Andrew St. SR8: Eas 1E 163
Anfield Ct. NE3: Ken 2A 56
Anfield Rd. NE3: Ken 2A 56
Angel of the North 5A 98
Angerton Av. NE27: Shir 3D 46
        NE30: N Shi 4C 48
Angerton Gdns. NE5: Newc T 1H 67
Angerton Ter. NE23: Dud 3H 31
Anglesey Gdns. NE5: Cha P 5A 54
Anglesey Pl. NE4: Newc T 4D 68
Anglesey Rd. SR3: E Her 2F 131
Anglesey Sq. SR3: E Her 2F 131
Angle Ter. NE28: W'snd 5D 60
Angram Dr. SR2: Sund 6G 119
Angram Wlk. NE5: Cha P 5A 54
Angrove Gdns. SR4: Sund 2H 117
Angus DH2: Ous 5H 111
Angus Cl. NE12: Kil 2C 44
Angus Rd. NE8: Gate 3E 83
Angus Sq. DH7: B'don 4F 159
        SR3: E Her 2F 131
Angus St. DH7: B'don 3G 159
        SR8: Eas 1E 163
Angus Ter. SR8: Eas 2F 163
Anker's House Mus. 6D 126
Annand Rd. DH1: Dur 4F 155
Anne Dr. NE12: Longb 5G 45
Annfield Pl. DH9: Ann P 5E 121
ANNFIELD PLAIN 6F 121
Annfield Plain By-Pass
        DH9: Ann P 5C 120
Annfield Rd. NE23: Cra 5B 16
Annfield Ter. DH9: Ann P 4E 121
Annie St. SR6: Monk 1D 104
ANNITSFORD 2B 32
Annitsford Dr. NE23: Dud 3B 32
Annitsford Pond Nature Reserve
        .2B 32
Anscomb Gdns. NE7: Newc T 5A 58
Anson Cl. NE33: S Shi 1D 74
Anson Pl. NE5: Newc T 5A 54
Anson St. NE8: Gate 2B 84
Anstead Cl. NE23: Cra 3B 22
Anthony Ct. DH9: Stly 2C 122
Anthony Rd. SR3: E Her 1F 131

Anthony St. DH9: Stly 2C 122
        SR8: Eas 1F 163
Antliff Ter. DH9: Ann P 5F 121
Antonine Wlk. NE15: Hed W 5H 51
Anton Pl. NE23: Cra 4B 22
Antrim Cl. NE5: Newc T 4G 55
Antrim Gdns. SR7: S'hm 3A 142
Antwerp Rd. SR3: E Her 2E 131
Anvil Ct. DH1: Dur 6A 144
Apperley NE5: Newc T 6C 54
Apperley Av. DH1: H Shin 5H 161
        NE3: Ken 3G 55
Appian Pl. NE9: Gate 4B 84
        NE15: Thro 5D 52
        (not continuous)
Appleby Ct. DH4: Hou S 2B 136
        NE12: Longb 1A 58
        NE29: N Shi 2B 62
Appleby Gdns. NE9: Gate 2A 98
        NE28: W'snd 3E 61
Appleby Pk. NE29: N Shi 1B 62
Appleby Pl. NE40: Ryton 5A 64
Appleby Rd. SR3: E Her 2F 131
Appleby Sq. SR3: E Her 2F 131
Appleby St. NE29: N Shi 3C 62
Appleby Way SR8: Pet 4A 164
Apple Cl. NE15: Lem 1A 66
Apple Ct. NE25: Sea D 3B 24
Appledore Gdns.
        DH3: Ches S 4D 126
        NE9: Gate 2H 97
Appledore Rd. NE24: News 2C 18
Appleforth Av. SR2: Sund 6G 119
Appleton Cl. NE11: Gate 3C 82
Appletree Gdns. NE6: Walk 1E 71
        NE25: Whit B 2A 48
Applewood NE12: Kil 2F 45
Appley Ter. SR6: Monk 3E 105
Apsley Cres. NE3: Ken 2A 56
Aquila Dr. NE15: Hed W 5F 51
Arbeia Roman Fort & Mus. 3E 63
Arbroath DH2: Ous 6H 111
Arbroath Rd. SR3: E Her 1F 131
Arcade Pk. NE30: N Shi 6F 49
Arcade, The NE24: Bly 6C 12
        (off Waterloo Rd.)
Arcadia DH2: Ous 6H 111
Arcadia Av. DH3: Ches S 4C 126
Arcadia Ter. NE24: Bly 1C 18
Archbold Ter.
        NE2: Newc T 2G 69 (1F 5)
Archer Rd. SR3: E Her 1F 131
Archer Sq. SR3: E Her 1F 131
Archer St. NE28: W'snd 4B 60
Archer Vs. NE28: W'snd 4B 60
Archery Ri. DH1: Dur 1A 160
Archibald St. NE3: Gos 2E 57
Arcot Av. NE23: Nel V 1G 21
        NE25: Whit B 2A 48
Arcot Dr. NE5: Newc T 1D 66
        NE25: Whit B 2A 48
Arcot La. NE23: Dud, Sea D 1D 30
Arcot Ter. NE24: Bly 5B 12
Ardale Ho. NE3: Ken 3A 56
Arden Av. NE3: Gos 4D 42
Arden Cl. NE28: W'snd 6B 46
Arden Cres. NE5: Newc T 6H 55
Arden Ho. NE3: Gos 1E 57
Arden Sq. SR3: E Her 1G 131
Ardrossan DH2: Ous 6H 111
Ardrossan Rd. SR3: E Her 2F 131
Arena Bus. Pk. DH4: Hou S . . .4G 137

Arena Way NE4: Newc T 6E **69**
Argent St. SR8: Eas 1F **163**
Argus Cl. NE11: Gate 4D **82**
Argyle Ct. DH9: Stly 6E **109**
Argyle Pl. DH6: S Het 5H **149**
  NE29: N Shi 5C **48**
Argyle Sq. SR2: Sund 2C **118** (6F **7**)
Argyle St. NF1: Newc T 4G **69** (4F **5**)
  NE24: Bly 4B **12**
  NE30: N Shi 5F **49**
  NE31: Heb 3B **72**
  SR2: Sund 2C **118** (6F **7**)
Argyle Ter. NE29: N Shi 5C **48**
Argyll DH2: Ous 6H **111**
Arisaig DH2: Ous 6H **111**
Arklecrag NE37: Wash 1A **114**
Arkle Rd. SR3: E Her 2F **131**
Arkleside Pl. NE5: Cha P 6B **54**
Arkle St. NE8: Gate 3E **83**
  NE13: Bru V 1C **42**
Arkwright St. NE8: Gate 4F **83**
Arlington Av. NE3: Ken 4B **56**
Arlington Cl. DH4: Hou S 6C **128**
Arlington Ct. NE3: Ken 4C **56**
Arlington Gro. NE16: Whi 5E **81**
  NE23: Cra 5B **16**
Arlington St. NE31: Heb 5D **72**
Arlington St. SR4: Sund 1H **117**
Arlott Ho. NE29: N Shi 4H **61**
Armitage Gdns. NE9: Spri 4C **98**
ARMSTRONG 6G **99**
Armstrong Av. NE6: Newc T 6B **58**
  NE34: S Shi 3G **75**
Armstrong Bldg. NE1: Newc T 1C **4**
Armstrong Dr. NE12: Kil 3B **44**
Armstrong Ho. NE37: Wash 6G **99**
Armstrong Ind. Est.
  NE37: Wash 6G **99**
Armstrong Ind. Pk.
  NE4: Newc T 6C **68**
    (not continuous)
Armstrong Rd. NF4: Newc T 5H **67**
  NE15: Newc T 4D **66**
  NE28: W'snd 6E **61**
  NE37: Wash 6F **99**
  SR8: Pet 4D **162**
Armstrong St. NE5: Cal 6H **39**
  NF8: Gate 4E **83**
    (not continuous)
Armstrong Ter. NE33: S Shi 2E **75**
Arncliffe Av. SR4: Sund 3G **117**
Arncliffe Gdns. NE5: Cha P 5A **54**
Arndale Arc. NE32: Jar 2F **73**
Arndale Ho. NE3: Ken 2A **56**
  NE12: Longb 1A **58**
Arndale Sq. *NE12: Longb* 1A *58*
    (off Greyfriars La.)
Arnham Gro. SR4: Sund 5B **116**
Arnison Retail Cen. DH1: Dur . . .5B **144**
Arnold Cl. DH9: Stly 3E **123**
Arnold Rd. SR3: E Her 1F **131**
Arnold St. NE35: Bol C 3B **88**
Arnside Wlk. NE5: Cha P 5A **54**
    (not continuous)
Arran Ct. SR3: New S 3A **132**
Arran Dr. NE32: Jar 6A **74**
Arran Gdns. NE10: Gate 4C **84**
Arran Pl. NE29: N Shi 5G **47**
Arras La. SR1: Sund 6E **105**
Arrol Pk. SR4: Sund 1B **118**
Arrow Cl. NE12: Kil 3B **44**
Arthington Way NE34: S Shi 4G **75**
Arthur Av. SR2: Ryh 3G **133**

Arthur Cook Av. NE16: Whi 5G **81**
ARTHURS HILL 3C **68**
Arthur St. DH2: Beam 2C **124**
  DH7: Ush M 5B **152**
  NE8: Gate 1H **83**
  NE24: Bly 5C **12**
    (not continuous)
  NE32: Jar 3F **73**
  SR2: Ryh 3G **133**
  SR6: Whit 5F **77**
Arthur Ter. SR6: Whit 5F **77**
Arun Cl. SR8: Pet 2C **164**
Arundale Ho's. DH3: Bir 3C **112**
Arundel Cl. NE13: Wide O 6C **30**
  NE22: Bed 2C **10**
Arundel Ct. NE3: Ken 6G **41**
  NE12: Longb 1A **58**
Arundel Dr. NE15: Lem 2C **66**
  NE25: Whit B 1F **47**
Arundel Gdns. NE9: Gate 6A **84**
  SR3: E Her 2E **131**
Arundel Rd. SR3: F Her 1F **131**
Arundel Wlk. DH2: Ous 2H **125**
  NE16: Whi 6E **81**
Arundel Way DH7: B'don 5E **159**
Asama Ct. NE4: Newc T 6C **68**
    (not continuous)
Ascot Cl. NE20: W'snd 1B **60**
Ascot Ct. NE3: Ken 6G **41**
  SR3: E Her 2F **131**
    (not continuous)
Ascot Cres. NE8: Gate 3E **83**
Ascot Gdns. NE34: S Shi 2F **75**
Ascot Pl. DH2: Ous 1H **125**
Ascot St. SR8: Eas 1F **163**
Ascott Ct. NE12: Longb 1A **58**
Ascot Wlk. NE3: Ken 6G **41**
Ash Av. DH1: Dur 6G **155**
  DH7: Ush M 5C **152**
  NE13: Din 4F **29**
Ashberry Gro. SR6: Monk 4D **104**
Ashbourne Av. NE6: Walk 3F **71**
Ashbourne Cl. NE27: Back 6A **34**
Ashbourne Rd. NE32: Jar 4G **73**
Ashbrook Cl. DH7: B'don 6B **158**
ASHBROOKE 3C **118**
Ashbrook Cl. NE25: Whit B 6A **36**
Ashbrooke Cl. NE25: Whit B 6A **36**
Ashbrooke Cres. SR2: Sund 3D **118**
Ashbrooke Cross SR2: Sund 4C **118**
Ashbrooke Gdns. NE28: W'snd . . .4C **60**
Ashbrooke Mt. SR2: Sund 3C **118**
Ashbrooke Range SR2: Sund 4C **118**
Ashbrooke Rd. SR2: Sund 3C **118**
Ashbrooke St. NE3: Ken 4A **56**
Ashbrooke Ter. NE36: E Bol 4F **89**
  SR2: Sund 3D **118**
Ashburne Ct. SR2: Sund 3D **118**
Ashburn Rd. NE28: W'snd 1C **60**
Ashburton Rd. NE3: Gos 3C **56**
Ashbury NE25: Whit B 5G **35**
Ashby St. SR2: Sund 4F **119**
Ash Ct. NE29: N Shi 4A **48**
Ash Cres. SR7: S'hm 6A **142**
  SR8: Pet 1G **165**
Ashcroft Dr. NE12: Longb 6E **45**
Ashdale DH4: Pen 1C **128**
  NE20: Pon 2C **38**
Ashdale Ct. SR6: Monk 3E **105**
Ashdale Cres. NE5: Cha P 5B **54**
Ashdown Av. DH1: Dur 4H **155**
Ashdown Cl. NE12: Longb 6B **44**

Ashdown Rd. SR3: E Her 1F **131**
Ashdown Way NE12: Longb 6B **44**
Asher St. NE10: Gate 2C **84**
Ashfield NE32: Jar 2H **87**
Ashfield Av. NE16: Whi 3G **81**
Ashfield Cl. NE4: Newc T 5C **68**
Ashfield Ct. NE39: H Spen 1A **92**
Ashfield Gdns. NE28: W'snd 4F **59**
Ashfield Gro. NE26: Whit B 5C **36**
  NE29: N Shi 1C **62**
Ashfield Lodge NE4: Newc T 5C **68**
Ashfield Pk. NE16: Whi 3F **81**
Ashfield Ri. NE16: Whi 6F **81**
Ashfield Rd. NE3: Gos 3C **56**
  NE16: Whi 6F **81**
Ashfield Ter. DH3: Ches S 1D **134**
  NE9: Spri 4F **99**
  NE10: Gate 2F **85**
  NE40: Ryton 4C **64**
Ashford NE9: Gate 3A **98**
Ashford Cl. NE24: News 2C **18**
  NE29: N Shi 4B **48**
Ashford Gro. NE5: Cha P 3H **53**
Ashford Rd. SR3: E Her 2F **131**
Ashgill NE37: Wash 1H **113**
Ash Gro. NE11: Dun 2A **82**
  NE28: W'snd 6B **60**
  NE40: Ryton 3C **64**
  SR6: Whit 2G **91**
Ashgrove NE34: S Shi 4H **75**
  NE8: Gate 2G **83**
Ashgrove Ter. DH3: Bir 2B **112**
  NE8: Gate 2G **83**
Ash Hill Ct. SR2: Sund 3D **118**
Ashkirk NE23: Dud 3A **32**
  SR3: E Her 1G **131**
Ashkirk Cl. DH2: Ches S 2A **134**
Ashkirk Way NE25: Sea D 1B **34**
Ashlea Cl. SR3: E Her 1F **131**
Ashlea Pk. SR3: E Her 1F **131**
Ashleigh DH2: Ches S 4A **126**
Ashleigh Av. DH1: Dur 2B **154**
Ashleigh Cl. NE21: Bla T 2C **80**
Ashleigh Cres. NE5: Newc T 1C **67**
Ashleigh Gdns. SR6: Cle 1A **90**
Ashleigh Gro. NE2: Newc T 5F **57**
  NE12: Longb 6D **44**
  NE30: N Shi 5E **49**
  SR6: Monk 1E **105**
Ashleigh Rd. NE5: Newc T 1E **67**
Ashleigh Ter. SR6: Monk 1E **105**
Ashleigh Vs. NE36: E Bol 4F **89**
Ashley Cl. NE12: Kil 1F **45**
  NE30: Wash 4C **114**
Ashley Ct. DH9: Tan L 1A **122**
Ashley Rd. NE34: S Shi 3E **75**
Ashley Ter. DH3: Ches S 5C **126**
Ashmead Cl. NE12: Kil 1E **45**
Ash Mdws. NE38: Wash 2E **127**
Ashmore St.
  SR2: Sund 2D **118** (6G **7**)
Ashmore Ter.
  SR2: Sund 2D **118** (6G **7**)
Asholme NE5: Newc T 6C **54**
Ashridge Cl. NE34: S Shi 1B **76**
Ashridge Ct. NE10: Gate 4H **85**
Ash Sq. NE38: Wash 3C **114**
Ash St. NE21: Bla T 2A **80**
Ash Ter. DH9: Ann P 4E **121**
  DH9: Stly 6F **123**
  DH9: Tan L 5H **107**
  NE13: Bru V 6C **30**
  SR7: Mur 2D **150**
Ashton Cl. NE5: Cha P 3H **53**

Ashton Ct. NE40: Ryton 5D **64**
Ashton Downe DH2: Ches S 1C **134**
Ashton Ri. DH2: Ches S 1C **134**
   SR8: Pet 6E **163**
Ashton St. SR8: Eas 1F **163**
Ashton Way NE26: Whit B 4A **36**
   SR3: E Her 3E **131**
Ashtree Cl. NE4: Newc T 5B **68**
   NE39: Row G 2F **93**
Ashtree Dr. NE22: Bed 3H **9**
Ashtree Gdns. NE25: Whit B 2A **48**
Ashtree La. NE21: Bla T 1A **92**
   NE39: H Spen, Row G 1A **92**
Ashtrees Gdns. NE9: Gate 4H **83**
Ashvale Av. NE11: Kib 1E **111**
Ash Way DH4: Hou S 2E **137**
Ashwell Rd. SR3: E Her 2F **131**
Ashwood *DH3: Ches S* *1D* **134**
   (off George St.)
   DH6: S Het 6A **150**
Ashwood Av. SR5: S'wck 3H **103**
Ashwood Cl. NE12: Longb 5E **45**
   NE23: Cra 5B **16**
Ashwood Cres. NE6: Walk 6F **59**
Ashwood Cft. NE31: Heb 2B **72**
Ashwood Gdns. NE9: Gate 2A **98**
Ashwood Gro. NE13: Wide O 6D **30**
   SR5: C'twn 4D **102**
Ashwood Ho. NE7: Newc T 3A **58**
Ashwood St. SR2: Sund 2B **118**
Ashwood Ter. SR2: Sund 2B **118**
Askern Av. SR2: Sund 6G **119**
Askerton Dr. SR8: Pet 4A **164**
Askew Rd. NE8: Gate 3D **82**
   (Derwentwater Rd.)
   NE8: Gate 1F **83**
   (St Cuthbert's Rd.)
Askew Rd. W. NE8: Gate 2E **83**
   (not continuous)
Askrigg Av. NE28: W'snd 6B **46**
   SR2: Sund 6F **119**
Askrigg Cl. DH2: Ous 5G **111**
Askrigg Wlk. NE5: Cha P 6A **54**
Aspen Av. SR8: Pet 1H **165**
Aspen Cl. DH1: Dur 4G **155**
   DH4: Hou S 4D **128**
Aspen Ct. DH3: Gt Lum 4G **135**
   SR3: New S 3G **131**
Aspenlaw NE9: Gate 1C **98**
Aspen Ter. NE5: Newc T 6A **56**
Aspen Way NE24: News 3A **18**
Aspley Cl. SR3: New S 3A **132**
Asquith Ter. DH9: Ann P 4E **121**
Association Rd.
   SR6: Monk 3E **105**
Astbury Cl. NE38: Wash 1H **127**
Aster Pl. NE4: Newc T 2G **67**
Aster Ter. DH4: Hou S 5F **129**
Astley Ct. NE12: Kil 2D **44**
Astley Dr. NE26: Whit B 2A **36**
Astley Gdns. NE25: Sea D 6A **24**
Astley Gro. NE26: Sea S 2F **25**
Astley Rd. NE25: Sea D 5A **24**
Astley Vs. NE23: E Har 4B **16**
Astley Vs. NE26: Sea S 2F **25**
Aston Sq. SR3: E Her 2F **131**
Aston St. NE33: S Shi 2F **75**
Aston Wlk. NE6: Walk 3G **71**
Aston Way NE16: Whi 6D **80**
Astral Ho. SR1: Sund 3G **7**
Athelhampton NE38: Wash 2E **115**
Athelstan Rigg SR2: Ryh 2G **133**

Athenaeum St.
   SR1: Sund 1D **118** (4H **7**)
Atherton Dr. DH4: Hou S 4E **137**
   NE4: Newc T 5A **68**
Atherton St. DH1: Dur 6B **154**
Athlone Ct. NE24: Bly *5C* **12**
   (off Disraeli St.)
Athlone Pl. DH3: Bir 6D **112**
Athol Gdns. NE9: Gate 4B **84**
   NE25: Whit B 2H **47**
   SR2: Ryh 3G **133**
Athol Grn. NE11: Dun 2C **82**
Athol Gro. SR3: New S 2A **132**
Athol Ho. *NE20: Pon* *5F* **27**
   (off Callerton La.)
Atholl DH2: Ous 5H **111**
Athol Pk. SR2: Sund 2E **119**
Athol Rd. SR2: Sund 2E **119**
Athol St. NE11: Dun 2C **82**
Athol Ter. SR2: Sund 2E **119**
Atkinson Gdns. NE29: N Shi 4C **62**
Atkinson Rd. DH3: Ches S 4D **126**
   NE4: Newc T 5H **67**
   SR6: Monk 1D **104**
Atkinson's Bldgs. *SR4: Sund* *6B* **104**
   (off Trimdon St.)
Atkinson St. NE28: W'snd 6H **59**
Atkinson Ter. NE4: Newc T 4H **67**
   NE28: W'snd 6H **59**
Atkin St. NE12: Kil 1B **44**
Atlantis Fitness Cen. *3D* **84**
   (off Coldwell St.)
Atlantis Rd. SR3: E Her 1E **131**
Atlas Gym *5B* **100**
   (off Front St.)
Atley Way NE23: Nel V 5G **15**
Atmel Way NE28: W'snd 6D **46**
Attlee Cl. NE23: Dud 6B **32**
Attlee Gro. SR2: Ryh 1E **133**
Attlee Sq. DH6: Sher 5D **156**
Attwood Gro. SR5: S'wck 4B **104**
Aubone Av. NE15: Newc T 3G **67**
Auburn Cl. NE28: W'snd 5E **61**
Auburn Gdns. NE4: Newc T 1A **68**
Auckland DH2: Ches S 1A **134**
Auckland Av. NE34: S Shi 3B **76**
Auckland Rd. DH1: Dur 6D **144**
   NE31: Heb 2D **72**
Auckland Ter. NE32: Jar 5A **74**
Auden Gro. NE4: Newc T 3A **68**
Audland Wlk. NE5: Cha P 6A **54**
Audley Cl. NE2: Newc T 5H **57**
Audley Gdns. SR3: Sund 4B **118**
Audley Rd. NE3: Gos 3G **57**
Audouins Row NE8: Gate 3F **83**
Augusta Cl. NE13: Bru V 5C **30**
Augusta Ct. NE28: W'snd 1C **60**
Augusta Sq. SR3: E Her 2F **131**
   (not continuous)
Augusta Ter. SR6: Whit 2F **91**
Augustine Cl. DH1: Dur 1A **154**
August Pl. NE33: S Shi 6F **63**
Augustus Dr. NE22: Bed 3G **9**
Austen Av. NE34: S Shi 6D **74**
Austen Pl. DH9: Stly 5F **123**
Austerfield Pk. DH5: Hett H 2D **148**
Austin Sq. SR5: S'wck 3B **104**
Australia Gro. NE34: S Shi 6B **74**
Australia Twr. SR3: E Her 1G **131**
Austral Pl. NE13: Wide O 6C **30**
Austwick Wlk. NE5: Cha P 6A **54**
Auton Cl. DH7: Ush M 4D **152**
Auton Ct. DH7: Ush M 4E **153**

Auton Fld. DH7: Ush M 4E **153**
Auton Fld. Ter. DH7: Ush M 4E **153**
Auton Stile DH7: Ush M 4D **152**
Autumn Cl. NE38: Wash 1B **114**
Avalon Dr. NE15: Lem 1C **66**
Avalon Rd. SR3: E Her 1F **131**
Avebury Dr. NE38: Wash 2C **114**
Avebury Pl. NE23: Cra 6C **16**
Avenue Cres. NE25: Sea D 5A **24**
Avenue Rd. NE8: Gate 3H **83**
   NE25: Sea D 6A **24**
Avenues, The NE11: Gate 2G **97**
Avenue St. DH1: H Shin 5H **161**
Avenue Ter. NE25: Sea D 6B **24**
   SR2: Sund 3C **118**
Avenue, The DH1: Dur 6A **154**
   (Crossgate Peth)
   DH1: Dur 6A **144**
   (Hudspeth Cres.)
   DH2: Ches S 6B **126**
   DH2: Pelt 2G **125**
   DH3: Bir 3C **112**
   DH3: Lam P 4C **128**
   DH5: Hett H 1D **148**
   DH9: Ann P 6E **121**
   (Chirnside Ter.)
   DH9: Ann P, Dip 2D **120**
   (Fondlyset La.)
   NE9: Gate 4A **84**
   NE10: Gate 2D **84**
   NE21: Bla T 1C **80**
   NE25: Sea D 5B **24**
   NE26: Sea D, Sea S 5B **24**
   NE26: Whit B 6C **36**
   NE28: W'snd 6H **59**
   NE38: Wash 2C **114**
   NE39: Row G 4F **93**
   SR2: Sund 2D **118**
   SR7: Mur 2D **150**
   SR7: S'hm 5F **141**
Avenue Vivian DH4: Hou S 2D **136**
Aviemore Rd. NE36: W Bol 4D **88**
Avison Ct. NE4: Newc T 3D **68**
Avison Pl. NE4: Newc T 3D **68**
Avison St. NE4: Newc T 4D **68**
Avocet Cl. NE24: News 4C **18**
Avolon Ct. NE4: Newc T 3D **68**
Avolon Pl. NE4: Newc T 3D **68**
Avolon Wlk. NE4: Newc T 4D **68**
Avon Av. NE29: N Shi 3A **62**
   NE32: Jar 1G **87**
Avon Cl. NE28: W'snd 1B **60**
   NE39: Row G 2F **93**
Avon Ct. NE25: Sea D 3B **24**
Avon Cres. DH4: Hou S 4E **137**
Avoncroft Cl.
   SR7: S'hm, Sea 3D **140**
Avondale SR4: Sund 2C **116**
Avondale Av. DH4: Pen 2F **129**
   NE12: Longb 5D **44**
   NE24: Cow 5E **11**
Avondale Cl. NE24: Cow 5F **11**
Avondale Ct. NE3: Gos 3F **57**
Avondale Gdns. NE36: W Bol 5C **88**
Avondale Ri. NE6: Newc T 4C **70**
Avondale Rd. NE6: Newc T 4C **70**
   NE20: Pon 2A **38**
Avondale Ter. DH3: Ches S 6C **126**
   NE8: Gate 2G **83**
   NE36: W Bol 4C **88**
Avonlea Way NE5: Newc T 4G **55**
Avonmouth Rd. SR3: E Her 2F **131**
Avonmouth Sq. SR3: E Her 2F **131**

Avon Rd. DH9: Stly 4D **122**
  NE31: Heb 5C **72**
  SR8: Pet 2C **164**
Avon St. NE8: Gate 2A **84**
  SR1: Sund 1F **119**
  SR8: Eas 1E **163**
Avon Ter. NE38: Wash 3C **114**
Awnless Ct. NE34: S Shi 4E **75**
Axbridge Gdns. NE4: Newc T . . .4A **68**
Axminster Cl. NE23: Cra 6C **16**
Axwell Dr. NE24: Cow 6H **11**
AXWELL PARK 2C **80**
Axwell Pk. Cl. NE16: Whi 4E **81**
Axwell Pk. Rd. NE21: Bla T 2C **80**
Axwell Pk. School Ho's.
  NE21: Bla T 2C **80**
Axwell Pk. Vw. NE15: Newc T . . .4F **67**
Axwell Ter. NE16: Swa 2E **81**
Axwell Vw. NE16: Whi 4E **81**
  NE21: Bla T 2A **80**
Aycliffe Av. NE9: Gate 1D **98**
Aycliffe Cres. NE9: Gate 1D **98**
Aycliffe Pl. NE9: Gate 1E **99**
Aydon Gdns. NE12: Longb 1H **57**
Aydon Gro. NE32: Jar 6F **73**
Aydon Ho. NE3: E Her 2G **131**
Aydon Rd. NE30: N Shi 4E **49**
Aydon Wlk. NE5: Newc T 6C **54**
Aykley Ct. DH1: Dur 3A **154**
Aykley Grn. DH1: Dur 3A **154**
Aykley Heads Bus. Cen.
  DH1: Dur 3B **154**
Aykley Heads Sports Cen. 3C **154**
Aykley Rd. DH1: Dur 1B **154**
Aykley Va. DH1: Dur 2A **154**
Aylesbury Dr. SR3: New S 4A **132**
Aylesbury Pl. NE12: Longb 6B **44**
Aylesford Sq. NE24: News 2C **18**
Aylsham Cl. NE5: Cha P 3H **53**
Aylsham Ct. SR3: New S 5A **132**
Aylward Pl. DH9: Stly 4F **123**
Aylyth Pl. NE3: Ken 4B **56**
Ayr Dr. NE32: Jar 6H **73**
AYRE'S QUAY 5B **104**
Ayre's Quay Rd.
  SR1: Sund 6C **104** (3F **7**)
Ayre's Ter. NE29: N Shi 1C **62**
Ayrey Av. NE34: S Shi 5B **74**
Aysgarth Av. NE28: W'snd 6B **46**
  SR2: Sund 5F **119**
Aysgarth Grn. NE3: Ken 3B **56**
AYTON .4F **113**
Ayton Av. SR2: Sund 6F **119**
Ayton Cl. NE5: Newc T 4C **54**
Ayton Ct. NE22: Bed 3F **9**
Ayton Ri. NE6: Newc T 4C **70**
Ayton Rd. NE38: Wash 3F **113**
Ayton St. NE6: Newc T 4C **70**
Azalea Av. SR2: Sund 2C **118**
Azalea Ter. SR8: Pet 1H **165**
Azalea Ter. Nth.
  SR2: Sund 2C **118** (6F **7**)
Azalea Ter. Sth.
  SR2: Sund 2C **118** (6F **7**)
Azalea Way NE15: Thro 1E **65**

B

Bk. Albion Rd. NE30: N Shi 1C **62**
Bk. Albion St. SR4: Sund 1C **116**
Bk. Beach Rd. NE33: S Shi 5F **63**
Bk. Beaumont Ter NE3: Gos 2F **57**

Bk. Bridge St. SR1: Sund 3G **7**
Bk. Chapman St. NE6: Walk 2C **70**
Bk. Croft Rd. NE24: Bly 6C **12**
Bk. Ecclestone Rd.
  NE33: S Shi 6G **63**
             (off Mowbray Rd.)
Bk. Frederick St. Nth.
  DH7: B'don 6E **159**
                (Leesfield Dr.)
  DH7: B'don 5C **158**
            (St Brandon's Gro.)
Bk. Frederick St. Sth.
  DH7: B'don 6E **159**
Bk. George St. NE4: Newc T 5E **69**
Bk. Goldspink La. NE2: Newc T . .1H **69**
Bk. Hawthorn Rd. W.
  NE3: Gos 3E **57**
Bk. Heaton Pk. Rd.
  NE6: Newc T 3B **70**
Bk. High St. NE3: Gos 3C **57**
Bk. Hylton Rd. SR4: Sund 6B **104**
Bk. John St. Nth. DH7: B'don . . .5F **159**
Back La. DH3: Gt Lum 2G **135**
  DH4: Pen 1F **129**
  NE21: Bla T 1H **79**
  NE25: Whit B 6A **36**
Bk. Lodge Ter. SR1: Sund 1F **119**
Bk. Loud Ter. DH9: Ann P 5D **120**
Bk. Maling St. NE6: Newc T 4A **70**
               (off Maling St.)
Bk. Mitford St. NE4: Newc T 6D **68**
Bk. Mount Joy
  DH1: Dur 1D **160** (6D **6**)
Bk. New Bri. St.
  NE1: Newc T 3H **69** (3G **5**)
Bk. North Bri. St. SR5: Monk . . .5D **104**
Bk. Nth. Railway St.
  SR7: S'hm 3B **142**
Bk. North Ter. SR7: S'hm 3B **142**
Bk. Percy Gdns. NE30: N Shi . . .5F **49**
Bk. Prudhoe Ter. NE30: N Shi . . .5F **49**
           (off Percy Pk. Rd.)
Bk. Prudoe St. NE29: N Shi 2C **62**
Bk. Rothesay Ter. NE22: Bed . . .3B **10**
Back Row NE16: Whi 4E **81**
Bk. Ryhope St. SR2: Ryh 2E **133**
Bk. St George's Ter.
  NE2: Newc T 6G **57**
Bk. Seaburn Ter. SR6: Monk 1E **92**
Bk. Shipley Rd. NE30: N Shi 6F **49**
Bk. Silver St. DH1: Dur 2B **6**
Bk. Sth. Railway St.
  SR7: S'hm 4B **142**
Bk. Stephen St. NE6: Newc T . . .3A **70**
Back St. NE21: Bla T 2H **79**
Bk. Victoria Ter. DH9: Ann P 4F **121**
Backview Ct. SR5: S'wck 2C **104**
Bk. Western Hill DH1: Dur 4B **154**
Bk. Westoe Rd. NE33: S Shi 5F **63**
            (off Halstead Pl.)
Bk. Woodbine St. NE8: Gate 2G **83**
BACKWORTH 6A **34**
Backworth Bus. Pk.
  NE27: Back 1A **46**
Backworth La. NE27: Seg 2F **33**
Backworth Ter. NE27: Shir 4B **46**
               (off West St.)
Backworth Workshops
  NE27: Back 1A **46**
Baden Cres. SR5: C'twn 2C **102**
Baden Powell St. NE9: Gate 4A **84**
Baden St. DH3: Ches S 1C **134**
Bader Ct. NE24: Bly 1D **18**

Badger Cl. SR3: New S 4A **132**
Badger M. NE9: Spri 3F **99**
Badgers Wood DH9: Stly 6E **109**
Badminton Cl. NE35: Bol C 2H **87**
Baffin Ct. SR3: New S 3H **131**
Baildon Cl. NE28: W'snd 3A **60**
Bailey Ct. DH1: Dur 3B **6**
Bailey Ind. Est. NE32: Jar 1F **73**
Bailey Ri. SR8: Pet 5D **162**
Bailey Sq. SR5: C'twn 1C **102**
Bailey St. DH9: Tan L 5H **107**
Bailey Way DH5: Hett H 4D **140**
Bainbridge Av. NE34: S Shi 5B **74**
  SR3: Sund 4B **118**
Bainbridge Bldgs. NE9: Spri 3C **98**
Bainbridge Holme Cl.
  SR3: Sund 4B **118**
Bainbridge Holme Rd.
  SR3: Sund 4C **118**
Bainbridge St. DH1: Carr 2B **156**
Bainford Av. NE15: Newc T 3E **67**
Baird Av. NE28: W'snd 5G **61**
Baird Cl. NE37: Usw 3C **100**
Baird Ct. NE10: Gate 2C **84**
Baird St. SR5: C'twn 2C **102**
Bakehouse La.
  DH1: Dur 5D **154** (2D **6**)
Baker Gdns. NE10: Gate 3H **85**
  NE11: Dun 2B **82**
Baker Rd. NE23: Nel V 6F **15**
Baker Sq. SR5: C'twn 2C **102**
Baker St. DH5: Hou S 2A **138**
  SR5: C'twn 2C **102**
Bakewell Ter. NE6: Walk 5D **70**
Baldersdale Gdns. SR3: Sund . . .5B **118**
Baldwin Av. NE4: Newc T 2B **68**
  NE36: E Bol 4G **89**
Baldwin St. SR8: Eas 1F **163**
Balfour Rd. NE15: Newc T 4E **67**
             (not continuous)
Balfour St. DH5: Hou S 2A **138**
  NE8: Gate 2F **83**
  NE24: Bly 4B **12**
Balgonie Cotts. NE40: Ryton . . .4C **64**
Baliol Sq. DH1: Dur 2A **160**
Balkwell Av. NE29: N Shi 1H **61**
Balkwell Grn. NE29: N Shi 1A **62**
Ballast Hill NE24: Bly 5D **12**
Ballast Hill Rd. NE29: N Shi 4C **62**
Ballater Cl. DH9: Stly 3F **123**
Balliol Av. NE12: Longb 4C **44**
Balliol Bus. Pk. NE12: Longb . . .5A **44**
             (not continuous)
Balliol Cl. SR8: Pet 2B **164**
Balliol Gdns. NE7: Longb 2B **58**
Ballston Cl. NE38: Wash 4C **114**
Balmain Rd. NE3: Ken 3A **56**
Balmlaw NE9: Gate 1D **98**
Balmoral DH3: Gt Lum 3G **135**
Balmoral Av. NE3: Gos 3G **57**
  NE32: Jar 6A **74**
Balmoral Cl. NE22: Bed 3C **10**
Balmoral Ct. SR5: C'twn 2C **102**
Balmoral Cres. DH5: Hou S 4B **138**
Balmoral Dr. NE10: Gate 3C **84**
  SR8: Pet 4A **164**
Balmoral Gdns. NE26: Whit B . . .5B **36**
  NE29: N Shi 6B **48**
Balmoral St. NE28: W'snd 5H **59**
Balmoral Ter. NE3: Gos 3G **57**
  NE6: Newc T 2B **70**
  SR2: Sund 5F **119**
  SR3: E Her 2E **131**

Balmoral Way NE10: Gate 4C **84**
  NE24: News 3A **18**
Balroy Ct. NE12: Longb 6E **45**
Baltic Bus. Cen. NE8: Gate 6B **70**
Baltic Cen. for Contemporary Art
  ....5H **69** (6H **5**)
Baltic Ind. Pk. NE29: N Shi 4A **62**
Baltic Quay
  NE8: Gate 5H **69** (6H **5**)
Baltic Rd. NE10: Gate 6D **70**
Baltimore Av. SR5: C'twn 2A **102**
Baltimore Ct. NE37: Wash 5A **100**
Baltimore Sq. SR5: C'twn 2B **102**
  (not continuous)
Bamborough Ct. NE23: Dud 3A **32**
Bamborough Ter. NE30: N Shi ...6C **48**
Bambro St. SR2: Sund 2E **119**
Bamburgh Av. NE33: S Shi 6H **63**
  NE34: S Shi 6H **63**
  SR8: Pet 5F **163**
Bamburgh Cl. NE24: Bly 6A **12**
  NE38: Wash 2G **113**
Bamburgh Ct. NE4: Newc T 6A **68**
  NE7: Newc T 2H **57**
  NE11: Gate 4E **83**
Bamburgh Cres. DH4: Hou S ...4F **129**
  NE27: Shir 2D **46**
Bamburgh Dr. NE10: Gate 1H **85**
  NE28: W'snd 5D **60**
Bamburgh Gdns. SR3: Sund 4B **118**
Bamburgh Gro. NE32: Jar 6E **73**
  NE34: S Shi 1B **76**
Bamburgh Ho. NE5: Newc T 4C **54**
Bamburgh Rd. DH1: Dur 6C **144**
  NE5: Newc T 4C **54**
  NE12: Longb 5F **45**
Bamburgh Ter. NE6: Newc T ...3C **70**
Bamburgh Wlk. NE3: Gos 1C **56**
Bamford Ter. NE12: Longb 4F **45**
Bamford Wlk. NE34: S Shi 4A **75**
Bampton Av. SR6: Monk 6C **90**
Banbury NE37: Usw 5C **100**
Banbury Av. SR5: C'twn 1C **102**
Banbury Gdns. NE28: W'snd 2B **60**
Banbury Rd. NE3: Ken 2B **56**
Banbury Ter. NE33: S Shi 1F **75**
  NE34: S Shi 2F **75**
Banbury Way NE24: News 2C **18**
  NE29: N Shi 3H **61**
Bancroft Ter. SR4: Sund 1H **117**
Banesley La. NE11: Gate, Kib ...5C **96**
Banff St. SR5: C'twn 1C **102**
Bangor Sq. NE32: Jar 2E **87**
Bank Av. NE16: Whi 4E **81**
Bank Cotts. NE22: E Sle 2F **11**
Bank Ct. NE21: Bla T 5D **66**
  NE30: N Shi 2D **62**
Bankdale Gdns. NE24: Cow 6G **11**
Bank Foot DH1: H Shin 3G **161**
Bank Foot Station (Metro) 1F **55**
Bankhead Rd. NE15: Thro 6F **53**
Bankhead Ter. DH4: Hou S 2E **137**
Banks Bldgs. DH4: Hou S 3G **129**
Banks Holt DH2: Ches S 1A **134**
Bankside Cl. SR2: Ryh 2E **133**
Bankside La. NE34: S Shi 4E **75**
Bankside Rd. NF15: Newc T 4D **66**
Bank, The SR6: Whit 3F **91**
BANK TOP 5C **52**
Bank Top NE25: Well 5E **35**
  NE30: N Shi 2E **49**
  NE40: G'sde 6B **64**
Bank Top Hamlet NE16: Whi 4E **81**

Bannatyne's Health & Squash Club
  ....4H **155**
Bannerman Ter. DH6: Sher 6G **157**
  DH7: Ush M 5B **152**
Bannister Dr. NE12: Longb 5F **45**
Bannockburn NE12: Kil 1C **44**
Barbara St. SR2: Sund 5F **119**
Barbary Cl. DH2: Pelt 2G **125**
Barbary Dr. SR6: Monk 3F **105**
Barbondale Lonnen
  NE5: Cha P 5A **54**
Barbour Av. NE34: S Shi 2A **76**
Barclay Pl. NE5: Newc T 6F **55**
Barclay St. SR6: Monk 5D **104** (1G **7**)
Barcusclose La. DH9: Tan L ...1A **108**
  NE16: Burn 1A **108**
Bardolph Rd. NE29: N Shi 1H **61**
Bardon Cl. NE5: Newc T 3D **54**
Bardon Ct. NE34: S Shi 4G **75**
Bardon Cres. NE25: H'wll 1D **34**
Bardsey Pl. NE12: Longb 6B **44**
Barehirst St. NE33: S Shi 2D **74**
Barents Cl. NE5: Newc T 5D **54**
Baret Rd. NE6: Walk 1E **71**
Barford Cl. NE9: Gate 3A **98**
Barford Dr. DH2: Ches S 2A **134**
Baring St. NE33: S Shi 3E **63**
Barkers Haugh DH1: Dur 4D **154**
Barker St. NE2: Newc T ...3H **69** (2G **5**)
Barking Cres. SR5: C'twn 2B **102**
Barking Sq. SR5: C'twn 2B **102**
Barkwood Rd. NE39: Row G 3C **92**
Barleycorn Pl. SR1: Sund 5H **7**
BARLEY MOW 6D **112**
BARLOW 5C **78**
Barlow Cres. NE21: Bla T 5C **78**
Barlow Fell Rd. NE21: Bla T ...6C **78**
Barlowfield Cl. NE21: Bla T 3G **79**
Barlow La. NE21: Bla T 4E **79**
Barlow La. End NE40: G'sde ...2B **78**
Barlow Rd. NE21: Bla T 5C **78**
Barlow Vw. *NE40: G'sde* *2B 78*
  (off Dyke Heads La.)
BAR MOOR 4B **64**
Barmoor Dr. NE3: Gos 4B **42**
Barmoor La. NE40: Ryton 4B **64**
Barmoor Ter. NE40: Ryton 4A **64**
Barmouth Cl. NE28: W'snd 2B **60**
Barmouth Rd. NE29: N Shi 2G **61**
BARMSTON 1D **114**
Barmston Cen. NE38: Wash 1D **114**
Barmston Cl. NE38: Wash 3D **114**
Barmston Ct. NE38: Wash 3D **114**
Barmston Ferry NE38: Wash ...4F **115**
Barmston La. NE37: Wash 4E **101**
  NE38: Wash 3F **115**
  (not continuous)
  SR5: Wash 6F **101**
Barmston Mere Training Cen.
  SR5: Wash 6F **101**
Barmston Rd. NE38: Wash 3E **115**
Barmston Way NE38: Wash 1D **114**
  (not continuous)
Barnabas Pl. SR2: Sund 2F **119**
Barnard Cl. DH1: Dur 6D **144**
  NE22: Bed 4G **9**
Barnard Ct. DH4: Hou S 2B **136**
Barnard Cres. NE31: Heb 2G **72**
Barnard Grn. NE3: Ken 6A **42**
Barnard Gro. NE32: Jar 5H **73**
Barnard Pk. DH5: Hett H 1C **148**
Barnard St. NE24: Bly 6C **12**
  SR4: Sund 2H **117**

Barnard Wynd SR8: Pet 4B **164**
Barnesbury Rd. NE4: Newc T ...4A **68**
Barnes Ct. SR4: Sund 2H **117**
Barnes Pk. Rd. SR4: Sund 3A **118**
Barnes Rd. NE33: S Shi 2D **74**
  SR7: Mur 2B **150**
Barnes St. DH5: Hett H 1C **148**
Barnes Vw. SR4: Sund 3H **117**
Barnett Ct. SR5: S'wck 3B **104**
Barn Hill DH9: Stly 2C **122**
Barn Hollows SR7: Eas 5H **151**
Barningham NE38: Wash 2E **115**
Barningham Cl. SR3: Sund 5B **118**
Barns Cl. NE32: Jar 5E **73**
Barnstaple Cl. NE28: W'snd ...2A **60**
Barnstaple Rd. NE29: N Shi ...4G **47**
Barns, The DH9: Stly 1C **122**
Barnton Rd. NE10: Gate 5E **85**
BARNWELL 1F **129**
Barnwood Cl. NE28: W'snd 2A **60**
Baroness Dr. NE15: Newc T ...2E **67**
Barons Quay Rd. SR5: C'twn ...5D **102**
Baronswood NE3: Gos 3D **56**
Barrack Cl. NE4: Newc T ..3E **69** (3A **4**)
Barrack Rd.
  NE2: Newc T 2C **68** (3A **4**)
  NE4: Newc T 3E **69**
Barrack Row DH4: Hou S 3E **129**
Barrack St. SR1: Sund 5F **105**
Barrack Ter. NE11: Kib 1F **111**
Barras Av. NE23: Dud 2B **32**
  NE23: Seg 2E **33**
  NE24: News 2B **18**
Barras Av. W. NE24: News 3B **18**
Barras Bri. NE1: Newc T ..3F **69** (2D **4**)
Barras Dr. SR3: Sund 4B **118**
Barrasford Cl. NE3: Gos 3C **56**
Barrasford Dr. NE13: Wide O ...6E **31**
Barrasford Rd. DH1: Dur 1D **154**
  NE23: Cra 4C **22**
Barrasford St. NE28: W'snd ...6G **61**
Barras Gdns. NE23: Dud 2B **32**
Barras M. NE23: Seg 2F **33**
Barr Cl. NE28: W'snd 2C **60**
Barrie Sq. SR5: S'wck 3B **104**
Barrington Av. NE30: N Shi ...3B **48**
Barrington Ct. DH5: Hett H 1C **148**
  NE22: Bed 5A **10**
Barrington Dr. NE38: Wash 2B **114**
Barrington Ind. Est. NE22: Bed ...1A **10**
Barrington Pk. NE22: E Sle 2F **11**
Barrington Pl. NE4: Newc T ...3D **68**
  NE8: Gate 1F **83**
  (Chester Pl.)
  NE8: Gate *1G 83*
  (off Bensham Rd.)
Barrington Rd.
  NE22: Bed, Sco G 1H **9**
Barrington St. NE33: S Shi 4E **63**
Barron St. Sth. SR5: C'twn 4E **103**
Barrowburn Pl. NE23: Seg 2G **33**
Barrow St. SR5: C'twn 1B **102**
Barry St. NE8: Gate 4F **83**
  NE11: Dun 2B **82**
Barsloan Gro. SR8: Pet 5B **162**
Barton Cl. NE28: W'snd 2B **60**
  NE30: N Shi 4D **48**
  NE37: Usw 3D **100**
Barton Ct. SR6: Monk 6C **90**
Barton Pk. SR2: Ryh 2D **132**
Bartram Gdns. NE8: Gate 4G **83**
Bartram St. SR5: Monk 2C **104**
Barwell Cl. NE28: W'snd 2B **60**

Barwell Ct. NE7: Newc T 5E 59
Barwick St. SR7: Mur 4D 150
SR8: Eas 1F 163
Basildon Gdns. NE28: W'snd 2A 60
Basil Way NE34: S Shi 6G 75
Basingstoke Pl. NE12: Longb 6C 44
Basingstoke Rd. SR8: Pet 6C 162
Baslow Gdns. SR3: Sund 4B 118
Bassenfell Ct. NE37: Wash 1H 113
Bassenthwaite Av.
DH2: Ches S 2B 134
Bassington Av. NE23: Cra 2G 21
Bassington Cl. NE4: Newc T 3D 68
Bassington Dr. NE23: Cra 1F 21
Bassington Ind. Est.
NE23: Cra 2G 21
Bassington La. NE23: Cra 1F 21
Bates Ho's. NE21: Bla T 2D 80
Bates La. NE21: Bla T 1D 80
Batey St. DH9: Ann P 4E 121
Bath Cl. NE28: W'snd 2C 60
Bathgate Av. SR5: C'twn 1B 102
Bathgate Cl. NE28: W'snd 2C 60
Bathgate Sq. SR5: C'twn 2B 102
Bath La. NE4: Newc T 4E 69 (4A 4)
NE24: Bly 6D 12
Bath La. Ter.
NE4: Newc T 4F 69 (4A 4)
Bath Rd. NE10: Gate 1D 84
NE31: Heb 6C 72
Bath Sq. NE32: Jar 2E 87
Bath St. NE6: Walk 3H 71
Bath St. Ind. Est. NE6: Walk 3H 71
Bath Ter. NE3: Gos 2F 57
NE24: Bly 6D 12
NE30: N Shi 6F 49
SR7: S'hm 3B 142
Batley St. SR5: C'twn 1B 102
BATTLE FIELD 4A 70 (4H 5)
Battle Grn. DH2: Pelt 4G 125
BATTLE HILL 2B 60
Battle Hill Dr. NE28: W'snd 3A 60
Battle Hill Est. NE28: W'snd 1D 60
Baugh Cl. NE37: Wash 6G 99
Baulkham Hills DH4: Pen 3F 129
Bavington NE10: Gate 6G 85
Bavington Dr. NE5: Newc T 6G 55
Bavington Gdns. NE30: N Shi 4C 48
Bavington Rd. NE25: Sea D 6B 24
Bawtry Cl. NF28: W'snd 2A 60
Bawtry Gro. NE29: N Shi 2A 62
Baxter Av. NE4: Newc T 3A 68
SR5: C'twn 1B 102
Baxter Pl. NE25: Sea D 6B 24
Baxter Rd. SR5: C'twn 1B 102
Baxter Sq. SR5: C'twn 1B 102
Baxterwood Ct. NE4: Newc T 3C 68
Baxterwood Gro. NE4: Newc T . . .3C 68
Bay Av. SR8: Pet 1H 165
Baybridge Rd. NE5: Newc T 4C 54
Bay Ct. DH7: Ush M 6D 152
Bayfield Gdns. NE8: Gate 2B 84
Baysdale DH4: Pen 1C 128
Bayswater Av. SR5: C'twn 2C 102
Bayswater Rd. NE2: Newc T 5G 57
NE8: Gate 3B 84
Bayswater Sq. SR5: C'twn 2C 102
Baytree Gdns. NE25: Whit B 2B 48
Baytree Ter. DH2: Beam 2D 124
Baywood Gro. NE28: W'snd 2A 60
Beach Av. NE26: Whit B 6C 36
Beachborough Cl. NE29: N Shi . . .4B 48

Beach Cft. Av. NE30: N Shi 3D 48
Beachcross Rd. SR4: Sund 2B 118
Beach Gro. SR8: Pet 6H 163
Beach Rd. NE29: N Shi 6A 48
NE30: N Shi 5C 48
NE33: S Shi 5F 63
Beach St. SR4: Sund 5B 104
Beachville St. SR4: Sund 2B 118
Beach Way NE30: N Shi 4C 48
Beachway NF24: Bly 3E 19
Beacon Ct. NF9: Gate 6B 84
NE13: Wide O 5C 30
Beacon Dr. NE13: Wide O 5C 30
SR6: Monk 4F 105
Beacon Glade NE34: S Shi 4C 76
Beacon Ho. NE26: Whit B 3B 36
Beacon La. NE23: Cra, Dud 3F 21
BEACON LOUGH 6B 84
Beacon Lough Rd. NE9: Gate . . .1H 97
Beacon M. NE23: Cra 3G 21
Beacon Ri. NE9: Gate 6B 84
Beaconsfield Av. NE9: Gate 6A 84
Beaconsfield Cl. NE25: Whit B 4H 35
Beaconsfield Cres. NE9: Gate 6A 84
Beaconsfield Rd. NE9: Gate 6H 83
Beaconsfield St. DH9: Stly 2D 122
NE4: Newc T 4C 68
NE24: Bly 6D 12
Beaconsfield Ter. DH3: Bir 3D 112
Beacon Shop. Cen.
NE29: N Shi 2D 62
Beaconside NE34: S Shi 3C 76
Beacon St. NE9: Gate 6H 83
NE30: N Shi 1E 63
NE33: S Shi 3E 63
Beadling Gdns. NE4: Newc T 3A 68
Beadnell Av. NE29: N Shi 3H 61
Beadnell Cl. DH2: Ches S 2A 134
NE21: Bla T 3G 79
Beadnell Cl. NE28: W'snd 2C 60
Beadnell Gdns. NE27: Shir 2D 46
Beadnell Pl.
NE2: Newc T 3H 69 (3G 5)
Beadnell Rd. NE24: Bly 2H 17
Beadnell Way NF3: Gos 2C 56
Beagle Sq. SR3: New S 2A 132
Beal Cl. NE24: Bly 6A 12
Beal Dr. NE12: Longb 4F 45
Beal Gdns. NE28: W'snd 2D 60
Beal Grn. NE3: Ken 3G 55
Beal Rd. NE27: Shir 2D 46
Beal Ter. NE6: Walk 5F 71
Beal Wlk. DH1: H Shin 4H 161
Beal Way NE3: Gos 2D 56
Beaminster Way NE3: Ken 2G 55
Beaminster Way E. NE3: Ken 2G 55
BEAMISH 1A 124
Beamishburn Rd.
DH9: Beam, Stly 6E 109
NE16: Sun 3F 109
Beamish Cl. NE28: W'snd 2A 60
Beamish Ct. DH2: Pelt 3E 125
DH9: Stly 3C 122
NE25: Whit B 2A 48
Beamish Gdns. NE9: Gate 1D 98
Beamish Hills DH9: Beam 2H 123
Beamish (North of England
Open Air Mus., The) 5H 109
Beamish Red Row
DH9: Beam 4F 109
Beamish St. DH9: Stly 3C 122
Beamish Vw. DH3: Bir 2D 112
DH9: Stly 2F 123

Beaney La. DH2: Plaw 4A 134
Beanley Av. NE15: Lem 3A 66
(off Shirley St.)
NE31: Heb 5B 72
Beanley Cres. NE30: N Shi 6F 49
Beanley Pl. NE7: Newc T 4A 58
BEARPARK 4D 152
Beatrice Av. NE24: News 3H 17
Beatrice Gdns. NE34: S Shi 3H 75
NE36: E Bol 4F 89
Beatrice Ho. SR2: Sund 6F 7
Beatrice Rd. NE6: Newc T 6R 58
Beatrice St. SR6: Monk 3E 105
Beatrice Ter. DH4: Hou S 3F 129
DH4: Pen 6C 114
Beattie St. NE34: S Shi 4D 74
Beatty Av. NE2: Gos 4G 57
SR5: C'twn 2B 102
Beatty Rd. NE22: Bed 5B 10
Beatty St. SR8: Eas 1F 163
Beaufort Cl. DH4: Hou S 4F 129
NE5: Newc T 4H 55
Beaufort Gdns. NE28: W'snd 2B 60
Beaufront Cl. NE10: Gate 5H 85
Beaufront Gdns. NE5: Newc T . . .6G 55
NE8: Gate 2B 84
Beaufront Ter. NE32: Jar 6F 73
NF33: S Shi 1E 75
NE36: W Bol 4D 88
Beauly NE38: Wash 4B 114
Beaumaris DH4: Hou S 6B 128
Beaumaris Ct. NF12: Longb 1A 58
Beaumaris Gdns. SR3: E Her 2E 131
Beaumaris Way NE5: Newc T 3F 55
Beaumont Cl. DH1: Dur 6A 144
Beaumont Ct. NE25: Whit B 5H 35
Beaumont Cres. SR8: Pet 4E 163
Beaumont Dr. NE25: Whit B 4G 35
NE38: Wash 2B 114
Beaumont Ho. NE5: Newc T 5G 55
Beaumont Mnr. NE24: Cow 6F 11
Beaumont Pl. SR8: Pet 1E 165
Beaumont St. NE4: Newc T 6B 68
NE24: Bly 5B 12
NE29: N Shi 2C 62
SR2: Sund 3E 119
SR5: S'wck 2A 104
SR7: S'hm 5B 142
Beaumont Ter. NE3: Gos 2F 57
NE5: Newc T 5D 54
NE13: Bru V 5C 30
NE32: 4E 73
Beaurepaire DH7: Ush M 4C 152
Beaver Cl. DH1: Dur 5C 144
Bebdon Ct. NE24: Bly 2A 18
BEBSIDE 6D 10
Bebside Furnace Rd.
NE24: Cow 4D 10
Bebside Rd. NE24: Cow 6C 10
Beckenham Av. NE36: E Bol 3F 89
Beckenham Cl. NE36: E Bol 3G 89
Beckenham Gdns.
NE28: W'snd 3A 60
Beckett St. NE8: Gate 5A 70
Beckfoot Cl. NE5: Newc T 6F 55
Beckford NE38: Wash 3E 115
Beckford Cl. NE28: W'snd 2A 60
Beck Pl. SR8: Pet 6D 162
Beckside Gdns. NE5: Cha P 6H 53
Beckwith Rd. SR3: E Her 1E 131
Beda Hill NE21: Bla T 6A 66
Bedale Cl. DH1: Carr 3B 156
NE28: W'snd 2A 60

Bedale Ct. NE9: Gate 3B **98**
   NE34: S Shi 4C **74**
Bedale Cres. SR5: C'twn 2C **102**
Bedale Dr. NE25: Whit B 2B **48**
Bedale Grn. NE5: Newc T 4H **55**
Bedale St. DH5: Hett H 3C **148**
Bedburn NE38: Wash 6F **113**
Bedburn Av. SR5: C'twn 3E **103**
Bede Av. DH1: Dur 6G **155**
   (not continuous)
Bedeburn Foot NE5: Newc T 2D **54**
Bedeburn Rd. NE5: Newc T 3D **54**
Bede Burn Vw. NE32: Jar 4F **73**
Bede Cl. DH9: Stly 2F **123**
   NE12: Longb 5A **46**
Bede Ct. DH3: Ches S 6C **126**
   NE8: Gate 1A **84**
   NE30: N Shi 2E **49**
Bede Cres. NE28: W'snd 3B **60**
   NE38: Wash 1A **114**
Bede Gallery 5F **73**
Bede Ho. NE8: Gate 1H **83**
   SR3: E Her *2F* ***131***
   (off Castle Grn.)
Bede Ind. Est. NE32: Jar 3A **74**
Bede Pct. NE32: Jar 2F **73**
Bede Station (Metro) 3A **74**
Bede St. SR6: Monk 3E **105**
   SR8: Eas 1F **163**
Bedesway NE32: Jar 3A **74**
Bede's World Mus. 2H **73**
Bede Ter. DH2: Ches S 6B **126**
   NE32: Jar 4G **73**
   NE36: E Bol 4F **89**
Bede Twr. SR2: Sund 2D **118** (6H **7**)
Bede Trad. Est. NE32: Jar 3A **74**
Bede Wlk. NE3: Gos 2G **57**
   NE31: Heb 4D **72**
Bede Way DH1: Dur 1C **154**
Bedeway SR8: Pet 1D **164**
Bedewell Ind. Pk. NE31: Heb 4E **73**
Bedford Av. DH3: Bir 1C **126**
   (not continuous)
   NE28: W'snd 4G **59**
   NE33: S Shi 6E **63**
Bedford Ct. NE30: N Shi 2D **62**
Bedford Ho. *NE29: N Shi* *2D* ***62***
   (off Saville St.)
Bedford Pl. NE5: Cha P 6A **54**
   NE8: Gate 1G **83**
   SR3: New S 1A **132**
   SR8: Pet 5C **162**
Bedfordshire Dr. DH1: Carr 4B **156**
Bedford St. DH5: Hett H 1B **148**
   NE29: N Shi 1C **62**
   SR1: Sund 6D **104** (2H **7**)
Bedford Ter. *NE29: N Shi* *2C* ***62***
   (off Bedford St.)
Bedford Way NE29: N Shi 2D **62**
BEDLINGTON 5H **9**
Bedlington Bank NE22: Bed 5A **10**
Bedlington Country Pk. 1B **16**
BEDLINGTON STATION 3C **10**
Bedson Bldg. NE1: Newc T 1C **4**
Beech Av. DH4: Hou S 2H **137**
   NE3: Ken 1B **56**
   NE13: Din 4F **29**
   NE16: Whi 3G **81**
   NE23: E Cram 4D **22**
   SR6: Whit 2F **91**
   SR7: Mur 2D **150**
Beechbrooke SR2: Ryh 3F **133**

Beechburn Wlk. NE4: Newc T 4D **68**
Beech Cl. DH1: Bras 5E **145**
   NE3: Gos 4F **43**
Beech Ct. NE20: Pon 4A **38**
   NE29: N Shi 1B **62**
   (Cedar Ct.)
   NE29: N Shi 1B **62**
   (Chase, The)
Beech Cres. SR7: S'hm 5A **142**
Beech Crest DH1: Dur 6B **154**
Beechcroft NE3: Gos 5D **56**
   NE37: Usw 3H **99**
Beechcroft Av. DH7: B'don 6B **158**
   NE3: Ken 4C **56**
Beechcroft Cl. DH1: Dur 4G **155**
Beechdale Rd. DH1: Carr 3B **156**
Beech Dr. NE11: Dun 2A **82**
Beecher St. NE24: Cow 5H **11**
Beeches, The NE4: Newc T 6C **68**
   NE12: Longb 1D **58**
   NE20: Pon 5D **26**
Beechfield Gdns. NE28: W'snd 4G **59**
Beechfield Rd. NE3: Gos 3D **56**
Beech Gdns. NE9: Gate 5H **83**
Beech Gro. DH7: Ush M 6D **152**
   DH9: Dip 2C **120**
   NE9: Spri 4F **99**
   NE12: Longb 1C **58**
   NE22: Bed 4A **10**
   NE26: Whit B 6B **36**
   NE28: W'snd 5H **59**
   NE34: S Shi 5H **75**
Beech Gro. Ct. NE40: Ryton 5A **64**
Beechgrove La. DH9: Edm 6B **124**
Beech Gro. Rd. NE4: Newc T 5C **68**
Beech Gro. Ter. NE40: Ryton 5A **64**
Beech Gro. Ter. Sth.
   NE40: Ryton 5A **64**
Beech M. NE3: Ken 5B **42**
Beecholm Ct. SR2: Sund 4D **118**
Beech Pk. DH7: B'don 6C **158**
Beech Rd. DH1: Dur 2B **154**
   DH6: Sher 5D **156**
Beech Sq. NE38: Wash 3C **114**
Beech St. NE4: Newc T 4A **68**
   NE8: Gate 2B **84**
   NE16: Sun 3F **95**
   NE32: Jar 2E **73**
Beech Ter. DH9: Ann P 4E **121**
   DH9: Stly 5C **122**
   (Hustledown Rd.)
   DH9: Stly 6F **123**
   (Oak Ter.)
   NE16: Burn 1A **108**
   NE21: Bla T 1A **80**
   SR8: Pet 1G **165**
Beech Way NE12: Kil 1C **44**
Beechway NE10: Gate 6F **85**
Beechways DH1: Dur 4H **153**
Beechwood NE39: H Spen 2A **92**
Beechwood Av. NE3: Gos 1G **57**
   NE9: Gate 2A **98**
   NE25: Whit B 1H **47**
   NE40: Ryton 4C **64**
Beechwood Cl. NE32: Jar 3H **73**
Beechwood Cres. SR5: S'wck 2H **103**
Beechwood Gdns. NE11: Gate 5D **82**
Beechwood Ho. NE7: Newc T 3A **58**
Beechwood Pl. NE20: Pon 4E **27**
Beechwoods DH2: Ches S 4B **126**
Beechwood St. SR2: Sund 2B **118**
Beechwood Ter. DH4: Hou S 6G **129**
   SR2: Sund 2B **118**

Beehive Workshops DH1: Dur . . .5H **155**
Beeston Av. SR5: C'twn 2B **102**
Beetham Cres. NE5: Newc T 1E **67**
Beethoven St. NE33: S Shi 5F **63**
Begonia Cl. NE31: Heb 6C **72**
Bek Rd. DH1: Dur 1C **154**
Beldene Dr. SR4: Sund 3G **117**
Belford Av. NE27: Shir 2D **46**
Belford Cl. NE28: W'snd 2B **60**
   SR2: Sund 4D **118**
Belford Ct. NE24: Cow 6H **11**
Belford Gdns. NE11: Gate 6C **82**
Belford Rd. SR2: Sund 4E **119**
Belford St. SR8: Pet 4F **163**
Belford Ter. NE6: Walk 4E **71**
   NE30: N Shi 6C **48**
Belford Ter. E. SR2: Sund 4E **119**
Belfry, The DH4: Hou S 5E **129**
Belgrade Cres. SR5: C'twn 1B **102**
Belgrade Sq. SR5: C'twn 2B **102**
Belgrave Ct. NE10: Gate 3D **84**
Belgrave Cres. NE24: Bly 1D **18**
Belgrave Gdns. NE34: S Shi 3H **75**
Belgrave Pde. NE4: Newc T 5D **68**
Belgrave Ter. NE10: Gate 3D **84**
   NE33: S Shi 4F **63**
Bellamy Cres. SR5: C'twn 2B **102**
Bellburn Ct. NE23: Cra 1D **22**
Belle Gro. Pl. NE2: Newc T 2D **68**
Belle Gro. Ter. NE2: Newc T 2D **68**
Belle Gro. Vs. NE2: Newc T 2D **68**
Belle Gro. W. NE2: Newc T 2D **68**
Bellerby Dr. DH2: Ous 4G **111**
Belle St. DH9: Stly 3D **122**
Belle Vw. NE39: H Spen 6A **78**
Belle Vue DH9: Tan L 2C **108**
Belle Vue Av. NE3: Gos 2F **57**
Belle Vue Bank NE9: Gate 6G **83**
Belle Vue Cotts. NE9: Gate 6G **83**
Belle Vue Cres. NE33: S Shi 3D **74**
   SR2: Sund 3C **118**
Bellevue Cres. NE23: Cra 5B **16**
Belle Vue Dr. SR2: Sund 3C **118**
Belle Vue Gro. NE9: Gate 6H **83**
Belle Vue La. NE36: E Bol 5E **89**
Belle Vue Pk. SR2: Sund 3C **118**
Belle Vue Pk. W. SR2: Sund 3C **118**
Belle Vue Rd. SR2: Sund 3C **118**
Belle Vue St. NE30: N Shi 2E **49**
Belle Vue Ter.
   DH1: Dur 4H **155**
   NE9: Gate 6G **83**
   NE9: Spri 4F **99**
   NE22: E Sle 2F **11**
   NE29: N Shi 2C **62**
Belle Vue Vs. NE36: E Bol 4E **89**
Bellfield Av. NE3: Ken 1B **56**
Bellgreen Av. NE3: Gos 4F **43**
Bell Gro. NE12: Kil 1B **44**
Bell Ho. Rd. SR5: S'wck 6A **90**
   (not continuous)
Bellingham Cl. NE28: W'snd 3B **60**
Bellingham Ct. NE3: Ken 2H **55**
Bellingham Dr. NE12: Longb 6F **45**
Bellingham Ho. SR4: Sund 3D **116**
Bellingham Vs. *NE22: Bed* 4A **10**
Bellister Gro. NE5: Newc T 2G **67**
Bellister Pk. SR8: Pet 3E **165**
Bellister Rd. NE29: N Shi 1H **61**
Bell Mdw. DH7: B'don 6C **158**
Belloc Av. NE34: S Shi 6D **74**
Bells Bldgs. DH9: Ann P 4F **121**
BELL'S CLOSE 3C **66**

Bells Cl. NE15: Lem 4C 66
NE24: Cow 5F 11
Bells Cl. Ind. Est. NE15: Lem . . .4C 66
Bell's Cotts. NE40: G'sde 2A 78
Bell's Ct. NE1: Newc T 4G 69 (4E 5)
Bell's Folly DH1: Dur 2A 160
Bellshill Est. NE28: W'snd 1C 60
Bell's Pl. NE22: Bed 5A 10
Bell St. DH4: Pen 1F 129
NE30: N Shi 2D 62
NE31: Heb 3B 72
NE38: Wash 3D 114
SR4: Sund 1H 117
Bell's Ville DH1: Dur 5G 155
Bell Vs. NE20: Pon 5F 27
Bellway Ind. Est. NE12: Longb . . .6F 45
BELMONT 4A 156
Belmont NE10: Gate 6G 85
Belmont Av. NE25: Whit B 1H 47
SR7: Eas 5H 151
Belmont Bus. Pk. DH1: Dur . . .3H 155
Belmont Cl. NE28: W'snd 2B 60
Belmont Cotts. NE5: Newc T 4D 54
Belmont Ind. Est. DH1: Dur 3H 155
Belmont Ri. DH5: Hett H 4C 148
Belmont Rd. DH1: Carr, Dur . . .3G 155
SR4: Sund 2H 117
Belmont St. NE6: Walk 6F 71
Belmont Ter. NE9: Spri 4E 99
Belmont Wlk. NE6: Walk 6F 71
Belmount Av. NE3: Gos 4F 43
Belper Cl. NE28: W'snd 2A 60
Belsay Av. NE13: Bru V 1C 42
NE25: Whit B 1D 48
NE34: S Shi 2A 76
SR8: Pet 5F 163
Belsay Cl. NE28: W'snd 1D 60
Belsay Ct. NE24: Cow 6A 12
Belsay Gdns. NE3: Ken 5B 42
NE11: Gate 6C 82
SR4: Sund 2H 117
Belsay Gro. NE22: Bed 2C 10
Belsay Pl. NE4: Newc T 3C 68
Belsfield Gdns. NE32: Jar 5F 73
Belsize Pl. NE6: Walk 1F 71
Beltingham NE5: Newc T 6C 54
Belvedere NE29: N Shi 6B 48
Belvedere Av. NE25: Whit B 1B 48
Belvedere Ct. NE6: Newc T 2C 70
Belvedere Gdns. NE12: Longb . . .1D 58
Belvedere Ho. NE6: Newc T 3B 70
(off Heaton Wlk.)
Belvedere Parkway NE3: Ken 1H 55
Belvedere Retail Pk. NE3: Ken . . .1H 55
Belvedere Rd.
SR2: Sund 2C 118 (6F 7)
Bemersyde Dr. NE2: Newc T 4G 57
Benbrake Av. NE29: N Shi 4A 48
Bendigo Av. NE34: S Shi 6B 74
Benedict Rd. SR6: Monk 3F 105
Benevente St. SR7: S'hm 5B 142
Benfield Bus. Pk. NE6: Walk 1E 71
Benfield Gro. NE26: Sea S 2F 25
Benfield Rd. NE6: Newc T 5D 58
Benfloot Av. SR5: C'twn 2B 102
Benjamin Rd. NE28: W'snd 4E 61
Bennett Ct. NE15: Lem 3A 66
SR2: Sund 4E 119
Bennett Gdns. NE10: Gate 1D 84
Benridge Bank DH4: W Rai 3E 147
Benridge Pk. NE24: News 4H 17
BENSHAM 2G 83

Bensham Av. NE8: Gate 2F 83
Bensham Ct. NE8: Gate 2F 83
NE34: S Shi 4E 75
Bensham Cres. NE8: Gate 2F 83
Bensham Rd. NE8: Gate 3F 83
Bensham St. NE35: Bol C 2B 88
Bensham Trad. Est. NE8: Gate . . .3E 83
Benson Pl. NE6: Newc T 3C 70
Benson Rd. NE6: Walk 3D 70
Benson St. DH3: Ches S 1C 134
DH9: Stly 2C 122
Benson Ter. NE10: Gate 3D 84
Bentall Bus. Pk. NE37: Wash . . .6D 100
Bent Ho. La. DH1: Dur 6H 155
Bentinck Cres. NE4: Newc T 5B 68
Bentinck Pl. NE4: Newc T 5B 68
Bentinck Rd. NE4: Newc T 5B 68
Bentinck St. NE4: Newc T 5B 68
Bentinck Ter. NE4: Newc T 4B 68
Bentinck Vs. NE4: Newc T 4B 68
BENTON 1D 58
Benton Av. SR5: C'twn 1B 102
Benton Bank NE7: Newc T 6A 58
(not continuous)
Benton Cl. NE7: Newc T 2B 58
Benton Hall Wlk. NE7: Newc T . .5D 58
Benton La. NE12: Longb 4B 44
(not continuous)
Benton Lodge Av. NE7: Newc T . .2B 58
Benton Pk. Rd.
NE7: Longb, Newc T 2H 57
Benton Rd. NE7: Newc T 2C 58
NE27: Shir 3B 46
NE34: S Shi 1E 89
BENTON SQUARE 4H 45
Benton Sq. Ind. Est. NE12: Kil . . .4H 45
Benton Station (Metro) 1D 58
Benton Ter. DH9: Stly 2D 122
NE2: Newc T 2H 69 (1G 5)
Benton Vw. NE12: Longb 5D 44
Benton Way NE28: W'snd 6H 59
(Brussels Rd.)
NE28: W'snd 1H 71
(Neptune Rd.)
Bents Cotts. NE33: S Shi 5G 63
Bents Cotts. App. NE33: S Shi . . .5G 63
Bents Pk. Rd. NE33: S Shi 1G 63
Bents, The SR6: Monk 4F 91
Benville Ter. DH7: New B 1A 158
BENWELL 4H 67
Benwell Cl. NE15: Newc T 4H 67
Benwell Dene Ter.
NE15: Newc T 4G 67
Benwell Grange NE15: Newc T . .4H 67
Benwell Grange Av.
NE15: Newc T 4H 67
Benwell Grange Rd.
NE15: Newc T 4G 67
Benwell Grange Ter.
NE15: Newc T 4G 67
Benwell Gro. NE4: Newc T 4A 68
Benwell Hall Dr. NE15: Newc T . .3F 67
Benwell Hill Gdns.
NE6: Newc T 2G 67
Benwell Hill Rd. NE5: Newc T . . .2F 67
Benwell La. NE15: Newc T 4F 67
(not continuous)
Benwell Village NE15: Newc T . . .3F 67
Benwell Village M.
NE15: Newc T 3G 67
Berberis Way NE15: Thro 1E 65
(off Lovaine St.)
Beresford Av. NE31: Heb 6B 72

Beresford Ct. NE26: Sea S 3H 25
Beresford Gdns. NE6: Newc T . . .4C 70
Beresford Pk. SR2: Sund 2B 118
Beresford Rd. NE26: Sea S 3H 25
NE30: N Shi 2C 48
Beresford St. NE11: Dun 2C 82
Bergen Cl. NE29: N Shi 3F 61
Bergen Sq. SR5: C'twn 1B 102
Bergen St. SR5: C'twn 1B 102
Berkdale Rd. NE9: Gate 2G 97
Berkeley Cl. NE12: Kil 1E 45
NE35: Bol C 1B 88
SR3: E Her 2E 131
Berkeley Sq. NE3: Gos 6D 42
Berkeley St. NE33: S Shi 5F 63
Berkhampstead Ct. NE10: Gate . .4A 86
Berkley Av. NE21: Bla T 1C 80
Berkley Cl. NE28: W'snd 2B 60
Berkley Rd. NE29: N Shi 1H 61
Berkley St. NE15: Thro 1F 65
Berkley Ter. NE15: Thro 1F 65
Berkley Way NE31: Heb 1D 72
Berkshire Cl. DH1: Carr 4A 156
NE5: Newc T 5D 54
Berkshire Rd. SR8: Pet 5C 162
Bermondsey St.
NE2: Newc T 3H 69 (3H 5)
Bernard Shaw St. DH4: Hou S . . .3H 137
Bernard St. DH4: Hou S 3H 137
NE6: Walk 5H 71
Bernard Ter. DH2: Pelt 3G 125
Berrington Dr. NE5: Newc T 4F 55
Berrishill Gro. NE25: Whit B 5G 35
Berry Cl. NF6: Walk 4G 71
NE28: W'snd 2A 60
Berryfield Cl. SR3: New S 4A 132
Berry Hill NE40: G'sde 2B 78
Berryhill Cl. NE21: Bla T 2B 80
Bertha Ter. DH4: Hou S 5H 129
Bertram Cres. NE15: Newc T 3G 67
Bertram Pl. NE27: Shir 1D 46
Bertram St. DH3: Bir 3C 112
NE33: S Shi 1E 75
Berwick NE38: Wash 3F 113
Berwick Av. SR5: C'twn 1B 102
Berwick Chase SR8: Pet 4B 164
Berwick Cl. NE15: Lem 2G 65
Berwick Ct. NE20: Pon 4F 27
Berwick Dr. NE28: W'snd 2B 60
Berwick Hill Rd.
NE20: Pon, Wool 3F 27
Berwick Sq. SR5: C'twn 2B 102
Berwick St. NE31: Heb 3B 72
Berwick Ter. NE29: N Shi 3H 61
Besford Gro. SR1: Sund 1E 119
Bessemer Rd. DH6: S Het 6H 149
Bessie Surtees Ho. 6E 5
Bessie Ter. NE21: Bla T 1G 79
Best Vw. DH4: Pen 3F 129
Bethany Gdns. DH9: Ann P 4F 121
Bethany Ter. DH9: Ann P 4F 121
Bethel Av. NE6: Walk 2D 70
Bethune Av. SR7: S'hm 4G 141
(not continuous)
Betjeman Cl. DH9: Stly 3C 120
Better Bodies Health & Fitness Club
. . . . .4D 22
Betts Av. NE15: Newc T 4F 67
Bevan Av. SR2: Ryh 2E 133
Bevan Dr. NE12: Longb 1H 57
Bevan Gdns. NE10: Gate 3G 85
Bevan Gro. DH1: Dur 5H 155
Bevan Sq. SR7: Mur 1C 150

Beverley Cl. NE3: Gos 3D **42**
Beverley Ct. NE9: Gate 5A **84**
　　NE32: Jar 2F **73**
　　NE37: Wash 6B **100**
Beverley Cres. NE9: Gate 5A **84**
Beverley Dr. NE16: Swa, Whi . . .2G **81**
　　NE21: Bla T 3F **79**
Beverley Gdns. DH3: Ches S . . .1D **134**
　　NE30: N Shi 2E **49**
　　NE40: Ryton 4A **64**
Beverley Pk. NE25: Whit B 1A **48**
Beverley Pl. NE28: W'snd 4D **60**
Beverley Rd. NE9: Gate 5A **84**
　　NE25: Whit B 1A **48**
　　SR2: Sund 5F **119**
Beverley Ter. DH9: Ann P 4E **121**
　　NE6: Walk 4G **71**
　　NE15: Thro 5G **53**
　　NE30: N Shi 2E **49**
Beverley Vs. NE30: N Shi 2E **49**
Beverley Way SR8: Pet 6C **162**
Bevin Sq. DH6: S Het 6B **150**
Beweshill Cres. NE21: Bla T 2G **79**
Beweshill La. NE21: Bla T 1F **79**
　　　(not continuous)
Bewick Cl. DH2: Ches S 3A **134**
Bewick Ct. NE1: Newc T 3E **5**
Bewick Cres. NE15: Lem 2B **66**
Bewicke Lodge NE28: W'snd 5E **61**
Bewicke Rd. NE28: W'snd 6E **61**
　　　(not continuous)
Bewicke Rd. Ind. Est.
　　NE28: W'snd 6E **61**
Bewicke St. NE28: W'snd 6F **61**
Bewicke Vw. DH3: Bir 2D **112**
Bewick Main Cvn. Pk.
　　DH2: Kib 2G **111**
Bewick Pk. NE28: W'snd 1D **60**
Bewick Rd. NE8: Gate 2G **83**
Bewick St. NE1: Newc T . . .5E **69 (6B 4)**
　　NE33: S Shi 1E **75**
Bewley Gro. SR8: Pet 4A **164**
Bewley Ter. DH7: New B 1A **158**
Bexhill Rd. SR5: C'twn 2B **102**
Bexhill Sq. NE24: News 2C **18**
　　SR5: C'twn 1B **102**
Bexley Av. NE15: Newc T 3E **67**
Bexley Gdns. NE28: W'snd 2B **60**
Bexley Pl. NE16: Whi 6E **81**
Bexley St. SR4: Sund 1H **117**
Biceps Fitness Cen. 6G **163**
Bickerton Wlk. NE5: Newc T 6C **54**
Bickington Ct. DH4: Hou S 6G **129**
BIDDICK HALL 1D **88**
Biddick Hall Dr. NE34: S Shi 5D **74**
Biddick Inn Ter. NE38: Wash 1C **128**
Biddick La. NE38: Wash 1B **128**
Biddick Ter. NE38: Wash 4C **114**
Biddick Vw. NE38: Wash 4C **114**
Biddick Village Cen.
　　NE38: Wash 4B **114**
Biddick Vs. NE38: Wash 4C **114**
Biddlestone Cres. NE29: N Shi . . .2H **61**
Biddlestone Rd. NE6: Newc T . . .6C **58**
Bideford Gdns. NE9: Gate 2H **97**
　　NE26: Whit B 5B **36**
　　NE32: Jar 4A **74**
　　NE34: S Shi 6H **63**
Bideford Gro. NE16: Whi 6E **81**
Bideford Rd. NE3: Ken 3A **56**
Bideford St. SR2: Sund 5F **119**
Bigbury Cl. DH4: Hou S 5G **129**
Bigges Gdns. NE28: W'snd 3F **59**

BIGGES MAIN 5F **59**
Bigg Mkt. NE1: Newc T . . . .4F **69 (5D 4)**
Big Waters Nature Reserve 4B **30**
Bilbrough Gdns. NE4: Newc T . . .5H **67**
BILL QUAY 1H **85**
Bill Quay Farm 1G **85**
Bill Quay Ind. Est. NE10: Gate . . .6H **71**
BILLY MILL 6H **47**
Billy Mill Av. NE29: N Shi 1A **62**
Billy Mill La. NE29: N Shi 5G **47**
Bilsdale SR6: Monk 4F **91**
Bilsdale Pl. NE12: Longb 1H **57**
Bilsmoor Av. NE7: Newc T 5B **58**
Bilton Hall Rd. NE32: Jar 3H **73**
Binchester St. NE34: S Shi 5C **74**
Bingfield Gdns. NE5: Newc T . . .6G **55**
Bingley Cl. NE28: W'snd 2C **60**
Bingley St. SR5: C'twn 2B **102**
Bink Moss NE37: Wash 1G **113**
Binsby Gdns. NE9: Gate 3B **98**
Binswood Av. NE5: Newc T 6F **55**
Bircham Dr. NE21: Bla T 1B **80**
Bircham St. DH9: Stly 4B **122**
Birch Av. NE10: Gate 4G **85**
　　SR6: Whit 2F **91**
Birch Ct. SR3: New S 3G **131**
Birch Cres. DH4: Hou S 1G **137**
　　NE16: Burn 1F **107**
Birches, The DH5: Eas L 4E **149**
　　DH9: Stly 1D **122**
　　　(not continuous)
　　NE16: Sun 3G **95**
Birchfield NE16: Whi 5F **81**
　　NE38: Wash 5C **114**
Birchfield Gdns. NE9: Gate 3A **98**
　　NE15: Lem 2C **66**
Birchfield Rd. SR2: Sund 3B **118**
Birchgate Cl. NE21: Bla T 2G **79**
Birch Gro. NE28: W'snd 2A **60**
　　NE32: Jar 2E **73**
Birchgrove Av. DH1: Dur 4H **155**
Birchington Av. NE33: S Shi 2E **75**
Birch Rd. NE21: Bla T 1B **80**
Birch St. NE32: Jar 2E **73**
Birch Ter. DH3: Bir 2B **112**
　　NE6: Walk 4G **71**
Birchtree Gdns. NE25: Whit B . . .2B **48**
Birchvale Av. NE5: Newc T 5E **55**
Birchwood Av. NE7: Newc T 4C **58**
　　NE13: Wide O 6D **30**
　　NE16: Whi 6E **81**
Birchwood Cl. DH9: Beam 1A **124**
　　NE23: Seg 2F **33**
Birdhill Pl. NE34: S Shi 4E **75**
Birds Nest Rd.
　　NE6: Newc T, Walk 5D **70**
　　　(not continuous)
Bird St. NE30: N Shi 1E **63**
Birkdale NE25: Whit B 6H **35**
　　NE33: S Shi 6G **63**
Birkdale Av. SR6: Monk 4E **91**
Birkdale Cl. NE7: Newc T 3C **58**
　　NE28: W'snd 3H **59**
　　NE37: Usw 3H **99**
Birkdale Dr. DH4: Hou S 5E **129**
Birkdale Gdns. DH1: Carr 4B **156**
Birkhead Cottages,
　　Garden & Nursery 1H **109**
BIRKHEADS 1H **109**
Birkheads La. NE11: Kib, Sun . . .1H **109**
Birkland La. DH9: Beam 1A **110**
　　NE11: Beam, Kib 1A **110**
　　NE16: Kib, Sun 4G **95**

Birkshaw Wlk. NE5: Newc T 6C **54**
Birks Rd. NE15: Hed W, Thro 2B **52**
Birling Pl. NE5: Newc T 5H **55**
Birnam Gro. NE32: Jar 1A **88**
Birney Edge NE20: Pon 4C **38**
Birnham Pl. NE3: Ken 4B **56**
Birnie Cl. NE4: Newc T 5A **68**
Birrell Sq. SR5: C'twn 1B **102**
Birrell St. SR5: C'twn 1B **102**
BIRTLEY 3C **112**
Birtley Av. NE30: N Shi 5F **49**
　　　(not continuous)
　　SR5: C'twn 1B **102**
Birtley By-Pass DH3: Bir 6C **98**
Birtley Cl. NE3: Gos 3C **56**
Birtley Crematorium DH3: Bir . . .1B **112**
Birtley La. DH3: Bir 2C **112**
Birtley Leisure Cen. 4C **112**
Birtley Rd. NE38: Wash 6F **113**
Birtley Sports Complex 5C **112**
Birtley Vs. DH3: Bir 2C **112**
Birtwhistle Av. NE31: Heb 6B **72**
Biscop Ter. NE32: Jar 4G **73**
Bishopbourne Ct. NE29: N Shi . . .4B **48**
Bishop Cres. NE32: Jar 1G **73**
Bishopdale DH4: Pen 1C **128**
　　　(not continuous)
　　NE28: W'snd 2F **59**
Bishopdale Av. NE24: Cow 1G **17**
Bishop Morton Gro.
　　SR1: Sund 1E **119**
Bishop Ramsey Ct.
　　NE34: S Shi 3A **76**
Bishop Rock Dr. NE12: Longb . . .1A **58**
Bishop's Av. NE4: Newc T 4C **68**
Bishops Cl. NE28: W'snd 5C **60**
Bishops Ct. DH1: H Shin 3F **161**
　　NE5: Newc T 1D **66**
Bishops Dr. NE40: Ryton 5D **64**
Bishops Mdw. NE22: Bed 4G **9**
Bishop's Rd. NE15: Newc T 5H **67**
Bishops Way DH1: Dur 6B **144**
　　SR3: New S 4G **131**
Bishops Wynd DH5: Hou S 4A **138**
Bishopton St. NE24: Bly 1C **18**
　　SR1: Sund 1E **119**
BISHOPWEARMOUTH . . .6C **104 (2E 7)**
Bisley Ct. NE28: W'snd 2B **60**
Bisley Dr. NE34: S Shi 2F **75**
Bittern Cl. NE11: Dun 1B **82**
　　NE28: W'snd 1E **61**
Blackberries, The NE9: Spri 4F **99**
Black Boy Rd. DH4: Hou S 5B **136**
Black Boy Yd.
　　NE1: Newc T . . . . .4F **69 (5D 4)**
Blackburn Cl. DH7: Ush M 3C **152**
Blackburn Grn. NE10: Gate 4C **84**
BLACK CALLERTON 5H **39**
Blackcap Cl. NE38: Wash 4F **113**
Blackcliff Way DH7: Ush M 3C **152**
Blackdown Cl. SR8: Pet 2B **164**
Black Dr. DH3: Lam P 4H **127**
Blackettbridge NE1: Newc T 3C **4**
Blackett Pl.
　　NE1: Newc T . . . . .4F **69 (4D 4)**
Blackett St. DH9: Ann P 5E **121**
　　NE1: Newc I . . . . .4F **69 (4C 4)**
　　NE31: Heb 1D **72**
Blackett Ter. SR4: Sund 1A **118**
BLACKFELL 1G **113**
Blackfell Rd. NE37: Wash 1F **113**
Blackfell Village Cen.
　　NE37: Wash 1G **113**

Blackfell Way DH3: Bir 2D **112**
Blackfriars 5B **4**
Blackfriars Ct. NE1: Newc T 5B **4**
Blackfriars Way NE12: Longb 1A **58**
Blackheath Cl. NE37: Usw 3A **100**
Blackheath Ct. NE3: Ken 2F **55**
Blackhill Av. NE28: W'snd 6C **46**
Blackhill Cres. NE9: Gate 1D **98**
Blackhills Rd. SR8: Pet 5G **163**
Blackhills Ter. SR8: Pet 6G **163**
Blackhouse La. NF40: Ryton 4B **64**
Black La. NE5: Newc T 1D **54**
 NE9: Gate 3B **98**
 NE9: Spri 4B **98**
 NE13: Wool 1D **54**
 NE21: Bla T 2G **79**
Blackpool Pde. NE31: Heb 6E **73**
Black Rd. DH7: B'don 3G **159**
 NE31: Heb 2D **72**
 SR2: Ryh 2F **133**
Blackrow La. NE9: Gate 2A **98**
 NE15: Hed W, Thro 4H **51**
Blackstone Ct. NE21: Bla T 1G **79**
Black Thorn Cl. DH7: B'don 6C **158**
Blackthorn Cl. NE16: Sun 3E **95**
Blackthorn Dr. NE24: News 3A **18**
 NE28: W'snd 2A **60**
Blackthorne NE10: Gate 6F **85**
Blackthorne Av. SR8: Pet 1H **165**
Blackthorn Pl. NE4: Newc T 6D **68**
Blackwater Ho. SR3: New S 3A **132**
Blackwell Av. NE6: Walk 3F **71**
Blackwood Rd. SR5: C'twn 2B **102**
Bladen St. NE32: Jar 2E **73**
Bladen St. Ind. Est. NE32: Jar . . .2E **73**
Blagdon Av. NE34: S Shi 1G **75**
Blagdon Cl.
 NF1: Newc T 4H **69** (4G **5**)
Blagdon Ct. NF22: Bed 3C **10**
Blagdon Cres. NE23: Nel V 1G **21**
Blagdon Dr. NE24: News 4A **18**
Blagdon Ter. NE13: Sea B 3D **30**
 NE23: Cra 3B **22**
Bloidwood Dr. DH1: Dur 4A **160**
Blair Cl. NE23: Cra 6D **156**
Blair Ct. DH7: B'don 4G **159**
Blake Av. NE16: Whi 4F **81**
Blake Cl. DH9: Stly 3E **123**
BLAKELAW 5G **55**
Blakelaw Rd. NE5: Newc T 5F **55**
 (Bonnington Way)
 NE5: Newc T 5C **55**
 (Cragston Cl.)
Blakemoor Pl. NE5: Newc T 6G **55**
Blake St. SR8: Eas 1F **163**
Blaketown NE23: Seg 2G **33**
Blake Wlk. NE8: Gate 1A **84**
Blanche Gro. SR8: Pet 2D **164**
Blanche Ter. DH9: Tan L 5H **107**
Blanchland NE38: Wash 6C **114**
Blanchland Av. DH1: Dur 1E **155**
 NE13: Wide O 5D **30**
 NE15: Lem 2A **66**
Blanchland Dr. NE28: W'snd 3B **46**
Blanchland Dr. NE25: H'wll 1D **34**
 SR5: S'wck 2C **104**
Blanchland Ter.
 NE30: N Shi 6D **48**
Blandford Ct.
 NE4: Newc T 5E **69** (6A **4**)
Blandford Pl. SR7: S'hm 4B **142**
Blandford Rd. NE29: N Shi 4H **47**

Blandford Sq.
 NE1: Newc T 5E **69** (6A **4**)
 (not continuous)
Blandford St.
 NE1: Newc T 5E **69** (6A **4**)
 SR1: Sund 1D **118** (4G **7**)
Blandford Way NE28: W'snd . . .2B **60**
Bland's Opening DH3: Ches S . . .6C **126**
Blaxton Pl. NE16: Whi 6D **80**
BLAYDON 6B **66**
Blaydon Av. SR5: C'twn 1C **102**
Blaydon Bank NE21: Bla T 2H **79**
BLAYDON BURN 1G **79**
Blaydon Bus. Cen. NE21: Bla T . .6C **66**
Blaydon Bus. Pk. NE21: Bla T . . .5D **66**
Blaydon Haughs Ind. Est.
 NE21: Bla T 5C **66**
Blaydon Highway NE21: Bla T . . .6A **66**
Blaydon Ind. Pk. NE21: Bla T . . .6B **66**
Blaydon Station (Rail) 5A **66**
Blaydon Swimming Pool 1C **80**
Blaydon Trade Pk. NE21: Bla T . . .6C **66**
Blaykeston Cl. SR7: S'hm 2E **141**
Blayney Row NE15: Thro 1C **64**
Bleachfield NE10: Gate 5F **85**
BLEACH GREEN 2A **80**
Bleach Grn. DH5: Hett H 2C **148**
Bleasdale Cres. DH4: Pen 2F **129**
Blehelm Cl. NE24: News 4B **18**
Blencathra NE30: N Shi 3G **48**
 NE37: Wash 1A **114**
Blencathra Way NE21: Bla T 3A **80**
Blenheim NE12: Kil 1D **44**
Blenheim Cl. NE10: Gate 5D **84**
Blenheim Dr. NE22: Bed 2C **10**
Blenheim Pl. NE11: Dun 2A **82**
Blenheim Wlk. NE33: S Shi 4F **63**
Blenkinsop Gro. NE32: Jar 6F **73**
Blenkinsop M. NE3: Gos 4C **42**
Blenkinsop Ct. SR8: Pet 4B **164**
Blenkinsopp St. NE28: W'snd . . .5H **59**
Bletchley Av. SR5: C'twn 1B **102**
Blezard Bus. Pk. NE13: Sea B . . .2D **30**
Blezard Ct. NE21: Bla T 5C **66**
Blind La. DH1: Dur 6D **164**
 DH3: Ches S 3D **126**
 DH4: Hou S 5F **129**
 SR3: New S 1A **132**
Blindy La. DH5: Eas L 4E **149**
Bloemfontein Pl. DH9: Stly 6F **123**
 (off Middles Rd.)
Bloom Av. DH9: Stly 3C **122**
Bloomfield Ct. SR6: Monk 3F **105**
Bloomfield Dr. DH5: W Rai 2H **147**
Bloomsbury Ct. NE3: Gos 3D **56**
Blossom Gro. DH4: Hou S 5F **129**
Blossom St. DH5: Hett H 6D **138**
Blount St. NE6: Walk 3D **70**
Blucher Colliery Rd.
 NE15: Thro 6H **53**
Blucher Rd. NE12: Kil 4C **44**
 NE29: N Shi 4B **62**
Blucher Ter. NE15: Thro 6H **53**
BLUCHER VILLAGE 6H **53**
Blue Anchor Ct. NE1: Newc T . . .6F **5**
Bluebell Cl. NE9: Gate 6B **84**
Bluebell Dene NE5: Newc T 2C **55**
Bluebell Way NE34: S Shi 4D **74**
Blueburn Dr. NE12: Kil 1F **45**
Blue Carpet, The 4E **5**
Blue Coat Bldgs.
 DH1: Dur 5D **154** (2C **6**)

Blue Coat Ct.
 DH1: Dur 5D **154** (2C **6**)
Blue Ho. Bank DH2: Edm, Pelt . .6B **124**
 DH9: Edm 6B **124**
Blue Ho. Ct. NE37: Usw 5H **99**
Blue Ho. La. NE37: Wash 5H **99**
 SR6: Cle, S'wck 4H **89**
Blue Ho. Rd. NE31: Heb 6B **72**
Blue Quarries Rd. NE9: Gate . . .5B **84**
Blue Reef Aquarium 3E **49**
Blue Top Cotts. NE23: Cra 3D **22**
Blumer St. DH4: Hou S 3E **137**
BLYTH 5C **12**
Blyth Cl. NE23: Dud 3H **31**
Blyth Ct. NE15: Lem 2A **66**
 NE34: S Shi 4E **75**
Blyth Crematorium NE24: Cow . . .5A **12**
Blyth Dr. NE61: Hep 4A **8**
Blythe Ter. DH3: Bir 3B **112**
Blyth Ind. Est. NE24: Cow 4H **11**
Blyth Rd. NE26: Sea S, Whit B
 . . . . .5H **25** & 1A **36**
Blyth Spartans AFC (Croft Pk.) . . .1C **18**
Blyth Sports Cen. 6B **12**
Blyth Sq. SR5: C'twn 2C **102**
Blyth St. NE25: Sea D 5A **24**
 SR5: C'twn 2C **102**
Blythswood NE2: Newc T 1G **69**
Blyton Av. NE34: S Shi 4B **74**
 SR2: Ryh 2E **133**
Bobby Shafto Cvn. Pk.
 DH9: Beam 6C **110**
Bodlewell Ho. SR1: Sund 6E **105**
 (off High St. E.)
Bodlewell La. SR1: Sund 6E **105**
Bodley Cl. NE3: Ken 2H **55**
Bodmin Cl. NE28: W'snd 2C **60**
Bodmin Ct. NE9: Gate 3A **98**
Bodmin Rd. NE29: N Shi 5G **47**
Bodmin Sq. SR5: C'twn 1C **102**
Bodmin Way NE3: Ken 1B **56**
Body Line Health & Fitness Studio
 . . . . .5F **119**
 (off Ryhope Rd.)
Bodywork Health Club 6F **159**
Body Zone Health & Fitness Club
 . . . . .4E **5**
Bog Ho's. NE23: E Har 5C **16**
Boghouse La. DH9: Stly 5E **109**
Bognor St. SR5: C'twn 1B **102**
Bog Row DH5: Hett H 2C **148**
Bohemia Ter. NE24: Bly 1C **18**
Boker La. NE36: E Bol 3D **88**
Bolam NE38: Wash 3F **113**
Bolam Av. NE24: Bly, Cow 6B **12**
 NE30: N Shi 4C **48**
Bolam Bus. Cen. NE23: Cra 1G **21**
Bolam Ct. NE15: Thro 6D **52**
Bolam Coyne NE6: Newc T 4C **70**
Bolam Gdns. NE28: W'snd 4F **61**
Bolam Gro. NE30: N Shi 4C **48**
Bolam Ho. NE4: Newc T 4D **68**
Bolam Pl. NE22: Bed 3C **10**
Bolam Rd. NE12: Kil 2C **44**
Bolams Bldgs. DH9: Tan L 6G **107**
Bolam St. NE6: Newc T 4C **70**
 NF8: Gate 3D **82**
 SR8: Eas 1F **163**
Bolam Way NE6: Newc T 4C **70**
 NE25: Sea D 6A **24**
Bolbec Rd. NE4: Newc T 2A **68**
Bolburn NE10: Gate 4G **85**
BOLDON 3E **89**

Boldon Bus. Pk.—Bracknell Cl.

Boldon Bus. Pk. NE35: Bol C 3A **88**
  (Brooklands Way)
  NE35: Bol C 4B **88**
  (Didcot Way)
Boldon Cl. NE28: W'snd 2B **60**
BOLDON COLLIERY 2A **88**
Boldon Colliery Workshops 2B **88**
Boldon Dr. NE36: W Bol 4B **88**
Boldon Gdns. NE9: Gate 2C **98**
Boldon Ho. DH1: Dur 4C **144**
Boldon La. NE34: S Shi 3D **74**
  (not continuous)
  NE36: E Bol 3E **89**
  NE36: S Shi 2E **89**
  SR6: Cle 2G **89**
Boldon UGC Cinema 3A **88**
Bolingbroke Rd. NE29: N Shi 1H **61**
Bolingbroke St. NE6: Newc T 3A **70**
  NE33: S Shi 5F **63**
Bollihope Dr. SR3: Sund 5B **118**
Bolton Cl. DH1: Dur 6C **144**
Bonaventure DH4: Pen 1G **129**
Bonchester Cl. NE22: Bed 3H **9**
Bonchester Ct. NE28: W'snd 2C **60**
Bonchester Pl. NE23: Cra 1D **22**
Bond Cl. SR5: S'wck 4C **104**
Bond Ct. NE4: Newc T 4A **68**
Bondene Av. NE10: Gate 3E **85**
Bondene Av. W. NE10: Gate 3D **84**
Bondene Way NE23: Cra 5B **16**
Bondfield Cl. NE28: W'snd 4D **60**
Bondfield Gdns. NE10: Gate 3G **85**
Bondicarr Pl. NE5: Newc T 6H **55**
Bondicar Ter. NE24: Bly 6B **12**
Bond St. NE4: Newc T 4H **67**
Bone La. DH9: Dip 6D **106**
Bonemill La. NE38: Wash 1E **127**
Bonner's Fld.
  SR6: Monk 5D **104** (1G **7**)
Bonnington Way NE5: Newc T 5F **55**
Bonnivard Gdns. NE23: Seg 2G **33**
Bonsall Ct. NE34: S Shi 4F **75**
Booth St. NE10: Gate 3D **84**
  SR4: Sund 1A **118**
Bootle St. SR5: C'twn 2C **102**
Bordeaux Cl. SR3: New S 3G **131**
Border Rd. NE28: W'snd 6H **59**
Boreham Cl. NE28: W'snd 2B **60**
Borough Ct. SR1: Sund 6E **105**
Borough Rd. NE29: N Shi 2C **62**
  NE32: Jar 3F **73**
  NE34: S Shi 4H **75**
  SR1: Sund 1D **118** (4H **7**)
Borrowdale Av. NE6: Walk 2F **71**
  NE24: Cow 5G **11**
  SR6: Monk 6C **90**
Borrowdale Cl. NE36: E Bol 3E **89**
Borrowdale Cres. DH4: Pen 1E **129**
  NE21: Bla T 3H **79**
Borrowdale Dr. DH1: Carr 3A **156**
Borrowdale Gdns. NE9: Gate 2B **98**
Borrowdale Ho. NE34: S Shi 4E **75**
Borrowdale St. DH5: Hett H 3C **148**
Boscombe Dr. NE28: W'snd 3A **60**
Boston Av. NE7: Newc T 2B **58**
  NE38: Wash 1A **114**
  (not continuous)
Boston Cl. NE28: W'snd 2B **60**
Boston Ct. NE12: Longb 5F **45**

Boston Cres. SR5: C'twn 1A **102**
Boston St. SR5: C'twn 1A **102**
  SR8: Eas 1F **163**
Boswell Av. NE34: S Shi 6D **74**
Bosworth NE12: Kil 1D **44**
Bosworth Gdns. NE6: Newc T 5C **58**
Bothal Cl. NE24: Bly 6A **12**
Bothal St. NE6: Newc T 3D **70**
Botham Ho. NE29: N Shi 4H **61**
Bottle Bank NE8: Gate 5G **69**
Bottlehouse St. NE6: Newc T 5C **70**
Bottle Works Rd. SR7: S'hm 4C **142**
Boulby Cl. SR3: New S 2C **132**
Boulevard, The NE11: Dun 2G **81**
  NE12: Longb 1A **58**
Boulmer Av. NE23: Cra 5B **16**
Boulmer Cl. NE3: Ken 5B **42**
Boulmer Ct. DH2: Ches S 1C **134**
Boulmer Gdns. NE13: Wide O 5D **30**
Boulsworth Rd. NE29: N Shi 4A **48**
Boult Ter. DH4: Hou S 3F **129**
Boundary Cl. DH7: Ush M 6C **152**
Boundary Gdns. NE7: Newc T 4A **58**
BOUNDARY HOUSES 5E **129**
Boundary Ho's DH4: Hou S 4D **128**
Boundary Mill Stores
  NE27: Shir 3D **46**
Boundary St. SR5: S'wck 3C **104**
Boundary Way NE26: Sea S 3H **25**
Bourdon Ho.
  SR1: Sund 1D **118** (5H **7**)
Bourne Av. NE4: Newc T 2A **68**
Bourne Cl. DH9: Stly 2E **123**
  (not continuous)
Bournemouth Ct. NE28: W'snd ..2B **60**
Bournemouth Dr. SR7: Mur 5F **141**
Bournemouth Gdns.
  NE5: Newc T 4D **54**
  NE26: Whit B 5B **36**
Bournemouth Pde. NE31: Heb 6E **73**
  (not continuous)
Bournemouth Rd. NE29: N Shi ...2G **61**
Bourne St. SR8: Eas 1F **163**
Bourne Ter. DH9: Ann P 5F **121**
Bourn Lea DH4: Hou S 4E **129**
BOURNMOOR 6C **128**
Bournmoor DH4: Hou S 6C **128**
Bourtree Cl. NE28: W'snd 3A **60**
Bowbank Cl. SR3: Sund 5B **118**
Bowburn Av. SR5: C'twn 3E **103**
Bowburn Cl. NE10: Gate 4A **86**
Bower St. SR6: Monk 1D **104**
Bower, The NE32: Jar 3F **87**
Bowes Av. DH5: Eas L 4D **148**
  SR7: Mur 5E **141**
Bowes Cl. NE16: Sun 3F **95**
Bowes Ct. DH1: Dur 6D **144**
  NE3: Gos 2G **57**
  NE24: Bly 6C **12**
Bowes Cres. NE16: Burn 5B **94**
Bowes Ho. SR3: E Her 2F **131**
  (off Castle Grn.)
Bowes Lea DH4: Hou S 5D **128**
Bowes Lyon Cl. NE39: Row G 5D **92**
Bowes Lyon Ct. NE9: Gate 3H **83**
Bowes Manor Equestrian Cen. ...6D **98**
Bowes Railway Cen. 3E **99**
Bowes St. NE3: Gos 2G **57**
  NE24: Bly 6B **12**
  (not continuous)
Bowes Ter. DH9: Dip 1D **120**
Bowesville NE16: Burn 2H **107**
Bowes Wlk. NE12: Longb 6C **44**

Bowfell Av. NE5: Newc T 3H **55**
Bowfell Cl. NE5: Newc T 4H **55**
Bowfield Av. NE3: Gos 4E **43**
Bowland Cres. NE21: Bla T 1A **80**
Bowland Ter. NE21: Bla T 6A **66**
Bow La. DH1: Dur 6C **154** (4B **6**)
Bowlynn Cl. SR3: New S 3G **131**
Bowman Dr. NE23: Dud 3B **32**
Bowman Pl. NE33: S Shi 6E **63**
Bowman St. SR6: Whit 2F **91**
Bowmont Dr. DH9: Tan L 1A **122**
  NE23: Cra 1D **22**
Bowmont Wlk. DH2: Ches S 2A **134**
Bowness Av. NE28: W'snd 1C **60**
Bowness Cl. NE36: E Bol 4E **89**
  SR8: Pet 6E **163**
Bowness Pl. NE9: Gate 1B **98**
Bowness Rd. NE5: Newc T 6E **55**
  NE16: Whi 4G **81**
Bowness St. SR5: C'twn 1C **102**
Bowness Ter. NE28: W'snd 2C **60**
Bowsden Cl. NE3: Gos 2G **57**
Bowsden Ter. NE3: Gos 2G **57**
Bowtrees SR2: Sund 4D **118**
Boxlaw NE9: Gate 6C **84**
Boyd Cres. NE28: W'snd 5A **60**
Boyd Rd. NE28: W'snd 5A **60**
Boyd St. DH1: Dur 1D **160** (5C **6**)
  NE2: Newc T 3H **69** (3H **5**)
  NE15: Thro 1E **65**
  SR8: Eas 1F **163**
Boyd Ter. DH9: Stly 4C **122**
  NE5: Newc T 4D **54**
  NE15: Thro 6H **53**
Boyne Ct. DH7: B'don 4F **159**
  NE24: Bly 5C **12**
  (off Regent St.)
Boyne Gdns. NE27: Shir 2C **46**
Boyne Ter. NE37: Usw 5A **100**
Boyntons DH2: Plaw 1A **144**
Boystones Ct. NE37: Wash 1H **113**
Brabourne Gdns. NE29: N Shi 4B **48**
Brabourne St. NE34: S Shi 3E **75**
Bracken Av. NE28: W'snd 3A **60**
Brackenbeds Cl. DH2: Pelt 3G **125**
Brackenbeds La.
  DH2: Ous, Pelt 2H **125**
  (not continuous)
Brackenburn Cl. DH4: Hou S 2G **137**
Bracken Cl. DH9: Stly 3C **122**
  NE13: Din 5F **29**
Bracken Ct. DH7: Ush M 4C **152**
  (not continuous)
Brackendale Rd. DH1: Carr 4B **156**
Brackendene Dr. NE9: Gate 6G **83**
Brackendene Pk. NE9: Gate 6G **83**
Bracken Dr. NE11: Dun 5B **82**
Bracken Fld. Rd. DH1: Dur 2B **154**
Brackenfield Rd. NE3: Gos 3D **56**
Bracken Hill SR8: Pet 2A **164**
Bracken Hill Bus. Pk.
  SR8: Pet 2A **164**
Brackenlaw NE9: Gate 1C **98**
Brackenpath M. NE3: Gos 4D **42**
Bracken Pl. NE4: Newc T 2H **67**
Brackenridge NE16: Burn 1E **107**
Brackenside NE3: Gos 4E **43**
Bracken Way NE40: Ryton 6A **64**
Brackenway NE37: Wash 6H **99**
Brackenwood Gro. SR2: Sund ...5C **118**
Brackley NE37: Usw 4C **100**
Brackley Gro. NE29: N Shi 3H **61**
Bracknell Cl. SR3: New S 1C **132**

Bracknell Gdns. NE5: Cha P 6H 53
Brack Ter. NE10: Gate 1H 85
Bradbury Cl. DH9: Tan L 1A 122
NE10. Gate 4A 86
Bradbury Ct. NE20: Pon 5F 27
(off Thornhill Rd.)
NE25: Sea D 3B 24
Bradbury Pl. NE25: Sea D 3B 24
Bradford Av. NE28: W'snd 2B 60
SR5: C'twn 1C 102
Bradford Cres. DH1: Dur 4F 155
Bradley Av. DH5: Hou S 5A 138
NE34: S Shi 3A 76
Bradley Cl. DH2: Ous 5F 111
Bradley Lodge Dr. DH9: Dip ...1E 121
Bradley St. SR8: Eas 1F 163
Bradley Ter. DH5: Eas L 4E 149
DH9: Dip 2E 121
Bradman Dr. DH3: Ches S 1E 135
Bradman Sq. SR5: C'twn 1C 102
Bradman St. SR5: C'twn 1C 102
Bradshaw Sq. SR5: C'twn 2C 102
Bradshaw St. SR5: C'twn 2C 102
Bradwell Rd. NF3: News 2A 56
Bradwell Way DH4: Hou S 4G 129
Brady & Martin Ct.
NE1: Newc T 3G 69 (2E 5)
Brady Sq. NE38: Wash 3D 114
Brady St. SR4: Sund 6H 103
Braebridge Pl. NE3: Ken 4B 56
Braefell Ct. NE37: Wash 1H 113
Braemar Ct. NE10: Gate 1H 85
Braemar Dr. NE34: S Shi 1A 76
Braemar Gdns. NE25: Whit B ...1G 47
SR3: E Her 3E 131
SR3: Sund 4D 118
Braemar Ter. SR8: Pet 1H 165
Braeside NE11: Dun 4B 82
SR2: Sund 3B 118
Braeside Cl. NE30: N Shi 2C 48
Braeside Ter. NE26: Whit B 1E 49
Brae, The SR2: Sund 1B 118
Braham Rd. NE29: N Shi 3H 61
Braintree Gdns. NE3: Ken 3B 56
Braithwaite Rd. SR8: Pet 1F 165
Brakespeare Pl. SR8: Pet 2E 165
Brama Teams Ind. Pk.
NE8: Gate 2D 82
Bramble Cl. NE24: News 3A 18
Bramble Dykes NE15: Newc T ...4F 67
Bramblelaw NE9: Gate 1C 98
Brambles Leisure Cen. 4E 63
Brambles, The DH3: Bir 1D 112
NE40: Ryton 4B 64
Brambling Lea NE22: Bed 3C 10
Bramhall Dr. NE38: Wash 1H 127
Bramham Ct. NE34: S Shi 4G 75
Bramhope Grn. NE9: Gate 3B 98
Bramley Cl. SR4: Sund 4C 116
Bramley Ct. NE7: Newc T 4E 59
Brampton Av. NE6: Walk 5F 71
Brampton Ct. NE23: Cra 1C 22
SR8: Eas 2B 162
Brampton Gdns. NE9: Gate 2A 98
NE15: Thro 5D 52
NE28: W'snd 3E 61
Brampton Pl. NE29: N Shi 2H 61
Brampton Rd. NE34: S Shi 4C 74
Bramwell Cl. NE3: Gos 2F 57
Bramwell Rd. SR2: Sund 2E 119
Brancepeth Av. DH4: Hou S ...2E 137
NE4: Newc T 5A 68
Brancepeth Chare SR8: Pet 4B 164

Brancepeth Cl. DH1: Dur 1D 154
DH7: Ush M 6E 153
NE15: Lem 2A 66
Brancepeth Rd. NE31: Heb 2D 72
NE38: Wash 3G 113
Brancepeth Ter. NE32: Jar 6F 73
Brancepeth Vw. DH7: B'don 6B 158
Branch St. NE21: Bla T 2H 79
Brand Av. NE4: Newc T 2A 68
Brandling Ct. NE2: Newc T 1H 69
NE10: Gate 2D 84
(off William St.)
NE34: S Shi 5A 76
Brandling Dr. NE3: Gos 4F 43
Brandling La. NE10: Gate 2D 84
Brandling M. NE3: Gos 4F 43
Brandling Pk. NE2: Newc T 1F 69
Brandling Pl. NE10: Gate 2D 84
Brandling Pl. Sth.
NE2: Newc T 1G 69
Brandling St. NE8: Gate 5G 69
SR6: Monk 3E 105
(not continuous)
Brandling St. Sth.
SR6: Monk 4E 105
Brandlings Way SR8: Pet 6D 162
Brandling Ter. NE30: N Shi 1D 62
BRANDLING VILLAGE 1G 69
BRANDON 5D 158
Brandon Av. NE27: Shir 2C 46
Brandon Cl. DH2: Ches S 2A 134
DH4: Hou S 4H 137
NE21: Bla T 3G 79
NE24: Cow 5H 11
Brandon Gdns. NE9: Gate 2D 98
Brandon Gro.
NE2: Newc T 2H 69 (1H 5)
Brandon Ho. DH7: B'don 6C 158
Brandon La. DH7: B'don 5C 158
Brandon Rd. NE3: Ken 1B 56
NE29: N Shi 1H 61
Brandon Vw. DH7: Ush M 1E 159
BRANDON VILLAGE 4C 158
Brandy La. NE37: Wash 6H 99
Brandywell NE10: Gate 5F 85
Brannen St. NE29: N Shi 2A 62
Bransdale DH4: Pen 1C 120
Bransdale Av. SR6: Monk 4F 91
Branston St. SR5: S'wck 3B 104
Branton Av. NE31: Heb 6B 72
Brantwood DH2: Ches S 6H 125
Brantwood Av. NE25: Whit B ...1H 47
Brantwood Ct. NE21: Bla T 1B 80
Branxton Cres. NE6: Walk 4F 71
Brasher St. NE33: S Shi 3E 63
BRASSIDE 5F 145
Brass Thill DH1: Dur 6B 154
Braunespath Est. DH7: New B ..1B 158
Bray Cl. NE28: W'snd 2B 60
Braydon Dr. NE29: N Shi 4A 62
Brayside NE32: Jar 2H 87
Breackneck Stairs NE1: Newc T ..6D 4
Breamish Dr. NE38: Wash 6F 113
Breamish Ho. NE1: Newc T 4A 70
Breamish Quays
NE1: Newc T 4A 70 (4H 5)
Breamish St.
NE1: Newc T 4A 70 (4H 5)
NE32: Jar 4E 73
Brearley Way NE10: Gate 3C 84
Breckenbeds Rd. NE9: Gate ...1G 97
Brecken Ct. NE9: Gate 1G 97
Brecken Way DH7: B'don 5E 159

Brecon Cl. NE5: Newc T 3F 55
SR8: Pet 2B 164
Brecon Pl. DH2: Ous 1H 125
Brecon Rd. DH1: Dur 6E 145
Bredon Cl. NE38: Wash 4H 113
Brendale Av. NE5: Newc T 4B 54
Brendon Pl. SR8: Pet 6B 162
BRENKLEY 6A 20
Brenkley Av. NE27: Shir 3C 46
Brenkley Cl. NE13: Din 4F 29
Brenkley Cl. NE13: Sea D 3D 30
Brenkley Way NE13: Sea B 2D 30
Brenlynn Cl. SR3: New S 3G 131
Brennan Cl. NE15: Newc T 3F 67
Brentford Av. SR5: C'twn 2C 102
Brentford Sq. SR5: C'twn 2C 102
Brentwood Av. NE2: Newc T ...5F 57
Brentwood Cl. NE25: Sea D ...1C 34
Brentwood Gdns. NF2: Newc T ..5F 57
NE16: Whi 6F 81
SR3: Sund 4B 118
Brentwood Gro. NE28: W'snd ...6B 60
Brentwood Pl. NE33: S Shi 5F 63
Brentwood Rd. DH4: Hou S 4E 129
Brettanby Gdns. NE40: Ryton ...3C 64
Brettanby Rd. NE10: Gate 4C 84
Brett Cl. NE7: Newc T 4D 58
Bretton Gdns. NE7: Newc T ...5C 58
Brewers La. NE29: N Shi 5G 61
Brewer Ter. SR2: Ryh 3G 133
Brewery Bank NE16: Swa 2E 81
Brewery Bond NE29: N Shi 3D 62
Brewery La. NE10: Gate 1D 84
NE16: Swa 2E 81
(off Brewery Bank)
NE20: Pon 5E 27
NE33: S Shi 5D 62
Brewery Sq. DH9: Stly 2D 122
Brewery Stables NE1: Newc T ...5A 4
(off Blandford Sq.)
Brewery St. NE24: Bly 5D 12
(off Sussex St.)
Brewhouse Bank NE30: N Shi ...1E 63
Brian Ct. NE26: Whit B 6B 36
Briar Av. DH4: Hou S 3H 137
DH7: D'don 6C 158
NE26: Whit B 4B 36
Briar Bank DH1: Dur 5B 144
Briar Cl. DH2: Plaw 2A 144
DH4: Hou S 5D 128
(Boundary Houses)
DH4: Hou S 2C 136
(Woodstone Village)
NE21: Bla T 1G 79
NE28: W'snd 2A 60
Briardale NE13: Din 4F 29
NE22: Bed 4G 9
Briardale Rd. NE24: Cow 6G 11
Briardene DH1: Dur 6B 154
NE16: Burn 1E 107
Briardene Cl. SR3: E Her 3E 131
Briardene Cres. NE3: Ken 4C 56
Briardene Dr. NE10: Gate 3B 86
Briar Edge NE12: Longb 5D 44
Briarfield NE38: Wash 6B 114
Briarfield Rd. NE3: Gos 3D 56
Briar Glen SR7: Mur 2H 149
Briarhill DH2: Ches S 4A 126
Briar La. NE15: Thro 6E 53
Briar Lea DH4: Hou S 5D 128
Briarlea NE61: Hep 1A 8
Briar Pl. NE15: Newc T 4E 67

Briar Rd. DH1: Carr 3B 156
NE39: Row G 3D 92
Briarside NE5: Newc T 4E 55
Briars, The SR5: C'twn 4D 102
Briarsyde NE12: Longb 1E 59
Briarsyde Cl. NE16: Whi 6C 80
Briar Ter. NE16: Burn 1A 108
Briar Va. NE25: Whit B 2H 47
Briarwood Av. DH2: Pelt 6G 125
NE3: Gos 1G 57
Briarwood Cres. NE6: Walk 6F 59
NE11: Dun 3B 82
Briarwood Rd. NE24: Bly 1D 18
Briarwood St. DH4: Hou S 2C 136
Briary, The NE15: Thro 5C 52
Brick Gth. DH5: Eas L 5D 148
Brick Row SR2: Ryh 2E 133
Bridekirk NE37: Wash 6A 100
(not continuous)
Bridge App. SR5: Sund 4A 104
Bridge Cotts. NE23: Dud 3B 32
Bridge Cres.
SR1: Sund 6D 104 (2G 7)
Bridge End DH3: Ches S 5C 126
Bridge Ho. SR1: Sund 3G 7
Bridgemere Dr. DH1: Dur 1A 154
Bridge Pk. NE3: Gos 5E 43
Bridge Rd. Sth NE29: N Shi 3A 62
Bridge Row DH1: Carr 1B 156
Bridges Shop. Cen., The
SR1: Sund 1C 118 (4F 7)
Bridges, The SR1: Sund 3F 7
Bridge St. DH1: Dur 5B 154
DH9: Stly 5C 122
NE8: Gate 5G 69
NE13: Sea B 3D 30
NE21: Bla T 5H 65
NE24: Bly 5C 12
(not continuous)
SR1: Sund 6D 104 (3G 7)
Bridges Vw. NE8: Gate 1F 83
Bridge Ter. NE22: Bed 2C 10
NE27: Shir 1D 46
Bridgewater Cl. NE15: Lem 2A 66
NE28: W'snd 3A 60
Bridgewater Rd. NE37: Wash . . .6C 100
Bridle Path NE3: Gos 6G 43
NE36: E Bol 4E 89
SR3: E Her 1E 131
Bridle, The NE27: Shir 3F 47
Bridlington Av. NE9: Gate 2H 97
Bridlington Cl. NE28: W'snd 2B 60
Bridlington Pde. NE31: Heb 6E 73
Bridport Rd. NE29: N Shi 4H 47
Brier Av. SR8: Pet 5F 163
Brier Dene Cl. NE26: Whit B 3B 36
Brierdene Ct. NE26: Whit B 3A 36
Brier Dene Cres. NE26: Whit B . . .3A 36
Brierdene Rd. NE26: Whit B 2B 36
Brierdene Vw. NE26: Whit B 3A 36
Brierfield Gro. SR4: Sund 3F 117
Brierley Cl. NE24: Cow 6H 11
Brierley Rd. NE24: Cow 6H 11
Briermede Av. NE9: Gate 1H 97
Briermede Pk. NE9: Gate 1H 97
Brierville DH1: Dur 6R 154
Brieryside NE5: Newc T 6H 55
Briery Va. Cl. SR2: Sund 2C 118
Briery Va. Rd. SR2: Sund 2C 118
Brigham Av. NE3: Ken 4A 56
Brigham Pl. NE33: S Shi 4E 63
Brightlea DH3: Bir 2E 113

Brightman Rd. NE29: N Shi 1C 62
Brighton Cl. NE28: W'snd 2C 60
Brighton Gdns. NE8: Gate 4G 83
Brighton Gro. NE4: Newc T 3C 68
NE26: Whit B 5B 36
NE29: N Shi 1B 62
Brighton Pde. NE31: Heb 6E 73
Brighton Rd. NE8: Gate 2F 83
Brighton Ter. DH6: Sher 6H 157
Bright St. NE33: S Shi 5F 63
SR6: Monk 4D 104
Brignall Cl. DH3: Gt Lum 4H 135
Brignall Gdns. NE15: Newc T 2E 67
Brignall Ri. SR3: Sund 5B 118
Brigside Cotts. NE13: Sea B 3E 31
(not continuous)
Brindley Rd. NE37: Wash 1B 114
SR8: Pet 1A 164
Brinkburn DH2: Ches S 6A 126
NE38: Wash 5C 114
Brinkburn Av. NE3: Gos 1D 56
NE8: Gate 3G 83
NE16: Swa 3E 81
NE23: Cra 3C 22
NE24: Bly 1D 18
Brinkburn Cl. NE6: Newc T 4B 70
NE21: Bla T 3G 79
Brinkburn Ct. NE6: Newc T 3B 70
(off Brinkburn Cl.)
NE30: N Shi 1D 62
Brinkburn Cres. DH4: Hou S 1G 137
Brinkburn La. NE6: Newc T 4B 70
(off Brinkburn St.)
Brinkburn Pl. NE6: Newc T 3B 70
Brinkburn Sq. NE6: Newc T 4B 70
(not continuous)
Brinkburn St. NE6: Newc T 4B 70
(not continuous)
NE28: W'snd 6G 61
NE34: S Shi 4D 74
SR4: Sund 2A 148
Brisbane Av. NE34: S Shi 6B 74
Brisbane Ct. NE8: Gate 6G 69
Brisbane St. SR5: C'twn 2C 102
Brislee Av. NE30: N Shi 6E 49
(not continuous)
Brislee Gdns. NE3: Ken 3A 56
Bristlecone SR3: New S 4G 131
Bristol Av. NE37: Usw 5H 99
SR5: C'twn 2B 102
Bristol Dr. NE28: W'snd 2B 60
Bristol St. NE25: Sea D 4A 24
Bristol Ter. NE4: Newc T 5C 68
Bristol Wlk. NE25: Sea D 3B 24
Bristol Way NE32: Jar 2G 87
Britannia Ct. NE4: Newc T 5C 68
Britannia Pl. NE4: Newc T 4C 68
Britannia Rd. SR3: New S 2A 132
Britannia Ter. DH4: Hou S 3E 137
Britten Cl. DH9: Stly 4E 123
Brixham Av. NE9: Gate 2H 97
Brixham Cl. SR7: Mur 5G 141
Brixham Cres. NE32: Jar 4H 73
Brixham Gdns. SR3: Sund 4B 118
Broadbank NE10: Gate 3H 85
Broad Chare
NE1: Newc T 4G 69 (5F 5)
Broad Cl., The SR8: Pet 1D 164
Broadfield Pl. NE34: S Shi 4F 75
Broadfield Wlk. NE5: Newc T 3E 55
Broad Gth. NE1: Newc T 5G 69 (6F 5)
Broad Landing NE33: S Shi 4D 62
Broadlands SR6: Cle 4A 90

Broadlea NE10: Gate 3H 85
Broadmayne Av. SR4: Sund 3F 117
Broadmayne Gdns. SR4: Sund . . .3F 117
Broad Mdws. NE3: Ken 4B 56
SR2: Sund 3B 118
Broadmeadows NE38: Wash 5C 114
SR3: E Her 3D 130
Broadmeadows Cl. NE16: Swa 2E 81
Broadmead Way NE15: Newc T 4D 66
Broadoak NE10: Gate 2H 85
Broadpark NE10: Gate 3H 85
Broadpool Grn. NE16: Whi 5G 81
Broadpool Ter. NE16: Whi 5G 81
(Broom Ter.)
NE16: Whi 5G 81
(Southfield Ter.)
Broadshaw Wlk. NE15: Thro 6D 52
Broadsheath Ter. SR5: S'wck . . .4H 103
(not continuous)
Broadside NE10: Gate 3H 85
Broadstairs Ct. SR4: Sund 3F 117
Broadstone Gro. NE5: Cha P 6A 54
Broadstone Way NE28: W'snd 3A 60
Broadviews DH3: Gt Lum 3G 135
Broadview Vs. DH6: Sher 6E 157
Broadwater NE10: Gate 2H 85
Broadway DH3: Ches S 4C 126
NE9: Gate 5B 84
NE15: Lem 2B 66
NE16: Whi 6D 80
NE20: Pon 2C 38
NE24: Bly 1C 18
Broadway Circ. NE24: Bly 6B 12
Broadway Cl. NE30: N Shi 2D 48
Broadway Ct. NE3: Gos 6E 43
NE28: W'snd 1C 60
Broadway Cres. NE24: Bly 1C 18
Broadway E. NE3: Gos 6E 43
Broadway, The DH4: Hou S 3A 138
NE30: N Shi 2D 48
NE33: S Shi 5H 63
SR4: Sund 4D 116
(not continuous)
Broadway Vs. NE15: Newc T 4F 67
Broadway W. NE3: Gos 6D 42
Broadwell Ct. NE3: Newc T 3H 57
Broadwood Rd. NE15: Newc T 2D 66
Broadwood Vw. DH3: Ches S 1D 134
Brockenhurst Dr. SR4: Sund 5C 116
Brock Farm Ct. NE30: N Shi 1C 62
Brockhampton Cl. NE35: Bol C . . .1A 88
Brock La. NE22: E Sle, W Sle 1F 11
Brockley Av. NE34: S Shi 5D 74
Brockley St. SR5: C'twn 2C 102
Brockley Ter. NE35: Bol C 2A 88
BROCKLEY WHINS 6B 74
Brockley Whins Station (Metro)
. . . . .1B 88
Brock Sq. NE6: Newc T 4B 70
Brock St. NE6: Newc T 4B 70
Brockwade NE10: Gate 6F 85
Brockwell Cen., The NE23: Cra . . .1B 22
Brockwell Cl. NE21: Bla T 2G 79
Brockwell Ct. NE24: Bly 2A 18
Brockwell Dr. NE39: Row G 2E 93
Brockwell Ho. NE5: Newc T 5G 55
Brockwell Rd. NE38: Wash 2F 113
Brockwell St. NE24: Bly 3A 18
Broderick Ter. DH4: Hou S 6H 129
Brodie NE34: S Shi 5E 75
Brodrick Cl. NE3: Ken 2H 55
Brodrick St. NE33: S Shi 4F 63

Brokenheugh NE5: Newc T 6D 54
Bromarsh Ct. SR6: Monk 4F 105
Bromford Rd. NE3: Ken 2H 55
Bromley Av. NE25: Whit B 2A 48
Bromley Cl. DH1: H Shin ..5H 161
Bromley Ct. NE3: Ken 6H 41
Bromley Gdns. NE24: News 2C 18
   NE28: W'snd 2B 60
Brompton Cl. DH2: Ous ...5G 111
Brompton Pl. NE11: Dun 3C 82
Brompton Ter. DH4: Hou S ...5H 129
Bromsgrove Cl. NE28: W'snd ..2B 60
Bronte Pl. DH9: Stly 5F 123
Bronte St. NE8: Gate 2B 84
Brookbank Cl. SR3: New S ..4H 131
Brook Ct. NE22: Bed 4A 10
Brookdale DH1: Carr 3C 156
Brooke Av. NE16: Whi 3E 81
   NE35: Bol C 3D 88
Brooke Cl. DH9: Stly 3E 123
Brooke Ho. DH5: Hou S 4A 138
Brookes Ri. DH7: B'don 4F 159
Brooke St. SR5: Monk ...5C 104 (1F 7)
Brookes Wlk. NE34: S Shi 1C 88
Brookfield NE3: Gos 5D 56
Brookfield Cres. NE5: Cha P ..6A 54
Brookfield Ter. NE10: Gate ...2G 85
   (off Shields Rd.)
Brook Gdns. NE26: Whit B 5D 36
Brookland Dr. NE12: Kil 2E 45
Brookland Rd. SR4: Sund ...1H 117
Brooklands NE20: Pon 2A 38
Brooklands Way NE35: Bol C ...3H 87
Brookland Ter. NE29: N Shi 4F 47
   (not continuous)
Brooklyn St. SR7: Mur 3D 150
Brooklyn Ter. SR7: Mur 3D 150
Brook Rd. SR4: Sund 2B 118
Brookside DH5: Hou S 5H 137
   NE23: Dud 4A 32
Brookside Av. NE13: Bru V 6C 30
   NE24: Cow 6H 11
Brookside Cotts. SR2: Sund 3C 118
Brookside Cres. NE5: Newc T ...6H 55
Brookside Gdns. SR2: Sund 3C 118
Brookside Ter. SR2: Sund 3C 118
Brookside Wood NE38: Wash ..6B 114
Brooksmead NE28: W'snd 3G 59
Brook St. NE6: Newc T 4D 70
   NE26: Whit B 6D 36
Brookvale Av. NE3: Ken 3B 56
Brook Vw. SR7: S'hm 3F 141
Brook Wlk. SR3: New S 4H 131
Broom Cl. DH9: Stly 2F 123
   NE16: Whi 5G 81
   NE21: Bla T 3H 79
Broom Ct. NE9: Spri 5F 99
Broom Cres. DH7: Ush M 5C 152
Broome Cl. NE3: Ken 1B 56
Broome Ct. DH7: Ush M 1F 159
Broome Rd. DH1: Carr 3B 156
Broom Farm W. DH7: Ush M ...1E 159
Broomfield NE32: Jar 1G 87
Broomfield Av. NE6: Walk 6E 59
   NE28: W'snd 2A 60
Broomfield Rd. NE3: Gos 3D 56
Broom Grn. NE16: Whi 5G 81
Broom Hall Dr. DH7: Ush M ...6D 152
BROOM HILL 5B 138
Broom Hill DH9: Stly 2B 122
Broomhill Est. DH5: Hett H 5B 138
Broomhill Gdns. NE5: Newc T ..6H 55
Broomhill Ter. DH5: Hett H 6B 138

Broom La. DH1: Dur 6C 152
   DH7: Ush M 6C 152
   NE16: Whi 6F 81
Broomlaw NE9: Gate 1C 98
Broomlea NE29: N Shi 4F 47
Broomlea Ct. NE21: Bla T 6A 66
Broomlee Cl. NE7: Newc T 4D 58
Broomlee Rd. NE12: Kil 2C 44
Broomley Ct. NE3: Ken 6B 42
Broomley Wlk. NE3: Ken 6B 42
BROOMPARK 1E 159
Broomridge Av. NE15: Newc T ..3H 67
Broomshields Av. SR5: S'wck ..2B 104
Broomshields Cl. SR5: S'wck ..2B 104
BROOMSIDE 3C 156
Broomside Cl. DH1: Carr 3B 156
Broomside La. DH1: Carr 3A 156
Broomside Pk. DH1: Dur 3G 155
Brooms La. DH8: Con, Lead 5A 120
Brooms, The DH2: Ous 5H 111
Broom Ter. NE16: Burn 1H 107
   NE16: Whi 5G 81
Broomy Hill Rd. NE15: Thro ...5C 52
Broomylinn Pl. NE23: Cra 1C 22
Brotherlee Rd. NE3: Ken 6B 42
Brougham Ct. SR8: Pet 4A 164
Brougham St.
   SR1: Sund 1D 118 (4G 7)
Brough Ct. NE6: Newc T 2C 70
Brough Gdns. NE28: W'snd 3E 61
Brough Pk. Stadium (Speedway)
   ....3D 70
Brough Pk. Way NE6: Walk ...3D 70
Brough St. NE6: Newc T 2C 70
Broughton Rd. NE33: S Shi ...5F 63
Brough Way NE6: Newc T 2C 70
Brown Cres. NE9: Spri 4C 98
Browne Rd. SR6: Monk 2D 104
BROWNEY 6F 159
Browney La. DH7: B'don 6E 159
Browning Cl. DH9: Stly 3F 123
   NE34: S Shi 1D 88
   (not continuous)
Browning Sq. NE8: Gate 1A 84
Browning St. SR8: Eas 1F 163
Brownlow Cl. NE7: Newc T ...4F 59
Brownlow Rd. NE34: S Shi 3E 75
Brownrigg Dr. NE23: Cra 4C 22
Brownriggs Ct. NE37: Wash ..1H 113
Brown Rd. SR5: C'twn 4D 102
Browns Bldgs. DH3: Bir 6C 112
   NE22: Red 5G 9
Brownsea Pl. NE9: Gate 4A 84
Browntop Pl. NE34: S Shi 4E 75
Brow, The NE6: Newc T 4C 70
Broxbourne Ter. SR4: Sund ...1A 118
Broxburn Cl. NE28: W'snd 2C 60
Broxburn Ct. NE5: Newc T 4G 55
Broxholm Rd. NE6: Newc T ...6B 58
Bruce Cl. NE5: Newc T 5D 54
   NE34: S Shi 5E 75
Bruce Gdns. NE5: Newc T 2G 67
Bruce Kirkup Rd. SR8: Pet 5F 163
Bruce Pl. SR8: Pet 5C 162
Bruce St. SR5: S'wck 3C 104
Brundon Av. NE26: Whit B 4B 36
Brunel Dr. SR6: Monk 3F 105
Brunel Lodge NE4: Newc T ...6C 68
   (off Brunel St.)
Brunel St. NE4: Newc T 6D 68
   NE8: Gate 3F 83
Brunel Ter. NE4: Newc T 6C 68
Brunel Wlk. NE4: Newc T 6C 68

Brunswick Gro. NE13: Bru V 5C 30
Brunswick Ind. Est. NE13: Bru V ..5B 30
Brunswick Pk. Ind. Est.
   NE13: Bru V 5B 30
Brunswick Pl.
   NE1: Newc T 4F 69 (3D 4)
   SR5: C'twn 1C 102
Brunswick Rd. NE27: Shir 3D 46
   SR5: C'twn 1C 102
Brunswick Sq. NE27: Shir 3D 46
Brunswick St. NE33: S Shi 6E 63
BRUNSWICK VILLAGE 5C 30
Brunton Av. NE3: Ken 1B 56
   NE28: W'snd 4F 61
Brunton Cl. NE27: Shir 3D 46
Brunton Gro. NE3: Ken 1B 56
Brunton La. NE3: Gos 3H 41
   NE3: Ken 2G 55
   NE13: Bru V, Wide O, Wool ..3H 41
Brunton M. NE13: Bru V 3B 42
Brunton Rd. NE13: Wool 6F 41
Brunton St. NE29: N Shi 4H 61
Brunton Ter. SR4: Sund 1A 118
Brunton Wlk. NE3: Ken 1G 55
   (not continuous)
Brunton Way NE10: Gate 1H 85
   NE23: Cra 5B 16
Brussels Rd. NE28: W'snd 6H 59
   SR4: Sund 6F 103
BRYAN'S LEAP 1G 107
Bryans Leap NE16: Burn 6G 93
Bryden Ct. NE34: S Shi 4F 75
Brydon Cres. DH6: S Het 6B 150
Bryers St. SR6: Whit 2F 91
Buchanan Grn. NE11: Dun 2C 82
Buchanan St. NE31: Heb 4B 72
Buckingham SR3: E Her 1G 131
Buckingham Cl. SR6: Whit 3F 91
Buckingham Rd. SR8: Pet 5B 162
Buckinghamshire Rd.
   DH1: Carr 4A 156
Buckingham St. NE4: Newc T ...4D 68
   NE38: Wash 4B 114
Buck's Hill DH1: Dur 3C 160
Buck's Hill Vw. NE16: Whi 5G 81
Buckthorne Gro. NE7: Newc T ..4C 58
Buddle Arts Cen. 5H 59
Buddle Cl. SR8: Pet 5D 162
Buddle Ct. NE4: Newc T 5A 68
Buddle Gdns. NE40: G'side ...2A 78
Buddle Ind. Est. NE28: W'snd ..1A 72
Buddle Rd. NE4: Newc T 5H 67
Buddle St. NE28: W'snd 6A 60
   SR2: Sund 2E 119
Bude Ct. NE28: W'snd 2A 60
Bude Gdns. NE9: Gate 2H 97
Bude Gro. NE29: N Shi 4H 47
Bude Sq. SR7: Mur 1D 150
Budle Cl. NE3: Gos 1D 56
   NE24: Bly 6A 12
Budleigh Rd. NE3: Ken 2B 56
Budworth Av. NE26: Sea S 4H 25
Bugatti Ind. Pk. NE29: N Shi ...2G 61
Bullfinch Dr. NE16: Whi 4E 81
Bullion La. DH2: Ches S 6B 126
Bull La. SR1: Sund 6E 105
Bulman Ho. NE3: Gos 2E 57
Bulman's La. NE29: N Shi 5C 48
Bulmer Ho. NE34: S Shi 2A 76
Bulmer Rd. NE34: S Shi 2A 76
Bungalows, The DH3: Bir 1B 112
   DH5: Hett H 5B 138

Bungalows, The DH6: S Het 6B 150
　DH7: New B 1B 158
　DH9: Tan L 1A 122
　NE10: Gate 3E 85
　NE11: Kib 5G 97
　NE21: Bla T 1G 79
　NE28: W'snd 4D 60
　SR8: Pet 5F 163
Bunyan Av. NE34: S Shi 6C 74
Burdale Av. NE5: Newc T 6E 55
BURDON 6B 132
Burdon Av. DH5: Hou S 3C 138
　NE23: Nel V 2H 21
Burdon Cl. SR6: Cle 2G 89
Burdon Cres. SR2: Ryh 3E 133
　SR6: Cle 2G 89
　SR7: S'hm 2F 141
Burdon La. SR2: New S, Ryh . . .4C 132
　SR3: New S 6H 131
Burdon Lodge NE16: Sun 3G 95
Burdon Main Row NE29: N Shi . .3C 62
Burdon Pk. NE16: Sun 3G 95
Burdon Pl. NE2: Newc T 1G 69
　SR8: Pet 1E 165
　　　　(not continuous)
Burdon Plain NE16: Sun 1F 109
Burdon Rd. SR1: Sund . . .2D 118 (6H 7)
　SR2: Sund 2D 118 (6H 7)
　SR3: New S 4B 132
　SR6: Cle 2G 89
Burdon St. NE29: N Shi 4H 61
Burdon Ter. NE2: Newc T 1G 69
　NE22: Bed 4G 9
Burford Ct. NE3: Newc T 3A 58
Burford Gdns. SR3: Sund 4B 118
Burghley Rd. NE10: Gate 5C 84
Burgoyne Ct. NE37: Usw 5B 100
Burke St. SR5: C'twn 2C 102
Burlawn Cl. SR2: Ryh 1F 133
Burleigh St. NE33: S Shi 6F 63
Burlington Cl. SR2: Sund 2E 119
Burlington Ct. NE2: Newc T 5H 57
　NE28: W'snd 6C 46
Burlington Gdns. NE6: Newc T . . .1B 70
Burlison Gdns. NE10: Gate 1C 84
Burnaby Dr. NE40: Ryton 5B 64
Burnaby St. SR4: Sund 2A 118
Burn Av. NE12: Longb 5D 44
　　　　(not continuous)
　NE28: W'snd 5H 59
Burnbank NE10: Gate 5G 85
　NE13: Sea B 3D 30
　SR5: S'wck 3B 104
Burnbank Av. NE25: Well 6F 35
Burnbridge NE13: Sea B 3D 30
Burn Closes Cres. NE28: W'snd . .4C 60
Burn Crook DH5: Hou S 5H 137
Burnden Gro. DH4: Hou S 4D 128
Burnet Cl. NE28: W'snd 2A 60
Burney Vs. NE8: Gate 2A 84
Burnfoot Ter. NE26: Whit B 1D 48
Burnfoot Way NE3: Ken 4A 56
Burn Gdns. SR8: Eas 1C 162
Burnhall Dr. SR7: S'hm 2G 141
Burnham Av. NE15: Lem 2G 65
Burnham Cl. DH4: Pen 3F 129
　NE24: News 2C 18
Burnham Gro. NE6: Walk 5E 71
　NE36: E Bol 4F 89
Burnham St. NE34: S Shi 3E 75
Burn Heads Rd. NE31: Heb 5B 72
Burnhills Gdns. NE40: G'sde 2A 78
Burnhills La. NE21: G'sde 3B 78

Burnhope Dr. SR5: S'wck 2B 104
Burnhope Gdns. NE9: Gate 2D 98
Burnhope Rd. NE38: Wash 1C 114
Burnhope Way SR8: Pet 6B 162
Burnigill DH7: B'don 6E 159
Burnip Rd. SR7: Mur 1C 150
Burn La. DH5: Hett H 2C 148
Burnlea Gdns. NE23: Seg 1H 33
Burnley St. NE21: Bla T 1A 80
Burnmoor Gdns. NE9: Gate 2D 98
BURNOPFIELD 1F 107
Burnopfield Gdns.
　NE15: Newc T 3E 67
Burnopfield Rd. NE39: Row G . . .4F 93
Burnop Ter. NE39: Row G 3A 92
Burn Pk. Rd. DH4: Hou S 3G 137
　SR2: Sund 2B 118
Burn Prom. DH4: Hou S 2H 137
　　　　(not continuous)
Burn Rd. NE21: Bla T 2F 79
Burns Av. NE24: Bly 2A 18
　NE35: Bol C 3D 88
Burns Av. Nth. DH5: Hou S 4A 138
　　　　(not continuous)
Burns Av. Sth. DH5: Hou S 4A 138
Burns Cl. DH4: W Rai 3E 147
　DH9: Stly 3E 123
　NE16: Whi 6F 81
Burns Ct. NE34: S Shi 6D 74
Burns Cres. NE16: Swa 3E 81
BURNSIDE 1G 137
Burn Side SR8: Pet 1D 164
Burnside NE2: Newc T 2D 68
　　　　(off Richardson Rd.)
　NE10: Gate 4E 85
　NE20: Pon 2B 38
　NE22: Bed 2D 10
　NE25: H'wll 2D 34
　NE32: Jar 5G 73
　NE36: E Bol 4G 89
Burnside Av. DH4: Hou S 2G 137
　NE23: Dud 3B 32
　SR8: Pet 1G 165
Burnside Cl. NE16: Whi 1E 95
　NE23: Seg 2E 33
　NE24: Cow 5H 11
Burnside Cotts. NE23: Dud 3B 32
　SR7: Mur 6G 141
Burnside Rd. NE3: Gos 6E 43
　NE25: Whit B 2D 48
　NE30: Whit B 2D 48
　NE39: Row G 3D 92
Burnside, The NE5: Newc T 6C 54
Burnside Vw. NE23: Seg 2E 33
Burns St. NE32: Jar 2F 73
Burnstones NE5: Newc T 6C 54
Burn Ter. DH4: Hou S 3G 129
　NE28: W'snd 5D 60
　NE31: Heb 1A 86
Burnthouse Bank DH2: Pelt 5H 125
Burnt Ho. Cl. NE21: Bla T 3G 79
Burnthouse La.
　NE16: Sun, Whi 1E 95
　NE16: Whi 6E 81
　　　　(Fairfield Av.)
Burnt Ho. Rd. NE25: Whit B 2A 48
Burntland Av. SR5: S'wck 3H 103
Burn Vw. NE23: Dud 3B 32
　NE32: Jar 3G 87
Burnville NE6: Newc T 2A 70
Burnville Rd. SR4: Sund 2B 118
Burnville Rd. Sth.
　SR4: Sund 2B 118

Burnway NE37: Wash 5H 99
　SR7: S'hm 3G 141
BURRADON 5C 32
Burradon NE23: Dud 6C 32
Burradon Rd. NE23: Dud 5C 32
　　　　(Cheviot Grange)
　NE23: Dud 3C 32
　　　　(Seaton Cft.)
Burrow St. NE33: S Shi 4E 63
Burscough Cres. SR6: Monk 3D 104
Burstow Av. NE6: Walk 6E 71
Burt Av. NE29: N Shi 2A 62
Burt Cl. SR8: Pet 5D 162
Burt Cres. NE23: Dud 3B 32
Burtree NE38: Wash 5H 113
Burt Rd. NE22: Bed 2E 11
Burt St. NE24: Bly 5C 12
Burt Ter. NE15: Thro 5G 53
Burwell Av. NE5: Newc T 1D 66
Burwood Cl. NE6: Walk 6G 71
Burwood Rd. NE6: Walk 6F 71
　NE29: N Shi 5G 47
Bushblades La.
　DH9: Ann P, Dip, Tan L 1E 121
Bus. & Innovation Cen.
　SR5: Sund 4H 103
Buston Ter. NE2: Newc T 6H 57
Busty Bank NE16: Burn 4F 93
　NE39: Burn 4F 93
Butcher's Bri. Rd. NE32: Jar 4F 73
Bute Cotts. NE11: Dun 2A 82
Bute Ct. SR3: New S 3A 132
Bute Dr. NE39: H Spen 1A 92
Buteland Rd. NE15: Newc T 2D 66
Bute Rd. Nth. NE39: H Spen 1A 92
Bute Rd. Sth. NE39: H Spen 2A 92
Bute St. DH9: Tan L 5G 107
Butler St. SR8: Eas 1F 163
Butsfield Gdns. SR3: Sund 5B 118
Butterburn Cl. NE7: Newc T 3E 59
Butterfield Cl. NE40: Ryton 6A 64
Buttermere NE10: Gate 3G 85
　SR6: Cle 2A 90
　SR8: Pet 4A 164
Buttermere Av. DH5: Eas L 5E 149
　NE16: Whi 4G 81
Buttermere Cl. DH2: Ches S 1C 134
　NE5: Newc T 6F 55
　NE12: Kil 2C 44
Buttermere Cres. DH6: S Het 5G 149
　NE21: Bla T 3H 79
Buttermere Gdns. NE9: Gate 6A 84
　NE34: S Shi 3G 75
Buttermere Rd. NE30: N Shi 3C 48
Buttermere St. SR2: Sund 5E 119
Buttermere Way NE24: Cow 4H 11
Buttsfield Ter. DH4: Pen 1F 129
Buxton Cl. NE28: W'snd 2B 60
　NE32: Jar 4G 73
Buxton Gdns. NE5: Newc T 4D 54
　SR3: Sund 4B 118
Buxton Grn. NE5: Newc T 4D 54
Buxton St. NE1: Newc T . . .4H 69 (4G 5)
Byer Bank DH5: Hou S 4C 138
BYERMOOR 6B 94
Byermoor Ind. Est. NE16: Burn . . .6B 94
Byers Ct. SR3: New S 1B 132
Byer Sq. DH5: Hett H 5C 138
Byer St. DH5: Hett H 5C 138
Byeways, The NE12: Longb 1B 58
Bygate Cl. NE3: Ken 4A 56
Bygate Rd. NE25: Whit B 1A 48
BYKER 4C 70

Byker Bank NE1: Newc T 4A 70
  NE6: Newc T 4A 70
Byker Bri. NE1: Newc T . . .3A 70 (3H 5)
  NE6: Newc T 3A 70
Byker Bus. Development Cen.
  NE6: Newc T 4B 70
Byker Cres. NE6: Newc T 3C 70
Byker Lodge NE6: Newc T 4C 70
Byker Station (Metro) 3B 70
Byker St. NE6: Walk 3F 71
Byker Ter. NE6: Walk 3F 71
Byker Wall Baths 3B 70
Byland Cl. DH4: Hou S 1G 137
Byland Ct. DH7: Ush M 4D 152
  NE38: Wash 2A 114
Byland Rd. NE12: Longb 1H 57
Bylands Gdns. SR3: Sund 4B 118
Byony Toft SR2: Ryh 2G 133
Byrness NE5: Newc T 6C 54
Byrness Cl. NE3: Ken 3G 55
Byrness Ct. NE28: W'snd 2C 60
Byrness Row NE23: Cra 1C 22
Byrne Ter. W. SR3: New S 2B 132
Byron Av. DH2: Pelt 6G 125
  NE24: Bly 2A 18
  NE28: W'snd 6E 61
  NE31: Heb 3D 72
  NE35: Bol C 3C 88
Byron Cl. DH2: Ous 6H 111
  DH9: Stly 3E 123
Byron Ct. NE5: Cha P 5A 54
  NE16: Swa 3E 81
Byron Lodge Est. SR7: S'hm . . .3E 141
Byron Rd. SR5: S'wck 3A 104
Byrons Ct. SR7: S'hm 1A 142
Byron St. DH2: Ous 6H 111
  NE2: Newc T 3C 69 (2F 5)
  NE33: S Shi 1F 75
  SR5: S'wck 4C 104
  SR8: Eas 1F 163
Byron Ter. DH5: Hou S 4A 138
  SR7: S'hm 2F 141
Byron Wlk. NE8: Gate 1A 84
By-Way, The NE15: Thro 6D 52
Bywell Av. NE3: Ken 5B 42
  NE15: Lem 2C 66
  NE34: S Shi 2A 76
  SR5: S'wck 2C 104
Bywell Dr. SR8: Pet 4C 164
Bywell Gdns. NE10: Gate 5B 84
  NE11: Gate 6C 82
Bywell Gro. NE27: Shir 2E 47
Bywell Rd. SR6: Cle 3H 89
Bywell St. NE6: Newc T 4D 70
  (not continuous)
Bywell Ter. NE26: Sea S 3H 25
  NE32: Jar 6F 73

C

Cadlestone Ct. NE23: Cra 1D 22
Cadwell La. SR8: Eas 1B 162
Caedmon Live Theatre 3H 83
Caernarvon Cl. NE5: Newc T 3F 55
Caernarvon Dr. SR3: E Her 3E 131
Caer Urfa Cl. NE33: S Shi 3E 63
Caesar's Wlk. NE33: S Shi 3E 63
Caesar Way NE28: W'snd 3C 60
Cairncross SR5: C'twn 4C 102
Cairnglass Grn. NE23: Cra 1D 22
Cairngorm Av. NE38: Wash 4G 113
Cairnhill Ter. DH4: Hou S 5H 129

Cairnside SR3: E Her 2E 131
  SR7: Sea 2D 140
Cairnside Sth. SR3: E Her 2D 130
Cairnsmore Cl. NE6: Walk 1H 71
  NE23: Cra 5B 22
Cairnsmore Dr. NE38: Wash . . .4H 113
Cairns Rd. SR5: Monk 1C 104
  SR7: Mur 2A 150
Cairns Sq. SR5: Monk 1C 104
Cairns Way NE3: Ken 6B 42
Cairo St. SR2: Sund 3E 119
Caithness Rd. SR5: C'twn 3B 102
Caithness Sq. SR5: C'twn 3B 102
Calais Rd. SR5: C'twn 4B 102
Calandra Chase NE2: Newc T . . .1D 68
Caldbeck Av. NE6: Walk 6F 71
Caldbeck Cl. NE6: Walk 6F 71
Calderbourne Av. SR6: Monk 1E 105
Calder Cl. SR3: New S 3H 131
Calderdale NE28: W'snd 2F 59
Calderdale Av. NE6: Walk 2F 71
Calder Grn. NE32: Jar 1G 87
Calder's Cres. NE38: Wash 6B 114
Calder Wlk. NE16: Sun 3E 95
Calderwood Cres. NE9: Gate . . .2A 98
Calderwood Pk. NE9: Gate 2A 98
Caldew Cl. DH5: Eas L 3D 148
Caldew Cres. NE5: Newc T 1E 67
Caldwell Rd. NE3: Ken 5B 42
Caledonia DH3: Gt Lum 3G 135
  NE21: Bla T 3G 79
Caledonian Rd. SR5: C'twn 2B 102
Caledonian St. NE31: Heb 2B 72
Caledonia St. NE6: Walk 5G 71
Calfclose Dr. NE32: Jar 1F 87
Calfclose La. NE32: Jar 1F 87
Calfclose Wlk. NE32: Jar 6G 73
California NE21: Bla T 2H 79
Callaley Av. NE16: Whi 5D 80
Callaly Av. NE23: Cra 3C 22
Callaly Way NE6: Walk 5D 70
Callander DH2: Ous 5A 112
Callendar Ct. NE9: Gate 6B 84
Callerdale Rd. NE24: Cow 5G 11
CALLERTON 1H 53
Callerton NE12: Kil 6D 32
Callerton Av. NE29: N Shi 1G 61
Callerton Cl. NE23: Cra 3C 22
Callerton Ct. NF5: Newc T 4E 55
  NE20: Pon 1E 39
Callerton La. NE5: Cal 3E 39
  NE20: Cal, Pon 3E 39
CALLERTON LANE END 6E 39
Callerton La. End Cotts.
  NE5: Cal 6E 39
Callerton Parkway Station (Metro)
  . . . . .4C 40
Callerton Pl. DH9: Stly 6H 123
  NE4: Newc T 4C 68
Callerton Rd. NF15: Thro 5D 52
Callerton Vw. NE5: Cha P 3H 53
Calley Cl. SR8: Pet 4C 164
Callington Cl. DH4: Hou S 1C 136
Callington Dr. SR2: Ryh 2F 133
Callum Dr. NE34: S Shi 1A 76
Calow Way NE16: Whi 6D 80
Calstock Cl. SR7: Mur 3D 150
Calthwaite Cl. SR5: C'twn 3C 102
Calver St. NE34: S Shi 4G 75
  (not continuous)
Calvert Ter. SR7: Mur 2C 150
Calvus Dr. NE15: Hed W 5H 51
Camberley Cl. SR3: New S 1C 132

Camberley Dr. DH7: B'don 6B 158
Camberley Rd. NE28: W'snd 3E 61
Camberwell Cl. NE11: Gate 5D 82
Camberwell Way
  SR3: E Her, New S 3F 131
Cambo Av. NE22: Bed 4C 16
  NE25: Whit B 2H 47
Cambo Cl. NE3: Gos 2F 57
  NE24: Bly 6A 12
  NE28: W'snd 1B 60
Cambo Dr. NE23: Cra 4C 22
Cambo Grn. NE5: Newc T 5G 55
CAMBOIS 1B 12
Cambo Pl. NE30: N Shi 4C 48
Camborne Gro. NE8: Gate 2H 83
Camborne Pl. NE8: Gate 2H 83
Cambourne Av. SR6: Monk 1E 105
Cambria Grn. SR4: Sund 1C 116
Cambrian Cl. NE38: Wash 4H 113
Cambrian St. NE32: Jar 2G 73
Cambrian Way NE38: Wash 3H 113
Cambria St. SR4: Sund 1C 116
Cambridge Av. NE12: Longb 5D 44
  NE26: Whit B 6C 36
  NE28: W'snd 4G 59
  NE31: Heb 3D 72
  NE37: Usw 5H 99
Cambridge Cres. DH4: Hou S . . .3E 129
Cambridge Dr. DH3: Gt Lum 4G 135
Cambridge Pl. DH3: Bir 6C 112
Cambridge Rd. SR3: New S 2A 132
  SR8: Pet 5C 162
Cambridgeshire Dr. DH1: Carr . . .5A 156
Cambridge St. NE4: Newc T 6D 68
Cambridge Ter. NE8: Gate 2G 83
Camden Sq. NE30: N Shi 2D 62
  SR7: S'hm 5A 142
Camden St.
  NE2: Newc T 3G 69 (2F 5)
  NE30: N Shi 2D 62
  SR5: S'wck, Sund 4A 104
Camelford Ct. NE15: Lem 1A 66
Camelot Cl. SR7: S'hm 3A 142
Cameron Cl. NE34: S Shi 6E 75
Cameron Wlk. NE11: Dun 1G 81
Camerton Pl. NE28: W'snd 6C 46
Camilla Rd. NE15: Hed W 5H 51
Camilla St. NE8: Gate 2H 83
Cam Mead SR3: New S 5A 132
CAMPBELL PARK 4D 72
Campbell Pk. Rd. NE31: Heb 3C 72
Campbell Pl. NE4: Newc T 4C 68
Campbell Rd. SR5: C'twn 3B 102
Campbell Sq. SR5: C'twn 3B 102
Campbell St. NE31: Heb 2C 72
  SR8: Eas 1F 163
Campbell Ter. DH5: Eas L 4D 148
CAMPERDOWN 6B 32
Camperdown NE5: Newc T 6D 54
Camperdown Av.
  DH3: Ches S 4D 126
  NE12: Kil 1B 44
Camperdown Ind. Est.
  NE12: Kil 6B 32
Campion Dr. DH9: Tan L 1B 122
Campion Gdns. NE10: Gate 6D 84
Campsie Cl. NE38: Wash 4H 113
Campsie Cres. NE30: N Shi 4C 48
Camp St. SR8: Eas 1F 163
Camp Ter. NE29: N Shi 1C 62
Campus Martius NE15: Hed W . . .5F 51
Campville NE29: N Shi 1C 62
Camsey Cl. NE12: Longb 1H 57

Camsey Pl. NE12: Longb 1H 57
CANADA 5C 126
Canberra Av. NE25: Whit B 2H 47
Canberra Dr. NE34: S Shi 5A 74
Canberra Rd. SR4: Sund 3F 117
Candelford Cl. NE7: Newc T 4D 58
Candlish St. NE33: S Shi 5F 63
Candlish Ter. SR7: S'hm 5C 142
Canning St. NE4: Newc T 4A 68
(Farndale Rd.)
NE4: Newc T 4A 68
(Wellfield Rd.)
NE31: Heb 4B 72
Cannock DH2: Ous 5H 111
NE12: Kil 1D 44
Cannock Dr. NE7: Newc T 3A 58
Cannon St. NE8: Gate 5G 69
Cann Rd. SR8: Pet 5D 162
Cann St. SR8: Eas 1C 162
Canonbie Sq. NE23: Cra 1D 22
Canon Cockin St. SR2: Sund ..3E 119
Canon Gro. NE32: Jar 2G 73
Canonsfield Cl. NE15: Cha P ...4H 53
SR3: New S 4H 131
Canterbury Av. NE28: W'snd 1B 60
Canterbury Cl. DH3: Gt Lum ...5G 135
NE12: Longb 1A 58
Canterbury Rd. DH1: Dur 5D 144
SR5: C'twn 3C 102
Canterbury St. NE6: Walk 3D 70
(not continuous)
NE33: S Shi 1F 75
Canterbury Way NE13: Wide O ..5D 30
NE32: Jar 2E 87
Capercaillie Lodge NE23: Dud ..2C 32
Capetown Rd. SR5: C'twn 3B 102
Capetown Sq. SR5: C'twn 3B 102
Caplestone Cl. NE38: Wash ...4H 113
Capstan La. NE9: Gate 3C 98
Captains Row, The
NE33: S Shi 1D 74
Captains Wharf NE33: S Shi 4D 62
Capulet Gro. NE34: S Shi 4C 74
Capulet Ter. SR2: Sund 3E 119
Caradoc Cl. NE38: Wash 4H 113
Caragh Rd. DH2: Ches S 2B 134
Caraway Wlk. NE34: S Shi 1G 89
(not continuous)
Carden Av. NE34: S Shi 4B 76
Cardiff Sq. SR5: C'twn 4B 102
Cardiff St. SR8: Eas 1F 163
Cardigan Gro. NE30: N Shi 2C 48
Cardigan Rd. SR5: C'twn 3B 102
Cardigan Ter. NE6: Newc T 2B 70
Cardinal Cl. NE12: Longb 1A 58
NE15: Cha P 4H 53
Cardinals Cl. SR3: New S 4H 131
Cardonnel St. NE29: N Shi 3C 62
Cardwell St. SR6: Monk 4D 104
(not continuous)
Careen Cres. SR3: E Her 2D 130
Carew Ct. NE23: Cra 4B 22
Carham Av. NE23: Cra 3C 22
Carham Cl. NE3: Gos 1F 57
Carisbrooke NE22: Bed 3H 9
Carisbrooke Cl. NE37: Usw 5B 100
Caris St. NE8: Gate 3A 84
Carlby Way NE23: Cra 5H 15
Carlcroft SR6: Monk 4E 105
Carlcroft Pl. NE23: Cra 4C 22
CARLEY HILL 1A 104
Carley Hill Rd. SR5: S'wck 2B 104
Carley Rd. SR5: S'wck 3B 104

Carley Sq. SR5: S'wck 3B 104
Carlile Ho NE4: Newc T 4C 68
(off Cookson St.)
Carlingford Rd. DH2: Ches S ...2B 134
Carliol Pl. NE1: Newc T 4G 69 (4E 5)
Carliol Sq. NE1: Newc T 4G 69 (4E 5)
(not continuous)
Carliol St. NE1: Newc T 4G 69 (4E 5)
Carlisle Cl. NE27: Longb 5A 46
Carlisle Ct. NE10: Gate 2D 84
Carlisle Cres. DH4: Pen 2E 129
Carlisle Ho. SR3: E Her 2F 131
(off Ashford Rd.)
Carlisle Pl. NE9: Gate 1B 98
Carlisle Rd. DH1: Dur 6E 145
Carlisle St. NE10: Gate 2D 84
Carlisle Ter. NE27: Shir 4C 46
SR5: S'wck 3A 104
Carlisle Way NE27: Longb 4A 46
Carlton Av. NE24: News 4A 18
Carlton Cl. DH2: Ous 5G 111
NE3: Ken 4C 56
Carlton Ct. NE11: Gate 6E 83
NE29: N Shi 2B 62
Carlton Cres. SR3: E Her 2E 131
Carlton Gdns. NE15: Lem 2C 66
Carlton Grange NE3: Ken 4C 56
Carlton Ho. NE22: Bed 4H 9
Carlton Rd. NE12: Longb 1D 58
Carlton St. NE24: Bly 6D 12
Carlton Ter. NE9: Gate 6G 83
NE9: Spri 4F 99
NE24: Bly 5B 12
NE29: N Shi 2B 62
SR2: Sund 2D 118
(off Mowbray Rd.)
SR8: Eas 2B 162
Carlyle Cl. NE28: W'snd 6E 61
Carlyle Cres. NE16: Swa 3E 81
Carlyle St. NE28: W'snd 6E 61
Carlyon St. SR2: Sund ...2D 118 (6G 7)
Carmel Gro. NE23: Cra 6A 16
Carmel Rd. DH9: Stly 3B 122
Carnaby Rd. NE6: Walk 5F 71
Carnation Av. DH4: Hou S 6C 128
Carnation Ter. NE16: Whi 4F 81
Carnegie Cl. NE34: S Shi 5E 75
Carnegie St. SR2: Sund 5F 119
Carnforth Cl. NE28: W'snd 6C 46
Carnforth Gdns. NE9: Gate 1B 98
Carnforth Grn. NE3: Ken 3A 56
Carnoustie DH2: Ous 6A 112
NE37: Usw 2A 100
Carnoustie Cl. NE7: Newc T ...3C 58
Carnoustie Ct. NE10: Gate 5H 85
NE25: Whit B 6G 35
Carnoustie Dr. NE34: S Shi 6H 75
Carol Gdns. NE7: Newc T 4B 58
Caroline Cotts. NE5: Newc T ...1F 67
Caroline Gdns. NE28: W'snd ...4E 61
Caroline St. DH5: Hett H 1C 148
NE4: Newc T 5A 68
NE32: Jar 2E 73
SR7: S'hm 4B 142
Caroline Ter. NE21: Bla T 5H 65
Carol St. SR4: Sund 6B 104
Carolyn Cl. NE12: Longb 1C 58
Carolyn Cres. NE26: Whit B ...4A 36
Carolyn Way NE26: Whit B 4A 36
Carpenters St. NE33: S Shi 5D 62
Carr Av. DH7: B'don 5D 158
Carr-Ellison Ho. NE4: Newc T ..6B 68

Carr Fld. NE20: Pon 4F 27
Carrfield Rd. NE3: Ken 2B 56
CARR HILL 4B 84
Carr Hill Rd. NE9: Gate 3A 84
NE10: Gate 3A 84
Carr Ho. Dr. DH1: Dur 1C 154
Carrhouse La. SR7: Hett H 6G 139
Carrick Cl. NE24: News 3B 18
Carrick Dr. NE24: News 2B 18
Carrigill Dr. NE12: Longb 1A 58
Carrington Cl. NE23: Seg 2F 33
Carrisbrooke Ct. SR1: Sund 1B 118
Carrmere Rd. SR2: Sund 6E 119
Carrmyers DH9: Ann P 3E 121
Carrock Cl. SR8: Pet 4D 164
Carrock Ct. SR3: New S 3H 131
Carroll Wlk. NE34: S Shi 1C 88
Carrowmore Rd. DH2: Ches S ..2C 134
Carr Row DH4: Leam 2C 146
Carrsdale DH1: Carr 2B 156
Carrside DH1: Dur 1B 154
Carrs, The DH1: Dur 6C 144
Carr St. NE24: Bly 3A 18
NE31: Heb 2B 72
(not continuous)
Carrsway DH1: Carr 2B 156
Carrsyde Cl. NE16: Whi 6D 80
Carr Vw. NE20: Wool 6A 28
CARRVILLE 3A 156
Carrville Link Rd. DH1: Dur ...5E 155
Carsdale Rd. NE3: Ken 2H 55
Carter Av. NE31: Heb 3C 72
Cartington Av. NE27: Shir 3C 46
Cartington Cl. SR8: Pet 4D 164
Cartington Ct. NE3: Ken 6A 42
Cartington Rd. DH1: Dur 2C 154
NE29: N Shi 2A 62
Cartington Ter. NE6: Newc T ...6B 58
Cartmel Bus. Cen. NE10: Gate ..2G 85
Cartmel Ct. DH2: Ches S 1A 134
Cartmel Grn. NE5: Newc T 6E 55
Cartmel Gro. NE8: Gate 4F 83
Cartmel Pk. NE10: Gate 2G 85
Cartmel Ter. DH2: Beam 2D 124
Cartwright Rd. SR5: C'twn 4D 102
Carville Gdns. NE28: W'snd ...1H 71
Carville Ri. NE6: Newc T 3C 70
Carville Rd. NE28: W'snd 6H 59
(not continuous)
Carville Sta. Cotts.
NE28: W'snd 6A 60
Carville St. NE10: Gate 1B 84
Carvis Cl. DH7: B'don 6C 158
Carwarding Pl. NE5: Newc T ...5G 55
Caseton Cl. NE25: Whit B 5G 35
Caspian Cl. NE32: Jar 4G 73
Caspian Rd. SR5: C'twn 4B 102
Caspian Sq. SR5: C'twn 4B 102
Cassie Bldg.
NE2: Newc T 2F 69 (1D 4)
Castellain Rd. SR5: C'twn 4E 103
Casterton Gro. NE5: Cha P 4H 53
Castle Chare DH1: Dur ...5C 154 (2A 6)
(not continuous)
Castle Cl. DH3: Ches S 1D 134
DH5: Hett H 3D 148
NE3: Ken 2H 55
NE16: Whi 4E 81
Castle Ct. DH9: Ann P 5F 121
NE20: Pon 5E 27
(off Merton Rd.)
Castledale Av. NE24: Cow 1G 17
CASTLE DENE 2G 135

Castledene Ct. NE3: Newc T 3H **57**
  SR5: C'twn 3C **102**
Castle Dene Gro. DH4: Hou S . . .3H **137**
CASTLE EDEN 6C **164**
Castle Eden Dene Nature Reserve
  .3E **165**
Castle Farm M. NE2: Gos 4H **57**
Castle Flds. DH4: Hou S 6B **128**
Castletord Rd. SR5: C'twn 3R **102**
Castle Gth. NE1: Newc T . . .5G **69** (6E **5**)
Castlegate Gdns. NE8: Dun 2C **82**
Castle Keep 5G **69** (6E **5**)
Castlemain Cl. DH4: Hou S 6B **128**
Castle M. SR3: E Her 2F **131**
Castlenook Pl. NE15: Newc T . . .2D **66**
Castlereagh Homes, The
  SR7: S'hm 2B **142**
Castloreagh Rd. SR7: S'hm 4B **142**
Castlereagh St. SR3: New S . . .2A **132**
Castlereigh Cl. DH4: Hou S 6B **128**
Castle Riggs DH2: Ches S 6B **126**
Castles Farm Rd. NE2: Gos 4G **57**
  NE3: Gos 4G **57**
Castles Grn. NE12: Kil 2E **45**
  SR3: E Her 2F **131**
Castleside Rd. NF15: Newc T . . .3E **67**
Castle Sq. NE27: Back 6H **33**
Castle Stairs
  NE1: Newc T 5G **69** (6E **5**)
Castle St. NE13: Bru V 1C **42**
  SR1: Sund 6C **104** (3F **7**)
  SR8: Eas 1F **163**
Castle St. Sth. SR5: C'twn 4E **103**
Castleton Cl. NE2: Newc T 5H **57**
  NE23: Cra 6A **16**
Castleton Gro. NE2: Newc T 5H **57**
Castleton Lodge NE4: Newc T . . .4B **68**
Castleton Rd. NE32: Jar 4G **73**
CASTLETOWN 4C **102**
Castletown Way
  SR5: C'twn, S'wck 3F **103**
Castle Vw. DH3: Ches C 5C **126**
  DH4: Pen 1F **129**
  DH7: Ush M 6E **153**
  SR5: C'twn 4D **102**
Castleway NE13: Din 5F **29**
Castlewood Cl. NE5: Newc T 5B **54**
Catcheside Cl. NE16: Whi 6C **81**
CATCHGATE 4E **121**
Catchwell Rd. DH9: Dip 1D **120**
Cateran Way NE23: Cra 4B **22**
Caterhouse Rd. DH1: Dur 1B **154**
Catharine St. W. SR4: Sund . . .1A **118**
Cathedral Ct. NE8: Gate 6A **70**
Cathedral Stairs
  NE1: Newc T 4G **69** (5E **5**)
Cathedral Vw. DH4: Hou S 6H **129**
Catherine Cookson Bldg.
  NE2: Newc T 1B **4**
Catherine Cookson Ct.
  NE33: S Shi 6G **63**
Catherine Rd. DH4: Hou S 3H **129**
Catherine St. NE33: S Shi . . .4F **63**
Catherine Ter. DH9: Ann P 5H **121**
  DH9: Stly 1D **122**
  NE10: Gate 3C **84**
Catholic Row NE22: Bed 5G **9**
Catkin Wlk. NE40: Ryton 6A **64**
Cato Sq. SR5: S'wck 3A **104**
Cato St. SR5: S'wck 3A **104**
  (not continuous)

Catrail Pl. NE23: Cra 1C **22**
Catton Gro. NE16: Sun 2F **95**
Catton Pl. NE28: W'snd 1C **60**
CAULDWELL 1G **75**
Cauldwell Av. NE25: Whit B 2H **47**
  NE34: S Shi 2G **75**
Cauldwell Cl. NE25: Whit B 1A **48**
Cauldwell La. NE25: Whit B 1H **47**
Cauldwell Pl. NE34: S Shi 2G **75**
Cauldwell Vs. NE34: S Shi 2G **75**
Causeway NE9: Gate 4R **84**
Causeway, The NE9: Gate 3A **84**
  NE15: Thro 6D **52**
  SR6: Monk 5D **104**
CAUSEY 2F **109**
Causey Arch DH9: Tan L 3E **109**
Causey Bank
  NE1: Newc T 4H **69** (5F **5**)
Causey Bldgs. NE3: Gos 3E **57**
Causey Dr. DH9: Stly 1E **123**
Causey Rd.
  DH9: Stly, Sun, Tan L 6E **109**
  NE16: Sun 6E **109**
Causey Row NE16: Sun 2F **109**
Causey St. NE3: Gos 3E **57**
Causey Vw. DH9: Stly 2F **123**
Causey Way DH9: Stly 6E **109**
Cavalier Vw. NE31: Heb 2B **72**
Cavalier Way DH6: Now S 2H **131**
Cavel Burrs SR2: Ryh 3C **132**
Cavell Pl. DH9: Stly 4E **123**
Cavell Rd. SR5: C'twn 3C **102**
Cavel Sq. SR8: Eas 1D **162**
Cavendish Ct. DH7: B'don 6C **158**
Cavendish Pl. NE2: Newc T 6H **57**
  NE16: Burn 3G **107**
  SR3: New S 2H **131**
Cavendish Rd. NE2: Newc T 6H **57**
Coversham Rd. NE5: Cha P 4H **53**
Cawburn Cl. NE7: Newc T 4E **59**
Cawdell Ct. NE30: N Shi 2D **62**
Cawnpore Sq. SR4: Sund 6G **103**
Cawthorne Ter. NE16: Burn 3G **107**
  (off Cragless)
  NE29: N Shi 5C **48**
  (off Front St.)
Caxton Wlk. NE34: S Shi 1C **88**
Caxton Way DH3: Ches S 1D **126**
  (not continuous)
Caynham Cl. NE29: N Shi 5A **48**
Cayton Gro. NE5: Cha P 5H **53**
Cecil Ct. NE20: Pon 5F **27**
  NE28: W'snd 1H **71**
Cecil St. NE29: N Shi 2C **62**
Cedar Av. DH2: Plaw 1A **144**
Cedar Cl. DH1: Dur 4G **155**
  NE22: Bed 3H **9**
  NE25: Whit B 2B **48**
Cedar Ct. DH6: S Het 6H **149**
  NE29: N Shi 4A **48**
Cedar Cres. NE9: Gate 1H **97**
  NE11: Dun 4B **82**
  NE16: Burn 1F **107**
Cedar Dr. DH1: Dur 4B **160**
  NE32: Jar 3G **87**
Cedar Gro. NE24: News 3A **18**
  NE28: W'snd 5B **60**
  NE31: Heb 6C **72**
  NE34: S Shi 4H **75**
  NE40: Ryton 3B **64**
  SR6: Whit 1F **91**
Cedar Rd. NE4: Newc T 2G **67**
  NE21: Bla T 1A **80**

Cedars DH2: Ches S 4B **126**
Cedars Ct. SR2: Sund 3D **118**
Cedars Cres. SR2: Sund 4E **119**
  SR7: Mur 2D **150**
Cedars Grn. NE9: Gate 2A **98**
Cedars Pk. SR2: Sund 4E **119**
Cedars, The DH4: Pen 1F **129**
  NE4: Newc T 6D **68**
  NE9: Spri 3C **98**
  NE16: Whi 1F **95**
  SR2: Sund 4D **118**
Cedar St. SR8: Pet 1H **165**
Cedar Ter. DH4: Hou S 3E **137**
  (not continuous)
  NE38: Wash 6H **113**
Cedartree Gdns. NE25: Whit B . .2A **48**
Cedar Way NE12: Longb 5E **45**
Cedarway NE10: Gate 6E **85**
Cedarwood DH4: Hou S 2C **136**
  NE9: Gate 6C **84**
Cedarwood Av. NE6: Walk 6G **59**
Cedarwood Gro. SR2: Sund 5C **118**
Cedric Cres. SR2: Sund 3B **118**
Celadon Cl. NE15: Lem 1A **66**
Celandine Cl. NE3: Gos 6F **43**
Celandine Way NE10: Gate 5D **84**
Cellar Hill Ter. DH4: Hou S 1H **137**
Celtic Cl. SR6: Cle 2G **89**
Celtic Cres. SR6: Cle 2G **89**
Cemetery App. NE34: C Shi 1G **75**
Cemetery Rd. DH9: Stly 2D **122**
  NE8: Gate 2H **83**
  NE32: Jar 3G **73**
Centenary Av. NE34: S Shi 4A **76**
Centenary Cotts. NE22: Bed 5H **9**
Centenary Ct. NE4: Newc T 5B **68**
Central Arc. NE1: Newc T 4D **4**
Central Av. DH7: B'don 6E **159**
  NE29: N Shi 1H **61**
  NE34: S Shi 3H **75**
  SR6: Whit 3E **91**
Central Gdns. NE34: S Shi 3H **75**
Central Lwr. Prom.
  NE26: Whit B 5D **36**
Central Sq. NE1: Newc T 6D **4**
  NE8: Gate 6D **4**
Central Station (Metro) . . .5F **69** (6C **4**)
Central Way SR4: Sund 6G **103**
Centralway NE11: Dun 1F **97**
Centrium Ct. NE28: W'snd 3C **60**
Conturian Way NE22: Bed 3G **9**
Centurion Rd. NE15: Lem 1D **66**
Centurion Way NE9: Gate 5B **84**
  NE15: Hed W 5G **51**
Century Ter. DH9: Ann P 4E **121**
Ceolfrid Ter. NE32: Jar 5G **73**
Chacombe NE38: Wash 4A **114**
Chadderton Dr. NE5: Cha P 5H **53**
Chad Ho. NE8: Gate 1H **83**
Chadwick St. NE28: W'snd 6H **59**
Chadwick Wlk. NE8: Gate 1E **83**
Chaffinch Rd. SR5: C'twn 4E **103**
Chaffinch Way NE12: Kil 1C **44**
Chainbridge Rd NE21: Bla T 6B **66**
  (Cowen Rd.)
  NE21: Bla T 1F **80**
  (Factory Rd.)
Chainbridge Rd. Ind. Est.
  NE21: Bla T 5D **66**
Chains, The DH1: Dur . . .5D **154** (2D **6**)
Chalfont Gro. SR4: Sund 5C **106**
Chalfont Rd. NE6: Walk 5F **71**
Chalfont Way DH7: B'don 5E **159**

Chalford Rd. SR5: S'wck 3B 104
Chamberlain St. NE24: Bly 1D 18
Chambers Cres. NE9: Spri 4C 98
Chancery La. NE24: Bly 6B 12
Chandler Cl. DH1: Dur 6G 155
Chandler Ct. NE2: Newc T 5H 57
    SR8: Eas 1F 163
Chandlers Ford DH4: Pen 1C 128
Chandlers Quay NE6: Newc T 6C 70
Chandless St. NE8: Gate 6H 69
    (off High St.)
Chandos SR3: New S 5A 132
Chandos St. NE8: Gate 3H 83
Chandra Pl. NE5: Newc T 5F 55
Chantry Cl. SR3: New S 4G 131
Chantry Dr. NE13: Wide O 4D 30
Chantry Pl. DH4: W Rai 3E 147
Chapel Av. NE16: Burn 1H 107
Chapel Cl. NE3: Gos 4F 43
    NE11: Kib 1F 111
Chapel Ct. DH6: Sher 6E 157
    NE13: Sea B 3D 30
    NE15: Thro 1E 65
    NE39: H Spen 6A 78
Chapel Hill Rd. SR8: Pet 6F 163
Chapel Ho. Dr. NE5: Cha P 6A 54
Chapel Ho. Gro. NE5: Cha P 6A 54
Chapel Ho. Rd. NE5: Cha P 6A 54
Chapel La. NE25: Whit B 1A 48
CHAPEL PARK 3B 54
Chapel Pk. Shop. Cen.
    NE5: Cha P 3B 54
Chapel Pl. NE13: Sea B 3D 30
Chapel Rd. NE32: Jar 2F 73
Chapel Row DH3: Bir 4E 113
    DH4: Hou S 5C 128
    (Bournmoor)
    DH4: Hou S 6A 128
    (Philadelphia)
Chapel St. DH5: Hett H 1D 148
    DH9: Tan L 5H 107
    NE29: N Shi 2A 62
Chapel Vw. DH4: W Rai 4D 146
    NE13: Bru V 5C 30
    NE39: Row G 2E 93
Chapelville NE13: Sea B 3D 30
Chaplin St. SR7: S'hm 6B 142
Chapman St. SR6: Monk 1E 105
Chapter Row NE33: S Shi 4E 63
Chare, The NE1: Newc T . . .3F 69 (3C 4)
    SR8: Pet 1D 164
Charlbury Cl. NE9: Spri 4F 99
Charlcote Cres. NE36: E Bol 4F 89
Charles Av. NE3: Ken 1A 56
    NE12: Longb 5D 44
    NE26: Whit B 6D 36
    NE27: Shir 1D 46
Charles Baker Wlk.
    NE34: S Shi 2B 76
Charles Ct. NE6: Newc T 2C 70
    (off Elvet Cl.)
Charles Dr. NE23: Dud 3B 32
Charles Perkins Memorial
    Cott. Homes DH3: Bir 4C 112
Charles St. DH4: Hou S 5H 129
    DH9: Stly 5C 122
    NE8: Gate 1H 83
    NE13: Bru V 1C 42
    NE35: Bol C 3B 88
    SR1: Sund 6D 104 (2H 7)
    SR2: Ryh 3G 133
    SR3: New S 1A 132
    SR6: Monk 5D 104 (1H 7)

Charles St. SR7: S'hm 4B 142
    SR8: Eas 1F 163
Charles Ter. DH2: Pelt 4G 125
Charleswood NE3: Gos 5F 43
Charlie St. NE40: G'sde 2A 78
Charlotte Cl. NE4: Newc T 6D 68
Charlotte M. NE1: Newc T 5B 4
Charlotte Sq.
    NE1: Newc T 4E 69 (5B 4)
Charlotte St. DH9: Stly 5C 122
    NE28: W'snd 5A 60
    (not continuous)
    NE30: N Shi 2D 62
    NE33: S Shi 5E 63
Charlton Ct. NE25: Whit B 2A 48
Charlton Gro. SR6: Cle 3A 90
Charlton Rd. SR5: Monk 2C 104
Charlton St. NE15: Lem 3B 66
    NE24: Bly 6B 12
Charlton Vs. NE40: G'sde 2B 78
    (off Lead Rd.)
Charlton Wlk. NE8: Gate 2E 83
Charman St.
    SR1: Sund 6D 104 (3G 7)
Charminster Gdns.
    NE6: Newc T 5C 58
Charnwood DH9: Stly 1C 122
Charnwood Av. NE12: Longb 1A 58
Charnwood Ct. NE33: S Shi 5G 63
Charnwood Gdns. NE9: Gate 5B 84
Charter Dr. SR3: E Her 2E 131
Charters Cres. DH6: S Het 6H 149
Chase Ct. DH6: Sher 6E 157
    NE16: Whi 4F 81
Chasedale Cres. NE24: Cow 6G 11
CHASE FARM 6F 11
Chase Farm Dr. NE24: Cow 5F 11
Chase Mdws. NE24: Cow 1F 17
Chase M. NE24: Cow 6F 11
Chase, The NE12: Kil 3A 44
    NE29: N Shi 1C 62
    NE38: Wash 6F 113
Chatham Cl. NE25: Sea D 2B 34
Chatham Rd. SR5: C'twn 3C 102
Chathill Cl. NE25: Whit B 6H 35
Chathill Ter. NE6: Walk 4F 71
Chatsworth NE3: Gos 5E 57
Chatsworth Ct. NE33: S Shi 4F 63
Chatsworth Cres. SR4: Sund 3A 118
Chatsworth Dr. NE22: Bed 2C 10
Chatsworth Gdns.
    NE5: Newc T 4D 54
    NE6: Newc T 5D 70
    NE25: Whit B 2A 48
Chatsworth Pl. NE16: Whi 6E 81
Chatsworth Rd. NE32: Jar 4G 73
Chatsworth St. SR4: Sund 2A 118
Chatsworth St. Sth.
    SR4: Sund 3A 118
Chatterton St. SR5: S'wck 3A 104
Chatton Av. NE23: Cra 3C 22
    NE34: S Shi 1B 76
Chatton Cl. DH2: Ches S 2A 134
Chatton St. NE28: W'snd 6G 61
Chatton Wynd NE3: Ken 6C 42
Chaucer Av. NE34: S Shi 6C 74
Chaucer Cl. DH9: Stly 3E 123
    NE8: Gate 1A 84
Chaucer Rd. NE16: Whi 3F 81
Chaucer St. DH4: Hou S 3H 137
Chaytor Gro. SR1: Sund 1E 119
Chaytor St. NE32: Jar 1F 73
Chaytor Ter. Nth. DH9: Stly 6F 123

Chaytor Ter. Sth. DH9: Stly 6G 123
Cheadle Av. NE23: Cra 5A 16
Cheadle Rd. SR5: C'twn 3C 102
Cheam Cl. NE16: Whi 6F 81
Cheam Rd. SR5: C'twn 3C 102
Cheddar Gdns. NE9: Gate 2H 97
Chedder Cl. DH9: Ann P 6F 121
Cheeseburn Gdns.
    NE5: Newc T 1G 67
Cheldon Cl. NE25: Whit B 5G 35
Chelford Cl. NE28: W'snd 6C 46
Chelmsford Gro.
    NE2: Newc T 2A 70 (1H 5)
Chelmsford Rd. SR5: C'twn 3C 102
Chelmsford Sq. SR5: C'twn 2C 102
Chelmsford St. SR3: New S 1A 132
Chelsea Gdns. NE8: Gate 3B 84
Chelsea Gro. NE4: Newc T 4C 68
Chelsea Ho. DH9: Stly 2D 122
    (off Quarry Rd.)
Cheltenham Dr. NE35: Bol C 1A 88
Cheltenham Rd. SR5: C'twn 3C 102
Cheltenham Sq. SR5: C'twn 3C 102
Cheltenham Ter. NE6: Newc T . . .2B 70
Chelton Cl. NE13: Bru V 1D 42
Chepstow Gdns. NE8: Gate 4F 83
Chepstow Rd. NE15: Newc T 3D 66
Chepstow St. SR4: Sund 1B 118
Cherribank SR2: Ryh 3E 133
Cherry Av. SR8: Pet 1H 165
Cherry Banks DH3: Ches S 4D 126
Cherry Blossom Way
    SR5: Wash 4F 101
Cherryburn Gdns. NE4: Newc T . . .1A 68
Cherry Cotts. DH9: Tan L 5H 107
Cherry Gro. NE12: Kil 1C 44
Cherry Pk. DH7: B'don 6C 158
Cherrytree Cl. NE12: Kil 3F 45
Cherrytree Ct. NE22: Bed 3D 10
Cherry Tree Dr. NE22: Bed 4H 9
Cherrytree Dr. NE16: Whi 3G 81
Cherrytree Gdns. NE9: Gate 1A 98
    NE25: Whit B 2B 48
Cherrytree Rd. DH2: Ches S 4A 126
Cherry Trees NE24: Bly 1A 18
Cherrytree Sq. SR2: Ryh 1E 133
Cherry Tree Wlk. NE31: Heb 5C 72
Cherry Way DH4: Hou S 2F 137
    NE12: Kil 1C 44
Cherrywood NE6: Walk 6E 59
Cherrywood Gdns.
    SR3: New S 2B 132
Cherwell NE37: Usw 5D 100
Cherwell Rd. SR8: Pet 2B 164
Cherwell Sq. NE12: Longb 4C 44
Chesham Gdns. NE5: Cha P 5H 53
Chesham Grn. NE3: Ken 2B 56
Cheshire Av. DH3: Bir 6C 112
Cheshire Ct. NE31: Heb 4B 72
Cheshire Dr. DH1: Carr 5A 156
Cheshire Gdns. NE28: W'snd 4G 59
Cheshire Gro. NE34: S Shi 2B 76
Chesils, The NE12: Longb 2A 58
Chesmond Dr. NE21: Bla T 6A 66
Chessar Av. NE5: Newc T 5F 55
Chester Av. NE28: W'snd 4D 60
Chester Cl. NE20: Pon 1B 38
Chester Cres.
    NE2: Newc T 2H 69 (1G 5)
    SR1: Sund 1B 118
Chesterfield Rd. NE4: Newc T 5B 68
Chester Gdns. NE34: S Shi 2G 75

Chester Gro. NE23: Seg 2E 33
  NE24: Bly 1A 18
Chesterhill NE23: Cra 5B 22
CHESTER-LE-STREET 6C 126
Chester-le-Street Leisure Cen.
  ....6D 126
Chester-le-Street Station (Rail)
  ....6C 126
Chester M. SR4: Sund 2B 118
CHESTER MOOR 4A 134
Chester Oval SR1: Sund 1B 118
  (off Chester Rd.)
Chester Pl. NE8: Gate 1F 83
  SR8: Pet 6B 162
Chester Rd.
  DH3: Gt Lum, Lam P 4E 127
  DH4: Pen 3F 129
  DH9: Stly 2E 123
  SR1: Sund 1D 118 (5E 7)
  SR2: Sund 1B 118
  SR4: Pen 4C 116
  SR4: Sund 4C 116
  (Sevenoaks Dr.)
  SR4: Sund 2G 117
  (West Mt.)
Chester Rd. Est. DH9: Stly 2E 123
Chesters Av. NE12: Longb 1H 57
Chesters Ct. NE12: Longb 1B 58
Chesters Pk. NE9: Gate 5H 83
Chesters, The NE5: Cha P 6A 54
Chester St. DH4: Hou S 4H 7
  NE2: Newc T 2H 69 (1G 5)
  SR4: Sund 1A 118
Chester St. E. SR4: Sund 1B 118
Chester St. W. SR4: Sund 1A 118
Chester Ter. SR1: Sund 1B 118
  SR8: Fas 1D 162
Chester Ter. Nth. SR4: Sund 1B 118
Chesterton Rd. NE34: S Shl 5D 74
Chester Way NE32: Jar 2E 87
Chesterwood Dr. NE28: W'snd 5G 59
Chesterwood Ter. NE10: Gate 1H 85
Chestnut Av. NE5: Newc T 5H 55
  NE16: Whi 6F 81
  NE24: Bly 4D 12
  NE25: Whit B 1B 48
  NE38: Wash 6H 113
Chestnut Cl. NE12: Kil 1B 44
  NE32: Jar 2H 87
Chestnut Cres. SR5: S'wck 2H 103
Chestnut Gdns. NE8: Gate 3E 83
Chestnut Gro. DH7: Ush M 6C 152
  NE34: S Shi 5H 75
Chestnut St. NE28: W'snd 6A 60
Chestnut Ter. DH4: Hou S 1G 137
Cheswick Dr. NE3: Gos 1F 57
Cheswick Rd. NE25: Sea D 1C 34
Cheveley Pk. Shop. Cen.
  DH1: Carr 3B 156
Cheveley Wlk. DH1: Carr 4B 156
Chevin Cl. NE6: Walk 6G 59
Chevington NE10: Gate 6G 85
Chevington Gdns. NE5: Newc T ...6H 55
Chevington Gro. NE25: Whit B ...4H 35
Cheviot Cl. DH2: Ches S 3A 134
  NE21: Bla T 2A 80
  (not continuous)
  NE29: N Shi 3B 48
  NE37: Wash 1G 113
Cheviot Ct. DH9: Ann P 6F 121
  NE7: Newc T 3A 58
  NE21: Bla T 6A 66

Cheviot Ct. NE26: Whit B 1E 49
  SR7: S'hm 3G 141
Cheviot Gdns. NE11: Gate 4C 82
  SR7: S'hm 3G 141
Cheviot Grange NE23: Dud 5C 32
Cheviot Grn. NE11: Dun 3C 82
Cheviot Ho. NE37: Wash 3A 114
Cheviot La. SR2: Ryh 2D 132
Cheviot Mt. NE6: Newc T 3C 70
Cheviot Pl. SR8: Pet 6B 162
  (not continuous)
Cheviot Rd. DH2: Ches S 2B 134
  (not continuous)
  NE32: Jar 5E 73
  NE34: S Shi 1A 76
Cheviot St. SR4: Sund 6H 103
Cheviot Ter. DH9: Stly 4E 123
Cheviot Vw. NE10: Gate 5D 84
  NE12: Longb 1D 58
  NE13: Bru V 5C 30
  NE20: Pon 5G 27
  NE23: Seg 2F 33
  NE26: Whit B 1D 48
  NE27: Shir 4B 46
Chevron, The NE6: Newc T 4B 70
  (off Gordon Sq.)
Chevy Chase NE1: Newc T 3C 4
Chevychase Ct. SR7: Sea 1F 141
Cheyne, The SR3: New S 4A 132
Chichester Av. NE23: Nel V 1H 21
Chichester Cl. NE3: Ken 6H 41
  NE8: Gate 1G 83
Chichester Gro. NE22: Bed 3H 9
Chichester Pl. NE33: S Shi 1E 75
Chichester Rd. DH1: Dur 6D 144
  NE33: S Shi 1E 75
  SR6: Monk 1E 105
Chichester Rd. E. NE33: S Shi ...6F 63
Chichester Station (Metro) 1E 75
Chichester Way NE32: Jar 2F 87
Chicken Rd. NE28: W'snd 4G 59
Chicks La. SR6: Whit 3F 91
Chigwell Cl. DH4: Pen 2F 129
Chilcote NE10: Gate 4D 84
Chilcrosso NE10: Gate 5F 85
  (not continuous)
Childhood Memories Toy Mus. 4F 49
Chilham Ct. NE29: N Shi 5F 47
  NE38: Wash 3H 113
Chillingham Cl. NE24: Bly 2H 17
Chillingham Ct. NE6: Newc T 2C 70
Chillingham Dr. DH2: Ches S ...3A 134
  NE29: N Shi 3H 61
Chillingham Gro. SR8: Pet 4A 164
Chillingham Ho. SR6: Monk 5E 105
  (off Mulgrave Dr.)
Chillingham Ind. Est.
  NE6: Walk 2C 70
Chillingham Rd. DH1: Dur 1D 154
  NE6: Newc T, Walk 6C 58
Chillingham Road Station (Metro)
  ....2D 70
Chillingham Ter. NE32: Jar 5H 73
Chilside Rd. NE10: Gate 4D 84
Chiltern Av. DH2: Ches S 1B 134
  (not continuous)
Chiltern Cl. NE38: Wash 4H 113
Chiltern Dr. NE12: Longb 4B 44
Chiltern Gdns. DH9: Stly 4F 123
  NE11: Gate 4C 82
Chiltern Rd. NE29: N Shi 3A 48
Chilton Av. DH4: Hou S 2D 136
Chilton Gdns. DH4: Hou S 3E 137

Chilton Gth. SR8: Pet 2F 165
CHILTON MOOR 4E 137
Chilton St. SR5: S'wck 4C 104
Chimney Mills NE2: Newc T 1E 69
China St. SR2: Sund 3E 119
Chingford Cl. DH4: Pen 2G 129
Chipchase NE38: Wash 3F 113
Chipchase Av. NE23: Cra 3B 22
Chipchase Cl. NE22: Bed 4F 9
Chipchase Ct. DH4: Hou S 2B 136
  NE25: Sea D 3A 24
  SR7: Sea 1F 141
Chipchase Cres. NE5: Newc T ...4C 54
Chipchase M. NE3: Gos 4C 42
Chipchase Ter. NE32: Jar 6F 73
Chippendale Pl. NE2: Newc T 2D 68
Chirnside NE23: Cra 5B 22
Chirnside Ter. DH9: Ann P 6E 121
CHIRTON 2B 62
Chirton Av. NE29: N Shi 2B 62
  NE34: S Shi 3C 76
Chirton Dene Quay
  NE29: N Shi 5B 62
Chirton Dene Way
  NE29: N Shi 5B 62
Chirton Grn. NE24: Bly 2H 17
  NE29: N Shi 2B 62
Chirton Gro. NE34: S Shi 3C 76
Chirton Hill Dr. NE29: N Shi ...6G 47
Chirton La. NE29: N Shi 1A 62
Chirton Lodge NE29: N Shi 2A 62
Chirton W. Vw. NE29: N Shi 2B 62
Chirton Wynd NE6: Newc T 4C 70
Chislehurst Rd. DH4: Pen 2F 129
Chiswick Gdns. NE8: Gate 3A 84
Chiswick Rd. SR5: C'twn 3C 102
Chiswick Sq. SR5: C'twn 3C 102
Chollerford Av. NE25: Whit B ...1D 48
  NE29: N Shi 1G 61
Chollerford Cl. NE3: Gos 3C 56
Chollerford M. NE25: H'wll 1D 34
Chollerton Dr. NE12: Longb 5G 45
  NE22: Bed 4A 10
Choppington Rd. NE22: Bed 4H 9
  NE62: Sco G 4H 9
Chopwell Gdns. NE9: Gate 3D 98
Chopwell Woods Rd.
  NE39: H Spen 3A 92
Chorley Pl. NE6: Walk 4E 71
CHOWDENE 2H 97
Chowdene Bank NE9: Gate 3G 97
  NE11: Gate 3G 97
Chowdene Ter. NE9: Gate 1H 97
Christal Ter. SR6: Monk 2D 104
Christchurch Ct. SR7: S'hm 3G 141
Christchurch Pl. SR8: Pet 2C 164
Christie Ter. NE6: Walk 4F 71
Christon Cl. NE3: Gos 2G 57
Christon Rd. NE3: Gos 2E 57
Christon Way NE10: Gate 1H 85
Christopher Rd. NE6: Walk 2E 71
Chudleigh Gdns. NE5: Cha P 5H 53
Chudleigh Ter. NE21: Bla T 1A 80
Church Av. NE3: Gos 2F 57
  NE62: Sco G 1G 9
Church Bank DH9: Stly 2D 122
  NE15: Thro 2F 65
  NE28: W'snd 5B 60
  NE32: Jar 2H 73
  SR5: S'wck 4A 104
Church Chare DH3: Ches S 6D 126
  NE16: Whi 4F 81
  NE20: Pon 4F 27

Church Cl. DH4: Hou S 5C **128**
NE13: Din 4F **29**
NE22: Bed 5H **9**
NE25: Whit B 1G **47**
SR7: S'hm 3A **142**
SR8: Pet 2E **165**
Church Ct. NE10: Gate 2D **84**
NE13: Bru V 1C 42
(off Church La.)
NE22: Bed 5H **9**
Churchdown Cl. NE35: Bol C 1A **88**
Church Dr. NE9: Gate 5A **84**
Churcher Gdns. NE28: W'snd 3G **59**
Church Flatt NE20: Pon 4F **27**
Church Grn. NE16: Whi 4F **81**
SR7: S'hm 3A **142**
Churchill Av. DH1: Dur 5F **155**
NE25: Whit B 2A **48**
SR5: S'wck 3A **104**
Churchill Gdns. NE2: Newc T . . .6A **58**
Churchill M. NE6: Newc T 5C **70**
Churchill Sq. DH1: Dur 4F **155**
DH4: Hou S 3F **137**
Churchill St.
NE1: Newc T 5E **69** (6A **4**)
NE28: W'snd 2D **60**
SR1: Sund 1E **119**
Church La. DH1: Dur 5E **155**
(Gilesgate)
DH1: Dur 1D **160** (5C **6**)
(Hallgarth St.)
NE3: Gos 2F **57**
NE9: Gate 5B **84**
NE22: Bed 5A **10**
SR1: Sund 1C **118** (4F **7**)
SR6: Whit 3F **91**
SR7: Mur 2B **150**
Church La. Nth. SR7: Mur 2B **150**
Church Mdw. DH7: B'don 4F **159**
Church M. NE27: Back 6A **34**
Church Pl. NE10: Gate 2D **84**
Church Ri. NE16: Whi 4F **81**
NE40: Ryton 4E **65**
(not continuous)
Church Rd. DH2: Pelt 3F **125**
DH5: Hett H 5C **138**
NE3: Gos 2E **57**
NE9: Gate 6A **84**
NE15: Thro 2F **65**
NE27: Back, H'wll 6A **34**
Church Row *NE10: Gate 5C 84*
(off Windy Nook Rd.)
Church Side DH3: Gt Lum 4G **135**
Churchside NE13: Din 4F **29**
Church St. DH1: Dur 1D **160** (5C **6**)
DH3: Bir 3C **112**
DH4: Hou S 3A **138**
DH4: W Rai 3E **147**
DH5: Hou S 3A **138**
DH9: Ann P 5F **121**
DH9: Stly 2D **122**
NE6: Walk 5G **71**
(Caledonia St.)
NE6: Walk 4G **71**
(Church Wlk.)
NE8: Gate 5G **69**
NE10: Gate 3D **84**
NE11: Dun 2C **82**
NE16: Sun 5E **95**
NE21: Bla T 2H **79**
NE23: Cra 3B **22**
NE24: Bly 5C **12**
NE30: N Shi 1D **62**

Church St. NE31: Heb 2B **72**
NE32: Jar 2F **73**
SR4: Sund 1C **116**
SR5: S'wck 3B **104**
SR7: Mur 3C **150**
SR7: S'hm 4B **142**
TS27: Hes 6G **165**
Church St. E. SR1: Sund 6E **105**
Church St. Head
DH1: Dur 1D **160** (6C **6**)
Church St. Nth. SR6: Monk 4D **104**
Church St. Vs.
DH1: Dur 1D **160** (6C **6**)
Church Ter. NE21: Bla T 6A **66**
Church Va. DH6: H Pitt 3G **157**
Church Vw. DH1: Carr 3B **156**
DH2: Plaw 2A **144**
DH3: Bir 3C **112**
NE25: Well 6D **34**
NE28: W'snd 5B **60**
NE35: Bol C 2A **88**
NE37: Wash 6B **100**
SR3: New S 2A **132**
Church Vw. Vs. DH5: Hett H 6C **138**
Church Wlk. NE6: Walk 4G **71**
(not continuous)
NE8: Gate 5G **69** (6F **5**)
SR1: Sund 6F **105**
Churchwalk Ho. NE6: Walk 4G **71**
Church Ward SR2: Ryh 3G **133**
Church Way NE25: Well 5E **35**
NE29: N Shi 1C **62**
NE33: S Shi 4E **63**
Church Wood NE23: Cra 3B **22**
Church Wynd DH6: Sher 6D **156**
Churston Cl. DH4: Hou S 5G **129**
Cicero Ter. SR5: S'wck 3A **104**
Cinderford Cl. NE35: Bol C 1A **88**
Circle, The NE32: Jar 5F **73**
Cirencester St. SR4: Sund 6B **104**
Cirus Ho. SR3: New S 3A **132**
Citadel E. NE12: Kil 2D **44**
Citadel W. NE12: Kil 2D **44**
Citygate NE1: Newc T 4E **69** (4B **4**)
City Library 4H **7**
City Pool 3G **69** (2E **5**)
City Rd. NE1: Newc T 4G **69** (5E **5**)
City Stadium 3A **70** (2H **5**)
City Theatre (Durham) 6C **154** (3B **6**)
City Way SR3: E Her 4D **130**
Civic Ct. NE31: Heb 4D **72**
Clacton Rd. SR5: C'twn 4B **102**
Clanfield Ct. NE3: Newc T 3H **57**
Clanny Ho. SR4: Sund 1H **117**
Clanny St. SR1: Sund 1C **118** (4E **7**)
(St Michaels Way)
SR1: Sund 1B **118**
(Westbourne Rd.)
Clapham Av. NE6: Newc T 4D **70**
Clappersgate SR8: Eas 2A **162**
Clara Av. NE27: Shir 1D **46**
Clarabad Ter. NE12: Longb 4G **45**
Clara St. NE4: Newc T 5H **67**
NE21: Bla T 2H **79**
SR7: S'hm 3H **141**
Claremont Av. NE15: Lem 1B **66**
SR6: Monk 2E **105**
Claremont Bri. NE2: Newc T 1D **4**
Claremont Ct. *NE26: Whit B 3A 36*
(off Claremont Cres.)
Claremont Cres.
NE26: Whit B 4A **36**
Claremont Dr. DH4: Hou S 3E **129**

Claremont Gdns. NE26: Whit B . . .5B **36**
NE36: E Bol 4F **89**
Claremont Ho.
NE1: Newc T 2E **69** (1B **4**)
Claremont Nth. Av. NE8: Gate 1G **83**
Claremont Pl. NE2: Newc T 2E **69**
NE8: Gate 2G **83**
Claremont Rd. NE2: Newc T 1C **68**
NE26: Whit B 3A **36**
SR6: Monk 2E **105**
Claremont Sth. Av. NE8: Gate 2G **83**
Claremont Sports Hall 2E **69**
Claremont St. NE2: Newc T 2E **69**
NE8: Gate 2G **83**
Claremont Ter. NE2: Newc T 2E **69**
NE9: Spri 4F **99**
NE10: Gate 1H **85**
NE24: Bly 6B **12**
SR2: Sund 2C **118** (6F **7**)
Claremont Twr. NE1: Newc T 1C **4**
Claremont Wlk. NE8: Gate 2G **83**
(Bk. Woodbine St.)
NE8: Gate 2G **83**
(St Cuthbert's Pl.)
Claremount Ct. NE36: W Bol 4D **88**
Clarence Cres. NE26: Whit B 1D **48**
Clarence Ho.
NE2: Newc T 3H **69** (2G **5**)
Clarence Pl. NE3: Gos 2G **57**
Clarence St. DH9: Tan L 5H **107**
NE2: Newc T 3H **69** (3G **5**)
NE26: Sea S 4H **25**
SR5: S'wck 3H **103**
(not continuous)
SR7: S'hm 4B **142**
Clarence Ter. DH3: Ches S 6C **126**
Clarence Wlk.
NE2: Newc T 3H **69** (2G **5**)
Clarendon M. NE3: Gos 3E **43**
Clarendon Rd. NE6: Newc T 6C **58**
Clarendon Sq. SR5: S'wck 2B **104**
Clare Rd. SR8: Pet 2B **164**
Clarewood Av. NE34: S Shi 1A **76**
Clarewood Ct. NE4: Newc T 3C **68**
Clarewood Grn. NE4: Newc T 3C **68**
Clarewood Pl. NE5: Newc T 1G **67**
Clarke's Ter. NE23: Dud 4A **32**
Clarke Ter. NE10: Gate 3C **84**
SR7: Mur 2C **150**
Clarks Hill Wlk. NE15: Thro 2F **65**
Clark's Ter. SR7: S'hm 2E **141**
Clark Ter. DH9: Stly 1D **122**
Clarty La. NE11: Kib 3F **111**
Clasper Cl. NE33: S Shi 3E **63**
Clasper St. NE4: Newc T 6D **68**
Clasper Way NE16: Swa 6E **67**
Claude Gibb Hall
NE1: Newc T 2G **69** (1F **5**)
Claude St. DH5: Hett H 2C **148**
Claude Ter. SR7: Mur 2D **150**
Claudius Ct. NE33: S Shi 3E **63**
Claverdon St. NE5: Cha P 3H **53**
Clavering Cen. NE16: Whi 6D **80**
Clavering Pl. DH9: Ann P 6F **121**
NE1: Newc T 5F **69** (6D **4**)
Clavering Rd. NE16: Swa 3E **81**
NE21: Bla T 2A 80
(off Shibdon Bank)
Clavering Sq. NE11: Dun 3B **82**
Clavering St. NE28: W'snd 6F **61**
(not continuous)
Clavering Way NE21: Bla T 2C **80**
Claverley Dr. NE27: Back 6A **34**

Claxheugh Rd. SR4: Sund 6D 102
Claxton St. SR8: Pet 6G 163
Clay La. DH1: Dur 1A 160
(not continuous)
Claymere Rd. SR2: Sund 6E 119
Claypath DH1: Dur 5D 154 (2C 6)
  NE10: Gate 1F 69
Claypath Ct. DH1: Dur ...5D 154 (2C 6)
Claypath La. NE33: S Shi 5E 63
(not continuous)
Claypath Rd. DH5: Hett H 3C 148
Claypath St. NE6: Newc T 3A 70
Claypool Cl. NE34: S She 4E 75
Clayside Ho. NE33: S Shi 6F 63
Clayton Pk. Sq. NE2: Newc T 1G 69
Clayton Rd. NE2: Newc T 1F 69
Clayton St. NE1: Newc T ...4F 69 (5C 4)
  NE22: Bed 3D 10
  NE23: Dud 3H 31
  NE32: Jar 2F 73
Clayton St. W.
  NE1: Newc T 5E 69 (6B 4)
Clayton Ter. NE10: Gate 2C 84
Clayworth Rd. NE3: Gos 4D 42
CLEADON 2A 90
Cleadon Gdns. NE9: Gate 2D 98
  NE28: W'snd 2E 61
Cleadon Hill Dr. NE34: S Shi 5A 76
Cleadon Hill Rd. NE34: S Shi 5B 76
Cleadon La. NE36: E Bol 2G 89
  SR6: Cle, Whit 2B 90
Cleadon La. Ind. Est.
  NE36: E Bol 3F 89
Cleadon Lea SR6: Cle 2H 89
Cleadon Mdws. SR6: Cle 2A 90
CLEADON PARK 5A 76
Cleadon St. NE6: Walk 3E 71
Cleadon Towers NE34: S Shi 5B 76
Cleasby Gdns. NE9: Gate 5H 83
Cleaside Av. NE34: S Shi 5A 76
Cleehill Dr. NE29: N Shi 4B 48
Cleeve Dr. NE38: Wash 2B 114
Cleghorn St. NE6: Newc T 1C 70
Clegwell Ter. NE31: Heb 3D 72
Clematis Cres. NE9: Spri 3D 98
Clement Av. NE22: Bed 4C 10
Clementhorpe NE29: N Shi 6C 48
Clementina Cl. SR2: Sund 2E 119
Clement St. NE9: Gate 6H 83
Clennel Ho. NE4: Newc T 4A 68
Clennell Av. NE31: Heb 4B 72
Clent Way NE12: Longb 1A 58
Clephan St. NE11: Dun 2R 82
Clervaux Ter. NE32: Jar 3G 73
Cleveland Av. DH2: Ches S 1B 134
  NE29: N Shi 1B 62
Cleveland Ct. NE32: Jar 2E 73
  NE33: S Shi 3E 63
Cleveland Cres. NE29: N Shi 1C 62
Cleveland Dr. NE38: Wash 4H 113
Cleveland Gdns. NE7: Newc T 4A 58
  NE28: W'snd 4F 61
Cleveland Pl. SR8: Pet 1B 164
Cleveland Rd. NE20: N Shi 1R 62
  SR4: Sund 3H 117
Cleveland St. NE33: S Shi 3F 63
Cleveland Ter. DH9: Stly 4E 123
  NE29: N Shi 1C 62
  SR4: Sund 2A 118
Cleveland Vw. SR6: Monk 5E 91
Cliff Cotts. NE32: Jar 1H 73
Cliffe Ct. SR6: Monk 1F 105
Cliffe Pk. SR6: Monk 1F 105

Clifford Rd. DH9: Stly 3C 122
  NE6: Newc T 4D 70
Clifford's Fort Moat
  NE30: N Shi 2E 63
(not continuous)
Clifford St. DH3: Ches S 2C 134
  NE6: Newc T 3B 70
  NE21: Bla T 6A 66
  NE30: N Shi 1E 63
  SR4: Sund 1A 118
Clifford Ter. DH3: Ches S 1C 134
Cliff Rd. SR2: Ryh 3G 133
Cliff Row NE30: Whit B 1E 49
Cliffside NE34: S Shi 3C 76
Cliff Ter. SR2: Ryh 3G 133
  SR8: Eas 2B 162
Cliff Vw. SR2: Ryh 3G 133
Clifton Av. NE28: W'snd 5H 59
  NE34: S Shi 2G 75
Cliftonbourne Av. SR6: Monk 1E 105
Clifton Cl. NE40: Ryton 5E 65
Clifton Ct. NE3: Ken 6H 41
  NE9: Spri 4E 99
  NE25: Whit B 4A 36
Clifton Gdns. NE9: Gate 4H 83
  NE24: News 3B 18
  NE29: N Shi 4A 62
(not continuous)
Clifton Gro. NE25: Whit B 4A 36
Clifton Rd. NE4: Newc T 4A 68
  NE23: Cra 4C 22
  SR6: Monk 2E 105
Clifton Sq. SR8: Pet 6D 162
Clifton Ter. NE12: Longb 6D 44
  NE26: Whit B 6D 36
  NE33: S Shi 2E 75
Cliftonville Av. NE4: Newc T 4A 68
Cliftonville Gdns. NE26: Whit B 5C 36
Clifton Wlk. NE5: Cha P 5H 53
Clintburn Ct. NE23: Cra 1C 22
Clinton Pl. NE3: Gos 3D 42
  SR3: E Her 3E 131
Clipsham Cl. NE12: Longb 1B 58
Clipstone Av. NE6: Walk 6E 71
Clipstone Cl. NE15: Thro 5C 52
Clitheroe Gdns. NE22: Bed 3F 9
Clive Pl. NE6: Newc T 4B 70
Clive St. NE29: N Shi 2D 62
  NE34: S Shi 5C 74
Clockburn Lonnen NE16: Whi 6B 80
Clockburnsyde Cl. NE16: Whi 6C 80
Clockmill Rd. NE11: Dun 2C 82
Clockstand Cl. SR6: Monk 3E 105
Clockwell St. SR5: S'wck 4H 103
Cloggs, The NE20: Pon 4F 27
Cloister Av. NE34: S Shi 4C 74
Cloister Ct. NE8: Gate 6H 69
Cloister Gth. NE7: Newc T 2H 57
Cloisters, The NE7: Newc T 2H 57
  NE34: S Shi 2H 75
  SR2: Sund 2D 118
Cloister Wlk. NE32: Jar 2G 73
Close NE1: Newc T 5F 69 (6D 4)
Closeburn Sq. SR3: New S 3B 132
Close E., The DH2: Ches S 4B 126
Closefield Gro. NE25: Whit B 1A 48
Close Ho. Est. NE15: Hed W 6F 51
Close St. SR4: Sund 6A 104
  SR5: S'wck 4B 104
Close, The DH1: Carr 4B 156
  DH2: Ches S 4C 126
  DH5: Hou S 3B 138
  NE5: Newc T 1C 66

Close, The NE16: Burn 6A 94
  NE20: Pon 6E 27
  NE21: Bla T 2G 79
  NE23: Seg 2F 33
  NE24: Bly 4C 12
  SR6: Cle 2H 89
Cloth Mkt. NE1: Newc T ...4F 69 (5D 4)
CLOUGH DENE 4G 107
Clough Dene
  NE16: Burn, Tan L 4G 107
Clough La. NE1: Newc T 5D 4
Clousden Dr. NE12: Longb 4E 45
Clousden Grange NE12: Kil 4E 45
Clousden Hill NE12: Longb 4E 45
Clovelly Gdns. NE22: Bed 5H 9
  NE26: Whit B 5C 36
Clovelly Pl. NE20: Pon 3C 38
  NE32: Jar 4A 74
Clovelly Rd. SR5: C'twn 2B 102
Clovelly Sq. SR5: C'twn 2C 102
Clover Av. DH4: Hou S 4F 129
  NE10: Gate 1B 84
  NE21: Bla T 5A 80
Cloverdale NE22: Bed 4G 9
Cloverdale Gdns. NE7: Newc T 4B 58
  NE16: Whi 6F 81
Cloverfield Av. NE3: Ken 1B 56
Clover Hill NE16: Sun 3F 95
(not continuous)
  NE32: Jar 2G 87
Cloverhill Av. NE31: Heb 6B 72
Cloverhill Cl. NE23: Dud 2A 32
Cloverhill Dr. NE40: Ryton 5A 64
Clover Laid DH7: B'don 6C 158
Clowes Ter. DH9: Ann P 5F 121
Clowes Wlk. DH9: Stly 2F 123
Club La. DH1: Dur 4H 153
Clumber St. NE4: Newc T 6C 68
(not continuous)
Cluny Gallery, The 3A 70
Clyde Av. NE31: Heb 6C 72
Clyde Ct. SR3: New S 3H 131
Clydedale Av. NE12: Longb 6C 44
Clydesdale Av. DH4: Pen 2F 129
Clydesdale Gth. DH1: Dur 5C 144
Clydesdale Mt. NF6: Newc T 4C 70
Clydesdale Rd. NE6: Newc T 4C 70
Clydesdale St. DH5: Hett H 3C 148
Clyde St. DH9: Stly 2F 123
  NE8: Gate 3A 84
Clyvedon Ri. NE34: S Shi 6A 76
Coach La. NE7: Newc T 2C 58
  NE12: Newc T 2C 58
  NE13: Bru V 1C 41
  NE29: N Shi 2C 62
Coach Open NE28: W'snd 6F 61
Coach Rd. NE11: Gate 6D 82
  NE15: Thro 5C 52
  NE28: W'snd 6A 60
  NE37: Usw 4A 100
Coach Rd. Est. NE37: Usw 4A 100
Coach Rd. Grn. NE10: Gate 1C 84
Coalbank Rd. DH5: Hett H 3B 148
Coalbank Sq. DH5: Hett H 3B 148
Coalburn Ter. NE61: Hep 1A 8
Coaley La. DH4: Hou S 6G 129
Coalford La. DH6: H Pitt 2G 157
Coalford Rd. DH6: Sher 5D 156
Coalway Dr. NE16: Whi 3F 81
Coalway La. NE16: Swa, Whi 3F 81
  NE16: Whi 3F 81
Coalway La. Nth. NE16: Swa 2F 81
Coanwood Bungs. NE23: Cra 4B 22

Coanwood Dr. NE23: Cra 4B 22
Coanwood Gdns. NE11: Gate 6D 82
Coanwood Rd. NE15: Newc T 5F 67
Coanwood Way NE16: Sun 2F 95
Coast Rd. NE7: Newc T 6B 58
  NE28: W'snd 4G 59
  NE29: N Shi 1H 61
  NE34: S Shi . . . . . .6H 63 & 1A 76
  SR6: Whit 2D 76
  SR8: Pet 1G 165
  TS27: B Col 1G 165
Coates Cl. DH9: Stly 4E 123
Coatsworth Ct. NE8: Gate 1G 83
Coatsworth Rd. NE8: Gate 1G 83
Cobalt Cl. NE15: Lem 1A 66
Cobbett Cres. NE34: S Shi 6D 74
Cobden Rd. NE23: Cra 5C 22
Cobden St. NE8: Gate 2A 84
  NE28: W'snd 5H 59
Cobden Ter. NE8: Gate 2A 84
Cobham Pl. NE6: Walk 5G 71
Cobham Sq. SR5: S'wck 3B 104
Cobledene NE29: N Shi 4A 62
Coblehouse NE26: Whit B 1E 49
Coble Landing NE33: S Shi 4D 62
Coburg St. NE8: Gate 1H 83
  NE24: Bly 6D 12
  NE30: N Shi 1D 62
Coburn Cl. NE23: Dud 6C 32
Cochrane Ct. NE4: Newc T 4A 68
Cochrane Pk. Av. NE7: Newc T . .4C 58
Cochrane St. NE4: Newc T 4A 68
Cochrane Ter. DH7: Ush M . . .6C 152
  NE13: Din 4F 29
Cochran St. NE21: Bla T 6A 66
Cockburn Ter. NE29: N Shi 4H 61
Cocken La. DH3: Gt Lum 4H 135
Cocken Lodge Farm Cvn. Pk.
  DH4: Leam 2A 146
Cocken Rd. DH1: Gt Lum 2A 146
  DH3: Gt Lum, Leam, Plaw . .2D 144
  DH4: Leam 2A 146
Cockermouth Grn. NE5: Newc T . .1E 67
Cockermouth Rd. SR5: C'twn . . .2B 102
Cockhouse La. DH7: Ush M 5A 152
Cohen Ct. NE8: Gate 3G 83
Colbeck Av. NE16: Sun 2F 81
Colbeck Ter. NE30: N Shi 6F 49
Colbourne Av. NE23: Nel V 6G 15
Colbourne Cres. NE23: Nel V 6G 15
Colbury Cl. NE23: Cra 5A 16
Colby Ct. NE4: Newc T 5D 68
Colchester St. NE34: S Shi 5C 74
Colchester Ter. SR4: Sund 2H 117
Coldbeck Ct. NE23: Cra 4C 22
COLD HESLEDON 3G 151
Cold Hesledon Ind. Est.
  SR7: Mur 2G 151
Coldingham Gdns.
  NE5: Newc T 5H 55
Coldside Gdns. NE5: Cha P 4H 53
Coldstream DH2: Ous 5A 112
Coldstream Av. SR5: S'wck 3B 104
Coldstream Cl. DH4: Hou S 4F 129
Coldstream Dr. NE21: Bla T 3G 79
Coldstream Gdns.
  NE28: W'snd 4D 60
Coldstream Rd. NE15: Newc T . . .3F 67
Coldstream Way NE29: N Shi 5G 47
Coldwell Cl. DH6: S Het 6G 149
Coldwell La. NE10: Gate 4C 84
Coldwell Pk. Av. NE10: Gate 4C 84

Coldwell Pk. Dr. NE10: Gate 4C 84
Coldwell St. NE10: Gate 3D 84
Coldwell Ter. NE10: Gate 4C 84
Colebridge Cl. NE5: Newc T 4G 55
Colebrooke DH3: Bir 5D 112
Cole Gdns. NE10: Gate 3G 85
Colegate NE10: Gate 4F 85
Colegate W. NE10: Gate 4F 85
Colepeth NE10: Gate 4E 85
Coleridge Av. NE9: Gate 1G 97
  NE33: S Shi 6G 63
Coleridge Gdns. DH9: Dip 1D 120
Coleridge Pl. DH2: Pelt 6G 125
Coleridge Rd. SR5: C'twn 3D 102
Coleridge Sq. NE31: Heb 3C 72
Coley Grn. NE5: Cha P 3H 53
Coley Hill Cl. NE5: Cha P 3A 54
Coley Ter. SR6: Monk 2E 105
Colgrove Pl. NE3: Ken 2A 56
Colgrove Way NE3: Ken 2B 56
Colima Av. SR5: Sund 5D 102
Colin Ct. NE21: Bla T 5C 66
Colin Pl. NE6: Walk 1G 71
Colin Ter. SR2: Ryh 3F 133
College Burn Rd. SR3: New S 4G 131
College Dr. NE33: S Shi 1G 75
College Ho. NE1: Newc T 2E 5
College La.
  NE1: Newc T 3G 69 (2E 5)
  NE12: Longb 1C 58
College Rd. NE31: Heb 6B 72
College St. NE1: Newc T . . .3G 69 (2E 5)
College, The DH1: Dur . . .6C 154 (4A 6)
College Vw. DH7: Ush M 3C 152
  SR5: S'wck 4C 104
Collier Cl. NE15: Thro 6D 52
Collierley La. DH9: Dip 6C 106
Colliery La. DH5: Hett H 3D 148
  NE4: Newc T 4D 68 (4A 4)
Colliery Rd. DH7: Ush M 3D 152
  NE11: Dun 1B 82
COLLIERY ROW 3F 137
Collin Av. NE34: S Shi 4B 76
Colling Av. SR7: S'hm 4G 141
  (not continuous)
Collingdon Grn. NE39: H Spen . . .1A 92
Collingdon Rd. NE39: H Spen 1A 92
Collingwood Av. NE28: W'snd . . .3H 59
Collingwood Bldgs. NE1: Newc T . .5D 4
  (off Collingwood St.)
Collingwood Cen. NE29: N Shi . . .4B 48
Collingwood Cl. NE23: Nel V 1G 21
Collingwood Cotts. NE20: Pon . . .4B 26
Collingwood Ct. NE37: Usw 5D 100
Collingwood Cres. NE20: Pon 1D 38
Collingwood Dr. DH4: Hou S 3E 129
Collingwood Gdns. NE10: Gate . . .1D 84
Collingwood Mans.
  NE29: N Shi 3D 62
Collingwood M. NE3: Gos 2E 57
Collingwood Rd. NE25: Well 6E 35
Collingwood St. DH5: Hett H 5C 138
  NE1: Newc T 5F 69 (6D 4)
  NE10: Gate 2D 84
  NE31: Heb 1E 75
  NE33: S Shi 1E 75
  SR5: S'wck 3B 104
  (not continuous)
Collingwood Ter. NE2: Newc T . . .6H 57
  NE11: Dun 2C 82
  NE24: Bly 6C 12
  NE26: Whit B 1E 49
  NE30: N Shi 6F 49

Collingwood Vw. NE29: N Shi 2B 62
Collingwood Wlk. NE37: Usw . . .5D 100
  (off Collingwood Ct.)
Collywell Bay Rd. NE26: Sea S . .3H 25
Collywell Ct. NE26: Sea S 3H 25
Colman Av. NE34: S Shi 3C 74
Colmet Ct. NE11: Gate 1F 97
Colnbrook Cl. NE3: Ken 6H 41
Colombo Rd. SR5: C'twn 4B 102
Colpitts Ter. DH1: Dur 6B 154
Colston Pl. NE12: Longb 6D 44
Colston Ri. SR8: Pet 6C 162
Colston St. NE4: Newc T 6C 68
Colston Way NE25: Whit B 4H 35
Coltere Av. NE36: E Bol 4G 89
Colton Gdns. NE9: Gate 2A 98
Coltpark NE5: Newc T 6D 54
Coltpark Pl. NE23: Cra 4B 22
Coltsfoot Gdns. NE10: Gate 6C 84
Coltspool NE11: Kib 1F 111
Columba St. SR5: S'wck 3B 104
Columba Wlk. NE3: Gos 2F 57
  (not continuous)
COLUMBIA 3D 114
Columbia Grange NE3: Ken 2A 56
Columbia Ter. NE24: Bly 1C 18
Column of Liberty 2H 93
Colville Ct. DH9: Stly 3F 123
Colwell Pl. NE5: Newc T 2A 54
Colwell Rd. NE27: Shir 3D 46
  NE29: N Shi 4B 48
Colwyne Pl. NE5: Newc T 5F 55
Colwyn Pde. NE31: Heb 1E 87
Combe Dr. NE15: Lem 2H 65
Comet Dr. SR8: Eas 1C 162
Comet Row NE12: Kil 3C 44
Comet Sq. SR3: New S 2A 132
Comma Ct. NE11: Gate 4D 82
Commerce Way DH4: Hou S 4G 137
Commercial Bldgs. NE24: Bly 5C 12
  (off Church St.)
Commercial Rd. NE3: Gos 2G 57
  NE6: Newc T 4C 70
  NE24: Bly 5C 12
  NE32: Jar 1G 73
  (not continuous)
  NE33: S Shi 6D 62
  SR2: Sund 2F 119
Commercial Sq. DH7: B'don 5E 159
Commercial St. DH7: B'don 4E 159
  NE21: Bla T 2H 79
Commercial Way NE23: Cra 3A 22
Commissioners Wharf
  NE29: N Shi 5C 62
Community North Sports Complex
  . . . . .1E 103
Community Recreation Cen. 3B 54
Compton Av. NE34: S Shi 2F 75
Compton Ct. NE38: Wash 2H 113
Compton Rd. NE29: N Shi 2B 62
CONCORD 4B 100
Concorde Ho. NE25: H'wll 2C 34
Concorde Sq. SR3: New S 2A 132
Concorde Way NE32: Jar 3F 73
Concord Ho. NE5: Newc T 5D 54
  NE37: Usw 5B 100
Concordia Leisure Cen. 3A 22
Condercum Ct. NE15: Newc T 4G 67
Condercum Ind. Est.
  NE4: Newc T 4H 67
Condercum Rd. NE4: Newc T 4H 67
Condercum Rd. Bk.
  NE4: Newc T 4H 67

Cone St. NE33: S Shi 5D 62
Cone Ter. DH3: Ches S 6D 126
Conewood Ho. NE3: Ken 1B 56
Conhope La. NE4: Newc T 4H 67
Conifer Cl. DH1: Dur 4G 155
  NE21: Bla T 3H 79
Conifer Ct. NE12: Longb 5F 45
Coningsby Cl. NE3: Gos 5F 43
Coniscliffe Av. NE3: Ken 4B 56
Coniscliffe Pl. SR6: Monk 4E 105
Coniscliffe Rd. DH9: Stly 3D 122
Coniscliffe Ter. SR8: Eas 2B 162
  (off Thorpe Rd.)
Conishead Ter. DH6: S Het 5H 149
Coniston DH3: Bir 5D 112
  NE10: Gate 3G 85
Coniston Av. DH5: Eas L 5E 149
  NE2: Newc T 5G 57
  NE16: Whi 4H 81
  NE31: Heb 4D 72
  SR5: Monk 1C 104
Coniston Cl. DH1: Carr 3C 156
  DH2: Ches S 1C 134
  NE12: Kil 2C 44
  NE15: Thro 2E 65
  SR8: Pet 1E 165
Coniston Ct. NE5: Newc T 1F 67
Coniston Cres. NE21: Bla T 3H 79
Coniston Dr. NE32: Jar 6H 73
Coniston Gdns. NE9: Gate 6B 84
Coniston Grange NE36: E Bol . . .3D 88
Coniston Ho. NE38: Wash 1A 114
Coniston Pl. NE9: Gate 6B 84
Coniston Rd. NE24: Cow 4F 11
  NE28: W'snd 3D 60
  NE30: N Shi 3B 48
Connaught Cl. DH4: Hou S 4G 129
Connaught Gdns. NE12: Longb . .6D 44
Connaught M. NE2: Newc T 6G 57
  (off Bk. St George's Ter.)
Connaught Ter. NE32: Jar 3F 73
Connolly Ho. NE34: S Shi 6F 75
Consett Rd. NE11: Gate 6B 82
Constable Cl. DH9: Stly 3D 122
  NE40: Ryton 5D 64
Constable Gdns. NE34: S Shi . . .6E 75
Constables Gth. DH3: Bir 3C 112
Constance St. DH2: Pelt 2G 125
Constitutional Hill DH1: Dur 5E 155
Content St. NE21: Bla T 2A 80
Convent Rd. NE4: Newc T 6F 57
  (not continuous)
Conway Cl. NE22: Bed 4F 9
  NE40: Ryton 5D 64
Conway Dr. NE7: Newc T 3A 58
Conway Gdns. NE28: W'snd 3G 59
  SR3: E Her 2F 131
Conway Gro. NE26: Sea S 2F 25
Conway Pl. DH2: Ous 1H 125
Conway Rd. SR5: C'twn 3B 102
  SR5: C'twn 3B 102
Conway Sq. NE9: Gate 3A 84
  SR5: C'twn 3B 102
Conyers Av. DH2: Ches S 4B 126
Conyers Cres. SR8: Pet 4E 163
Conyers Gdns. DH2: Ches S 4B 126
Conyers Pl. DH2: Ches S 4B 126
Conyers Rd. DH2: Ches S 4B 126
  NE6: Newc T 3B 70
Cook Av. DH7: Ush M 4C 152
Cook Cl. NE33: S Shi 1D 74
Cook Cres. SR7: Mur 2B 150
Cooke's Wood DH7: Ush M 1E 159
Cook Gdns. NE10: Gate 3H 85

Cook Gro. SR8: Pet 4E 163
Cook's Cotts. DH7: Ush M 5B 152
Cookshold La.
  DH6: H Pitt, Sher 6E 157
Cookson Cl. NE4: Newc T 4D 68
Cookson Ho. NE33: S Shi 4E 63
Cookson Pl. DH9: Stly 4F 123
Cookson's La. NE1: Newc T 5F 69
Cookson St. NE4: Newc T 4C 68
Cookson Ter. DH2: Ches S 6B 126
Cook Sq. SR5: C'twn 3C 102
Cooks Wood NE38: Wash 4B 114
Coomassie Rd. NE24: Bly 6C 12
Coomside NE23: Cra 5C 22
Coop Bldgs. DH3: Bir 3C 112
Co-operative Bldgs. DH9: Dip . . .1C 120
  NE25: Sea D 6B 24
Co-operative Cres. NE10: Gate . .4C 84
Cooperative St. DH3: Ches S . . .5C 126
Co-operative Ter. DH2: Beam . . .2C 124
  DH2: Pelt 5C 124
  DH4: Hou S 2D 136
  DH5: Hett H 1C 148
  DH7: New B 1A 158
  DH9: Dip 1C 120
  NE10: Gate 4C 84
  NE12: Longb 4G 45
  NE13: Bru V 5C 30
  NE16: Burn 1H 107
  NE27: Shir 4C 40
  (Cramlington Ter.)
  NE27: Shir 2C 40
  (St Mark's Ct.)
  NE37: Usw 5C 100
  NE39: H Spen 6A 78
  SR4: Sund 2A 118
Co-operative Ter. E. DH9: Dip . . .1D 120
Co-operative Ter. W.
  DH9: Dip 1C 120
Co-operative Vs. DH7: B'don 4G 159
Cooperative Vs. DH6: Sher 6H 157
Cooper Sq. DH1: Dur 4F 155
Cooper St. SR6: Monk 3C 105
Copeland Ct. DH1: Dur 1A 160
Copenhagen Ho. NE1: Newc T 5G 5
Copland Ter.
  NE2: Newc T 3H 69 (3G 5)
Copley Av. NE34: S Shi 1E 89
Copley Dr. SR3: Sund 5B 118
Copperas La. NE15: Newc T 2D 66
Copperfield DH1: Dur 2A 160
Coppergate Ct. NE31: Heb 2D 72
Coppers Cl. NE11: Gate 4D 82
Coppice, The NE26: Sea S 3G 25
Coppice Way
  NE2: Newc T 3H 69 (2G 5)
Coppy La. DH9: Beam 2F 109
  NE16: Beam, Sun 2F 109
Copse, The NE3: Gos 5F 43
  NE12: Longb 4E 45
  NE16: Burn 1F 107
  NE21: Bla T 1D 80
  NE37: Usw 3H 99
Coptleigh DH5: Hou S 4C 138
Coquet NE38: Wash 6F 113
Coquet Av. NE3: Gos 1D 56
  NE24: News 2C 18
  NE26: Whit B 6C 36
  NE34: S Shi 1B 76
Coquet Bldgs. NE15: Thro 6H 53
Coquet Cl. SR8: Pet 2C 164
Coquetdale Av. NE6: Walk 3G 71
Coquetdale Pl. NE22: Bed 4C 10

Coquetdale Vs. SR6: Monk 3E 105
Coquet Dr. DH2: Ous 1G 125
Coquet Gdns. DH9: Stly 5C 122
Coquet Gro. NE15: Thro 5C 52
Coquet Ho. SR3: New S 3H 131
Coquet St. NE1: Newc T 4A, 70 (4H 5)
  NE31: Heb 3B 72
  NE32: Jar 4E 73
Coquet Ter. NE6: Newc T 6C 58
  NE23: Dud 3H 31
Corbett St. SR7: S'hm 3H 141
  (not continuous)
  SR8: Eas 1F 163
Corbiere Cl. SR3: New S 3G 131
Corbitt St. NE8: Gate 2E 83
Corbridge Av. NE13: Wide O 5D 30
Corbridge Cl. NE28: W'snd 1C 60
Corbridge Ct. NE12: Longb 1H 57
Corbridge Rd. NE6: Newc T 3C 70
Corbridge St. NE6: Newc T 3B 70
Corby Gdns. NE6: Walk 3F 71
Corby Ga. SR2: Sund 3D 118
Corby Gro. SR8: Pet 4A 164
Corby Hall Dr. SR2: Sund 3D 118
Corby M. SR2: Sund 3D 118
Corchester Rd. NE22: Bed 3G 9
Corchester Wlk.
  NE7: Newc T 3B 58
Corcyra St. SR7: S'hm 5B 142
Corfu Rd. SR5: C'twn 3C 102
Corinthian Sq. SR5: C'twn 3C 102
Cork St. SR1: Sund 6E 105
Cormorant Cl. NE24: News 3D 18
  NE38: Wash 4F 113
Cormorant Dr. NE11: Dun 1C 82
Cornbank Cl. SR3: New S 4A 132
Corndean NE38: Wash 3E 115
Cornelia Cl. SR3: New S 2A 132
Cornelia St. SR3: New S 2A 132
Cornelia Ter. SR7: S'hm 4A 142
Cornel M. NE7: Newc T 4C 58
Cornel Rd. NE7: Newc T 4B 58
Corney St. NE33: S Shi 2D 74
Cornfield Gth. SR8: Pet 2F 165
Cornfields, The NE31: Heb 3C 72
Cornforth Cl. NE10: Gate 5A 86
Cornhill NE5: Newc T 6D 54
  NE32: Jar 2G 87
Cornhill Av. NE3: Ken 6B 42
Cornhill Cen., The
  SR5: S'wck 3B 104
  (off Goschen St.)
Cornhill Cl. NE29: N Shi 6H 47
Cornhill Cres. NE29: N Shi 6H 47
  (not continuous)
Cornhill Rd. NE23: Cra 3C 22
  SR5: S'wck 3B 104
Corn Mill Dr. DH5: Hou S 5H 137
Cornmoor Gdns. NE16: Whi 6F 81
Cornmoor Rd. NE16: Whi 5F 81
Cornsay Cres. DH2: Ous 5H 111
Cornthwaite Dr. SR6: Whit 2E 91
Cornwall Ct. SR7: Mur 2D 150
Cornwallis NE37: Usw 4C 100
Cornwallis Sq. NE33: S Shi 6D 62
Cornwallis St. NE33: S Shi 4E 63
Cornwall Rd. NE31: Heb 6D 72
Cornwall St. SR8: Eas 1F 163
Cornwall Wlk. DH1: Carr 4B 156
Cornwell Ct. NE3: Newc T 3H 57
Cornwell Cres. NE22: Bed 5B 10
Coronation Av. DH1: Carr 3B 156
  NE16: Sun 3F 95

Coronation Av. SR2: Ryh 3F **133**
  SR8: Pet 1G **165**
Coronation Bungs. NE3: Gos 2F **57**
Coronation Cl. SR1: Sund 6E **105**
Coronation Cres. DH4: Hou S . . .1G **137**
  DH6: H Pitt 1F **157**
  NE25: Whit B 6B **36**
Coronation Grn. DH5: Eas L 5F **149**
Coronation Rd. NE5: Cha P 4H **53**
  NE16: Sun 3F **95**
  NE25: Sea B 6A **24**
Coronation Sq. DH6: S Het 6B **150**
Coronation St. DH2: Pelt 3E **125**
  DH3: Ches S 2D **134**
  NE23: Dud 2B **32**
  NE24: Bly 1C **18**
  NE28: W'snd 5A **60**
  NE29: N Shi 3C **62**
  NE33: S Shi 5E **63**
  NE40: Ryton 5E **65**
  SR1: Sund 6E **105** (3H **7**)
    (not continuous)
Coronation Ter. DH1: Dur 6A **156**
  DH2: Pelt 5D **124**
  DH3: Ches S 2C **134**
  DH5: Hett H 3C **148**
  DH9: Ann P 5H **121**
  NE9: Spri 4F **99**
  NE11: Kib 1E **111**
  NE29: N Shi 4F **47**
  NE35: Bol C 2A **88**
  SR4: Sund 1D **116**
Corporation Rd. SR2: Sund 3F **119**
Corporation St.
  NE4: Newc T 4D **68** (5A **4**)
Corporation Yd. NE15: Thro 1F **65**
Corriedale Cl. DH1: Dur 5C **144**
Corrighan Ter. DH5: W Rai 1G **147**
Corrofell Gdns. NE10: Gate 1E **85**
Corry Ct. SR4: Sund 3G **117**
Corsair NE16: Whi 5D **80**
Corsenside NE5: Newc T 6D **54**
Corstophine Town NE33: S Shi . . .1D **74**
Cortina Av. SR4: Sund 3F **117**
Corvan Ter. DH9: Tan L 5G **107**
Cosford Ct. NE3: Ken 6G **41**
Cossack Ter. SR4: Sund 6G **103**
Cosserat Pl. NE31: Heb 2B **72**
Cosser St. NE24: News 3H **17**
Coston Dr. NE33: S Shi 4E **63**
    (not continuous)
Cosyn St. NE6: Newc T 4A **70**
Cotehill Dr. NE20: Pon 1B **38**
Cotehill Rd. NE5: Newc T 6F **55**
Cotemede NE10: Gate 5G **85**
Cotemede Ct. NE10: Gate 5G **85**
Cotfield Wlk. NE8: Gate 4E **85**
Cotgarth, The NE10: Gate 4E **85**
Cotherstone Ct. SR3: Sund 5B **118**
Cotherstone Rd. DH1: Dur 1D **154**
Cotman Gdns. NE34: S Shi 1F **89**
Cotsford Cres. SR8: Pet 1G **165**
Cotsford Grange SR8: Pet 1H **165**
Cotsford La. SR8: Pet 1G **165**
Cotsford Pk. Est. SR8: Pet 1H **165**
Cotswold Dr. DH2: Ches S 1A **134**
    (not continuous)
  NE12: Longb 4B **44**
Cotswold Cl. NE38: Wash 3H **113**
Cotswold Dr. NE25: Whit B 2B **48**
Cotswold Gdns. NE7: Newc T 4A **58**
  NE11: Gate 4C **82**
Cotswold Pl. SR8: Pet 6B **162**

Cotswold Rd. NE29: N Shi 3A **48**
  SR5: C'twn 3C **102**
Cotswolds La. NE35: Bol C 2A **88**
Cotswold Sq. SR5: C'twn 2C **102**
Cotswold Ter. DH9: Stly 4E **123**
Cottage Farm NE7: Newc T 4D **58**
Cottage Gdns. SR6: Cle 2A **90**
Cottage La. NE5: Newc T 6H **55**
Cottages Rd. SR7: S'hm 5B **142**
Cottages, The NE11: Kib 4G **97**
  SR8: Pet 4E **163**
Cottenham Chare NE4: Newc T . .4D **68**
Cottenham St. NE4: Newc T 4D **68**
Cotterdale NE28: W'snd 2F **59**
Cotterdale Av. *NE8: Gate* 3H **83**
    (off Patterdale Ter.)
Cotter Riggs Pl. NE5: Cha P 5H **53**
Cotter Riggs Wlk. NE5: Cha P . . .5H **53**
Cottersdale Gdns. NE5: Cha P . . .4H **53**
Cottingham Cl. SR8: Pet 6B **162**
Cottingwood Ct. NE4: Newc T . . .3D **68**
Cottingwood Gdns.
  NE4: Newc T 3D **68**
Cottingwood Grn. NE24: News . . .4A **18**
Cottonwood DH4: Hou S 3D **128**
  SR3: New S 4G **131**
Coulthards La. NE8: Gate 6H **69**
Coulthards Pl. NE8: Gate 5A **70**
Coulton Dr. NE36: E Bol 4F **89**
Council Av. DH4: Hou S 3F **129**
Council Ter. NE37: Wash 6B **100**
Counden Rd. NE5: Newc T 4C **54**
Countess Av. NE26: Whit B 6C **36**
Countess Cl. SR7: S'hm 3A **142**
Countess Dr. NE15: Newc T 2E **67**
Counts House 1C **160** (5B **6**)
County Hall Bldgs. DH1: Dur 4B **154**
County Show Ground (Agricultural)
  . . . . .5B **128**
Coupland Gro. NE32: Jar 6F **73**
Courtfield Rd. NE6: Walk 1F **71**
Court La. DH1: Dur 6D **154** (4C **6**)
Courtney Cl. NE3: Ken 6G **41**
Courtney Dr. DH2: Ous 2H **125**
  SR3: New S 1H **131**
Court Rd. NE22: Bed 4H **9**
Court St. SR8: Eas 1F **163**
Court, The NE16: Whi 5G **81**
Courtyard, The DH9: Tan L 1A **122**
Cousin St. SR1: Sund 6E **105**
Coutts Rd. NE6: Walk 1E **71**
Coventry Gdns. NE4: Newc T 5A **68**
  NE29: N Shi 3A **62**
Coventry Rd. DH1: Dur 6E **145**
Coventry Way NE32: Jar 1F **87**
Coverdale NE10: Gate 5G **85**
  NE28: W'snd 2F **59**
Coverdale Av. NE24: Cow 6G **11**
  NE37: Usw 5A **100**
Coverdale Wlk. NE33: S Shi 2E **75**
Coverley DH3: Gt Lum 3G **135**
Coverley Rd. SR5: C'twn 3D **102**
Covers, The NE12: Longb 1E **59**
  NE16: Swa 2D **80**
  NE28: W'snd 4H **59**
Cove, The DH4: Hou S 3F **129**
Cowan Cl. NE21: Bla T 5G **65**
Cowans Av. NE12: Kil 1C **44**
Cowan Ter. SR1: Sund . . .1D **118** (5G **7**)
Cowdray Ct. NE3: Ken 6G **41**
Cowdray Rd. SR5: C'twn 3D **102**
Cowdrey Ho. *NE29: N Shi* 4H **61**
    (off St John's Grn.)

Cowell Gro. NE39: Row G 3C **92**
Cowell St. SR8: Pet 6F **163**
Cowen Gdns. NE9: Gate 4A **98**
Cowen Rd. NE21: Bla T 6B **66**
Cowen St. NE6: Walk 3F **71**
  NE21: Bla T 3H **79**
Cowen Ter. NE39: Row G 2F **93**
COWGATE 6H **55**
Cowgate NE1: Newc T 4G **69** (5F **5**)
Cowgate Leisure Cen. 4H **55**
Cowley Cres. DH5: W Rai 1G **147**
Cowley Pl. NE24: Cow 5H **11**
Cowley Rd. NE24: Cow 4H **11**
Cowpath Gdns. NE10: Gate 2G **85**
COWPEN 3H **11**
Cowpen Hall Rd. NE24: Cow 5G **11**
COWPEN NEW TOWN 4G **11**
Cowpen Rd. NE24: Bly, Cow 5F **11**
    (not continuous)
Cowpen Sq. NE24: Bly 4B **12**
Cowper Ter. NE12: Longb 4C **44**
Cox Chare NE1: Newc T . . .4H **69** (5G **5**)
Coxfoot Cl. NE34: S Shi 4E **75**
COX GREEN 4F **115**
Coxgreen Rd. DH4: Pen 1E **129**
  SR4: Pen 6E **115**
COXLODGE 2C **56**
Coxlodge Rd. NE3: Gos 2C **56**
Coxlodge Ter. NE3: Gos 2C **56**
Coxon St. NE10: Gate 1H **85**
  SR2: Sund 2E **119**
Coxon Ter. NE10: Gate 2C **84**
Cradock Av. NE31: Heb 5B **72**
Cragdale Gdns. DH5: Hett H 3B **148**
Craggyknowe NE37: Wash 1F **113**
Craghall Dene NE3: Gos 3G **57**
Craghall Dene Av. NE3: Gos 3G **57**
CRAGHEAD 6G **123**
Craghead La. DH9: Stly 6G **123**
Craghead Rd. DH2: Pelt 5G **123**
Cragleas NE16: Burn 3G **107**
Cragside DH2: Ches S 5A **126**
  NE7: Newc T 4B **58**
  NE13: Wide O 5D **30**
  NE23: Cra 5B **22**
  NE26: Whit B 4A **36**
  NE34: S Shi 4B **76**
  NE37: Wash 6G **99**
Cragside Av. NE29: N Shi 5H **47**
Cragside Ct. DH5: Hou S 3B **138**
  DH9: Ann P 6F **121**
  NE4: Newc T 6A **68**
Cragside Gdns. NE11: Gate 6C **82**
  NE12: Kil 1F **45**
  NE22: Bed 2B **10**
  NE28: W'snd 4D **60**
Cragston Av. NE5: Newc T 4G **55**
Cragston Cl. NE5: Newc T 5G **55**
Cragston Ct. NE5: Newc T 5G **55**
Cragston Way NE5: Newc T 5G **55**
Cragton Gdns. NE24: Cow 6H **11**
Craigavon Rd. SR5: C'twn 4D **102**
Craig Cres. NE23: Dud 3A **32**
Craigend NE23: Cra 4C **22**
Craighill DH4: Hou S 3E **129**
Craiglands, The *SR2: Sund* 4C **118**
    (off Tunstall)
Craigmillar Av. NE5: Newc T 4G **55**
Craigmillar Cl. NE5: Newc T 4F **55**
Craigmill Pk. NE24: Cow 5G **11**
Craigmont Ct. *NE12: Longb* 1D **58**
    (off West Av.)
Craigshaw Rd. SR5: C'twn 2B **102**

Craigshaw Sq. SR5: C'twn 2B **102**
Craigside Ct. NE11: Gate 6C **82**
Craig St. DH3: Bir 3C **112**
Craig Ter. SR8: Eas 2B **162**
Craigwell Dr. SR3: New S 5A **132**
Crake Way NE38: Wash 5F **113**
Cramer St. NE8: Gate 2H **83**
CRAMLINGTON 3A **22**
Cramlington Rd. NE23: Dud 2A **32**
    SR5: C'twn 4B **102**
Cramlington Sports Cen. 5A **22**
Cramlington Sq. SR5: C'twn 3B **102**
Cramlington Station (Rail) 2H **21**
Cramlington Ter. NE24: News . . .3A **18**
    NE27: Shir 4C **46**
CRAMLINGTON VILLAGE 2B **22**
Cramond Ct. NE9: Gate 2G **97**
Cramond Way NE23: Cra 5B **22**
Cranberry Dr. NE38: Wash 4C **114**
Cranberry Rd. SR5: C'twn 3C **102**
Cranberry Sq. SR5: C'twn 3C **102**
Cranborne SR3: E Her 3E **131**
Cranbourne Grn. NE30: N Shi . . .2D **48**
Cranbrook SR3: Sund 4A **118**
Cranbrook Av. NE3: Gos 6E **43**
Cranbrook Ct. NE3: Ken 6A **42**
Cranbrook Rd. NE15: Newc T 5F **67**
Cranesville NE9: Gate 6C **84**
    (not continuous)
Craneswater Av. NE26: Whit B . . .2B **38**
Cranfield Pl. NE15: Lem 2A **66**
Cranford Gdns. NE15: Lem 2C **66**
Cranford St. NE34: S Shi 3E **75**
Cranford Ter. SR4: Sund 2A **118**
    SR8: Eas 1B **162**
Cranham Cl. NE12: Kil 1F **45**
Cranlea NE3: Ken 1G **55**
Cranleigh DH3: Gt Lum 4G **135**
Cranleigh Av. NE3: Ken 6G **41**
Cranleigh Pl. NE25: Whit B 5H **35**
Cranleigh Rd. SR5: C'twn 3C **102**
Cranshaw Pl. NE23: Cra 4B **22**
Cranston Pl. SR2: Ryh 3G **133**
Crantock Rd. NE3: Ken 2B **56**
Cranwell Ct. NE3: Ken 6G **41**
Cranwell Dr. NE13: Wide O 5D **30**
Craster Av. NE12: Longb 4F **45**
    NE27: Shir 2C **46**
    NE34: S Shi 1B **76**
Craster Cl. DH2: Ches S 2A **134**
    NE24: Bly 6A **12**
    NE25: Whit B 5H **35**
Craster Ct. NE11: Gate 5E **83**
    NE23: Cra 3A **22**
Craster Gdns. NE28: W'snd 4D **60**
Craster Rd. NE29: N Shi 2H **61**
Craster Sq. NE3: Gos 1C **56**
Craster Ter. NE7: Newc T 5B **58**
Crathie DH3: Bir 6C **98**
Craven Ct. SR6: Monk 4F **105**
CRAWCROOK 5A **64**
Crawfields Ct. NE12: Longb 1H **57**
Crawford Av. CR8: Pet 5D **162**
Crawford Av. W. SR8: Pet 5C **162**
Crawford Cl. DH6: Sher 6D **156**
Crawford Ct. SR3: New S 3H **131**
Crawford Gdns. NE40: Ryton . . .5A **64**
Crawford Pl. NE25: Whit B 1A **48**
Crawford Ter. NE24: Bly 4B **12**
Crawford Ter. NE6: Walk 4F **71**
Crawhall Rd.
    NE1: Newc T 4H **69** (4H **5**)
Crawlaw Bungs. SR8: Eas 1E **163**

Crawlaw Rd. SR8: Eas 1D **162**
Crawley Av. NE31: Heb 6B **72**
Crawley Gdns. NE16: Whi 4G **81**
Crawley Rd. NE28: W'snd 6H **59**
Crawley Sq. NE31: Heb 6B **72**
Craythorne Gdns.
    NE6: Newc T 5C **58**
Creeverlea NE38: Wash 4A **114**
Creighton Av. NE3: Ken 4A **56**
Creland Way NE5: Newc T 4G **55**
Crescent Cl. DH6: Sher 6D **156**
Crescent, The DH2: Ches S 4A **134**
    (Chester Moor)
    DH2: Ches S 6B **126**
    (Chester-le-Street)
    DH2: Ous 1H **125**
    DH4: Hou S 5H **129**
    DH4: W Rai 3D **146**
    DH5: Hett H 2C **148**
    DH6: Sher 6D **156**
    DH9: Tan L 1B **122**
    NE7: Newc T 2B **58**
    NE11: Dun 3B **82**
    NE11: Kib 1E **111**
    NE13: Wool 1F **55**
    NE15: Thro 5D **52**
    NE16: Sun 3F **95**
    NE16: Whi 5G **81**
    NE20: Pon 2A **38**
    NE23: Seg 2F **33**
    NE26: Whit B 1D **48**
    NE28: W'snd 4H **59**
    NE30: N Shi 5E **49**
    NE32: Jar 5E **73**
    NE34: S Shi 5H **75**
    NE39: H Spen 2A **92**
    NE39: Row G 3F **93**
    NE40: Ryton 4D **64**
    SR3: New S 6A **118**
    SR6: Cle 3H **89**
Crescent Va. NE26: Whit B 1C **48**
    (off Jesmond Ter.)
Crescent Way NE12: Longb 5E **45**
Cres. Way Nth. NE12: Longb 5E **45**
Cres. Way Sth. NE12: Longb 5E **45**
Creslow NE10: Gate 5E **85**
Cressbourne Av. SR6: Monk 1E **105**
Cresswell Av. NE12: Longb 5C **44**
    NE26: Sea S 3G **25**
    NE29: N Shi 6B **48**
    SR8: Pet 1G **165**
Cresswell Cl. NE21: Bla T 3G **79**
    NE25: Whit B 2A **48**
Cresswell Dr. NE3: Ken 6A **42**
    NE24: Bly 2A **18**
Cresswell Rd. NE28: W'snd 6G **59**
Cresswell St. NE6: Walk 3D **70**
    (not continuous)
Cresswell Ter.
    SR2: Sund 2C **118** (6F **7**)
Cresthaven NE10: Gate 5E **85**
Crest, The NE13: Din 4F **29**
    NE22: Bed 4G **9**
    NE26: Sea S 5H **25**
Crewe Av. DH1: Dur 6H **155**
Crichton Av. DH3: Ches S 2D **134**
Cricket Ter. NE16: Burn 1G **107**
Cricklewood Dr. DH4: Pen 2F **129**
Cricklewood Rd. SR5: C'twn 4B **102**
Criddle St. NE8: Gate 5A **70**
Crieff Gro. NE32: Jar 6H **73**
Crieff Sq. SR5: C'twn 3B **102**
Crigdon Hill NE5: Newc T 6D **54**

Crighton NE38: Wash 2G **113**
Crimdon Gro. DH4: Hou S 4G **137**
Crimea Rd. SR5: C'twn 3B **102**
Crindledykes NE38: Wash 5C **114**
Cripps Av. NE10: Gate 3H **85**
Crispin Ct. NE5: Newc T 4D **54**
Crocus Cl. NE21: Bla T 1G **79**
Croft Av. NE12: Longb 6E **45**
    NE28: W'snd 5A **60**
    SR4: Sund 1A **118**
Croft Cl. NE40: Ryton 5D **64**
Croftdale Rd. NE21: Bla T 1A **80**
Crofter Cl. NE23: Dud 2A **32**
Crofthead Dr. NE23: Cra 5B **22**
Crofton Mill Ind. Est.
    NE24: Bly 1D **18**
Crofton St. NE24: Bly 6C **12**
    NE34: S Shi 3E **75**
Crofton Way NE15: Lem 2H **65**
Croft Pk. 1C **18**
Croft Rigg DH7: B'don 6C **150**
Croft Rd. NE24: Bly 6C **12**
Croftside DH3: Bir 2C **112**
Croftside Av. SR6: Whit 2F **91**
Croftside Ho. SR3: New S 4H **131**
Crofts Pk. NE61: Hep 1A **8**
Croft Stairs NE1: Newc T . . .4G **69** (5F **5**)
Crofts, The NE20: Pon 5F **27**
Croft St. NE1: Newc T 4G **69** (4E **5**)
Croftsway NE4: Newc T 5B **68**
Croft Ter. DH9: Ann P 5G **121**
    NE32: Jar 3F **73**
Croft, The DH6: Sher 6H **157**
    NE3: Ken 3C **56**
    NE12: Kil 1E **45**
    NE22: H Bri 5C **8**
    NE40: Ryton 5D **64**
    SR7: Mur 3D **150**
    (off Grasmere Ter.)
Croft Vw. NE12: Kil 3E **45**
Croft Vs. NE40: G'sde 1A **70**
Croftwell Cl. NE21: Bla T 2B **80**
Cromarty DH2: Ous 5H **111**
Cromarty St. SR6: Monk 3D **104**
Cromdale Pl. NE5: Newc T 6F **55**
Cromer Av. NE10: Gate 2H **97**
Cromer Ct. NE9: Gate 2A **98**
Cromer Gdns. NE2: Gos 4G **57**
    NE26: Whit B 5C **36**
Crompton Rd. NE6: Newc T 6B **58**
Cromwell Av. NE21: Bla T 1H **79**
Cromwell Ct. NE10: Gate 1A **86**
    (off Richmond Av.)
    NE21: Bla T 5G **65**
Cromwell Pl. NE21: Bla T 2G **79**
Cromwell Rd. NE10: Gate 1H **85**
    NE16: Whi 3G **81**
Cromwell St. NE8: Gate 2A **84**
    NE21: Bla T 5G **65**
    SR4: Sund 6A **104**
Cromwell Ter. NE10: Gate 1H **85**
    NE29: N Shi 1B **62**
Crondall St. NE33: S Shi 2F **75**
Cronin Av. NE34: S Shi 5D **74**
CROOKGATE BANK 1A **100**
Crook Hall Gardens 4C **154**
Crookham Way NE23: Cra 5C **22**
CROOKHILL 5E **65**
Crookhill Ter. NE40: Ryton 5E **65**
Cropthorne NE10: Gate 5H **85**
Crosby Ct. SR2: Sund 2F **119**
Crosby Gdns. NE9: Gate 2B **98**
Crosland Pk. NE23: Nel V 6H **15**

Crosland Way NE23: Nel V 5H **15**
Cross Av. NE28: W'snd 3F **59**
Crossbank Rd. NE5: Newc T 4H **55**
Crossbrook Rd. NE5: Newc T 5H **55**
Cross Carliol St.
   NE1: Newc T 4G **69** (4E **5**)
Cross Dr. NE40: Ryton 3C **64**
Crossfell NE20: Pon 1C **38**
Crossfield Pk. NE10: Gate 5C **84**
Crossfield Ter. NE6: Walk 5G **71**
Crossgate DH1: Dur 6B **154** (3A **6**)
   NE33: S Shi 5E **63**
CROSSGATE MOOR 5A **154**
Crossgate Moor Gdns.
   DH1: Dur 4H **153**
Crossgate Peth DH1: Dur 6A **154**
Crossgate Rd. DH5: Hett H 3C **148**
Crossgill NE37: Wash 6H **99**
Crosshill Rd. NE15: Newc T 5F **67**
Cross Keys La. NE9: Gate 6H **83**
Cross La. NE11: Dun 1H **81**
   NE11: Gate 2C **96**
   NE16: Dun, Swa, Whi 3G **81**
Crosslaw NE5: Newc T 6D **54**
Crosslea Av. SR3: Sund 4B **118**
Crossley Ter. NE4: Newc T 3B **68**
   NE12: Longb 4F **45**
Cross Morpeth St. NE2: Newc T . .1D **68**
Cross Pde. NE4: Newc T 5C **68**
Cross Pl. SR1: Sund 6E **105**
Cross Rigg Cl. DH4: Pen 2E **129**
Cross Row DH1: Dur 6C **144**
   NE10: Gate 2B **84**
   NE40: Ryton 5E **65**
Cross Sheraton St.
   *NE2: Newc T 1D **68***
   (off Sheraton St.)
Cross St. DH4: Hou S 3E **137**
   (Front St.)
   DH4: Hou S 2H **137**
   (Station Rd.)
   DH6: H Pitt 3H **157**
   NE1: Newc T 4E **69** (5B **4**)
   NE6: Newc T 4A **70**
   NE8: Gate 2H **83**
   SR8: Eas 1F **163**
Cross Ter. NE39: Row G 4D **92**
   NE40: Ryton 3C **64**
Cross Va. Rd. SR2: Sund 3C **118**
Cross Valley Ct. DH1: Dur 6A **154**
Cross Vw. Ter. DH1: Dur 1A **160**
Cross Villa Pl. No. 2
   NE4: Newc T 4E **69** (5A **4**)
Cross Villa Pl. No. 3
   NE4: Newc T 4E **69** (5A **4**)
Cross Villa Pl. No. 4
   NE4: Newc T 4D **68** (5A **4**)
Cross Villa Pl. No. 5
   NE4: Newc T 4D **68** (5A **4**)
Cross Way NE34: S Shi 4A **76**
Crossway NE2: Newc T 4G **57**
   NE9: Gate 5B **84**
   (Broadway)
   NE9: Gate 5A **84**
   (Sheriff's Highway)
   NE30: N Shi 5E **49**
Crossway Ct. NE3: Ken 4B **56**
Crossways NE32: Jar 2G **87**
   NE36: E Bol 4G **89**
   SR3: New S 2H **131**
Crossways, The NE13: Bru V 1C **42**
Crossway, The NE3: Ken 3B **56**
   NE15: Lem 2B **66**

Crosthwaite Gro.
   SR5: C'twn 4C **102**
Croudace Row NE10: Gate 3D **84**
Crow Bank NE28: W'snd 5A **60**
Crow Hall La. NE23: Cra, Nel V . .5H **15**
Crowhall La. NE10: Gate 3D **84**
Crow Hall Rd. NE23: Nel V 6H **15**
Crowhall Towers NE10: Gate 3D **84**
Crow La. SR3: E Her 2D **130**
Crowley Av. NE16: Whi 4G **81**
Crowley Gdns. NE21: Bla T 1A **80**
Crowley Rd. NE16: Swa 2E **81**
Crowley Vs. *NE16: Swa 2E **81***
   (off Crowley Rd.)
Crown Rd. SR5: Sund 5A **104**
Crown St. NE24: Bly 6D **12**
Crown Ter. NE40: G'sde 2B **78**
Crowther Ind. Est.
   NE38: Wash 2F **113**
Crowther Rd. NE38: Wash 2F **113**
Crowtree Leisure Cen. . . .1C **118** (4F **7**)
Crowtree Rd.
   SR1: Sund 1C **118** (3F **7**)
   (not continuous)
Croxdale Ct. NE34: S Shi 4C **74**
Croxdale Gdns. NE10: Gate 2G **85**
Croxdale Ter. NE10: Gate 2G **85**
   NE40: G'sde 2C **78**
Croydon Rd. NE4: Newc T 3C **68**
Crozier St. SR5: S'wck 4C **104**
Cruddas Pk. Shop. Cen.
   NE4: Newc T 6C **68**
Crudwell Cl. NE35: Bol C 1A **88**
Crummock Av. SR6: Monk 1C **104**
Crummock Ct. NE28: W'snd 3E **61**
Crummock Rd. NE5: Newc T 1F **67**
Crumstone Ct. NE12: Kil 1E **45**
Crusade Wlk. NE32: Jar 4F **73**
Cuba St. SR2: Sund 3E **119**
Cuillin Cl. NE38: Wash 4H **113**
Culford Pl. NE28: W'snd 1C **60**
CULLERCOATS 2E **49**
Cullercoats Rd. SR5: C'twn 4B **102**
Cullercoats Sq. SR5: C'twn 4B **102**
Cullercoats Station (Metro) 2E **49**
Cullercoats St. NE6: Walk 3E **71**
   (not continuous)
Culloden Ter. SR8: Eas 2F **163**
Culloden Wlk. NE12: Kil 1D **44**
Cumberland Av. NE22: Bed 4G **9**
Cumberland Pl. DH3: Bir 6D **112**
   NE34: S Shi 2B **76**
Cumberland Rd. NE29: N Shi 6F **47**
   SR3: New S 1A **132**
Cumberland St. NE28: W'snd 6F **61**
   (George St.)
   NE28: W'snd 5A **60**
   (Richardson St.)
   SR1: Sund 6D **104** (2G **7**)
   (not continuous)
Cumberland Wlk. NE7: Newc T . . .3B **58**
   (not continuous)
Cumberland Way NE37: Usw 3B **100**
Cumbrian Av. DH2: Ches S 1C **134**
   (not continuous)
   SR6: Monk 6C **90**
Cumbrian Gdns. NE11: Gate 5C **82**
Cumbrian Way SR8: Pet 1E **165**
Cumbria Pl. DH9: Stly 2E **123**
Cumbria Wlk. NE4: Newc T 4C **68**
Cummings Av. DH6: Sher 5D **156**
Cummings St. NE24: Bly 5C **12**
Cunningham Pl. DH1: Dur 4F **155**

Curlew Cl. NE12: Longb 6A **44**
   NE38: Wash 5G **113**
   NE40: Ryton 5E **65**
Curlew Rd. NE32: Jar 1G **73**
   (not continuous)
Curlew Way NE24: News 3C **18**
Curran Ho. NE32: Jar 1G **73**
Curren Gdns. NE10: Gate 1C **84**
Curtis Rd. NE4: Newc T 2B **68**
Curzon Pl. NE5: Newc T 5F **55**
   NE8: Gate 5G **69**
Curzon Rd. W. NE28: W'snd 6H **59**
Curzon St. NE8: Gate 3G **83**
Cushat Cl. NE6: Newc T 4C **70**
Cushycow La. NE40: Ryton 5D **64**
Customs House, The 5D **62**
Cut Bank NE1: Newc T 4A **70**
Cuthbert Av. DH1: Dur 6G **155**
Cuthbert Cl. DH1: Dur 6H **155**
   (Cuthbert Av.)
   DH1: Dur 6H **155**
   (Dragon Villa)
Cuthbertson Ct. SR6: Monk 6E **91**
Cuthbert St. NE8: Gate 1F **83**
   NE16: Sun 4E **95**
   NE31: Heb 3B **72**
   (not continuous)
Cuthbert Wlk. NE3: Gos 2G **57**
Cutting St. NE7: S'hm 2F **141**
Cygnet Cl. NE5: Cha P 3B **54**
Cyncopa Way NE5: Newc T 5H **55**
Cypress Av. NE4: Newc T 1H **67**
Cypress Ct. DH7: B'don 6D **158**
Cypress Cres. NE11: Dun 3B **82**
   NE24: Bly 6C **12**
Cypress Dr. NE24: Bly 6C **12**
Cypress Gdns. NE12: Kil 1C **44**
   NE24: Bly 6C **12**
Cypress Gro. DH1: Dur 4G **155**
   NE40: Ryton 3B **64**
Cypress Rd. NE9: Spri 3D **98**
   NE21: Bla T 1A **80**
Cypress Sq. SR3: New S 1A **132**
Cyprus Gdns. NE9: Gate 5A **84**

D

Dachet Rd. NE25: Whit B 4H **35**
Dacre Rd. SR6: Monk 1D **104**
Dacre St. NE33: S Shi 1E **75**
   (not continuous)
Daffodil Av. SR8: Pet 6F **163**
Daffodil Cl. NE21: Bla T 1H **79**
Dahlia Ct. SR4: Sund 6B **104**
Dahlia Cres. SR8: Eas 2D **162**
Dahlia Pl. NE4: Newc T 2H **67**
Dahlia Way NE31: Heb 5C **72**
   (not continuous)
Dainton Cl. DH4: Hou S 5G **129**
Dairnbrook NE37: Wash 1G **113**
Dairy La. DH4: Hou S 3G **137**
   NE2: Newc T 1D **68**
Dairy Wlk. DH3: Lam P 3H **127**
Daisy Cotts. DH3: Bir 3C **112**
Dalamere Cl. NE38: Wash 2I **127**
Dalden Gro. SR7: S'hm 3B **142**
Dalegarth Gro. SR6: Monk 6C **90**
Dale Rd. NE25: Whit B 1H **47**
Dales, The NE5: Newc T 5A **56**
Dale St. DH7: Ush M 5B **152**
   NE24: Bly 4C **12**
   NE33: S Shi 4F **63**

Dale Ter. SR6: Monk 2E **105**
 SR7: Mur 6G **141**
Dale Top NE25: H'wll 2C **34**
Dalla St. SR4: Sund 6C **102**
Dally M. NE3: Gos 4D **42**
Dalmahoy NE37: Usw 2B **100**
Dalmatia Ter. NE24: Bly 1C **18**
Dalston Pl. NE24: News 3C **18**
Dalton Av. SR7: S'hm 4H **141**
 (not continuous)
Dalton Cl. NE23: Cra 3B **22**
Dalton Ct. NE28: W'snd 2F **59**
Dalton Cres. NE6: Newc T 3B **70**
Dalton Hgts. SR7: Mur 5E **141**
 (not continuous)
DALTON-LE-DALE 6F **141**
Dalton Pk. SR7: Mur 3E **151**
Dalton Pl. NE5: Cha P 4A **54**
Daltons La. NE33: S Shi 5D **62**
Dalton St. NE6: Newc T 3B **70**
 (not continuous)
Dalton Ter. SR7: Mur 3D **150**
Dalton Way DH4: Pen 2E **129**
Dame Dorothy Cres.
 SR6: Monk 4E **105**
 (off Dame Dorothy St.)
Dame Dorothy St.
 SR6: Monk 5D **104** (1G **7**)
Dama Flora Robson Av.
 NE34: S Shi 5B **74**
Damson Way DH1: Dur 5H **155**
Danby Cl. NE38: Wash 1F **127**
 SR3: New S 3B **132**
Danby Gdns. NE6: Newc T 5D **58**
Dance City 6B **4**
Danelaw DH3: Gt Lum 3G **135**
Danville Rd. SR6: Monk 1D **104**
Daphne Cres. SR7: S'hm 5A **142**
D'Arcy Cl. SR1: Sund 1F **119**
D'Arcy Sq. SR7: Mur 1E **151**
D'Arcy St. SR1: Sund 1E **119**
Darden Cl. NE12: Kil 1F **45**
Darden Lough NE5: Newc T 5D **54**
Darenth St. NE34: S Shi 3E **75**
Darien Av. SR6: Monk 1D **104**
Darley Ct. DH2: Plaw 1A **144**
 SR3: New S 3H **131**
Darley Pl. NE15: Newc T 4E **67**
Darling Pl. DH9: Stly 4F **123**
Darlington Av. SR8: Pet 5F **163**
Darlington Rd. DH1: Dur 1A **160**
Darnell Pl. NE4: Newc T 3D **68**
Darras Cl. NE33: S Shi 6F **63**
Darras Dr. NE29: N Shi 6G **47**
DARRAS HALL 2C **38**
Darras M. NE20: Pon 2C **38**
Darras Rd. NE20: Pon 2A **38**
Darrell St. NE13: Bru V 5C **30**
Dartford Cl. NE25: Sea D 6B **24**
Dartford Rd. NE33: S Shi 5H **63**
 SR6: Monk 1D **104**
Dartmouth Av. NE9: Gate 2H **97**
Dartmouth Cl. SR7: Mur 5G **141**
Darvall Cl. NE25: Whit B 4H **35**
Darwin Cres. NE3: Ken 4B **56**
Darwin St. SR5: S'wck 4H **103**
Daryl Cl. NE21: Bla T 2G **79**
Daryl Way NE10: Gate 3B **86**
Davenport Dr. NE3: Gos 4D **42**
David Gdns. SR6: Monk 2F **105**
David Lloyd Tennis Cen. 4H **57**
Davidson Cotts. NE2: Gos 4G **57**
Davidson Rd. NE10: Gate 1H **85**

Davidson St. NE10: Gate 3D **84**
David St. NE28: W'snd 6H **59**
Davies Hall NE31: Heb 2B **72**
Davies Wlk. SR8: Pet 5E **163**
Davison Av. NE26: Whit B 5B **36**
 SR3: New S 2B **132**
Davison Cres. SR7: Mur 1B **150**
Davison St. NE15: Thro 1E **65**
 NE24: Bly 5C **12**
 NE35: Bol C 2A **88**
Davison Ter. SR5: S'wck 3A **104**
 (off Nth. Hylton Rd.)
Davis Ter. SR8: Eas 1D **162**
Davy Bank NE28: W'snd 6B **60**
Davy Dr. SR8: Pet 5A **162**
DAWDON 6B **142**
Dawdon Bus. Pk. SR7: S'hm 6C **142**
Dawdon Cres. SR7: S'hm 5B **142**
Dawlish Cl. NE29: N Shi 5H **47**
 SR7: S'hm 5F **141**
Dawlish Gdns. NE9: Gate 2H **97**
Dawlish Pl. NE5: Cha P 4A **54**
Dawson Sq. NE30: N Shi 6F **49**
Dawson St. NE6: Walk 3G **71**
Dawson Ter. SR4: Sund 6C **102**
Daylesford Dr. NE3: Newc T 3H **57**
Daylesford Rd. NE23: Cra 5A **16**
Dayshield NE5: Newc T 6D **54**
Deacon Cl. NE15: Cha P 5H **53**
Deacon Ct. NE12: Longb 1A **58**
Deaconsfield Cl. SR3: New S 4H **131**
Deal Cl. NE24: News 3C **18**
Dean Cl. SR8: Pet 2F **165**
Deanery St. NE22: Bed 4H **9**
Deanham Gdns. NE5: Newc T . . .1G **67**
Dean Ho. NE6: Walk 1G **71**
Dean Rd. NE33: S Shi 2D **74**
DEANS 2E **75**
Deans Cl. NE16: Whi 3F **81**
Deansfield Gro. NE15: Cha P 4H **53**
Deansgate Ho.
 DH1: Dur 6D **154** (4C **6**)
Dean St. NE1: Newc T 4G **69** (5E **5**)
 NE9: Gate 6H **83**
Deans Wlk. DH1: Dur 4F **155**
Dean Ter. NE33: S Shi 2D **74**
 NE40: Ryton 4C **64**
 SR5: S'wck 4H **103**
Dearham Gro. NE23: Cra 5A **16**
Debdon Gdns. NE6: Newc T 6C **58**
Debdon Pl. NE23: Cra 3B **22**
Debussy Ct. NE32: Jar 3G **73**
DECKHAM 3A **84**
Deckham St. NE8: Gate 3A **84**
Deckham Ter. NE8: Gate 3A **84**
Deepbrook Rd. NE5: Newc T 6G **55**
Deepdale NE28: W'snd 2F **59**
 NE38: Wash 6G **113**
Deepdale Cl. NE16: Whi 1D **94**
Deepdale Cres. NE5: Newc T 5H **55**
Deepdale Gdns. NE12: Kil 2C **44**
Deepdale Grn. NE5: Newc T 5A **56**
Deepdale Rd. NE30: N Shi 3D **48**
Deepdale St. DH5: Hett H 3C **148**
Deepdene Gro. SR6: Monk 6E **91**
Deepdene Rd. SR6: Monk 6D **90**
Deerbolt Pl. NE12: Longb 6C **44**
Deerbush NE5: Newc T 6D **54**
Deerness Ct. DH7: B'don 5E **159**
Deerness Hgts. DH7: B'don 4D **158**
Deerness Leisure Cen. 6D **152**
Deerness Rd. SR2: Sund 2E **119**

Dee Rd. NE31: Heb 6D **72**
Deer Pk. Way NE21: Bla T 2C **80**
Dees Av. NE28: W'snd 4H **59**
Dee St. NE32: Jar 2G **73**
Defender Ct. SR5: Sund 5E **103**
Defoe Av. NE34: S Shi 6E **75**
De Grey St. NE4: Newc T 6C **68**
Deighton Wlk. NE5: Newc T 6D **54**
Delacour Rd. NE21: Bla T 6A **66**
Delamere Ct. SR3: New S 3A **132**
Delamere Cres. NE23: Cra 5A **16**
Delamere Gdns. SR8: Eas 1C **162**
Delamere Rd. NE3: Ken 2B **56**
DELAVAL 5F **67**
Delaval DH2: Ches S 6A **126**
Delaval Av. NE25: Sea D 6A **24**
 NE29: N Shi 1A **62**
Delaval Ct. NE22: Bed 3C **10**
 NE33: S Shi 6F **63**
Delaval Cres. NE24: News 3H **17**
Delavale Cl. SR8: Pet 1F **165**
Delaval Gdns. NE15: Newc T 5F **67**
 NE24: News 3H **17**
Delaval Rd. NE12: Longb 5D **44**
 NE15: Newc T 5F **67**
 (not continuous)
 NE26: Whit B 1E **49**
Delaval St. NE24: News 3H **17**
Delaval Ter. NE3: Gos 3C **56**
 NE24: Bly 5B **12**
 (not continuous)
Delaval Trad. Est. NE25: Sea D . .4A **24**
Deleval Ct. NE12: Longb 4E **45**
 (off Deleval Rd.)
Delhi Cres. NE40: G'sde 6A **64**
Delhi Gdns. NE40: G'sde 6A **64**
Delhi Vw. NE40: G'sde 6A **64**
Delight Bank DH9: Dip 2D **120**
Delight Ct. DH9: Dip 1D **120**
Delight Row DH9: Dip 1D **120**
Dellfield Dr. SR4: Sund 3C **116**
Dell, The DH4: Hou S 6H **129**
Delta Bank Rd. NE11: Dun 6G **67**
Delta Pk. NE11: Dun 6G **67**
Delton Cl. NE38: Wash 4C **114**
Demesne Dr. NE22: Bed 5H **9**
Dempsey Rd. NE13: Bru V 1D **42**
Denbeigh Pl. NE12: Longb 6C **44**
Denbigh Av. NE28: W'snd 3E **61**
 SR6: Monk 1D **104**
Denby Cl. NE23: Cra 5A **16**
Denby Wlk. NE5: Cha P 4A **54**
Dene Av. DH5: Hou S 4C **138**
 NE3: Gos 3G **57**
 NE12: Kil 3A **44**
 NE13: Bru V 5C **30**
 NE15: Lem 3B **66**
 NE39: Row G 4D **92**
Denebank NE25: Whit B 6A **36**
Dene Bank Av. SR8: Pet 1G **165**
Dene Bank Vw. NE3: Ken 4A **56**
Deneburn NE10: Gate 4G **85**
Dene Cl. NE7: Newc T 6A **58**
 NE40: Ryton 4D **64**
Dene Ct. DH3: Bir 1C **112**
 NE7: Newc T 6B **58**
 NE15: Lem 1C **66**
 NE38: Wash 1A **114**
Dene Cres. NE3: Gos 3G **57**
 NE26: Whit B 5B **36**
 NE28: W'snd 5B **60**
 NE39: Row G 4D **92**
 NE40: Ryton 4D **64**

Dene Dr. DH1: Carr 2B **156**
Deneford NE9: Gate 4A **98**
Dene Gdns. DH5: Hou S 4B **138**
  NE10: Gate 2H **85**
  NE15: Lem 3B **66**
  NE25: Whit B 6A **36**
Dene Gro. NE3: Gos 3G **57**
  NE23: Seg 1G **33**
Deneholm NE25: Whit B 5A **36**
  NE28: W'snd 4B **60**
Dene Ho. Rd. SR7: S'hm 3A **142**
Dene La. SR6: Monk 1D **104**
  (Dykelands La.)
  SR6: Monk, Whit 4C **90**
  (Moor La.)
Dene M. SR5: C'twn 4E **103**
Dene Pk. NE20: Pon 2B **38**
  SR5: C'twn 4E **103**
Dene Rd. NE21: Bla T 6A **66**
  NE30: N Shi 5E **49**
  NE39: Row G 4D **92**
  SR5: C'twn 4E **103**
  SR7: Mur, S'hm 6F **141**
DENESIDE 5G **141**
Dene Side NE21: Bla T 1B **80**
Deneside NE5: Newc T 3D **54**
  NE11: Dun 4B **82**
  NE15: Newc T 2E **67**
  NE23: Seg 1G **33**
  NE32: Jar 2G **87**
  NE34: S Shi 3C **76**
Deneside Av. NE9: Gate 1G **97**
Deneside Cl. NE15: Thro 5D **52**
Deneside Ct. NE2: Newc T 1A **70**
  NE26: Whit B 3A **36**
Dene St. DH5: Hett H 5C **138**
  DH9: Stly 4B **122**
  NE25: H'wll 1D **34**
  SR3: New S 6A **118**
  SR4: Sund 6H **103**
  SR8: Pet 6G **163**
Dene Ter. NE3: Gos 3G **57**
  NE15: Thro 6F **53**
  NE21: Bla T *1H* **79**
  (off Park Av.)
  NE32: Jar 5E **73**
  SR6: Monk 1D **104**
  SR7: S'hm 3B **142**
  SR8: Pet 1G **165**
Dene, The DH2: Ches S 4B **134**
  DH4: W Rai 3E **147**
  NE25: Whit B 6A **36**
  SR7: Mur 6G **141**
Dene Vw. DH9: Stly 2G **123**
  NE3: Gos 3G **57**
  NE16: Burn 1G **107**
  NE22: Bed 4C **10**
  NE25: H'wll 1D **34**
  NE39: H Spen 2A **92**
  NE39: Row G 3C **92**
Dene Vw. Ct. NE24: Cow 5H **11**
Dene Vw. Cres. SR4: Sund 1D **116**
Dene Vw. Dr. NE24: Cow 5H **11**
Dene Vw. E. NE22: Bed 5C **10**
Dene Vw. W. NE22: Bed 5B **10**
Dene Vs. DH3: Ches S 2D **134**
  SR8: Pet 1H **165**
Dene Wlk. NE29: N Shi 5A **62**
Dene Way SR7: S'hm 3A **142**
Deneway NE39: Row G 1G **93**
Denewell Av. NE7: Newc T 4A **58**
  NE9: Gate 6H **83**
Denewood NE12: Kil 3D **44**

Denewood Ct. DH9: Stly 5F **123**
  NE28: W'snd 5E **61**
Dene Wood (Nature Reserve)
  . . . . .5F **123**
Denham Av. SR6: Monk 1D **104**
Denham Dr. NE25: Sea D 1B **34**
Denham Gro. NE21: Bla T 3F **79**
Denham Wlk. NE5: Cha P 4H **53**
Denhill Pk. NE15: Newc T 3H **67**
Denholm Av. NE23: Cra 5A **16**
Denholme Lodge NE11: Dun 2B **82**
Denmark Cen. NE33: S Shi 4E **63**
Denmark Ct. NE6: Newc T 2C **70**
Denmark St. NE6: Newc T 2C **70**
  (not continuous)
  NE8: Gate 1H **83**
Dennison Cres. DH3: Bir 1C **112**
Denshaw Cl. NE23: Cra 5A **16**
Dentdale DH4: Pen 1C **128**
Denton Av. NE15: Lem 3B **66**
  NE29: N Shi 1G **61**
DENTON BURN 1D **66**
Denton Chare
  NE1: Newc T 5F **69** (6D **4**)
Denton Ct. NE5: Newc T 2E **67**
Denton Gdns. NE15: Newc T 4G **67**
Denton Ga. NE5: Newc T 4E **55**
Denton Gro. NE5: Newc T 4E **55**
Denton Hall Turret 2D **66**
Denton Pk. Ho. NE5: Newc T 5C **54**
Denton Pk. Shop. Cen.
  NE5: Newc T 5C **54**
Denton Park Swimming Pool 5C **54**
Denton Rd. NE15: Newc T 3D **66**
Denton Vw. NE21: Bla T 1H **79**
Dent St. NE24: Bly 1D **18**
  SR6: Monk 1D **104**
Denver Gdns. NE6: Walk 4E **71**
Denway Gro. NE26: Sea S 2F **25**
Denwick Av. *NE15: Lem* *3A* **66**
  (off Shirley St.)
Denwick Cl. DH2: Ches S 3A **134**
Denwick Ter. NE30: N Shi 6E **49**
Depot Rd. NE6: Walk 2D **70**
DEPTFORD 5B **104**
Deptford Rd. NE8: Gate 5A **70**
  SR4: Sund 6B **104**
Deptford Ter. SR4: Sund 5A **104**
Derby Ct. NE4: Newc T 3D **68**
Derby Cres. NE31: Heb 4B **72**
Derby Gdns. NE28: W'snd 4G **59**
Derby Rd. DH9: Stly 4C **122**
Derbyshire Dr. DH1: Carr 5B **156**
Derby St. NE4: Newc T 3D **68**
  NE32: Jar 2G **73**
  NE33: S Shi 5E **63**
  SR2: Sund 1C **118** (5E **7**)
Derby Ter. NE33: S Shi 5F **63**
Dereham Cl. NE26: Sea S 4H **25**
Dereham Ct. NE5: Newc T 3F **55**
Dereham Rd. NE26: Sea S 5H **25**
Dereham Way NE29: N Shi 5F **47**
Derry Av. SR6: Monk 1E **105**
Derwent Av. NE11: Gate 6F **83**
  NE15: Thro 2E **65**
  NE31: Heb 6C **72**
  NE39: Row G 4E **93**
Derwent Cl. SR7: S'hm 3A **142**
Derwent Ct. NE7: Newc T 3A **58**
  NE11: Gate 6F **83**
Derwent Cres. DH3: Gt Lum 4H **135**
  NE16: Swa 3E **81**
Derwent Crook Dr. NE9: Gate . . .6G **83**

Derwent Crookfoot Rd.
  NE9: Gate 6G **83**
Derwentdale Gdns.
  NE7: Newc T 4B **58**
Derwent Gdns. NE9: Gate 6A **84**
  NE28: W'snd 3E **61**
DERWENTHAUGH 1E **81**
Derwenthaugh Ind. Est.
  NE16: Swa 6D **66**
Derwenthaugh Marina
  NE21: Bla T 6E **67**
Derwenthaugh Riverside Pk.
  NE16: Swa 1E **81**
Derwenthaugh Rd.
  NE21: Bla T, Swa 5D **66**
Derwent Ho. NE37: Wash 3H **113**
Derwent Pk. NE39: Row G 3F **93**
Derwent Pl. NE21: Bla T 2H **79**
Derwent Rd. NE26: Sea S 3F **25**
  NE30: N Shi 3D **48**
  SR8: Pet 6E **163**
Derwentside NE16: Swa 3E **81**
Derwent St. DH4: Hou S 3F **129**
  DH5: Eas L 3D **148**
  DH9: Stly 1C **122**
  NE15: Newc T 4F **67**
  SR1: Sund 1C **118** (5F **7**)
Derwent Ter. DH6: S Het 5G **149**
  DH9: Ann P 6E **121**
  NE16: Burn 1H **107**
  (not continuous)
  NE38: Wash 3C **114**
Derwent Twr. NE11: Dun 2C **82**
Derwent Valley Cotts.
  NE39: Row G 4F **93**
Derwent Vw. NE16: Burn 1H **107**
  NE21: Bla T 2H **79**
Derwent Vw. Ter. DH9: Dip 6D **106**
Derwentwater Av.
  DH2: Ches S 2B **134**
Derwentwater Ct. NE8: Gate 2F **83**
Derwentwater Gdns.
  NE16: Whi 4H **81**
Derwentwater Rd. NE8: Gate 3D **82**
Derwentwater Ter. NE33: S Shi . . .1E **75**
Derwent Way NE12: Kil 2C **44**
  NE21: Bla T 2C **80**
Deuchar Ho. NE2: Newc T 1G **5**
Deuchar St. NE2: Newc T 1H **69**
Devon Av. NE16: Whi 4G **81**
Devon Cres. DH3: Bir 1B **112**
Devon Dr. SR3: New S 1A **132**
Devon Gdns. NE9: Gate 4H **83**
  NE34: S Shi 2B **76**
Devonport DH4: Hou S 6G **129**
Devon Rd. NE29: N Shi 4H **47**
  NE31: Heb 6D **72**
Devonshire Dr. NE27: Kil 4A **46**
Devonshire Gdns. NE28: W'snd . . .4G **59**
Devonshire Pl. NE2: Newc T 6H **57**
Devonshire Rd. DH1: Carr 4B **156**
Devonshire St. NE33: S Shi 2D **74**
  SR5: S'wck 4C **104**
Devonshire Ter.
  NE2: Newc T 2F **69** (1D **4**)
  NE26: Whit B 1D **48**
Devonshire Twr. SR5: S'wck 4D **104**
Devon St. DH4: Hou S 3G **129**
  DH5: Hett H 1B **148**
Devon Wlk. NE37: Usw 4B **100**
Devonworth Pl. NE24: Cow 6G **11**
Dewhurst Ter. NE16: Sun 3F **95**
Dewley NE23: Cra 4B **22**

Dewley Ct. NE23: Cra 4B 22
Dewley Pl. NE5: Newc T 4C 54
Dewley Rd. NE5: Newc T 6E 55
Dewsgreen NE23: Cra 3B 22
Dexter Ho. NE29: N Shi 4A 62
Dexter Way NE10: Gate 3C 84
Deyncourt DH1: Dur 3A 160
NE20: Pon 3D 38
Deyncourt Cl. NE20: Pon 4D 38
Diamond Ct. NE3: Ken 2G 55
Diamond St. NE28: W'snd 5H 59
Diamond Ter. DH1: Dur . . .5C 154 (1A 6)
Diana St. NE4: Newc T 4D 68 (4A 4)
Dibley Sq. NE6: Newc T 4B 70
Dibley St. NE6: Newc T 4B 70
Dickens Av. NE16: Swa 3E 81
NE34: S Shi 6D 74
Dickens St. DH4: Hou S 3H 137
SR5: S'wck 4A 104
Dickens Wlk. NE5: Cha P 4A 54
Dickens Wynd DH1: Dur 2A 160
Dickins Wlk. SR8: Pet 2E 165
Didcot Av. NF29: N Shi 3A 62
Didcot Way NE35: Bol C, W Bol 4A 88
Dillon St. NE32: Jar 4E 73
SR7: S'hrm 4B 142
Dilston Av. NE25: Whit B 1D 48
Dilston Cl. NE27: Shir 3D 46
NE38: Wash 3G 113
SR8: Pet 4C 164
Dilston Dr. NE5: Newc T 5C 54
Dilston Gdns. SR4: Sund 2H 117
Dilston Rd. DH1: Dur 1D 154
NE4: Newc T 4C 68
(not continuous)
Dilston Ter. NE3: Gos 3G 57
NE32: Jar 6F 73
Dimbula Gdns. NE7: Newc T 5D 58
Dinmont Pl. NE23: Cra 4B 22
DINNINGTON 4F 29
Dinnington Rd.
  NE13: Bru V, Din 5G 29
  NE13: Din 5G 29
  NE29: N Shi 1G 61
Dinsdale Av. NE28: W'snd 3A 60
Dinsdale Cotts. SR2: Ryh 3F 133
Dinsdale Dr. DH1: Carr 3B 156
Dinsdale Pl.
  NE2: Newc T 2H 69 (1H 5)
Dinsdale Rd.
  NE2: Newc T 2H 69 (1H 5)
  SR6: Monk 3E 105
Dinsdale St. SR2: Ryh 3F 133
Dinsdale St. Sth. SR2: Ryh 3F 133
Dinting Cl. SR8: Pet 2B 164
Dipe La. NE36: E Bol, W Bol 5C 88
DIPTON 1D 120
Dipton Av. NE4: Newc T 5A 68
Dipton Gdns. SR3: Sund 5B 118
Dipton Gro. NE23: Cra 3B 22
Dipton Rd. NE25: Whit B 4H 35
Dipwood Rd. NE39: Row G 5D 92
Dipwood Way NE39: Row G 5D 92
Discovery Ct. SR3: New S 3H 101
Dishforth Grn. NE9: Gate 4B 98
Dispensary La.
  NE1: Newc T 4F 69 (5B 4)
Disraeli St. DH4: Hou S 3F 137
NE24: Bly 5B 12
(not continuous)
DISSINGTON MARCH 5B 38
Dissington Pl. NE5: Newc T 1G 67
NE16: Whi 6E 81

Ditchburn Ter. SR4: Sund 5H 103
Dixon Pl. NE11: Dun 3B 82
Dixon Ri. SR8: Pet 1H 165
Dixon Rd. DH5: Hou S 5H 137
Dixons Sq. SR6: Monk 4D 104
Dixon St. NE8: Gate 2E 83
NE33: S Shi 6E 63
Dobson Cl. NE4: Newc T 6D 68
Dobson Cres. NE6: Newc T 5C 70
Dobson Ho. NE3: Gos 1E 57
NE12: Kil 3B 44
Dobson Ter. SR7: Mur 2C 150
Dockendale La. NE16: Whi 4G 81
Dockendale M. NE16: Whi 4G 81
Dock Rd. NE29: N Shi 3C 62
Dock Rd. Sth. NE29: N Shi 4C 62
Dock St. NE33: S Shi 3D 74
SR6: Monk 5E 105
Dockwray Cl. NE30: N Shi 2D 62
Dockwray Sq. NE30: N Shi 2D 62
Doctor Pit Cotts. NE22: Bed 4H 9
Doctor Ryan Ho. NE6: Walk 4G 71
Doctor Winterbottom Hall
  NE33: S Shi 6H 63
Doddfell Cl. NE37: Wash 1G 113
Doddington Cl. NE15: Lem 2H 65
Doddington Dr. NE23: Cra 3B 22
Doddington Vs. NE10: Gate 4C 84
Dodd's Bldgs. NE35: Bol C 2A 88
Dodd's Ct. SR5: C'twn 2C 102
Dodds Ter. DH3: Bir 1C 112
Dodd Ter. DH9: Ann P 6F 121
Dodsworth Nth. NE40: G'sde 2B 78
Dodsworth Ter. NE40: G'sde 2B 78
Dodsworth Vs. NE40: G'sde 2B 78
Dog Bank NE1: Newc T 5G 69 (6F 5)
Dog Leap Stairs NE1: Newc T 6E 5
Dolphin Ct. NE4: Newc T 4H 67
Dolphin Quay NE29: N Shi 2D 62
Dolphin St. NF4: Newc T 4H 67
Dolphin Vs. NE13: Bru V 1D 42
Dominies Cl. NE39: Row G 2F 93
Dominion Rd. DH7: B'don 6D 158
Donald Av. DH6: S Het 5G 149
Donald St. NE3: Gos 2G 57
Doncaster Rd.
  NE2: Newc T 2H 69 (1H 5)
Don Cres. DH3: Gt Lum 4H 135
Doncrest Rd. NE37: Usw 4H 99
Don Dixon Dr. NE32: Jar 2F 87
Donerston Gro. SR8: Pet 3A 164
Don Gdns. NE36: W Bol 4B 88
NE37: Usw 4B 100
Donkin Rd. NE37: Wash 6G 99
Donkins St. NE35: Bol C 2A 88
Donkin Ter. NE30: N Shi 6E 49
Donnington Cl. SR5: C'twn 4C 102
Donnington Ct.
  NE3: Newc T 3H 57
Donnini Ho. SR8: Eas 1C 162
Donnini Pl. DH1: Dur 4F 155
Donnison Gdns. SR1: Sund 6E 105
Donridge NE37: Usw 4H 99
Don Rd. NE32: Jar 2H 73
Donside NE10: Hew 1F 99
Don St. NE11: Gate 1E 97
Donvale Rd. NE37: Usw 4G 99
Don Vw. NE36: W Bol 4B 88
DONWELL 4H 99
Dorcas Av. NE15: Newc T 4G 67
Dorcas Ter. NE37: Usw 5B 100
Dorchester Cl. NE5: Cha P 4H 53
Dorchester Ct. NE25: Sea D 3A 24

Dorchester Gdns. NE9: Gate 3H 97
Doreen Av. SR7: Mur 5F 141
Doric Rd. DH7: New B 2B 158
Dorking Av. NE29: N Shi 3A 62
Dorking Cl. NE24: News 3C 18
Dorking Rd. SR6: Monk 1E 105
Dorlonco Vs. DH7: B'don 6E 159
Dormand Dr. SR8: Pet 4D 164
Dornoch Cres. NE10: Gate 5E 85
Dorrington Rd. NE3: Ken 1A 56
Dorset Av. DH3: Bir 6D 112
NE28: W'snd 5G 59
NE31: Heb 4D 72
NE34: S Shi 2B 76
SR6: Monk 1E 105
Dorset Gro. NE29: N Shi 4H 47
Dorset Rd. NE8: Gate 5A 70 (6H 5)
NE15: Newc T 3D 66
Dorset St. DH5: Eas L 5E 149
Double Row NE25: Sea D 5H 23
Douglas Av. NE3: Gos 1C 56
SR8: Pet 6F 163
Douglas Bader Ho. NE24: Bly 1D 18
(off Twizell St.)
Douglas Cl. NE34: S Shi 5E 75
Douglas Ct. DH9: Ann P 6E 121
NE11: Gate 3G 97
Douglas Gdns. DH1: Dur 2A 160
(not continuous)
NE11: Dun 4C 82
Douglas Pde. NE31: Heb 1E 87
Douglas Rd. SR6: Monk 1E 105
Douglas Sq.
  SR1: Sund 6E 105 (2H 7)
Douglass St. NE28: W'snd 5H 59
Douglas St. NE28: W'snd 6E 61
Douglas Ter. DH4: Pen 1G 129
DH9: Dip 3A 120
NE4: Newc T 4D 68
NE37: Usw 3B 100
Douglas Vs. DH1: Dur 5F 155
Douglas Way NE1: Newc T 3C 4
Doulting Cl. NE12: Longb 1B 58
Douro Ter. SR2: Sund . . .2D 110 (6C 7)
Dove Av. NE32: Jar 6G 73
Dove Cl. DH7: B'don 5C 158
NE12: Kil 1C 44
Dovecote Cl. NE25: Whit B 5G 35
Dovecote Farm DH2: Ches S 6H 125
Dovecote Rd. NE12: Longb 6E 45
Dove Ct. DH3: Bir 2C 112
NE30: N Shi 2E 49
Dovecrest Ct. NE28: W'snd 3D 60
Dovedale Av. NE24: Cow 6G 11
Dovedale Ct. NE34: S Shi 4C 74
Dovedale Gdns. NE7: Newc T 4A 58
NE9: Gate 1A 98
Dovedale Rd. SR6: Monk 6C 90
Dover Cl. NE5: Cha P 4A 54
NE22: Bed 4F 9
Dovercourt Rd. NE6: Walk 5G 71
Dove Row NE30: N Shi 2E 49
Dowling Av. NE25: Whit B 1B 48
Downe Cl. NE24: News 3C 18
Downend Rd. NE5: Newc T 4B 54
Downfield NE37: Usw 2B 100
Downham NE5: Newc T 6D 54
Downham Ct. NE33: S Shi 6E 63
DOWNHILL 2D 102
Downhill La. NE36: W Bol 1G 101
Downs La. DH5: Hett H 6D 138
(not continuous)
Downs Pit La. DH5: Hett H 1D 148

Downswood NE12: Kil 2F **45**
Dowsey Rd. DH6: Sher 5D **156**
Dowson Sq. SR7: Mur 2A **150**
Doxford Av. DH5: Hett H 5B **138**
Doxford Cotts. DH5: Hett H 5B **138**
Doxford Dr. SR8: Pet 1A **164**
Doxford Gdns. NE5: Newc T 6H **55**
Doxford Intl. Bus. Pk.
  SR3: E Her 4E **131**
DOXFORD PARK 4A **132**
Doxford Pk. Way SR3: E Her . . .3F **131**
  SR3: New S 3G **131**
Doxford Pl. NE23: Cra 4B **22**
Doxford Ter. DH5: Hett H 5C **138**
Doxford Ter. Nth. SR7: Mur 2A **150**
Doxford Ter. Sth. SR7: Mur 2A **150**
Dragon La. DH1: Dur 4H **155**
Dragon Villa DH1: Dur 6H **155**
Dragonville Ind. Est.
  DH1: Dur 4H **155**
  (not continuous)
Dragonville Pk. DH1: Dur 5H **155**
Drake Cl. NE33: S Shi 1D **74**
Drayton Rd. NE3: Ken 3A **56**
  SR6: Monk 1D **104**
Drey, The NE20: Pon 2B **38**
Drivecote NE10: Gate 3E **85**
Drive, The DH3: Bir 5D **112**
  NE3: Gos 4E **57**
  NE5: Newc T 1D **66**
  NE7: Newc T 3B **58**
  NE9: Gate 4H **83**
  NE10: Gate 3E **85**
  NE16: Whi 5G **81**
  NE28: W'snd 5H **59**
  NE30: N Shi 5F **49**
  NE37: Usw 4A **100**
Dronfield Cl. DH2: Ches S 2A **134**
Drove Rd. NE15: Thro 3B **52**
Drumaldrace NE37: Wash 1G **113**
Drum Ind. Est. DH2: Ches S 2B **126**
Drummond Bldg. NE2: Newc T . . .1D **4**
Drummond Cres. NE34: S Shi 4B **74**
Drummond Rd. NE3: Ken 4B **56**
Drummond Ter. NE30: N Shi 6D **48**
Drumoyne Cl. SR3: E Her 3D **130**
Drumoyne Gdns. NE25: Whit B . . .2H **47**
Drum Rd. DH2: Ches S 1B **126**
  DH3: Ches S 1B **126**
Drumsheugh Pl. NE5: Newc T . . .5F **55**
Druridge Av. SR6: Monk 6E **91**
Druridge Cres. NE24: Bly 1H **17**
  NE34: S Shi 1B **76**
Druridge Dr. NE5: Newc T 6G **55**
  NE24: Bly 1H **17**
Drury La. DH1: Dur 6C **154** (3B **6**)
  NE1: Newc T 4F **69** (5D **4**)
  NE29: N Shi 6G **47**
  NE32: Jar 1G **73**
  SR1: Sund 6E **105**
Drybeck Ct. NE4: Newc T 4D **68**
  NE23: Cra 1D **22**
Drybeck Sq. SR3: New S 3B **132**
Drybeck Wlk. NE23: Cra 1D **22**
Dryborough St. SR4: Sund 6B **104**
Dryburgh NE38: Wash 2B **114**
Dryburgh Cl. NE29: N Shi 5A **48**
Dryburn Hill DH1: Dur 2A **154**
Dryburn Pk. DH1: Dur 2A **154**
Dryburn Rd. DH1: Dur 3A **154**
Dryburn Vw. DH1: Dur 2A **154**
Dryden Cl. DH9: Stly 3E **123**
  NE34: S Shi 1D **88**

Dryden Ct. NE9: Gate 3H **83**
Dryden Rd. NE9: Gate 3H **83**
Dryden St. SR5: S'wck 3A **104**
Drysdale Cl. NE13: Bru V 5C **30**
Drysdale Cres. NE13: Bru V 5C **30**
Dubmire Cotts. DH4: Hou S 3E **137**
Dubmire Ct. DH4: Hou S 3E **137**
Dubmire Ind. Est. DH4: Hou S . . .2F **137**
Duchess Cres. E. NE32: Jar 6F **73**
Duchess Cres. W. NE32: Jar 6F **73**
Duchess Dr. NE15: Newc T 2E **67**
Duchess St. NE26: Whit B 6C **36**
Duckpool La. NE16: Whi 4G **81**
Duckpool La. Nth. NE16: Whi 3G **81**
Duddon Cl. SR8: Pet 1E **165**
Duddon Pl. NE9: Gate 1B **98**
DUDLEY 3A **32**
Dudley Av. SR6: Monk 1D **104**
Dudley Bus. Cen. NE23: Dud 1H **31**
Dudley Ct. NE23: Cra 3A **22**
Dudley Dr. NE23: Dud 3A **32**
Dudley Gdns. SR3: E Her 2E **131**
Dudley Ho. *NE4: Newc T* 2C **60**
  (off Barrack Rd.)
Dudley La. NE13: Sea B 3E **31**
  NE23: Cra, Dud 1A **32**
  NE23: Dud, Sea B 3E **31**
Dudley La. Cotts.
  NE13: Sea B 3D **30**
Duffy Ter. DH9: Ann P 6G **121**
Dugdale Ct. NE3: Ken 2H **55**
Dugdale Rd. NE3: Ken 2H **55**
Duke of Northumberland Ct.
  NE28: W'snd 2C **60**
Duke's Av. NE31: Heb 5B **72**
Dukes Cotts. NE15: Thro 2F **65**
  NE27: Back 6A **34**
Dukes Dr. NE3: Gos 4D **42**
Dukesfield NE23: Cra 3B **22**
Duke's Gdns. NE24: Cow 5A **12**
Dukes Mdw. NE13: Wool 5C **40**
Duke St. DH9: Ann P 4E **121**
  NE1: Newc T 5E **69** (6A **4**)
  NE10: Gate 2G **85**
  NE26: Whit B 4C **36**
  NE29: N Shi 3D **62**
  SR4: Sund 1A **118**
  SR7: S'hm 3H **141**
Duke St. Nth. SR6: Monk 3D **104**
Dukes Wlk. NE26: Whit B 4C **36**
Dukesway NE11: Gate 6D **82**
Dukesway Ct. NE11: Gate 2E **97**
Dukesway W. NE11: Gate 3E **97**
Duke Wlk. NE8: Gate 2E **83**
Dulverston Cl. NE5: Cha P 4A **54**
Dulverton Av. NE33: S Shi 2F **75**
Dulverton Ct. NE2: Newc T 4H **57**
Dumas Wlk. NE5: Cha P 4A **54**
Dumfries Cres. NE32: Jar 6A **74**
Dunbar Cl. NE5: Cha P 4A **54**
Dunbar Gdns. NE28: W'snd 3E **61**
Dunbar St. SR4: Sund 2H **117**
Dunblane Cres. NE5: Newc T 1D **66**
Dunblane Dr. NE24: News 3C **18**
Dunblane Rd. SR6: Monk 6E **91**
Dunbreck Gro. SR4: Sund 3A **118**
Duncairn *DH9: Stly* 2D **122**
  (off View La.)
Duncan St. NE6: Walk 3G **71**
  NE8: Gate 2B **84**
  SR4: Sund 6H **103**
Duncombe Cres. DH9: Stly 1D **122**
Duncow La. DH1: Dur 6C **154** (4B **6**)

Dun Cow St.
  SR1: Sund 6C **104** (3F **7**)
Dundas St. SR6: Monk . . .5D **104** (1G **7**)
Dundas Way NE10: Gate 3C **84**
Dundee Cl. NE5: Cha P 4A **54**
Dundee Ct. NE32: Jar 6A **74**
Dundrennan NE38: Wash 4A **114**
Dunedin Cl. DH9: Ann P 4F **121**
Dunelm SR2: Sund 3A **118**
  (not continuous)
Dunelm Cl. DH3: Bir 3C **112**
Dunelm Ct. DH1: Dur 6C **154** (3A **6**)
  DH7: B'don 6C **158**
  NE31: Heb 4B **72**
Dunelm Dr. DH4: Hou S 3G **137**
  NE36: W Bol 4D **88**
Dunelm Rd. DH5: Hett H 1B **148**
Dunelm Sth. SR2: Sund 3B **118**
Dunelm St. NE33: S Shi 5F **63**
Dunelm Ter. SR7: Mur 1F **151**
Dunelm Wlk. NE37: Pet 6D **162**
Dunford Gdns. NE5: Cha P 3B **54**
Dunholm Cl. DH5: Hou S 4A **138**
Dunholme Cl. DH1: Dur 2B **154**
Dunholme Rd. NE4: Newc T 4B **68**
Dunira Cl. NE2: Newc T 5H **57**
Dunkeld Cl. DH4: Hou S 4D **128**
  NE10: Gate 3H **85**
  NE24: News 3C **18**
Dunkirk Av. DH5: Hou S 4B **138**
Dunlin Cl. NE40: Ryton 5E **65**
Dunlin Dr. NE24: News 3C **18**
  NE38: Wash 4F **113**
Dunlop Cl. NE7: Newc T 3C **58**
Dunlop Cres. NE34: S Shi 3A **76**
Dunmoor Cl. NE3: Gos 3C **56**
Dunmoor Ct. DH2: Ches S 2A **134**
Dunmore Av. SR6: Monk 6E **91**
Dunmorlie St. NE6: Newc T 3D **70**
Dunn Av. SR3: New S 6A **118**
Dunne Rd. NE21: Bla T 5C **66**
Dunning St. SR1: Sund . . .6C **104** (3F **7**)
Dunnlynn Cl. SR3: New S 3G **131**
Dunnock Dr. NE16: Sun 2E **95**
  NE38: Wash 5F **113**
Dunn's Ter. NE2: Newc T 1D **68**
Dunn St. DH9: Ann P 5F **121**
  NE4: Newc T 6D **68**
Dunns Yd. DH9: Ann P 4G **121**
Dunn Ter. NE6: Newc T 3B **70**
Dunnykirk Av. NE3: Ken 2H **55**
Dunraven Cl. DH4: Hou S 4G **129**
Dunsany Ter. DH2: Pelt 5G **125**
Dunscar DH4: Hou S 2F **137**
Dunsdale Dr. NE23: Cra 1D **22**
Dunsdale Rd. NE25: H'will 1C **34**
Dunsgreen NE20: Pon 6E **27**
Dunsgreen Ct. NE20: Pon 6E **27**
Dunsley Gdns. NE13: Din 4F **29**
Dunsmuir Gro. NE8: Gate 3F **83**
Dunstable Pl. NE5: Cha P 4H **53**
Dunstanburgh Cl. NE6: Newc T . . .4D **70**
  NE22: Bed 4F **9**
  NE38: Wash 3H **113**
Dunstanburgh Ct. DH4: Hou S . . .2B **136**
  NE10: Gate 4H **85**
Dunstanburgh Rd.
  NE6: Newc T, Walk 4D **70**
Dunstan Cl. DH2: Ches S 2A **134**
Dunstan Wlk. NE5: Newc T 6D **54**
DUNSTON 2C **82**
Dunston Activity Cen. 3C **82**
Dunston Bank NE11: Dun 4A **82**

Dunston Ent. Pk. NE11: Dun 1A **82**
DUNSTON HILL 4B **82**
Dunston Pl. NE24: Cow 6H **11**
Dunston Pool & Squash Club 4A **82**
Dunston Rd. NE11: Dun 1B **82**
        (not continuous)
Dunston Station (Rail) 3C **82**
Dunston Workshops NE11: Dun . . .1B **82**
        (off Colliery Rd.)
Dunvegan DH3: Bir 5E **113**
Dunvegan Av. DH2: Ches S 2B **134**
Durant Rd. NE1: Newc T . .3G **69** (3E **5**)
Durban St. NE24: Bly 5B **12**
DURHAM 6C **154** (4B **6**)
Durham Av. NE37: Usw 5H **99**
        SR8: Pet 5F **163**
Durham Castle 6C **154** (3B **6**)
Durham Cathedral 6C **154** (4B **6**)
Durham City Swimming Baths
        . . . . .6D **154** (3D **6**)
Durham Cl. NE22: Bed 3F **9**
Durham County Cricket Ground
        .1E **135**
Durham Ct. NE31: Heb 4B **72**
Durham Crematorium
        DH1: Dur 4B **160**
Durham Dr. NE32: Jar 2E **87**
Durham Gro. NE32: Jar 1E **87**
Durham Heritage Con. & Mus.
        . . . . .6C **154** (4C **6**)
Durham La.
        DH6: H Pitt, Shad, Sher 6H **157**
        SR8: Eas 2A **162**
        (not continuous)
Durham Light Infantry Mus.
        & Arts Cen. 4C **154**
Durham Moor DH1: Dur 2A **154**
Durham Moor Cres. DH1: Dur . . .2A **154**
Durham Pl. DH3: Bir 6C **112**
        DH4: Hou S 6H **129**
        (off Front St.)
        NE8: Gate 2H **83**
Durham Rd. DH1: Dur 2A **154**
        (Aykley Va.)
        DH1: Dur 4E **153**
        (Toll Ho. Rd.)
        DH2: Ches S 3C **134**
        DH3: Bir, Ches S 1C **112**
        DH3: Ches S 3C **134**
        DH4: E Her 6B **130**
        DH4: Hou S 3A **138**
        DH5: Hou S 1B **138**
        (Houghton Cut)
        DH5: Hou S 2H **137**
        (North Rd.)
        DH5: W Rai 2G **147**
        (not continuous)
        DH7: Ush M 4E **153**
        (Bearpark)
        DH7: Ush M 5B **152**
        (Ushaw Moor)
        DH9: Ann P 6G **121**
        DH9: Sfly 4E **123**
        NE8: Gate 2H **83**
        NE9: Gate, Spri 1H **97**
        NE23: Cra 6C **16**
        SR2: Sund 1B **118**
        (New Durham Rd.)
        SR2: Sund 3B **118**
        (Silksworth La.)
        SR3: E Her, Sund 3D **130**
Durham Rd. Trad. Est.
        DH3: Bir 1C **126**

Durham Station (Rail) . . .5C **154** (1A **6**)
Durham St. DH4: Hou S 3E **137**
        NE4: Newc T 5B **68**
        (not continuous)
        NE10: Gate 2F **85**
        NE28: W'snd 5A **60**
        SR7: S'hm 3H **141**
Durham St. W. NE28: W'snd 5A **60**
Durham Ter. DH1: Dur 1A **154**
        SR3: New S 6A **118**
Durham University Mus.
        of Archaeology 6C **154** (4A **6**)
Durham University
        Oriental Mus. 2B **160**
Durham Way SR8: Pet 3B **164**
Dutton Ct. NE21: Bla T 5D **66**
Duxbury Pk. NE38: Wash 1B **128**
Duxfield Rd. NE7: Newc T 4B **58**
Dwyer Cres. SR2: Ryh 3F **133**
Dyer Sq. SR5: S'wck 3B **104**
Dykefield Av. NE3: Ken 6A **42**
DYKE HEADS 1B **78**
Dyke Heads La.
        NE40: G'sde 1B **78**
Dykelands Rd. SR6: Monk 1D **104**
Dykelands Way NE34: S Shi 6B **74**
Dykenook Cl. NE16: Whi 1E **95**
Dykes Way NE10: Gate 6D **84**
Dymock Ct. NE3: Ken 2F **55**

E

Eaglescliffe Dr. NE7: Newc T 5D **58**
Eaglesdene DH5: Hett H 1C **148**
Ealing Ct. NE3: Ken 1F **55**
Ealing Dr. NE30: N Shi 4E **49**
Ealing Sq. NE23: Cra 3F **21**
Eardulph Av. DH3: Ches S 6D **126**
Earl Grey's Monument . . .4F **69** (4D **4**)
Earl Grey Way NE29: N Shi 4B **62**
Earlington Ct. NE12: Longb 4E **45**
Earls Cl. NE13: Wool 5D **40**
Earls Ct. NE11: Gate 6F **83**
        SR5: S'wck 1A **104**
Earls Court Health Club 4G **7**
        (off Dlandford St.)
Earls Dene NE9: Gate 1H **97**
Earls Dr. NE9: Gate 1H **97**
        NE15: Newc T 2E **67**
Earl's Gdns. NE24: Cow 5A **12**
Earls Grn. DH5: W Rai 2H **147**
Earls Pk. Nth. NE11: Gate 4E **83**
Earlston St. SR5: S'wck 1A **104**
Earlston Way NE23: Cra 5C **16**
Earl St. DH9: Ann P 4F **121**
        SR4: Sund 1B **118**
        SR7: S'hm 3G **141**
Earls Way NE1: Newc T 3D **4**
Earlsway NE11: Gate 4E **83**
Earlswood Av. NE9: Gate 1H **97**
Earlswood Gro. NE24: News 4B **18**
Earlswood Pk. NE9: Gate 1H **97**
Earnshaw Way NE25: Whit B 4H **35**
EARSDON 6E **35**
Earsdon Cl. NE5: Newc T 6E **55**
Earsdon Ct. NE25: Whit B 1H **47**
Earsdon Grange Rd.
        DH5: Hou S 2B **138**
Earsdon Rd. DH5: Hou S 3B **138**
        NE3: Ken 4A **56**
        NE25: Well, Whit B 6E **35**
        NE27: Back, Shir 3B **46**

Earsdon Ter. NE27: Shir 4C **46**
        SR2: Ryh 3F **133**
Earsdon Vw. NE27: Shir 1D **46**
Easby Cl. NE3: Gos 5F **43**
Easby Rd. NE38: Wash 3B **114**
Easedale NE26: Sea S 3G **25**
Easedale Av. NE3: Gos 4E **43**
Easedale Gdns. NE9: Gate 1A **98**
EASINGTON 2B **162**
Easington Av. NE9: Gate 2C **98**
        NE23: Cra 5C **16**
EASINGTON COLLIERY 1E **163**
EASINGTON LANE 4E **149**
Easington St.
        SR5: Monk 5C **104** (1F **7**)
        SR8: Eas 1D **162**
Easington St. Nth.
        SR5: Monk 5C **104** (1F **7**)
East Acres NE13: Din 3G **29**
        NE21: Bla T 1B **80**
E. Atherton St. DH1: Dur 6B **154**
East Av. DH2: Ches S 4A **134**
        NE12: Longb 1D **58**
        NE25: Whit B 6A **36**
        NE34: S Shi 3A **76**
        (not continuous)
        NE38: Wash 6H **113**
E. Back Pde. SR2: Sund 2F **119**
East Bailey NE12: Kil 1D **44**
FAST BOLDON 4G **89**
E. Boldon Rd. SR6: Cle 3B **89**
East Boldon Station (Metro) 4G **89**
Eastbourne Av. NE6: Walk 3G **71**
        NF8: Gate 3G **83**
Eastbourne Ct. NE6: Walk 3G **71**
Eastbourne Gdns. NE6: Walk 3G **71**
        NE23: Cra 3F **21**
        NE26: Whit B 5B **36**
Eastbourne Gro. NE33: S Shi 4F **63**
Eastbourne Pde. NE31: Heb 1E **87**
Eastbourne Sq. SR5: S'wck 1B **104**
E. Bridge St. DH4: Pen 6C **114**
Eastburn Gdns. NE10: Gate 1G **85**
Eastcheap NE6: Newc T 6C **58**
E. Cleft Rd. SR1: Sund 1B **118**
Eastcliffe Av. NE3: Ken 4C **56**
F. Cliff Rd. SR7: S'hm 6C **142**
East Cl. NE34: S Shi 3A **76**
Eastcombe Cl. NE35: Bol C 1A **88**
E. Coronation St. SR7: Mur 2D **150**
Eastcote Ter. NE6: Walk 5F **71**
EAST CRAMLINGTON 4D **22**
E. Cramlington Ind. Est.
        NE23: E Cram 5E **23**
East Cramlington Pond
        (Nature Reserve) 5G **23**
East Cres. NE22: Bed 3E **11**
E. Cross St.
        SR1: Sund 6D **104** (2H **7**)
Eastdene Rd. SR7: S'hm 4F **141**
Eastdene Way SR8: Pet 2F **165**
EAST DENTON 1E **67**
East Dr. NE24: News 3A **18**
        SR6: Cle 3H **89**
E. Ellen St. SR7: Mur 3D **150**
        (off W. Ellen St.)
East End Swimming Pool 3C **70**
Easten Gdns. NE10: Gate 2D **84**
Eastern Av. NE9: Gate 1F **97**
        NE11: Gate 1F **97**
Eastern Ter. NE28: W'snd 6G **61**
Eastern Way NE5: Newc T 5H **55**
        NE20: Pon 6D **26**

E. Farm Ct. NE16: Sun 2G 95
NE23: Cra 3B 22
E. Farm Ter. NE23: Cra 3B 22
Eastfield NE8: Pet 2F 165
Eastfield Av. NE6: Walk 1G 71
NE25: Whit B 1H 47
Eastfield Ho. NE6: Walk 1G 71
Eastfield Rd. NE12: Longb 1C 58
NE34: S Shi 1H 75
East Flds. SR6: Whit 3F 91
Eastfields DH9: Stly 4C 122
Eastfield St. SR4: Sund 2H 117
Eastfield Ter. NE12: Longb 1D 58
E. Forest Hall Rd.
NE12: Longb 5E 45
East Front NE2: Newc T 1G 69
Eastgarth NE5: Newc T 2E 55
Eastgate NE8: Gate 6H 69
NE62: Sco G 1H 9
Eastgate Gdns. NE4: Newc T 5B 68
EAST GATESHEAD 1A 84
E. George Potts St.
NE33: S Shi 6F 63
E. George St. NE30: N Shi 1E 63
East Grange NE25: H'wll 1D 34
SR5: S'wck 2C 104
E. Grange Ct. SR8: Eas 2B 162
East Gro. SR4: Sund 2D 116
EAST HARTFORD 4B 16
E. Hendon Rd. SR1: Sund 1F 119
EAST HERRINGTON 2D 130
E. Hill Rd. NE8: Gate 2B 84
E. Holburn NE33: S Shi 5D 62
EAST HOLYWELL 4B 34
EAST HOWDON 5G 61
E. Howdon By-Pass
NE28: W'snd 6G 61
NE29: N Shi 6G 61
EAST JARROW 3H 73
EAST KYO 3H 121
Eastlands DH5: Hett H 2B 148
NE7: Newc T 4A 58
NE21: Bla T 2H 79
NE38: Wash 2E 127
East Lea NE21: Bla T 3A 80
Eastlea Cres. SR7: S'hm 4G 141
Eastlea Rd. SR7: S'hm 4F 141
Eastleigh Cl. NE35: Bol C 3A 88
E. Moffett St. NE33: S Shi 6F 63
E. Moor Rd. SR4: Sund 6H 103
Eastmoor Rd. SR7: Mur 3E 151
E. Norfolk St. NE30: N Shi 2D 62
Easton Homes NE22: Bed 3C 10
East Pde. DH2: Plaw 2A 144
DH9: Stly 2E 123
NE26: Whit B 5D 36
E. Park Gdns. NE21: Bla T 2A 80
E. Park Rd. NE9: Gate 5G 83
E. Park Vw. NE23: Bly 6E 13
E. Percy St. NE30: N Shi 1E 63
EAST RAINTON 1G 147
East Riggs NE22: Bed 5H 9
E. Side Av. DH7: Ush M 4C 152
EAST SLEEKBURN 2F 11
East Sq. NE23: Cra 3A 22
E. Stainton St. NE33: S Shi 6F 63
EAST STANLEY 2E 123
E. Stanley By-Pass DH9: Stly 2F 123
E. Stevenson St. NE33: S Shi 6F 63
East St. DH2: Pelt 4C 124
DH9: Stly 2F 123
NE8: Gate 6H 69
NE30: N Shi 5G 49

East St. NE31: Heb 2D 72
(not continuous)
NE33: S Shi 4E 63
NE39: H Spen 1A 92
SR4: Sund 6G 103
SR6: Whit 3F 91
East Ter. TS27: Hes 6G 165
East Thorp NE5: Newc T 2D 54
East Vw. DH2: Plaw 3A 144
DH6: Sher 6H 157
DH7: B'don 6E 159
DH9: Dip 1D 120
DH9: Stly 6C 122
NE10: Gate 5F 85
NE13: Wide O 4D 30
NE16: Burn 1G 107
NE21: Bla T 6B 66
NE22: Bed 2D 10
NE23: Seg 2F 33
NE25: Sea D 4A 24
NE31: Heb 5B 72
NE35: Bol C 3B 88
NE36: W Bol 4C 88
NE39: Row G 3C 92
SR2: Ryh 3E 133
SR5: C'twn 4E 103
SR6: Monk 2E 105
SR7: Mur 3D 150
SR7: S'hm 2F 141
SR8: Pet 6G 163
E. View Av. NE23: Cra 3B 22
E. View Sth. SR5: C'twn 4E 103
E. View Ter. NE10: Gate 5F 85
NE16: Swa 3F 81
NE23: Dud 3A 32
East Vines SR1: Sund 6F 105
Eastward Grn. NE25: Whit B 1H 47
Eastway NE34: S Shi 4B 76
East-West Link Rd.
NE23: Cra 2B 22
Eastwood Av. NE24: News 4B 18
Eastwood Cl. NE23: Dud 6C 32
Eastwood Cl. NE12: Longb 6D 44
Eastwood Gdns. NE3: Ken 3B 56
NE9: Gate 5A 84
NE10: Gate 2C 84
Eastwood Pl. NE23: Cra 5C 16
Eaton Cl. NE38: Wash 1H 127
Eaton Pl. NE4: Newc T 4B 68
Eavers Ct. NE34: S Shi 4E 75
Ebba Wlk. NE3: Gos 2F 57
Ebchester Av. NE9: Gate 2D 98
Ebchester Ct. NE3: Ken 2G 55
Ebchester St. NE34: S Shi 4C 74
Ebdon La. SR6: Monk 1D 104
Ebor St. NE6: Newc T 1C 70
NE34: S Shi 5C 74
Eccles Ct. NE27: Back 6A 34
Eccles Ter. NE27: Shir 4C 46
Eccleston Cl. NE27: Back 1A 46
Eccleston Rd. NE33: S Shi 5G 63
Ecgfrid Ter. NE32: Jar 4G 73
Eco Cen., The NE31: Heb 1D 72
Eddison Rd. NE38: Wash 3D 114
Eddleston NE38: Wash 6G 113
Eddleston Av. NE3: Ken 4C 56
Eddrington Gro. NE5: Cha P 4A 54
Ede Av. NE11: Dun 3B 82
NE34: S Shi 3B 76
Eden Av. NE16: Burn 1G 107
Eden Cl. NE5: Cha P 5A 54
Eden Cotts. TS27: Hes 6G 165

Eden Ct. NE22: Bed 5A 10
NE28: W'snd 6H 59
Edencroft DH9: Stly 3C 124
Edendale Av. NE6: Walk 3G 71
NE12: Longb 6C 44
NE24: Cow 5H 11
Edendale Cl. NE24: Cow 5H 11
NE34: S Shi 5C 74
Edendale Ter. NE8: Gate 3H 83
SR8: Pet 1F 165
Edenfield DH9: Stly 2C 124
Edengarth NE30: N Shi 3B 48
Edenhill Rd. SR8: Pet 6E 163
Eden Ho. Rd. SR4: Sund 2B 118
Eden La. SR8: Pet 5D 162
Eden Pl. NE30: N Shi 4C 48
Eden Rd. DH1: Dur 1C 154
Eden St. NE28: W'snd 6H 59
SR8: Pet 6G 163
Eden St. W. SR1: Sund . . .6C 104 (3E 7)
Eden Ter. DH1: Dur 4A 156
DH4: Hou S 3F 129
DH9: Stly 4B 122
SR2: Sund 2B 118
Eden Va. SR2: Sund 2B 118
Edenvale Est. SR8: Pet 1F 165
Eden Vs. NE38: Wash 3C 114
Eden Wlk. NE32: Jar 6G 73
Edgar St. NE3: Newc T 2H 57
Edgecote NE37: Usw 5D 100
Edge Ct. DH1: Dur 5F 155
(not continuous)
Edgefield Av. NE3: Ken 2B 56
Edgefield Dr. NE23: Cra 5C 16
Edge Hill NE20: Pon 4B 38
Edgehill Cl. NE20: Pon 4C 38
Edgemount NE12: Kil 1E 45
Edgeware Ct. SR5: S'wck 2A 104
Edgeware Rd. NE8: Gate 3A 84
Edgeware Wlk. NE4: Newc T 6A 68
Edgewood NE20: Pon 3D 38
Edgewood Av. NE22: Bed 4C 10
Edgeworth Cl. NE35: Bol C 1A 88
Edgeworth Cres. SR6: Monk 3D 104
Edgmond Ct. SR2: Ryh 1E 133
Edhill Av. NE34: S Shi 4B 74
Edhill Gdns. NE34: S Shi 5B 74
Edinburgh Ct. NE3: Ken 5H 41
Edinburgh Dr. NE22: Bed 3F 9
Edinburgh Rd. NE32: Jar 5A 74
Edinburgh Sq. SR5: S'wck 2A 104
Edington Gro. NE30: N Shi 4C 48
Edington Rd. NE30: N Shi 4C 48
Edison Gdns. NE8: Gate 4G 83
Edison St. SR7: Mur 2C 150
Edith Av. NE21: Bla T 1A 80
Edith Moffatt Ho. NE29: N Shi 1C 62
(off Albion Rd.)
Edith St. NE30: N Shi 5E 49
NE32: Jar 2E 73
SR2: Sund 3E 119
SR7: S'hm 6C 142
Edith Ter. DH4: Hou S 5H 129
NE16: Whi 4E 81
(off Swalwell Bank)
Edlingham Cl. NE3: Gos 3H 57
Edlingham Ct. DH5: Hou S 3B 138
Edlingham Rd. DH1: Dur 2C 154
Edmonton Sq. SR5: S'wck 2A 104
Edmund Cl. DH7: Ush M 3C 152
Edmund Pl. NE9: Gate 6H 83
Edmund Rd. NE27: Longb 4B 46
Edna Ter. NE5: Newc T 4E 55

Edrich Ho. NE29: N Shi 4A 62
Edward Av. SR8: Pet 6F 163
Edward Burdis St.
   SR5: S'wck 3B 104
Edward Cain Ct. SR8: Pet 6G 163
Edward Ho. SR2: Sund 5E 7
Edward Pl. NE4: Newc T 4D 68
Edward Rd. DH3: Bir 2B 112
   NE22: Bed 3D 10
   NE28: W'snd 4D 60
Edwardson Rd. DH7: B'don 6F 159
Edwards Rd. NE26: Whit B 1E 49
Edward St. DH1: Dur 5F 155
   DH3: Ches S 6C 126
   DH5: Hett H 1C 148
   DH9: Stly 6G 123
   NE3: Gos 2E 57
   NE16: Burn 3G 107
   NE24: Bly 5B 12
   NE31: Heb 3A 72
   SR3: New S 2A 132
   SR7: S'hm 5B 142
Edward's Wlk.
   NE1: Newc T 3F 69 (2C 4)
Edward Ter. DH2: Pelt 3F 125
   DH7: New B 1B 158
   DH9: Ann P 5H 121
Edwina Gdns. NE29: N Shi 6A 48
Edwin Gro. NE28: W'snd 4E 61
Edwin's Av. NE12: Longb 5E 45
Edwin's Av. Sth. NE12: Longb 5E 45
Edwin St. DH5: Hou S 2A 138
   NE6: Newc T 3B 70
   NE13: Bru V 5C 30
   SR4: Sund 6G 103
Edwin Ter. NE40: G'sde 1C 78
Egerton Rd. NE34: S Shi 3E 75
Egerton St. NE4: Newc T 5H 67
   (not continuous)
   SR2: Sund 2E 119 (6H 7)
Eggleston Cl. DH1: Dur 1C 155
   DH3: Gt Lum 4H 135
Eggleston Dr. SR3: Sund 5A 118
Egham Rd. NE5: Cha P 5A 54
Eglesfield Rd. NE33: S Shi 1E 75
Eglingham Av. NE30: N Shi 4E 49
Eglinton St. SR5: S'wck 4C 104
Eglinton St. Nth. SR5: S'wck 4C 104
Eglinton Twr. SR5: S'wck 4D 104
Egremont Dr. NE9: Gate 5A 84
Egremont Gdns. NE9: Gate 5A 84
Egremont Gro. SR8: Pet 4A 164
Egremont Pl. NE26: Whit B 1D 48
Egremont Way NE23: Cra 5C 16
Egton Ter. DH3: Bir 2C 112
Eider Cl. NE24: News 4C 18
Eider Wlk. NE12: Kil 1C 44
Eighteenth Av. NE24: Bly 2A 18
   (not continuous)
Eighth Av. DH2: Ches S 6B 126
   NE6: Newc T 1C 70
   NE11: Gate 2E 97
   NE24: Bly 2B 18
Eighth St. SR8: Pet 6G 163
EIGHTON BANKS 3D 90
Eighton Ter. NE9: Gate 2E 99
Eishort Way NE12: Longb 1B 58
Eland Cl. NE3: Ken 2H 55
Eland Edge NE20: Pon 4F 27
Eland Grange NE20: Pon 4E 27
Eland La. NE20: Pon 5F 27
Eland Vw. NE20: Pon 5F 27
Elberfield Ct. NE32: Jar 3F 73

Elder Cl. DH7: Ush M 6D 152
Elder Gdns. NE9: Spri 4C 98
Elder Gro. NE9: Gate 6H 83
   NE34: S Shi 6H 75
Elders Wlk. SR6: Whit 3F 91
Elderwood Gdns. NE11: Gate 6D 82
Eldon Ct. NE1: Newc T 3F 69 (3C 4)
   NE28: W'snd 6F 61
   (off Eldon St.)
Eldon Gdns.
   NE1: Newc T 3F 69 (3C 4)
Eldon Ho. NE3: Gos 1E 57
Eldon La. NE1: Newc T 4F 69 (4D 4)
Eldon Leisure Cen. 4C 4
Eldon Pl. NE1: Newc T 2F 69 (1D 4)
   NE15: Lem 2B 66
   NE33: S Shi 2D 74
Eldon Rd. NE15: Lem 2B 66
Eldon Sq. NE1: Newc T 4F 69 (4C 4)
Eldon Sq. Bus Concourse
   NE1: Newc T 3C 4
   (off Percy St.)
Eldon Sq. Shop. Cen.
   NE1: Newc T 3F 69 (3C 4)
Eldon St. NE8: Gate 6A 70
   NE28: W'snd 5E 61
   NE33: S Shi 6D 62
   SR4: Sund 1A 118
Eldon Way NE1: Newc T 3F 69 (3D 4)
Eleanor St. NE30: N Shi 1E 49
   NE33: S Shi 4F 63
Eleanor Ter. NE16: Whi 4E 81
   (off Swalwell Bank)
   NE40: Ryton 5A 64
Electric Cres. DH4: Hou S 5G 129
Elemore La. DH5: Eas L 6C 148
   (not continuous)
   DH6: Eas L, H Pitt
   . . . . .6A 148 & 2G 157
Elemore St. DH6: H Pitt 2F 157
ELEMORE VALE 5D 148
Elemore Vw. DH6: S Het 6H 149
Elenbel Av. NE22: Bed 4C 10
Eleventh Av. DH2: Ches S 6D 126
   NE11: Gate 3F 97
   NE24: Bly 1C 18
Eleventh Av. Nth. NE11: Gate 2G 97
Eleventh St. NE8: Gate 8F 103
Elford Cl. NE25: Whit B 6H 35
Elfordleigh DH4: Hou S 5G 129
Elgar Av. NE5: Cha P 5A 54
Elgar Cl. DH9: Stly 4E 123
Elgen Vs. NE39: Row G 4D 92
Elgin Av. NE28: W'snd 3D 60
   SR7: S'hm 4F 141
Elgin Cl. NE22: Bed 3D 10
   NE23: Cra 3F 21
   NE29: N Shi 5G 47
Elgin Ct. NE10: Gate 1H 85
Elgin Gdns. NE6: Walk 3F 71
Elgin Gro. DH9: Stly 3F 123
Elgin Pl. DH3: Bir 5D 112
Elgin Rd. NE9: Gate 4B 84
Elgin St. NE32: Jar 5A 74
Elgy Rd. NE3: Coo 4D 56
Elisabeth Av. DH3: Bir 1B 112
Elite Bldgs. DH9: Stly 2D 122
Elizabeth Ct. DH6: H Pitt 2G 157
   NE12: Longb 5G 45
Elizabeth Cres. NE23: Dud 3A 32
Elizabeth Diamond Gdns.
   NE33: S Shi 1D 74
Elizabeth Dr. NE12: Longb 5G 45

Elizabeth Rd. NE28: W'snd 4E 61
Elizabeth St. DH5: Hou S 2A 138
   DH9: Ann P 5G 121
   NE6: Newc T 3A 70
   NE23: E Cram 4F 23
   NE33: S Shi 5F 63
   SR5: C'twn 4D 102
   SR5: Monk 2C 104
   SR7: S'hm 4A 142
Elizabeth Woodcock Maritime
   Almshouses, The
   SR2: Sund 2D 118
   (off Gorse Rd.)
Ella McCambridge Ho.
   NE6: Walk 4G 71
Ellam Av. DH1: Dur 1A 160
Ell-Dene Cres. NE10: Gate 4E 85
Ellen Ct. NE32: Jar 2F 73
Ellen Ter. NE37: Usw 5D 100
Ellerbeck Cl. NE10: Gate 3C 84
Ellerby Ho. NE6: Walk 6E 71
   (off McCutcheon Ct.)
Ellersmere Gdns. NE30: N Shi . . .3D 48
Ellerton Way NE10: Gate 3C 84
   NE23: Cra 5C 16
Ellesmere DH4: Hou S 6B 128
   (not continuous)
Ellesmere Av. NE3: Gos 3G 57
   NE5: Newc T 5E 55
   NE6: Walk 2F 71
Ellesmere Ct. SR2: Sund 6E 119
Ellesmere Dr. SR7: S'hm 4F 141
Ellesmere Rd. NE4: Newc T 4A 68
Ellesmere Ter. SR6: Monk 2E 105
Ellie Bldgs. DH9: Stly 2C 122
   (off Royal Rd.)
Ellington Cl. DH2: Ous 5G 111
   NE15: Lem 2H 65
   SR2: Ryh 4F 133
Elliot Rd. NE10: Gate 1B 84
   (not continuous)
Elliott Cl. DH4: Pen 2F 129
Elliott Dr. NE10: Gate 3D 84
Elliott Gdns. NE28: W'snd 3G 59
   NE34: S Shi 1F 89
Elliott Rd. SR8: Pet 6D 162
Elliott St. NE24: Bly 3H 17
Elliott Ter. NE4: Newc T 1B 68
   NE37: Usw 5C 100
Elliott Wlk. NE13: Bru V 1B 42
Ellis Leazes DH1: Dur 5E 155
Ellison Bldg.
   NE1: Newc T 3G 69 (3E 5)
Ellison Pl. NE1: Newc T . . .3G 69 (3E 5)
   NE9: Gate 1H 97
   NE32: Jar 1F 73
Ellison Rd. NE11: Dun 3B 82
   SR8: Pet 6E 163
Ellison St. NE8: Gate 6G 69
   NE31: Heb 2A 72
   (not continuous)
   NE32: Jar 1F 73
   (not continuous)
Ellison Ter. NE1: Newc T . . .3G 69 (3E 5)
Ellison Vs. NE8: Gate 2A 84
Ellis Rd. SR5: S'wck 2A 104
Ellis Sq. SR5: S'wck 2B 104
Ellwood Gdns. NE9: Gate 3H 83
Ellwoods Gym
   Peterlee 1H 165
   (off Windsor Cnr.)
   Sunderland 1E 119
   (off Murton St.)

Elm Av. DH2: Pelt 3E 125
  DH7: B'don 6D 158
  NE11: Dun 3B 82
  NE13: Din 4F 29
  NE16: Whi 3G 81
  NE34: S Shi 5H 75
Elm Cl. NE23: Cra 5C 16
Elm Ct. NE16: Whi 6F 81
Elms Cres. DH2: Plaw 2A 144
Elm Cft. Rd. NE12: Longb 6E 45
Elm Dr. NE22: Bed 5H 9
  SR6: Whit 2G 91
Elmfield DH5: Hett H 5C 138
Elmfield Av. DH1: Dur 4H 155
Elmfield Cl. SR3: E Her 3E 131
Elmfield Gdns. NE3: Gos 3D 56
  NE25: Whit B 2H 47
  NE28: W'snd 4F 59
Elmfield Gro. NE3: Gos 3D 56
Elmfield Pk. NE3: Gos 4D 56
Elmfield Rd. NE3: Gos 4D 56
  NE15: Thro 5E 53
  NE31: Heb 6D 72
Elmfield Ter. NE10: Gate 2G 85
  NE31: Heb 5D 72
Elm Gro. DH4: Hou S 4G 129
  DH7: Ush M 6D 152
  NE3: Ken 6B 42
  NE12: Kil 4D 44
  NE16: Burn 1F 107
  NE34: S Shi 5H 75
Elm Pl. DH4: Hou S 6H 129
Elm Rd. NE20: Pon 6G 27
  NE21: Bla T 1B 80
  NE29: N Shi 6F 47
Elmsford Gro. NE12: Longb 1B 58
Elmsleigh Gdns. SR6: Cle 1A 90
Elms, The DH5: Eas L 5F 149
  NE3: Gos 4D 56
  SR2: Sund 2D 118
  SR4: Sund 1C 116
Elm St. DH3: Ches S 6C 126
  DH9: Stly 5B 122
  NE13: Sea B 3E 31
  NE16: Sun 3F 95
  NE32: Jar 2E 73
Elm St. W. NE16: Sun 3F 95
Elms W. SR2: Sund 2D 118
Elm Ter. DH3: Bir 2B 112
  DH9: Ann P 5E 121
  DH9: Stly 6F 123
  DH9: Tan L 5H 107
  NE28: W'snd 5A 60
  SR8: Pet 1G 165
Elm Tree Ct. SR7: S'hm 6A 142
Elm Tree Dr. NE40: G'sde 2B 78
Elmtree Gdns. NE25: Whit B 2A 48
  SR8: Pet 1F 165
Elmtree Gro. NE3: Gos 4D 56
Elm Trees NE24: Bly 1B 18
Elm Vs. NE13: Bru V 6C 30
Elmway DH2: Ches S 4A 126
Elmwood NE15: Lem 1A 66
Elmwood Av. NE13: Wide O 6E 31
  NE28: W'snd 5D 60
    (not continuous)
  SR5: S'wck 2H 103
Elmwood Cres. NE6: Walk 6F 59
Elmwood Dr. NE20: Pon 4E 27
Elmwood Gdns. NE11: Gate 5D 82
Elmwood Gro. NE26: Whit B 5C 36
Elmwood Ho. NE7: Newc T 3A 58

Elmwood Rd. NE25: Whit B 1A 48
Elmwood Sq. SR5: S'wck 3H 103
Elmwood St. DH4: Hou S 2C 136
  SR2: Sund 2B 118
Elrick Cl. NE5: Cha P 5A 54
Elrington Gdns. NE5: Newc T 1F 67
Elsdon Av. NE25: Sea D 6A 24
Elsdonburn Rd. SR3: New S 4G 131
Elsdon Cl. NE24: Bly 6A 12
  SR8: Pet 4C 164
Elsdon Ct. NE16: Whi 6E 81
Elsdon Dr. NE12: Longb 5F 45
Elsdon Gdns. NE11: Dun 3C 82
Elsdon M. NE31: Heb 2D 72
Elsdon Pl. NE29: N Shi 3C 62
Elsdon Rd. DH1: Dur 1D 154
  NE3: Gos 2E 57
  NE16: Whi 5E 81
Elsdon St. NE29: N Shi 3C 62
Elsdon Ter. NE28: W'snd 6H 59
  NE29: N Shi 3H 61
Elsham Grn. NE3: Ken 1A 56
Elsing Cl. NE5: Newc T 3F 55
Elstob Cotts. SR3: Sund 5A 118
Elstob Pl. NE6: Walk 5E 71
  SR3: Sund 5A 118
Elston Cl. NE5: Cha P 5A 54
Elstree Ct. NE3: Ken 6F 41
Elstree Gdns. NE24: News 4B 18
Elstree Sq. SR5: S'wck 1A 104
ELSWICK 5C 68
Elswick Ct. NE1: Newc T . . .3F 69 (3D 4)
Elswick Dene NE4: Newc T 6C 68
Elswick E. Ter.
  NE4: Newc T 5D 68 (6A 4)
Elswick Rd. NE4: Newc T 5A 68
  NE37: Wash 6G 99
Elswick Row NE4: Newc T 4D 68
Elswick St. NE4: Newc T 4D 68
Elswick Swimming Pool 5C 68
Elswick Way NE34: S Shi 3C 74
Elswick Way Ind. Est.
  NE34: S Shi 3C 74
Elsworth Grn. NE5: Newc T 4G 55
Elterwater Rd. DH2: Ches S 2B 134
Eltham St. NE33: S Shi 1D 74
Elton St. E. NE28: W'snd 6H 59
Elton St. W. NE28: W'snd 6H 59
Eltringham Cl. NE28: W'snd 5G 59
Elvaston Rd. NE40: Ryton 3C 64
Elvet Bri. DH1: Dur 6D 154 (3B 6)
Elvet Cl. NE6: Newc T 2C 70
  NE13: Wide O 5D 30
Elvet Ct. NE6: Newc T 2C 70
Elvet Cres. DH1: Dur 6D 154 (4C 6)
  DH2: Ches S 1C 134
  DH5: Hett H 4C 148
Elvet Hill Rd. DH1: Dur 2C 160
Elvet Moor DH1: Dur 2A 160
Elvet Waterside
  DH1: Dur 6D 154 (3C 6)
Elvet Way NE6: Newc T 2C 70
Elvington St. SR6: Monk 2E 105
Elwin Cl. NE26: Sea S 4H 25
Elwin Pl. DH2: Pelt 3G 125
  NE26: Sea S 4H 25
Elwin St. DH2: Pelt 2G 125
Elwin Ter. SR2: Sund . . .2C 118 (5E 7)
Ely Cl. NE7: Newc T 3D 58
Ely Rd. DH1: Dur 5D 144
Elysium La. NE8: Gate 2E 83
Ely St. NE8: Gate 2G 83
Ely Ter. DH9: Ann P 4A 122

Ely Way NE32: Jar 2F 87
Embankment Rd. SR7: S'hm 5B 142
    (Cottages Rd.)
  SR7: S'hm 3H 141
    (Stanley St.)
Embassy Gdns. NE15: Newc T . . .3F 67
Emblehope NE37: Wash 1G 113
Emblehope Dr. NE3: Gos 3C 56
Emblehope Ho. SR3: E Her 1F 131
Embleton Av. NE3: Gos 1C 56
  NE28: W'snd 2C 60
  NE34: S Shi 1B 76
Embleton Cl. DH1: Dur 6D 144
Embleton Cres. NE29: N Shi 5G 47
Embleton Dr. DH2: Ches S 2A 134
  NE24: Bly 2A 18
Embleton Gdns. NE5: Newc T 6H 55
  NE10: Gate 2D 84
Embleton Rd. NE10: Gate 1H 85
  NE29: N Shi 5G 47
Embleton St. SR7: S'hm 6B 142
Embleton Wlk. NE8: Gate 1F 83
    (off St Cuthbert's La.)
Emden Rd. NE3: Ken 1B 56
EMERSON 5F 113
Emerson Ct. NE27: Shir 2C 46
  SR8: Pet 6G 163
Emerson Pl. NE27: Shir 2C 46
Emerson Rd. NE38: Wash 3F 113
Emily St. DH4: Hou S 5H 129
  NE6: Walk 3E 71
  NE8: Gate 2B 84
Emily St. E. SR7: S'hm 4B 142
    (not continuous)
Emlyn Rd. NE34: S Shi 3E 75
Emma Ct. SR2: Sund 2E 119
Emmaville NE40: Ryton 5A 64
Emmbrook Cl. DH5: W Rai 1H 147
Emmerson Ter. NE38: Wash 2C 114
Emmerson Ter. W.
  SR3: New S 2B 132
Emperor Way SR3: E Her 4D 130
Empire Bldgs. DH1: Dur 5G 155
Empire Theatre
  Sunderland 6C 104 (3F 7)
Empress Rd. NE6: Walk 5H 71
Empress St. SR5: S'wck 4C 104
Emsworth Rd. SR5: S'wck 2A 104
Emsworth Sq. SR5: S'wck 2A 104
Enderby Rd. SR4: Sund 6B 104
Enfield Av. NE16: Swa 2F 81
Enfield Gdns. NE16: Whi 6F 81
Enfield Rd. NE8: Gate 3H 83
  SR7: S'hm 4F 141
Enfield St. SR4: Sund 6H 103
Engels Ter. DH9: Stly 4E 123
Engel St. NE39: Row G 3B 92
Engine Inn Rd. NE28: W'snd 3D 60
Engine La. NE9: Gate 1H 97
Englefield NE10: Gate 1F 99
Englefield Cl. NE3: Ken 6H 41
Englemann Way SR3: New S 4G 131
Enid Av. SR6: Monk 2D 104
Enid St. NE13: Bru V 1C 42
Ennerdale DH3: Bir 5E 113
  NE10: Gate 3G 85
  NE37: Wash 6A 100
  SR2: Sund 3C 118
Ennerdale Cl. DH1: Carr 3C 156
  SR7: S'hm 4F 141
  SR8: Pet 6D 162
Ennerdale Cres. DH4: Pen 1E 129
  NE21: Bla T 3H 79

Ennerdale Gdns. NE9: Gate 6A **84**
  NE28: W'snd 3E **61**
Ennerdale Pl. DH2: Ches S 2C **134**
Ennerdale Rd. NE6: Walk 3F **71**
  NE24: Cow 4F **11**
  NE30: N Shi 3C **48**
Ennerdale St. DH5: Hett H 3B **148**
Ennerdale Wlk. NE16: Whi 1D **94**
Ennismore Ct. NE12: Longb 1D **58**
Ensign Ho. NE30: N Shi 6F **49**
Enslin Gdns. NE6: Walk 6F **71**
Enslin St. NE6: Walk 6F **71**
Enterprise Ct. NE23: Nel V 6H **15**
  SR7: Sea 1E **141**
Enterprise Ho. NE11: Gate 1F **97**
Eothen Rest Ho. NE26: Whit B 1C **48**
Epinay Wlk. NE32: Jar 3G **73**
Epping Cl. SR7: S'hm 5F **141**
Epping Ct. NE23: Cra 3F **21**
Epping Sq. SR5: S'wck 2A **104**
EPPLETON 6C **138**
Eppleton Est. DH5: Hett H 6D **138**
Eppleton Hall Cl. SR7: S'hm 3E **141**
Eppleton Row DH5: Hett H 1D **148**
Eppleton Ter. DH2: Beam 2D **124**
Eppleton Ter. E. DH5: Hett H 1D **148**
Eppleton Ter. W. DH5: Hett H 1D **148**
Epsom Cl. NE29: N Shi 3B **62**
Epsom Ct. NE3: Ken 6G **41**
Epsom Sq. SR5: S'wck 2A **104**
Epsom Way NE24: News 4B **18**
Epwell Gro. NE23: Cra 5C **16**
Epworth DH9: Tan L 1A **122**
Epworth Gro. NE8: Gate 2F **83**
Equitable St. NE28: W'snd 3E **61**
Erick St. NE1: Newc T 4G **69** (4E **5**)
  (not continuous)
Erin Sq. SR5: S'wck 2D **104**
Erith Ter. SR4: Sund 1H **117**
Ermine Cres. NE9: Gate 5B **84**
Ernest Pl. DH1: Dur 5G **155**
Ernest St. DH2: Pelt 2G **125**
  NE35: Bol C 3C **88**
  SR2: Sund 3F **119**
Ernest Ter. DH9: Choo S 1C **134**
  DH9: Stly 1D **122**
  SR2: Ryh 3G **133**
Ernwill Av. SR5: C'twn 4D **102**
Errington Cl. NE20: Pon 3C **38**
Errington Dr. DH9: Tan L 1A **122**
Errington Rd. NE20: Pon 3B **38**
Errington St. NE24: Cow 6E **11**
Errington Ter. NE12: Longb 4E **45**
Errol Pl. DH3: Bir 5D **112**
Erskine Ct. NE2: Newc T 5H **57**
Erskine Rd. NE33: S Shi 5F **63**
Erskine Way NE33: S Shi 5F **63**
Escallond Dr. SR7: Mur 5F **141**
Escombe Ter. NE6: Newc T 4C **70**
  (off St Peter's Rd.)
Esdale SR2: Ryh 3E **133**
Esher Ct. NE3: Ken 6G **41**
Esher Gdns. NE24: News 4B **18**
Esher Pl. NE23: Cra 3F **21**
Eshmere Cres. NE5: Cha P 4A **54**
Eshott Cl. NE3: Ken 1C **56**
  NE5: Newc T 6E **55**
Eshott Cl. NE5: Newc T 6E **55**
Esh Wood Vw. DH7: Ush M 5B **152**
Esk Av. DH3: Gt Lum 4H **135**
Esk Ct. SR3: New S 3H **131**
Eskdale DH3: Bir 6E **113**
  DH4: Pen 1E **129**

Eskdale Av. NE24: Cow 5G **11**
  NE28: W'snd 2A **60**
Eskdale Cl. DH1: Carr 3C **156**
  SR7: S'hm 4F **141**
Eskdale Ct. NE34: S Shi 3E **75**
Eskdale Cres. NE37: Usw 5H **99**
Eskdale Dr. NE32: Jar 6H **73**
Eskdale Gdns. NE9: Gate 1A **98**
Eskdale Mans. NE2: Newc T 1G **69**
  (off Eskdale Ter.)
Eskdale Rd. SR6: Monk 5F **91**
Eskdale St. DH5: Hett H 3B **148**
  NE34: S Shi 4E **75**
Eskdale Ter. NE2: Newc T 1G **69**
  NE26: Whit B 1E **49**
  NE30: Whit B 1E **49**
Eskdale Wlk. SR8: Pet 1E **165**
Esk St. NE9: Gate 4B **84**
Esk Ter. DH3: Bir 2C **112**
Eslington Ct. NE0: Gate 3D **82**
Eslington Rd. NE2: Newc T 2G **69**
Eslington Ter. NE2: Newc T 1G **69**
Esmeralda Gdns. NE23: Seg 2G **33**
Esplanade NE26: Whit B 6D **36**
Esplanade Av. NE26: Whit B 6D **36**
Esplanade M.
  SR2: Sund 2D **118** (6G **7**)
Esplanade Pl. NE26: Whit B 6D **36**
Esplanade, The SR2: Sund 6G **7**
Esplanade W. SR2: Sund 2D **110**
Espley Cl. NE12: Longb 5G **45**
Espley Ct. NE3: Ken 6A **42**
Esporta
  Silksworth 4F **131**
Essen Way SR3: Sund 4B **118**
Essex Cl. NE4: Newc T 6D **68**
Essex Cres. SR7: S'hm 4F **141**
Essex Dr. NE37: Usw 3B **100**
Essex Gdns. NE9: Gate 4H **83**
  NE28: W'snd 4C **60**
  NE34: S Shi 2C **76**
Essex Gro. SR3: New S 1A **132**
Essex Pl. SR8: Pet 5C **162**
Essex St. DH5: Hett H 1B **148**
Essington Way SR8: Pet 4C **162**
Estate Ho's. DH4: Hou S 5C **128**
Esther Campbell Ct.
  NE2: Newc T 2E **69** (1A **4**)
Esther Sq. NE38: Wash 3C **114**
Esthwaite Av. DH2: Ches S 2B **134**
Eston Ct. NE24: Cow 5H **11**
  NE28: W'snd 2F **59**
Eston Gro. SR5: S'wck 2C **104**
Estuary Way SR4: Sund 6D **102**
Etal Av. NE25: Whit B 1D **48**
  NE29: N Shi 3H **61**
Etal Cl. NE27: Shir 2D **46**
Etal Ct. NE29: N Shi 1C **62**
Etal Cres. NE27: Shir 2D **46**
  NE32: Jar 5A **74**
Etal La. NE5: Newc T 4E **55**
Etal Pl. NE3: Ken 6C **42**
Etal Rd. NE24: News 4H **17**
Etal Way NE5: Newc T 3F **55**
Ethel Av. NE21: Bla T 1A **80**
  SR2: Ryh 3G **133**
Ethel St. NE4: Newc T 5H **67**
  NE23: Dud 5A **32**
Ethel Ter. NE34: S Shi 4D **74**
  NE39: H Spen 2A **92**
  SR5: C'twn 4D **102**
Etherley Cl. DH1: Dur 6D **144**
Etherley Rd. NE6: Walk 2D **70**

Etherstone Av. NE7: Newc T 5C **58**
Eton Cl. NE23: Cra 5C **16**
Eton Sq. NE31: Heb 3D **72**
Ettrick Cl. NE12: Kil 1C **44**
Ettrick Gdns. NE8: Gate 3B **84**
  SR4: Sund 3H **117**
Ettrick Gro. SR3: Sund 2G **117**
  SR4: Sund 2G **117**
Ettrick Lodge NE3: Gos 3F **57**
Ettrick Rd. NE32: Jar 4E **73**
Ettrick Ter. Nth. DH9: Stly 6F **123**
Ettrick Ter. Sth. DH9: Stly 6F **123**
European Way SR4: Sund 6F **103**
Euryalus Ct. NE33: S Shi 6H **63**
Eustace Av. NE29: N Shi 2A **62**
Euston Ct. SR5: S'wck 1A **104**
Evanlade NE10: Gate 5H **85**
Eva St. NE15: Lem 3A **66**
Evelyn St. SR2: Sund 2B **118**
Evelyn Ter. DH9: Stly 3C **122**
  NE21: Bla T 6A **66**
  SR2: Ryh 3F **133**
Evenwood Gdns. NE9: Gate 6B **84**
Everard St. NE23: E Har 4B **16**
Everest Gro. NE36: W Dol 1D **88**
Everest Sq. SR5: S'wck 1A **104**
Ever Ready Ind. Est.
  DH9: Tan L 5C **108**
Eversleigh Pl. NE15: Thro 5E **53**
Eversley Cres. SR5: S'wck 2A **104**
  (not continuous)
Eversley Pl. NE6: Newc T 2B **70**
  NE28: W'snd 4D **60**
Everton Dr. SR7: S'hm 4F **141**
Everton La. SR5: S'wck 2A **104**
Evesham SR4: Sund 1C **116**
Evesham Av. NE26: Whit B 5B **36**
Evesham Cl. NE35: Bol C 2B **88**
Evesham Gth. NE3: Ken 4A **56**
Evesham Pl. NE23: Cra 2F **21**
Evesham Rd. SR7: S'hm 4F **141**
Eve St. SR8: Pet 1H **165**
Evistones Gdns. NE6: Walk 6E **71**
Evistones Rd. NE9: Gate 5H **83**
Ewart Ct. NE3: Ken 6C **42**
Ewart Cres. NE34: S Shi 5A **74**
Ewbank Av. NE4: Newc T 2A **68**
Ewe Hill Cotts. DH4: Hou S 2D **136**
Ewe Hill Ter. DH4: Hou S 2D **136**
Ewe Hill Ter. W. DH4: Hou S 2D **136**
Ewehurst Cres. DH9: Dip 6E **107**
Ewehurst Gdns. DH9: Dip 6E **107**
Ewehurst Pde. DH9: Dip 6E **107**
Ewehurst Rd. DH9: Dip 6E **107**
  (not continuous)
Ewen Ct. NE29: N Shi 5F **47**
Ewesley NE38: Wash 1G **127**
Ewesley Cl. NE5: Newc T 6E **55**
Ewesley Gdns. NE13: Wide O 5D **30**
Ewesley Rd. SR4: Sund 2H **117**
Ewing Pl. SR4: Sund 2A **118**
Ewing Rd. SR4: Sund 2A **118**
Exchange Bldgs. NE1: Newc T 6F **5**
  (off King St.)
  NE26: Whit B 6D **36**
Exelby Cl. NE3: Gos 5F **43**
Exeter Av. SR7: S'hm 4H **141**
  (not continuous)
Exeter Cl. DH3: Gt Lum 5G **135**
  NE23: Cra 2G **21**
Exeter Ct. NE31: Heb 4B **72**
Exeter Rd. NE28: W'snd 2G **59**
  NE29: N Shi 4G **47**

Exeter St. NE6: Walk 5G 71
NE8: Gate 2G 83
SR4: Sund 6H 103
Exeter Way NE32: Jar 1F 87
Exhibition Pk. 1F 69
Exmouth Cl. SR7: S'hm 5G 141
Exmouth Rd. NE29: N Shi 2G 61
Exmouth Sq. SR5: S'wck 2A 104
Exmouth St. SR5: S'wck 2A 104
Extension Rd. SR1: Sund 1F 119
Eyemouth NE34: S Shi 4C 74
Eyemouth La. SR5: S'wck 2A 104
Eyemouth Rd. NE29: N Shi 2G 61
Eyre St. DH9: Stly 4B 122

F

Faber Rd. SR5: S'wck 2A 104
Factory Rd. NE21: Bla T 5B 66
Factory, The TS27: Cas E 6B 164
Fairbairn Rd. SR8: Pet 5D 162
Fairburn Av. DH5: Hou S 5A 138
NE7: Newc T 3C 58
Fairclough Ct. SR8: Pet 2B 164
Fairdale Av. NE7: Newc T 3C 58
Fairfalls Ter. DH7: New B 1A 158
Fairfield DH2: Pelt 2F 125
DH9: Ann P 4F 121
NE12: Longb 1H 57
Fairfield Av. NE12: Longb 5D 44
NE16: Whi 6E 81
NE24: News 3B 18
Fairfield Cl. NE11: Dun 2B 82
Fairfield Dr. NE25: Whit B 1G 47
NE30: N Shi 3D 48
SR6: Whit 1F 91
Fairfield Grn. NE25: Whit B 1G 47
Fairfield Ind. Est. NE10: Gate 1G 85
Fairfield Rd. NE2: Newc T 6F 57
Fairfields NE40: Ryton 5B 64
Fairfield Ter. NE10: Gate 2G 85
Fair Grn. NE25: Whit B 1G 47
Fairgreen Cl. SR3: New S 4H 131
Fairhaven NE9: Spri 3F 99
Fairhaven Av. NE6: Walk 3G 71
Fairhill Cl. NE7: Newc T 3C 58
Fairhills Av. DH9: Dip 2C 120
Fairholme Av. NE34: S Shi 3H 75
Fairholme Rd. SR3: Sund 4C 118
Fairholm Rd. NE4: Newc T 4A 68
Fairisle DH2: Ous 6A 112
Fairlands E. SR6: Monk 3D 104
Fairlands W. SR6: Monk 3D 104
Fairlawn Gdns. SR4: Sund 3G 117
Fairles St. NE33: S Shi 3F 63
Fairmead Way SR4: Sund 2C 116
Fairmile Dr. SR3: New S 4A 132
Fairmont Way NE7: Newc T 3C 58
Fairney Cl. NE20: Pon 5F 27
Fairney Edge NE20: Pon 5F 27
Fairnley Wlk. NE5: Newc T 5E 55
Fairport Ter. SR8: Eas 2F 163
Fairspring NE5: Newc T 5E 55
Fair Vw. DH4: W Rai 3D 146
NE16: Burn 1E 107
Fairview Av. NE34: S Shi 2H 75
Fairview Grn. NE7: Newc T 3C 58
Fairview Pk. DH5: Hett H 2D 148
Fairview Ter. DH9: Ann P 6E 121
Fairville Cl. NE23: Cra 5B 16
Fairville Cres. NE7: Newc T 3C 58
Fairway NE21: Bla T 5G 65

Fairway Cl. NE3: Gos 5D 42
Fairways NE25: Whit B 6G 35
SR3: New S 2B 132
Fairways Av. NE7: Newc T 2C 58
Fairways, The DH9: Stly 3C 124
(Green's Bank)
DH9: Stly 6C 122
(New Acres Rd.)
Fairway, The NE3: Gos 5D 42
NE37: Usw 2A 100
Fairy St. DH5: Hett H 1C 148
Falconars Ct.
NE1: Newc T 4F 69 (5C 4)
Falconar St.
NE1: Newc T 3G 69 (3F 5)
NE2: Newc T 3G 69 (3F 5)
Falcon Pl. NE12: Longb 6A 44
Falcon Way NE34: S Shi 5D 74
Faldonside NE6: Newc T 5D 58
Falkirk NE12: Kil 1D 44
Falkland Av. NE3: Ken 4B 56
NE31: Heb 3C 72
Falkland Rd. SR4: Sund 1G 117
Falla Pk. Cres. NE10: Gate 3C 84
Falla Pk. Rd. NE10: Gate 3C 84
Falloden Av. NE3: Ken 5B 42
Fallodon Gdns. NE5: Newc T 5H 55
Fallodon Rd. NE29: N Shi 2H 61
Fallowfield NE10: Gate 5G 85
Fallowfield Av. NE3: Ken 1B 56
Fallowfield Ter. DH6: S Het 6A 150
Fallowfield Way NE38: Wash . . .5C 114
Fallow Pk. Av. NE24: Bly 1A 18
Fallow Rd. NE34: S Shi 3D 76
Fallsway DH1: Carr 2B 156
Falmouth Cl. SR7: Mur 5G 141
Falmouth Dr. NE32: Jar 4H 73
Falmouth Rd. NE6: Newc T 2B 70
NE29: N Shi 4H 47
SR4: Sund 6G 103
Falmouth Sq. SR4: Sund 1G 117
Falmouth Wlk. NE23: Cra 1A 22
Falsgrave Pl. NE16: Whi 6D 80
Falstaff Rd. NE29: N Shi 1H 61
Falston Cl. NE12: Longb 5G 45
Falstone NE10: Gate 6F 85
NE38: Wash 5C 114
Falstone Av. NE15: Lem 1C 66
NE34: S Shi 3A 76
Falstone Dr. DH2: Ches S 2A 134
Falstone Sq. NE3: Ken 1C 56
Falston Rd. NE24: Bly 2A 18
Faraday Cl. NE38: Wash 2F 115
Faraday Gro. NE8: Gate 4F 83
SR4: Sund 1G 117
Faraday Rd. SR8: Pet 4E 163
Faraday St. SR7: Mur 2C 150
Farding Lake Ct. NE34: S Shi . . .3C 76
Farding Sq. NE34: S Shi 3D 76
Fareham Gro. NE35: Bol C 3H 87
Fareham Way NE23: Cra 2B 22
FAREWELL HALL 4B 160
Farewell Vw. DH7: B'don 3G 159
Farlam Av. NE30: N Shi 4C 48
Farlam Rd. NE5: Newc T 1F 67
Farleigh Ct. NE29: N Shi 5F 47
Farm Cl. NE16: Sun 3F 95
NE37: Usw 4H 99
Farmer Cres. SR7: Mur 2B 150
Farm Hill Rd. SR6: Cle 1A 90
Farm Rd. DH1: Dur 4D 160
NE23: E Har 4B 16
Farm St. SR5: S'wck 4B 104

Farm Wlk. SR3: New S 4A 132
Farnborough Cl. NE23: Cra 1B 22
Farnborough Dr. SR3: New S . . .1B 132
Farn Ct. NE3: Ken 5H 41
Farndale NE28: W'snd 2F 59
Farndale Av. SR6: Monk 5F 91
Farndale Cl. NE13: Din 4F 29
NE21: Bla T 3F 79
Farndale Ct. NE24: News 3B 18
Farndale Rd. NE4: Newc T 4A 68
Farne Av. NE3: Ken 6C 42
NE34: S Shi 2B 76
Farne Rd. NE12: Longb 5E 45
NE27: Shir 2D 46
Farne Sq. SR4: Sund 6F 103
Farne Ter. NE6: Walk 3E 71
Farnham Cl. DH1: Dur 2C 154
NE15: Lem 3B 66
Farnham Gro. NE24: News 3B 18
Farnham Lodge NE12: Longb 6B 44
Farnham Rd. DH1: Dur 1C 154
NE34: S Shi 3E 75
Farnham St. NE15: Lem 3B 66
Farnham Ter. SR4: Sund 2H 117
Farnley Hey Rd. DH1: Dur 6A 154
Farnley Mt. DH1: Dur 6A 154
Farnley Ridge DH1: Dur 6A 154
Farnley Rd. NE6: Newc T 6C 58
Farnon Rd. NE3: Gos 2C 56
Farnsworth Ct. NE2: Newc T 5H 57
Farquhar St. NE2: Newc T 1H 69
Farrfeld NE10: Gate 1F 99
Farrier Cl. DH1: Dur 5B 144
NE38: Wash 5C 114
FARRINGDON 2F 131
Farringdon Av. SR3: E Her 1E 131
Farringdon Rd. NE30: N Shi 3C 48
Farringdon Row
SR1: Sund 5B 104 (1E 7)
Farrington's Ct.
NE1: Newc T 4F 69 (5D 4)
Farrow Dr. SR6: Whit 2E 91
Farthings, The NE37: Usw 3H 99
FATFIELD 6B 114
Fatfield Pk. NE38: Wash 5B 114
Fatfield Rd. NE38: Wash 3C 114
Fatherly Ter. DH4: Hou S 3F 137
Faversham Ct. NE3: Ken 6H 41
Faversham Pl. NE23: Cra 1B 22
Fawcett St. SR1: Sund . .6D 104 (3G 7)
Fawcett Ter. SR2: Ryh 3G 133
Fawcett Way NE33: S Shi 4E 63
FAWDON 1B 56
Fawdon Cl. NE3: Ken 5B 42
Fawdon Ho. NE3: Ken 5B 42
Fawdon La. NE3: Ken 6B 42
Fawdon Pk. Cen. NE3: Ken 1B 56
Fawdon Pk. Ho. NE3: Ken 1B 56
(off Fawdon Pk. Rd.)
Fawdon Pk. Rd. NE3: Ken 6A 42
Fawdon Pl. NE29: N Shi 1G 61
Fawdon Station (Metro) 1B 56
Fawdon Wlk. NE3: Ken 6H 41
Fawlee Grn. NE3: Ken 3G 55
Fawley Cl. NE35: Bol C 2A 88
Fawn Rd. SR4: Sund 1E 117
Fearon Wlk. DH1: Dur . . .6D 154 (3C 6)
Featherbed La. DH1: Dur 3G 133
Featherstone DH3: Gt Lum 3H 135
NE38: Wash 2F 113
Featherstone Gro. NE3: Gos 4C 42
NE22: Bed 3G 9
NE32: Jar 6E 73

Featherstone Rd. DH1: Dur 2D 154
Featherstone St. SR6: Monk 3F 105
Featherstone Vs. SR6: Monk 3F 105
Federation Sq. SR7: Mur 3C 150
Federation Ter. DH9: Tan L 5H 107
Federation Way NE11: Dun 2A 82
Fee Ter. SR2: Ryh 3E 133
Feetham Av. NE12: Longb 5F 45
Feetham Ct. NE12: Longb 4G 45
Felixstowe Dr. NE7: Newc T 4C 58
Fell Bank DH3: Bir 3C 112
Fell Cl. DH3: Bir 4E 113
   NE16: Sun 3F 95
   NE37: Wash 6H 99
Fell Cotts. NE9: Spri 4F 99
   (off Fell Rd.)
Fell Ct. NE9: Gate 6B 84
Fellcross DH3: Bir 2C 112
Fell Dyke NE10: Gate 5C 84
Felldyke NE10: Gate 6E 85
FELLGATE 2F 87
Fellgate Av. NE32: Jar 2G 87
Fellgate Gdns. NE10: Gate 3A 86
Fellgate Station (Metro) 1G 87
FELLING 3D 84
Felling Bus. Cen. NE10: Gate . . .1D 84
Felling By-Pass NE10: Gate 2E 85
   (Abbotsford Rd.)
   NE10: Gate 1C 84
   (Grn. Lane Gdns.)
Felling Dene Gdns.
   NE10: Gate 2E 85
Felling Ga. NE10: Gate 2C 84
Felling Ho. Gdns. NE10: Gate . . .2D 84
Felling Ind. Est. NE10: Gate 1C 84
Felling Pool 5G 85
Felling Shore Ind. Est.
   NE10: Gate 6D 70
Felling Station (Metro) 2D 84
Felling Vw. NE6: Walk 6F 71
Fellmere Av. NE10: Gate 3G 85
Fell Pl. NE9: Spri 4F 99
Fell Rd. DH2: Pelt 6G 125
   NE9: Spri 4F 99
   SR4: Sund 6F 103
Fellrose Ct. DH2: Pelt 5C 125
Fellsdyke Ct. NE10: Gate 5C 84
FELLSIDE 3C 94
Fellside DH3: Bir 4D 112
   NE20: Pon 4B 38
   NE34: S Shi 4B 76
Fellside Av. NE16: Sun 2F 95
Fellside Cl. DH9: Stly 2F 123
   NE20: Pon 4B 38
Fellside Ct. NE16: Whi 4E 81
   NE37: Wash 1H 113
Fellside Gdns. DH1: Carr 3A 156
FELLSIDE PARK 5D 80
Fellside Rd. NE16: Burn 6A 94
   NE16: Whi 3C 94
Fell Side, The NE3: Ken 3B 56
Fell Sq. SR4: Sund 6E 103
Fells Rd. NE11: Gate 4F 83
Fells, The NE9: Gate 5A 84
Fell Ter. NE16: Burn 1H 107
Fell Vw. DH9: Stly 4C 122
   NE39: H Spen 2A 92
Fell Way, The NE5: Newc T 6B 54
Felsham Sq. SR4: Sund 1G 117
Felstead Cres. SR4: Sund 6F 103
Felstead Pl. NE24: News 3B 18
Felstead Sq. SR4: Sund 1F 117
Felthorpe Ct. NE5: Newc T 3F 55

Felton Av. NE3: Ken 1C 56
   NE25: Whit B 1D 48
   NE34: S Shi 3A 76
Felton Cl. NE27: Shir 2D 46
Felton Cres. NE8: Gate 4G 83
Felton Dr. NE12: Longb 4F 45
Felton Grn. NE6: Newc T 3C 70
Felton Ter. NE30: N Shi 5F 49
   (off Hotspur St.)
Felton Wlk. NE6: Newc T 3C 70
Fomwick Wlk NE8: Gate 1F 83
   (off St Cuthbert's Rd.)
FENCE HOUSES 2E 137
Fencer Ct. NE3: Gos 5E 43
Fencer Hill Pk. NE3: Gos 5E 43
Fence Rd. DH3: Lam P 3C 128
FENHAM 1H 67
Fenham Chase NE4: Newc T 1H 67
Fenham Ct. NE4: Newc T 1A 68
Fenham Hall Dr. NE4: Newc T . . .1H 67
Fenham Grn. NE4: Newc T 3C 68
   (not continuous)
Fenham Swimming Pool 1H 67
Fenkle St. NE1: Newc T . . .4F 69 (5B 4)
Fennel NE9: Gate 1C 98
Fennel Gro. NE34: S Shi 6G 75
   SR8: Eas 1B 162
Fenning Pl. NE6: Newc T 5C 70
Fenside Rd. SR2: Ryh 1F 133
Fenton Cl. DH2: Ches S 1A 134
Fenton Sq. SR4: Sund 1F 117
Fenton Ter. DH4: Hou S 3H 129
Fenton Wlk. NE5: Newc T 5E 55
Fenton Well La. DH3: Gt Lum . . .4E 135
Fenwick Av. NE24: News 2B 18
   NE34: S Shi 4C 74
Fenwick Cl. DH2: Ches S 2A 134
   DH4: Pen 2F 129
   NE2: Newc T 6H 57
Fenwick St. DH4: Pen 1F 129
   NE35: Bol C 2A 88
Fenwick Ter. DH1: Dur 1H 159
   NE2: Newc T 6H 57
   NE29: N Shi 1C 62
Fcrone Cl. DH1: Dur 4D 154 (1D 6)
Ferens Pk. DH1: Dur 6D 154
Ferguson Cres. NE13: Bru V 1C 42
Ferguson's La.
   NE15: Newc T 3E 67
Ferguson St. SR2: Sund 1F 119
Fern Av. DH9: Stly 4B 122
   NE2: Newc T 6G 57
   NE3: Ken 6R 42
   NE23: Cra 5B 16
   NE26: Whit B 6D 36
   NE29: N Shi 1B 62
   SR5: S'wck 3A 104
   SR6: Whit 1F 91
Fernbank NE26: Sea S 3F 25
Fern Ct. SR8: Pet 3A 164
Fern Cres. SR7: S'hm 6A 142
Ferndale DH1: Carr 4B 156
Ferndale Av. NE3: Gos 4F 43
   NE28: W'snd 5A 60
   NE36: E Bol 4F 89
Ferndale Cl. NE24: Cow 5G 11
Ferndale Gro. NE36: E Bol 4F 89
Ferndale La. NE36: E Bol 4F 89
Ferndale Rd. DH4: Pen 1E 129
Ferndale Ter. NE9: Spri 4F 99
   SR4: Sund 5G 103
Fern Dene NE28: W'snd 3C 60
Ferndene Av. DH2: Pelt 6G 125

Ferndene Ct. NE3: Gos 3F 57
Ferndene Cres. SR4: Sund 1H 117
Ferndene Gro. NE7: Newc T 4B 58
   NE40: Ryton 3D 64
Fern Dene Rd. NE8: Gate 3G 83
Ferndown Ct. NE10: Gate 4H 85
   NE40: Ryton 5D 64
Fern Dr. NE23: Dud 3A 32
   SR6: Cle 2H 89
Fern Gdns. NE9: Gate 5H 83
Ferngrove NE32: Jar 3G 87
Fernhill Av. NE16: Whi 4E 81
Fernlea NE23: Dud 3B 32
Fernlea Cl. NE38: Wash 5C 114
Fernlea Gdns. NE40: Ryton 5A 64
Fernlea Grn. NE3: Ken 2B 56
Fernleigh DH3: Gt Lum 4G 135
Fernley Vs. NE23: Cra 3C 22
Fernlough NE9: Gate 6C 84
Fern St. SR4: Sund 6B 104
Fernsway SR3: Sund 4D 118
Fern Ter. DH9: Tan L 6F 107
Fernville Av. NE16: Sun 3F 95
Fernville Rd. NE3: Gos 4D 56
Fernville St. SR4: Sund 2B 118
Fernwood NE2: Newc T 1G 69
Fernwood Av. NE3: Gos 1F 57
Fernwood Cl. SR3: New S 4A 132
Fernwood Rd. NE2: Newc T 1G 69
   NE15: Lem 3B 66
Ferrand Dr. DH4: Hou S 3H 137
Ferriby Cl. NE3: Gos 5F 43
Ferrisdale Way NE3: Ken 6B 42
Ferry App. NE33: S Shi 4D 62
Ferryboat La. SR5: C'twn 2B 102
Ferrydene Av. NE3: Ken 3B 56
Ferry M. NE29: N Shi 3D 62
Ferry St. NE32: Jar 1F 73
   NE33: S Shi 4D 62
Festival Cotts. NE12: Kil 6B 32
FESTIVAL PARK 4D 82
Festival Pk. Dr. NE11: Gate 4D 82
Festival Way NE11: Dun 2C 82
Fetcham Ct. NE3: Ken 6G 41
Fewster Sq. NE10: Gate 5G 85
Field Cl. NE3: Newc T . . .3H 69 (3H 5)
Fieldfare Cl. NE38: Wash 4F 113
Field Fare Ct. NE16: Burn 2A 108
Fieldhouse Cl. NE61: Hep 1A 8
Fieldhouse La. DH1: Dur 4A 154
   NE61: Hep 1A 8
Field Ho. Rd. NE8: Gate 4G 83
Fieldhouse Ter. DH1: Dur 4B 154
Fielding Ct. NE5: Newc T 3F 55
   NE34: S Shi 6C 74
Fielding Pl. NE9: Gate 3B 84
Field La. NE10: Gate 3F 85
Fieldside DH2: Pelt 2G 125
   DH5: W Rai 2G 147
   SR6: Whit 2E 91
Field Sq. SR4: Sund 1F 117
Field St. NE3: Gos 2G 57
   NE10: Gate 2D 84
Field Ter. NE15: Thro 5D 62
   NE32: Jar 4F 73
Field Vw. DH7: Ush M 4D 152
Fieldway NE32: Jar 2G 87
Fife Av. DH2: Ches S 6B 126
   NE32: Jar 6A 74
Fife St. NE8: Gate 2A 84
   SR7: Mur 3D 150
Fifteenth Av. NE24: Bly 1B 18

Fifth Av. DH2: Ches S 6B **126**
   NE6: Newc T 2C **70**
   NE11: Gate 6E **83**
          (Carlton Ct.)
   NE11: Gate 6F **83**
          (Earlsway)
   NE24: Bly 1B **18**
Fifth Av. Bus. Pk. NE11: Gate 1F **97**
Fifth Av. E. NE11: Gate 6F **83**
Fifth St. SR8: Pet 6G **163**
         (not continuous)
Filby Dr. DH1: Carr 2B **156**
Filey Cl. NE23: Cra 1B **22**
Filton Cl. NE23: Cra 1B **22**
Finchale NE38: Wash 4A **114**
Finchale Abbey Cvn. Pk.
   DH1: Bras 3G **145**
Finchale Av. DH1: Bras 5E **145**
Finchale Cl. DH4: Hou S 3H **137**
   NE11: Dun 5B **82**
   SR2: Sund 2E **119**
Finchale Ct. DH4: W Rai 3D **146**
Finchale Gdns. NE9: Gate 3C **98**
   NE15: Thro 4D **52**
Finchale Priory 2H **145**
Finchale Rd. DH1: Dur 5D **144**
         (Canterbury Rd.)
   DH1: Dur 2A **154**
         (Durham Moor)
   NE31: Heb 1C **86**
Finchale Ter. DH4: Hou S 2C **136**
   NE6: Newc T 4C **70**
   NE32: Jar 5H **73**
Finchale Vw. DH1: Dur 5B **144**
   DH4: W Rai 3C **146**
Finchdale Cl. NE29: N Shi 3B **62**
Finchdale Ter. DH3: Ches S 6C **126**
Finchley Ct. NE6: Walk 1G **71**
Finchley Cres. NE6: Walk 1G **71**
Findon Gro. NE29: N Shi 3A **62**
Fines Pk. DH9: Ann P 4G **121**
Finney Ter. DH1: Dur 5D **154** (1C **6**)
Finsbury Av. NE6: Walk 3E **71**
Finsbury St. SR5: S'wck 4C **104**
Finsmere Pl. NE5: Newc T 6F **55**
Finstock Ct. NE3: Newc T 3H **57**
Fir Av. DH1: Dur 6G **155**
   DH7: B'don 6D **158**
Firbank Av. NE30: N Shi 3D **48**
Firbanks NE32: Jar 2H **87**
Fire Sta. Cotts. SR6: Monk 1D **104**
Firfield Rd. NE5: Newc T 5G **55**
Fir Gro. NE34: S Shi 4H **75**
Fir Pk. DH7: Ush M 5D **152**
First Av. DH2: Ches S 1B **126**
   NE6: Newc T 2C **70**
   NE11: Gate 5E **83**
   NE24: Bly 1B **18**
   NE29: N Shi 3F **61**
Firs, The NE3: Gos 3D **56**
Fir St. NE32: Jar 2E **73**
First St. NE8: Gate 2F **83**
   SR8: Pet 6G **163**
Fir Ter. NE16: Burn 1H **107**
Firth Sq. SR4: Sund 6F **103**
Firtree Av. NE6: Walk 6G **59**
   NE12: Longb 4D **44**
   NE38: Wash 6H **113**
Fir Tree Cl. DH1: Dur 3G **155**
Fir Tree Copse NE61: Hep 1A **8**
Firtree Cres. NE12: Longb 4C **44**
Firtree Gdns. NE25: Whit B 2B **48**
Firtree Rd. NE16: Whi 5E **81**

Firtrees DH2: Ches S 4B **126**
   NE10: Gate 6E **85**
Firtrees Av. NE28: W'snd 4F **61**
Firwood Cres. NE39: H Spen 2A **92**
Firwood Gdns. NE11: Gate 6D **82**
Fisher Ind. Est. NE6: Walk 3H **71**
Fisher La. NE13: Sea B 1D **30**
   NE23: Cra, Nel V 4D **20**
Fisher Rd. NE27: Back 6H **33**
Fisher St. NE6: Walk 2H **71**
Fisherwell Rd. NE10: Gate 1G **85**
Fish Quay NE30: N Shi 2E **63**
Fitzpatrick Pl. NE33: S Shi 5G **63**
Fitzroy Ter. SR5: S'wck 3H **103**
Fitzsimmons Av. NE28: W'snd . . .4H **59**
Flag Chare NE1: Newc T 5G **5**
Flagg Ct. NE33: S Shi 4F **63**
Flagg Ct. Ho. NE33: S Shi 4F **63**
Flake Cotts. DH3: Ches S 5D **126**
Flambard Rd. DH1: Dur 2B **154**
Flass Av. DH7: Ush M 5B **152**
Flassburn Rd. DH1: Dur 4A **154**
Flass St. DH1: Dur 5B **154**
Flass Ter. DH7: Ush M 5B **152**
Flaunden Cl. NE34: S Shi 4B **76**
Flaxby Cl. NE3: Gos 5F **43**
Flax Cotts. NE62: Sco G 1G **9**
Flax Sq. SR4: Sund 6E **103**
Fleetham Cl. DH2: Ches S 2A **134**
Fleet St. SR1: Sund 1F **119**
Fleming Bus. Cen., The
   NE2: Newc T 1F **69**
Fleming Ct. NE8: Gate 1E **83**
Fleming Gdns. NE10: Gate 4C **84**
Fleming Pl. SR8: Pet 1D **164**
Fletcher Cres. DH4: E Her 3A **130**
Fletcher Ter. DH3: Hou S 5H **129**
Flexbury Gdns. NE9: Gate 3A **98**
   NE10: Gate 3C **84**
   NE15: Lem 2C **66**
Flight, The NE21: Bla T 2G **79**
FLINT HILL 6E **107**
Flint Hill Bank DH9: Dip 6E **107**
Flixton DH4: Hou S 2F **137**
Flock Sq. SR4: Sund 6F **103**
Flodden NE12: Kil 1D **44**
Flodden Cl. DH2: Ches S 2A **134**
Flodden Rd. SR4: Sund 1F **117**
Flodden St. NE6: Newc T, Walk . . .4D **70**
Floral Dene SR4: Sund 1C **116**
Floralia Av. SR2: Ryh 3G **133**
Flora St. NE6: Newc T 3B **70**
Florence Av. NE9: Gate 5A **84**
Florence Cres. SR5: S'wck 3H **103**
Florence St. NE21: Bla T 2H **79**
Florence Ter. DH5: Hett H 3C **148**
Florida St. SR4: Sund 6H **103**
Flotterton Gdns. NE5: Newc T . . .2G **67**
Flour Mill Rd. NE11: Dun 1B **82**
Flying Ho. SR3: New S 4H **131**
Folds Cl. DH7: New B 2A **158**
Folds, The DH4: Hou S 3F **137**
   DH5: W Rai 1H **147**
         (off North St.)
Fold, The NE6: Walk 1G **71**
   NE16: Burn 6G **93**
   NF25: Whit B 6A **36**
   SR3: New S 4B **132**
Folldon Av. SR6: Monk 2D **104**
FOLLINGSBY 6B **86**
Follingsby Av. NE10: Gate 6B **86**
Follingsby Cl. NE10: Gate 5B **86**
Follingsby Dr. NE10: Gate 4A **86**

Follingsby La.
   NE10: Gate, Usw, W Bol 6A **86**
   NE36: W Bol 1G **101**
Follingsby Pk. NE10: Gate 5B **86**
         (not continuous)
Follonsby La. NE36: W Bol 1H **101**
Follonsby Ter. NE36: W Bol 4C **86**
Folly Cotts. NE40: G'sde 2B **78**
Folly La. NE40: G'sde 1A **78**
Folly Ter. DH1: Dur 6A **144**
FOLLY, THE 1C **78**
Folly, The NE36: W Bol 4C **88**
Folly Yd. NE40: G'sde 1C **78**
Fondlyset La.
   DH9: Ann P, Dip 2D **120**
Fontaine Rd.
   SR1: Sund 6C **104** (2F **7**)
Fontburn Ct. NE29: N Shi 3A **62**
   SR5: S'wck 1H **103**
Fontburn Pl. NE7: Longb 2A **58**
Fontburn Rd. NE22: Bed 4C **10**
   NE25: Sea D 6B **24**
Fontburn Ter. NE30: N Shi 1D **62**
Fonteyn Pl. DH9: Stly 4F **123**
   NE23: Cra 5B **16**
Fontwell Dr. NE8: Gate 4F **83**
Forbeck Rd. SR4: Sund 1F **117**
Forber Av. NE34: S Shi 3B **76**
Forbes Ter. SR2: Ryh 3E **133**
Ford Av. NE29: N Shi 3H **61**
   SR4: Sund 1C **116**
Ford Cres. NE27: Shir 2C **46**
   NE32: Jar 6F **73**
   SR4: Sund 1C **116**
Ford Dr. NE24: Bly 6A **12**
Fordenbridge Cres.
   SR4: Sund 1F **117**
Fordenbridge Rd. SR4: Sund 1F **117**
Fordenbridge Sq. SR4: Sund 1G **117**
FORD ESTATE 1G **117**
Fordfield Rd. SR4: Sund 1E **117**
Ford Gro. NE3: Gos 6D **42**
Fordhall Dr. SR4: Sund 1G **117**
Fordham Rd. DH1: Dur 1C **154**
   SR4: Sund 6F **103**
Fordham Sq. SR4: Sund 1G **117**
Fordland Pl. SR4: Sund 1H **117**
FORDLEY 3B **32**
Fordmoss Wlk. NE5: Newc T 5E **55**
Ford Oval SR4: Sund 6D **102**
Ford Rd. DH1: Dur 6D **144**
Ford St. NE6: Newc T 4A **70**
   NE8: Gate 2B **84**
Ford Ter. NE28: W'snd 5D **60**
   SR4: Sund 1H **117**
Ford Vw. NE23: Dud 2A **32**
Forest Av. NE12: Longb 5E **45**
Forestborn Ct. NE5: Newc T 5D **54**
Forest Dr. NE38: Wash 1F **127**
Forest Ga. NE12: Kil 4G **45**
FOREST HALL 5D **44**
Forest Hall Rd. NE12: Longb 5E **44**
Fore St. NE2: Newc T 1A **70**
Forest Rd. NE15: Newc T 5G **67**
   NE33: S Shi 5E **63**
   SR4: Sund 6F **103**
Forest Rd. Ind. Est.
   NE33: S Shi 5E **63**
Forest Vw. DH7: B'don 6B **158**
Forest Way NE23: Seg 2F **33**
Forfar St. SR6: Monk 3D **104**
Forge La. DH3: Gt Lum 2H **135**
Forge Rd. NE8: Gate 3C **82**

Forge, The DH1: Dur 5A **144**
  SR4: Sund 6H **103**
Forge Wlk. NE15: Thro 6F **53**
Forres Ct. DH9: Stly 3F **123**
Forres Pl. NE23: Cra 1B **22**
Forrest Rd. NE28: W'snd 6G **59**
Forster Av. DH6: Sher 5D **156**
  NE22: Bed 4G **9**
  NE34: S Shi 2G **75**
  SR7: Mur 4E **161**
Forster Ct. NE9: Gate 1H **97**
Forster St. NE1: Newc T . . .4H **69** (5G **5**)
  NE24: Bly 6D **12**
  SR6: Monk 3E **105**
Forsyth Rd. NE2: Newc T 6F **57**
Forsyth St. NE29: N Shi 4F **47**
Forth Banks NE1: Newc T 5F **69**
Forth Cl. SR8: Pet 2D **164**
Forth Ct. NE34: S Shi 4E **75**
  SR3: New S 3H **131**
Forth La. NE1: Newc T 5F **69** (6C **4**)
Forth Pl. NE1: Newc T 5E **69** (6B **4**)
Forth St. NE1: Newc T 5E **69** (6C **4**)
Fortrose Av. SR3: Sund 4A **118**
Fort Sq. NE33: S Shi 3E **63**
Fort St. NE33: S Shi 3F **63**
Forum Ct. NE22: Bed 4H **9**
Forum, The NE15: Newc T . . .2D **66**
  NE28: W'snd 6H **59**
Forum Way NE23: Cra 3H **21**
Fossdyke NE10: Gate 6F **85**
Fossefeld NE10: Gate 4G **85**
Fosse Law NE15: Thro 6C **53**
Fosse Ter. NE9: Gate 5A **84**
Foss Way NE34: S Shi 4D **74**
Fossway NE6: Walk 2D **70**
Foster Cl. NE11: Gate 2E **97**
Foster Dr. NE8: Gate 1B **84**
Foster Memorial Homes
  NE24: Bly 6B **12**
Foster St. NE6: Walk 3H **71**
         (not continuous)
Foundation 5F **5**
Foundry Ct. NE6: Newc T 5C **70**
Foundry La. NE6: Newc T 3A **70**
  NE16: Swa 2F **81**
Foundry Rd. SR7: S'hm 4C **142**
Fountain Cl. NE22: Bed 4H **9**
Fountain Gro. NE34: S Shi 1H **75**
Fountain Head Bank
  NE26: Sea S 3F **25**
Fountain La. NE21: Bla T 6A **66**
         (not continuous)
Fountain Row NE2: Newc T 2D **68**
Fountains Cl. NE11: Dun 5B **82**
  NE38: Wash 3B **114**
Fountains Cres. DH4: Hou S . . .1G **137**
  NE31: Heb 6C **72**
Fouracres Rd. NE5: Newc T 5A **56**
Four La. Ends DH5: Hett H 3D **148**
Four Lane Ends Station (Metro)
  . . . . .2C **58**
Fourstones NE5: Newc T 5E **55**
Fourstones Cl. NE3: Ken 2H **55**
Fourstones Rd. SR4: Sund 6G **103**
Fourteenth Av. NE24: Bly 1B **18**
Fourth Av. DH2: Ches S 6B **126**
  NE6: Newc T 2C **70**
  NE11: Gate 6E **83**
  NE24: Bly 1B **18**
Fourth St. NE8: Gate 2F **83**
  SR8: Pet 6G **163**
         (not continuous)

Fowberry Cres. NE4: Newc T . . .2A **68**
Fowberry Rd. NE15: Newc T 5D **66**
Fowler Cl. DH4: Hou S 5G **129**
Fowler Gdns. NE11: Dun 2B **82**
Fowler St. NE33: S Shi 4E **63**
Fowlers Yd. DH1: Dur 3B **6**
Fox & Hounds La.
  NE15: Newc T 3G **67**
Fox & Hounds Rd.
  NE5: Newc T 2G **67**
Fox Av. NE34: S Shi 5B **74**
Foxcover Ct. SR7: S'hm 6A **142**
Foxcover La. SR3: E Her 2D **130**
Foxcover Rd. SR3: E Her 1C **130**
  SR4: Sund 5B **116**
Fox Covert La. NE20: Pon 5D **26**
Foxglove DH4: Hou S 4D **128**
Foxglove Cl. NE24: News 3A **18**
Foxglove Cl. NE34: S Shi 5D **74**
Foxhills Cl. NE38: Wash 5C **114**
Foxhills Covert NE16: Whi 6C **80**
Foxhills, The NE16: Whi 5C **80**
Foxhomes NE32: Jar 3H **87**
Foxhunters Light Ind. Est.
  NE25: Whit B 2B **48**
Foxhunters Rd. NE25: Whit B . . .2B **48**
Foxlair Cl. SR3: New S 5A **132**
Fox Lea Wlk. NE23: Seg 2F **33**
Foxley NE37: Usw 5C **100**
Foxley Cl. NE12: Kil 1F **45**
Foxpit La. DH9: Stly 4E **109**
Fox St. NE10: Gate 2C **84**
  SR2: Sund 2B **118**
  SR7: S'hm 5B **142**
Foxton Av. NE3: Ken 6B **42**
  NE30: N Shi 2D **48**
Foxton Cl. NE29: N Shi 4A **62**
Foxton Ct. SR6: Cle 2A **90**
Foxton Grn. NE3: Ken 2A **56**
Foxton Hall NE37: Usw 2B **100**
Foxton Way DH1: H Shin 4H **161**
  NE10: Gate 1H **85**
Foyle St. SR1: Sund 1D **118** (4H **7**)
Framlington Ho. NE2: Newc T . .2E **69**
Framlington Pl. NE2: Newc T . . .2E **69**
Framwelgate
  DH1: Dur 5C **154** (1A **6**)
Framwelgate Bridge
  DH1: Dur 6C **154** (3A **6**)
Framwelgate Peth
  DH1: Dur 4B **154** (1A **6**)
Framwelgate Waterside
  DH1: Dur 5C **154** (2B **6**)
FRAMWELLGATE MOOR 2A **154**
Framwellgate School Sports Cen.
  . . . . .1B **154**
Francesca Ter. NE5: Newc T 1F **67**
         (off Pooley Rd.)
Frances St. NE21: Bla T 1G **79**
  SR3: New S 2A **132**
Frances Ville NE62: Sco G 1G **9**
Francis St. SR6: Monk 3D **104**
Francis Way DH5: Hett H 1C **148**
  NE27: Longb 4B **46**
Frank Av. SR7: S'hm 4H **141**
         (not continuous)
Frankham St. NE5: Newc T 5D **54**
Frankland Dr. NE25: Whit B 2A **48**
Frankland La.
  DH1: Bras, Dur 4C **154** (1B **6**)
Frankland Mt. NE25: Whit B 2A **48**
Frankland Rd. DH1: Dur 2B **154**
Franklin Ct. NE37: Usw 5B **100**

Franklin St. NE33: S Shi 5E **63**
  SR4: Sund 6A **104**
Franklin Trad. Est. NE21: Bla T . .5C **66**
Franklyn Av. NE26: Sea S 2F **25**
Franklyn Rd. SR8: Pet 6C **162**
Frank Pl. DH3: Bir 4C **112**
  NE29: N Shi 1C **62**
Frank St. DH1: Dur 5G **155**
  NE28: W'snd 6H **59**
  NE40: G'sde 2A **78**
  SR6: S'wck 3B **104**
Fraser Cl. NE33: S Shi 1D **74**
Frater Ter. NE28: W'snd 5G **61**
Frazer Ter. NE10: Gate 2G **85**
Freda St. SR5: S'wck 4H **103**
Frederick Gdns. DH4: Pen 2E **129**
Frederick Pl. DH4: Hou S 3A **138**
Frederick Rd.
  SR1: Sund 6D **104** (3H **7**)
Frederick St. NE33: S Shi 1E **75**
  SR1: Sund 6D **104** (3H **7**)
  SR4: Sund 1C **116**
  SR7: S'hm 4B **142**
Frederick St. Nth. DH7: B'don . .6E **159**
Frederick St. Sth. DH7: B'don . .6E **159**
Frederick Ter. DH5: Eas L 4D **148**
  DH6: S Het 6H **149**
  SR6: Whit 2F **91**
Freehold St. NE24: Bly 5D **12**
Freeman Rd. NE3: Gos 3H **57**
Freemans Pl.
  DH1: Dur 5C **154** (2B **6**)
Freeman Way NE26: Whit B 4A **36**
Freesia Gdns. SR5: Monk 2C **104**
Freesia Grange NE38: Wash 4C **114**
Freezemoor Rd. DH4: Hou S . . .3H **129**
Freight Village NE13: Wool 3C **40**
Fremantle Rd. NE34: S Shi 4B **76**
Frenchmans Row NE15: Thro . . .5B **52**
Frenchmans Way NE34: S Shi . . .2B **76**
French St. NE24: Bly 6C **12**
Frensham NE38: Wash 3E **115**
Frensham Way DH7: B'don 5E **159**
Frenton Cl. NE5: Cha P 5A **54**
Friarage Av. SR6: Monk 2D **104**
Friar Rd. SR4: Sund 1F **117**
Friars NE1: Newc T 5B **4**
         (off Low Friar St.)
Friars Dene Rd. NE10: Gate 1C **84**
Friarsfield Cl. SR3: New S 4G **131**
FRIARS GOOSE 6D **70**
Friars Goose Water Sports Club
  . . . . .6D **70**
Friarside Cres. NE39: Row G 5D **92**
Friarside Gdns. NE16: Burn 1F **107**
  NE16: Whi 5E **81**
Friarside Rd. NE4: Newc T 1A **68**
Friar Sq. SR4: Sund 1F **117**
Friars Row DH1: Dur 4F **155**
  NE16: Burn 2F **107**
Friars St. NE1: Newc T 4E **69** (5B **4**)
Friars Way NE5: Newc T 1G **67**
Friar Way NE32: Jar 2G **73**
Friary Gdns. NE10: Gate 1C **84**
Friday Flds. La. NE2: Newc T . . .4G **57**
Friendly Bldgs. NE13: Din 4F **29**
Frinton Pk. SR3: Sund 4A **118**
Frobisher Ct. SR3: New S 3H **131**
Frobisher St. NE31: Heb 3D **72**
Frome Gdns. NE9: Gate 3H **97**
Frome Pl. NE23: Cra 1B **22**
Frome Sq. SR4: Sund 1E **117**
Front Rd. SR4: Sund 6F **103**

Front St. DH1: Dur 1A **154**
    (Durham Ter.)
DH1: Dur, Sher 6G **155**
    (Habgood Dr.)
DH2: Ous 1H **125**
DH2: Pelt 4D **124**
    (Grange Villa Rd.)
DH2: Pelt 4F **125**
    (North Vw.)
DH2: Pelt 2F **125**
    (Station La.)
DH3: Ches S 5C **126**
DH3: Gt Lum 4G **135**
DH4: Hou S 3E **137**
    (Cross St.)
DH4: Hou S 6H **129**
    (Houghton Rd.)
DH4: Pen 1G **129**
DH5: Hett H 1C **148**
    (Caroline St.)
DH5: Hett H 4A **148**
    (York St.)
DH6: H Pitt 1E **157**
DH6: S Het 5G **149**
DH6: Sher 6A **156**
DH7: B'don 3G **159**
DH9: Ann P 5F **121**
DH9: Dip 2C **120**
    (not continuous)
DH9: Stly 6G **123**
    (Craghead)
DH9: Stly 2E **123**
    (East Stanley)
DH9: Stly 3C **122**
    (Stanley)
DH9: Tan L 5H **107**
    (Tantobie)
DH9: Tan L 3B **108**
    (Tanfield)
NE7: Longb, Newc T 2C **58**
NE12: Kil 6B **32**
NE12: Longb, Newc T
    . . . . .2C **58**
NE13: Din 4F **29**
NE13: Sea B 2D **30**
NE15: Lem 4C **66**
NE16: Burn 1E **107**
NE16: C Dene 4F **107**
NE16: Swa 2E **81**
NE16: Whi 4E **81**
NE21: Bla T 2H **79**
NE23: Cra 4D **22**
    (High Pit Rd.)
NE23: Cra 3B **22**
    (Station Rd.)
NE23: Dud 2B **32**
NE23: Seg 2E **33**
NE24: Cow 6D **10**
NE25: Well 6E **35**
NE25: Whit B 1A **48**
NE29: N Shi 5C **48**
    (Bulman's La.)
NE29: N Shi 2A **62**
    (Quadrant, The)
NE30: N Shi 6F **49**
    (Bath Ter.)
NE30: N Shi 2E **49**
    (Victoria Cres.)
NE35: Bol C 2A **88**
NE36: E Bol 4E **89**
NE37: Usw 5B **100**
NE39: H Spen 6A **78**
SR6: Cle 2A **90**

Front St. SR6: Whit 3E **91**
TS27: Hes 6F **165**
Front St. E. DH4: Pen 1F **129**
NE22: Bed 5A **10**
Front St. W. DH4: Pen 1F **129**
NE22: Bed 5H **9**
Frosterley Cl. DH1: Dur 1D **154**
DH5: Eas L 5F **149**
Frosterley Dr. DH3: Gt Lum 4H **135**
Frosterley Gdns.
    DH9: Ann P 5F **121**
    SR3: Sund 5B **118**
Frosterley Pl. NE4: Newc T 3C **68**
Frosterley Wlk. NE16: Sun 2F **95**
Froude Av. NE34: S Shi 6E **75**
Fuchsia Gdns. NE31: Heb 6C **72**
Fuchsia Pl. NE5: Newc T 5H **55**
Fulbrook Cl. NE23: Cra 5B **16**
Fulbrook Rd. NE3: Ken 2B **56**
Fulforth Cl. DH7: Ush M 3C **152**
Fuller Rd. SR2: Sund 3E **119**
Fullerton Pl. NE9: Gate 3A **84**
Fulmar Dr. NE24: News 3C **18**
NE38: Wash 3F **113**
Fulmar Wlk. SR6: Whit 1F **91**
Fulton Pl. NE5: Newc T 5G **55**
FULWELL 1D **104**
Fulwell Av. NE34: S Shi 2B **76**
Fulwell Grn. NE5: Newc T 6F **55**
Fulwell Rd. SR6: Monk 1D **104**
SR8: Pet 1E **165**
Fulwell Windmill 2C **104**
Furnace Bank NE24: Bed 4D **10**
Furness Cl. SR8: Pet 1B **164**
Furness Ct. SR3: New S 3H **131**
Furrowfield NE10: Gate 6C **84**
Furzefield Rd. NE3: Gos 3D **56**
Fylingdale Dr. SR3: New S 2C **132**
Fynes Cl. SR8: Pet 5D **162**
Fynes St. NE24: Bly 5C **12**

G

Gables Ct. SR4: Sund 4E **117**
Gables, The NE13: Wool 1F **55**
NE24: Bly 5B **12**
NE38: Wash *3C 114*
    (off Fatfield Rd.)
Gadwall Rd. DH4: W Rai 5F **137**
Gainers Ter. NE28: W'snd 1A **72**
Gainford DH2: Ches S 6A **126**
NE9: Gate 3H **97**
Gainsborough Av. NE34: S Shi . . .6F **75**
NE38: Wash 3C **114**
Gainsborough Cl.
    NE25: Whit B 4G **35**
Gainsborough Cres.
    DH4: Hou S 4E **129**
    NE9: Gate 4B **84**
Gainsborough Gro.
    NE4: Newc T 3B **68**
Gainsborough Pl. NE23: Cra . . .6B **22**
Gainsborough Rd. DH9: Stly 4D **122**
SR4: Sund 5E **117**
Gainsborough Sq. SR4: Sund . . .5E **117**
Gainsford Av. NE9: Gate 1G **97**
Gair Ct. DH2: Plaw 1A **144**
Gairloch Cl. NE23: Cra 6B **16**
Gairloch Dr. DH2: Ous 2H **125**
NE38: Wash 4G **113**
Gairloch Rd. SR4: Sund 4E **117**
Gairsay Cl. SR2: Ryh 1E **133**

Gala Bingo
    Derwenthaugh 6F **67**
    Newcastle upon Tyne
    . . . . .4F **69** (5C **4**)
    Sunderland 6A **104**
    Willington Square 2D **60**
Galashiels Gro. DH4: Hou S . . .4F **129**
Galashiels Rd. SR4: Sund 4D **116**
Galashiels Sq. SR4: Sund 4E **117**
Gala Theatre 2B **6**
    (off Millennium Pl.)
Galen Ho. NE1: Newc T 4F **69** (5C **4**)
Gale St. DH9: Stly 4B **122**
Galfrid Cl. SR7: Mur 5F **141**
Gallagher Cres. SR8: Pet 1F **165**
Gallalaw Ter. NE3: Gos 2H **57**
Gallant Ter. NE28: W'snd 6G **61**
Galleria, The NE11: Dun 2G **81**
Galleries Retail Pk.
    NE38: Wash 1A **114**
Galleries Shop. Cen., The
    NE38: Wash 2A **114**
Galley's Gill Rd.
    SR1: Sund 6C **104** (3E **7**)
Galloping Grn. Cotts.
    NE9: Spri 3D **98**
Galloping Grn. Farm Cl.
    NE9: Spri 3D **98**
Galloping Grn. Rd.
    NE9: Gate, Spri 2D **98**
Galloway Rd. SR8: Pet 6D **162**
Gallowgate NE1: Newc T . .4E **69** (4B **4**)
Galsworthy Rd. NE34: S Shi 6C **74**
SR4: Sund 4E **117**
Galway Rd. SR4: Sund 4D **116**
Galway Sq. SR4: Sund 4D **116**
Gambia Rd. SR4: Sund 5D **116**
Gambia Sq. SR4: Sund 5D **116**
Ganton Av. NE23: Cra 5B **22**
Ganton Cl. NE37: Usw 3A **100**
Ganton Ct. NE34: S Shi 6H **75**
Garasdale Cl. NE24: News 3B **18**
Garcia Ter. SR6: Monk 1E **105**
    (not continuous)
Garden Av. DH1: Dur 1A **154**
Garden Cl. NE13: Sea B 3D **30**
Garden Cotts. NE9: Gate 6A **84**
Garden Cft. NE12: Longb 5E **45**
Garden Dr. NE31: Heb 5B **72**
Gardener St. NE4: Newc T 6C **68**
Garden Est. DH5: Hett H 1D **148**
Garden Ho. Cres. NE16: Whi . . .3G **81**
Garden La. NE33: S Shi 5E **63**
SR6: Cle 3H **89**
Garden Pk. NE28: W'snd 3D **60**
Garden Pl. DH4: Pen 2F **129**
    SR1: Sund 6C **104** (3F **7**)
Gardens, The DH2: Ches S 6B **126**
NE25: Whit B 1B **48**
NE38: Wash 3C **114**
Garden St. DH4: Hou S 6H **129**
NE3: Gos 2E **57**
NE21: Bla T 6A **66**
Garden Ter. DH4: Hou S 6H **129**
DH9: Stly 6F **123**
    (Middles, The)
DH9: Stly 4C **122**
    (Stanley)
NE21: Bla T *2H 79*
    (off Florence St.)
NE25: Well 6E **35**
NE40: G'sde 6A **64**
Garden Wlk. NE11: Dun 1G **81**

Gardiner Cres. DH2: Pelt 5G **125**
Gardiner Rd. SR4: Sund 4C **116**
Gardiner Sq. NE11: Kib 2E **111**
  SR4: Sund 4D **116**
Gardner Pk. NE29: N Shi 2B **62**
Gardner Pl. NE29: N Shi 2D **62**
Gardners Pl. DH7: B'don 4F **159**
Garesfield Gdns. NE16: Burn . . .1F **107**
  NE39: Row G 2E **93**
Garestield La. NE21: Bla T 6E **79**
Gareston Cl. NE24: Cow 6H **11**
Garfield St. SR4: Sund 6H **103**
Garforth Cl. NE23: Cra 5A **22**
Garland Ter. DH4: Hou S 3E **137**
Garleigh Cl. NE12: Kil 2G **45**
Garmondsway NE6: Newc T 4C **70**
Garner Cl. NE5: Cha P 4B **54**
Garnet St. SR4: Sund 6H **103**
Garnwood St. NE33: S Shi 1D **74**
Garrett Cl. NE28: W'snd 4D **60**
Garrick Cl. NE29: N Shi 6G **47**
Garrick St. NE33: S Shi 1E **75**
Garrigill NE38: Wash 6D **114**
Garron St. SR7: S'hm 5B **142**
Garsdale DH3: Bir 6E **113**
Garsdale Av. NE37: Usw 5A **100**
Garsdale Rd. NE26: Whit B 2A **36**
Garside Av. DH3: Bir 1C **112**
Garside Gro. SR8: Pet 5B **162**
Garstin Cl. NE7: Newc T 4E **59**
Garth Cres. NE21: Bla T 2H **79**
  NE34: S Shi 6H **63**
Gth. Farm Rd. NE21: Bla T 2H **79**
Garthfield Cl. NE5: Newc T 4E **55**
Garthfield Cnr. NE5: Newc T 4E **55**
Garthfield Cres. NE5: Newc T . . .4E **55**
Gth. Heads
  NE1: Newc T 4H **69** (5G **5**)
Garth, The DH2: Pelt 2G **125**
  NE3: Ken 3D **56**
  NE5: Newc T 6C **54**
  NE21: Bla T 2H **79**
Gth. Thirteen NE12: Kil 1C **44**
Gth. Sixteen NE12: Kil 1D **44**
Gth. Twenty NE12: Kil 2E **45**
Gth. Twenty One NE12: Kil 1E **45**
Gth. Twenty Two NE12: Kil 2E **45**
Gth. Twenty Four NE12: Kil 2E **45**
Gth. Twenty Five NE12: Kil 2F **45**
Gth. Twenty Seven NE12: Kil 2F **45**
Gth. Thirty Two NE12: Kil 2E **45**
Gth. Thirty Three NE12: Kil 2D **44**
Garland Rd. SR4: Sund 4C **116**
Garvey Vs. NE10: Gate 5B **84**
Gashouse Dr. DH3: Lam P 3A **128**
Gaskell Av. NE34: S Shi 6D **74**
Gas La. NE21: Bla T 5A **66**
Gas Works Rd. SR7: S'hm 5C **142**
Gatacre St. NE24: Bly 5C **12**
Gateley Av. NE24: News 3B **18**
Gatesgarth NE9: Gate 6A **84**
Gatesgarth Gro. SR6: Monk 6D **90**
GATESHEAD 1H **83**
Gateshead FC . . . . .GO **70**
Gateshead Highway NE8: Gate . .6H **69**
Gateshead Indoor Bowling Cen.
  . . . . .2H **83**
Gateshead International
  Stadium 6C **70**
Gateshead Leisure Cen. 3H **83**
Gateshead Millennium Bridge
  (Footbridge) 4H **69** (6G **5**)
Gateshead Quay Vis. Cen. 6F **5**

Gateshead Rd. NE16: Sun 4F **95**
Gateshead Stadium Station (Metro)
  . . . . .1A **84**
Gateshead Station (Metro) 6G **69**
Gateshead Western By-Pass
  NE9: Gate, Kib 3G **97**
  NE11: Gate 4D **82**
  NE16: Dun, Swa 2G **81**
Gate, The 4F **69** (4C **4**)
Gatwick Ct. NE3: Ken 6F **41**
Gatwick Rd. SR4: Sund 4D **116**
Gaughan Cl. NE6: Walk 6F **71**
Gaweswell Ter. DH4: Hou S 5H **129**
  (off North St.)
Gayfield Ter. SR8: Eas 2F **163**
Gayhurst Cres. SR3: New S 3A **132**
Gayton Rd. NE37: Usw 4C **100**
Geddes Rd. SR4: Sund 4D **116**
Gellesfield Chare NE16: Whi 1F **95**
Gelt Cres. DH5: Eas L 3D **148**
General Graham St.
  SR4: Sund 2A **118**
General Havelock Rd.
  SR4: Sund 6G **103**
General's Wood, The
  NE38: Wash 1H **127**
Geneva Rd. SR4: Sund 4D **116**
Genister Pl. NE4: Newc T 1H **67**
Geoffrey Av. DH1: Dur 1A **160**
Geoffrey St. NE34: S Shi 6E **75**
  SR6: Whit 2F **91**
Geoffrey Ter. DH9: Stly 4B **122**
George Pit La. DH3: Gt Lum 5H **135**
George Pl. NE1: Newc T . . .3F **69** (2C **4**)
George Rd. NE22: Bed 3D **10**
  NE28: W'snd 1H **71**
George Scott St. NE33: S Shi 3F **63**
George Smith Gdns.
  NE10: Gate 1C **84**
George Sq. NE30: N Shi 1D **62**
Georges Rd. NE4: Newc T 5B **68**
  (not continuous)
George Stephenson Way
  NE29: N Shi 4B **62**
George St. DH1: Dur 6A **154**
  DH3: Bir 3B **112**
  DH3: Ches S 1D **134**
  DH5: Hett H 6C **138**
  DH6: Sher 6D **156**
  DH9: Dip 1D **120**
  DH9: Stly 6G **123**
  NE3: Gos 2C **56**
  NE4: Newc T 5E **69** (6A **4**)
  NE10: Gate 2F **85**
  NE13: Bru V 5C **30**
  NE15: Thro 5F **53**
  NE16: Whi 4E **81**
  NE21: Bla T 6B **66**
  NE24: Bly 1C **18**
  NE28: W'snd 6F **61**
  NE30: N Shi 1D **62**
  SR2: Ryh 3G **133**
  SR7: Mur 3D **150**
  SR7: S'hm 4A **142**
George St. E. SR3: New S 1A **132**
George St. Ind. Est.
  SR7: S'hm 4A **142**
George St. Nth. SR6: Monk 5D **104**
George St. W. SR3: New S 1A **132**
George's Vw. NE23: Dud 4A **32**
George Ter. DH7: Ush M 4E **153**
George Way
  NE4: Newc T 5E **69** (6A **4**)

Georgian Ct. NE12: Longb 4B **44**
  SR4: Sund 3A **118**
Gerald St. NE4: Newc T 5H **67**
  NE34: S Shi 6E **75**
Gerrard Cl. NE23: Cra 5B **22**
  NE26: Whit B 2A **36**
Gerrard Rd. NE26: Whit B 2A **36**
  SR4: Sund 4D **116**
Gertrude St. DH4: Hou S 1H **137**
Ghyll Fld. Rd. DH1: Dur 2B **154**
Gibbons Wlk. NE34: S Shi 1C **88**
Gibbs Ct. DH2: Ches S 1C **134**
GIBSIDE 4A **94**
Gibside 3H **93**
Gibside DH2: Ches S 6A **126**
Gibside Cl. DH9: Stly 2F **123**
Gibside Ct. NE11: Dun 5B **82**
Gibside Cres. NE16: Burn 5B **94**
Gibside Gdns. NE15: Newc T 3F **67**
Gibside Ter. NE16: Burn 1H **107**
Gibside Vw. NE21: Bla T 2H **79**
Gibside Way NE11: Dun, Swa . . .1F **81**
Gibson Ct. NE35: Bol C 3B **88**
  (not continuous)
Gibsons Bldgs. NE40: Ryton 5A **64**
  (off Main St.)
Gibson St. NE1: Newc T . . .4H **69** (4G **5**)
  NE28: W'snd 2C **60**
Gibson Street Leisure Cen.
  . . . . .4H **69** (4H **5**)
Gibson Ter. NE40: Ryton 5A **64**
  (off Main St.)
Gifford Sq. SR4: Sund 3E **117**
Gilberdyke NE10: Gate 6G **85**
Gilbert Rd. SR4: Sund 4D **116**
  SR8: Pet 6C **162**
Gilbert Sq. SR4: Sund 5D **116**
Gilbert St. NE33: S Shi 1E **75**
Gildale DH4: Pen 1C **128**
Gilderdale Way NE23: Cra 6A **22**
GILESGATE 4G **155**
Gilesgate DH1: Dur 5D **154** (2D **6**)
Gilesgate Cl. DH1: Dur . . .5D **154** (1D **6**)
GILESGATE MOOR 5G **155**
Gilesgate Rd. DH5: Eas L 3D **148**
Gilhurst Grange SR1: Sund 1R **118**
Gilhurst Ho. SR1: Sund 6B **104**
Gillas La. DH5: Hou S 4C **138**
Gillas La. E. DH5: Hou S 4B **138**
Gillas La. W. DH5: Hou S 5A **138**
Gill Brl. Av. SR1: Sund . . .6C **104** (2F **7**)
Gill Burn NE39: Row G 2E **93**
Gill Cres. Nth. DH4: Hou S 1C **136**
Gill Cres. Sth. DH4: Hou S 1C **136**
GILLEY LAW 1G **131**
Gillies St. NE6: Newc T 3D **70**
Gilliland Cres. DH3: Bir 1C **112**
Gillingham Rd. SR4: Sund 4D **116**
Gill Rd. SR1: Sund 6C **104** (2F **7**)
Gillside Ct. NE34: S Shi 4C **74**
Gill Side Gro. SR6: Monk 3E **105**
Gill St. NE4: Newc T 4A **68**
Gill Ter. SR4: Sund 6C **102**
  (off Pottery La.)
Gilmore Cl. NE5: Cha P 4B **54**
Gilmore Ho. NE8: Gate 3G **83**
  (off Whitehall Rd.)
Gilpin Ho. DH4: Hou S 1G **137**
Gilpin St. DH4: Hou S 3H **137**
Gilsland Av. NE28: W'snd 4D **60**
Gilsland Gro. NE23: Cra 6B **16**
Gilsland St. SR4: Sund 1A **118**
Gilwell Way NE3: Gos 4D **42**

Gilwood Ct. DH4: Pen 3E **129**
Gingler La. NE40: G'sde 1A **78**
Girtin Rd. NE34: S Shi 1F **89**
Girton Cl. SR8: Pet 2B **164**
Girvan Cl. DH9: Stly 3F **123**
Girven Ter. DH5: Eas L 4E **149**
Girven Ter. W. DH5: Eas L 4D **148**
Gisburn Ct. NE23: Cra 6B **16**
Gishford Way NE5: Newc T 5F **55**
Givens St. SR6: Monk 3E **105**
Gladeley Way NE16: Sun 3E **95**
Glade, The NE15: Cha P 5G **53**
  NE32: Jar 2F **87**
Gladstonbury Pl.
  NE12: Longb 1C **58**
Gladstone Av. NE26: Whit B . . .5B **36**
Gladstone M. NE24: Bly 5B **12**
Gladstone Pl.
  NE2: Newc T 2G **69** (1F **5**)
Gladstone St. DH4: Hou S 3F **137**
  DH9: Beam 2H **123**
  DH9: Stly 4B **122**
  NE15: Lem 3A **66**
  NE24: Bly 5B **12**
  NE28: W'snd 6F **61**
  NE31: Heb 3E **73**
  SR6: Monk 4D **104**
Gladstone Ter. DH3: Bir 3B **112**
  DH4: Pen 1D **128**
  NE2: Newc T 2G **69** (1F **5**)
  NE8: Gate 2H **83**
  NE22: Bed 5A **10**
  NE26: Whit B 1D **48**
  NE35: Bol C 1A **88**
  NE37: Usw 5D **100**
Gladstone Ter. W. NE8: Gate . .2G **83**
Gladstone Vs.
  DH1: Dur 1D **160** (6C **6**)
Gladwyn Rd. SR4: Sund 5D **116**
Gladwyn Sq. SR4: Sund 5D **116**
Glaholm Rd. SR1: Sund 1F **119**
Glaisdale Ct. NE34: S Shi 5C **74**
Glaisdale Dr. SR6: Monk 5E **91**
Glaisdale Rd. NE7: Longb 2A **58**
Glamis Av. NE3: Gos 3E **43**
  SR4: Sund 3E **117**
Glamis Ct. DH4: Hou S 2B **136**
  NE34: S Shi 6H **75**
Glamis Cres. NE39: Row G 1G **93**
Glamis Ter. NE16: Sun 4E **95**
Glamis Vs. DH3: Bir 1C **112**
Glanmore Rd. SR4: Sund 4D **116**
Glantlees NE5: Newc T 5E **55**
Glanton Av. NE25: Sea D 6A **24**
Glanton Cl. DH2: Ches S 1A **134**
  NE6: Newc T 5C **70**
  NE10: Gate 4A **86**
  NE28: W'snd 4C **60**
Glanton Ct. NE11: Dun 2C **82**
Glanton Rd. NE29: N Shi 6H **47**
Glanton Sq. SR4: Sund 4E **117**
Glanton Ter. SR8: Pet 1H **165**
Glanton Wynd NE3: Gos 6D **42**
Glanville Cl. NE11: Gate 4D **82**
Glanville Rd. SR3: E Her 4F **131**
Glasbury Av. SR4: Sund 3E **117**
Glasgow Rd. NE32: Jar 5A **74**
Glassey Ter. NE22: Bed 4D **10**
Glasshouse Bri. NE1: Newc T . .4A **70**
  NE6: Newc T 4A **70**
Glasshouse St. NE6: Newc T . . .5C **70**
Glastonbury NE38: Wash 3B **114**
Glastonbury Gro. NE2: Newc T . .5H **57**

Glaston Ho. NE24: Cow 5H **11**
Glazebury Way NE23: Cra 6B **16**
Gleaston Ct. SR8: Pet 4B **164**
GLEBE 2B **114**
Glebe Av. NE12: Longb 6D **44**
  NE16: Whi 4F **81**
  SR8: Eas 1D **162**
Glebe Cen. NE38: Wash 2B **114**
Glebe Cl. NE5: Cha P 4B **54**
  NE20: Pon 4E **27**
Glebe Ct. NE22: Bed 4H **9**
Glebe Cres. NE12: Longb 4D **44**
  NE38: Wash 1C **114**
  SR8: Eas 1D **162**
Glebe Dr. SR7: S'hm 1F **141**
Glebe Est. SR7: S'hm 1F **141**
Glebe M. NE22: Bed 4H **9**
Glebe Mt. NE38: Wash 1C **114**
Glebe Ri. NE16: Whi 4E **81**
Glebe Rd. NE12: Longb 4D **44**
  NE22: Bed 4H **9**
Glebeside DH5: Hett H 6C **138**
Glebe Ter. DH4: Hou S 2H **137**
  NE11: Dun 3B **82**
  NE12: Longb 4D **44**
  NE62: Sco G 1G **9**
  SR8: Eas 1C **162**
  (not continuous)
Glebe Vw. SR7: Mur 1E **151**
  (not continuous)
Glebe Vs. NE12: Longb 4C **44**
Glebe Wlk. NE16: Whi 4F **81**
Glenallen Gdns. NE30: N Shi . . .4E **49**
Glenamara Ho. NE2: Newc T 2F **5**
Glenavon Av. DH2: Ches S 5B **126**
Glen Barr DH2: Ches S 5B **126**
Glenbrooke Ter. NE9: Gate 1H **97**
Glenburn Cl. NE38: Wash 4F **113**
Glencarron Cl. NE38: Wash 4G **113**
Glen Cl. NE39: Row G 2E **93**
Glencoe NE12: Kil 1D **44**
Glencoe Av. DH2: Ches S 5B **126**
  NE23: Cra 6B **22**
Glencoe Ri. NE39: Row G 4C **92**
Glencoe Rd. SR4: Sund 5D **116**
Glencoe Sq. SR4: Sund 4D **116**
Glencoe Ter. NE39: Row G 4C **92**
Glencot Gro. SR7: Eas 6G **151**
Glencourse NE36: E Bol 4G **89**
Glen Ct. NE31: Heb 3B **72**
Glendale Av. NE3: Gos 3C **56**
  NE16: Whi 5E **81**
  NE24: Cow 5E **11**
  NE26: Whit B 4C **36**
  NE28: W'snd 3H **59**
  NE29: N Shi 1A **62**
  NE37: Usw 5A **100**
Glendale Cl. NE5: Cha P 4B **54**
  NE21: Bla T 3F **79**
  SR3: E Her 3E **131**
Glendale Gdns. NE9: Gate 6B **84**
Glendale Gro. NE29: N Shi 1B **62**
Glendale Rd. NE27: Shir 2E **47**
Glendale Ter. NE6: Newc T 3C **70**
Glendford Pl. NE24: News 3B **18**
Glendower Av. NE29: N Shi 1H **61**
Glendyn Cl. NE7: Newc T 6A **58**
Gleneagle Cl. NE5: Cha P 4B **54**
Gleneagles NE25: Whit B 6H **35**
  NE33: S Shi 6H **63**
Gleneagles Cl. NE7: Newc T . . .2C **58**
Gleneagles Ct. NE25: Whit B . . .6H **35**
Gleneagles Dr. NE37: Usw 3H **99**

Gleneagles Rd. NE9: Gate 2G **97**
  SR4: Sund 5D **116**
Gleneagles Sq. SR4: Sund 5D **116**
Glenesk Gdns. SR2: Sund 5C **118**
Glenesk Rd. SR2: Sund 4C **118**
Glenfield Av. NE23: Cra 6B **16**
Glenfield Rd. NE12: Longb 6C **44**
  (Hailsham Av.)
  NE12: Longb 6B **44**
  (Ongar Way)
Glengarvan Cl. NE38: Wash 4G **113**
Glenholme Cl. NE38: Wash 4F **113**
Glenhurst Cotts. SR8: Eas 1D **162**
Glenhurst Dr. NE5: Cha P 4B **54**
  NE16: Whi 1D **94**
Glenhurst Gro. NE34: S Shi 3H **75**
Glenhurst Rd. SR8: Eas 1D **162**
Glenhurst Ter. SR7: Mur 2D **150**
Glenkerry Cl. NE38: Wash 4G **113**
Glenleigh Dr. SR4: Sund 3E **117**
Glenluce DH3: Bir 4E **113**
  (not continuous)
Glenluce Ct. NE23: Cra 5B **22**
Glen Luce Dr. SR2: Sund 5F **119**
Glenluce Dr. NE23: Cra 6A **22**
Glenmoor NE31: Heb 2B **72**
Glenmore Av. DH2: Ches S 5C **126**
Glenmuir Av. NE23: Cra 6A **22**
Glenorrin Cl. NE38: Wash 4G **113**
Glen Path SR2: Sund 4D **118**
Glenridge Av. NE6: Newc T 6B **58**
Glenroy Gdns. DH2: Ches S . . .5B **126**
Glens Flats DH6: H Pitt 2F **157**
Glenshiel Cl. NE38: Wash 4G **113**
Glenside NE32: Jar 1G **87**
Glenside Cl. NE9: Gate 1G **97**
Glenside Ter. DH2: Pelt 5H **125**
Glen St. NE31: Heb 4B **72**
Glen Ter. DH2: Ches S 5A **126**
  *DH4: Pen 1F **129***
  (off Rainton St.)
  NE38: Wash 3C **114**
Glen, The SR2: Sund 4D **118**
Glenthorne Rd. SR6: Monk 3E **105**
Glenthorn Rd. NE2: Newc T 5G **57**
Glen Thorpe Av. SR6: Monk . . .3E **105**
Glenthorpe Ho. NE33: S Shi 6F **63**
Glenwood Vs. NE5: Cha P 4B **54**
Gloria Av. NE25: Sea D 3B **24**
Glossop St. NE39: H Spen 1A **92**
Gloucester Av. SR6: Monk 1E **105**
Gloucester Ct. NE3: Ken 5G **41**
Gloucester Pl. NE34: S Shi 4A **76**
  SR8: Pet 6B **162**
Gloucester Rd. NE4: Newc T . . .4C **68**
  NE29: N Shi 6F **47**
Gloucestershire Dr. DH1: Carr . .4A **156**
Gloucester St. NE25: Sea D 4B **24**
Gloucester Ter. NE4: Newc T . . .5C **68**
Gloucester Way NE4: Newc T . . .5D **68**
  NE32: Jar 2F **87**
Glover Ind. Est. NE37: Wash . . .6C **100**
Glover Network Cen.
  NE37: Wash 6E **101**
Glover Rd. NE37: Usw 5D **100**
  SR4: Sund 5D **116**
Glover Sq. SR4: Sund 5D **116**
Glue Gth. DH1: Dur 5F **155**
Glynfellis NE10: Gate 6F **85**
Glynfellis Ct. NE10: Gate 6F **85**
Glynwood Cl. NE23: Cra 6B **16**
Glynwood Gdns. NE9: Gate 6A **84**

Goalmouth Cl. SR6: Monk 3E **105**
Goatbeck Ter. DH7: B'don 4F **159**
Goathland Av. NE12: Longb 1B **58**
Goathland Dr. SR3: New S 2B **132**
Godfrey Rd. SR4: Sund 4D **116**
Gofton Wlk. NE5: Newc T 5E **55**
Goldcrest Rd. NE38: Wash 4F **113**
Goldcrest Way NE15: Lem 4A **66**
Goldfinch Cl. NE4: Newc T 6B **68**
Goldlynn Dr. SR3: New S 3G **133**
Goldsbrough Ct. NE2: Newc T 2E **69**
Goldsmith Rd. SR4: Sund 5D **116**
Goldspink La. NE2: Newc T 2H **69**
Goldstone NE9: Gate 1H **97**
Goldstone Ct. NE12: Kil 1E **45**
Goldthorpe Cl. NE23: Cra 6B **16**
Golf Course Rd. DH4: Hou S 5D **128**
Gompertz Gdns. NE33: S Shi 1D **74**
Goodrich Cl. DH4: Hou S 4G **129**
Good St. DH9: Stly 1C **122**
Goodwood NE12: Kil 2E **45**
Goodwood Av. NE8: Gate 3E **83**
Goodwood Cl. NE5: Cha P 4A **54**
Goodwood Rd. SR4: Sund 4C **116**
Goodwood Sq. SR4: Sund 4C **116**
Goodyear Cres. DH1: Dur 6G **155**
Goole Rd. SR4: Sund 4E **117**
Gordon Av. NE3: Gos 3E **57**
   SR5: C'twn 5C **102**
   SR8: Pet 6F **163**
Gordon Ct. NE10: Gate 2D **84**
   (off Church Pl.)
Gordon Dr. NE36: E Bol 4F **89**
Gordon Ho. NF6· Newc T 4B **70**
   (off Dalton St.)
Gordon Rd. NE6: Newc T 4B **70**
   NE24: Bly 2D **18**
   NE34: S Shi 3E **75**
   SR4: Sund 5D **116**
Gordon Sq. NE6: Newc T 4B **70**
   NE26: Whit B 1E **49**
Gordon St. NE33: S Shi 1E **75**
Gordon Ter. DH4: Pen 1G **129**
   DH9: Stly 1D **122**
   NE22: Bed 5A **10**
   NE26: Whit B 6E **37**
   SR2: Ryh 3G **133**
   SR5: S'wck 3A **104**
Gorleston Way SR3: New S 5A **132**
Gorse Av. NE34: S Shi 4H **75**
Gorsedale Gro. DH1: Carr 4B **156**
Gorsedene Av. NE26: Whit B 2B **36**
Gorsedene Rd. NE26: Whit B 2A **36**
Gorsehill NE9: Gate 6C **84**
Gorse Hill Way NE5: Newc T 4G **55**
Gorse Rd. SR2: Sund 2D **118**
Gort Pl. DH1: Dur 4F **155**
Goschen St. NE8: Gate 3F **83**
   NE24: Bly 5B **12**
   (not continuous)
   SR5: S'wck 3A **104**
GOSFORTH 3E **57**
Gosforth Av. NE34: S Shi 5E **75**
Gosforth Bowling Club 3E **57**
Gosforth Bus. Pk. NE12: Longb . .6H **43**
Gosforth Cen., The NE3: Gos 3E **57**
Gosforth Ind. Est. NE3: Gos 2G **57**
Gosforth Pk. Vs. NE13: Wide O . . .1E **43**
Gosforth Pk. Way NE12: Longb . .6H **43**
Gosforth St.
   NE2: Newc T 3H **69** (2G **5**)
   (not continuous)
   NE10: Gate 2D **84**

Gosforth Swimming Pool 1E **57**
Gosforth Ter. NE3: Gos 2G **57**
   NE10: Gate 2F **85**
Gosport Way NE24: News 3B **18**
Gossington NE38: Wash 2E **115**
Goswick Av. NE7: Newc T 5B **58**
Goswick Dr. NE3: Ken 5B **42**
Gouch Av. NE22: Bed 1A **10**
Goundry Av. SR2: Ryh 3G **133**
Gourock Sq. SR4: Sund 4C **116**
Gowanburn NE23: Cra 6A **22**
Gowan Ter. NE2: Newc T 6H **57**
Gower Rd. SR5: S'wck 3A **104**
Gower St. NE6: Walk 5G **71**
Gower Wlk. NE8: Gate 3C **84**
Gowland Av. NE4: Newc T 3A **68**
   (not continuous)
Gowland Sq. SR7: Mur 2B **150**
Grace Ct. DH9: Ann P 6E **121**
Gracefield Cl. NE5: Cha P 4B **54**
Grace Gdns. NE28: W'snd 3G **59**
Grace Ho. NE29: N Shi 4A **62**
Grace St. NE6: Newc T 3C **70**
   (not continuous)
   NE11: Dun 3B **82**
Gradys Yd. NE15: Thro 4D **52**
Grafton Cl. NE6: Newc T 3B **70**
Grafton Ho. NE6: Newc T 3B **70**
Grafton Pl. NE6: Newc T 3B **70**
Grafton Rd. NE26: Whit B 1E **49**
Grafton St. NE6: Newc T 3B **70**
   SR4: Sund 6B **104**
Gragareth Way NE37: Wash 1G **113**
Graham Av. NE16: Whi 3F **81**
Graham Pk. Rd. NE3: Gos 4E **57**
Graham Rd. NE31: Heb 4B **72**
Grahamsley St. NE8: Gate 1H **83**
Graham St. NE33: S Shi 5F **63**
Graham Ter. DH6: H Pitt 2F **157**
   SR7: Mur 2D **150**
Graham Way, The
   SR7: Mur, S'hm 5F **141**
Grainger Arc.
   NE1: Newc T 4F **69** (4C **4**)
Grainger Mkt
   NE1: Newc T 4F **69** (4C **4**)
Grainger Pk. Rd.
   NE4: Newc T 5B **68**
Grainger St.
   NE1: Newc T 5F **69** (6C **4**)
Graingerville Nth. NE4: Newc T . . .4C **68**
   (off Westgate Rd.)
Graingerville Sth. NE4: Newc T . . .4C **68**
   (off Westgate Rd.)
Grampian Av. DH2: Ches S 1B **134**
   (not continuous)
Grampian Cl. NE29: N Shi 4B **48**
Grampian Ct. DH9: Ann P 6E **121**
Grampian Dr. SR8: Pet 2B **164**
Grampian Gdns. NE11: Gate 5D **82**
Grampian Gro. NE36: W Bol 4D **88**
Grampian Pl. NE12: Longb 4B **44**
Granaries, The NE39: H Spen . . .1A **92**
Granary, The DH4: Hou S 3F **137**
Granby Cl. NE16: Sun 2F **95**
   SR3: Sund 4B **118**
Granby Ter. NE16: Sun 3F **95**
Grand Pde. NE30: N Shi 3E **49**
Grandstand Rd.
   NE2: Gos, Newc T 6C **56**
   NE4: Newc T 1B **68**
   NE5: Gos, Newc T 6C **56**

Grange Av. DH4: Hou S 2E **137**
   NE12: Longb 1E **59**
   NE22: Bed 2E **11**
   NE27: Shir 1D **46**
   SR8: Eas 2B **162**
Grange Cl. NE24: News 3B **18**
   NE25: Whit B 1H **47**
   NE28: W'snd 5A **60**
   NE30: N Shi 3D **48**
   SR8: Pet 5C **162**
Grange Ct. DH2: Pelt 4D **124**
   NE10: Gate 3G **85**
   NE32: Jar 2F **73**
   NE40: Ryton 5C **64**
Grange Cres. NE10: Gate 4G **85**
   NE40: Ryton 5C **64**
   SR2: Sund 2D **118** (6G **7**)
Grange Dr. NE40: Ryton 5C **64**
Grange Est. NE11: Kib 1E **111**
Grange Farm DH1: H Shin 5H **161**
Grange Farm Dr. NE16: Whi 6E **81**
Grange La. NE16: Whi 6E **81**
Grange Lonnen
   NE40: Ryton 4B **64**
Grange Mnr. NE16: Whi 6F **81**
Grangemere Cl. SR2: Sund 6E **119**
Grange Nook NE16: Whi 6E **81**
GRANGE PARK 2E **11**
Grange Pk. NE25: Whit B 2G **47**
Grange Pk. Av. NE22: Bed 2D **10**
   SR5: S'wck 2C **104**
Grange Pl. NE32: Jar 2F **73**
Grange Rd. DH1: Carr 3A **156**
   DH9: Stly 3B **122**
   NE3: Gos 6E **43**
   NE4: Newc T 3G **67**
   NE10: Gate 4G **85**
   NE15: Thro 1E **65**
   NE20: Pon 4F **27**
   NE32: Jar 2F **73**
   (not continuous)
   NE40: Ryton 4C **64**
   SR5: C'twn 5C **102**
Grange Rd. W. NE32: Jar 2E **73**
Grange St. DH2: Pelt 2G **125**
Grange St. Sth. SR2: Sund 5F **119**
Grange Ter. DH2: Pelt 5F **125**
   NE9: Gate 3A **84**
   NE11: Kib 1E **111**
   NE36: E Bol 4F **89**
   SR2: Sund 2C **118** (6F **7**)
   SR5: S'wck 3B **104**
Grange, The DH9: Tan L 1A **122**
   NE22: H Bri 6C **8**
   NE25: Whit B 1G **47**
   NE36: E Bol 4F **89**
GRANGETOWN 5F **119**
Grange Vw. DH4: Hou S 6H **129**
   DH5: W Rai 6H **137**
   NE40: Ryton 5C **64**
   SR5: S'wck 2C **104**
GRANGE VILLA 4C **124**
Grange Villa Rd. DH2: Pelt 4D **124**
Grange Vs. NE28: W'snd 5A **60**
Grange Wlk. NE16: Whi 6E **81**
Grangeway NE29: N Shi 4B **48**
Grangewood Cl. DH4: Hou S 4E **129**
Grangewood Ct. DH4: Hou S 3E **129**
Grantham Av. SR7: S'hm 5H **141**
   (not continuous)
Grantham Dr. NE9: Gate 1G **97**
Grantham Pl. NE23: Cra 5A **22**
   (not continuous)

Grantham Rd.
NE2: Newc T 2H **69** (1G **5**)
SR6: Monk 3E **105**
Grantham St. NE24: Bly 1D **18**
Grants Cres. SR7: S'hm 4A **142**
Grant St. NE32: Jar 2E **73**
SR8: Pet 6G **163**
Granville Av. DH9: Ann P 5F **121**
NE12: Longb 4E **45**
NE26: Sea S 4H **25**
Granville Ct. NE2: Newc T 1H **69**
Granville Cres. NE12: Longb . . .6E **45**
Granville Dr. DH4: Hou S 4G **129**
NE5: Cha P 4B **54**
NE12: Longb 6E **45**
Granville Gdns. NE2: Newc T 1A **70**
Granville Lodge NE12: Longb . . .5E **45**
Granville Rd. NE2: Newc T 1H **69**
NE3: Gos 6F **43**
SR8: Pet 2F **165**
Granville St. NE8: Gate 2H **83**
SR4: Sund 6B **104**
Grape La. DH1: Dur 6C **154** (3A **6**)
(not continuous)
Grasmere DH3: Bir 5E **113**
SR6: Cle 2A **90**
Grasmere Av. DH5: Eas L 5E **149**
NE6: Walk 4E **71**
NE10: Gate 3F **85**
NE15: Thro 2E **65**
NE32: Jar 6H **73**
Grasmere Ct. NE12: Kil 2C **44**
NE15: Thro 2E **65**
Grasmere Cres. DH4: Hou S . . .3F **129**
NE21: Bla T 3H **79**
NE26: Whit B 4B **36**
SR5: Monk 2C **104**
Grasmere Gdns. NE34: S Shi 3G **75**
NE38: Wash 3C **114**
Grasmere Ho. NE6: Walk 4E **71**
Grasmere Pl. NE3: Gos 6E **43**
Grasmere Rd. DH2: Ches S . . .2B **134**
NE16: Whi 4G **81**
NE28: W'snd 6G **59**
NE31: Heb 4D **72**
SR8: Pet 6E **163**
Grasmere St. NE8: Gate 2G **83**
Grasmere St. W. NE8: Gate 2G **83**
Grasmere Ter. DH6: S Het 6B **150**
DH9: Stly 5B **122**
NE38: Wash 3C **114**
SR7: Mur 3D **150**
Grasmere Way NE24: Cow 5G **11**
Grasmoor Pl. NE15: Lem 2H **65**
Grassbanks NE10: Gate 5H **85**
Grassdale DH1: Carr 4B **156**
Grassholm Mdws.
SR3: Sund 5B **118**
Grassholm Pl. NE12: Longb 6A **44**
Grassington Dr. NE23: Cra 5A **22**
Grasslees NE38: Wash 1F **127**
GRASSWELL 1H **137**
Grasswell Cvn. Pk.
DH4: Hou S 1H **137**
Grasswell Dr. NE5: Newc T 4H **55**
Grasswell Ter. DH4: Hou S 1H **137**
Gravel Walks DH5: Hou S 2A **138**
Gravesend Rd. SR4: Sund 5D **116**
Gravesend Sq. SR4: Sund 5E **117**
Gray Av. DH1: Dur 2B **154**
DH2: Ches S 1B **134**
DH6: Sher 5D **156**
NE13: Wide O 4E **31**

Gray Av. SR7: Mur 2C **150**
TS27: Hes 6F **165**
Gray Ct. SR2: Sund 3D **118**
SR8: Eas 1D **162**
Graylands NE38: Wash 1E **127**
Grayling Ct. SR3: E Her 4E **131**
Grayling Rd. NE11: Gate 4D **82**
Gray Rd. SR2: Sund 3D **118**
Grays Cross SR1: Sund 6E **105**
(off High St. E.)
Grays Ter. DH1: Dur 6A **154**
NE35: Bol C 2A **88**
Graystones NE10: Gate 4H **85**
Gray St. NE24: Bly 4C **12**
NE32: Jar 2G **73**
Gray's Wlk. NE34: S Shi 1C **88**
Gray Ter. DH9: Ann P 4A **122**
Graythwaite DH2: Ches S 6H **125**
GREAT EPPLETON 6F **139**
Greathead St. NE33: S Shi 2D **74**
Gt. Lime Rd.
NE12: Dud, Gos, Kil, Longb . . .2A **44**
(not continuous)
GREAT LUMLEY 4H **135**
Gt. North Rd. DH1: Dur 1A **154**
NE2: Gos, Newc T 4F **57**
NE3: Gos 4E **43**
NE13: Wide O 5E **31**
Great Pk. NE13: Wide O 2C **42**
Grebe Cl. NE11: Dun 1C **82**
NE24: News 2C **18**
Grebe Ct. NE2: Newc T 6H **57**
Greely Rd. NE5: Newc T 5D **54**
Greenacre Pk. NE9: Gate 2H **97**
Greenacres DH2: Pelt 2F **125**
NE20: Pon 3C **38**
Greenacres Cl. NE40: Ryton 6A **64**
Green Av. DH4: Hou S 5H **129**
Greenbank NE21: Bla T 1A **80**
NE32: Jar 2F **73**
Greenbank Dr. SR4: Sund 2C **116**
Greenbank St. DH3: Ches S 5D **126**
Greenbank Ter. DH3: Ches S 5C **126**
Greenbourne Gdns. NE10: Gate . . .4C **84**
Green Cl. NE25: Whit B 1H **47**
NE30: N Shi 4D **48**
Green Ct. DH1: Dur 5F **155**
Green Cres. NE23: Dud 3G **31**
GREENCROFT 6E **121**
Greencroft DH6: S Het 6A **150**
Greencroft Av. NE6: Walk 1G **71**
Greencroft Ind. Pk.
DH9: Ann P 6E **121**
Greencroft Parkway
DH9: Ann P 6F **121**
Greencroft School Sports Cen.
. . . . .5E **121**
Greencroft Ter. DH9: Ann P 6D **120**
Greendale Cl. NE24: Cow 5G **11**
Greendale Gdns. DH5: Hett H . . .3B **148**
Green Dr. SR7: S'hm 6B **142**
Greendyke Ct. NE5: Newc T 2E **55**
Greenesfield Bus. Cen.
NE8: Gate 6G **69**
Greenfield Av. NE5: Newc T 5E **55**
Green Fld. Pl.
NE4: Newc T 4E **69** (5A **4**)
Greenfield Pl. NE40: Ryton 4C **64**
Greenfield Rd. NE3: Gos 3D **42**
Green Flds. NE40: Ryton 4B **64**
Greenfields DH2: Ous 5A **112**
Greenfield Ter. DH9: Ann P 5F **121**
NE10: Gate 2F **85**

Greenfinch Cl. NE38: Wash 4F **113**
Greenford NE11: Kib 1F **111**
Greenford La. DH2: Bir, Kib 1H **111**
NE11: Kib 5G **97**
Greenford Rd. NE6: Walk 6F **71**
Green Gro. NE40: G'sde 6B **64**
Greenhall Vw. NE5: Newc T 5A **56**
Greenhaugh NE12: Longb 4B **44**
Greenhaugh Rd. NE25: Well 6F **35**
Greenhead NE38: Wash 3F **113**
Greenhill SR7: Mur 2D **150**
Greenhills DH9: Stly 6C **122**
NE12: Kil 6C **32**
Greenhill Vw. NE5: Newc T 5A **56**
Grn. Hill Wlk. NE34: S Shi 3C **76**
Greenholme Cl. NE23: Cra 6B **16**
Greenhow Cl. SR2: Ryh 4F **133**
Greenlands DH9: Stly 5B **122**
NE32: Jar 1G **87**
Greenlands Ct. NE25: Sea D 5B **24**
Green La. DH1: Dur 5F **155**
(McNally Pl., not continuous)
DH1: Dur 6E **155**
(Old Elvet)
DH1: Sher 6C **156**
NE10: Gate 1D **84**
(Bath Rd.)
NE10: Gate 2G **85**
(Shields Rd.)
NE10: Gate 2C **84**
(Sunderland Rd.)
NE12: Kil 1E **45**
(not continuous)
NE13: Wool 5D **40**
NE23: Dud 3H **31**
NE34: S Shi 5C **74**
NE36: E Bol 5F **89**
SR7: Sea 5G **139**
Green La. Gdns. NE10: Gate 1C **84**
Greenlaw NE5: Newc T 1C **66**
Greenlaw Rd. NE23: Cra 6A **22**
Greenlea NE29: N Shi 4F **47**
Greenlea Cl. NE39: H Spen 2A **92**
SR4: Sund 4E **117**
Greenlee Dr. NE7: Newc T 4D **58**
Greenmarket
NE1: Newc T 4F **69** (4C **4**)
Greenmount DH4: Hou S 2F **137**
Green Pk. NE28: W'snd 4E **59**
Greenrigg NE21: Bla T 2B **80**
(not continuous)
NE26: Sea S 3G **25**
Greenrigg Gdns. SR3: Sund 4B **118**
Greenriggs Av. NE3: Gos 4F **43**
Green's Bank DH9: Stly 2C **124**
Greenshields Rd. SR4: Sund 5D **116**
Greenshields Sq. SR4: Sund 5D **116**
GREENSIDE 2A **78**
Greenside NE34: S Shi 3B **76**
Greenside Av. NE13: Bru V 5C **30**
NE28: W'snd 4D **60**
SR8: Pet 6F **163**
Greenside Ct. SR3: Sund 5E **117**
Greenside Cres. NE15: Newc T . . .2E **67**
Greenside Rd. NE40: G'sde 1A **78**
Green's Pl. NE33: S Shi 3E **63**
(not continuous)
Green Sq. NE25: Whit B 1H **47**
Green St. SR1: Sund 6D **104** (3G **7**)
SR7: S'hm 4B **142**
Green Ter. SR1: Sund 1C **118** (4F **7**)
Green, The DH1: H Shin 5H **161**
DH2: Ches S 6B **126**

Green, The DH5: Hou S 2B **138**
NE3: Ken 4B **56**
NE10: Gate 3E **85**
NE15: Thro 6F **53**
NE20: Pon 3F **27**
NE25: Whit B 5A **36**
NE28: W'snd 5H **59**
NE38: Wash 1C **114**
NE39: Row G 3C **92**
SR5: S'wck 4A **104**
SR7: Eas 6H **151**
SR8: Pel 3A **164**
Greentree La. DH9: Ann P 4E **121**
Greentree Sq. NE5: Newc T 5F **55**
Green Way NE25: Whit B 1H **47**
Greenway NE4: Newc T 1H **67**
NE5: Cha P 3A **54**
Greenway, The SR4: Sund 3E **117**
Greenwell Cl. NE21: Bla T 2G **79**
Greenwich Pl. NF8: Gate 5A **70**
Greenwood NE12: Kil 2F **45**
Greenwood Av. DH4: Hou S . . .3G **137**
NE6: Walk 6G **59**
NE22: Bed 2D **10**
Greenwood Cl. NE38: Wash . . .4D **114**
Greenwood Gdns. NE10: Gate . .2D **84**
NE11: Gate 6C **82**
Greenwood Rd. SR4: Sund 4D **116**
Greenwood Sq. SR4: Sund 5D **116**
Greetlands Rd. SR2: Sund 5C **118**
Gregory Rd. SR4: Sund 5D **116**
Gregory Ter. DH4: Hou S 2E **137**
Gregson St. NE15: Newc T 5E **67**
Gregson Ter. SR7: S'hm 2F **141**
Grenada Cl. NE26: Whit B 3B **36**
Grenada Dr. NE26: Whit B 3B **36**
Grenada Pl. NE26: Whit B 3B **36**
Grenfell Sq. SR4: Sund 5D **116**
Grenville Ct. NE20: Pon 1A **38**
NE23: Cra 4A **22**
Grenville Dr. NE3: Gos 4D **42**
Grenville Ter.
NE1: Newc T 4H **69** (4G **5**)
Grenville Way NE26: Whit B 4A **36**
Gresford St. NE33: S Shi 3E **75**
Gresham Cl. NE23: Cra 5D **22**
Greta Av. DH4: Pen 3E **129**
Greta Gdns. NE33: S Shi 1F **75**
Greta St. Nth. DH2: Pelt 3E **125**
Greta St. Sth. DH2: Pelt 3E **125**
Greta Ter. SR4: Sund 2A **118**
Gretna Dr. NE32: Jar 1B **88**
Gretna Rd. NE15: Newc T 2F **67**
Gretna Ter. NE10: Gate 3C **84**
Gretton Pl. NE7: Newc T 4A **58**
Grey Av. NE23: Cra 6A **22**
Greybourne Gdns. SR2: Sund . . .5C **118**
Greyfriars La. NE12: Longb 1A **58**
Grey Gables DH7: B'don 5E **159**
Greylingstadt Ter. DH9: Stly 6E **123**
Grey Ridges DH7: B'don 5E **159**
Grey's Ct. NE1: Newc T . . .4F **69** (5D **4**)
Greystead Cl. NE5: Cha P 4B **54**
Greystead Rd. NE5: Well 6F **35**
Greystoke Av. NE2: Newc T 2A **70**
NE16: Whi 5F **81**
SR2: Sund 5C **118**
Greystoke Gdns. NE2: Newc T . . .1A **70**
NE9: Gate 3B **98**
NE16: Whi 6F **81**
SR2: Sund 4C **118**
Greystoke Pk. NE3: Gos 5D **42**

Greystoke Pl. NE23: Cra 6A **22**
(not continuous)
Greystoke Wlk. NE16: Whi 6E **81**
Greystone Pl. SR5: S'wck 3A **104**
Grey St. DH4: Hou S 2H **137**
NE1: Newc T 4F **69** (4D **4**)
NE13: Bru V 5C **30**
NE28: W'snd 5A **60**
NE30: N Shi 1D **62**
Grey Ter. SR2: Ryh 3F **133**
Greywood Av. NE4: Newc T 2A **68**
Grieves Bldgs. DH4: Hou S 3G **129**
Grieves' Row NE23: Dud 2A **32**
Grieve's Stairs NE29: N Shi 2D **62**
(off Bedford St.)
Grieve St. NE24: Bly 4B **12**
Griffith Ter. NE27: Shir 4B **46**
Grimsby St. NE24: Bly 1C **18**
Grindleford Ct. NE34: S Shi 4G **75**
GRINDON 4D **116**
Grindon Av. SR4: Sund 2D **116**
Grindon Cl. NE23: Cra 6A **22**
NE25: Whit B 3A **48**
Grindon Ct. SR4: Sund 4E **117**
Grindon Gdns. SR4: Sund 4E **117**
Grindon La. SR3: Sund 4E **117**
SR4: Sund 4E **117**
(Glenleigh Dr.)
SR4: Sund 4E **117**
(Rowan Cl.)
Grindon Pk. SR4: Sund 4E **117**
Grindon Ter. SR4: Sund 2A **118**
Grinstead Cl. NE34: S Shi 2H **75**
Grinstead Way DH1: Carr 2B **156**
Grisedale Gdns. NE9: Gate 1A **98**
Grisedale Rd. SR8: Pet 1E **165**
Grizedale NE37: Wash 1H **113**
Grizedale Cl. SR6: Monk 5C **90**
Groat Mkt. NE1: Newc T 4F **69** (5D **4**)
Grosmont DH3: Gt Lum 3G **135**
Grosvenor Av. NE2: Newc T 6H **57**
NE16: Swa 3F **81**
Grosvenor Cl. NE23: Cra 6A **22**
Grosvenor Ct. NE5: Cha P 4B **54**
Grosvenor Cres. NE31: Heb 5D **72**
Grosvenor Dr. NE26: Whit B 1C **48**
NE34: S Shi 1H **75**
SR6: Cle 2G **89**
Grosvenor Gdns. NE2: Newc T . . .1A **70**
NE28: W'snd 4F **61**
NE34: S Shi 3H **75**
Grosvenor M. NE29: N Shi 1C **62**
NE33: S Shi 1G **75**
Grosvenor Pl. NE2: Newc T 6G **57**
NE24: Cow 1F **17**
NE29: N Shi 1C **62**
Grosvenor Rd. NE2: Newc T 6H **57**
NE33: S Shi 1G **75**
Grosvenor St. SR5: S'wck 3H **103**
Grosvenor Vs. NE2: Newc T 6H **57**
Grosvenor Way NE5: Cha P 5B **54**
Grotto Gdns. NE34: S Shi 4D **76**
Grotto Rd. NE34: S Shi 3D **76**
Grousemoor NE37: Wash 6G **99**
Grove Av. NE3: Gos 3F **57**
Grove Cotts. DH3: Bir 3C **112**
NE40: Ryton 5A **64**
Grove Ho. Dr. DH1: Dur 5E **155**
Grove Rd. DH7: B'don 6C **158**
NE9: Gate 5A **84**
NE15: Thro 6F **53**
Grove Rd. Shop. Units
DH7: B'don 6D **158**

Grove St. DH1: Dur 6B **154** (4A **6**)
Grove Ter. DH7: B'don 3G **159**
NE16: Burn 1H **107**
Grove, The DH1: Dur 4A **154**
DH5: Hou S 5H **137**
NE2: Newc T 5H **57**
(not continuous)
NE3: Gos 3E **57**
NE5: Newc T 6B **54**
NE12: Longb 1D **58**
NE16: Whi 5G **81**
NE20: Pon 6D **26**
NE25: Whit B 1B **48**
NE32: Jar 2F **87**
NE39: Row G 4F **93**
SR2: Ryh 3F **133**
SR2: Sund 3D **118**
SR5: C'twn 4D **102**
SR8: Eas 1A **162**
Guardians Ct. NE20: Pon 4F **27**
Guelder Rd. NE7: Newc T 4C **58**
Guernsey Rd. SR4: Sund 5D **116**
Guernsey Sq. SR4: Sund 5D **116**
Guildford Pl. NE6: Newc T 2B **70**
Guildford St. SR2: Sund 3E **119**
Guillemot Cl. NE24: News 2C **18**
Guillemot Row NE12: Kil 1C **44**
Guisborough Dr. NE29: N Shi 5F **47**
Guisborough St. SR4: Sund 2H **117**
Gulbenkian Studio Theatre 2D **4**
Gullane NE37: Usw 2B **100**
Gullane Cl. DH9: Stly 3F **123**
NE10: Gate 1A **86**
Gunnerston Gro. NE3: Ken 2H **55**
Gunnerton Cl. NE23: Cra 6B **22**
Gunnerton Pl. NE29: N Shi 1H **61**
Gunn St. NE11: Dun 3B **82**
Gut Rd. NE28: W'snd 5D **60**
Guyzance Av. NE3: Gos 1C **56**
Gypsies Green Sports Ground . . .5H **63**

H

Habgood Dr. DH1: Dur 6G **155**
Hackworth Rd. SR8: Eas, Pet 4A **162**
Hackworth Way NE29: N Shi 4B **62**
Haddington Rd. NE25: Whit B 4G **35**
Haddon Cl. NE25: Whit B 6F **35**
Haddon Grn. NE25: Well 6F **35**
Haddon Rd. SR2: Sund 5F **119**
Haddricksmill Ct. NE3: Gos 3G **57**
Haddricks Mill Rd. NE3: Gos 3G **57**
Hadleigh Ct. DH4: Hou S 3F **129**
Hadleigh Rd. SR4: Sund 2F **117**
Hadrian Av. DH3: Ches S 4D **126**
Hadrian Ct. NE12: Kil 2E **45**
NE15: Lem 1C **66**
NE20: Pon 4B **38**
Hadrian Gdns. NE21: Bla T 2B **80**
Hadrian Ho. NE15: Thro 5D **52**
Hadrian Lodge NE34: S Shi 4B **74**
Hadrian Pl. NE9: Gate 4A **84**
NE15: Thro 5D **52**
Hadrian Rd. NE4: Newc T 2H **67**
NE24: News 4A **18**
NE28: W'snd 6A **60**
NE32: Jar 5H **73**
(Finchale Ter.)
NE32: Jar 5H **73**
(Lindisfarne Rd.)
NE32: Jar 5A **74**
(Newcastle Rd.)

Hadrian Road Station (Metro) . . .6C 60
Hadrians Ct. NE11: Gate 1F 97
Hadrian Sq. NE6: Newc T 3C 70
Hadrian St. SR4: Sund 6A 104
Hadstone Pl. NE5: Newc T 6G 55
Hagan Hall NE32: Jar 2G 87
Haggerston Cl. NE5: Newc T 3F 55
Haggerston Ct. NE5: Newc T 3F 55
Haggerston Cres. NE5: Newc T . . .4F 55
Haggerstone Dr. SR5: C'twn 4C 102
Haggerston Ter. NE32: Jar 5A 74
Haggie Av. NE28: W'snd 4B 60
Haggs La. NE11: Kib 5C 96
Hahnemann Ct. SR5: S'wck 3B 104
Haig Av. NE25: Whit B 1A 48
Haig Cres. DH1: Dur 6G 155
NE15: Newc T 4E 67
Haigh Ter. NE9: Spri 4C 98
Haig Rd. NE22: Bed 5B 10
Haig St. NE11: Dun 3B 82
Hailsham Av. NE12: Longb 6C 44
Hailsham Pl. SR8: Pet 1D 164
HAINING 6D 130
Haininghead NE38: Wash 5C 114
Hainingwood Ter. NE10: Gate 1H 85
Haldane Ct. NE2: Newc T 1G 69
Haldane Ter. NE2: Newc T 1G 69
Haldon Pl. SR8: Pet 2B 164
Hale Ri. SR8: Pet 1E 165
Halewood Av. NE3: Ken 3A 56
Half Flds. Rd. NE21: Bla T 2H 79
Half Moon La. NE8: Gate 6G 69
(Hudson St.)
NE8: Gate 6G 69
(Mulgrave Ter.)
NE30: N Shi 6F 49
(off Front St.)
Half Moon Yd. NE1: Newc T 4F 69 (5D 4)
Halidon Rd. SR2: Sund 6D 118
Halidon Sq. SR2: Sund 6D 118
Halifax Pl. NE11: Dun 2A 82
SR2: Ryh 3F 133
Halifax Rd. NE11: Dun 2A 82
Halkirk Way NE23: Cra 6A 16
Hallam Rd. SR8: Pet 6D 162
Hall Av. DH7: Ush M 5B 152
NE4: Newc T 3A 68
Hall Cl. DH4: W Rai 3E 147
SR7: Sea 2D 140
Hall Cres. SR8: Pet 4F 163
Hall Dene Way SR7: Sea 2E 141
Hall Dr. NE12: Kil 6C 32
Halleypike Cl. NE7: Newc T 4D 58
Hall Farm DH1: H Shin 3F 161
Hall Farm Rd. SR3: New S 4H 131
Hallfield Cl. SR3: New S 4A 132
Hallfield Dr. SR8: Eas 2A 162
Hall Gdns. DH6: Sher 6E 157
NE10: Gate 4D 84
NE36: W Bol 4C 88
HALLGARTH 3F 157
Hall Gth. NE3: Gos 5E 43
Hallgarth NE10: Gate 4G 85
(not continuous)
Hallgarth Bungs. DH5: Hett H . . .3C 148
Hallgarth Ct. SR6: Monk 4F 105
Hallgarth Ho. NE33: S Shi 1E 75
Hallgarth La. DH6: H Pitt 3F 157
Hallgarth Rd. NE21: Bla T 1H 79
Hallgarth St. DH1: Dur . . .6D 154 (4C 6)
DH6: Sher 6D 156
Hallgarth, The
DH1: Dur 1D 160 (5D 6)

Hallgarth Vw.
DH1: Dur 1D 160 (5D 6)
DH6: H Pitt 2G 157
Hallgarth Vs. DH6: Sher 6E 157
Hall Grn. NE24: Cow 6H 11
Halliday Gro. DH7: B'don 4F 159
Halling Cl. NE6: Walk 5G 71
Hallington Dr. NE25: Sea D 6B 24
Hallington M. NE12: Kil 2C 44
Halliwell St. DH4: Hou S 2H 137
Hall La. DH1: H Shin 4F 161
DH4: W Rai 3E 147
DH5: Hou S 3A 138
Hallow Dr. NE15: Thro 6C 52
Hall Pk. NE21: Bla T 5G 65
Hall Rd. NE31: Heb 4C 72
NE37: Usw 5C 100
Hallside Rd. NE24: Cow 1H 17
Hall St. DH6: S Het 6H 149
Hall Ter. NE10: Gate 1H 85
NE24: Bly 5C 12
Hall Vw. SR6: Whit 3F 91
Hall Wlk. SR8: Eas 1A 162
Hall Walks SR8: Eas 1A 162
Hallwood Cl. NE22: H Bri 5C 8
Halstead Pl. NE33: S Shi 5F 63
(not continuous)
Halstead Sq. SR4: Sund 2F 117
Halterburn Cl. NE3: Gos 3C 56
Halton Dr. NE13: Wide O 5D 30
NE27: Back 2B 46
Halton Rd. DH1: Dur 2D 154
Halton Way NE3: Gos 4C 42
Hamar Cl. NE29: N Shi 3G 61
Hambard Way NE38: Wash 3B 114
Hambledon Av. DH2: Ches S 1B 134
(not continuous)
NE30: N Shi 2C 48
Hambledon Cl. NE35: Bol C 3A 88
Hambledon Gdns. NE7: Newc T . .4A 58
Hambledon Pl. SR8: Pet 2A 164
Hambledon St. NE24: Bly 5B 12
Hambleton Dr. SR7: S'hm 3H 141
Hambleton Grn. NE9: Gate 4B 98
Hambleton Rd. NE38: Wash 4H 113
Hamilton Ct. NE8: Gate 3A 84
SR6: Monk 3F 105
Hamilton Cres. NE4: Newc T 3D 68
NE29: N Shi 5G 47
Hamilton Dr. NE26: Whit B 3B 36
Hamilton Pl. NE4: Newc T 3D 68
Hamilton St. SR8: Pet 6F 163
Hamilton Ter. *NE36: W Bol 5C 88*
(off Dipe La.)
Hamilton Way NE26: Whit B 3B 36
Hammer Sq. Bank
DH9: Beam 1A 124
Hampden Rd. SR6: Monk 3E 105
Hampden St. NE33: S Shi 1E 75
Hampshire Ct. NE4: Newc T 1C 82
Hampshire Gdns.
NE28: W'snd 3C 60
Hampshire Pl. NE37: Usw 4B 100
SR8: Pet 6B 162
Hampshire Rd. DH1: Carr 4A 156
Hampshire Way NE34: S Shi 2C 76
Hampstead Cl. NE24: News 4A 18
Hampstead Gdns. NE32: Jar 1H 87
Hampstead Rd. NE4: Newc T 4A 68
SR4: Sund 3F 117
Hampstead Sq. SR4: Sund 3E 117
Hampton Cl. DH9: Ann P 5E 121
NE23: Cra 2D 22

Hampton Ct. DH3: Ches S 2D 126
NE16: Swa 2F 81
Hampton Dr. NE10: Gate 3C 84
Hampton Rd. NE30: N Shi 3B 48
Hamsterley Cl. DH3: Gt Lum 4H 135
Hamsterley Ct. SR3: New S 3A 132
Hamsterley Cres. DH1: Dur 1D 154
NE9: Gate 2C 98
NE15: Lem 2H 65
Hamsterley Dr. NE12: Kil 1C 44
Hamsterley Gdns. DH9: Ann P . .5E 121
HAMSTERLEY MILL 2A 106
Hanby Gdns. SR3: Sund 4A 118
Hancock Mus. 2F 69 (1D 4)
Hancock St.
NE2: Newc T 2F 69 (1D 4)
Handel St. NE33: S Shi 5F 63
Handley Cres. DH5: W Rai 1G 147
Handley St. SR8: Pet 6F 163
Handy Dr. NE11: Dun 1H 81
Handyside Pl.
NE1: Newc T 3F 69 (3C 4)
Hangingstone La. DH9: Ann P . . .6B 120
Hangmans La. DH5: Hou S 1G 139
SR3: New S 1G 139
Hanlon Ct. NE32: Jar 1D 72
Hannington Pl. NE6: Newc T 3A 70
Hannington St. NE6: Newc T 3A 70
Hann Ter. NE37: Usw 5D 100
Hanover Cl. NE5: Cha P 5A 54
Hanover Ct. DH1: Dur 6B 154 (3A 6)
(not continuous)
NE9: Gate 3A 98
NE23: Dud 2B 32
Hanover Dr. NE21: Bla T 2G 79
Hanover Gdns. *NE28: W'snd 6E 61*
(off Station Rd.)
Hanover Ho. NE32: Jar 5F 73
Hanover Pl. NE23: Cra 5A 16
SR4: Sund 5B 104
Hanover Sq.
NE1: Newc T 5F 69 (6D 4)
NE21: Bla T 2G 79
(off Waterloo St.)
Hanover Stairs *NE1: Newc T 5F 69*
(off Hanover St.)
Hanover St.
NE1: Newc T 5F 69 (6D 4)
Hanover Wlk. NE5: Cha P 5A 54
NE21: Bla T 3G 79
Harbord Ter. NE26: Sea D 4D 24
Harbottle Av. NE3: Gos 1C 56
NE27: Shir 3D 46
Harbottle Ct. NE6: Newc T 5C 70
Harbottle Cres. NE32: Jar 1F 87
Harbottle St. NE6: Newc T 5C 70
Harbour Dr. NE33: S Shi 3F 63
(not continuous)
Harbour, The DH4: Hou S 3F 129
Harbour Vw. NE22: E Sle 2H 11
NE30: N Shi 2D 62
(off Lit. Bedford St.)
NE33: S Shi 2E 63
SR6: Monk 3F 105
Harbour Wlk. SR7: S'hm 3A 142
Harcourt Pk. NE9: Gate 6A 84
Harcourt Rd. SR2: Sund 6D 118
Harcourt St. NE9: Gate 6A 84
Hardgate Rd. SR2: Sund 6D 118
Hardie Av. NE16: Whi 3E 81
Hardie Dr. NE36: W Bol 4C 88
Hardman Cl. NE40: Ryton 4D 64
Hardman Gdns. NE40: Ryton 4D 64

Hardwick Ct. NE8: Gate 2A 84
Hardwick Pl. NE3: Ken 4C 56
Hardwick Ri. SR6: Monk 5E 105
Hardwick St. SR8: Pet 1G 165
Hardyards Ct. NE34: S Shi 4E 75
Hardy Av. NE34: S Shi 6D 74
Hardy Ct. NE30: N Shi 1D 62
Hardy Gro. NE28: W'snd 2G 59
Hardy Sq. SR5: S'wck 3A 104
Hardy St. SR7: S'hm 4B 142
Hardy Ter. DH9: Ann P 5A 122
Harebell Rd. NE9: Gate 6C 84
Harehills Av. NE5: Newc T 4H 55
Harehills Twr. NE3: Ken 4A 56
HARELAW 3E 121
Harelaw Cl. DH2: Pelt 3F 125
Harelaw Dr. SR6: Monk 4E 105
Harelaw Gdns. DH9: Ann P 3E 121
Harelaw Gro. NE5: Newc T 6B 54
Harelaw Ind. Est. DH9: Ann P . . .2F 121
Hareshaw Rd. NE25: Well 6F 35
Hareshaw Ter. NE6: Newc T 5C 70
(off St Peter's Rd.)
Hareside NE23: Cra 4A 22
Hareside Cl. NE15: Thro 1F 65
Hareside Ct. NE15: Thro 1F 65
Hareside Foot Path NE15: Thro . .2F 65
Hareside Wlk. NE15: Thro 1F 65
Harewood Cl. NE16: Whi 1E 95
NE25: Whit B 1F 47
Harewood Ct. NE25: Whit B 1F 47
Harewood Cres. NE25: Whit B . . .1F 47
Harewood Dr. NE22: Bed 3C 10
Harewood Gdns. SR3: Sund 4A 118
Harewood Grn. NE9: Gate 3B 98
Harewood Rd. NE3: Gos 1F 57
Hareydene NE5: Newc T 1D 54
Hargill Dr. NE38: Wash 6G 113
Hargrave Ct. NE24: Bly 1A 18
Harland Way NE38: Wash 2B 114
Harlebury NE27: Back 6H 33
Harle Cl. NE5: Newc T 6C 54
Harlequin Lodge NE10: Gate 3D 84
Harleston Way NE10: Gate 5E 85
Harle St. DH7: B'don 0F 159
NE28: W'snd 6H 59
Harley Ter. DH6: Sher 5D 156
NE3: Gos 2F 57
Harlow Av. NE3: Ken 6B 42
NE27: Back 2B 46
Harlow Cl. NE23: Cra 6B 16
HARLOW GREEN 3A 98
Harlow Grn. La. NE9: Gate 3A 98
Harlow Pl. NE7: Newc T 4B 58
Harlow St. SR4: Sund 1B 118
Harnham Av. NE29: N Shi 2H 61
Harnham Gdns. NE5: Newc T . . .1G 67
Harnham Gro. NE23: Cra 4A 22
Harold Sq. SR2: Sund 2E 119
Harold St. NE32: Jar 2G 73
Harold Wilson Dr. TS27: Hes 6F 165
HARPERLEY 3G 121
Harperley Dr. SR3: Sund 5B 118
Harperley Gdns. DH9: Ann P . . .4E 121
Harperley La. DH9: Tan L 6H 107
Harperley Rd. DH9: Ann P 4F 121
Harper St. NE24: Bly 6B 12
Harraby Gdns. NE9: Gate 2A 98
Harras Bank DH3: Bir 4C 112
HARRATON 6H 113
Harraton Ter. DH3: Bir 3C 112
DH3: Lam P 2A 128

Harriet Pl. NE6: Newc T 3C 70
Harriet St. NE6: Newc T 3D 70
NE21: Bla T 1A 80
Harrington St. NE28: W'snd 5H 59
(off Blenkinsop St.)
Harriot Dr. NE12: Kil 3A 44
Harrison Cl. SR8: Pet 2E 165
Harrison Ct. DH3: Bir 4C 112
NE23: Dud 3B 32
Harrison Gdns. NE8: Gate 4F 83
Harrison Gth. DH6: Sher 5D 156
Harrison Pl. NE2: Newc T 1F 5
Harrison Rd. NE28: W'snd 4E 61
Harrison Ter. SR8: Eas 1D 162
Harrogate St. SR2: Sund 2E 119
Harrogate Ter. SR7: Mur 2C 150
Harrow Cres. DH4: Hou S 3E 129
Harrow Gdns. NE13: Wide O 6E 31
Harrow Sq. SR4: Sund 2F 117
Harrow St. NE27: Shir 1C 46
Hartburn NE10: Gate 6G 85
Hartburn Dr. NE5: Cha P 4B 54
Hartburn Pl. NE4: Newc T 2B 68
Hartburn Rd. NE30: N Shi 4B 48
Hartburn Ter. NE25: Sea D 6B 24
Hartburn Wlk. NE3: Ken 2H 55
(not continuous)
Hart Ct. SR1: Sund 6D 104 (2H 7)
Hartford NE12: Kil 6D 32
Hartford Bank NE22: H Bri 3E 15
NE23: H Bri 3E 15
HARTFORD BRIDGE 2E 15
Hartford Bri. Farm NE22: H Bri . . .2D 14
Hartford Cvn. Site NE22: H Bri . . .1D 14
Hartford Ct. NE22: Bed 5G 9
Hartford Cres. NE22: Bed 5G 9
Hartford Dr. NE22: H Bri 2F 15
Hartford Ho. NE4: Newc T 3D 68
(off Barrack Rd.)
Hartford Rd. NE3: Gos 6F 43
NE22: Bed, H Bri 2F 15
NE34: S Shi 4C 74
Hartford Rd. SR2: Sund 2F 117
Hartford Rd. E. NE22: Bed 5H 9
Hartford Rd. W. NE22: Bed 5H 9
Hartford St. NE6: Newc T 1C 70
Harthorpe NE10: Gate 1H 85
Harthope Av. SR5: C'twn 2E 103
Harthope Cl. NE38: Wash 1F 127
Harthope Dr. NE29: N Shi 4A 62
Hartington Rd. NE30: N Shi 4C 48
Hartington St. NE4: Newc T 4C 68
NE8: Gate 2H 83
SR6: Monk 3E 105
Hartington Ter. NE33: S Shi 1F 75
Hartland Dr. DH3: Bir 4D 112
Hartlands NE22: Bed 5G 9
Hartleigh Pl. NE24: Cow 6G 11
Hartlepool Av. SR8: Pet 5F 163
HARTLEY 5H 25
Hartley Av. NE26: Whit B 6A 36
Hartleyburn Av. NE31: Heb 6B 72
HARTLEYBURN ESTATE 6C 72
Hartley Cl. NE13: Bru V 5B 30
NE25: Sea D 6A 24
Hartley Gdns. NE25: Sea D 6A 24
SR5: S'wck 2C 104
Hartley La. NE25: Well, Whit B . . .5E 35
NE26: Sea S, Whit B 1G 35
Hartley Sq. NE26: Sea S 5H 25
Hartley St. NE25: Sea D 6A 24
SR1: Sund 6F 105
Hartley St. Nth. NE25: Sea D 6A 24

Hartley Ter. NE24: News 3A 18
Hartoft Cl. DH4: Hou S 6H 129
HARTON 3H 75
Harton Gro. NE34: S Shi 2G 75
Harton Ho. Rd. NE34: S Shi 2G 75
Harton Ho. Rd. E. NE34: S Shi . . .2A 76
Harton La. NE34: S Shi 4E 75
HARTON NOOK 4H 75
Harton Quay NE33: S Shi 5D 62
Harton Ri. NE34: S Shi 2H 75
Harton Vw. NE36: W Bol 4C 88
Hartside DH3: Bir 6D 112
NE15: Lem 2A 66
Hartside Cotts. DH9: Ann P 5F 121
Hartside Cres. NE21: Bla T 3G 79
NE23: Cra 5A 16
NE27: Back 1B 46
Hartside Gdns. DH5: Eas L 4E 149
NE2: Newc T 6H 57
Hartside Pl. NE3: Gos 4E 43
Hartside Rd. SR4: Sund 3F 117
Hartside Sq. SR4: Sund 3F 117
Hartside Vw. DH1: Dur 6A 144
DH7: Ush M 3C 152
Hart Sq. SR4: Sund 2G 117
Hartswood NE9: Gate 4A 98
Hart Ter. SR6: Monk 5F 91
Harvard Rd. NE3: Ken 2A 56
Harvest Cl. SR3: New S 4H 131
Harvey Cl. NE38: Wash 2F 113
SR8: Pet 6D 162
Harvey Combe NE12: Kil 2B 44
Harvey Cres. NE10: Gate 3H 85
Harwood Cl. NE23: Cra 4A 22
NE38: Wash 6G 113
Harwood Ct. NE23: Cra 4A 22
Harwood Dr. NE12: Kil 2F 45
Harwood Grn. NE3: Ken 1A 56
Hascombe Cl. NE25: Whit B 5H 35
Haslemere Dr. SR3: Sund 4A 118
Hassop Way NE22: Ded 3H 9
Hastings Av. DH1: Dur 2A 160
NE3: Ken 6H 41
NE12: Longb 6D 44
NE26: Sea S 2F 25
NE26: Whit B 3A 36
Hastings Ct. NE22: Bed 3C 10
NE25: Sea D 3B 24
Hastings Dr. NE30: N Shi 5E 49
Hastings Gdns. NE25: Sea D 3B 24
HASTINGS HILL 5C 116
Hastings Pde. NE31: Heb 6E 73
Hastings St. NE23: Cra 4C 22
SR2: Sund 3F 119
Hastings Ter. NE23: Cra 5D 16
NE25: Sea D 2B 24
SR2: Sund 4F 119
Hastings Wlk. NE37: Usw 5C 100
(off Hastings Ct.)
Haswell Cl. NE10: Gate 4B 86
Haswell Gdns. NE30: N Shi 1C 62
Haswell Ho. NE30: N Shi 6F 49
Hatfield Av. NE31: Heb 3D 72
Hatfield Cl. DH1: Dur 1A 154
Hatfield Dr. NE23: Seg 1F 33
Hatfield Gdns. NE25: Whit B 6F 35
SR3: Sund 4A 118
Hatfield Ho. NE29: N Shi 2C 62
Hatfield Pl. SR8: Pet 2E 165
Hatfield Sq. NE33: S Shi 4A 76
Hatfield Vw. DH1: Dur . . .6D 154 (4C 6)
Hathaway Gdns. SR3: Sund 4A 118
Hathersage Gdns. NE34: S Shi . . .4F 75

Hatherton Av. NE30: N Shi 2D 48
Hathery La. NE24: Bly, Cow 6D 10
Hatton Gallery 1C 4
Haugh La. NE21: Bla T 4G 65
  NE21: Thro 3E 65
Haughton Ct. NE4: Newc T 6C 68
Haughton Cres. NE5: Newc T 6C 54
  NE32: Jar 1F 87
Haughton Ter. NE24: Bly 6C 12
Hautmont Rd. NE31: Heb 5D 72
Hauxley NE12: Kil 6D 32
Hauxley Dr. DH2: Ches S 3A 134
  NE3: Ken 6A 42
  NE23: Cra 5H 15
Hauxley Gdns. NE5: Newc T 5H 55
Havanna NE12: Kil 6C 32
Havannah Cres. NE13: Din 4F 29
Havannah Nature Reserve 1A 42
Havannah Rd. NE37: Wash 6H 99
Havant Gdns. NE13: Wide O 4D 30
Havelock Cl. NE8: Gate 1G 83
Havelock Ct. SR4: Sund 1F 117
Havelock Cres. NE22: E Sle 2F 11
Havelock Ho. SR4: Sund 1F 117
Havelock M. NE22: E Sle 1F 11
Havelock Pl. NE4: Newc T 4D 68
Havelock Rd. NE27: Back 2B 46
  SR4: Sund 1G 117
Havelock St. NE24: Bly 5C 12
  NE33: S Shi 6E 63
   (Frederick St.)
  NE33: S Shi 6D 62
   (Rekendyke La.)
  SR1: Sund 6F 105
Havelock Ter. *DH9: Stly* *2D 122*
   (off High St.)
  DH9: Tan L 5H 107
  NE8: Gate 1G 83
  NE32: Jar 4F 73
  SR2: Sund 2B 118
Havelock Vs. NE22: E Sle 2F 11
Haven Ct. DH1: Dur 5C 144
  NE24: Bly 1A 18
  SR6: Monk 4F 105
Haven, The DH4: Hou S 3F 129
  NE29: N Shi 4C 62
Havercroft NE10: Gate 4H 85
Haverley Dr. SR7: S'hm 2E 141
Haversham Cl. NE7: Newc T ...2A 58
Haversham Pk. SR5: Monk 6C 90
Hawarden Cres. SR4: Sund 2A 118
Hawes Av. DH2: Ches S 2C 134
Hawes Ct. SR6: Monk 6C 90
Hawesdale Cres. NE21: Bla T ..3H 79
Hawes Rd. SR8: Pet 6D 162
Haweswater Cl. NE34: S Shi 3F 75
Hawick Ct. DH9: Stly 3F 123
Hawick Cres. NE6: Newc T 5B 70
Hawick Cres. Ind. Est.
  NE6: Newc T 5B 70
Hawkesley Rd. SR4: Sund 2F 117
Hawkey's La. NE29: N Shi 1B 62
Hawkhill Cl. DH2: Ches S 3A 134
Hawkhills Ter. DH3: Bir 2C 112
Hawkhurst NE38: Wash 5C 114
Hawkins Ct. SR3: New S 3H 131
Hawkins Rd. SR7: Mur 4E 151
Hawksbury NE16: Whi 4E 81
Hawksfeld NE10: Gate 1E 99
Hawkshead Cl. NE3: Ken 6H 41
Hawkshead Pl. NE9: Gate 6B 84
Hawksley NE5: Newc T 5D 54
Hawks Rd. NE8: Gate 5H 69 (6H 5)

Hawks St. NE8: Gate 5A 70
Hawk Ter. DH3: Bir 4E 113
Hawkwell Ri. NE15: Thro 6D 52
Hawsker Cl. SR3: New S 2C 132
HAWTHORN 6H 151
Hawthorn Av. NE13: Bru V 6C 30
  SR3: New S 1B 132
Hawthorn Cl. DH2: Plaw 2A 144
  NE16: Whi 6F 81
  SR7: Mur 3D 150
Hawthorn Cotts. DH6: S Het ...6B 150
Hawthorn Ct. DH2: Plaw 2A 144
Hawthorn Cres. DH1: Dur 4G 155
  NE38: Wash 6H 113
  SR8: Pet 1G 165
Hawthorn Dr. NE11: Dun 3B 82
Hawthorne Av. NE31: Heb 3D 72
  NE34: S Shi 5H 75
Hawthorne Dr. NE32: Jar 1H 87
Hawthorne Gdns. NE9: Gate ...5H 83
Hawthorne Rd. NE24: Bly 1D 18
Hawthorne Ter. DH9: Tan L 4A 108
Hawthorn Gdns. NE3: Ken 3B 56
  NE10: Gate 2D 84
  NE26: Whit B 6B 36
  NE29: N Shi 6B 48
  NE40: Ryton 5E 65
Hawthorn Gro. NE28: W'snd ...5H 59
Hawthorn M. NE3: Gos 3E 57
Hawthorn Pk. DH7: B'don 5D 158
Hawthorn Pl. DH1: Dur 5B 144
  NE4: Newc T 5D 68
  NE12: Kil 1C 44
Hawthorn Rd. DH1: Carr 2B 156
  DH6: S Het 6C 150
  NE3: Gos 3E 57
  NE21: Bla T 1A 80
Hawthorn Rd. W. NE3: Gos 3E 57
Hawthorn Sq. SR7: S'hm 3B 142
Hawthorns, The DH9: Ann P ...4F 121
  NE3: Gos 3E 57
  NE4: Newc T 6C 68
  NE9: Spri 4D 98
  NE36: E Bol 4F 89
Hawthorn St. DH4: Hou S 1G 137
  NE15: Thro 5F 53
  NE32: Jar 2E 73
  SR4: Sund 1A 118
  SR8: Eas 1D 162
Hawthorn Ter. DH1: Dur 6B 154
  DH2: Pelt 4G 125
  DH3: Ches S 1D 134
  DH7: New B 1A 158
  DH9: Ann P 5H 121
  NE4: Newc T 5C 68
  NE9: Spri 4F 99
   (Peareth Hall Rd.)
  NE9: Spri 4D 98
   (Sandy La.)
  NE15: Thro 5F 53
  SR6: Monk 5E 91
Hawthorn Vs. NE23: Cra 3C 22
  NE28: W'snd 5H 59
Hawthorn Wlk. NE4: Newc T ...5D 68
Hawthorn Way NE20: Pon 2D 38
Haydn St. NE8: Gate 3H 83
Haydock Dr. NE10: Gate 4A 86
Haydon NE38: Wash 6C 114
Haydon Cl. NE3: Ken 5B 42
Haydon Dr. NE25: Whit B 2B 48
Haydon Gdns. NE27: Back 2B 46
Haydon Pl. NE5: Newc T 1E 67
Haydon Sq. SR4: Sund 2F 117

Hayes Wlk. NE13: Wide O 5D 30
Hayfield La. NE16: Whi 5F 81
Hayhole Rd. NE29: N Shi 5A 62
Haylands Sq. NE34: S Shi 4G 75
Hayleazes Rd. NE15: Newc T ...2D 66
Haymarket NE1: Newc T ..3F 69 (3D 4)
Haymarket La.
  NE1: Newc T 3F 69 (2C 4)
Haymarket Station (Metro)
  ....3F 69 (2D 4)
Haynyng, The NE10: Gate 4E 85
Hayricks, The DH9: Tan L 3B 108
Hay St. SR5: Monk 5C 104 (1F 7)
Hayton Av. NE34: S Shi 4A 76
Hayton Cl. NE23: Cra 2C 22
Hayton Rd. NE30: N Shi 4B 48
Hayward Av. NE25: Sea D 6B 24
Hayward Pl. NE5: Newc T 5F 55
Hazard La.
  DH5: Hett H, W Rai 2H 147
Hazel Av. DH4: Hou S 3G 137
  DH7: B'don 6C 158
  NE29: N Shi 6B 48
  SR3: New S 1B 132
Hazel Cres. SR8: Eas 2D 162
Hazeldene NE25: Whit B 6H 35
  NE32: Jar 3G 87
Hazeldene Av. NE3: Ken 3G 55
Hazeldene Ct. NE30: N Shi 6E 49
Hazel Dr. TS27: Hes 6F 165
Hazeley Gro. NE3: Ken 2H 55
Hazeley Way NE3: Ken 2H 55
Hazel Gro. DH2: Ches S 4A 126
  NE12: Kil 3B 44
  NE16: Burn 1A 108
  NE34: S Shi 5H 75
Hazelgrove NE10: Gate 4H 85
Hazel Leigh DH3: Gt Lum 4G 135
Hazelmere Av. NE3: Gos 4F 43
  NE22: Bed 4G 9
Hazelmere Cres. NE23: Cra 1C 22
Hazelmere Dene NE23: Seg 2E 33
Hazelmoor NE31: Heb 2B 72
Hazel Rd. NE8: Gate 3E 83
  NE21: Bla T 1B 80
Hazel St. NE32: Jar 2E 73
Hazel Ter. DH4: Hou S 1G 137
  DH9: Stly 6F 123
Hazelwood NE12: Kil 2F 45
  NE32: Jar 3H 73
Hazelwood Av. NE2: Newc T ...5G 57
  SR5: S'wck 3H 103
Hazelwood Cl. NE9: Spri 3D 98
Hazelwood Gdns.
  NE38: Wash 6H 113
Hazelwood Ter. NE28: W'snd ...4E 61
Hazledene Ter. SR4: Sund 1H 117
HAZLERIGG 1C 42
Hazlitt Av. NE34: S Shi 6D 74
Hazlitt Pl. NE23: Seg 2G 33
Headlam Gdns. *NE6: Newc T* ...*3D 70*
   (off Grace St.)
Headlam St. NE6: Newc T 3C 70
Headlam Vw. NE28: W'snd 5E 61
Healey Dr. SR3: Sund 5B 118
Health Connection, The 2A 56
Healthlands Fitness & Leisure Cen.
  Washington 5B 100
  Whickham 4F 81
Heartsbourne Dr. NE34: S Shi ...6H 75
Heath Cl. NE11: Dur 4D 82
  SR8: Pet 2E 165
   (not continuous)

Heathcote Grn. NE5: Newc T 4F 55
Heath Ct. NE1: Newc T 4G 69 (5E 5)
Heath Cres. NE15: Newc T 5E 67
Heathdale Gdns. NE7: Newc T 4B 58
Heather Cl. SR6: Cle 1A 90
Heatherdale Cres. DH1: Carr . . .3B 156
Heatherdale Ter. NE9: Gate 2B 98
Heather Dr. DH5: Hett H 6C 138
Heather Hill NE9: Spri 4F 99
Heatherlaw NE9: Gate 6C 84
NE37: Wash 1F 113
Heather Lea DH9: Dip 5E 107
Heatherlea Gdns. SR3: Sund 4B 118
Heatherlea Pl. NE37: Usw 4B 100
Heather Pl. NE4: Newc T 1A 68
NE40: Ryton 5A 64
Heatherslaw Rd.
NE5: Newc T 1G 67
Heather Ter. NE16: Burn 1H 107
Heather Way DH9: Stly 3B 122
Heatherwell Grn.
NE10: Gate 4C 84
Heathery La. NE3: Gos 6G 43
Heathfield SR2: Sund 5C 118
Heathfield Cres. NE5: Newc T . . .4H 55
Heathfield Farm NE40: G'sde 2A 78
Heathfield Gdns. DH9: Ann P . . .4F 121
NE40: G'sde 2A 78
Heathfield Pl. NE3: Gos 4F 43
NE9: Gate 5H 83
Heathfield Rd. NE9: Gate 5H 83
Heath Grange DH5: Hou S 2A 138
Heathlands Fitness
and Leisure Cen. 1D 134
(off Front St.)
Heathlands Ladies Leisure Cen.
South Gosforth 2G 57
Whitley Bay 4A 36
(off Claremont Cres.)
Heathmeads DH2: Pelt 3F 125
Heath Sq. SR4: Sund 2C 117
Heathway NE32: Jar 1G 87
SR7: S'hm 6A 142
Heathways DH1: H Shin 4H 161
Heathwell Gdns. NE16: Swa 3F 81
Heathwell Rd. NE15: Newc T 2D 66
Heathwood Av. NE16: Whi 4E 81
HEATON .6C 58
Heaton Cl. NE6: Newc T 2B 70
Heaton Gdns. NE34: S Shi 1E 89
Heaton Gro. NE6: Newc T 2B 70
Heaton Hall Rd. NE6: Newc T 2B 70
Heaton Pk. Ct. NE6: Newc T 2B 70
Heaton Pk. Rd. NE6: Newc T 2B 70
Heaton Pk. Vw. NE6: Newc T 2B 70
Heaton Pl. NE6: Newc T 2B 70
Heaton Rd. NE6: Newc T 6B 58
Heaton Swimming Pool 6C 58
Heaton Ter. NE6: Newc T 3A 70
NE29: N Shi 1A 62
Heaton Wlk. NE6: Newc T 3B 70
Heaviside Pl. DH1: Dur 5E 155
HEBBURN 4B 72
Hebburn Baths 3D 72
HEBBURN COLLIERY 2D 72
HEBBURN NEW TOWN 4A 72
Hebburn Station (Metro) 3B 72
Hebburn St. SR8: Eas 1C 162
Heber St. NE4: Newc T 4E 69 (4A 4)
Hebron Way NE23: Cra 3A 22
Hector St. NE27: Shir 1D 46
Heddon Av. NE13: Bru V 1C 42
Heddon Banks NE15: Hed W 6F 51

Heddon Cl. NE3: Ken 1C 56
NE40: Ryton 4D 64
HEDDON-ON-THE-WALL 5G 51
Heddon Vw. NE21: Bla T 1H 79
NE40: Ryton 4D 64
Heddon Way NE34: S Shi 3C 74
Hedge Cl. NE11: Gate 4D 82
HEDGEFIELD 4F 65
Hedgefield Av. NE21: Bla T 4F 65
Hedgefield Cotts. NE21: Bla T 4F 65
Hedgefield Ct. NE21: Bla T 4F 65
Hedgefield Gro. NE24: News 4A 18
Hedgefield Vw. NE23: Dud 2A 32
Hedgehope NE37: Wash 1G 113
Hedgehope Rd. NE5: Newc T 3E 55
Hedgelea NE40: Ryton 4B 64
Hedgelea Rd. DH5: W Rai 2G 147
Hedgeley Rd. NE5: Newc T 1C 66
NE29: N Shi 6H 47
NE31: Heb 3B 72
Hedgeley Ter. NE6: Walk 3F 71
Hedley Av. NE24: Bly 1C 18
Hedley Cl. NE33: S Shi 3E 63
Hedley Ct. DH7: Ush M 3C 152
NE24: Bly 1D 18
Hedley La. NE16: Sun 1F 109
Hedley Pl. NE28: W'snd 6H 59
(Equitable St.)
NE28: W'snd 6H 59
(York Dr.)
Hedley Rd. NE25: H'wll 1C 34
NE29: N Shi 4B 62
Hedley St. NE3: Gos 2E 57
NE8: Gate 3F 83
NE33: S Shi 3E 63
Hedley Ter. DH6: S Het 6H 149
DH9: Dip 3A 120
NE3: Gos 2E 57
SR2: Ryh 3G 133
HEDWORTH 1H 87
Hedworth Av. NE34: S Shi 5C 74
Hedworth Ct. SR1: Sund 1E 119
Hedworth La. NE32: Jar 6G 73
NE35: Bol C 2H 87
Hedworth Pl. NE9: Gate 2C 98
Hedworth Sq. SR1: Sund 1E 119
Hedworth St. DH3: Ches S 5C 126
Hedworth Ter. DH4: Hou S 3F 129
SR6: Whit 3F 91
(off North Guards)
Hedworth Vw. NE32: Jar 6H 73
Heighley St. NE15: Newc T 4D 66
Helena Av. NE26: Whit B 6D 36
Helena Ho. SR2: Sund 2B 118
(off Albert Ct.)
Helen St. NE21: Bla T 1G 79
NE23: E Cram 4F 23
SR6: Monk 1E 105
Helford Rd. SR8: Pet 3C 164
Hellvellyn Ct. DH9: Ann P 6F 121
Helmdon NE37: Usw 5C 100
Helmsdale Av. NE10: Gate 2D 84
Helmsdale Rd. SR4: Sund 2F 117
Helmsley Cl. DH4: Pen 3E 129
Helmsley Ct. SR6: S'wck 2G 103
Helmsley Dr. NE28: W'snd 5D 60
Helmsley Grn. NE9: Gate 3B 98
Helmsley Rd. DH1: Dur 6C 144
NE2: Newc T 2H 69 (1G 5)
Helston Ct. NE15: Lem 2H 65
Helvellyn Av. NE38: Wash 4G 113
Helvellyn Cl. NE21: Bla T 3A 80
Helvellyn Rd. SR2: Sund 6D 118

Hemel St. DH3: Ches S 1C 134
Hemlington Cl. SR2: Ryh 3F 133
Hemmel Courts DH7: B'don 4E 159
Hemming St. SR2: Sund 5F 119
Hemsley Rd. NE34: S Shi 6H 63
Henderson Av. NE16: Whi 3E 81
Henderson Ct. NE29: N Shi 4B 62
Henderson Gdns. NE10: Gate 3H 85
Henderson Rd. NE28: W'snd 3H 59
NE34: S Shi 5B 74
SR4: Sund 1H 117
Hendersyde Cl. NE5: Newc T 4F 55
HENDON 3E 119
Hendon Burn Av. SR2: Sund 2E 119
Hendon Burn Av. W.
SR2: Sund 3E 119
Hendon Cl. NE29: N Shi 4C 62
SR1: Sund 1E 119
Hendon Gdns. NE32: Jar 1H 87
Hendon Rd. NE8: Gate 3B 84
SR1: Sund 6E 105
SR2: Sund 1E 119
Hendon St. SR1: Sund 1F 119
Hendon Valley Ct. SR2: Sund 3E 119
Hendon Valley Rd. SR2: Sund 2E 119
Henley Av. DH2: Pelt 6G 125
Henley Cl. NE23: Cra 2D 22
Henley Gdns. NE28: W'snd 3F 61
Henley Rd. NE30: N Shi 4E 49
SR4: Sund 2F 117
Henley St. NE6: Walk 2C 70
Henley Way NE35: Bol C 3A 88
Henlow Rd. NE15: Lem 2A 66
Henry Nelson St. NE33: S Shi 3F 63
Henry Robson Way
NE33: S Shi 5E 63
Henry Sq. NE2: Newc T . . .3H 69 (3G 5)
Henry St. DH4: Hou S 3F 129
DH5: Hett H 5C 138
DH5: Hou S 2A 138
NE3: Gos 2F 57
NE15: Thro 5G 53
NE29: N Shi 2C 62
NE33: S Shi 3F 63
SR7: S'hm 3B 142
Henry St. E. SR2: Sund 1F 119
Henry St. Nth. SR7: Mur 2D 150
(off Henry St. 3th.)
Henry St. Sth. SR7: Mur 2D 150
Henry Ter. DH4: Hou S 1D 136
Hensby Ct. NE5: Newc T 3F 55
Henshaw Gro. NE25: H'wll 1D 34
Henshaw Pl. NE5: Newc T 2F 67
Henshelwood Ter. NE2: Newc T . . .6G 57
Henson Cl. NE38: Wash 3B 114
Hepburn Gdns. NE10: Gate 2C 84
Hepburn Gro. SR5: C'twn 4B 102
Hepple Ct. NE24: Bly 1A 18
Hepple Way NE3: Gos 1C 56
HEPSCOTT 1A 8
Hepscott Dr. NE25: Whit B 5H 35
HEPSCOTT PARK 4A 8
Hepscott Ter. NE33: S Shi 2F 75
Herbert St. NE8: Gate 2A 84
Herbert Ter. SR5: S'wck 6B 90
SR7: S'hm 4B 142
Herd Cl. NE21: Bla T 2G 79
Herd Ho. La. NE21: Bla T 1F 79
Herdinghill NE37: Wash 1F 113
Herdlaw NE23: Cra 3A 22
Hereford Ct. NE3: Ken 5H 41
SR2: Sund 6D 118
Hereford Rd. SR2: Sund 6D 118

Herefordshire Dr. DH1: Carr 4A 156
Hereford Sq. SR2: Sund 6D 118
Hereford Way NE32: Jar 1F 87
    (not continuous)
Heritage Cl. NE8: Gate 2E 83
Hermiston NE25: Whit B 6A 36
Hermitage Gdns.
    DH2: Ches S 2B 134
Hermitage Pk. DH3: Ches S 2C 134
Hermitage, The DH2: Ches S 3B 134
Heron Cl. NE24: News 3C 18
    NE38: Wash 5G 113
Heron Dr. NE33: S Shi 3E 63
Heron Pl. NE12: Longb 6A 44
Heron Vs. NE34: S Shi 5D 74
Heron Way NE16: Whi 4F 81
Herrick St. NE5: Newc T 4E 55
Herring Gull Cl. NE24: News 4C 18
Herrington M. DH4: E Her 3A 130
Herrington Rd. DH4: E Her 3B 130
    SR3: E Her 2D 130
Herschel Bldg. NE1: Newc T 2C 4
Hersham CI. NE3: Ken 6H 41
Hertburn Gdns. NE37: Wash . . .6B 100
Hertburn Ind. Est.
    NE37: Wash 6C 100
Hertford NE9: Gate 3H 97
Hertford Av. NE34: S Shi 2C 76
Hertford CI. NE25: Whit B 5G 35
Hertford Cres. DH5: Hett H 1B 148
Hertford Gro. NE23: Cra 2C 22
Hertford Pl. SR8: Pet 5C 162
Herton Cl. SR8: Pet 6C 162
    (not continuous)
Hesket Ct. NE3: Ken 6A 42
HESLEDEN 6G 165
Hesleden Rd.
    TS27: B Col, Hes 5G 165
Hesledon La. SR7: Eas 4H 151
Hesledon Wlk. SR7: Mur 1E 151
Hesleyside Dr. NE5: Newc T 1F 67
Hesleyside Rd. NE25: Well 6F 35
Hester Av. NE25: Sea D 3B 24
Hester Bungs. NE25: Sea D 3B 24
    (off Hester Av.)
Hester Gdns. NE25: Sea D 3C 24
Heswall Rd. NE23: Cra 5A 16
HETTON DOWNS 5D 138
HETTON-LE-HOLE 1C 148
Hetton Lyons Country Pk. 1D 148
Hetton Lyons Ind. Est.
    DH5: Hett H 2D 148
Hetton Rd. DH5: Hou S 4A 138
Hetton Sports Complex 1C 148
Heugh Hill NE9: Spri 3G 99
Hewitson Ter. NE10: Gate 4C 84
Hewitt Av. SR2: Ryh 1E 133
Hewley Cres. NE15: Thro 6D 52
HEWORTH 3E 85
Heworth Av. NE10: Gate 2G 85
Heworth Burn Cres.
    NE10: Gate 3E 85
Heworth Ct. NE34: S Shi 4C 74
Heworth Cres. NE37: Usw 5B 100
Heworth Dene Gdns.
    NE10: Gate 2E 85
Heworth Gro. NE37: Usw 5A 100
Heworth Rd. NE37: Usw 3B 100
Heworth Station (Metro) 2F 85
Heworth Station (Rail) 3F 85
Heworth Way NE10: Gate 3G 85
Hewson Pl. NE9: Gate 5B 84
Hexham NE38: Wash 3F 113

Hexham Av. NE6: Walk 4F 71
    NE23: Cra 2C 22
    NE31: Heb 1C 86
    SR7: S'hm 5H 141
    (not continuous)
Hexham CI. NE29: N Shi 6G 47
Hexham Ct. NE6: Walk 3G 71
    NE11: Dun 5B 82
Hexham Dr. DH9: Ann P 4F 121
Hexham Ho. NE6: Walk 3G 71
Hexham Old Rd.
    NE40: Bla T, Ryton 4C 64
Hexham Rd.
    NE15: Hed W, Thro 5G 51
    NE16: Swa 2D 80
    SR4: Sund 2F 117
Hextol Gdns. NE15: Newc T 2D 66
Heybrook Av. NE29: N Shi 5B 48
Heyburn Gdns. NE15: Newc T . . .4H 67
Heywood's Ct.
    NE1: Newc T 4F 69 (5D 4)
Hibernian Rd. NE32: Jar 2F 73
Hibernia Rd. NE6: Walk 5G 71
Hickling Ct. NE5: Newc T 3G 55
Hickstead CI. NE28: W'snd 6C 46
Hickstead Gro. NE23: Cra 2D 22
Hiddleston Av. NE7: Newc T 2B 58
Higham Pl.
    NE1: Newc T 3G 69 (3E 5)
High Axwell NE21: Bla T 1B 80
High Back Cl. NE32: Jar 5E 73
HIGH BARNES 2H 117
High Barnes DH3: Gt Lum 4G 135
High Barnes Ter. SR4: Sund . . .2A 118
High Beacon Stairs
    NE30: N Shi 2E 63
    (off Union Quay)
High Bri. NE1: Newc T 4F 69 (5D 4)
Highbridge NE3: Gos 6E 43
Highburn NE23: Cra 5A 22
High Burn Ter. NE10: Gate 4E 85
Highbury NE2: Newc T 6F 57
    NE10: Gate 3E 85
    NE25: Whit B 6A 36
Highbury Av. NE9: Spri 3G 99
Highbury CI. NE9: Spri 3G 99
Highbury Pl. NE29: N Shi 2A 62
HIGH CALLERTON 3E 39
High Carr Cl. DH1: Dur 2B 154
High Carr Rd. DH1: Dur 2A 154
High Chare DH3: Ches S 6C 126
Highcliffe Gdns. NE8: Gate 3A 84
High Croft DH7: B'don 4D 158
    NE37: Usw 4H 99
High Cft. CI. NE31: Heb 5B 72
Highcroft Dr. SR6: Whit 2E 91
Highcroft Pk. SR6: Whit 2F 91
    (not continuous)
Highcross Rd. NE30: N Shi 2C 48
High Dene NE7: Newc T 6A 58
    NE34: S Shi 4D 74
High Dewley Burn NE15: Thro . . .4D 52
High Downs Sq. DH5: Hett H . . .6C 138
HIGH DUBMIRE 3F 137
HIGH FELL 5A 84
HIGHFIELD 3C 92
Highfield DH3: Bir 1C 112
    NE16: Sun 2F 95
    NE24: Cow 6F 11
Highfield Av. NE12: Longb 5D 44
Highfield CI. NE5: Newc T 4D 54
Highfield Ct. NE10: Gate 4E 85
Highfield Cres. DH3: Ches S 4C 126

Highfield Dr. DH4: Hou S 3F 137
    NE34: S Shi 1H 75
Highfield Gdns. DH3: Ches S 4C 126
Highfield Grange
    DH4: Hou S 4F 137
Highfield Pl. NE13: Wide O 6C 30
    SR4: Sund 1H 117
Highfield Ri. DH3: Ches S 4C 126
Highfield Rd. DH4: Hou S 3E 129
    NE5: Newc T 5D 54
    NE8: Gate 2A 84
    NE33: S Shi 6H 63
    NE34: S Shi 1H 75
    NE39: Row G 3C 92
Highfield Ter. DH7: Ush M 6B 152
    NE6: Walk 5F 71
High Flatworth NE29: N Shi 1F 61
High Friar La.
    NE1: Newc T 4F 69 (4D 4)
High Friars NE1: Newc T 4C 4
HIGH FRIARSIDE 1E 107
High Gth. SR1: Sund 6E 105
    (off High St. E.)
Highgate DH1: Dur 5C 154 (1A 6)
Highgate Gdns. NE32: Jar 1H 87
Highgate Rd. SR4: Sund 2F 117
High Ga., The NE3: Ken 3A 56
Highgreen Chase NE16: Whi 1E 95
High Grindon Ho. SR4: Sund . . .4E 117
High Gro. NE4: Newc T 4C 68
    NE40: Ryton 5D 64
Highgrove NE5: Cha P 5B 54
Highgrove Ct. SR8: Eas 3C 162
High Hamsterley Rd.
    NE39: Ham M 2A 106
HIGH HANDENHOLD 2D 124
Highheath NE37: Wash 1F 113
HIGH HEATON 5B 58
High Hedgefield Ter.
    NE21: Bla T 4E 65
HIGH HEWORTH 4E 85
High Heworth La. NE10: Gate . . .4E 85
High Horse CI. NE39: Row G 1G 93
High Horse CI. Wood
    NE39: Row G 1G 93
High Ho. Gdns. NE10: Gate 3E 85
    (not continuous)
Highland Rd. NE5: Newc T 4H 55
High La. DH4: E Her, Hou S 5A 130
High La. Row NE31: Heb 1D 72
High Lanes NE10: Gate 4F 85
High Laws NE3: Gos 3H 57
Highlaws Gdns. NE9: Gate 3B 98
High Level Rd. NE8: Gate 6G 69
High Mdw. NE34: S Shi 1H 75
High Mdws. DH7: B'don 4C 158
    NE3: Ken 4A 56
High Mill Rd. NE39: Ham M 2A 106
High Moor Ct. NE5: Newc T 5A 56
High Moor Pl. NE34: S Shi 4E 75
HIGH MOORSLEY 5H 147
HIGH NEWPORT 1A 132
High Pasture NE38: Wash 6C 114
High Pit Rd. NE23: Cra 4D 22
HIGH PITTINGTON 2F 157
High Primrose Hill
    DH4: Hou S 6B 128
High Quay NE1: Newc T 4A 70 (5H 5)
High Reach NE10: Gate 1G 85
High Ridge NE13: Bru V 1D 42
    NE22: Bed 4G 9
Highridge DH3: Bir 2C 112
High Rd., The NE34: S Shi 3H 75

High Row DH4: Hou S 2C 136
 NE15: Lem 3A 66
 NE37: Usw 4B 100
 NE40: Ryton 5E 65
High Sandgrove SR6: Cle 2A 90
High Shaws DH7: B'don 4E 159
HIGH SHIELDS 6E 63
HIGH SHINCLIFFE 4H 161
Highside Dr. SR3: Sund 4A 118
HIGH SOUTHWICK 2A 104
HIGH SPEN 1A 92
High Spen Ct. NE39: H Spon 1A 92
High Spen Ind. Est.
 NE39: H Spen 6A 78
Highstead Av. NE23: Cra 6A 16
High St. DH1: Carr 3A 156
 DH1: Dur 5C 154 (2B 6)
 DH1: H Shin 4H 161
            (High Shincliffe)
 DH1: H Shin 3F 161
            (Shincliffe)
 DH5. Eas L 4C 149
 DH6: H Pitt 1F 157
 DH7: B'don 4G 159
 DH9: Stly 2D 122
 NE3: Gos 2E 57
 NE8: Gate 5G 69
            (Bottle Bank)
 NE8: Gate 6H 69
            (Nelson St.)
 NE9. Gate 2C 90
 NE10: Gate 3D 84
 NE15: Thro 2F 65
 NE24: Bly 6B 12
            (Edward St.)
 NE24: Bly 6C 12
            (Thoroton St.)
 NE32: Jar 2H 73
            (Church Bank)
 NE32: Jar 2G 73
            (Monkton Rd.)
 SR4: Sund 1C 116
High St. E. NE28: W'snd 6A 60
 SR1: Sund 6E 105
High St. Nth. DH1: H Shin 3G 161
 DH7: D'don 4F 160
            (not continuous)
High St. Sth. DH1: H Shin 3G 161
 DH7: B'don 4G 159
High St. Sth. Bk.
 DH7: B'don 4G 159
High St. W. NE6: W'snd 6G 59
 SR1: Sund 1C 118 (4E 7)
            (St Michael's Way)
 SR1: Sund 6C 104 (3F 7)
            (West St.)
High Swinburne Pl.
 NE4: Newc T 4E 69 (5A 4)
Hightree Cl. SR3: New S 4H 131
HIGH URPETH 1D 124
High Vw. DH7: Ush M 5B 152
 NE20: Pon 3D 38
 NE28: W'snd 4H 59
High Vw. Nth. NE28: W'snd 3G 59
High Wlk. DH3: Lam P 3A 128
High Well Gdns. NE10: Gate 2E 85
Highwell La. NE5: Newc T 6C 54
High W. La. SR7: Eas 6G 151
High W. St. NE8: Gate 1H 83
Highwood Rd. NE15: Newc T ...2D 66
High Wood Ter. DH1: Dur 6C 6
High Wood Vw.
 DH1: Dur 1D 160 (6C 6)

Highworth Dr. NE7: Newc T 4D 58
 NE9: Spri 4F 99
High Yd. DH1: Dur 6D 154 (4C 6)
Hilda Av. DH1: Dur 6G 155
Hilda Cl. DH1: Dur 6H 155
Hilda Pk. DH2: Ches S 4B 126
Hilda St. DH9: Ann P 4E 121
 NE8: Gate 2F 83
 SR6: Monk 2D 104
            (not continuous)
Hilda Ter. DH2: Ches S 4B 126
            (not continuous)
 NE15: Thro 5D 52
Hilden Bldgs. NE7: Newc T 5C 58
Hilden Gdns. NE7: Newc T 5C 58
Hillary Av. NE12: Longb 5E 45
Hillary Pl. NE5: Newc T 4E 55
Hill Av. NE23: Seg 1G 33
Hill Brow SR3: New S 3B 132
Hill Ct. NE4: Newc T 4E 69 (4A 4)
Hill Cres. SR7: Mur 2B 150
 SR7: S'hm 6C 142
Hill Crest NE16: Burn 1H 107
Hillcrest DH1: Dur 5D 154 (1D 6)
 DH1: H Shin 4H 161
 NE10: Gate 5E 85
 NE25: Whit B 6A 36
 NE32: Jar 1H 87
 NE34: S Shi 4B 76
 SR3: E Her 2D 130
Hillcrest Dr. NE11: Dun 4A 82
Hill Crest Gdns. NE2: Gos 3G 57
Hillcrest M. DH1: Dur 5D 154 (1C 6)
Hillcrest Pl. TS27: Hes 6F 165
Hillcroft DH3: Bir 2C 112
 NE9: Gate 5A 84
 NE39: Row G 3C 92
Hill Dyke NE9: Gate, Spri 3C 98
Hillfield NE25: Whit B 6H 35
Hillfield Gdns. SR3: Sund 4B 118
Hillfield St. NE8: Gate 1G 83
Hillgate NE8: Gate 5G 69 (6F 5)
Hill Head Dr. NE5: Newc T 6B 54
Hillhead Gdns. NE11: Dun 5C 82
Hillhead La. NE16: Burn 4H 54
Hillhead Parkway NE5: Cha P ...5A 54
Hillhead Rd.
 NE5: Cha P, Newc T 6B 54
Hillheads Ct. NE25: Whit B 1C 48
Hillheads Rd. NE25: Whit B 2B 48
Hill Ho. Rd. NE5: Newc T 4C 54
Hill Ho. Rd. NE15: Thro 5C 52
Hillingdon Gro. SR4: Sund 5C 116
Hill La. DH4: Pen 6G 115
Hill Mdws. DH1: H Shin 4G 161
Hill Pk. NE20: Pon 3D 38
HILL PARK ESTATE 4G 73
Hill Pk. Rd. NE32: Jar 4G 73
Hill Ri. NE38: Wash 1B 114
 NE40: Ryton 6A 64
Hillrise Cres. SR7: Sea 3D 140
Hills Ct. NE21: Bla T 5C 66
Hillsden Rd. NE25: Whit B 4H 35
Hillside DH3: Bir 3D 112
 DH3: Ches S 5C 126
 NE11: Dun 4A 82
 NE12: Kil 3F 45
 NE20: Pon 4C 38
 NE21: Bla T 1H 79
 NE34: S Shi 5B 76
 NE36: W Bol 4C 88
 SR3: Sund 4C 118
Hillside Av. NE15: Lem 2C 66

Hillside Cl. NE39: Row G 2E 93
Hillside Cres. NE15: Newc T 5E 67
Hillside Dr. SR6: Whit 2E 91
Hillside Gdns. DH9: Stly 1E 123
            (not continuous)
 SR2: Sund 4C 118
Hillside Gro. DH6: H Pitt 2F 157
Hillside Pl. NE9: Gate 5A 84
Hillside Vw. DH6: Sher 5D 156
Hillside Vs. SR8: Pet 6F 163
Hillside Way DH4: Hou S 2A 138
Hillsleigh Rd. NE5: Newc T 4H 55
Hills St. NE8: Gate 6G 69
Hill St. NE32: Jar 2E 73
 NE33: S Shi 6D 62
 SR3: New S 2A 132
 SR7: S'hm 5B 142
Hillsview Av. NE3: Ken 2A 56
Hill Ter. DH4: E Her 3A 130
Hillthorne Cl. NE38: Wash 3C 114
Hill Top DH3: Bir 3D 112
 NE21: Bla T 2H 79
Hilltop DH9: Stly 2F 123
Hill Top Av. NE9: Gate 6A 84
Hill Top Gdns. NE9: Gate 6A 84
Hilltop Gdns. SR3: New S 2C 132
Hilltop Ho. NE5: Newc T 5E 55
Hilltop Rd. DH7: Ush M 3C 152
Hilltop Vw. SR6: Whit 1E 91
Hill Vw. DH7: Ush M 1E 159
 DH9: Beam 2H 123
Hillview SR3: E Her 2D 130
Hillview Cres. DH4: Hou S 6H 129
Hill Vw. Gdns. SR3: Sund 4B 118
Hillview Gro. DH4: Hou S 6H 129
Hill Vw. Rd. SR2: Sund 5D 118
Hillview Rd. DH4: Hou S 6H 129
Hill Vw. Sq. SR2: Sund 5D 118
Hilton Av. NE5: Newc T 5F 55
Hilton Cl. NE23: Cra 5A 16
Hilton Dr. SR8: Pet 2D 104
Hindley Gdns. NE4: Newc T 2H 67
Hindmarch Dr. NE35: Bol C 3D 88
 NE36: W Bol 4C 88
Hindson's Cres. Nth.
 DH4: Hou S 4F 129
Hindson's Cres. Sth.
 DH4: Hou S 4E 129
Hind St. SR1: Sund 1C 118 (4E 7)
Hinkley Cl. SR3: New S 3B 132
Hipsburn Dr. SR3: Sund 4A 118
Hiram Dr. NE36: E Bol 4F 89
Hirst Head NE22: Bed 4A 10
Hirst Tor. Nth NE22: Bed 4A 10
Hirst Vs. NE22: Bed 4A 10
Histon Cl. NE5: Newc T 4F 55
Histon Way NE5: Newc T 4F 55
Hi-Tec Village NE35: Bol C 4H 87
Hither Grn. NE32: Jar 1H 87
HMP Durham
 DH1: Dur 6D 154 (4D 6)
HMP Frankland DH1: Bras 5F 145
HMP Low Newton DH1: Bras 5F 145
Hobart NE26: Whit B 4B 36
Hobart Av. NE34: S Shi 6B 74
Hobart Gdns. NE7: Longb 2B 58
HOBSON 2G 107
Hobson Ind. Est. NE16: Burn ...2G 107
Hodgkin Pk. Cres.
 NE15: Newc T 4G 67
Hodgkin Pk. Rd. NE15: Newc T ..4G 67
Hodgson's Rd. NE24: Bly 5B 12
Hodgson Ter. NE37: Usw 5D 100

Hodkin Gdns. NE9: Gate 5B **84**
Hogarth Cotts. NE22: Bed 5A **10**
Hogarth Dr. NE38: Wash 4C **114**
Holbein Rd. NE34: S Shi 1E **89**
Holbein Rd. NE34: S Shi 6E **75**
Holborn Ct. DH7: Ush M 6D **152**
Holborn Pl. NE5: Newc T 6C **54**
Holborn Rd. SR4: Sund 3F **117**
Holborn Sq. SR4: Sund 3F **117**
Holburn Cl. NE40: Ryton 4D **64**
Holburn Cres. NE40: Ryton 4E **65**
Holburn Gdns. NE40: Ryton 4E **65**
Holburn La. NE40: Ryton 3D **64**
Holburn La. Ct. NE40: Ryton 3C **64**
Holburn Ter. NE40: Ryton 4E **65**
Holburn Wlk. NE40: Ryton 4E **65**
Holburn Way NE40: Ryton 4D **64**
Holden Pl. NE5: Newc T 5H **55**
Holder Ho. Way NE34: S Shi 6G **75**
Holderness Rd. NE6: Newc T 6B **58**
    NE28: W'snd 4E **61**
Hole La. NE16: Sun, Whi 1D **94**
Holeyn Hall Rd. NE41: Wylam . . .6B **50**
Holeyn Rd. NE15: Thro 6C **52**
Holland Dr. NE2: Newc T 2D **68**
Holland Pk. NE2: Newc T 2D **68**
    NE28: W'snd 4E **59**
Holland Pk. Dr. NE32: Jar 1H **87**
Hollinghill Rd. NE25: H'wll 1C **34**
Hollings Cres. NE28: W'snd 3H **59**
Hollingside La. DH1: Dur 2C **160**
Hollingside Way NE34: S Shi 4F **75**
Hollington Av. NE12: Longb 1B **58**
Hollington Cl. NE12: Longb 1B **58**
Hollinhill NE39: Row G 1G **93**
Hollinhill La. NE39: Row G 6F **79**
Hollin Hill Rd. NE37: Wash 6C **100**
Hollinside Cl. NE16: Whi 6E **81**
Hollinside Gdns. NE15: Newc T . . .3F **67**
Hollinside Rd. NE11: Dun 2F **81**
    NE16: Dun, Swa 2F **81**
    SR4: Sund 2F **117**
Hollinside Sq. SR4: Sund 2E **117**
Hollinside Ter. NE39: Row G 3D **92**
Hollowdene DH5: Hett H 2C **148**
Hollow, The NE32: Jar 2F **87**
Holly Av. DH5: Hou S 3A **138**
    NE2: Newc T 6G **57**
    NE3: Ken 1B **56**
    NE11: Dun 4B **82**
    NE12: Longb 4D **44**
    NE21: Bla T 5A **80**
    NE25: Well 6F **35**
    NE26: Whit B 6C **36**
    NE28: W'snd 6A **60**
    NE34: S Shi 4A **76**
    NE40: Ryton 3C **64**
    SR3: New S 1B **132**
    SR6: Whit 2F **91**
Holly Av. W. NE2: Newc T 6G **57**
Holly Bush Gdns. NE40: Ryton . . .5E **65**
Hollybush Rd. NE10: Gate 3C **84**
Hollybush Vs. NE40: Ryton 4E **65**
Hollycarrside Rd. SR2: Ryh 1E **133**
Holly Cl. NE12: Kil 1B **44**
Holly Ct. NE5: Newc T 5F **55**
    NE26: Whit B 6B **36**
    SR4: Sund 1A **118**
Holly Cres. NE38: Wash 6A **114**
Hollycrest DH2: Ches S 4B **126**
Hollydene NE11: Kib 1F **111**
    NE39: Row G 3F **93**
Holly Gdns. NE9: Gate 5H **83**

Holly Haven DH5: W Rai 1H **147**
Holly Hill NE10: Gate 3D **84**
Holly Hill Gdns. DH9: Stly 4D **122**
Holly Hill Gdns. E. DH9: Stly 4E **123**
Holly Hill Gdns. W. DH9: Stly . . .5D **122**
    (not continuous)
Hollyhock NE38: Wash 5C **114**
Hollyhock Gdns. NE31: Heb 6C **72**
Holly M. NE26: Whit B 6C **36**
Hollymount Av. NE22: Bed 5A **10**
Hollymount Sq. NE22: Bed 5A **10**
Hollymount Ter. NE22: Bed 5A **10**
Hollyoak Ho. NE24: Bly 2H **17**
Holly Pk. DH7: B'don 5D **158**
    DH7: Ush M 5C **152**
Holly Pk. Vw. NE10: Gate 3D **84**
Holly Rd. NE29: N Shi 6B **48**
Hollyside Cl. DH7: Ush M 3C **152**
Hollys, The DH3: Bir 6B **98**
Holly St. DH1: Dur 6B **154**
    NE32: Jar 2E **73**
Holly Ter. DH9: Ann P 4E **121**
    DH9: Stly 4B **122**
    NE16: Burn 1A **108**
Holly Vw. NE10: Gate 3C **84**
Hollywell Ct. DH7: Ush M 6D **152**
Hollywell Gro. NE13: Wool 5D **40**
Hollywell Rd. NE29: N Shi 1H **61**
Hollywood Av. NE3: Gos 1F **57**
    NE6: Walk 6G **59**
    SR5: S'wck 3H **103**
Hollywood Cres. NE3: Gos 1F **57**
Hollywood Gdns. NE11: Gate 6D **82**
Holman Ct. NE33: S Shi 5E **63**
Holme Av. NE6: Walk 4E **81**
    NE16: Whi 4E **81**
Holme Gdns. NE28: W'snd 5E **61**
    SR3: Sund 4B **118**
Holme Ri. NE16: Whi 4F **81**
Holmesdale Rd. NE5: Newc T 6H **55**
Holmeside SR1: Sund . . .1D **118** (4G **7**)
Holmeside Ter. NE16: Sun 3G **95**
Holmewood Dr. NE39: Row G 5D **92**
Holmfield Av. NE34: S Shi 2G **75**
Holm Grn. NE25: Whit B 1G **47**
Holmhill La. DH2: Ches S 4C **134**
    DH3: Ches S, Plaw 4C **134**
Holmland NE15: Newc T 5G **67**
Holmlands NE25: Whit B 6A **36**
Holmlands Cl. NE25: Whit B 6A **36**
Holmlands Cres. DH7: Ush M 2A **154**
Holmlands Pk. DH3: Ches S 1D **134**

Holmlands Pk. Nth.
    SR2: Sund 3C **118**

Holmlands Pk. Sth.
    SR2: Sund 3C **118**
Holmside Av. NE11: Dun 3C **82**
Holmside Pl. NE6: Newc T 2B **70**
Holmwood Av. NE25: Whit B 1H **47**
Holmwood Gro. NE2: Newc T 5F **57**
Holwick Cl. NE38: Wash 5G **113**
HOLY CROSS 4B **60**

Holy Cross Cemetery
    NE28: W'snd 4B **60**

Holy Cross Church
    (remains of) 4B **60**
Holyfields NE27: Shir 3B **46**
    (not continuous)
Holy Ho. SR1: Sund 6F **105**
    (off Adelaide Pl.)

Holy Jesus Bungs.
    NE2: Newc T 1D **68**
Holylake Sq. SR4: Sund 2F **117**

Holyoake Gdns. DH3: Bir 3C **112**
    NE9: Gate 3H **83**
Holyoake St. DH2: Pelt 3E **125**
Holyoake Ter. DH9: Stly 5C **122**
    NE37: Usw 5B **100**
    SR6: Monk 2E **105**
Holyrood DH3: Gt Lum 3G **135**
Holyrood Rd. SR2: Sund 5F **119**
HOLYSTONE 4A **46**
Holystone Av. NE3: Gos 1D **56**
    NE24: Bly 2A **18**
    NE25: Whit B 1D **48**
Holystone Cl. DH4: Hou S 1F **137**
    NE24: Bly 2H **17**
Holystone Ct. NE8: Gate 2F **83**
Holystone Cres. NE7: Newc T 4B **58**
Holystone Dr. NE27: Kil 3A **46**
Holystone Gdns. NE29: N Shi 5H **47**
Holystone Grange NE27: Longb . . .4A **46**
Holystone St. NE31: Heb 3B **72**

Holystone Trad. Est.
    NE31: Heb 3B **72**
Holystone Way NE12: Longb 5H **45**
    NE27: Longb 5A **46**
HOLYWELL 1D **34**
Holywell Av. NE6: Walk 6E **71**
    NE25: H'wll 1D **34**
    NE26: Whit B 5A **36**
Holywell Cl. NE4: Newc T 3D **68**
    NE21: Bla T 2B **80**
    NE25: H'wll 1D **34**
Holywell Dene Rd. NE25: H'wll . . .1D **34**
Holywell La. NE16: Sun 2F **95**
Holywell M. NE26: Whit B 5B **36**
Holywell Ter. NE27: Shir 4B **46**
Home Av. NE9: Gate 1H **97**
Homedowne Ho. NE3: Gos 2E **57**
Homeforth Ho. NE3: Gos 2E **57**
Homelea DH4: Hou S 5C **128**
Homeprior Ho. NE25: Whit B 1A **48**
Homer Ter. DH1: Dur 1A **160**
Homestall Cl. NE34: S Shi 4F **75**
Home Vw. NE38: Wash 2C **114**
Honeycomb Cl. SR3: New S 4H **131**
Honeycrook Dr. NE7: Newc T 4E **59**
Honeysuckle Av. NE34: S Shi 5D **74**
Honeysuckle Cl. SR3: New S 4A **132**
Honister Av. NE2: Gos 4G **57**
Honister Cl. NE15: Lem 2B **66**
Honister Dr. SR5: Monk 2C **104**
Honister Pl. NE15: Lem 2B **66**
Honister Rd. NE30: N Shi 3D **48**
Honister Way NE24: News 4A **18**
Honiton Cl. DH4: Hou S 5G **129**
Honiton Ct. NE3: Ken 1F **55**
Honiton Way NE29: N Shi 5F **47**
Hood Cl. SR5: S'wck 4C **104**
Hood Sq. NE21: Bla T 2G **79**
Hood St. NE1: Newc T 4F **69** (4D **4**)
    NE16: Swa 2E **81**
HOOKER GATE 2A **92**
Hookergate La. NE39: H Spen 1A **92**
    NE39: H Spen, Row G 2A **92**
Hope Av. SR8: Pet 1G **165**
Hopedene NE10: Gate 6G **85**
Hope Shield NE38: Wash 6F **113**
Hope St. DH6: Sher 6D **156**
    NE32: Jar 2G **73**
    SR1: Sund 1C **118** (4E **7**)
Hope Vw. SR2: Ryh 2F **133**
Hopgarth Ct. DH3: Ches S 5D **126**
Hopgarth Gdns. DH3: Ches S . . .5D **126**

Hopkins Ct. SR4: Sund 6H **103**
Hopkins Wlk. NE34: S Shi 1C **88**
Hopper Pl. DH1: Dur 2C **154**
  NE8: Gate 6H **69**
Hopper Rd. NE10: Gate 4C **84**
Hoppers Ct. *NE16: Swa* 2E **81**
           (off Quality Row Rd.)
Hopper St. NE8: Gate 6H **69**
  NE28: W'snd 5G **59**
  NE29: N Shi 2C **62**
  SR8: Eas 1B **162**
Hopper St. W. NE29: N Shi 2C **62**
Horatio Ho. NE30: N Shi 6F **49**
Horatio St. NE1: Newc T 4A **70**
  SR6: Monk 4E **105**
HORDEN 6G **163**
Hornbeam DH4: Hou S 4D **128**
Hornbeam Pl. NE4: Newc T 6D **68**
Horncliffe Gdns. NE16: Swa 3G **81**
Horncliffe Pl. NE15: Thro 5B **52**
Horncliffe Wlk. NE15: Lem 2G **65**
Horning Ct. NE5: Newc T 3F **55**
Hornsea Cl. NE13: Wide O 6D **30**
Hornsey Cres. DH5: Eas L 4D **148**
Hornsey Ter. DH5: Eas L 4D **148**
Horse Crofts NE21: Bla T 6A **66**
Horsham Gdns. SR3: Sund 4A **118**
Horsham Gro. NE29: N Shi 3A **62**
Horsham Ho. NE29: N Shi 3A **62**
Horsley Av. NE27: Shir 3D **46**
Horsley Ct. NE3: Ken 1A **56**
Horsley Gdns. NE11: Dun 3C **82**
  NE25: H'wll 1D **34**
  SR3: Sund 4A **118**
HORSLEY HILL 1A **76**
Horsley Hill Rd. NE33: S Shi 6G **63**
Horsley Hill Sq. NE34: S Shi 2B **76**
           (not continuous)
Horsley Ho. NE3: Gos 1E **57**
Horsley Rd. NE7: Newc T 6B **58**
  NE38: Wash 1E **115**
Horsley Ter. NE6: Walk 4F **71**
  NE30: N Shi 6F **49**
Horsley Va. NE34: S Shi 2H **75**
Horton Av. NE22: Bed 5H **9**
  NE27: Shir 3D **46**
  NE34: S Shi 6F **75**
Horton Cres. NE13: Din 4F **29**
Hortondale Gro. NE24: Cow 6H **11**
Horton Dr. NE23: Cra 6A **16**
Horton Mnr. NE24: Cow 6D **10**
Horton Pl. NE24: News 3H **17**
Horton Rd. NE22: Bed, Cow 6B **10**
  NE24: Cow 6D **10**
Horton St. NE24: Bly 6D **12**
Horwood Av. NE5: Newc T 5C **54**
Hospital Dr. NE31: Heb 5B **72**
Hospital La.
  NE15: Lem, Thro 2G **65**
Hospital of St Mary the Virgin, The
  NE4: Newc T 5D **68**
Hotch Pudding Pl.
  NE5: Newc T 1D **66**
Hotspur Av. NE22: Bed 5H **9**
  NE25: Whit B 1C **48**
  NE34: S Shi 2G **75**
Hotspur Rd. NE28: W'snd 2G **59**
Hotspur St. NE6: Newc T 2A **70**
  NE30: N Shi 5F **49**
Hotspur Way
  NE1: Newc T 3F **69** (3C **4**)
HOUGHALL 4D **160**
HOUGHTON 5F **51**

Houghton Av. NE5: Newc T 4A **56**
  NE30: N Shi 2D **48**
Houghton Cut DH5: Hou S 2A **138**
Houghton Ent. Cen.
  DH5: Hou S 3A **138**
Houghton Ga. DH3: Gt Lum 6H **127**
HOUGHTON-LE-SPRING 2H **131**
Houghton Rd. DH4: Hou S 6H **129**
  DH5: Hett H 5B **138**
Houghton Rd. W. DH5: Hett H . .1C **148**
Houghtonside DH4: Hou S 2A **138**
Houghton St. SR4: Sund 1A **118**
Houghwell Gdns.
  DH9: Stly, Tan L 1B **122**
Houlet Gth. NE6: Newc T 4C **70**
Houlskye Cl. SR3: New S 2C **132**
Hoults Ests. NE6: Newc T 2D **70**
Houndelee Pl. NE5: Newc T 6G **55**
Hounslow Gdns. NE32: Jar 1H **87**
Housesteads Gdns.
  NE12: Longb 1H **57**
House Ter. NE37: Usw 5B **100**
Houston Cl. NE4: Newc T 5D **68**
Houston St. NE4: Newc T 5D **68**
Houxty Rd. NE25: Well 6F **35**
Hovingham Cl. SR8: Pet 2E **165**
Hovingham Gdns. SR3: Sund 4A **118**
Howard Cl. NE27: Longb 4A **46**
Howard Ct. NE30: N Shi 2D **62**
Howardian Cl. NE38: Wash 4H **113**
Howard Pl. NE3: Gos 2E **57**
Howard St.
  NE1: Newc T 4H **69** (4H **5**)
  NE8: Gate 2B **84**
  NE10: Gate 5C **84**
  NE30: N Shi 2D **62**
  NE32: Jar 3G **73**
  SR5: S'wck 4D **104**
Howard Ter. NE39: H Spen 1A **92**
Howarth St. SR4: Sund 1A **118**
Howat Av. NE5: Newc T 6A **56**
Howdene Rd. NE15: Newc T 3D **66**
Howden Grn. Ind. Est.
  NE28: W'snd 5F **61**
Howden Rd. NE28: W'snd 6G **61**
HOWDON 3E **61**
Howdon La. NE28: W'snd 4E **61**
HOWDON PANS 6G **61**
Howdon Rd. NE28: W'snd 5G **61**
  NE29: N Shi 5E **61**
Howdon Station (Metro) 5E **61**
Howe Sq. SR4: Sund 2E **117**
Howe St. NE8: Gate 2B **84**
  NE31: Heb 3E **73**
Howick Av. NE3: Ken 6C **42**
Howick Pk. SR6: Monk . .5D **104** (1H **7**)
Howick Rd.
  SR6: Monk 5D **104** (1H **7**)
Howlcroft Vs. DH1: Dur 1A **160**
Howletch La. SR8: Pet 1C **164**
Howlett Hall Rd. NE15: Newc T . .2D **66**
Howley Av. SR5: C'twn 3E **103**
Hownam Cl. NE3: Gos 3C **56**
Hoy Cres. SR7: S hm 2F **141**
Hoylake Av. NE7: Newc T 2C **58**
Hoyle Av. NE4: Newc T 3A **68**
Hoyle Fold SR3: New S 5A **132**
Hoyson Vs. NE10: Gate 1H **85**
Hubert St. NE35: Bol D 3B **88**
Hucklow Gdns. NE34: S Shi 4F **75**
Huddart Ter. DH3: Bir 2C **112**
Huddlestone Ri. SR6: Monk . . .5E **105**

Huddleston Rd. NE6: Walk 2D **70**
Hudleston NE30: N Shi 1E **49**
Hudson Av. NE22: Bed 4B **10**
  NE23: Dud 3B **32**
  SR8: Pet 6F **163**
Hudson Rd. SR1: Sund 1E **119**
Hudson St. NE8: Gate 6G **69**
  NE30: N Shi 1D **62**
  NE34: S Shi 3D **74**
           (not continuous)
Hudspeth Cres. DH1: Dur 6A **144**
Hugar Rd. NE39: H Spen 2A **92**
Hugh Av. NE27: Shir 1D **46**
Hugh Gdns. NE4: Newc T 5A **68**
Hugh St. NE28: W'snd 6H **59**
  NE38: Wash 3D **114**
  SR6: Monk 1E **105**
Hull St. NE4: Newc T 4B **68**
Hulme Ct. SR8: Pet 2C **164**
Hulne Av. NE30: N Shi 6F **49**
Hulne Ter. NE15: Lem 3A **66**
Humber Ct. SR3: New S 3H **131**
Humber Gdns. NE8: Gate 2B **84**
Humber Hill DH9: Stly 4E **123**
Humbert St. NE32: Jar 3F **73**
Humbledon Pk. SR3: Sund 4A **118**
Humbledon Vw. SR2: Sund 3C **118**
Hume St. NE6: Newc T 4A **70**
  SR4: Sund 1A **118**
Humford Grn. NE24: Cow 6F **11**
Humford Way NE22: Bed 6A **10**
Humsford Gro. NE23: Cra 1C **22**
Humshaugh Cl. NE12: Longb 5G **45**
Humshaugh Rd. NE29: N Shi 1G **61**
Hunstanton Ct. NE9: Gate 2G **97**
Huntcliffe Av. SR6: Monk 5E **91**
Huntcliffe Gdns. NE6: Newc T . . .6C **58**
Hunter Av. DH7: Ush M 5B **152**
  NE24: Bly 1D **18**
Hunter Cl. NE36: E Bol 5F **89**
Hunter Ho. NE0: Walk 5G **71**
Hunter Pl. SR8: Eas 1D **162**
Hunter Rd. SR8: Pet 2A **164**
Hunters Ct. NE3: Gos 2G **57**
  NE28: W'snd 5A **60**
Hunters Hall Rd. SR4: Sund 2B **118**
Hunters Lodge NE28: W'snd 5A **60**
Hunters Moor Cl. NE2: Newc T . . .2D **68**
Hunters Pl. NE2: Newc T 1D **68**
Hunters Rd. NE2: Newc T 2C **68**
  NE3: Gos 2H **57**
Hunter's Ter. *NE9: Spri* 4F **99**
       (off Peareth Hall Rd.)
  NE33: S Shi 6F **63**
Hunter St. DH4: Hou S 4E **129**
  NE33: S Shi 6F **63**
Hunter Ter. SR2: Sund 3E **119**
Huntingdon Cl. NE3: Ken 5G **41**
Huntingdon Dr. NE23: Cra 2C **22**
Huntingdon Gdns. SR3: Sund . . .4A **118**
Huntingdon Pl. NE30: N Shi 6F **49**
Huntingdon Rd. SR8: Pet 5C **162**
Huntingdonshire Dr.
  DH1: Carr 4B **156**
Hunt Lea NE16: Whi 6C **80**
Huntley Av. SR7: Mur 2B **150**
Huntley Cres. NE21: Bla T 3G **79**
Huntley Sq. SR4: Sund 2F **117**
Huntley Ter. SR2: Ryh 3F **133**
Huntly Rd. NE25: Whit B 4G **35**
Huntscliffe Ho. NE34: S Shi 6E **75**
Hurst Ter. NE6: Walk 3E **71**
Hurstwood Rd. SR4: Sund 3A **118**

Hurworth Av. NE34: S Shi 3A 76
Hurworth Pl. NE32: Jar 3F 73
Hustledown Gdns. DH9: Stly ...5D 122
Hustledown Ho. DH9: Stly 3D 122
Hustledown Rd. DH9: Stly 5C 122
Hutton Cl. DH3: Ches S 2E 135
　NE4: Hou S 3G 137
　NE38: Wash 2F 113
Hutton Ho. NE29: N Shi 4A 62
Hutton St. NE3: Gos 2C 56
　NE35: Bol C 2B 88
　SR4: Sund 2B 118
Hutton Ter. NE2: Newc T ...2H 69 (1G 5)
　NE9: Gate 1H 97
Huxley Cl. NE34: S Shi 1D 88
Huxley Cres. NE8: Gate 4G 83
Hyacinth Ct. SR4: Sund 6B 104
Hybrid Cl. DH4: Hou S 4D 128
Hyde Pk. NE28: W'snd 4F 59
Hyde Pk. St. NE8: Gate 3F 83
Hyde St. NE33: S Shi 5F 63
　SR2: Sund 3F 119
Hyde Ter. NE3: Gos 2F 57
Hylton Av. NE34: S Shi 3B 76
Hylton Bank SR4: Sund 1D 116
HYLTON CASTLE 3C 102
Hylton Castle (restored) 3D 102
Hylton Castle Rd. SR5: C'twn ...4D 102
Hylton Cl. NE22: Bed 4F 9
Hylton Cl. NE38: Wash 2H 113
Hylton La. NE36: W Bol 5C 88
　SR5: C'twn 5C 88
Hylton Pk. SR5: Sund 4G 103
Hylton Pk. Rd. SR5: Sund 4F 103
HYLTON RED HOUSE 3E 103
Hylton Riverside Retail Pk.
　SR5: Sund 4F 103
Hylton Rd. DH1: Dur 1C 154
　NE32: Jar 5F 73
　SR4: Sund 3C 116
Hylton St. DH4: Hou S 1H 137
　NE8: Gate 2B 84
　NE29: N Shi 3C 62
　SR4: Sund 1A 118
Hylton Ter. DH2: Pelt 2G 125
　NE10: Gate 1H 85
　NE29: N Shi 2C 62
　SR2: Ryh 3E 133
Hylton Wlk. SR4: Sund 2C 116
　(not continuous)
Hymers Av. NE34: S Shi 5B 74
Hyperion Av. NE34: S Shi 4C 74

I

Ilchester St. SR7: S'hm 5B 142
Ilderton Pl. NE5: Newc T 1C 66
Ilford Av. NE23: Cra 6A 16
Ilford Pl. NE8: Gate 3A 84
Ilford Rd. NE2: Gos 4F 57
　NE28: W'snd 4D 60
Ilford Road Station (Metro) 4F 57
Ilfracombe Av. NE4: Newc T 4A 68
Ilfracombe Gdns. NE9: Gate ...2H 97
　NE26: Whit B 5B 36
Illingworth Ho. NE29: N Shi 4A 62
Ilminster Ct. NE3: Ken 1G 55
Imeary Gro. NE33: S Shi 6F 63
Imeary St. NE33: S Shi 6F 63
Imex Bus. Cen. DH3: Bir 3B 112
Imperial Bldgs. DH4: Hou S ...3A 138
Inchberry Cl. NE4: Newc T 5A 68

Inchcape Ter. SR8: Eas 2F 163
Inchcliffe Cres. NE5: Newc T ...5G 55
Independence Sq.
　NE38: Wash 2A 114
Industrial Rd. NE37: Usw 5C 100
　NE37: Wash 6C 100
Industrial St. DH2: Pelt 3E 125
Industry Rd. NE6: Newc T 5D 58
Ingham Grange NE33: S Shi 6F 63
Ingham Gro. NE23: Cra 6A 16
Ingham Pl.
　NE2: Newc T 3H 69 (3H 5)
Ingleborough Cl. NE37: Wash ...1G 113
Ingleby Ter. SR4: Sund 2A 118
Ingleby Way NE24: News 4A 18
Inglemere Pl. NE15: Newc T 3E 67
Ingleside NE16: Whi 5D 80
　NE34: S Shi 3B 76
Ingleside Rd. NE29: N Shi 6B 48
Ingleton Ct. SR4: Sund 2B 118
Ingleton Dr. NE15: Thro 5B 52
Ingleton Gdns. NE24: News 4A 18
Inglewood Cl. NE24: Cow 6F 11
Inglewood Pl. NE3: Gos 4E 43
Ingoe Av. NE3: Ken 6B 42
Ingoe Cl. NE24: Bly 6A 12
Ingoe St. NE15: Lem 3A 66
　NE28: W'snd 5G 61
Ingoldsby Ct. SR4: Sund 3G 117
Ingram Av. NE3: Ken 5B 42
Ingram Cl. DH2: Ches S 2A 134
　NE28: W'snd 2D 60
Ingram Dr. NE5: Cha P 3B 54
　NE24: Bly 6H 11
Ingram Ter. NE6: Walk 3G 71
Inkerman Rd. NE37: Usw 4B 100
Inkerman St. SR5: S'wck 4A 104
Inleborough Dr. NE40: Ryton ...5D 64
Innesmoor NE31: Heb 2B 72
Inskip Ho. NE34: S Shi 4E 75
Inskip Ter. NE8: Gate 3H 83
Institute Ter. DH7: Ush M 4E 153
Institute Ter. E. DH2: Ous 1H 125
Institute Ter. W. DH2: Ous 1H 125
Interchange Cen. NE8: Gate 6G 69
International Cen.
　for Life, The 5E 69 (6B 4)
Inverness Rd. NE32: Jar 6A 74
Inverness St. SR6: Monk 3D 104
Invincible Dr. NE4: Newc T 6C 68
Iolanthe Cres. NE6: Walk 2E 71
Iolanthe Ter. NE33: S Shi 5G 63
Iona Ct. NE28: W'snd 3D 60
Iona Pl. NE6: Walk 3G 71
Iona Rd. NE10: Gate 4B 84
　NE32: Jar 6A 74
Irene Av. SR2: Sund 6F 119
Iris Cl. NE21: Bla T 1G 79
Iris Cres. DH2: Ous 5H 111
Iris Pl. NE4: Newc T 2H 67
Iris Steadman Ho.
　NE4: Newc T 3C 68
　(off Thorpe Cl.)
Iris Ter. DH4: Hou S 6C 128
Ironside St. DH5: Hou S 2A 138
Irthing Av. NE6: Newc T 5D 70
Irton St. NE3: Gos 2E 57
Irvine Ho. NE12: Longb 5D 44
Irwin Av. NE28: W'snd 4A 60
Isabella Cl. NE4: Newc T 6A 68
Isabella Colliery Rd.
　NE24: Bly 1A 18
ISABELLA PIT 1A 18

Isabella Rd. NE24: Bly 1A 18
Isabella Wlk. NE15: Thro 6D 52
Isis Rd. SR8: Pet 2C 164
Islay Ho. SR3: New S 3A 132
Islestone NE9: Gate 1H 97
Ivanhoe NE25: Whit B 6A 36
Ivanhoe Cres. SR2: Sund 3B 118
Ivanhoe Ter. DH3: Ches S 1D 134
　DH9: Dip 6E 107
Ivanhoe Vw. NE9: Gate 3B 98
Iveagh Cl. NE4: Newc T 5H 67
Iveston Ter. DH9: Stly 2D 122
Ivor St. SR2: Sund 5G 119
Ivy Av. NE40: Ryton 3C 64
　SR7: S'hm 5H 141
　(not continuous)
Ivy Cl. NE4: Newc T 6D 68
　NE40: Ryton 3C 64
Ivy La. NE9: Gate 2A 98
Ivymount Rd. NE6: Newc T 6B 58
Ivy Pl. DH9: Tan L 4A 108
Ivy Rd. NE3: Gos 2E 57
　NE6: Walk 1F 71
　NE12: Longb 5E 45
Ivy St. NE13: Sea B 3E 31
Ivy Ter. DH4: Hou S 3F 129
　DH9: Stly 6F 123
　(Middles, The)
　DH9: Stly 5B 122
　(South Moor)
Ivyway DH2: Pelt 2G 125

J

Jack Common Ho.
　NE6: Newc T 2B 70
Jack Crawford Ho. SR2: Sund ...3F 119
Jackson Av. NE20: Pon 4F 27
Jackson St. NE6: Walk 3F 71
　NE8: Gate 6H 69
　NE30: N Shi 1D 62
　SR4: Sund 2A 118
Jackson St. W. NE30: N Shi 1D 62
Jack's Ter. NE34: S Shi 4E 75
Jacobins Chare
　NE1: Newc T 4E 69 (4B 4)
Jacques St. SR4: Sund 6H 103
Jacques Ter. DH2: Ches S 5B 126
Jade Cl. NE15: Lem 1A 66
James Armitage St.
　SR5: S'wck 3B 104
James Av. NE27: Shir 2D 46
James Bowman Ho. NE12: Kil ...2E 45
James Clydesdale Ho.
　NE15: Newc T 2E 67
James Mather St. NE33: S Shi ...4F 63
James Pl. St. NE6: Newc T 3A 70
James St. DH9: Ann P 5G 121
　DH9: Dip 2B 120
　DH9: Stly 6D 108
　NE4: Newc T 5B 68
　NE5: Newc T 5D 54
　NE16: Whi 4E 81
　SR5: S'wck 3A 104
　SR7: S'hm 5B 142
　SR8: Eas 1D 162
James St. Nth. SR7: Mur 2D 150
　(off Nth. Coronation St.)
James St. Sth. SR7: Mur 2D 150
James Ter. DH4: Hou S 3E 137
　DH5: Eas L 5D 148
　NE28: W'snd 6H 59

James Williams St.
SR1: Sund 6E **105**
Jamieson Ter. DH6: S Het 6B **150**
Jane Eyre Ter. NE8: Gate 2B **84**
Jane St. DH5: Hett H 5C **138**
DH9: Stly 5B **122**
NE6: Newc T 3C **70**
Jane Ter. NE6: Walk 4G **71**
Janet Sq. NE6: Newc T 4C **70**
Janet St. NE6: Newc T 4C **70**
(Bolam Way)
NE6: Newc T 5C **70**
(St Peter's Rd., not continuous)
Janus Cl. NE5: Cha P 3A **54**
JARROW 2F **73**
Jarrow Riverside Pk.
NE32: Jar 1G **73**
Jarrow Rd. NE34: Jar, S Shi 3B **74**
Jarrow Station (Metro) 2F **73**
Jarvis Rd. SR8: Pet 5D **162**
Jasmin Av. NE5: Cha P 3A **54**
Jasmine Cl. NE6: Walk 6E **59**
Jasmine Ct. SR4: Sund 6B **104**
Jasmine Cres. SR7: S'hm 6A **142**
Jasmine Ter. DH3: Bir 3D **112**
Jasmine Vs. *NE16: Whi* 4E **81**
(off Front St.)
Jasper Av. NE40: G'sde 2B **78**
SR7: S'hm 5H **141**
(not continuous)
Jaycroft Ct. *NE30: N Shi* 2D **62**
(off Stephenson St.)
Jedburgh Cl. NE5: Cha P 3A **54**
NE8: Gate 2H **83**
NE29: N Shi 5A **48**
SR7: Mur 3A **150**
Jedburgh Ct. NE11: Gate 3G **97**
Jedburgh Gdns. NE15: Newc T 3F **67**
Jedburgh Rd. DH4: Hou S 3F **129**
NE2: Newc T 6A **56**
NE4: Newc T 6A **56**
NE5: Newc T 6A **56**
Jedmoor NE31: Heb 2B **72**
Jefferson Cl. SR5: Monk 1C **104**
Jefferson Pl. NE4: Newc T 3D **68**
Jellicoe Rd. NE6: Walk 6F **71**
Jellico Ter. DH4: Leam 2B **146**
Jenifer Gro. NE7: Newc T 4A **58**
Jenison Av. NE15: Newc T 4G **67**
Jennifer Av. SR5: C'twn 4D **102**
Jervis St. NE31: Heb 3D **72**
JESMOND 6H **57**
Jesmond Dene Rd.
NE2: Gos, Newc T 5F **57**
Jesmond Dene Ter.
NE2: Newc T 6A **58**
Jesmond Gdns. NE2: Newc T 6H **57**
NE34: S Shi 6E **75**
Jesmond Pk. Ct. NE7: Newc T 6B **58**
Jesmond Pk. E. NE7: Newc T 5B **58**
Jesmond Pk. M. NE7: Newc T 6A **58**
Jesmond Pk. W. NE7: Newc T 5A **58**
Jesmond Pl. NE2: Newc T 6G **57**
Jesmond Rd. NE2: Newc T 2H **69**
Jesmond Rd. W.
NE2: Newc T 2F **69** (1D **4**)
Jesmond Station (Metro) 2G **69**
Jesmond Swimming Pool 5G **57**
Jesmond Ter. NE26: Whit B 1D **48**
JESMOND VALE 1B **70**
Jesmond Va. NE2: Newc T 2A **70**
(not continuous)
Jesmond Va. La. NE6: Newc T . . .1B **70**

Jesmond Va. Ter. NE6: Newc T . . .1B **70**
(not continuous)
Jessel St. NE9: Gate 1H **97**
Jetty, The NE10: Gate 1G **85**
Joan Av. SR2: Sund 6F **119**
Joannah St. SR5: Monk 2C **104**
Joan St. NE4: Newc T 5H **67**
(not continuous)
Jobling Av. NE21: Bla T 1G **79**
Joel Ter. NE10: Gate 1H **85**
John Av. NE40: G'sde 2B **78**
John Brown Ct. NE22: Bed 4H **9**
John Candlish Rd. SR4: Sund . . .6A **104**
John Clay St. NE33: S Shi 1F **75**
(Dean Rd.)
NE33: S Shi 6F **63**
(Victoria Rd.)
John Dobson St.
NE1: Newc T 3F **69** (2D **4**)
John F Kennedy Est.
NE38: Wash 2C **114**
(not continuous)
John George Joicey Mus.
. . . . .4G **69** (5E **5**)
John Reid Rd. NE34: S Shi 5A **74**
(not continuous)
Johnson Cl. SR8: Pet 5D **162**
Johnson St. NE8: Gate 2D **82**
NE11: Dun 2B **82**
NE15: Lem 3A **66**
NE33: S Shi 2E **75**
SR1: Sund 6B **104** (3E **7**)
Johnson Ter. DH9: Ann P 6G **121**
NE37: Usw 5D **100**
NE39: H Spen 1A **92**
Johnston Av. NE31: Heb 6B **72**
John St. DH1: Dur 6B **154**
DH4: Hou S 3E **137**
DH5: Hett H 1C **148**
DH5: Hou S 3B **138**
DH9: Beam 2H **123**
DH9: Stly 6G **123**
(Craghead)
DH9: Stly 5B **122**
(South Moor)
NF3: Gos 2G **57**
(Bowes St.)
NE3: Gos 2C **56**
(Kenton Rd.)
NE8: Gate 2B **84**
NE10: Gate 2F **85**
NE24: Cow 5H **11**
NE25: Well 6E **35**
NE28: W'snd 5H **59**
NE30: N Shi 1E **49**
NE35: Bol C 3B **88**
SR1: Sund 6D **104** (3H **7**)
SR2: Ryh 3G **133**
SR4: Sund 6C **102**
SR8: Eas 1E **163**
John St. Nth. DH7: B'don 5F **159**
John St. Sth. DH7: B'don 5F **159**
John Taylor Ct. SR5: S'wck 2A **104**
John Williamson St.
NE33: S Shi 2D **74**
John Wilson Ct. SR8: Pet 6G **163**
Joicey Gdns. DH9: Stly 2D **122**
Joicey Pl. NE9: Gate 5A **84**
Joicey Rd. NE9: Gate 5H **83**
Joicey St. NE10: Gate 2G **85**
Joicey Ter. DH9: Tan L 1B **122**
Jolliffe St. DH3: Ches S 2D **134**
Jonadab Rd. NE10: Gate 1G **85**

Jonadab St. NE10: Gate 2G **85**
Jones St. DH3: Bir 3C **112**
Jonquil Cl. NE5: Cha P 3A **54**
Joseph Cl. NE4: Newc T 5A **68**
Joseph Hopper Aged
Miners Homes DH3: Bir 6C **98**
Joseph Hopper
Memorial Homes 5B **84**
Joseph St. DH9: Stly 4C **122**
Jowett Sq. SR5: S'wck 3A **104**
Joyce Cl. NE10: Gate 3B **86**
Joyce Gro. SR8: Pet 4A **164**
Joyce Ter. SR5: C'twn 4D **102**
Jubilee Av. NE9: Spri 4C **98**
SR7: Mur 5F **141**
Jubilee Cen. SR7: S'hm 4B **142**
Jubilee Cl. DH7: New B 2B **158**
Jubilee Cotts. DH4: Hou S 3H **137**
Jubilee Ct. NE8: Gate 3E **83**
NE23: Dud 2B **32**
NE24: Bly 1B **18**
NE31: Heb 3F **73**
Jubilee Cres. DH6: Sher 6H **157**
(not continuous)
NE3: Gos 2C **56**
Jubilee Ho. DH5: Eas L 4E **149**
Jubilee Lodge NE23: Cra 5B **22**
Jubilee M. NE3: Gos 2D **56**
Jubilee Pl. DH1: H Shin 3F **161**
Jubilee Rd.
NE1: Newc T 4H **69** (4G **5**)
NE3: Ken 1C **56**
NE24: Bly 1C **18**
Jubilee Sq. DH5: Eas L 5E **149**
DH6: S Het 6H **149**
NE38: Wash 2A **114**
Jubilee St. NE28: W'snd 5H **59**
Jubilee Ter. DH9: Ann P 5H **121**
DH9: Tan L 5G **107**
NE6: Newc T 3D **70**
(not continuous)
NE13: Sea B 3D **30**
NE16: Swa 2E **81**
NE22: Bed 3D **10**
NE38: Wash 5E **115**
Jude Pl. SR8: Pet 5C **162**
Jude St. SR8: Eas 1C **162**
Judson Rd. SR8: Pet 6A **162**
Julian Av. NE6: Walk 2E **71**
NE33: S Shi 3F **63**
Julian Rd. NE10: Gate 3B **86**
Julian St. NE33: S Shi 3F **63**
Juliet Av. NE29: N Shi 1H **61**
Julius Caesar St. SR5: S'wck 3A **104**
June Av. NE21: Bla T 5A **80**
Juniper Cl. NE3: Gos 4E **43**
NE24: News 3A **18**
SR2: Sund 3E **119**
Juniper Ct. NE21: Bla T 6A **66**
Juniper Wlk. NE5: Cha P 3B **54**
Jupiter Ct. SR8: Eas 1C **162**
Jupiter Health & Fitness Cen.
. . . . .1B **162**
Jutland Av. NE31: Heb 4C **72**
Jutland Ter. DH9: Tan L 1B **122**

K

Kane Gdns. NE10: Gate 5C **84**
Karting North East (Go-Kart Track)
. . . . .2G **139**
Kascada Bowl 5C **154** (1B **6**)

Kateregina DH3: Bir 3D **112**
Katrine Cl. DH2: Ches S 1B **134**
Katrine Ct. SR3: New S 4A **132**
Kayll Rd. SR4: Sund 1H **117**
Kay's Cotts. NE10: Gate 4C **84**
Kay St. DH9: Stly 2D **122**
Kearsley Cl. NE25: Sea D 6B **24**
Kearton Av. NE5: Cha P 4A **54**
Keats Av. NE24: Bly 2A **18**
  NE35: Bol C 3D **88**
  SR5: S'wck 3A **104**
Keats Cl. DH9: Stly 3E **123**
Keats Rd. NE15: Lem 3G **65**
Keats Wlk. NE8: Gate 1A **84**
  NE34: S Shi 6C **74**
Keebledale Av. NE6: Walk 2F **71**
Keele Dr. NE23: Cra 3F **21**
Keelman's Ho. NE24: Bly 5C **12**
  (off Summers St.)
Keelmans La. SR4: Sund 6E **103**
Keelman Sq. NE1: Newc T 5G **5**
Keelman's Rd. SR4: Sund 6D **102**
Keelmans Ter. NE24: Bly 5C **12**
Keelman's Way NE8: Gate 1E **83**
Keelmen's Hospital
  NE1: Newc T 4H **69** (5G **5**)
Keel Row NE11: Swa 6F **67**
  NE24: Bly 5C **12**
Keighley Av. SR5: C'twn 1D **102**
Keighley Sq. SR5: C'twn 1C **102**
Keir Hardie Av. DH9: Stly 4D **122**
  NE10: Gate 3G **85**
Keir Hardie St. DH4: Hou S 3F **137**
  NE39: Row G 3B **92**
Keir Hardie Ter. DH3: Bir 1B **112**
Keith Cl. NE4: Newc T 5A **68**
Keith Sq. SR5: C'twn 1D **102**
Keldane Gdns. NE4: Newc T 4A **68**
Kelfield Gro. NE23: Cra 5B **16**
Kelham Sq. SR5: C'twn 1C **102**
Kell Cres. DH6: Sher 6G **157**
Kellfield Av. NE9: Gate 5A **84**
Kellfield Rd. NE9: Gate 6A **84**
Kell Rd. SR8: Pet 1F **165**
Kells Bldgs. DH1: Dur 1H **159**
Kells Gdns. NE9: Gate 6A **84**
Kells La. NE9: Gate 1H **97**
Kells Way NE39: Row G 4E **93**
Kellsway NE10: Gate 6F **85**
Kellsway Ct. NE10: Gate 6F **85**
Kelly Rd. NE31: Heb 6C **72**
Kelpie Gdns. SR6: Monk 4E **105**
Kelsey Way NE23: Cra 5B **16**
Kelso Cl. NE5: Cha P 3A **54**
Kelso Dr. NE29: N Shi 5A **48**
Kelso Gdns. NE15: Newc T 3F **67**
  NE22: Bed 4C **10**
  NE28: W'snd 3E **61**
Kelso Gro. DH4: Hou S 3E **129**
Kelson Way NE5: Cha P 3A **54**
Kelso Pl. NE8: Gate 2D **82**
Kelston Way NE5: Newc T 5G **55**
Kelvin Gdns. NE11: Dun 2B **82**
Kelvin Gro. NE2: Newc T 2H **69**
  NE8: Gate 3F **83**
  NE29: N Shi 5C **48**
  NE33: S Shi 6H **63**
  SRG: Cle 2G **89**
  SR6: Monk 3E **105**
Kelvin Pl. NE12: Longb 4G **45**
Kemble Cl. NE23: Cra 5B **16**
Kemble Sq. SR5: C'twn 1D **102**
Kemp Rd. SR8: Pet 6C **162**

Kempton Gdns. NE8: Gate 4E **83**
Kendal DH3: Bir 5E **113**
  (not continuous)
Kendal Av. NE24: Bly 1B **18**
  NE30: N Shi 3D **48**
Kendal Cl. SR8: Pet 4A **164**
Kendal Cres. NE9: Gate 1B **98**
Kendal Dr. NE23: Cra 1C **22**
  NE36: E Bol 4E **89**
Kendale Wlk. NE5: Newc T 4C **54**
Kendal Gdns. NE28: W'snd 2E **61**
Kendal Grn. NE6: Newc T 4B **70**
  (off Kendal St.)
Kendal Ho. NE6: Newc T 3B **70**
Kendal Pl. NE6: Newc T 4B **70**
Kendal St. NE6: Newc T 4B **70**
Kenilworth DH3: Gt Lum 3G **135**
  NE12: Kil 1D **44**
Kenilworth Ct. NE4: Newc T 5C **68**
  NE37: Usw 5D **100**
Kenilworth Rd. NE4: Newc T 5C **68**
  NE25: Whit B 6B **36**
Kenilworth Sq. SR5: C'twn 1E **103**
Kenilworth Vw. NE9: Gate 3A **98**
Kenley Rd. NE5: Newc T 1E **67**
  SR5: C'twn 1D **102**
Kenmoor Way NE5: Cha P 4A **54**
Kenmore Cl. NE10: Gate 3H **85**
Kenmore Cres. NE40: G'sde 1B **78**
Kennersdene NE30: N Shi 4E **49**
Kennet Av. NE32: Jar 6G **73**
Kennet Sq. SR5: C'twn 1D **102**
Kennford NE9: Gate 3A **98**
Kennington Gro. NE6: Walk 4E **71**
Kenny Pl. DH1: Dur 4F **155**
Kensington Av. NE3: Gos 6E **43**
Kensington Cl. NE25: Whit B 6B **36**
Kensington Ct. NE10: Gate 3C **84**
  NE31: Heb 4B **72**
  NE33: S Shi 1G **75**
Kensington Gdns.
  NE25: Whit B 6B **36**
  NE28: W'snd 1E **59**
  NE30: N Shi 1D **62**
Kensington Gro. NE30: N Shi 6D **48**
Kensington Ter. NE2: Newc T 2F **69**
  NE11: Dun 3B **82**
Kensington Vs. NE5: Newc T 4C **54**
Kent Av. NE11: Dun 3C **82**
  NE28: W'snd 5D **60**
  NE31: Heb 4B **72**
Kentchester Rd. SR5: C'twn 1E **103**
Kent Ct. NE3: Ken 5H **41**
Kent Gdns. DH5: Hett H 1B **148**
Kentmere Av. NE6: Walk 3F **71**
  SR6: Monk 6C **90**
Kentmere Cl. NE23: Seg 1G **33**
Kentmere Ho. DH4: Hou S 1G **137**
Kentmere Pl. SR8: Pet 1E **165**
KENTON 3A **56**
Kenton Av. NE3: Ken 4C **56**
KENTON BANKFOOT 1F **55**
KENTON BAR 3H **55**
Kenton Ct. NE33: S Shi 6F **63**
Kenton Cres. NE3: Ken 3B **56**
Kenton Gro. SR6: Monk 4D **104**
Kenton La. NE3: Ken, Newc T . . .3H **55**
Kenton Pk. Shop. Cen.
  NE3: Ken 4C **56**
Kenton Rd. NE3: Gos, Ken 2C **56**
  NE29: N Shi 6G **47**
Kent Pl. NE34: S Shi 3A **76**

Kent St. NE32: Jar 3E **73**
Kentucky Rd. SR5: C'twn 1C **102**
Kent Vs. NE32: Jar 3E **73**
Kent Wlk. SR8: Pet 5C **162**
Kenwood Gdns. NE9: Gate 3A **98**
  (not continuous)
Kenya Rd. SR5: C'twn 1E **103**
Kepier Chare NE40: Ryton 5A **64**
Kepier Ct. DH1: Dur 5D **154** (1D **6**)
Kepier Cres. DH1: Dur 4G **155**
  (not continuous)
Kepier Gdns. SR4: Sund 1C **116**
Kepier Hgts. DH1: Dur . . .5D **154** (1D **6**)
Kepier La. DH1: Dur 4E **155**
  (not continuous)
Kepier Ter. DH1: Dur 5D **154** (1D **6**)
Kepier Vs. DH1: Dur 1D **6**
Keppel St. NE11: Dun 2B **82**
  NE33: S Shi 4E **63**
Kerry Cl. NE24: Bly 5C **12**
Kerryhill Dr. DH1: Dur 5C **144**
Kerry Sq. SR5: C'twn 1D **102**
Kestel Cl. NE40: Ryton 5A **64**
Kesteven Sq. SR5: C'twn 1D **102**
Keston Dr. NE23: Cra 5B **16**
Kestrel Cl. NE38: Wash 5G **113**
Kestrel Ct. DH3: Bir 3C **112**
Kestrel Lodge Flats
  NE33: S Shi 4F **63**
Kestrel M. NE16: Whi 4E **81**
Kestrel Pl. NE12: Longb 6A **44**
Kestrel Sq. SR5: C'twn 1D **102**
Kestrel Way NE29: N Shi 4C **62**
  NE34: S Shi 5D **74**
Keswick Av. SR6: Monk 1C **104**
Keswick Dr. NE30: N Shi 3D **48**
Keswick Gdns. NE28: W'snd 4E **61**
Keswick Gro. NE5: Newc T 1E **67**
Keswick Rd. DH9: Stly 5B **122**
  SR8: Pet 6E **163**
Keswick St. NE8: Gate 2G **83**
Keswick Ter. DH6: S Het 5G **149**
Kettering Pl. NE23: Cra 1C **22**
Kettering Sq. SR5: C'twn 1D **102**
Kettlewell Ter. NE30: N Shi 1D **62**
Ketton Cl. NE12: Longb 1B **58**
Kew Gdns. NE26: Whit B 5B **36**
Kew Sq. SR5: C'twn 1C **102**
Keyes Gdns. NE2: Gos 4G **57**
KIBBLESWORTH 1E **111**
Kibblesworth Bank NE11: Kib . . .2C **110**
Kicks Leisure Club 6H **59**
  (off Warwick Rd.)
Kidd Av. DH6: Sher 6D **156**
Kidderminster Dr. NE5: Cha P . . .4A **54**
Kidderminster Rd.
  SR5: C'twn 2D **102**
Kidderminster Sq. SR5: C'twn . . .2D **102**
Kidd Sq. SR5: C'twn 1D **102**
Kidlandlee Grn. NE5: Newc T 3E **55**
Kidlandlee Pl. NE5: Newc T 3E **55**
Kidsgrove Sq. SR5: C'twn 1D **102**
Kielder NE38: Wash 3F **113**
Kielder Av. NE23: Cra 3F **21**
Kielder Cl. NE5: Newc T 4E **55**
  NE12: Kil 1C **44**
  NE24: Bly 2H **17**
Kielder Gdns. NE32: Jar 6F **73**
Kielder Ho. SR3: New S 3A **132**
Kielder Pl. NE25: Well 6F **35**
Kielder Rd. NE15: Lem 2H **65**
  NE25: Well 6F **35**
Kielder Ter. NE30: N Shi 1D **62**

Kielder Way NE3: Gos 6D **42**
Kier Hardie Way SR5: S'wck 4B **104**
Kilburn Cl. SR2: Ryh 3G **133**
Kilburn Dr. SR8: Pet 4F **163**
Kilburne Cl. NE7: Newc T 4E **59**
Kilburn Gdns. NE29: N Shi 4H **61**
Kilburn Grn. NE9: Gate 4B **98**
  (not continuous)
Kildale DH4: Pen 1C **128**
Kildare Sq. SR5: C'twn 1D **102**
Killarney Av. SR5: C'twn 1D **102**
Killarney Sq. SR5: C'twn 1D **102**
Killiebrigs NE15: Hed W 5F **51**
Killin Cl. NE5: Cha P 3A **54**
KILLINGWORTH 2D **44**
Killingworth Av. NE27: Back 1G **45**
Killingworth Dr. NE12: Kil 3B **44**
  SR4: Sund 3F **117**
Killingworth Ind. Area
  NE12: Kil 2B **44**
Killingworth La. NE12: Kil 3E **45**
  NE27: Back 1G **45**
Killingworth Leisure Cen. 2D **44**
Killingworth Pl.
  NE1: Newc T 3F **69** (3C **4**)
Killingworth Rd.
  NE3: Gos, Newc T 2H **57**
  NE12: Kil 4E **45**
Killingworth Shop. Cen.
  NE12: Kil 2D **44**
Killingworth Swimming Pool . . .2D **44**
KILLINGWORTH VILLAGE 3E **45**
Killingworth Way NE12: Kil 1A **44**
  NE23: Kil 1A **44**
  NE27: Back, Kil 1A **44**
Killowen St. NE9: Gate 1G **97**
Kilnhill Wlk. SR8: Pet 1E **165**
Kiln Ri. NE16: Whi 1E **95**
Kilnshaw Pl. NE3: Gos 4F **43**
Kilsyth Av. NE29: N Shi 3A **48**
Kilsyth Sq. SR5: C'twn 2D **102**
Kimberley NE38: Wash 2E **115**
Kimberley Av. NE29: N Shi 1A **62**
Kimberley Gdns. DH9: Stly 6G **123**
  NE2: Newc T 1A **70**
Kimberley St. NE24: Bly 5B **12**
  SR4: Sund 1H **117**
Kimberley Ter. NE24: Bly 5C **12**
KIMBLESWORTH 2A **144**
Kimblesworth Ind. Est.
  DH1: Plaw 3A **144**
Kinfauns Ter. NE9: Gate 6A **84**
Kingarth Av. SR6: Monk 6F **91**
King Charles Ct. SR6: C'twn 1C **102**
King Charles Twr.
  NE2: Newc T 3H **69** (2G **5**)
Kingdom Pl. NE29: N Shi 4C **62**
King Edward Bri. Arches
  NE1: Newc T 6F **69**
King Edward Pl. NE8: Gate 2B **84**
King Edward Rd. NE6: Newc T 6B **58**
  NE30: Shi 6E **49**
  NE40: Ryton 5E **65**
  SR4: Sund 1D **116**
  SR7: S'hm 6B **142**
King Edward St. DH9: Tan L 6A **108**
  NE8: Gate 2B **84**
King Edward VIII Ter.
  DH9: Stly 1E **123**
Kingfisher Blvd. NE15: Lem 4A **66**
Kingfisher Ct. NE11: Dun 1C **82**
Kingfisher Ind. Est.
  SR7: S'hm 3G **141**

Kingfisher Lodge NE32: Jar 3E **73**
Kingfisher Rd. NE12: Longb 6A **44**
Kingfisher Way NE24: News 3D **18**
  NE28: W'snd 1E **61**
King George Av. NE11: Dun 4B **82**
King George VI Bldg.
  NE1: Newc T 2C **4**
King George Rd. NE3: Ken 1A **56**
  NE34: S Shi 2G **75**
Kingham Ct. NE3: Newc T 3H **57**
King Henry Ct. SR5: C'twn 1C **102**
Kinghorn Sq. SR5: C'twn 1D **102**
King James Ct. SR5: C'twn 1C **102**
King James St. NE8: Gate 2H **83**
King John's Ct. NE20: Pon 1A **38**
King John's Palace (remains) . . .1B **70**
King John St. NE6: Newc T 1B **70**
King John Ter. NE6: Newc T 1B **70**
Kings Av. NE31: Heb 4D **72**
  SR6: Monk 6E **91**
Kingsbridge NE12: Longb 6H **43**
Kingsbridge Cl. NE29: N Shi 3A **62**
Kingsbury Cl. SR5: C'twn 1D **102**
Kingsbury Ct. NE12: Longb 1A **58**
Kingsclere Av. SR5: C'twn 1D **102**
Kingsclere Sq. SR5: C'twn 2D **102**
Kings Cl. NE8: Gate 2B **84**
Kings Ct. NE11: Gate 2F **97**
  NE32: Jar 2E **73**
Kingsdale Av. NE24: Cow 6G **11**
  NE37: USW 5H **99**
Kingsdale Rd. NE12: Longb 6H **43**
Kings Dr. NE26: Whit B 6C **36**
  NE40: G'side 2B **78**
King's Gdns. NE24: Cow 5A **12**
Kings Gro. DH1: Dur 2A **160**
Kingsland NE2: Newc T 1G **69**
Kingsland Sq. SR5: C'twn 2D **102**
King's La. DH2: Pelt 2F **125**
  (not continuous)
Kingsley Av. NE3: Gos 4E **43**
  NE25: Whit B 1B **48**
  NE34: S Shi 6C **74**
Kingsley Cl. DH9: Stly 2F **123**
  SR5: S'wck 4A **104**
Kingsley Pl. NE6: Newc T 2B **70**
  NE11: Dun 2B **82**
  NE16: Whi 3F **81**
  NE28: W'snd 4D **60**
Kingsley Ter. NE4: Newc T 4C **68**
King's Mnr.
  NE1: Newc T 4G **69** (4F **5**)
Kings Mdw. NE32: Jar 2G **87**
Kings Mdw. NE4: Newc T 6C **68**
Kingsmere DH3: Ches S 2C **126**
Kingsmere Gdns. NE6: Walk 5G **71**
Kings Pk. NE62: Sco G 1G **9**
King's Pl. SR4: Sund 6A **104**
Kings Rd. NE1: Newc T 3F **69** (2C **4**)
  NE12: Longb 4C **44**
  NE22: Bed 3D **10**
  NE26: Whit B 5B **36**
Kings Rd. Nth. NE28: W'snd 3H **59**
Kings Rd. Sth. NE28: W'snd 4H **59**
King's Rd., The SR6: S'wck 3A **104**
Kings Ter. NE9: Spri 4F **99**
  SR4: Sund 6H **103**
Kingston Av. DH7: Ush M 4C **152**
  NE6: Newc T, Walk 4D **70**
  SR7: S'hm 5H **141**
Kingston Cl. NE26: Whit B 3B **36**
Kingston Ct. NE26: Whit B 3B **36**
  (off Kingston Dr.)

Kingston Dr. NE26: Whit B 3B **36**
Kingston Grn. NE6: Walk 4D **70**
Kingston M. DH4: Hou S 4G **129**
KINGSTON PARK 1G **55**
Kingston Pk. 6F **41**
Kingston Pk. Av. NE3: Ken 1G **55**
Kingston Pk. Rd.
  NE3: Ken, Wool 5G **41**
Kingston Pk. Shop. Cen.
  NE3: Ken 1G **55**
Kingston Park Station (Metro) . . .1G **55**
Kingston Pl. NE8: Gate 3A **84**
Kingston Rd. NE8: Gate 3A **84**
Kingston Ter. SR6: Monk 3D **104**
Kingston Way NE26: Whit B 3B **36**
King St. DH3: Bir 3B **112**
  DH6: Sher 6D **156**
  DH9: Ann P 4F **121**
  NE1: Newc T 5G **69** (6F **5**)
  NE8: Gate 3E **83**
  NE10: Gate 1C **85**
  NE24: Bly 5C **12**
  NE30: N Shi 1D **62**
  NE33: S Shi 4E **63**
  SR1: Sund 6D **104** (3G **7**)
  SR6: Monk 1D **104**
Kings Va. NE28: W'snd 3A **60**
Kings Wlk. NE1: Newc T . . .2F **69** (1C **4**)
  NE5: Cha P 3H **53**
Kingsway DH5: Hou S 3B **138**
  NE4: Newc T 1A **68**
  NE16: Sun 2E **95**
  NE20: Pon 5E **27**
  NE24: Bly 1C **18**
  NE30: N Shi 5E **49**
  NE33: S Shi 5H **63**
Kingsway Av. NE3: Gos 6E **43**
Kingsway Nth. NE11: Gate 5E **83**
Kingsway Rd. SR5: C'twn 1C **102**
Kingsway Sth. NE11: Gate 1F **97**
Kingsway Vs. DH2: Pelt 2F **125**
Kingswood Av. NE2: Gos 4F **57**
Kingswood Cl. NE35: Bol C 2A **88**
Kingswood Ct. NE30: N Shi 6F **49**
Kingswood Dr. NE20: Pon 1C **38**
Kingswood Gro. SR4: Sund 5B **116**
Kingswood Rd. NE23: Cra 1C **22**
Kingswood Sq. SR5: C'twn 2D **102**
King Ter. DH9: Stly 4B **122**
Kinlet NE38: Wash 2E **115**
Kinley Rd. DH1: Carr 2B **156**
Kinloch Ct. DH2: Ches S 2B **134**
Kinloss Sq. NE23: Cra 1C **22**
Kinnaird Av. NE15: Newc T 3E **67**
Kinnock Cl. DH6: Sher 6E **157**
Kinross Cl. DH3: Bir 5D **112**
Kinross Ct. NE10: Gate 1H **85**
Kinross Dr. DH9: Stly 3F **123**
  NE3: Ken 2A **56**
Kinsale Sq. SR5: C'twn 2D **102**
Kinver Dr. NE5: Cha P 4A **54**
KIP HILL 6E **109**
Kip Hill Ct. DH9: Stly 1E **123**
Kipling Av. NE16: Swa, Whi 3F **01**
  NE31: Heb 3D **72**
  NE35: Bol C 3D **88**
Kipling Cl. DH9: Stly 3E **123**
Kipling Ct. NE16: Swa 3F **81**
Kiplings Ter. DH1: Dur 2H **159**
Kipling St. SR5: S'wck 4A **104**
Kipling Wlk. NE8: Gate 1A **84**
Kira Dr. DH1: Dur 5C **144**

Kirby Av. DH1: Dur 2A **154**
Kirby Cl. NE34: S Shi 5B **74**
Kirkbride Pl. NE23: Cra 1C **22**
    (not continuous)
Kirkdale Ct. NE23: Dud 6C **32**
  NE34: S Shi 5C **74**
Kirkdale Grn. NE4: Newc T 5D **68**
Kirkdale Sq. SR5: C'twn 2D **102**
Kirkdale St. DH5: Hett H 3B **148**
Kirkfield Gdns. DH9: Ann P 4E **121**
Kirkham NE38: Wash 3B **114**
Kirkham Av. NE3: Ken 6G **41**
Kirkham Rd. DH1: Dur 1D **154**
Kirkheaton Pl. NE5: Newc T 1G **67**
Kirkland Hill SR8: Pet 6E **163**
Kirklands NE23: Dud 6C **32**
Kirkland Wlk. NE27: Shir 2C **46**
Kirklea Rd. DH5: Hou S 3B **138**
Kirkleatham Gdns.
  NE6: Newc T 5D **58**
Kirkley Av. NE34: S Shi 3A **76**
Kirkley Cl. NE3: Gos 1D **56**
Kirkley Dr. NE20: Pon 4E **27**
Kirkley Lodge NE3: Gos 1D **56**
Kirkley Rd. NE27: Shir 3D **46**
Kirklinton Rd. NE30: N Shi 3C **48**
Kirknewton Cl. DH5: Hou S 3B **138**
Kirkside DH4: E Her 3A **130**
Kirkston Av. NE15: Lem 2B **66**
Kirkstone DH3: Bir 5D **112**
Kirkstone Av. NE30: N Shi 3C **48**
  NE32: Jar 6H **73**
  SR5: Monk 2C **104**
  SR8: Pet 1E **165**
Kirkstone Cl. DH5: Hou S 3B **138**
  NE21: Bla T 3A **80**
Kirkstone Dr. DH1: Carr 2A **156**
Kirkstone Gdns. NE7: Newc T 4A **58**
Kirkstone Rd. NE10: Gate 2F **85**
Kirk St. NE6: Newc T 4C **70**
    (Bolam Way)
  NE6: Newc T 4D **70**
    (Clifford Rd.)
Kirk Vw. DH4: Hou S 6H **129**
Kirkwall Cl. SR5: C'twn 4C **102**
Kirkwood NE23: Dud 6C **32**
Kirkwood Av. SR4: Sund 5C **116**
Kirkwood Dr. NE3: Ken 2A **56**
Kirkwood Gdns. NE10: Gate 2H **85**
Kirkwood Pl. NE3: Gos 4D **42**
Kirton Av. NE4: Newc T 3A **68**
Kirton Pk. Ter. NE29: N Shi 6C **48**
Kirton Way NE23: Cra 1C **22**
Kismet St. SR5: S'wck 3A **104**
Kitchener Rd. SR6: Whit 5E **77**
Kitchener St. NE9: Gate 4A **84**
  SR4: Sund 3H **117**
Kitchener St. DH4: E Her 3H **129**
  NE30: N Shi 6E **49**
  NE32: Jar 4F **73**
  SR2: Sund 6F **119**
Kitching Rd. SR8: Eas 4A **162**
Kittiwake Cl. NE24: News 4C **18**
  NE28: W'snd 6E **47**
Kittiwake Dr. NE38: Wash 4F **113**
Kittiwake Ho. NE26: Whit B 6D **36**
Kitty Brewster Ind. Est.
  NE24: Cow 4F **11**
Kitty Brewster Rd. NE24: Cow . . .5F **11**
Knaresborough Cl. NE22: Bed 3F **9**
Knaresborough Rd.
  SR7: Mur 2C **150**

Knaresborough Sq.
  SR5: C'twn 1E **103**
Knaresdale DH3: Bir 6D **112**
Knarsdale Av. NE29: N Shi 1H **61**
Knarsdale Pl. NE5: Newc T 6C **54**
Kneller Cl. DH9: Stly 3D **122**
Knightsbridge NE3: Gos 1E **57**
  SR3: E Her 1G **131**
Knightsbridge Ct. *NE3: Gos* *1E 57*
    (off Knightsbridge)
Knightside Gdns. NE11: Dun 5B **82**
Knightside Wlk. NE5: Cha P 4A **54**
Knivestone Ct. NE12: Kil 1E **45**
Knobbyends La. NE21: Bla T 3F **79**
Knoll Ri. NE11: Dun 4B **82**
Knollside Cl. SR3: New S 4H **131**
Knoll, The SR2: Sund 2B **118**
Knott Flats NE30: N Shi 1F **63**
Knott Pl. NE15: Newc T 4F **67**
Knoulberry NE37: Wash 1G **113**
Knoulberry Rd. NE37: Wash 1F **113**
Knowledge Hill NE21: Bla T 2H **79**
Knowle Pl. NE12: Longb 2B **58**
Knowles, The NE16: Whi 4G **81**
Knowsley Ct. NE3: Ken 2F **55**
Knox Cl. NE22: Bed 3D **10**
Knox Rd. NE22: Bed 5B **10**
Knox Sq. SR5: S'wck 3A **104**
Knutsford Wlk. NE23: Cra 1C **22**
Kristin Av. NE32: Jar 5G **73**
Kyffin Vw. NE34: S Shi 4B **76**
Kyle Cl. NE4: Newc T 5D **68**
Kyle Rd. NE8: Gate 3E **83**
Kyloe Av. NE25: Sea D 1B **34**
Kyloe Cl. NE3: Ken 6A **42**
Kyloe Pl. NE5: Newc T 4E **55**
Kyloe Vs. NE5: Newc T 4E **55**
Kyo Heugh Rd.
  DH9: Ann P, Tan L 3G **121**
Kyo La. DH9: Tan L 3H **121**
Kyo Rd. DH9: Ann P 4F **121**

L

Laburnum Av. DH1: Dur 6B **154**
  NE6: Walk 1F **71**
  NE10: Gate 4G **85**
  NE24: Bly 5B **12**
  NE26: Whit B 6C **36**
  NE28: W'snd 5H **59**
  NE38: Wash 6H **113**
Laburnum Cl. SR4: Sund 1C **116**
Laburnum Ct. DH7: Ush M 5D **152**
  NE12: Kil 1C **44**
Laburnum Cres. NE11: Kib 1E **111**
  SR7: S'hm 6A **142**
  SR8: Eas 1C **162**
Laburnum Gdns. NE9: Gate 5H **83**
  NE10: Gate 2D **84**
  NE32: Jar 5E **73**
Laburnum Gro. NE16: Sun 2F **95**
  NE16: Whi 4E **81**
  NE31: Heb 6C **72**
  NE34: S Shi 4H **75**
  SR5: C'twn 5C **102**
  SR6: Cle 2A **90**
Laburnum Ho. NE28: W'snd 6A **60**
Laburnum Pk. DH7: B'don 6B **158**
Laburnum Rd. NE21: Bla T 1A **80**
  SR6: Monk 2D **104**
Laburnum Ter. DH9: Ann P 4E **121**

Lacebark DH4: Hou S 3D **128**
  SR3: New S 5G **131**
Ladock Cl. SR2: Ryh 1G **133**
Lady Anne Rd. DH6: Sher 5D **156**
Ladybank NE5: Cha P 4H **53**
Lady Beatrice Ter. DH4: E Her . . .2A **130**
Lady Durham Cl. DH6: Sher 6C **156**
Ladyhaugh Dr. NE16: Whi 1E **95**
Lady in Leisure
  Kingston Park 1G **55**
Ladykirk Rd. NE4: Newc T 4A **68**
Ladykirk Way NE23: Cra 3G **21**
LADY PARK 3E **97**
Ladyrigg NE20: Pon 1D **38**
Ladysmith Ct. DH9: Stly 4E **123**
    (not continuous)
Ladysmith St. NE33: S Shi 5F **63**
Ladysmith Ter. DH7: Ush M 5B **152**
Lady's Piece La. DH6: H Pitt 1E **157**
Lady St. DH5: Hett H 6C **138**
Lady's Wlk. NE33: S Shi 3E **63**
Ladywell Rd. NE21: Bla T 1A **80**
Ladywell Way NE20: Pon 4D **26**
Ladywood Pk. DH4: Pen 1D **128**
Laet St. NE29: N Shi 2D **62**
Laindon Av. SR6: Monk 1D **104**
Laing Art Gallery . . . . .3G **69 (3E 5)**
Laing Gro. NE28: W'snd 4E **61**
Laing Ho. NE37: Wash 3H **113**
Laith Rd. NE3: Ken 2A **56**
Lake App. NE21: Bla T 2C **80**
Lake Av. NE34: S Shi 3C **76**
Lake Ct. SR3: New S 3A **132**
Lakeland Dr. SR8: Pet 6E **163**
Lakemore SR8: Pet 2C **164**
Lake Rd. DH5: Hou S 3A **138**
Lakeside NE21: Bla T 2D **80**
  NE34: S Shi 3D **76**
Lakeside Ct. NE11: Gate 6F **83**
Lake Vw. NE31: Heb 5B **72**
Laleham Ct. NE3: Ken 6H **41**
Lamara Dr. SR5: Monk 2C **104**
Lambden Cl. NE29: N Shi 4A **62**
Lambert Rd. NE37: Wash 6F **99**
Lambert Sq. NE3: Gos 2C **56**
Lambeth Pl. NE8: Gate 3A **84**
Lamb Farm Cl. NE12: Kil 1E **45**
Lambley Av. NE30: N Shi 3D **48**
Lambley Cl. NE16: Sun 3E **95**
Lambley Cres. NE31: Heb 6B **72**
Lambourn Av. NE29: N Shi 3H **61**
Lambourne Av. NE12: Longb 6C **44**
Lambourne Cl. DH4: Hou S 6C **128**
Lambourne Rd. SR2: Sund 4C **118**
Lamb St. NE6: Walk 4G **71**
  NE23: E Cram 4E **23**
Lamb Ter. NE27: Shir 4B **46**
LAMBTON 4H **113**
Lambton Av. NE16: Whi 4G **81**
Lambton Cen. NE38: Wash 4H **113**
Lambton Cl. NE40: Ryton 6A **64**
Lambton Ct. NE22: Bed 3C **10**
  NE38: Wash 1E **127**
  SR3: E Her 2E **131**
  SR8: Pet 4C **164**
Lambton Dr. DH5: Hett H 3C **148**
Lambton Gdns. NE16: Burn 2E **107**
    (not continuous)
Lambton La. DH4: Hou S 1D **136**
Lambton Lea DH4: Hou S 5E **129**
LAMBTON PARK 3H **127**
Lambton Pl. DH4: Pen 1F **129**

Lambton Rd. NE2: Newc T 1G **69**
NE31: Heb 2D **72**
Lambton St. DH1: Dur 5B **154**
DH3: Ches S 1D **134**
NE8: Gate 6G **69**
SR1: Sund 6D 128 (2H **7**)
Lambton Ter. DH4: Pen 1D **128**
DH9: Stly 6H **123**
NE32: Jar 5F **73**
Lambton Twr. SR1: Sund 6E **105**
(off High St. E.)
Lambton Wlk. DH1: Dur 3A **6**
LAMESLEY 5G **97**
Lamesley Rd. DH3: Bir, Kib 6A **98**
NE11: Kib 4G **97**
Lamonby Way NE23: Cra 5A **22**
Lampeter Cl. NE5: Newc T 4F **55**
Lamplight Arts Cen. 3C **122**
Lamport St. NE31: Heb 2A **72**
Lanark Cl. NE29: N Shi 5G **47**
Lanark Dr. NE32: Jar 6A **74**
Lancashire Dr. DH1: Carr 4D **156**
Lancaster Ct. NE3: Ken 6H **41**
Lancaster Dr. NE28: W'snd 6B **46**
Lancaster Hill SR8: Pet 5B **162**
(not continuous)
Lancaster Ho. NE4: Newc T 6C **68**
NE23: Cra 4D **22**
Lancaster Pl. NE11: Dun 2A **82**
Lancaster Rd. NE11: Dun 2A **82**
Lancaster St. NE4: Newc T 4D **68**
Lancaster Ter. DH3: Ches S 1D **134**
Lancaster Way NE32: Jar 2E **87**
(not continuous)
Lancastrian Rd. NE23: Cra 4A **22**
Lancefield Av. NE6: Walk 5F **71**
Lancet Ct. NE8: Gate 1H **83**
Lanchester NE38: Wash 5C **114**
Lanchester Av. NE9: Gate 2D **98**
Lanchester Cl. NE10: Gate 5A **86**
Lanchester Grn. NE22: Bed 3H **9**
Lanchester Rd. DH1: Dur 1F **153**
Lancing Ct. NE3: Ken 6G **41**
Land of Green Ginger
NE30: N Shi 6F **49**
(off Front St.)
Landsale Cotts. NE40: G'sde 2A **70**
Landscape Ter. NE40: G'sde 2D **78**
Landseer Cl. DH9: Stly 3D **122**
Landseer Gdns. NE9: Gate 3B **84**
NE34: S Shi 1F **89**
Landswood Ter. NE21: Bla T 4B **80**
Lane Cor. NE34: S Shi 4E **75**
Lane Head NE40: Ryton 4C **64**
Lanercost NE38: Wash 2B **114**
Lanercost Av. NE21: Bla T 1H **79**
Lanercost Dr. NE5: Newc T 1F **67**
Lanercost Gdns. NE10: Gate 5C **84**
NE15: Thro 5D **52**
Lanercost Pk. NE23: E Cram 4D **22**
Lanercost Rd. NE29: N Shi 2A **62**
Lanesborough Ct. NE3: Gos 3C **56**
Langdale DH3: Bir 6E **113**
NE26: Whit B 4A **36**
NE37: Wash 6A **100**
Langdale Cl. NE12: Longb 1A **58**
Langdale Cres. DH1: Carr 2A **156**
NE21: Bla T 3H **79**
Langdale Dr. NE23: Cra 2G **21**
Langdale Gdns. NE6: Walk 3G **71**
NE28: W'snd 2E **61**
Langdale Pl. SR8: Pet 1E **165**

Langdale Rd. DH4: Pen 1E **129**
NE9: Gate 6A **84**
Langdale St. DH5: Hett H 3B **148**
Langdale Way NE36: E Bol 3E **89**
Langdon Cl. NE29: N Shi 4B **48**
Langdon Gdns. DH9: Ann P 4E **121**
Langdon Rd. NE5: Newc T 5B **54**
Langeeford Pl. SR6: Monk 4E **105**
Langford Dr. NE35: Bol C 1B **88**
Langham Rd. NE15: Newc T 4D **66**
Langholm Av. NE29: N Shi 5G **47**
Langholm Cl. NE36: E Bol 4G **89**
(off Station Rd.)
Langholm Rd. NE3: Gos 6E **43**
NE36: E Bol 3F **89**
Langhorn Cl. NE6: Newc T 2B **70**
Langhurst SR2: Ryh 1E **133**
Langleeford Rd. NE5: Newc T 3E **55**
Langley Av. NE10: Gate 5H **85**
NE24: Cow 5H **11**
NE25: Whit B 2H **47**
NE27: Shir 3E **47**
Langley Cl. NE38: Wash 3H **113**
Langley Cres. DH7: B'don 4F **159**
Langley Gro. SR8: Pet 3A **164**
Langley Mere NE12: Longb 5D **44**
LANGLEY MOOR 3G **159**
Langley Moor Ind. Est.
DH7: B'don 4G **159**
(not continuous)
Langley Rd. DH1: Dur 1C **154**
NE5: Newc T 1D **66**
NE6: Walk 3F **71**
NE29: N Shi 1G **61**
SR3: Sund 5B **118**
Langley St. DH4: Hou S 3H **129**
Langley Tarn NE29: N Shi 3C **62**
Langley Ter. DH9: Ann P 5G **121**
NE32: Jar 6F **73**
Langley Vw. DH9: Ann P 6A **122**
Langport Rd. SR2: Sund 4D **118**
Langthorne Av. SR8: Pet 1H **165**
Langton Cl. SR4: Sund 1B **118**
Langton Ct. NE20: Pon 1B **38**
Langton Dr. NE23: Cra 5C **16**
Langton Lea DH1: H Shin 4H **161**
Langton St. NE8: Gate 1H **83**
(not continuous)
Langton Ter. DH4: Hou S 1C **136**
NE7: Newc T 5B **58**
Lanivet Cl. SR2: Ryh 1F **133**
Lannerwood NE29: N Shi 3C **62**
(off Coach La.)
Lansbury Cl. DH3: Bir 1B **112**
Lansbury Ct. NE12: Longb 2A **58**
Lansbury Dr. DH3: Bir 1B **112**
SR7: Mur 2C **150**
Lansbury Gdns. NE10: Gate 3G **85**
Lansbury Rd. NE16: Whi 5G **81**
Lansbury Way SR5: C'twn 4D **102**
Lansdowne SR2: Ryh 2E **133**
Lansdowne Cl. NE3: Gos 2E **57**
Lansdowne Cres. NE3: Gos 1E **57**
Lansdowne Gdns.
NE2: Newc T 1A **70**
Lansdowne Pl. NE3: Gos 2E **57**
Lansdowne Pl. W. NE3: Gos 2E **57**
Lansdowne Rd. NE12: Longb 5D **44**
Lansdowne St. SR4: Sund 6B **104**
Lansdowne Ter. NE3: Gos 2E **57**
NE29: N Shi 1B **62**
Lansdowne Ter. E. NE3: Gos 2E **57**

Lansdowne Ter. W.
NE29: N Shi 1A **62**
Lanthwaite Rd. NE9: Gate 6A **84**
Lanton St. DH4: Hou S 3H **129**
Lapford Dr. NE23: Cra 6C **16**
Lapwing Cl. NE24: News 3C **18**
NE38: Wash 4F **113**
Lapwing Ct. NE16: Burn 2A **108**
NE34: S Shi 4G **75**
L'Arbre Cres. NE16: Whi 4D **80**
Larch Av. DH4: Hou S 2G **137**
NE34: S Shi 1A **76**
SR6: Whit 2G **91**
Larch Cl. NE9: Spri 3D **98**
Larches Rd. DH1: Dur 4A **154**
Larches, The NE4: Newc T 6C **68**
NE16: Burn 6H **93**
Larch Gro. NE24: News 3A **18**
Larchlea NE20: Pon 3C **38**
Larchlea Sth. NE20: Pon 3C **38**
Larch Rd. NE21: Bla T 6B **66**
Larch St. NE16: Sun 3F **95**
Larch Ter. DH9: Stly 6F **123**
DH9: Tan L 6G **107**
Larchwood NE38: Wash 6H **113**
Larchwood Av. NE3: Ken 6B **42**
(not continuous)
NE6: Walk 1E **71**
NE13: Wide O 6E **31**
Larchwood Gdns. NE11: Gate . . .6D **82**
Larchwood Gro. SR2: Sund 5C **118**
Larkfield Cres. DH4: Hou S 4E **129**
Larkfield Rd. SR2: Sund 4C **118**
Larkhill SR2: Ryh 2F **133**
Larkrise Cl. NE7: Newc T 4D **58**
Larkspur NE9: Gate 6C **84**
Larkspur Cl. DH9: Tan L 1B **122**
Larkspur Rd. NE16: Whi 4F **81**
Larkspur Ter. NE2: Newc T 6G **57**
Larkswood NE34: S Shi 2B **76**
Larne Cres. NE3: Gate 6A **84**
Larriston Pl. NE23: Cra 3H **21**
Lartington Ct. DH3: Gt Lum 5H **135**
Lartington Gdns.
NE3: Newc T 2H **57**
Larwood Ct. DH3: Ches S 2E **135**
DH9: Ann P 6E **121**
Lascelles Av. NE34: S Shi 4G **75**
Laski Gdns. NE10: Gate 3H **85**
Latimer St. NE30: N Shi 5F **49**
Latrigg Ct. SR3: New S 3H **131**
Latton Cl. NE23: Cra 5A **22**
Laudordale Av. NE28: W'snd 3H **59**
Launceston Cl. NE3: Ken 5H **41**
Launceston Ct. SR3: E Her 2F **131**
Launceston Dr. SR3: E Her 2E **131**
Laura St. SR1: Sund 1D 118 (4H **7**)
SR7: S'hm 5B **142**
Laurel Av. DH1: Dur 6G **155**
NE3: Ken 1C **56**
NE12: Kil 4G **45**
SR7: S'hm 4H **141**
Laurel Ct. DH2: Ches S 4B **126**
NE30: N Shi 2D **62**
Laurel Cres. DH2: Beam 2D **124**
DH4: Hou S 1G **137**
NE6: Walk 6F **59**
Laurel End NE12: Kil 4G **45**
Laurel Gro. SR2: Sund 5C **118**
Laurel Pl. NE12: Kil 4F **45**
NE23: Cra 2B **22**
Laurel Rd. NE21: Bla T 1B **80**

Laurels, The SR3: New S 1A 132
(off Chelmsford St.)
Laurel St. NE15: Thro 4D 52
NE28: W'snd 6A 60
Laurel Ter. NE16: Burn 1F 107
NE25: H'wll 1C 34
Laurel Wlk. NE3: Gos 2E 57
Laurel Way NE40: Ryton 6A 64
Laurelwood Gdns. NE11: Gate ...6D 82
Lauren Ct. SR8: Eas 1C 162
Laurens Ct. NE37: Usw 5B 100
Lavender Gdns. NE2: Newc T 6F 57
NE9: Gate 5H 83
Lavender Gro. SR5: C'twn 4C 102
Lavender La. NE34: S Shi 4D 74
Lavender Rd. NE16: Whi 5E 81
Lavender Row NE9: Gate 6B 84
Lavender St. SR4: Sund 1C 116
Lavender Wlk. NE31: Heb 6C 72
Lavendon Cl. NE23: Cra 5A 22
Laverick NE10: Gate 5F 85
Laverick La. NE36: W Bol 4D 86
Laverick Ter. DH9: Ann P 6G 121
Laverock Hall Rd.
NE24: Bly, News 5E 17
Laverock Pl. NE3: Ken 2H 55
NE24: News 4H 17
Lavers Rd. DH3: Bir 2C 112
Lavington Rd. NE34: S Shi 1G 75
Lawe Rd. NE33: S Shi 3F 63
LAWE, THE 3F 63
Lawn Cotts. SR3: New S 3H 131
Lawn Dr. NE36: W Bol 5B 88
Lawnhead Sq. SR3: New S 3B 132
Lawnside SR7: S'hm 5G 141
Lawns, The DH5: Eas L 4E 149
SR3: New S 3H 131
SR6: Whit 3F 91
SR7: S'hm 5G 141
Lawnsway NE32: Jar 2G 87
Lawnswood DH5: Hou S 4B 138
Lawn, The NE40: Ryton 3C 64
Lawrence Av. NE21: Bla T 6A 66
NE34: S Shi 6F 75
Lawrence Ct. NE21: Bla T 6A 66
Lawrence Hill Ct. NE10: Gate ...3H 85
Lawrence St. SR1: Sund 1E 119
Lawson Av. NE32: Jar 6G 73
Lawson Ct. DH2: Ches S 1C 134
DH9: Stly 3C 124
NE35: Bol C 4B 88
Lawson Cres. NE3: Monk 1D 104
Lawson St. NE28: W'snd 6A 60
NE29: N Shi 3C 62
Lawson St. W. NE29: N Shi 3C 62
Lawson Ter. DH1: Dur 6B 154
DH5: Eas L 4D 148
NE4: Newc T 5A 68
Laws St. SR6: Monk 1D 104
Laxey St. DH9: Stly 3C 122
Laxford DH3: Bir 5D 112
Laxford Ct. SR3: New S 4A 132
Laybourn Gdns. NE34: S Shi 5C 74
(not continuous)
Layburn Gdns. NE15: Lem 1C 66
Layburn Pl. SR8: Pet 6C 162
Laycock Gdns. NE23: Seg 2E 33
Layfield Rd. NE3: Gos 4E 43
Laygate NE33: S Shi 6D 62
(not continuous)
Laygate Pl. NE33: S Shi 6E 63

Laygate St. NE33: S Shi 6D 62
Lea Av. NE32: Jar 1G 87
Leabank NE15: Lem 1B 66
Lead Rd. NE21: Bla T, G'sde 1C 78
NE40: G'sde 2A 78
Leafield Cres. NE34: S Shi 1A 76
Lea Grn. DH3: Ches S 6E 113
Leagreen Ct. NE3: Gos 2C 56
Leaholme Cres. NE24: Bly 1A 18
Lealholm Rd. NE7: Longb 2A 58
Leam Gdns. NE10: Gate 3A 86
Leamington St. SR4: Sund 1B 118
Leam La. NE10: Gate 3C 86
NE10: Gate 2E 99
NE32: Jar 6F 73
NE32: S Shi 4A 74
LEAM LANE ESTATE 6G 85
LEAMSIDE 3C 146
Leamside NE10: Gate 5F 85
NE32: Jar 5G 73
Leander Av. DH3: Ches S 1D 126
Leander Dr. NE35: Bol C 3A 88
Leaplish NE38: Wash 5D 114
Leap Mill 6H 93
Lea Rigg DH4: W Rai 3E 147
(not continuous)
Leas, The DH4: Hou S 6H 129
NE25: Whit B 1H 47
Leasyde Wlk. NE16: Whi 6C 80
Leatham SR2: Ryh 1E 133
Leat Ho. NE38: Wash 3F 115
Lea Vw. NE34: S Shi 1B 76
LEAZES 1F 107
Leazes Arc.
NE1: Newc T 3F 69 (3C 4)
Leazes Ct. DH1: Dur 5D 154 (2C 6)
NE4: Newc T 3D 68
Leazes Cres.
NE1: Newc T 3E 69 (3B 4)
Leazes La. DH1: Dur 5E 155
NE1: Newc T 3F 69 (3C 4)
Leazes Pde. NE2: Newc T 3D 68
Leazes Pk. Rd.
NE1: Newc T 3E 69 (3B 4)
Leazes Parkway NE15: Thro 6C 52
Leazes Pl. DH1: Dur 5D 154 (2C 6)
Leazes Ri. SR8: Pet 1F 165
Leazes Rd. DH1: Dur 5C 154 (2A 6)
Leazes Sq. NE1: Newc T ..3F 69 (3C 4)
Leazes Ter. NE1: Newc T ..3E 69 (2B 4)
Leazes, The NE15: Thro 6C 52
NE16: Burn 1F 107
NE34: S Shi 3H 75
SR1: Sund 1B 118
Leazes Vw. NE39: Row G 3D 92
Leazes Vs. NE16: Burn 1G 107
Lecondale NE10: Gate 1F 99
Lecondale Ct. NE10: Gate 1F 99
Ledbury Rd. SR2: Sund 4D 118
Leechmere Cres. SR7: S'hm 2E 141
Leechmere Ind. Est.
SR2: Sund 6E 119
Leechmere Rd. SR2: Sund 5C 118
Leechmere Vw. SR2: Ryh 1F 133
Leechmere Way SR2: Ryh 1E 133
(not continuous)
Lee Cl. NE38: Wash 2F 115
Leeds St. SR6: Monk 3D 104
Leeholme DH5: Hou S 4B 138
Leeholme Ct. DH9: Ann P 6G 121
Leeming Gdns. NE9: Gate 5B 84
Leesfield Dr. DH7: B'don 6E 159

Leesfield Gdns. DH7: B'don 6E 159
Leesfield Rd. DH7: B'don 6E 159
Lees St. DH9: Stly 2D 122
Lee St. SR5: S'wck 4B 104
SR6: Monk 1D 104
Lee Ter. DH5: Hett H 3C 148
SR8: Eas 1C 162
Legg Av. NE22: Bed 2E 11
Legges Dr. NE13: Sea B 3A 20
Legion Gro. NE15: Newc T 2D 66
Legion Rd. NE15: Newc T 2D 66
Leicester Cl. NE28: W'snd 2G 59
Leicestershire Dr.
DH1: Carr 5B 156
Leicester St. NE6: Walk 4E 71
Leicester Wlk. SR8: Pet 5C 162
Leicester Way NE32: Jar 2E 87
Leighton Rd. SR2: Sund 5D 118
Leighton St. NE6: Newc T 3A 70
NE33: S Shi 5G 63
Leighton Ter. DH3: Bir 2B 112
Leith Ct. NE34: S Shi 4E 75
Leith Gdns. DH9: Tan L 6B 108
LEMINGTON 3A 66
Lemington Gdns.
NE5: Newc T 2G 67
Lemington Rd. NE15: Lem 2G 65
Lemon St. NE33: S Shi 3D 74
Lena Av. NE25: Whit B 1A 48
Lenin Ter. DH9: Stly 5D 122
Lenore Ter. NE40: G'sde 1B 78
Leominster Rd. SR2: Sund 5D 118
Leonard Ho. SR3: New S 2A 132
Leopold Ho. SR2: Sund 2B 118
(off Albert Ct.)
Leopold St. NE32: Jar 3F 73
Lesbury Av. NE27: Shir 2C 46
NE28: W'snd 4D 60
Lesbury Chase NE3: Gos 6D 42
Lesbury Cl. DH2: Ches S 2A 134
Lesbury Gdns. NE13: Wide O 5E 31
Lesbury Rd. NE6: Newc T 6B 58
Lesbury St. NE15: Lem 3A 66
NE28: W'snd 6G 61
Leslie Av. NE31: Heb 4C 72
Leslie Cl. NE40: Ryton 5E 65
Leslie Cres. NE3: Gos 4E 57
Letch Av. SR7: Eas 5G 151
Letch Path NE15: Lem 2A 66
Letch, The NE12: Longb 4D 44
Letch Way NE15: Lem 2A 66
Letchwell Vs. NE12: Longb 4E 45
Leuchars Ct. DH3: Bir 4C 112
Leven Av. DH2: Ches S 2B 134
Leven Ho. SR3: New S 3A 132
Levens Wlk. NE23: Cra 2G 21
Leven Wlk. SR8: Pet 3C 164
Levisham Cl. SR3: New S 2C 132
Lewis Cres. SR2: Sund 2F 119
Lewis Dr. NE4: Newc T 3B 68
Lewis Gdns. NE34: S Shi 6E 75
Lexington Ct. DH7: B'don 6C 158
Leybourne Av. NE12: Kil 4D 44
Leybourne Dene NE12: Kil 3D 44
Leybourne Hold DH3: Bir 1C 112
Leyburn Cl. DH2: Ous 6F 111
DH4: Hou S 2H 137
Leyburn Ct. NE23: Cra 5A 22
Leyburn Dr. NE7: Newc T 4A 58
Leyburn Gro. DH4: Hou S 2G 137
Leyburn Pl. DH3: Bir 1B 112
Leyfield Cl. SR3: New S 4B 132

Leyton Pl. NE8: Gate 3A 84
Liberty Ter. DH9: Tan L 5H 107
Liberty Way SR6: Monk 5E 105
Library Stairs NE30: N Shi 2D 62
Library Ter. DH9: Ann P 5F 121
Library Wlk. DH9: Ann P 4F 121
Lichfield Av. NE6: Walk 5E 71
Lichfield Cl. DH3: Gt Lum 5G 135
NE3: Ken 6A 42
Lichfield Ho. SR5: S'wck 2B 104
Lichfield Rd. DH1: Dur 5D 144
SR5: S'wck 2A 104
Lichfield Way NE32: Jar 2E 87
(not continuous)
Lidcombe Cl. SR3: New S 2B 132
Liddell Ct. SR6: Monk 3F 105
Liddells Fell Rd. NE21: Bla T 1F 79
Liddell St. NE30: N Shi 2D 62
SR6: Monk 5D 104 (1H 7)
Liddell Ter. NE8: Gate 2F 83
NE11: Kib 1E 111
Liddle Av. DH6: Sher 6D 156
Liddle Cl. SR8: Pet 5B 162
Liddle Ct. NE4: Newc T 4C 68
Liddle Rd. NE4: Newc T 4C 68
Liddles St. NE22: Bed 2D 10
Lieven St. NE13: Bru V 1C 42
Life Science Cen. 5E 69 (6B 4)
Liffey Rd. NE31: Heb 6D 72
Lighthourne Rd. NE6: Walk 3G 71
Lightfoot Sports Cen. 5F 71
Lightwood Av. NE15: Newc T 5E 67
Lilac Av. DH1: Dur 2B 154
DH5: Hou S 3B 138
NE12: Longb 5F 45
NE24: Bly 5B 12
NE34: S Shi 4H 75
SR3: New S 1B 132
SR6: Whit 6F 77
Lilac Cl. NE5: Cha P 3H 53
Lilac Cres. NE16: Burn 1G 107
Lilac Gdns. DH2: Beam 2D 124
NE9: Gate 5H 83
NE16: Whi 4E 81
NE38: Wash 6A 114
SR6: Cle 1A 90
Lilac Gro. DH2: Ches S 4A 126
SR6: Monk 2D 104
Lilac Pk. DH7: Ush M 6C 152
Lilac Rd. NE6: Walk 6G 59
Lilac Sq. DH4: Hou S 6C 128
Lilac St. SR4: Sund 1C 116
Lilac Ter. DH9: Ann P 4E 121
Lilac Wlk. NE31: Heb 6C 72
Lilburn Cl. DH2: Ches S 3A 134
NE6: Newc T 5C 70
NE36: E Bol 3E 89
Lilburne Cl. SR1: Sund 6E 105
Lilburn Gdns. NE3: Newc T 3H 57
Lilburn Pl. SR5: S'wck 4A 104
Lilburn Rd. NE27: Shir 3C 46
Lilburn St. NE29: N Shi 2B 62
Lilian Av. NE28: W'snd 6G 59
SR2: Ryh 1E 133
Lilleycroft NE39: Row G 3F 93
Lilley Gro. SR5: C'twn 4D 102
Lilley Ter. NE39: Row G 2F 93
Lily Av. NE2: Newc T 6G 57
NE22: Bed 5B 10
Lily Bank NE28: W'snd 5H 59
Lily Bungs. DH9: Dip 1E 121
Lily Cl. NE21: Bla T 1G 79

Lily Cres. NE2: Newc T 6G 57
SR6: Whit 6F 77
Lily Est. NE15: Thro 4D 52
Lily Gdns. DH9: Dip 1E 121
Lily St. SR4: Sund 6B 104
Lily Ter. DH4: Hou S 5H 129
NE5: Newc T 4E 55
Lilywhite Ter. DH5: Eas L 3D 148
Lime Av. DH4: Hou S 2G 137
Limecrag Av. DH1: Dur 4H 155
Limecroft NE32: Jar 2G 87
Lime Gro. NE40: Ryton 4B 64
Limekiln Rd. NE28: W'snd 5B 60
Lime Pk. DH7: B'don 5D 158
Limes Av. NE24: Bly 4B 12
Limes, The DH4: Pen 1F 129
SR2: Sund 3D 118
SR6: Whit 3E 91
(off Front St.)
Limestone La. NE20: Pon 5A 26
Lime St. DH9: Stly 6B 122
NE1: Newc T 3A 70
NE15: Thro 4D 52
NE21: Bla T 2B 80
SR4: Sund 6B 104
Limetree NE38: Wash 5C 114
Limetrees Gdns. NE9: Gate 4H 83
Limewood Ct. NE2: Newc T 1D 68
Limewood Gro. NE13: Wide O . . .6D 30
Linaoro Cl. NE3: Kon 1E 119
Linacre Ct. SR8: Pet 2B 164
Linbridge Dr. NE5: Newc T 6B 54
Linburn NE38: Wash 1H 127
SR3: New S 1A 132
Lincoln Ct. NE31: Heb 4B 72
Lincoln Cres. DH5: Hett H 1B 148
Lincoln Grn. NE3: Gos 4E 43
Lincoln Rd. DH1: Dur 6D 144
NE23: Cra 5C 16
NE34: S Shi 2D 76
Lincolnshire Cl. DH1: Carr 4A 156
Lincoln St. NE8: Gate 2G 83
SR4: Sund 6H 103
Lincoln Wlk. DH3: Gt Lum 4G 135
SR8: Pet 5C 162
Lincoln Way NE32: Jar 2F 87
(not continuous)
Lincrest Ct. NE5: Newc T 5D 54
Lindale Av. NE16: Whi 6F 81
Lindale Rd. NE4: Newc T 1A 68
Lindean Pl. NE23: Cra 3H 21
Linden NE9: Gate 1D 98
Linden Av. NE3: Gos 3E 57
NE4: Newc T 2H 67
Linden Gdns. SR2: Sund 4C 118
Linden Gro. DH4: Hou S 3H 137
NE11: Dun 3C 82
Linden Pk. DH7: B'don 5D 158
Linden Rd. DH7: Ush M 4D 152
NE3: Gos 3E 57
NE12: Longb 1D 58
NE26: Whit B 6D 36
Linden Ter. NE9: Spri 4F 99
NE12: Longb 6D 44
NE26: Whit B 6D 36
Linden Way NE9: Spri 3C 98
(not continuous)
NE20: Pon 2C 38
Lindfield Av. NE5: Newc T 6F 55

Lindisfarne DH1: H Shin 4H 161
NE38: Wash 3A 114
SR2: Ryh 3E 133
SR8: Pet 3C 164
Lindisfarne Av. DH3: Ches S 6D 126
Lindisfarne Cl. DH2: Ches S 2A 134
DH4: Hou S 1G 137
NE2: Newc T 5H 57
NE5: Newc T 6D 54
Lindisfarne Ct. NE32: Jar 3B 74
Lindisfarne Dr. NE8: Gate 1H 83
Lindisfarne Pl. NE28: W'snd 4B 60
Lindisfarne Recess
NE32: Jar 5H 73
Lindisfarne Ri. DH1: Dur 2D 154
Lindisfarne Rd. DH1: Dur 2D 154
NE2: Newc T 5H 57
NE31: Heb 6C 72
NE32: Jar 5H 73
Lindisfarne Ter. NE30: N Shi 6C 48
Lindom Av. DH3: Ches S 6D 126
Lindon Mnr. NE12: Kil 1C 44
Lindon Rd. DH9: Stly 4C 122
Lindrick Ct. NE10: Gate 4A 86
Lindrick Pk. DH5: Hett H 2D 148
Lindsay Av. NE24: Cow 5A 12
Lindsay Cl. SR2: Sund 2E 119
Lindsay Ct. SR6: Whit 1F 91
Lindsay Rd. SR1: Sund 1E 119
SR2: Sund 1E 119
Lindsay St. DH5: Hett H 5D 138
Lindsey Cl. NE23: Cra 3G 21
Lindum Rd. NE9: Gate 3H 83
Linfield SR2: Ryh 2E 133
Lingcrest NE9: Gate 6C 84
Lingdale DH1: Carr 4B 156
Lingdale Av. SR6: Monk 5E 91
Lingey Gdns. NE10: Gate 3A 86
Lingey La. NE10: Gate 4H 85
Lingfield DH5: Hou S 4B 138
Lingholme DH2: Ches S 5A 126
Lingmell NE37: Wash 1H 113
Lingshaw NE10: Gate 4H 85
Lingside NE32: Jar 1G 87
Linhope Av. NE3: Ken 6B 42
Linhope Rd. NE5: Newc T 5D 54
Link Av. NE22: Bed 4F 9
Link Rd. NE5: Newc T 5A 56
NE13: Bru V 1C 42
Links Av. NE26: Whit B 4B 36
NE30: N Shi 3E 49
Links Ct. NE26: Whit B 4C 36
Links Grn. NE3: Gos 1F 57
Links Grn. Wlk. NE3: Gos 1F 57
Links Ho. Gdns. Cvn. Pk.
NE24: Bly 3D 18
Links Rd. NE24: Bly 3D 18
NE26: Sea S 3G 25
NE30: N Shi 2E 49
Links, The DH1: Carr 3B 156
NE26: Sea S 3G 25
NE26: Whit B 2B 36
Links Vw. NE24: News 3A 18
Links Wlk. NE5: Newc T 5D 54
Linkway NE32: Jar 2H 87
Linley Hill NE16: Whi 6C 80
Linnel Dr. NE15: Lem 2C 66
Linnet Cl. NE38: Wash 4G 113
Linnet Gro. SR5: C'twn 4E 103
Linnetsfield NE6: Walk 1F 71
(off Northmoor Rd.)
Linney Gdns. NE34: S Shi 5C 74

Linskell SR2: Ryh 1E **133**
Linskill Pl. NE3: Ken 4B **56**
  NE30: N Shi 6D **48**
Linskill St. NE30: N Shi 2D **62**
Linskill Ter. NE30: N Shi 1D **62**
Linslade Wlk. NE23: Cra 3H **21**
Lintfort NE38: Wash 2E **127**
Linthorpe Cl. NE34: S Shi 4C **74**
Linthorpe Rd. NE3: Gos 6E **43**
  NE30: N Shi 4D **48**
Linton NE12: Kil 6D **32**
Linton Rd. NE9: Gate 2H **97**
  NE26: Whit B 2A **36**
LINTZ 1F **107**
LINTZFORD 6C **92**
Lintzford Cl. NE39: Row G 5D **92**
Lintzford Gdns. NE15: Lem 2C **66**
  NE39: Row G 5D **92**
Lintzford La.
  NE39: C'wl, Row G 3A **92**
Lintzford Rd.
  NE39: Ham M, Row G 2A **106**
LINTZ GREEN 2C **106**
Lintz Grn. La. NE39: Ham M 1C **106**
Lintz La. NE16: Burn 2C **106**
Lintz Ter. DH9: Stly 4A **122**
  NE16: Burn 1F **107**
Linum Pl. NE4: Newc T 1A **68**
Linwood Pl. NE3: Gos 4E **43**
Lion Wlk. NE29: N Shi 4B **62**
Lipman Bldg.
  NE1: Newc T 2G **69** (1E **5**)
Lisa Av. SR4: Sund 2C **116**
Lisburn Ter. SR4: Sund 6A **104**
Lish Av. NE26: Whit B 1E **49**
Lishman Ter. NE40: Ryton 5A **64**
Lisle Ct. NE28: W'snd 5H **59**
Lisle Gro. NE28: W'snd 4E **61**
Lisle Rd. NE34: S Shi 2H **75**
Lisle St. NE1: Newc T . . .3F **69** (3D **4**)
  NE28: W'snd 5H **59**
Lismore Av. NE33: S Shi 2F **75**
Lismore Pl. NE15: Newc T 3H **67**
Lismore Ter. NE9: Spri 4F **99**
Lister Av. NE11: Dun 2B **82**
Lister Cl. DH5: Hou S 5H **137**
Lister Rd. SR8: Pet 5A **162**
Listers La. NE9: Gate 3A **84**
Lister St. NE15: Newc T 5D **66**
Litchfield Cres. NE21: Bla T 2H **79**
Litchfield La. NE21: Bla T 2H **79**
Litchfield St. NE21: Bla T 2H **79**
Litchfield Ter. NE21: Bla T 2H **79**
Lit. Bedford St. NE29: N Shi 2C **62**
Littlebridge Ct. DH1: Dur 6A **144**
LITTLEBURN 4G **159**
Littleburn Cl. DH4: Hou S 1G **137**
Littleburn Ind. Est.
  DH7: B'don 5H **159**
Littleburn La. DH7: B'don 4G **159**
Littleburn Rd. DH7: B'don 4G **159**
Little Dene NE2: Gos 4F **57**
Littledene NE9: Gate 4H **83**
Little Eden SR8: Pet 6D **162**
Little Mus. of Gilesgate, The . . .5F **155**
Little Theatre, The 3H **83**
LITTLE THORPE 3C **162**
LITTLETOWN 4H **157**
Littletown La. DH6: H Pitt 5H **157**
Lit. Villiers St.
  SR1: Sund 6E **105** (3H **7**)
    (not continuous)

Little Way NE15: Newc T 5F **67**
Litton Ct. SR3: New S 3H **131**
Littondale NE28: W'snd 3F **59**
Liverpool St.
  NE1: Newc T 3F **69** (3C **4**)
Live Theatre 5G **69** (6F **5**)
Livingstone Pl. NE33: S Shi 3E **63**
Livingstone Rd.
  SR1: Sund 6C **104** (3E **7**)
Livingstone St. NE33: S Shi 3F **63**
Livingstone Vw. NE30: N Shi 6E **49**
Lizard La. NE34: S Shi 3D **76**
  SR6: Whit 6E **77**
Lizard La. Cvn. & Camping Site
  NE34: S Shi 3D **76**
Lizard Vw. SR6: Whit 6E **77**
Lloyd Av. DH5: W Rai 1G **147**
Lloyd Ct. NE11: Dun 1A **82**
Lobban Av. NE31: Heb 6B **72**
Lobelia Av. NE10: Gate 1B **84**
Lobelia Cl. NE5: Cha P 4H **53**
Lobley Gdns. NE11: Dun 5C **82**
LOBLEY HILL 5C **82**
Lobley Hill DH7: B'don 5F **159**
Lobley Hill Rd. NE8: Gate 5D **82**
  NE11: Gate 5C **82**
Lobleyhill Rd. NE16: Burn, Sun . .6A **94**
Local Av. DH6: Sher 6G **157**
Lochcraig Pl. NE23: Cra 3G **21**
Lochfield Gdns. NE11: Kib 1E **111**
Lochmaben Ter. SR5: Monk 3D **104**
Lockerbie Gdns. NE15: Lem 2C **66**
Lockerbie Rd. NE23: Cra 3H **21**
LOCKHAUGH 1G **93**
Lockhaugh Rd. NE39: Row G . . .2F **93**
Locksley Cl. NE29: N Shi 4F **47**
Locomotion Way NE12: Kil 6B **32**
  NE29: N Shi 4C **62**
Lodge Cl. NE39: Ham M 2A **106**
Lodgeside Mdw. SR3: New S . . .4B **132**
Lodges Rd., The NE9: Gate 2G **97**
Lodge Ter. NE28: W'snd 5B **60**
Lodore Ct. SR3: New S 3H **131**
Lodore Gro. NE32: Jar 6H **73**
Lodore Rd. NE2: Gos 4F **57**
Lodsworth Dr. NE23: Cra 5A **22**
Loefield DH3: Gt Lum 3G **135**
Lofthill SR3: New S 4G **131**
Logan Rd. NE6: Walk 6F **59**
Logan St. DH5: Hett H 2C **148**
Logan Ter. DH6: S Het 5G **149**
    (off Front St.)
Lola St. NE13: Bru V 1B **42**
Lombard Dr. DH3: Ches S 2C **126**
Lombard Pl. DH3: Gt Lum 4G **135**
Lombard St.
  NE1: Newc T 5G **69** (6F **5**)
  SR1: Sund 6E **105**
Lomond Cl. NE38: Wash 4H **113**
Lomond Ct. SR3: New S 3A **132**
Lomond Pl. DH2: Ches S 2B **134**
London Av. NE37: Usw 4H **99**
Londonderry Bungs.
  SR8: Eas 1D **162**
Londonderry Ct. SR7: S'hm 3B **142**
Londonderry St. SR3: New S 2A **132**
  SR7. S'hm 0C **142**
Londonderry Ter. SR3: New S . . .2B **132**
  SR8: Eas 1D **162**
Londonderry Way DH4: Pen 2E **129**
Longacre DH4: Hou S 3G **137**
  NE38: Wash 6C **114**

Long Acres DH1: Dur 4F **155**
Long Bank DH3: Bir 6C **98**
  NE9: Gate, Spri 5B **98**
LONGBENTON 1A **58**
Longbenton Station (Metro) 2A **58**
Longborough Ct. NE3: Newc T . . .3A **58**
Long Burn Dr. DH2: Ches S 1A **134**
Long Cl. Rd. NE39: Ham M 2A **106**
Long Crag NE37: Wash 2G **113**
Long Dale DH2: Ches S 1A **134**
Longdean Cl. NE31: Heb 4A **72**
Longdean Pk. DH3: Ches S 3C **126**
Longfellow St. DH5: Hou S 4A **138**
Long Fld. Cl. NE34: S Shi 5F **75**
Longfield Rd. SR6: Monk 2D **104**
Longfield Ter. NE6: Walk 5G **71**
Long Gair NE21: Bla T 3G **79**
Long Gth. DH1: Dur 3H **153**
Long Headlam NE6: Newc T 3C **70**
Longhirst NE5: Newc T 5D **54**
  NE10: Gate 4G **85**
  NE12: Kil 6D **32**
Longhirst Dr. NE13: Wide O 6D **30**
  NE23: Cra 5A **22**
Longlands Dr. DH5: Hou S 4A **138**
Longleat Gdns. NE33: S Shi 4F **63**
Longley St. NE4: Newc T 3C **68**
Long Mdw. Cl. NE40: Ryton 6A **64**
Longmeadows NE20: Pon 2B **38**
  SR3: E Her 3E **131**
Longnewton St. SR7: S'hm 6B **142**
Longniddry NE37: Usw 2A **100**
Longniddry Ct. NE9: Gate 2G **97**
Longridge NE21: Bla T 2G **79**
Longridge Av. NE7: Newc T 4D **58**
  NE38: Wash 4G **113**
Longridge Dr. NE26: Whit B 4A **36**
Longridge Rd.
  NE21: Bla T, G'side 1C **78**
Longridge Sq. SR2: Sund 5D **118**
Longridge Way NE22: Bed 1A **10**
  NE23: Cra 3H **21**
Longrigg NE10: Gate 4F **85**
  NE16: Swa 1E **81**
Long Row NE33: S Shi 3D **62**
LONG SANDS 4F **49**
Longshank La. DH3: Bir 1A **112**
Longstaff Gdns. NE34: S Shi 5B **74**
Long Stairs
  NE1: Newc T 5G **69** (6E **5**)
Longston Av. NE30: N Shi 2D **48**
Longstone NE9: Gate 1H **97**
Longstone Cl. NE12: Kil 1E **45**
Longstone Sq. NE5: Newc T 6B **54**
Longwood Cl. NE16: Sun 2F **95**
Lonnen Av. NE4: Newc T 1H **67**
Lonnen Dr. NE16: Swa 3E **81**
Lonnen, The NE34: S Shi 4B **76**
  NE40: Ryton 4E **65**
Lonsdale DH3: Bir 6E **113**
Lonsdale Av. NE24: Cow 5E **11**
  SR6: Monk 5E **91**
Lonsdale Ct. NE2: Newc T 5G **57**
  NE34: S Shi 5C **74**
Lonsdale Gdns. NE28: W'snd 3E **61**
Lonsdale Rd. SR6: Monk 3E **105**
Lonsdale Ter. NE2: Newc T 5G **57**
Lookout Farm NE26: Sea S 3F **25**
Loraine Ter. NE15: Lem 3A **66**
Lord Armstrong Memorial 1D **4**
Lord Byrons Wlk. SR7: S'hm 2F **141**
Lordenshaw NE5: Newc T 5D **54**

Lord Gort Cl. SR5: S'wck 4A **104**
Lord Nelson St. NE33: S Shi 3D **74**
Lord St. NE1: Newc T 5E **69** (6A **4**)
  NE33: S Shi 6G **63**
  SR3: New S 2B **132**
  SR7: S'hm 4B **142**
Lorimers Cl. SR8: Pet 3B **164**
Lorne St. DH5: Eas L 5D **148**
Lorne Ter. SR2: Sund 2C **118**
Lorrain Rd. NE34: S Shi 1F **89**
Lort Ho. NE2: Newc T 3H **69** (2G **5**)
Lorton Av. NE30: N Shi 3C **48**
Lorton Rd. NE9: Gate 1A **98**
Losh Ter. NE6: Walk 4F **71**
Lossiemouth Rd. NE29: N Shi . . .2G **61**
Lothian Cl. DH3: Bir 6D **112**
Lothian Ct. NE5: Newc T 4G **55**
Lotus Cl. NE5: Cha P 4H **53**
Lotus Pl. NE4: Newc T 2H **67**
Loudon St. NE34: S Shi 4E **75**
Loud Ter. DH1: Dur 5D **120**
Loud Vw. Ter. DH9: Ann P 6F **121**
Loughborough Av. NE30: N Shi . .4E **49**
  SR2: Sund 4C **118**
Lough Ct. NE9: Gate 6B **84**
Loughrigg Av. NE23: Cra 3G **21**
Louie Ter. NE9: Gate 6A **84**
Louisa Cen., The 3C **122**
Louisa Ter. DH9: Stly 3G **121**
Louis Av. SR6: Monk 2D **104**
Louise Ho. SR2: Sund 6E **7**
Louise Ter. DH3: Ches S 6C **126**
Louisville NE20: Pon 4F **27**
Loup St. NE21: Bla T 6A **66**
Loup Ter. NE21: Bla T 6A **66**
Louvain Ter. DH5: Hett H 6C **138**
Louvain Ter. W. DH5: Hett H . . .6C **138**
Lovaine Av. NE25: Whit B 1C **48**
  NE29: N Shi 2C **62**
Lovaine Hall
  NE1: Newc T 2G **69** (1F **5**)
Lovaine Pl. NE29: N Shi 2C **62**
Lovaine Pl. W. NE29: N Shi 2B **62**
Lovaine Row NE30: N Shi 5F **49**
Lovaine St. DH2: Pelt 3E **125**
  NE16: Marl 1C **66**
Lovaine Ter. NE29: N Shi 1C **62**
Love Av. NE23: Dud 4B **32**
Love Av. Cotts. NE23: Dud 3B **32**
Lovelady Cl. NE30: N Shi 6F **49**
       (off St Oswin's Pl.)
Love La. NE1: Newc T 4H **69** (5G **5**)
  NE21: Bla T 2H **79**
Loveless Gdns. NE10: Gate 3H **85**
Lovett Wlk. NE8: Gate 1E **83**
Lowbiggin NE5: Newc T 2C **54**
Low Bri. NE1: Newc T 4G **69** (5E **5**)
Low Carrs Cvn. Pk. DH1: Dur . . .6B **144**
Low Chare DH3: Ches S 6C **126**
Low Chu. St. DH9: Ann P 4F **121**
Lowden Ct. NE2: Newc T 2E **69**
Lowdham Av. NE29: N Shi 3A **62**
Low Downs Rd. DH5: Hett H 5C **138**
Low Downs Sq. DH5: Hett H 5D **138**
Lwr. Crone St. NE27: Shir 1D **46**
      (off Up. Crone St.)
Lwr. Dundas St. SR6: Monk 5D **104**
Lower Prom. NE30: N Shi 5G **49**
Lwr. Rudyerd St. NE29: N Shi . . .2D **62**
Lowerson Av. DH4: Hou S 4E **129**
LOWE'S BARN 2H **159**
Lowe's Barn Bank DH1: Dur . . .2H **159**

Lowes Ct. DH1: Dur 1A **160**
Lowes Fall DH1: Dur 1A **160**
Lowes Ri. DH1: Dur 1A **160**
Loweswater Av. DH2: Ches S . . .2B **134**
  DH5: Eas L 5E **149**
Loweswater Cl. NE24: Cow 4F **11**
Loweswater Rd. NE5: Newc T . . .1F **67**
  NE9: Gate 1A **98**
Loweswood Cl. NE7: Newc T . . .6A **58**
Lowes Wynd DH1: Dur 1A **160**
LOW FELL 6H **83**
Lowfield Ter. NE6: Walk 5F **71**
Lowfield Wlk. NE16: Whi 4E **81**
Low Flatts Rd. DH3: Ches S . . .3C **126**
Low Fold NE6: Newc T 4B **70**
LOW FRIARSIDE 6D **92**
Low Friar St.
  NE1: Newc T 4F **69** (5C **4**)
Lowgate NE15: Thro 6D **52**
Low Gosforth Ct. NE3: Gos 4F **43**
Low Grn. DH1: H Shin 3F **161**
LOW GREENSIDE 1A **78**
Low Haugh NE20: Pon 4F **27**
Low Heworth La. NE10: Gate 1F **85**
Lowhills Rd. SR8: Pet 5B **162**
Lowick Cl. DH3: Bir 6D **112**
Lowick Ct. NE3: Gos 3G **57**
Lowland Cl. SR3: New S 4A **132**
Lowland Ho. DH7: B'don 5D **158**
Lowland Rd. DH7: B'don 5D **158**
Low La. NE34: S Shi 4E **75**
Lowleam Ct. NE5: Newc T 6D **54**
Low Level Bri. NE1: Newc T 4A **70**
  NE6: Newc T 4A **70**
LOW LIGHTS 1E **63**
Low Mann Pl. NE23: Cra 3B **22**
Low Mdws. SR6: Cle 2A **90**
Low Moor Cotts. DH1: Dur 4D **144**
LOW MOORSLEY 4A **148**
Lownds Ter. NE6: Walk 3E **71**
LOW PITTINGTON 1F **157**
Lowrey's La. NE9: Gate 6H **83**
Low Rd. DH1: H Shin 3F **161**
Low Rd. E. DH1: H Shin 3F **161**
Low Rd. W. DH1: H Shin 3F **161**
Low Row NE40: Ryton 6C **66**
  SR1: Sund 1C **118** (4F **7**)
  SR8: Eas 1B **162**
Lowry Gdns. NE34: S Shi 1F **89**
Lowry Rd. SR6: Monk 6E **91**
LOW SOUTHWICK 4B **104**
Low Sta. Rd. DH4: Leam 3C **140**
Low St. SR1: Sund 6E **105**
Lowther Av. DH2: Ches S 1B **134**
      (not continuous)
Lowther Cl. SR8: Pet 6D **162**
Lowther Ct. SR8: Pet 5B **164**
Lowther Sq. NE23: Cra 3G **21**
Lowthian Cres. NE6: Walk 4E **71**
Lowthian Ter. NE38: Wash 3D **114**
LOW WALKER 3H **71**
Low Well Gdns. NE10: Gate 2E **85**
Low Westow Rd. NE39: Row G . . .4C **92**
Loxton Sq. NE23: Cra 6A **22**
Lucknow St. SR1: Sund 6F **105**
Lucock St. NE34: S Shi 4D **74**
Lucombe Cl. DH4: Hou S 4D **128**
Lucy St. DH3: Ches S 5C **126**
  NE21: Bla T 6B **66**
Ludlow Av. NE29: N Shi 5A **48**
Ludlow Ct. NE3: Ken 6A **42**
Ludlow Dr. NE25: Whit B 6F **35**

Ludlow Rd. SR2: Sund 5D **118**
Luffness Dr. NE34: S Shi 6H **75**
Luke Ct. SR8: Pet 3D **164**
Luke Cres. SR7: Mur 2B **150**
Lukes La. NE31: Gate, Heb 1D **86**
Lulsgate SR5: C'twn 4C **102**
Lulworth Av. NE32: Jar 4H **73**
Lulworth Ct. SR3: E Her 2E **131**
Lulworth Gdns. SR2: Sund 4C **118**
Lumley Av. NE16: Swa 2F **81**
  NE34: S Shi 3B **76**
Lumley Cl. DH2: Ches S 6B **126**
  NE38: Wash 2H **113**
Lumley Ct. NE22: Bed 3C **10**
  NE31: Heb 1D **72**
  SR3: E Her 2E **131**
Lumley Cres. DH4: Hou S 5G **129**
Lumley Dr. SR8: Pet 4D **164**
Lumley Gdns. NE8: Gate 2B **84**
  NE16: Burn 2E **107**
      (not continuous)
Lumley New Rd.
  DH3: Ches S, Gt Lum 1F **135**
  DH3: Gt Lum 1F **135**
  DH4: Hou S 1F **135**
Lumley Rd. DH1: Dur 6C **144**
Lumley Sixth Pit DH4: Hou S . . .1B **136**
Lumley St. DH4: Hou S 1H **137**
  SR4: Sund 1A **118**
Lumley Ter. DH3: Ches S 1D **134**
  NE32: Jar 6F **73**
  SR2: Ryh 3F **133**
LUMLEY THICKS 2A **136**
Lumley Twr. SR1: Sund 6E **105**
Lumley Wlk. NE11: Dun 2C **82**
Lumley Way NE3: Gos 4C **42**
Lumsden Sq. SR7: Mur 2B **150**
Lumsden Ter. DH9: Ann P 4E **121**
Lund Av. DH1: Dur 1B **154**
Lund Ct. DH1: Dur 1B **154**
Lunedale Av. SR6: Monk 6C **90**
Lunedale Cl. DH3: Gt Lum 5H **135**
Lune Grn. NE32: Jar 1G **87**
Lunesdale St. DH5: Hett H 3C **148**
Lupin Cl. NE5: Cha P 3A **54**
Lupo Av. NE32: Jar 6A **74**
Luton Cres. NE29: N Shi 3H **61**
Lutterworth Cl. NE12: Longb 2B **58**
Lutterworth Pl. NE12: Longb 2B **58**
Lutterworth Rd. NE12: Longb . . .2B **58**
  SR2: Sund 4C **118**
Luxembourg Rd. SR4: Sund 0F **103**
Lychgate NE8: Gate 6H **69**
Lydbury Cl. NE23: Cra 6C **16**
Lydcott NE38: Wash 2F **115**
Lydford Ct. DH4: Hou S 6G **129**
  NE3: Ken 1G **55**
Lydford Way DH3: Bir 4D **112**
Lydney Cl. NE15: Thro 6C **52**
Lyncroft Rd. NE29: N Shi 1A **62**
Lyndale NE23: Cra 6C **16**
Lynden Gdns. NE5: Newc T 4E **55**
Lynden Ga. NE9: Gate 2A **98**
Lynden Rd. SR2: Ryh 1F **133**
LYNDHURST 1H **97**
Lyndhurst Av. DH3: Ches S 3C **126**
  NE2: Newc T 5G **57**
  NE9: Gate 1H **97**
Lyndhurst Cl. NE21: Bla T 3G **79**
Lyndhurst Cres. NE9: Gate 1A **98**
Lyndhurst Dr. DH1: Dur 6A **154**
  NE9: Gate 1A **98**

Lyndhurst Gdns. NE2: Newc T 5F 57
Lyndhurst Grn. NE9: Gate 1H 97
Lyndhurst Gro. NE9: Gate 1A 98
Lyndhurst Rd. DH9: Stly 3B 122
　NE12: Longb 6D 44
　NE25: Whit B 6A 36
Lyndhurst St. NE33: S Shi 5F 63
Lyndhurst Ter. NE16: Swa 2E 81
　SR4: Sund 5G 103
Lyndon Cl. NE36: E Bol 4D 88
Lyndon Dr. NE36: E Bol 4D 88
Lyndon Gro. NE36: E Bol 4D 88
Lyndon Wlk. NE24: Cow 5F 11
Lyne Cl. DH2: Ous 1H 125
Lyne's Dr. DH7: B'don 4F 159
Lynfield NE26: Whit B 4A 36
Lynfield Ct. NE5: Newc T 4F 55
Lynfield Pl. NE5: Newc T 4F 55
Lynford Gdns. SR2: Sund 4C 118
Lyngrove SR2: Ryh 1F 133
Lynholm Gro. NE12: Longb 5D 44
Lynmouth Pl. NE7: Newc T 4B 58
Lynmouth Rd. NE9: Gate 2H 97
　NE29: N Shi 2G 61
Lynndale Av. NE24: Cow 6G 11
Lynneholm Ct. NE8: Gate 3A 84
Lynnholm Cl. NE7: Newc T 5B 58
Lynnholme Gdns. NE9: Gate 3H 83
　(not continuous)
Lynn Rd. NE28: W'snd 6G 59
　NE29: N Shi 6H 47
Lynn St. DH3: Ches S 1C 134
　NE24: Bly 6B 12
Lynnwood Av. NE4: Newc T 4B 68
Lynnwood Bus. Development Cen.
　NE4: Newc T 4C 68
Lynnwood Ter. NE4: Newc T 4B 68
Lynthorpe SR2: Ryh 1F 133
Lynthorpe Gro. SR6: Monk 1E 105
Lynton Av. NE32: Jar 4A 74
Lynton Cl. DH4: Hou S 6G 129
　NE5: Newc T 4F 55
Lynton Pl. NE5: Newc T 4F 55
Lynton Way NE5: Newc T 4F 55
Lynwood Av. NE21: Bla T 6A 66
　SR4: Sund 5C 116
Lynwood Cl. NE20: Pon 3C 38
LYONS 3D 148
Lyons Av. DH5: Eas L 3D 148
Lyons La. DH5: Eas L 4E 149
Lyons, The DH5: Eas L 3D 148
Lyon St. NE31: Heb 3B 72
Lyric Cl. NE29: N Shi 5G 47
Lysdon Av. NE25: Sea D 3B 24
Lyster Cl. SR7: S'hm 2E 141
Lytchfeld NE10: Gate 4G 85
　(not continuous)
Lytham Cl. NE23: Cra 3G 21
　NE28: W'snd 6C 46
　NE37: Usw 3A 100
Lytham Dr. NE25: Whit B 6H 35
Lytham Grange DH4: Hou S 5E 129
Lytham Grn. NE10: Gate 1H 85
Lytham Pl. NE6: Walk 4E 71
Lythe Way NE12: Longb 1C 58

M

Mabel St. NE21: Bla T 6A 66
Macadam St. NE8: Gate 4F 83
McAnany Av. NE34: S Shi 4F 75

Macbeth Wlk. SR8: Pet 1H 165
McClaren Way DH4: E Her 2B 130
McCracken Cl. NE3: Gos 5E 43
McCracken Dr. NE13: Wide O 4E 31
McCutcheon Ct. NE6: Walk 6E 71
McCutcheon St. SR7: S'hm 2E 141
MacDonald Rd. NE4: Newc T 5H 67
McErlane Sq. NE10: Gate 2G 85
McEwan Gdns. NE4: Newc T 4B 68
Mcewans Indoor Cricket Cen.
　. . . . . .5H 137
McGowen Ct. NE6: Newc T 4C 70
McGuinness Av. SR8: Pet 4E 163
　(not continuous)
McIlvenna Gdns.
　NE28: W'snd 3G 59
McIntyre Hall NE31: Heb 2D 72
McIntyre Rd. NE31: Heb 2D 72
McKendrick Vs. NE5: Newc T 6H 55
MacKintosh Ct. DH1: Dur 5F 155
McLennan St. NE38: Wash 1B 114
Maclynn Cl. SR3: New S 3G 131
Macmerry Cl. SR5: C'twn 5B 102
Macmillan Gdns. NE10: Gate 3G 85
McNally Pl. DH1: Dur 5F 155
McNamara Rd. NE28: W'snd 4G 60
McNulty Ct. NE23: Dud 3H 31
Maddison Cl. SR1: Sund 6F 105
Maddison Gdns. NE23: Seg 2E 33
Maddison St. NE24: Bly 5C 12
Maddox Rd. NE12: Longb 1D 58
Madeira Av. NE26: Whit B 4B 36
Madeira Cl. NE5: Cha P 3A 54
Madeira Ter. NE33: S Shi 6F 63
Madras St. NE34: S Shi 5C 74
Madrona Cl. DH4: Hou S 4D 128
Mafeking Pl. NE29: N Shi 4F 47
Mafeking St. NE6: Walk 6F 71
　NE9: Gate 3A 84
　SR4: Sund 6H 103
Magdalene Av. DH1: Carr 3A 156
Magdalene Ct. DH1: Dur 5E 155
　(off Leazes La.)
　NE2: Newc T 1D 68
　SR7: S'hm 3B 142
Magdalene Hgts. DH1: Dur 5E 155
　(off Leazes La.)
Magdalene Pl. SR4: Sund 6H 103
Magdalene St. DH1: Dur 5E 155
Magenta Cres. NE5: Cha P 2A 54
Maglona St. SR7: S'hm 5B 142
Magnolia Cl. NE4: Newc T 2H 67
Magnolia Gro. NE16: Burn 1H 107
Mahogany Row DH9: Beam 6H 109
Maidenhair Cl. NE4: Newc T 4D 128
Maiden La. NE40: G'sde 1A 78
Maiden Law DH4: Hou S 4E 137
Maiden St. NE4: Newc T 6D 68
Maidens Wlk. NE8: Gate 5H 69
Maidstone Cl. SR3: New S 3F 131
Maidstone Ter. DH4: Hou S 5H 129
Main Cres. NE28: W'snd 3F 59
Maingate NE11: Gate 4E 83
Main Rd. NE13: Din 4F 29
　NE13: Wool 6F 41
　NE40: Ryton 4A 64
Mains Ct. DH1: Dur 2A 154
Mainsforth Ter. SR2: Sund 2F 119
Mainsforth Ter. W.
　SR2: Sund 3E 119
Mains Pk. Rd. DH3: Ches S 6D 126
Mainstone Cl. NE23: Cra 3A 22

Main St. NE20: Pon 5E 27
　NE40: Ryton 5A 64
Main St. Nth. NE23: Seg 2F 33
Main St. Sth. NE23: Seg 2F 33
Makendon St. NE31: Heb 2C 72
Makepeace Ter. NE9: Spri 4F 99
Malaburn Way SR5: S'wck 4A 104
Malaga Cl. NE5: Cha P 3H 53
Malaya Dr. NE6: Walk 4H 71
Malcolm Ct. NE25: Whit B 1H 47
Malcolm St. NE6: Newc T 3A 70
　SR7: S'hm 5B 142
Malden Cl. NE23: Cra 3H 21
Maling Pk. SR4: Sund 6D 102
Malings Cl. SR1: Sund 1F 119
Maling St. NE6: Newc T 4A 70
Mallard Cl. NE38: Wash 3F 113
Mallard Ct. NE12: Kil 1C 44
Mallard Lodge NE10: Gate 3D 84
Mallard Way DH4: W Rai 5F 137
　NE24: News 4D 18
　NE28: W'snd 1E 61
Mallowburn Cres. NE3: Ken 3G 55
Malmo Cl. NE29: N Shi 2F 61
Malone Gdns. DH3: Bir 1C 112
Malory Pl. NE8: Gate 1H 83
Maltby Cl. NE38: Wash 3B 114
　SR3: New S 4G 131
Malt Cres. SR8: Pet 6F 163
Malthouse Way NE5: Newc T 3F 55
Maltings, The DH1: Dur 3A 6
　SR3: New S 2C 132
Malton Cl. NE15: Lem 3C 66
　NE24: Cow 6H 11
Malton Ct. NE32: Jar 2E 73
Malton Cres. NE29: N Shi 3A 62
Malton Gdns. NE28: W'snd 3H 59
Malton Grn. NE9: Gate 4B 98
Malvern Av. DH2: Ches S 1B 134
　(not continuous)
Malvern Cl. SR8: Pet 2B 164
Malvern Ct. NE11: Gate 5C 82
　NE15: Lem 2H 65
　SR6: Cle 2H 89
Malvern Cres. SR7: S'hm 4G 141
Malvern Gdns. NE11: Gate 5C 82
　(not continuous)
　SR6: Monk 2E 105
Malvern Rd. NE26: Sea S 4H 25
　NE28: W'snd 4D 60
　NE29: N Shi 5A 48
　NE38: Wash 4H 113
Malvern St. NE4: Newc T 5C 68
　NE33: S Shi 2E 75
Malvern Ter. DH9: Stly 4E 123
Malvern Vs. DH1: Dur 5F 155
Malvins Cl. Rd. NE24: Cow 6A 12
Malvins Rd. NE24: Cow 5H 11
Mandale Cres. NE30: N Shi 2C 48
Mandarin Cl. NE5: Cha P 3H 53
Mandarin Lodge NE10: Gate 3D 84
　(off Crowhall La.)
Mandarin Way NE38: Wash 1F 115
Mandela Cl. DH9: Stly 4B 122
　SR1: Sund 6F 105
Mandela Way NE11: Dun 6G 67
Manderville Pk. DH5: Hett H 2D 148
Mandeville NE37: Usw 5D 100
Manet Gdns. NE34: S Shi 5F 75
Mangrove Cl. NE5: Cha P 3H 53
Manila St. SR2: Sund 3E 119
Manisty Ho. NE4: Newc T 5A 68

Manisty Ter. SR8: Eas 1C **162**
Mann Cres. SR7: Mur 1D **150**
Manners Gdns. NE25: Sea D ...5A **24**
Manningford CI. NE23: Cra 4A **22**
Manningford Dr. SR3: New S ...4G **131**
Manor Av. NE7: Newc T 2C **58**
   NE15: Thro 1F **65**
Manor Chare
   NE1: Newc T 4G **69** (5F **5**)
Manor CI. DH1: H Shin 3G **161**
   NE3: Gos 2F **57**
Manor Ct. NE33: S Shi 6H **63**
Manor Dr. DH9: Ann P 4F **121**
   NE7: Newc T 2C **58**
Manor Farm NE23: Dud 1A **32**
Manorfields NE12: Newc T 1D **58**
Manor Gdns. NE7: Newc T 2C **58**
   NE10: Gate 3H **85**
Manor Gro. DH4: E Her 2B **130**
   NE7: Newc T 2C **58**
   NE15: Thro 2F **65**
Manor Hall CI. SR7: S'hm 3E **141**
Manor Ho. CI. NE6: Newc T 4C **70**
Manor Ho. Farm Cotts.
   NE3: Ken 3H **55**
Manor Ho. Rd. NE2: Newc T 6H **57**
Manor Pk. NE37: Usw 5B **100**
Manor PI. NE7: Newc T 2C **58**
Manor Rd. DH9: Stly 2D **122**
   NE7: Newc T 3C **58**
   NE30: N Shi 5F **49**
   NE37: Usw 5B **100**
Manors Station (Metro) ..4G **69** (4F **5**)
Manors Station (Rail) 4G **69** (4F **5**)
Manor Ter. NE21: Bla T 2G **79**
   (Winlaton)
   NE21: Bla T 4A **80**
   (Winlaton Moor)
Manor Vw. DH6: H Pitt 3F **157**
   NE37: Usw 5C **100**
Manor Vw. E. NE37: Usw 5C **100**
Manor Wlk. NE7: Newc T 2C **58**
Mnr. Walks Shop. Cen.
   NE23: Cra 3A **22**
Manor Way SR8: Pet 2E **165**
Manorway NE30: N Shi 5F **49**
   NE32: Jar 2G **87**
Mansell Cres. SR8: Pet 6E **163**
Mansell PI. NE3: Ken 4A **56**
Mansel Ter. NE24: Cow 6E **11**
Mansfield Ct. NE36: W Bol 4C **88**
Mansfield Cres. SR6: Monk ...2E **105**
Mansfield PI. NE4: Newc T 4D **68**
Mansfield St. NE4: Newc T 4D **68**
Mansion Ho. NE36: W Bol 4C **88**
Manston CI. SR3: New S 3F **131**
Manx Sq. SR5: S'wck 2B **104**
Maple Av. DH1: Dur 5G **155**
   NE11: Dun 4C **82**
   NE25: Whit B 2B **48**
   SR3: New S 1B **132**
Maplebeck CI. SR3: New S 4F **131**
Maple CI. NE15: Lem 3C **66**
   NE22: Bed 4H **9**
Maple Ct. DH7: B'don 6B **158**
   NE12: Kil 1C **44**
   NE25: Sea D 3B **24**
Maple Cres. NE24: Cow 5F **11**
   SR7: S'hm 6A **142**
Mapledene NE38: Wash 5C **114**
Mapledene Rd. NE3: Ken 1B **56**
Maple Gdns. DH9: Stly 5C **122**

Maple Gro. DH9: Stly 5B **122**
   NE8: Gate 4G **83**
   NE10: Gate 3E **85**
   NE34: S Shi 5H **75**
   SR6: Whit 2F **91**
Maple Pk. DH7: Ush M 6D **152**
Maple Rd. NE21: Bla T 1A **80**
Maple Row NE11: Dun 1F **81**
Maple St. DH9: Stly 5B **122**
   NE4: Newc T 5D **68**
   NE32: Jar 2E **73**
Maple Ter. DH4: Hou S 4E **129**
   DH9: Ann P 4E **121**
   (off Pine Ter.)
   NE4: Newc T 5D **68**
   NE16: Burn 1F **107**
Maplewood DH2: Ches S 4A **126**
   NE6: Walk 1E **71**
Maplewood Av. SR5: S'wck ...2H **103**
Maplewood Cres.
   NE38: Wash 6H **113**
Maplewood St. DH4: Hou S ...2C **136**
Mapperley Dr. NE15: Lem 2C **66**
Marblet Ct. NE11: Gate 4D **82**
Marbury CI. SR3: New S 3F **131**
March Rd. NE23: Dud 3B **32**
March Ter. NE13: Din 4E **29**
Marcia Av. SR6: Monk 2D **104**
Marconi Way NE11: Dun, Swa ..2F **81**
Marcross CI. NE15: Cha P 5H **53**
Marcross Dr. SR3: New S 4F **131**
Mardale NE37: Wash 6H **99**
Mardale Gdns. NE9: Gate 2A **98**
Mardale Rd. NE5: Newc T 6F **55**
Mardale St. DH5: Hett H 3C **148**
MARDEN 1C **48**
Marden Av. NE30: N Shi 2E **49**
Marden Bridge Sports Cen. 1C **48**
Marden Ct. NE26: Sea S 2F **25**
Marden Cres. NE26: Whit B 1E **49**
Marden Farm Dr. NE30: N Shi ...2D **48**
Marden Quarry Nature Reserve
   ....2C **48**
Marden Rd. NE26: Whit B 6C **36**
   (not continuous)
Marden Rd. Sth. NE25: Whit B ...1C **48**
   (not continuous)
Marden Ter. NE30: N Shi 2E **49**
Mareburn Cres. NE10: Gate 3E **85**
Mare CI. NE23: Seg 6G **23**
Maree CI. SR3: New S 4G **131**
Margaret Alice St.
   SR4: Sund 6G **103**
Margaret Collins Ho.
   NE6: Walk 3E **71**
Margaret Cotts. *NE25: N Shi* ...3B **48**
   (off Zetland Dr.)
Margaret Dr. NE12: Longb 5G **45**
Margaret Gro. NE34: S Shi 4C **74**
Margaret Rd. NE26: Whit B 1E **49**
Margaret St. SR2: Sund 5G **119**
   SR7: S'hm 5B **142**
Margaret Ter. DH4: Hou S 3G **129**
   DH9: Tan L 6A **100**
   NE39: Row G 4C **92**
Margate St. SR3: New S 1A **132**
Margery La. DH1: Dur 6B **154**
Marguerite Ct. SR4: Sund 6B **104**
Marian Ct. NE8: Gate 2E **83**
Marian Dr. NE10: Gate 1H **85**
Marian Way NE20: Pon 3B **38**
   NE34: S Shi 6H **75**

Maria St. NE4: Newc T 5A **68**
   SR3: New S 2A **132**
   SR7: S'hm 4B **142**
Marie Curie Dr. NE4: Newc T ...5B **68**
Marigold Av. NE10: Gate 1B **84**
Marigold Ct. SR4: Sund 6B **104**
Marigold Cres. DH4: Hou S 6C **128**
Marigold Wlk. NE34: S Shi 4D **74**
Marina Av. SR6: Monk 2C **104**
   NE26: Sea S 2D **104**
Marina Dr. NE25: Whit B 1F **47**
   NF33: S Shi 4G **63**
Marina Gro. SR6: Monk 2D **104**
Marina Ter. SR2: Ryh 3F **133**
   SR6: Whit 2F **91**
Marina Vw. NE28: W'snd 5D **60**
   NE31: Heb 3A **72**
Marine App. NE33: S Shi 5F **63**
Marine Av. NE26: Whit B 6B **36**
Marine Ct. E. NE26: Whit B 5C **36**
Marine Ct. W. NE26: Whit B 5C **36**
Marine Dr. NE31: Heb, Jar 6E **73**
   SR2: Ryh 1F **133**
Marine Gdns. NE26: Whit B 6C **36**
Mariner's Cotts. NE33: S Shi ...4G **63**
   (not continuous)
Mariners' La. NE30: N Shi 6E **49**
Mariners Point NE30: N Shi 6F **49**
Mariner Sq. SR1: Sund 5F **105**
Mariners Wharf NE1: Newc T ..1A **70**
Marine Ter. NE24: Bly 6C **12**
Marine Ter. E. NE24: Bly 6C **12**
Marine Vw. NE26: Sea S 2F **25**
Marine Wlk. SR6: Monk 2F **105**
Marion St. SR2: Sund 3E **119**
Maritime Cres. SR8: Eas 3F **163**
Maritime St.
   SR1: Sund 1D **118** (4G **7**)
Maritime Ter.
   SR1: Sund 1C **118** (4F **7**)
Marius Av. NE15: Hed W 5H **51**
Mariville E. SR2: Ryh 4G **133**
Mariville W. SR2: Ryh 4G **133**
Marjorie St. NE23: E Cram 4E **23**
Markby CI. SR3: New S 4G **131**
Market Cres. DH4: Hou S 3G **129**
Market Hall DH9: Stly 2C **122**
Market La. NE1: Newc T ...4G **69** (5E **5**)
   NE11: Dun 3A **82**
   NE16: Dun, Swa, Whi 2F **81**
Market PI. DH1: Dur 2B **6**
   DH3: Ches S 5C **126**
   DH5: Hou S 3B **138**
   NE22: Bed 5H **9**
   NE24: Bly 5C **12**
   NE33: S Shi 4E **63**
Market PI. Ind. Est.
   DH5: Hou S 2B **138**
Market Sq. NE32: Jar 2F **73**
   SR1: Sund 1D **118** (4G **7**)
Market St. DH5: Hett H 6D **138**
   NE1: Newc T 4F **69** (4D **4**)
   NE23: Dud 3H **31**
   NE24: Bly 5C **12**
Market Way NE11: Gate 5F **83**
Markham Av. SR6: Whit 3G **91**
Markham St. SR2: Sund 5F **119**
Markington Dr. SR2: Ryh 3F **133**
Markle Gro. DH5: W Rai 6H **137**
Mark Ri. DH5: Hett H 6C **138**
Mark's La. DH4: Leam, W Rai ...1C **146**
Marlboro Av. NE16: Swa 3F **81**

Marlborough SR7: S'hm 4B 142
Marlborough App. NE3: Gos 6E 43
Marlborough Av. NE3: Gos 6D 42
Marlborough Ct. DH5: Hou S 5A 138
  NE3: Ken 6H 41
  NE32: Jar 4F 73
Marlborough Cres.
  NE1: Newc T 5E 69 (6B 4)
  NE9: Gate 2C 98
  SR8: Pet 1H 165
Marlborough Ho. NE26: Whit B . .5B 36
Marlborough Rd. NE37: Usw 4C 100
  SR4: Sund 4B 116
Marlborough St. Nth.
  NE33: S Shi 1F 75
Marlborough St. Sth.
  NE33: S Shi 1F 75
Marlborough Ter. NE62: Sco G . . .1H 9
Marlbro Health & Fitness Club
  . . . . .3B 142
  (off Vane Ter.)
Marleen Av. NE6: Newc T 1C 70
Marleen Ct. NE6: Newc T 1C 70
Marlesford Cl. SR3: New S 3F 131
Marley Cres. SR5: S'wck 2H 103
MARLEY HILL 4E 95
MARLEY POTS 2H 103
Marlfield Cl. NE5: Newc T 4F 55
Marlow Dr. SR3: New S 4F 131
Marlowe Gdns. NE8: Gate 2H 83
Marlowe Pl. DH5: Hou S 4A 138
Marlowe Wlk. NE34: S Shi 6C 74
Marlow Pl. NE12: Longb 1C 58
Marlow St. NE24: Bly 6B 12
Marlow Way NE16: Whi 6D 80
Marmion Rd. NE6: Walk 1F 71
Marmion Ter. NE25: Whit B 1B 48
Marne St. DH4: Hou S 3G 129
Marondale Av. NE6: Walk 2F 71
Marquis Av. NE5: Cha P 2A 54
Marquis Cl. NE12: Newc T 2D 58
Marquis Ct. NE11: Gate 2F 97
Marquisway NE11: Gate 2F 97
Marquisway Cen. NE11: Gate . . .2E 97
Marr Rd. NE31: Heb 4D 72
MARSDEN 4B 76
Marsden Av. SR6: Whit 6F 77
Marsden Cl. DH4: Hou S 3G 137
Marsden Gro. NE9: Gate 2D 98
  SR6: Whit 2F 91
Marsden La. NE5: Newc T 4E 55
  NE34: S Shi 2B 76
Marsden Rd. NE34: S Shi 2H 75
  SR6: Cle 3H 89
Marsden St. NE33: S Shi 1F 75
Marsden Vw. SR6: Whit 6F 77
Marshall's Ct.
  NE1: Newc T 4F 69 (5C 4)
Marshall St. SR6: Monk 1D 104
Marshall Ter. DH1: Dur 4H 155
Marshall Wallis Rd.
  NE33: S Shi 1E 75
  (not continuous)
Marsham Cl. NE15: Lem 2C 66
  SR6: Cle 1A 90
Marsham Rd. NE5: Newc T 4C 54
Marsh Ct. NE11: Gate 4D 82
Marshmont Av. NE30: N Shi 4E 49
Marske Ter. NE6: Walk 3E 71
Marston NE12: Kil 1D 44
Marston Wlk. NE16: Whi 6D 80
Martello Gdns. NE7: Newc T 5D 58

Martha St. DH9: Tan L 5H 107
Martin Ct. NE38: Wash 5F 113
Martindale Av. SR6: Monk 1C 104
Martindale Pk. DH5: Hou S 3A 138
Martindale Pl. NE25: Sea D 6C 24
Martindale Wlk. NE12: Kil 2C 44
Martin Hall NE32: Jar 3G 73
Martin Rd. NE28: W'snd 5D 60
Martin Ter. SR4: Sund 6H 103
Martin Way NE13: Bru V 5C 30
Marwell Dr. NE37: Usw 3C 100
Marwood Ct. NE25: Whit B 5H 35
Marwood Gro. SR8: Pet 4C 164
Marx Cres. DH9: Stly 4D 122
  (not continuous)
Mary Agnes St. NE3: Gos 2C 56
Mary Av. DH3: Bir 1B 112
Maryhill Cl. NE4: Newc T 5A 68
Mary Magdalene Bungs.
  NE2: Newc T 1D 68
Mary's Pl. NE6: Walk 3H 71
Mary St. DH9: Ann P 5G 121
  DH9: Stly 3C 122
  NE21: Bla T 1D 79
  (Black La.)
  NE21: Bla T 6A 66
  (Murray St.)
  SR1: Sund 1C 118 (5F 7)
  SR3: New S 1A 132
  SR7: S'hm 4C 142
Mary Ter. NE5: Newc T 5E 55
Masefield Av. NE16: Swa 2F 81
Masefield Cl. DH9: Stly 2F 123
Masefield Dr. NE34: S Shi 6C 74
Masefield Pl. NE8: Gate 1H 83
Masefields DH2: Pelt 6G 125
Maslin Gro. SR8: Pet 4A 164
MASON .3F 29
Mason Av. NE26: Whit B 6D 36
Mason Cres. SR8: Pet 1F 165
Mason Rd. NE28: W'snd 3G 59
Mason St. NE6: Newc T 4C 70
  NE13: Bru V 5C 30
Mason Vw. NE13: Sea B 3D 30
Massingham Way NE34: S Shi . . .4D 74
Master Mariner's Homes
  NE30: N Shi 6E 49
Mast La. NE30: N Shi 2D 48
Matamba Ter. SR4: Sund 1B 118
Matanzas St. SR2: Sund 4E 119
Matfen Av. NE13: Bru V 1C 42
  NE27: Shir 3E 47
Matfen Cl. NE15: Lem 3C 66
  NE24: Bly 6A 12
Matfen Ct. DH2: Ches S 6A 126
Matfen Dr. SR3: New S 3F 131
Matfen Gdns. NE28: W'snd 2D 60
Matfen Pl. NE3: Ken 1C 56
  NE4: Newc T 2B 68
Mather Rd. NE4: Newc T 5D 68
Matlock Gdns. NE5: Newc T 4D 54
Matlock Rd. NE32: Jar 4G 73
Matlock St. SR1: Sund . . .6D 104 (2G 7)
Matterdale Rd. SR8: Pet 1F 165
Matthew Bank NE2: Gos 4G 57
Matthew Cl. NE6: Newc T 3B 70
Matthew Rd. NE24: Bly 2D 18
Matthews Rd. SR7: Mur 4E 151
Matthew St. NE6: Newc T 3B 70
Maude Gdns. NE28: W'snd 6H 59
Maudlin Pl. NE5: Newc T 6H 55
Maudlin St. DH5: Hett H 5D 138

Mauds La. SR1: Sund 6E 105
Maud St. NE15: Lem 3A 66
  SR6: Monk 1E 105
Maud Ter. DH9: Tan L 4B 108
  NE27: Shir 4C 46
Maughan St. NE24: Bly 6D 12
Maureen Ter. DH1: Dur 1A 156
  SR7: S'hm 4A 142
Maurice Rd. NE28: W'snd 1H 71
Maurice Rd. Ind. Est.
  NE28: Walk 1H 71
Mautland Sq. DH4: Hou S 2A 138
Mautland St. DH4: Hou S 2A 138
Mavin St. DH1: Dur 1D 160 (5D 6)
Maxton Cl. SR3: New S 4F 131
Maxwell St. NE8: Gate 4F 83
  NE33: S Shi 5E 63
  SR4: Sund 6H 103
May Av. NE21: Bla T 4A 80
  NE40: Ryton 3C 64
Maybury Vs. NE12: Longb 2A 58
Maydown Cl. SR5: C'twn 5B 102
Mayfair Ct. NE31: Heb 4B 72
Mayfair Gdns. NE8: Gate 3A 84
  NE20: Pon 5F 27
  NE34: S Shi 2G 75
Mayfair Health Club 2B 118
  (off Durham Rd.)
Mayfair Rd. NE2: Newc T 5F 57
Mayfield NE16: Whi 6F 81
Mayfield Av. NE15: Thro 6E 53
  NE23: Cra 3C 22
Mayfield Ct. SR6: Monk 2D 104
Mayfield Dr. SR6: Cle 3B 90
Mayfield Gdns. NE15: Thro 6E 53
  NE28: W'snd 4F 59
  NE32: Jar 3E 73
Mayfield Gro. SR4: Sund 5C 116
Mayfield Pl. NE13: Wide O 6C 30
Mayfield Rd. NE3: Gos 3D 56
  SR4: Sund 1C 116
Mayfield Ter. NE5: Newc T 6A 56
May Gro. SR6: Whit 6F 77
Maynards Row DH1: Dur 5F 155
Maynes Way DH9: Stly 2F 123
Mayo Dr. SR3: New S 4G 131
Mayoral Way NE11: Gate 2F 97
Mayorswell Cl.
  DH1: Dur 5D 154 (1D 6)
Mayorswell Fld.
  DH1: Dur 5E 155 (1D 6)
Mayorswell St.
  DH1: Dur 5D 154 (1D 6)
Maypole Cl. SR5: S'wck 4B 104
May St. DH1: Dur 6B 154
  DH3: Bir 3C 112
  NE21: Bla T 2H 79
  NE33: S Shi 6F 63
  SR4: Sund 6B 104
Mayswood Rd. SR6: Monk 2D 104
Maythorne Dr. DH6: S Het 6B 150
Maytree Ho. NE4: Newc T 5C 68
Maywood Cl. NE3: Ken 3A 56
Meaburn St. SR1: Sund 1E 119
Meaburn Ter. SR1: Sund 1E 119
Meacham Way NE16: Whi 6E 81
Mead Av. NE12: Longb 5E 45
Mead Cres. NE12: Longb 5E 45
Meadowbank NE23: Dud 3A 32
Meadowbrook Dr. NE10: Gate . . .4A 86
Meadow Cl. DH5: Hou S 4B 138
  NE11: Dun 2A 82

Meadow Cl. NE12: Longb 6B 44
NE21: Bla T 2F 79
NE23: Seg 1F 33
NE40: Ryton 4D 64
Meadow Ct. NE20: Pon 6E 27
NE22: Bed 4G 9
Meadowcroft M. NE8: Gate 2F 83
Meadowdale Cres.
NE5: Newc T 4H 55
NE22: Bed 4F 9
Meadow Dr. DH2: Ches S 1A 134
NE13: Sea D 3E 31
SR3: E Her 3D 130
SR4: Sund 2D 116
MEADOWFIELD 6E 159
Meadowfield NE9: Spri 4F 99
NE20: Pon 4E 27
NE25: Whit B 6H 35
Meadowfield Av. NE3: Ken 1C 56
Meadowfield Ct. NE20: Pon 4D 26
Meadowfield Cres.
NE40: Ryton 5A 64
Meadowfield Dr. SR6: Cle 2A 90
Meadowfield Gdns. NE6: Walk . . .6G 59
Meadowfield Ind. Est.
DH7: B'don 6F 159
(Edwardson Rd.)
DH7: B'don 6G 159
(St John's Rd.)
NE20: Pon 5E 27
Meadowfield Leisure Cen. 5F 159
Meadowfield Pk. NE20: Pon 5E 27
(off Meadowfield)
Meadowfield Pl. DH7: B'don 5F 159
Meadowfield Rd. NE3: Gos 3D 56
Meadowfield Ter. NE12: Longb . . .4F 45
Meadowfield Way DH9: Tan L . . .1A 122
Meadow Gdns. SR3: Sund 4B 118
Meadow Grange DH4: Hou S 1C 136
Meadow Gro. SR4: Sund 2D 116
Meadow La. DH1: Dur 2A 156
NE11: Dun 2A 82
NE40: Ryton 5A 64
SR3: E Her 3D 130
Meadow Laws NE34: S Shi 5A 76
Meadow Ri. NE5: Newc T 3F 55
NE9: Gate 6C 84
Meadow Rd. NE15: Lem 1B 66
NE25: Whit B 1H 47
NE26: Sea S 3F 25
NE28: W'snd 6D 60
Meadowside SR2: Sund 3B 118
Meadows La. DH4: W Rai 1F 147
Meadows, The DH4: Hou S 6B 128
DH4: W Rai 3E 147
NE3: Ken 1B 56
NE16: Burn 3G 107
NE40: Ryton 4D 64
Meadow St. DH5: W Rai 2G 147
Meadowsweet Cl. NE24: News . . .3A 18
Meadow Ter. DH4: Hou S 3G 129
Meadow Va. SR2: Sund 3C 118
Meadowvale NE20: Pon 3A 38
Meadow Vw. DH9: Dip 6E 107
NE25: Sea D 3B 24
NE29: N Shi 3A 62
NE32: Jar 3H 87
NE40: G'sde 1A 78
SR3: E Her 3D 130
Meadow Wlk. NE40: Ryton 4D 64
SR3: New S 4H 131
Meadow Well Station (Metro) . . .3A 62

Mdw. Well Way NE29: N Shi 3A 62
Mead Wlk. NE6: Walk 3F 71
Mead Way NE12: Longb 5E 45
Meadway Dr. NE12: Longb 6F 45
Meadway Ho. NE12: Longb 5F 45
Means Ct. NE23: Dud 5B 32
Means Dr. NE23: Dud 5B 32
Mecca Bingo
Blyth 5D 12
Gateshead 6H 69
Sunderland 1D 118 (4G 7)
Modburn Av. NE30: N Shi 3E 49
Medburn Rd. NE15: Lem 2H 65
NF25: H'wll 1C 34
Medina Cl. SR3: New S 4G 131
Mediterranean Village
NE11: Dun 1G 81
(off Metro Cen.)
Medlar NE9: Gate 1C 98
Medlar Cl. DH4: Hou S 3D 128
Medomsley Gdns. NE9: Gate 1E 98
Medomsly St. SR4: Sund 6A 104
Medway DH3: Gt Lum 4G 135
NE32: Jar 1G 87
Medway Av. NE31: Heb 6C 72
Medway Cl. SR8: Pet 3C 164
Medway Cres. NE8: Gate 2B 84
Medway Gdns. DH9: Stly 5C 122
NE29: N Shi 6C 48
SR4: Sund 3F 117
Medway Pl. NE23: Cra 6C 16
Medwood Cl. NE3: Ken 2A 56
Medwyn Cl. DH4: Hou S 6C 128
NE24: News 2B 18
Megstone NE9: Gate 1H 97
Megstone Av. NE23: Cra 4A 22
Megstone Ct. NE12: Kil 1E 45
Melbeck Dr. DH2: Ous 5G 111
Melbourne Ct.
NE1: Newc T 4H 69 (4H 5)
NE8: Gate 6C 69
Melbourne Cres. NE25: Whit B . . .2A 48
Melbourne Gdns. NE34: S Shi . . .6B 74
Melbourne Pl. SR4: Sund 3G 117
Melbourne St.
NE1: Newc T 4G 69 (5F 5)
Melbury NE25: Whit B 5G 35
Melbury Ct. SR6: Monk 2D 104
Melbury Rd. NE7: Newc T 6A 58
Melbury St. SR7: S'hm 6B 142
Meldon Av. DH6: Sher 6F 157
NE3: Ken 6B 42
NE34: S Shi 3G 75
Meldon Cl. NE28: W'snd 4C 60
Meldon Gdns. NE11: Gate 6C 82
Meldon Ho. NE24: Cow 5H 11
Meldon Rd. SR4: Sund 6H 103
Meldon St. NE4: Newc T 5C 68
NE28: W'snd 6G 61
Meldon Ter. NE6: Newc T 1B 70
Meldon Way DH1: H Shin 4H 161
DH9: Ann P 5H 121
NE21: Bla T 3F 79
Melgarve Dr. SR3: New S 4G 131
Melkington Ct. NE5: Newc T 4F 55
Melkridge Gdns. NE7: Newc T . . .4D 58
Melkridge Pl. NE23: Cra 4H 21
Mellendean Cl. NE5: Newc T 4F 55
Melling Rd. NE23: Cra 3H 21
Melmerby Cl. NE3: Gos 6F 43
Melness Rd. NE13: Bru V 6C 30
Melock Ct. NE13: Bru V 6C 30

Melrose NE38: Wash 4B 114
Melrose Av. NE9: Gate 6A 84
NE22: Bed 4D 10
NE25: Sea D 1B 34
NE25: Whit B 1B 48
NE27: Back 6A 34
NE30: N Shi 3C 48
NE31: Heb 6C 72
SR7: Mur 3A 150
Melrose Cl. NE3: Gos 3D 42
NE15: Lem 3C 66
Melrose Ct. NE22: Bed 3D 10
Melrose Cres. SR7: S'hm 3F 141
Melrose Gdns. DH4: Hou S 6G 129
NE28: W'snd 2E 61
SR6: Monk 2E 105
Melrose Gro. NE32: Jar 5A 74
Melrose Ter. NE22: Bed 3D 10
Melrose Vs. NE22: Bed 3D 10
Melsonby Cl. SR3: New S 3F 131
Meltham Ct. NE15: Cha P 5H 53
Meltham Dr. SR3: New S 4G 131
Melton Av. NE6: Walk 4F 71
Melton Cres. NE26: Sea S 5H 25
Melton Dr. NE25: Sea D 3B 24
Melton Ter. NE25: Sea D 3B 24
Melvaig Cl. SR3: New S 4G 131
Melville Av. NE24: News 2B 18
Melville Gdns. NE25: Whit B 1G 47
Melville Gro. NE7: Newc T 4A 58
Melville St. DH3: Ches S 1C 134
Melvin Pl. NE5: Newc T 5F 55
Melvyn Gdns. SR6: Monk 2E 105
Membury Cl. SR3: New S 4G 131
Memorial Av. SR8: Eas 1E 163
Memorial Homes DH9: Tan L 1B 122
Menceforth Cotts.
DH2: Ches S 5B 126
Mendham Cl. NE10: Gate 5E 85
Mendip Av. DH2: Ches S 1B 134
(not continuous)
Mendip Cl. NE20: N Shi 4B 48
SR8: Pet 1B 164
Mendip Dr. NE38: Wash 4H 113
Mendip Gdns. NE11: Gate 5D 82
Mendip Ho. DH2: Ches S 1C 134
Mendip Ter. DH9: Stly 4E 123
Mendip Way NE12: Longb 1H 57
Mentieth Cl. NE38: Wash 4H 113
Menvill Pl. SR1: Sund 1E 119
Mercantile Rd. DH4: Hou S 4G 137
Merchants Wharf NE6: Newc T . . .6C 70
Mercia Retail Pk. DH1: Dur 5C 144
Mercia Way NE15: Lem 4C 66
Meredith Gdns. NE8: Gate 2H 83
Mere Dr. DH1: Dur 6B 144
Mere Knolls Rd. SR6: Monk 6E 91
Meresyde NE10: Gate 5G 85
Meresyde Ct. NE10: Gate 4G 85
Merevale Cl. NE37: Usw 3C 100
Merganser Lodge NE10: Gate 3D 84
(off Crowhall La.)
Meridian Way NE7: Newc T 4D 58
Merlay Dr. NE13: Din 5F 29
Merlay Hall NE6: Walk 5G 71
Merle Gdns. NE6: Newc T 4C 70
Merle Ter. SR4: Sund 5H 103
Merlin Cl. SR7: S'hm 3A 142
Merlin Ct. NE10: Gate 3D 84
(off High St.)
Merlin Cres. NE28: W'snd 4D 60

Merlin Dr. DH3: Ches S 2D **126**
Merlin Pl. NE12: Longb 6A **44**
Merlin Way NE27: Shir 4E **47**
Merrick Ho. SR3: New S 3H **131**
Merrington Cl. NE25: Sea D 2B **24**
  SR3: New S 3F **131**
Merrion Cl. SR3: New S 3F **131**
Merryfield Gdns. SR6: Monk 2E **105**
MERRYOAKS 2A **160**
Mersey Ct. SR3: New S 3H **131**
Mersey Pl. NE8: Gate 3B **84**
Mersey Rd. NE8: Gate 3B **84**
  NE31: Heb 6C **72**
Merton Ct. NE4: Newc T 5A **68**
Merton Rd. NE6: Walk 6F **71**
  NE20: Pon 5E **27**
Merton Sq. NE24: Bly 5C **12**
  (off Regent St.)
Merton Way NE20: Pon 5E **27**
Merz Ct. NE1: Newc T 1C **4**
Metcalfe Cres. SR7: Mur 2B **150**
Metcalfe Ho. DH1: Dur . . 5B **154** (2A **6**)
Methold Ho's. DH9: Beam . . .1A **124**
Methuen St. NE9: Gate 3A **84**
Methven Way NE23: Cra 5C **16**
Metro Cen. NE11: Dun 1G **81**
Metrocentre E. Bus. Pk.
  NE11: Dun 1A **82**
Metro Centre Station (Rail) 1H **81**
Metroland & Superbowl 1G **81**
Metro Pk. W. NE11: Dun 1F **81**
Metro Retail Pk. NE11: Dun 1F **81**
Mews Ct. DH5: Hou S 3A **138**
Mews, The DH1: H Shin 3F **161**
  DH2: Plaw 6A **134**
  DH4: Hou S 4E **137**
  NE1: Newc T 3F **69** (3C **4**)
  NE3: Gos 4F **43**
  NE10: Gate 3H **85**
  NE21: Bla T 1C **80**
  NE30: N Shi 5G **49**
  SR3: E Her 2D **130**
Michaelgate NE6: Newc T 4C **70**
Mickle Cl. NE37: Wash 1G **113**
Mickle Hill Rd.
  TS27: B Col, Hes 6G **165**
Mickleton Cl. DH3: Gt Lum 4H **135**
Mickleton Gdns. SR3: Sund 5B **118**
Mid Cross St. NE4: Newc T 6D **68**
Middlebrook NE20: Pon 2B **38**
Middle Chare DH3: Ches S 6C **126**
Middle Cl. NE38: Wash 6H **113**
Middle Dr. NE13: Wool 3D **40**
  (not continuous)
  NE20: Pon 3B **38**
Middle Engine La.
  NE27: N Shi 2D **60**
  NE28: N Shi, W'snd 2D **60**
  NE29: N Shi, W'snd 2D **60**
Middlefield DH2: Pelt 2G **125**
Middlefields Ind. Est.
  NE34: S Shi 3D **74**
Middlefield Ter. DH7: Ush M 6B **152**
Middle Gth. NE5: Newc T 5H **55**
Middle Ga. NE5: Newc T 6B **54**
Middle Grn. NE25: Whit B 1G **47**
Middle Gro. DH7: B'don 6C **158**
Middleham Cl. DH2: Ous 6F **111**
Middleham Ct. SR5: S'wck 2G **103**
Middleham Rd. DH1: Dur 6D **144**
MIDDLE HERRINGTON 1E **131**
MIDDLE RAINTON 2F **147**

Middle Row DH4: Hou S 2C **136**
  NE40: Ryton 6E **65**
Middles Rd. DH9: Stly 5D **122**
MIDDLES, THE 6F **123**
Middle St. NE6: Walk 3F **71**
  NE24: News 3H **17**
  NE30: N Shi 6F **49**
  (not continuous)
  SR1: Sund 6C **104** (3F **7**)
  (not continuous)
Middle St. E. NE6: Walk 3G **71**
Middleton Av. NE4: Newc T 3A **68**
  NE39: Row G 4F **93**
Middleton Cl. SR7: S'hm 2E **141**
Middleton Ct. NE2: Newc T 2H **69**
Middleton St. NE24: Bly 6C **12**
Middlewood DH7: Ush M 5C **152**
Middlewood Pk. NE4: Newc T . . .2A **68**
Mid Farm Ct. NE23: Cra 2B **22**
Midfield Dr. SR6: Monk 3E **105**
Midgley Dr. SR3: New S 4G **131**
Midhill Cl. DH7: B'don 5D **158**
Midhurst Av. NE34: S Shi 1H **75**
Midhurst Cl. SR3: New S 3F **131**
Midhurst Rd. NE12: Longb 6D **44**
Midmoor Rd. SR4: Sund 6G **103**
Midsomer Cl. SR3: New S 4F **131**
Midway NE6: Walk 3G **71**
Milbanke Cl. DH2: Ous 6H **111**
Milbanke St. DH2: Ous 6H **111**
Milburn Cl. DH3: Ches S 1E **135**
Milburn Dr. NE15: Newc T 3F **67**
Milburn St. SR4: Sund 6B **104**
Milcombe Cl. SR3: New S 3F **131**
Mildmay Rd. NE2: Newc T 5F **57**
Mildred St. DH5: Hou S 2A **138**
Milecastle Ct. NE5: Newc T 5B **54**
Mile End Rd. NE33: S Shi 3E **63**
  (not continuous)
Milfield Av. NE27: Shir 2D **46**
  NE28: W'snd 3A **60**
Milford Gdns. NE3: Gos 4D **42**
Milford Rd. NE15: Newc T 4G **67**
Military Rd. NE15: Hed W 3C **50**
  NE30: N Shi 1D **62**
Military Vehicle Mus. 1F **69**
Milk Mkt. NE1: Newc T 4H **69** (5G **5**)
Millais Gdns. NE34: S Shi 1E **89**
Mill Bank SR5: Monk 1C **104**
Millbank Ct. DH1: Dur 5B **154**
Millbank Cres. NE22: Bed 4A **10**
Millbank Ho. SR7: S'hm 3F **141**
Millbank Ind. Est. NE33: S Shi . . .5E **63**
Millbank Pl. NE22: Bed 5B **10**
Millbank Rd. NE6: Walk 5G **71**
  NE22: Bed 4B **10**
Millbank Ter. NE22: Bed 4A **10**
Millbeck Gdns. NE9: Gate 2B **98**
Millbeck Gro. DH5: Hou S 5H **137**
Millbrook NE10: Gate 4E **85**
  NE29: N Shi 2A **62**
Millbrook Rd. NE23: Cra 6C **16**
Millburngate DH1: Dur . . .5C **154** (2A **6**)
Millburngate Shop. Cen.
  DH1: Dur 5C **154** (2A **6**)
Millburn Ho. NE5: Newc T 5A **56**
Millburn Ter. DH4: Hou S 3F **129**
Mill Cl. NE29: N Shi 2A **62**
Mill Ct. DH4: Hou S 1C **136**
Mill Cres. DH4: Pen 3F **129**
  NE31: Heb 1A **86**
Milldale SR7: S'hm 3F **141**

Milldale Av. NE24: Cow 6G **11**
MILL DAM 5D **62**
Milldam NE33: S Shi 5D **62**
Milldene Av. NE30: N Shi 5E **49**
Mill Dene Vw. NE32: Jar 4G **73**
Milldyke Cl. NE25: Whit B 5G **35**
Millennium Pl.
  DH1: Dur 5C **154** (2B **6**)
Millennium Way
  SR5: Monk 5C **104** (1F **7**)
Miller Gdns. DH2: Pelt 5F **125**
Millers Bank NE28: W'snd 5D **60**
Millers Hill DH4: Hou S 3G **129**
Miller's La. NE16: Swa 2F **81**
Millers Rd. NE6: Walk 2C **70**
Miller St. NE8: Gate 3F **83**
Miller Ter. SR3: New S 1A **132**
Mill Farm Cl. NE4: Newc T 4D **68**
Mill Farm Rd. NE39: Ham M 1A **106**
MILLFIELD 6A **104**
Millfield NE22: Bed 6A **10**
  NE26: Sea S 4H **25**
Millfield Av. NE3: Ken 4A **56**
Millfield Cl. DH2: Ches S 2A **134**
  NE15: Thro 2F **65**
Millfield Ct. NE16: Whi 4G **81**
  NE22: Bed 5A **10**
  NE26: Sea S 4H **25**
Millfield E. NE22: Bed 6A **10**
Millfield Gdns. NE10: Gate 3C **84**
  NE24: Bly 4B **12**
  NE30: N Shi 5E **49**
Millfield Gro. NE30: N Shi 4E **49**
Millfield La. NE15: Thro 1F **65**
Millfield Nth. NE22: Bed 5A **10**
Millfield Rd. NE16: Whi 5F **81**
Millfield Sth. NE22: Bed 6A **10**
Millfield Station (Metro) 6A **104**
Millfield Ter. SR6: Whit 6F **77**
Millfield W. NE22: Bed 5A **10**
Millford NE10: Gate 4H **85**
Millford Ct. NE10: Gate 5H **85**
Mill Gro. NE30: N Shi 5E **49**
  NE34: S Shi 5B **76**
Millgrove Vw. NE3: Ken 4B **56**
Mill Hill DH5: Hou S 5H **137**
  SR8: Eas, Pet 4A **162**
Mill Hill La. DH1: Dur 2A **160**
Mill Hill Rd. NE5: Newc T 1D **66**
  SR3: New S 3H **131**
Mill Hill Wlk. SR3: New S 3A **132**
Mill Ho. NE2: Newc T 1D **68**
Mill Ho. DH1: Dur 5G **155**
Milling Ct. NE8: Gate 1E **83**
Mill La. DH1: Dur 5G **155**
  (St Josephs Cl.)
  DH1: Dur, H Shin 2G **161**
  (Willow Tree Av.)
  DH2: Plaw 1A **144**
  DH3: Plaw 1A **144**
  DH6: Sher 6E **157**
  DH7: New B 1C **158**
  DH9: Beam 5F **111**
  NE4: Newc T 5C **68**
  NE15: Hed W 4H **51**
  NE21: Bla T 4H **79**
  NE23: Seg 2C **32**
  NE29: N Shi 3D **62**
  NE31: Heb 6B **72**
  SR6: Whit 5F **77**
Mill La. Nth NE4: Newc T 4C **68**
Millne Ct. NE22: Bed 4H **9**

Millom Ct. SR8: Pet	4A 164
Millom Pl. NE9: Gate	1B 98
Mill Pit DH4: Hou S	3F 129
Mill Ri. NE3: Gos	3G 57
Mill Rd. DH7: B'don	4G 159
NE8: Gate	5H 69 (6H 5)
SR7: S'hm	3F 141
Mills Gdns. NE28: W'snd	4H 59
Mill St. SR4: Sund	1B 118
Mill Ter. DH4: Hou S	3F 129
SR8: Eas	1A 162
Millthorp Cl. SR2: Sund	6G 119
Millum Ter. SR6: Monk	4E 105
Mill Vw. NE10: Gate	4C 84
NE36: W Bol	4C 88
Mill Vw. Av. SR6: Monk	2D 104
Millview Dr. NE30: N Shi	4D 48
Mill Vs. NE36: W Bol	4C 88
Millway NE9: Gate	4A 84
NE26: Sea S	4H 25
Millway Gro. NE26: Sea S	4H 25
Millwood Grn. NE21: Bla T	5A 80
Milner Cres. NE21: Bla T	2G 79
Milner St. NE33: S Shi	5G 63
Milne Way NE3: Ken	2B 56
Milrig Cl. SR3: New S	4G 131
Milsted Cl. SR3: New S	4F 131
Milsted Ct. NE15: Cha P	5H 53
Milton Av. DH5: Hou S	4A 138
(not continuous)	
NE31: Heb	3C 72
Milton Cl. DH9: Stly	3F 123
NE2: Newc T	2H 69 (1G 5)
SR7: S'hm	4G 141
Milton Grn.	
NE2: Newc T	2H 69 (1G 5)
Milton Gro. NE29: N Shi	1B 62
(not continuous)	
Milton La. SR8: Eas	1C 162
Milton Pl. NE2: Newc T	2H 69 (1G 5)
NE9: Spri	4F 99
NE29: N Shi	1B 62
Milton Rd. NE16: Swa, Whi	3E 81
Milton Sq. NE8: Gate	1A 84
(not continuous)	
Milton St. NE32: Jar	1F 73
NE33: S Shi	1F 75
SR4: Sund	6A 104
Milton Ter. DH2: Pelt	6G 125
NE29: N Shi	1D 62
Milvain Av. NE4: Newc T	3A 68
Milvain Cl. NE8: Gate	2H 83
Milvain St. NE8: Gate	2H 83
Milverton Ct. NE3: Ken	1G 55
Mimosa Dr. NE31: Heb	6C 72
Mimosa Pl. NE4: Newc T	1H 67
Minden St. NE1: Newc T	4G 69 (4F 5)
Mindrum Ter. NE6: Walk	5F 71
NE29: N Shi	3H 61
Mindrum Way NE25: Sea D	6B 24
Minehead Gdns. SR3: New S	1A 132
Miners Cotts. NE15: Newc T	2E 67
Minerva Cl. NE5: Cha P	3A 54
Mingarry DH3: Bir	5E 113
Mingary Cl. DH5: W Rai	1G 147
Minorca Cl. SR1: Sund	1E 119
Minorca Pl. NE3: Ken	4B 56
Minskip Cl. SR3: New S	4G 131
Minster Cl. DH1: Carr	4A 156
NE8: Gate	6H 69
Minster Gro. NE15: Cha P	4H 53
Minsterley DH3: Gt Lum	4G 135

Minster Pde. NE32: Jar	2G 73
Minting Pl. NE23: Cra	3H 21
Minton Ct. NE29: N Shi	3B 62
Minton La. NE29: N Shi	3B 62
Minton Sq. SR4: Sund	6G 103
Mirlaw Rd. NE23: Cra	4H 21
Mistletoe Rd. NE2: Newc T	6G 57
Mistletoe St. DH1: Dur	6B 154
Mitcham Cres. NE7: Newc T	4B 58
Mitchell Av. NE2: Newc T	4G 57
NE25: Whit B	1H 47
Mitchell Cl. SR8: Pet	5D 162
Mitchell Gdns. NE34: S Shi	2H 75
Mitchell St. DH1: Dur	5B 154
DH3: Bir	3B 112
DH9: Ann P	5G 121
DH9: Stly	5B 122
NE6: Walk	3G 71
(not continuous)	
Mitchell Ter. DH9: Tan L	5H 107
Mitford Av. NE24: Bly	1A 18
NE25: Sea D	6A 24
Mitford Cl. DH1: H Shin	4H 161
DH3: Ches S	1D 126
NE38: Wash	3H 113
Mitford Ct. SR8: Pet	3D 164
Mitford Dr. DH6: Sher	6E 157
NE5: Newc T	4C 54
Mitford Gdns. NE11: Gate	6C 82
NE13: Wide O	4E 31
NE28: W'snd	2D 60
Mitford Pl. NE3: Ken	1C 56
Mitford Rd. NE34: S Shi	3G 75
Mitford St. NE28: W'snd	5G 61
SR6: Monk	1E 105
Mitford Ter. NE32: Jar	1F 87
Mitford Way NE13: Din	5F 29
Mithras Gdns. NE15: Hed W	5G 51
Mitre Pl. NE33: S Shi	1D 74
Moat Gdns. NE10: Gate	3A 86
Moatside Ct. DH1: Dur	6C 154 (3B 6)
Moatside La. DH1: Dur	6C 154 (3B 6)
Modder St. NE6: Walk	6F 71
Model Dwellings	
NE38: Wash	3C 114
Model Ter. DH4: Pen	1E 129
Moffat Av. NE32: Jar	5A 74
Moffat Cl. NE29: N Shi	5G 47
Moine Gdns. SR6: Monk	2E 105
Moir Ter. SR2: Ryh	3G 133
(off Robson Pl.)	
Molesdon Cl. NE30: N Shi	4C 48
Molineux Cl. NE6: Newc T	3B 70
Molineux Ct. NE6: Newc T	3B 70
Molineux St. NE6: Newc T	3B 70
Mollyfair Cl. NE40: Ryton	5A 64
Monarch Av. SR3: E Her	4E 131
Monarch Rd. NE4: Newc T	6C 68
Monarch Ter. NE21: Bla T	1A 80
Monastery Ct. NE32: Jar	2F 73
Mona St. DH9: Stly	2D 122
Moncreiff Ter. SR8: Eas	1D 162
Monday Cres. NE4: Newc T	3D 68
(not continuous)	
Monday Pl. NE4: Newc T	3D 68
Money Slack DH1: Dur	4B 160
Monkchester Grn. NE6: Walk	4E 71
Monkchester Rd. NE6: Walk	4E 71
Monk Ct. NE8: Gate	1H 83
SR8: Pet	4B 164
Monkdale Av. NE24: Cow	1G 17
Monkhouse Av. NE30: N Shi	4C 48

Monkridge NE15: Cha P	5H 53
NE26: Whit B	4A 36
Monkridge Ct. NE3: Gos	3G 57
Monkridge Gdns. NE11: Dun	4B 82
Monks Av. NE25: Whit B	2H 47
Monks Cres. DH1: Dur	4F 155
MONKSEATON	6B 36
Monkseaton Dr. NE25: Whit B	6G 35
NE26: Whit B	5A 36
Monkseaton Rd. NE25: Well	6E 35
Monkseaton Station (Metro)	6B 36
Monksfeld NE10: Gate	1E 85
Monksfield Cl. SR3: New S	4H 131
Monkside NE6: Newc T	1D 70
NE23: Cra	4H 21
Monkside Cl. NE38: Wash	5G 113
Monks Pk. Way NE12: Longb	1A 58
Monks Rd. NE25: Whit B	2G 47
Monkstone Av. NE30: N Shi	5E 49
Monkstone Cl. NE30: N Shi	5E 49
Monkstone Cres. NE30: N Shi	5E 49
Monkstone Grange	
NE30: N Shi	4D 48
Monk St. NE1: Newc T	4E 69 (5B 4)
SR6: Monk	4D 104
Monks Way NE30: N Shi	4E 49
Monksway NE32: Jar	3A 74
Monks Wood NE29: N Shi	5A 48
Monkswood Sq. SR3: New S	3B 132
Monk Ter. NE32: Jar	2Q 70
MONKTON	6F 73
Monkton NE10: Gate	5F 85
Monkton Av. NE34: S Shi	5B 74
Monkton Bus. Pk. NE31: Heb	1C 86
Monkton Dene NE32: Jar	5E 73
Monkton Hall NE31: Heb	5D 72
Monkton La. NE31: Heb	1C 86
NE32: Jar	6D 72
Monkton Rd. NE32: Jar	2F 73
(not continuous)	
Monkton Stadium	5E 73
Monkton Ter. NE32: Jar	2G 73
MONKWEARMOUTH	5D 104
Monkwearmouth Station Mus.	
	5D 104 (1G 7)
Monmouth Gdns.	
NE28: W'snd	3E 61
Monroe Pl. NE5: Newc T	5H 55
Mons Av. NE31: Heb	3C 72
Mons Cres. DH4: Hou S	3G 129
Montagu Av. NE3: Ken	4C 56
Montagu Ct. NE3: Ken	5C 56
Montague St. NE9: Gate	3H 83
Montague St. NE15: Lem	3B 66
SR6: Monk	2D 104
Monterey NE37: Usw	4B 100
SR3: New S	4G 131
Montfalcon Cl. SR8: Pet	1C 164
Montford Cl. SR3: New S	4F 131
Montgomery Rd. DH1: Dur	4F 155
Montorosso NE20: Wool	6A 28
Montpelier Ter. SR2: Sund	3E 119
Montpellier Pl. NE3: Ken	4B 56
Montrose Cl. NE25: Sea D	3B 24
Montrose Cres. NE9: Gate	4B 84
Montrose Dr. NE10: Gate	4H 85
Montrose Gdns. SR3: Sund	4A 118
Monument Ct. DH1: Dur	1A 160
Monument Mall Shop. Cen.	
NE1: Newc T	4F 69 (4D 4)
Monument Station (Metro)	
	4F 69 (4D 4)

Monument Ter. DH3: Bir 3C 112
  DH4: Pen 1E 129
Monument Vw. DH4: Pen 1F 129
MOOR 5F 45
Moor Cl. NE29: N Shi 5G 47
  SR1: Sund 6F 105
Moor Ct. DH4: Hou S 6C 128
  NE3: Gos 5D 56
  SR6: Whit 3E 91
Moor Cres. DH1: Dur 4G 155
  NE3: Gos 5E 57
Moor Crest Ter. NE29: N Shi 5B 48
  (off Walton Av.)
Moorcroft Cl. NE15: Lem 2B 66
Moorcroft Rd. NE15: Lem 2C 66
Moordale Av. NE24: Cow 1G 17
Moore Av. NE11: Dun 3B 82
  NE34: S Shi 3G 75
Moore Ct. NE15: Thro 2C 64
Moore Cres. DH3: Bir 1C 112
Moore Cres. Nth. DH5: Hou S . .4A 138
Moore Cres. Sth. DH5: Hou S . .4A 138
Moor Edge DH1: Dur 5H 153
  DH7: B'don 6D 158
Moor Edge Rd. NE27: Shir 1C 46
MOOR END 3A 156
Moor End Ter. DH1: Carr 3A 156
Moore Pk. NE8: Gate 2A 84
Moore St. DH9: Stly 4C 122
  NE8: Gate 2A 84
Moore St. Vs. NE8: Gate 2A 84
  (off Moore St.)
Moorfield NE2: Gos 4F 57
Moorfield Gdns. SR6: Cle 4A 90
Moorfoot Av. DH2: Ches S 1C 134
  (not continuous)
Moorfoot Gdns. NE11: Gate 4C 82
Moor Gdns. NE29: N Shi 5G 47
Moorhead NE5: Newc T 6A 56
Moorhead Ct. NE5: Newc T 6A 56
Moorhead M. NE5: Newc T 6A 56
Moorhouse Cl. NE34: S Shi 4F 75
Moorhouse Gdns.
  DH5: Hett H 3C 148
  (not continuous)
Moorhouses Rd. NE29: N Shi 5G 47
Moorings, The NE6: Newc T 5C 70
Moorland Av. NE22: Bed 2E 11
Moorland Cotts. NE22: Bed 2D 10
Moorland Ct. NE22: Bed 2E 11
Moorland Cres. NE6: Walk 2E 71
  NE22: Bed 2E 11
Moorland Dr. NE22: Bed 3E 11
Moorlands DH9: Dip 6E 107
  NE32: Jar 2H 87
Moorlands, The DH1: Dur 5G 155
Moorland Vs. NE22: Bed 2E 11
Moorland Way NE23: Nel V 6G 15
Moor La. NE3: Ken 3H 55
  NE20: Pon 1B 38
  NE34: S Shi 3G 75
  NE36: E Bol 3G 89
  SR6: Cle 4A 90
Moor La. E. NE34: S Shi 3H 75
Moormill NE11: Kib 1E 111
Moormill La. NE11: Kib 1F 111
Moor Pk. Ct. NE29: N Shi 6G 47
Moor Pk. Rd. NE29: N Shi 6F 47
  (not continuous)
Moor Pl. NE3: Gos 4E 57
Moor Rd. Nth NE3: Gos 2F 57
Moor Rd. Sth. NE3: Gos 4F 57

Moorsburn Dr. DH4: Hou S 2G 137
Moors Cl. DH4: Hou S 3F 137
Moorsfield DH4: Hou S 3F 137
MOORSIDE 4G 131
Moorside NE12: Longb 3B 44
  NE32: Jar 2G 87
  NE37: Wash 6H 99
Moorside Ct. NE5: Newc T 6A 56
Moorside Ind. Est. SR3: E Her . . .4F 131
Moorside Nth. NE4: Newc T 6A 56
Moorside Pl. NE4: Newc T 1B 68
Moorside Rd.
  SR3: E Her, New S 3F 131
Moorside Sth. NE4: Newc T 2B 68
Moorsley Rd. DH5: Hett H 4A 148
  DH5: Hett H, H Pitt 6F 147
Moor St. SR1: Sund 6E 105
  (Coronation St.)
  SR1: Sund 1F 119
  (Woodbine St.)
Moor Ter. SR1: Sund 6F 105
Moorvale La. NE5: Newc T 5A 56
Moor Vw. NE3: Ken 3H 55
  NE12: Kil 6C 32
  NE40: Ryton 5A 64
  SR6: Whit 3E 91
Moorview Cres. NE5: Newc T 5A 56
Moor Vw. Ter. DH9: Ann P 6E 121
Moor Vw. Wlk. NE12: Kil 1C 44
Moorway NE37: Wash 6H 99
Moorway Dr. NE15: Lem 2C 66
Moralee Cl. NE7: Newc T 4D 58
Moran St. SR6: Monk 1D 104
Moray Cl. DH3: Bir 6D 112
  SR8: Pet 2C 164
Moray St. SR6: Monk 3D 104
Morcott Gdns. NE29: N Shi 3A 62
Morden St. NE1: Newc T . . .3F 69 (3C 4)
Mordey Cl. SR2: Sund 2E 119
Mordue Ter. DH9: Ann P 6G 121
Morecambe Pde. NE31: Heb 1E 87
Moreland St. SR6: Monk 3D 104
Moresby Rd. NE23: Cra 5C 16
Morgan Bus. Cen. NE12: Kil 6B 32
Morgan St. SR5: S'wck 3B 104
Morgans Way NE21: Bla T 1G 79
Morgan Vs. NE28: W'snd 5A 60
  (off North Vw.)
Morinda Cl. DH4: Hou S 4D 128
Morland Av. NE38: Wash 4C 114
Morland Gdns. NE9: Gate 4B 84
Morley Av. NE10: Gate 1H 85
Morley Ct. NE6: Newc T 2C 70
Morley Hill Rd. NE5: Newc T 1D 66
Morley La. DH7: New B 5A 158
Morley Pl. NE27: Shir 1D 46
Morley Ter. DH4: Hou S 2E 137
  NE10: Gate 3D 84
Morningside NE38: Wash 1E 127
Morningside Ct. DH3: Ches S . . .5C 126
Mornington Av. NE3: Ken 4B 56
Morpeth Av. NE13: Wide O 4E 31
  NE32: Jar 6F 73
  NE34: S Shi 2F 75
Morpeth Cl. NE38: Wash 3G 113
Morpeth Dr. SR3: New S 3F 131
Morpeth St. NE2: Newc T 1D 68
  SR8: Pet 4F 163
Morpeth Ter. NE29: N Shi 3H 61
Morris Av. NE34: S Shi 6D 74
Morris Ct. NE23: Dud 3B 32

Morris Cres. NE35: Bol C 3C 88
Morris Gdns. NE10: Gate 3H 85
Morrison Ind. Est.
  DH9: Ann P 6G 121
Morrison Rd. DH9: Ann P 6G 121
Morrison Rd. Nth. Ind. Est.
  DH9: Ann P 6G 121
Morrison St. Sund 1E 83
Morris Rd. NE16: Whi 3F 81
Morris Sq. SR8: Eas 2C 162
Morris St. DH3: Bir 3B 112
  NE8: Gate 3E 83
  NE37: Usw 5A 100
Morris Ter. DH5: Hou S 4B 138
Morrit Ct. NE7: Newc T 2C 58
Morston Dr. NE15: Lem 3C 66
Mortimer Av. NE5: Newc T 4D 54
  NE29: N Shi 1H 61
Mortimer Chase NE23: E Har 4B 16
Mortimer Rd. NE33: S Shi 1F 75
  NE34: S Shi 1F 75
Mortimer St. SR4: Sund 6H 103
Mortimer Ter. NE25: H'wll 1C 34
  (off Laurel Ter.)
Morton Cl. NE38: Wash 3B 114
Morton Cres. DH4: Hou S 2D 136
  NE5: Cal 1H 53
Morton Grange Ter.
  DH4: Hou S 2C 136
Morton Sq. SR8: Pet 6C 162
Morton St. NE6: Newc T, Walk . . .3D 70
  NE33: S Shi 3E 63
Morton Wlk. NE33: S Shi 3E 63
Morval Cl. SR3: New S 4F 131
Morven Dr. NE10: Gate 2H 85
Morven Lea NE21: Bla T 1H 79
Morwick Cl. NE23: Cra 4H 21
Morwick Pl. NE5: Newc T 6H 55
Morwick Rd. NE29: N Shi 5H 47
Mosley St. NE1: Newc T 4F 69 (5D 4)
Mossbank NE9: Gate 2B 98
Moss Cl. NE15: Lem 1A 66
Moss Cres. NE40: Ryton 5A 64
Mossdale DH1: Carr 3C 156
Moss Side NE9: Gate 2C 98
Mosspool NE21: Bla T 1G 79
Mossway DH2: Pelt 2F 125
Mostyn Grn. NE3: Ken 2B 56
Motcombe Way NE23: Cra 5C 16
Moulton Ct. NE5: Newc T 5G 55
Moulton Pl. NE5: Newc T 5G 55
Mountbatten Av. NE31: Heb 5C 72
Mount Cl. NE12: Kil 1D 44
  NE25: Whit B 2H 47
  SR4: Sund 1D 116
Mountfield Gdns. NE3: Ken 3B 56
Mountford Rd. NE25: Sea D 2B 24
Mount Gro. NE11: Dun 4B 82
  SR4: Sund 3A 118
Mt. Joy Cres.
  DH1: Dur 1D 160 (6D 6)
Mount La. NE9: Spri 5E 99
Mt. Lonnen NE9: Spri 5E 99
MOUNT PLEASANT
  Gateshead 2B 84
  Houghton-le-Spring 1C 128
Mt. Pleasant DH3: Bir 2C 112
  DH5: Hou S 3B 138
  DH9: Dip 6E 107

Mt. Pleasant NE21: Bla T 2H 79
   SR5: S'wck 4A 104
Mt. Pleasant Bungs. DH3: Bir . . .2C 112
Mt. Pleasant Ct. NE15: Thro 5D 52
Mt. Pleasant Gdns. NE8: Gate . . .2A 84
Mt. Pleasant Rd. DH3: Bir 2C 112
Mount Rd. DH3: Bir 2C 112
   NE9: Spri 5E 99
   SR4: Sund 3H 117
Mountsett Crematorium
   DH9: Dip 5E 107
Mountside Gdns. NE11: Dun 4B 82
Mt. Stewart St. SR7: S'hm 6B 142
Mount Ter. NE33: S Shi 5E 63
Mount, The NE15: Thro 5C 52
   NE40: Ryton 4C 64
Mount Vw. NE16: Swa 3F 81
Mourne Gdns. NE11: Gate 5C 82
Moutter Cl. SR8: Pet 5E 163
Mowbray Cl. SR2: Sund 2D 118
Mowbray Rd. NE12: Longb 5D 44
   NE29: N Shi 1H 61
   NE33: S Shi 6F 63
   SR2: Sund 3D 118
Mowbray St. DH1: Dur 5B 154
   NE6: Newc T 3A 70
Mowbray Ter. DH4: Hou S 1H 137
Mowlam Dr. DH9: Stly 3E 123
Moyle Ter. NE16: Burn 3G 107
Mozart St. NE33: S Shi 5F 63
Muirfield NE25: Whit B 6H 35
   NE33: S Shi 6H 63
Muirfield Dr. NE10: Gate 5D 84
   NE37: Usw 3A 100
Muirfield Rd. NE7: Newc T 2C 58
Muirston Av. NE23: Cra 5C 16
Mulben Cl. NE4: Newc T 5A 68
Mulberry Cl. NF24: News 3B 18
Mulberry Gdns. NE10: Gate 1C 84
Mulberry Gro. NE16: Burn 3G 107
Mulberry Pk. NE9: Gate 6H 83
Mulberry Pl. NE4: Newc T 6D 68
Mulberry St. NE10: Gate 2C 84
Mulberry Ter. DH9: Ann P 5H 121
Mulberry Trad. Est. NE10: Gate . . .2C 84
Mulberry Way DH4: Hou S 2F 137
Mulcaster Gdns. NE28: W'snd . . .4G 59
Mulgrave Dr. SR6: Monk 5E 105
Mulgrave Ter. NE8: Gate 6G 69
Mulgrave Vs. NE8: Gate 1G 83
Mullen Dr. NE40: Ryton 5C 64
Mullen Gdns. NE28: W'snd 3G 59
Mullen Rd. NE28: W'snd 3G 59
Mull Gro. NE32: Jar 6A 74
Mullin Cl. DH7: Ush M 4D 152
Muncaster M. SR8: Pet 4A 164
Mundella Ter. NE6: Newc T 2B 70
Mundell St. DH9: Stly 5C 122
Mundle Av. NE21: Bla T 5A 80
Mundles La. NE36: E Bol 4F 89
Municipal Ter. NE37: Wash 1B 100
Munslow Rd. SR3: E Her 1E 131
Muriel St. DH9: Stly 6C 122
Murphy Gro. SR2: Ryh 2E 133
Murray Av. DH4: Hou S 2E 137
Murray Ct. DH2: Ches S 6B 126
Murrayfield NE23: Seg 1F 33
Murrayfield Dr. DH7: B'don 6C 158
Murrayfield Rd. NE5: Newc T 5H 55
Murrayfields NE27: Shir 4B 46
Murray Gdns. NE11: Dun 4C 82
Murray Pl. DH2: Ches S 6B 126

Murray Rd. DH2: Ches S 6B 126
   NE28: W'snd 4D 60
Murray St. NE21: Bla T 6A 66
   SR8: Pet 1G 165
Murray Ter. DH9: Dip 1C 120
Murtagh Diamond Ho.
   NE34: S Shi 4E 75
MURTON
   Houghton-le-Spring 2C 150
   Newcastle upon Tyne 3F 47
Murton Ho. NE29: N Shi 4G 47
Murton La. DH6: Eas L 4E 149
   NE27: N Shi, Shir 4E 47
Murton St. SR1: Sund . . .1E 119 (5H 7)
   SR7: Mur 3D 150
Muscott Gro. NE15: Newc T 3E 67
Mus. of Antiquities 2C 4
Musgrave Gdns. DH1: Dur 5G 155
Musgrave Rd. NE9: Spri 5H 83
Musgrave Ter. NE6: Walk 3E 71
   NE10: Gate 2G 85
   NE38: Wash 1B 114
Muswell Hill NE15: Newc T 4E 67
Mutual St. NE28: W'snd 6H 59
Mylord Cres. NE12: Kil 6B 32
Myra Av. TS27: Hes 6G 165
Myre Hall DH5: Hou S 3A 138
Myrella Cres. SR2: Sund 5C 118
Myreside Pl. NE12: Longb 6B 44
Myrtle Av. NE11: Dun 3B 82
   SR6: Whit 2F 91
Myrtle Cres. NE12: Longb 4D 44
Myrtle Gro. NE2: Newc T 5G 57
   NE9: Gate . . . . .GH 83
   NE16: Burn 1F 107
   NE28: W'snd 6B 60
   NE34: S Shi 5H 75
Myrtle Rd. NE21: Bla T 2A 80
Myrtles DH2: Ches S 4B 126

N

Nafferton Pl. NE5: Newc T 1G 67
Nailor's Bank NE8: Gate 5A 70
Nailsworth Cl. NE35: Bol C 1A 88
Nairn Cl. DH3: Bir 6D 112
   NE37: Usw 3A 100
Nairn Rd. NE23: Cra 2B 22
Nairn St. NE32: Jar 6A 74
Naisbitt Av. SR8: Pet 5E 163
Nansen Cl. NE5: Newc T 5D 54
Napier Cl. DH3: Ches S 1D 126
Napier Ct. NE16: Whi 1F 95
Napier Rd. NE16: Swa 2E 81
   SR7: S'hm 3G 141
Napier St. NE2: Newc T . . .3H 69 (2G 5)
   NE32: Jar 2F 73
   (not continuous)
   NE33: S Shi 3D 74
Napier Way NE21: Bla T 1C 80
Napoleon Cl. SR2: Ryh 2F 133
Narvik Way NE29: N Shi 2F 61
Nash Av. NE34: S Shi 0F 75
Nater's Bank NE30: N Shi 2E 63
   (off Union Quay)
Naters St. NE26: Whit B 1A 48
National Glass Cen. 5E 105
Natley Av. NE36: E Bol 4G 89
Navenby Cl. NE33: Gos 5F 43
   SR7: S'hm 2G 141
Naworth Av. NE30: N Shi 4C 48

Naworth Ct. SR8: Pet 4B 164
Naworth Dr. NE5: Newc T 4B 54
Naworth Ter. NE32: Jar 5H 73
Nawton Av. SR5: S'wck 3C 104
Nayland Rd. NE23: Cra 2A 22
Naylor Av. NE21: Bla T 5A 80
Naylor Ct. NE21: Bla T 5C 66
Naylor Pl. NE26: Sea S 2F 25
Nazareth M. NE2: Newc T 1H 69
Neale St. DH9: Ann P 5G 121
   DH9: Tan L 5H 107
   SR6: Monk 2D 104
Neale Ter. DH3: Bir 3C 112
Neale Wlk. NE3: Ken 4A 56
Nearlane Cl. NE13: Sea B 3E 31
Neasdon Cres. NE30: N Shi 4D 48
Neasham Rd. SR7: S'hm 2G 141
NEDDERTON 5C 8
Nedderton Cl. NE5: Cha P 3H 53
Needham Pl. NE23: Cra 2B 22
Neighbourhood Cen., The
   NE5: Newc T 3E 55
Neill Dr. NE16: Sun 3F 95
Neilson Rd. NE10: Gate 1B 84
Neil St. DH5: Eas L 4E 149
Nellie Gormley Ho. NE12: Kil 3B 44
Nell Ter. NE39: Row G 4C 92
Nelson Av. NE3: Gos 2C 56
   NE23: Nel V 1G 21
   NE33: S Shi 6H 63
Nelson Cl. SR2: Sund 2E 119 (6H 7)
   SR8: Pet 6G 163
   (not continuous)
Nelson Cres. NE29: N Shi 4H 61
Nelson Dr. NE23: Cra, Nel V 2F 21
Nelson Ho. NE30: N Shi 6F 49
Nelson Ind. Est. NE23: Nel V 6G 15
Nelson Pk. NE23: Nel V 6G 15
Nelson Pk. E. NE23: Nel V 6H 15
Nelson Pk. W. NE23: Nel V 6F 15
Nelson Rd. NE6: Walk 5H 71
   NE23: Nel V 6F 15
   NE25: Well 6F 36
Nelson St. DH3: Ches S 1C 134
   DH5: Hett H 2C 148
   NE1: Newc T 4F 69 (4D 4)
   NE8: Gate 0G 09
   NE29: N Shi 2C 62
   NE33: S Shi 4E 63
   NE38: Wash 3C 114
   NE40: G'sde 2A 78
   SR2: Ryh 2F 133
   SR7: S'hm 3H 141
Nelson Ter. DH6: Sher 6E 157
   NE29: N Shi 4H 61
NELSON VILLAGE 1G 21
Nelson Way NE23: Nel V 5F 15
Nene Ct. NE37: Usw 5C 100
Nenthead Cl. DH3: Gt Lum 4H 135
Neptune Rd. NE15: Lem 2C 66
   NE28: W'snd 1H 71
Neptune Way SR8: Eas 1C 162
Nesbit Rd. SR8: Pet 2E 165
Nesburn Rd. SR4: Sund 3A 110
Nesham Pl. DH5: Hou S 3A 138
Nesham St. NE4: Newc T 6C 68
Nesham Ter. SR1: Sund 6F 105
Ness Cl. NE21: Bla T 1G 79
Nest Rd. NE10: Gate 1D 84
Netherburn Rd. SR5: S'wck 3C 104
Netherby Cl. NE5: Newc T 1H 67
Netherby Dr. NE5: Newc T 1G 67

Netherdale NE22: Bed 4F **9**
Nether Farm Rd. NE10: Gate 2F **85**
Nether Riggs NE22: Bed 5H **9**
Netherton NE12: Kil 6C **32**
Netherton Av. NE29: N Shi 5H **47**
Netherton Cl. DH2: Ches S 1A **134**
Netherton Gdns. NE13: Wide O . . .5D **30**
Netherton Gro. NE29: N Shi 6H **47**
Netherton La. NE22: Bed 3E **9**
Netherwitton Way NE3: Gos 4D **42**
Nettleham Rd. SR5: S'wck 3C **104**
Nettles La. SR3: New S 3B **132**
NETTLESWORTH 1A **144**
Neville Ct. NE37: Usw 5D **100**
Neville Cres. DH3: Bir 1C **112**
Nevilledale Ter. *DH1: Dur* *6B* **154**
    (off Summerville)
Neville Dene DH1: Dur 6H **153**
Neville Rd. NE15: Lem 2B **66**
    SR4: Sund 6H **103**
    SR8: Pet 6C **162**
Nevilles Ct. DH1: Dur 6A **154**
Neville's Cross Bank
    DH1: Dur 2H **159**
Neville's Cross Rd.
    NE31: Heb 4D **72**
Neville's Cross Vs. DH1: Dur . . .1A **160**
Neville Sq. DH1: Dur 2A **160**
Neville St. *DH1: Dur* *3A* **6**
    NE1: Newc T 5F **69** (6B **4**)
Neville Ter. DH1: Dur 5A **154**
Neville Wlk. *NE37: Usw* *4D* **100**
    (off Marlborough Rd.)
Nevinson Av. NE34: S Shi 6F **75**
Nevis Cl. NE26: Whit B 3A **36**
Nevis Ct. NE26: Whit B 3A **36**
Nevis Gro. NE36: W Bol 4D **88**
Nevis Way NE26: Whit B 4A **36**
New Acres DH7: Ush M 5C **152**
New Acres Rd. DH9: Stly 6C **122**
Newark Cl. NE22: Bed 3F **9**
    SR8: Pet 6C **162**
    (not continuous)
Newark Cres. SR7: S'hm 2G **141**
Newark Dr. SR6: Whit 3F **91**
Newark Sq. NE29: N Shi 3B **62**
Newarth Cl. NE15: Lem 2C **66**
Newbank Wlk. NE21: Bla T 2G **79**
NEWBIGGIN HALL ESTATE 3D **54**
Newbiggin La. NE5: Newc T 3D **54**
New Blackett St. DH9: Ann P 4E **121**
Newbold Av. SR5: S'wck 3C **104**
Newbold St. NE6: Walk 4D **70**
Newbolt Ct. NE8: Gate 1A **84**
NEWBOTTLE 6H **129**
Newbottle La. DH4: Hou S 4D **136**
Newbottle St. DH4: Hou S 2H **137**
NEW BRANCEPETH 2B **158**
Newbridge Av. SR5: S'wck 3C **104**
Newbridge Bank DH3: Lam P 4F **127**
Newbridge Banks DH2: Pelt 5C **124**
New Bri. St.
    NE1: Newc T 4G **69** (4F **5**)
New Bri. St. W.
    NE1: Newc T 4F **69** (4D **4**)
    (not continuous)
Newbrough Cres. NE2: Newc T . . .5G **57**
Newburgh Av. NE25: Sea D 1A **34**
NEWBURN 2F **65**
Newburn Av. SR5: S'wck 3C **104**
Newburn Bri. Rd.
    NE21: Bla T, Thro 3E **65**

Newburn Ct. NE33: S Shi 6F **63**
Newburn Cres. DH4: Hou S 2H **137**
Newburn Hall Motor Mus. 1F **65**
Newburn Haugh Ind. Est.
    NE15: Lem 3H **65**
Newburn Ind. Est. NE15: Lem . . .3G **65**
Newburn La. End NE15: Thro 5D **52**
Newburn Leisure Cen. 1E **65**
Newburn Riverside Ind. Pk.
    NE15: Lem 5A **66**
Newburn Rd. DH9: Stly 1D **122**
    NE15: Thro 5D **52**
Newbury NE12: Kil 1D **44**
Newbury Av. NE8: Gate 3F **83**
    (not continuous)
Newbury Cl. NE15: Lem 2B **66**
Newbury St. NE33: S Shi 2F **75**
    SR5: Monk 2C **104**
Newby Cl. NE22: Bed 2C **10**
Newby La. DH6: H Pitt 2G **157**
Newby Pl. NE9: Gate 1B **98**
Newcastle Arts Cen. 5F **69** (6C **4**)
Newcastle Av. SR8: Pet 5F **163**
Newcastle Bank DH3: Bir 6B **98**
Newcastle Bus. Pk.
    NE4: Newc T 6B **68**
    (not continuous)
Newcastle Coll.
    NE1: Newc T 2G **69** (1E **5**)
Newcastle Discovery Mus.
    . . . . .5E **69** (6A **4**)
Newcastle Falcons Rugby
    Football Ground (Kingston Pk.)
    . . . . .6F **41**
Newcastle Football Cen. 3F **67**
NEWCASTLE INTERNATIONAL AIRPORT
    . . . . .2B **40**
Newcastle Opera House
    . . . . .4E **69** (5B **4**)
Newcastle Playhouse 2F **69** (1D **4**)
Newcastle Race Course 3F **43**
Newcastle Rd. DH1: Dur 3H **153**
    DH3: Bir 1C **112**
    DH3: Ches S 5C **126**
    DH4: Hou S 3G **137**
    NE24: News 3A **18**
    NE34: S Shi 5A **74**
    (not continuous)
    NE36: W Bol 4C **86**
    SR5: Monk 1C **104**
    SR5: S'wck 6A **90**
Newcastle Road Baths 3D **104**
Newcastle Science Pk.
    NE1: Newc T 4G **69** (4F **5**)
Newcastle Station (Rail)
    . . . . .5F **69** (6C **4**)
Newcastle St. NE29: N Shi 2C **62**
Newcastle Ter. DH1: Dur 1A **154**
    NE30: N Shi 6F **49**
Newcastle United FC (St James' Pk.)
    . . . . .3E **69** (3B **4**)
NEWCASTLE UPON TYNE
    . . . . .4F **69** (4C **4**)
Newcastle Western By-Pass
    NE3: Gos 4B **42**
    NE5: Newc T 4F **55**
    NE13: Bru V 4B **42**
    NE15: Lem, Newc T 3C **66**
New Coliseum Cinema 6D **36**
NEW DELAVAL 4A **18**
Newdene Wlk. NE15: Lem 2B **66**
New Dr. SR7: S'hm 2H **141**

New Durham Rd.
    DH9: Ann P 6G **121**
    SR2: Sund 1B **118** (5E **7**)
New Elvet DH1: Dur 6D **154** (2C **6**)
NEWFIELD 4E **125**
Newfield Rd. DH2: Pelt 4E **125**
Newfield Ter. DH2: Pelt 4E **125**
Newfield Wlk. NE16: Whi 5E **81**
New Front St. DH9: Ann P 5F **121**
    DH9: Tan L 6B **108**
Newgate NE1: Newc T 4F **69** (5C **4**)
Newgate St.
    NE1: Newc T 4F **69** (4C **4**)
New George St. NE33: S Shi 1E **75**
New Grange Ter. DH2: Pelt 5F **125**
New Grn. St. NE33: S Shi 6E **63**
Newham Av. NE13: Bru V 1C **42**
NEW HARTLEY 3B **24**
Newhaven Av. SR5: S'wck 3C **104**
NEW HERRINGTON 3H **129**
New Herrington Country Pk. . . .1H **129**
New Herrington Ind. Est.
    DH4: Hou S 3H **129**
Newington Ct. NE37: Usw 5A **100**
    SR5: S'wck 4C **104**
Newington Dr. NE29: N Shi 4B **48**
Newington Rd.
    NE2: Newc T 2H **69** (1H **5**)
    (not continuous)
    NE6: Newc T 2A **70**
NEW KYO 5H **121**
NEW LAMBTON 1C **136**
Newland Ct. NE34: S Shi 4E **75**
Newlands NE30: N Shi 3C **48**
Newlands Av. NE3: Gos 4E **43**
    NE24: Bly 2B **18**
    NE25: Whit B 2H **47**
    SR3: Sund 4B **118**
Newlands Pl. NE24: Bly 2B **18**
Newlands Rd. DH1: Carr 3A **156**
    NE2: Gos 4F **57**
    NE24: Bly 2B **18**
Newlands Rd. E. SR7: S'hm 3H **141**
Newlands Rd. W. SR7: S'hm 3G **141**
Newlyn Cres. NE29: N Shi 2A **62**
Newlyn Dr. NE23: Cra 2A **22**
    NE32: Jar 3H **73**
Newlyn Rd. NE3: Ken 2A **56**
Newman La. NE38: Wash 4C **114**
Newman Pl. NE8: Gate 3A **84**
Newman Ter. NE8: Gate 3A **84**
Newmarch St. NE32: Jar 2E **73**
Newmarket Wlk. NE33: S Shi 5E **63**
    (not continuous)
New Mills NE4: Newc T 3D **68**
Newminster Cl. DH4: Hou S 1F **137**
Newminster Rd. NE4: Newc T . . .3G **67**
Newmin Way NE16: Whi 6D **80**
Newport Gro. SR3: New S 1A **132**
New Quay NE29: N Shi 3D **62**
Newquay Gdns. NE9: Gate 3H **97**
New Rainton *DH4: Pen* *1F* **129**
    (off Rainton St.)
New Rainton St. *DH4: Pen* *1F* **129**
    (off Rainton St.)
New Redheugh Bri. Rd.
    NE1: Newc T 6E **69**
    NE8: Gate 6E **69**
Newriggs NE38: Wash 5B **114**
New Rd. DH2: Beam 2B **124**
    DH9: Beam 2B **124**
    NE11: Gate 5D **82**

New Rd. NE16: Burn 6G 93
NE35: Bol C 3B 88
NE36: E Bol 3B 88
NE38: Wash 1A 128
(not continuous)
NEWSHAM 3H 17
Newsham Cl. NE5: Cha P 3H 53
Newsham Rd. NE24: Bly 2A 18
NEW SILKSWORTH 2H 131
New Sth. Ter. DH3: Bir 3D 112
Newstead NE38: Wash 2A 114
Newstead Rd. DH4: Hou S 1G 137
Newsteads Cl. NE25: Whit B 6H 35
Newsteads Dr. NE25: Whit B 6G 35
Newsteads Farm Cotts.
NE25: Whit B 1G 47
Newstead Sq. SR3: New S 3A 132
New Strangford Rd.
SR7: S'hm 3H 141
New St. DH1: Dur 5B 154 (2A 6)
DH6: Sher 6E 157
SR4: Sund 1C 116
Newton Av. NE28: W'snd 4D 60
NE30: N Shi 2D 48
Newton Cl. NE15: Lem 2C 66
Newton Dr. DH1: Dur 2B 154
Newton Gro. NE34: S Shi 4C 74
NEWTON HALL 6C 144
Newton Hall NE7: Newc T 5B 58
Newton Ho. NE4: Newc T 3D 68
(off Barrack Rd.)
Newton Pl. NE7: Newc T 5B 58
Newton Rd. NE7: Newc T 4A 58
Newton St. NE8: Gate 3F 83
NE11: Dun 2B 82
NEW TOWN
Boldon Colliery 3B 88
Houghton-le-Spring 3B 138
Newtown Ind. Est. DH3: Bir 5C 112
NEW YORK 4F 47
New York By-Pass NE29: N Shi . . .4F 47
New York Ind. Pk. NE27: N Shi . . .5E 47
NE27: Shir 4E 47
New York Rd. NE27: Back, Shir . . .2C 46
(not continuous)
NE29: N Shi 4E 47
New York Way NE27: N Shi 5E 47
(not continuous)
Nicholas Av. SR6: Whit 3F 91
Nicholas St. DH5: Hett H 6D 138
Nichol Ct. NE4: Newc T 4H 67
Nicholson Cl. SR1: Sund 1E 119
Nicholson's Ter. DH9: Beam 1B 124
Nicholson Ter. NE12: Kil 4E 45
Nichol St. NE4: Newc T 4H 67
Nickleby Chare DH1: Dur 2B 160
Nidderdale Av. DH5: Hett H 3B 148
Nidderdale Cl. NE24: Cow 5G 11
Nidsdale Av. NE6: Walk 2G 71
Nightingale Cl. SR4: Sund 3C 116
Nightingale Pl. DH9: Stly 4F 123
Nile Cl. NE15: Lem 1A 66
Nile Ct. NE8: Gate 2A 84
Nile Ct. NE20: N Shi 1C 62
NE33: S Shi 5D 62
SR1: Sund 6E 105 (3H 7)
Nilverton Av. SR2: Sund 4D 118
Nimbus Ct. SR3: New S 3A 132
Nine Lands DH4: Hou S 3G 137
Nine Pins NE8: Gate 4F 83
NE9: Gate 5G 83
Ninnian Ter. DH9: Dip 1C 120

Ninth Av. DH2: Ches S 6B 126
NE6: Newc T 1C 70
NE11: Gate 2F 97
NE24: Bly 1B 18
Ninth Av. E. NE11: Gate 2F 97
Ninth St. SR8: Pet 6G 163
Nissan Way SR5: Wash 6F 101
Nithdale Cl. NE6: Walk 1H 71
Nixon St. NE8: Gate 5A 70
Nixon Ter. NE21: Bla T 2H 79
NE24: Bly 1D 18
Noble Gdns. NE34: S Shi 5B 74
Noble's Bank Rd. SR2: Sund 2F 119
Noble St. NE4: Newc T 6B 68
NE10: Gate 2D 84
SR2: Sund 2F 119
SR8: Eas 1E 163
Noble St. Ind. Est.
NE4: Newc T 6B 68
Noble Ter. SR2: Sund 2F 119
Noel Av. NE21: Bla T 5A 80
Noel St. DH9: Stly 2F 123
Noel Ter. NE21: Bla T 4B 80
Nolrmont Way SR3: New S 3G 131
Nookside SR4: Sund 3E 117
Nookside Ct. SR4: Sund 3E 117
Nook, The NE25: Whit B 1B 48
NE29: N Shi 2B 62
NO PLACE 2H 123
Nora St. NE34: S Shi 4E 75
SR4: Sund 3H 117
Norbury Gro.
NE6: Newc T, Walk 4D 70
Nordale Way NE24: Cow 5G 11
Norfolk Av. DH3: Bir 6C 112
SR3: New S 1H 131
Norfolk Cl. SR7: S'hm 2G 141
Norfolk Dr. NE37: Usw 3B 100
Norfolk Gdns. NE28: W'snd 3C 60
Norfolk M. NE30: N Shi 1C 62
Norfolk Pl. DH3: Bir 6D 112
Norfolk Rd. NE8: Gate 5A 70
NE34: S Shi 2C 76
Norfolk Sq. NE6: Newc T 3B 70
Norfolk St. DH5: Hett H 1B 148
NE30: N Shi 1D 62
SR1: Sund 6D 104 (3H 7)
Norfolk Wlk. SR8: Pet 5C 162
Norfolk Way NE15: Lem 2C 66
Norgas Ho. NE12: Kil 3C 44
Norham Av. Nth. NE34: S Shi 1A 76
Norham Av. Sth. NE34: S Shi 1A 76
Norham Cl. NE13: Wide O 6C 30
NE24: Bly 6A 12
Norham Ct. DH4: Hou S 2B 136
NE38: Wash 3H 113
Norham Dr. NE5: Newc T 4C 54
SR8: Pet 4C 164
Norham Pl. NE2: Newc T 6G 57
Norham Rd. DH1: Dur 6D 144
NE3: Gos 1D 56
NE26: Whit B 6B 36
NE29: N Shi 1G 61
Norham Rd. Nth. NE29: N Shi 5F 47
Norham Ter. NE21: Bla T 1H 79
NE32: Jar 5F 73
Norhurst NE16: Whi 6C 80
Norland Rd. NE15: Newc T 3D 66
Norley Av. SR5: S'wck 3C 104
Norma Cres. NE26: Whit B 1E 49
Norman Av. SR3: New S 2B 132
Normanby Cl. SR7: S'hm 2G 141

Normanby Ct. SR6: Monk 4F 105
Normandy Cres. DH5: Hou S 3B 138
Norman Rd. NE39: Row G 4E 93
Norman Ter. DH6: H Pitt 2G 157
NE28: W'snd 5F 61
Normanton Ter. NE4: Newc T 4C 68
Normount Av. NE4: Newc T 4A 68
Normount Gdns. NE4: Newc T . . .4A 68
Normount Rd. NE4: Newc T 4A 68
Northampton Rd. SR8: Pet 5C 162
Northamptonshire Dr.
DH1: Carr 4B 156
North App. DH2: Ches S 5B 126
North Av. NE3: Gos 3D 56
NE5: Newc T 5D 54
NE12: Longb 1D 58
NE34: S Shi 3H 75
NE37: Usw 4A 100
SR8: Pet 6F 163
North Bailey DH1: Dur . .6C 154 (4B 6)
Nth. Balkwell Farm Ind. Est.
NE29: N Shi 6F 47
Nth. Bank Ct. SR5: S'wck 3B 104
NORTH BLYTH 4C 12
Northbourne Rd. NE32: Jar 3E 73
Northbourne St. NE4: Newc T . . .5B 68
NE8: Gate 3H 83
Nth. Brancepeth Cl.
DH7: B'don 3G 159
Nth. Brancepeth Ter.
DH7: B'don 3G 159
Nth. Bridge St.
SR5: Monk 5D 104 (1G 7)
North Burns DH3: Ches S 5C 126
Nth. Church St. NE30: N Shi 1D 62
North Cl. NE6: Newc T 2C 70
NE34: S Shi 3H 75
NE40: Ryton 4C 64
Northcote Av. NE5: Cha P 6A 54
NE25: Whit B 1H 47
SR1: Sund 1E 119
Northcote St. NE4: Newc T 4C 68
NE33: S Shi 1F 75
Northcott Gdns. NE23: Seg 2E 33
North Ct. NE32: Jar 2F 73
North Cres. DH1: Dur 4A 154
NE38: Wash 6H 113
SR8: Eas 2B 162
Nth. Croft NE12: Longb 6E 45
Nth. Cross St. NE3: Gos 2E 57
Northdene DH3: Bir 6C 98
Northdene Av. SR7: S'hm 3B 142
North Dr. NE31: Heb 4A 72
NE38: Ches S, Wash 2D 126
SR6: Cle 2G 89
Nth. Durham St. SR1: Sund 6E 105
North East Aircraft Mus. 2A 102
Nth. Eastern Ct. NE11: Dun 4A 82
North East Exhibition Cen. 2F 43
Nth. E. Fruit & Vegetable Mkt.
NE11: Gate 5F 83
Nth. East Ind. Est. SR8: Pet 4D 162
NORTH END 4A 154
North End DH1: Dur 4A 154
DH7: B'don 4C 158
Northern Gallery for Contemporay Art
. . . . .4H 7
Northern Prom. NE26: Whit B 3C 36
Northern Ter. NE23: Dud 2A 32
Northern Way SR5: S'wck 3A 104

North Farm NE22: H Bri 5C **8**
Nth. Farm Av. SR4: Sund 5D **116**
Nth. Farm Rd. NE31: Heb 4B **72**
Northfield NE22: E Sle 1H **11**
Northfield Cl. NE16: Whi 6D **80**
Northfield Dr. NE12: Kil 3B **44**
SR4: Sund 5D **116**
Northfield Gdns. NE34: S Shi . . .1H **75**
Northfield Rd. NE3: Gos 3D **56**
NE33: S Shi 6H **63**
Northfields Cl. NE6: Newc T 2C **70**
Northfields Ho. *NE6: Newc T* *2C 70*
(off North Vw.)
Northgate DH9: Ann P 6F **121**
NE12: Kil 1D **44**
North Grange NE20: Pon 3E **27**
North Gro. NE40: Ryton 4D **64**
SR6: Monk 2E **105**
North Guards SR6: Whit 3E **91**
Nth. Hall Rd. SR4: Sund 3F **117**
North Haven SR7: S'hm 3H **141**
NORTH HYLTON 6C **102**
Nth. Hylton Rd.
SR5: C'twn, S'wck 3F **103**
Nth. Hylton Rd. Ind. Est.
SR5: C'twn 3F **103**
Nth. Jesmond Av. NE2: Newc T . . .4G **57**
Nth. King St. NE30: N Shi 1D **62**
Northland Cl. SR4: Sund 5D **116**
Northlands DH3: Ches S 4C **126**
NE21: Bla T 2H **79**
NE30: N Shi 4D **48**
North La. DH5: Hett H 5G **139**
NE36: E Bol 4E **89**
NORTHLEA 3H **141**
Northlea NE15: Lem 1C **66**
(not continuous)
Northlea Rd. SR7: S'hm 3G **141**
North Leigh DH9: Tan L 6B **108**
NORTH LODGE 2C **126**
North Lodge DH3: Ches S 2C **126**
Nth. Mason Lodge NE13: Din 3F **29**
Nth. Milburn St. SR4: Sund 6B **104**
Nth. Moor Cotts. SR3: E Her 6G **117**
Nth. Moor Ct. SR3: Sund 6G **117**
Nth. Moor La.
SR3: E Her, New S, Sund . . .6G **117**
Northmoor Rd. NE6: Walk 1E **71**
Nth. Moor Rd. SR3: Sund 6G **117**
Nth. Nelson Ind. Est.
NE23: Nel V 5G **15**
Northolt Av. NE23: Cra 2B **22**
North Pde. NE26: Whit B 6D **36**
NE29: N Shi 5A **62**
Nth. Railway St. SR7: S'hm 4B **142**
Nth. Ravensworth St.
SR4: Sund 6B **104**
North Ridge NE22: Bed 4G **9**
(Forster Av.)
NE22: Bed 4F **9**
(Meadowdale Cres.)
NE25: Whit B 6G **35**
North Rd. DH1: Dur 4B **154** (2A **6**)
DH3: Ches S 2C **126**
DH5: Hett H, Hou S 5H **137**
DH9: Ann P, Dip 2E **121**
NF13: Wide O 5E **31**
NE20: Pon 2E **27**
NE28: W'snd 5H **59**
NE29: N Shi 5B **48**
NE35: Bol C 2A **88**
(Boldon Colliery)

North Rd. NE35: Bol C, W Bol 3B **88**
(New Town)
NE36: E Bol 4E **89**
(not continuous)
NE36: W Bol 3B **88**
SR7: S'hm 2B **142**
Nth. Sands Bus. Cen.
SR6: Monk 5E **105**
NORTH SHIELDS 2C **62**
North Shields Station (Metro) . .2C **62**
North Side DH3: Bir 1D **112**
(not continuous)
Northside Pl. NE25: H'wll 1C **34**
North St. DH3: Bir 4E **113**
DH4: Hou S 5H **129**
DH4: W Rai 3D **146**
DH5: W Rai 1H **147**
NE1: Newc T 3F **69** (3D **4**)
NE21: Bla T 1G **79**
NE32: Jar 2F **73**
NE33: S Shi 4E **63**
SR3: New S 1A **132**
SR5: S'wck 4C **104**
SR6: Cle 2A **90**
North St. Ct. NE1: Newc T 3E **5**
North St. E.
NE1: Newc T 3G **69** (3E **5**)
North Ter. DH1: Dur 1A **154**
DH9: Ann P 4A **122**
NE2: Newc T 2E **69**
NE27: Shir 4C **46**
NE28: W'snd 5B **60**
SR3: New S 1B **132**
SR7: S'hm 3B **142**
SR8: Eas 2B **162**
North Thorn DH9: Stly 2D **122**
Nth. Tyne Ind. Est.
NE12: Longb 5G **45**
Northumberland Annexe
NE1: Newc T 2E **5**
Northumberland Av. NE3: Gos . . .3C **56**
NE12: Longb 6D **44**
NE22: Bed 4G **9**
NE28: W'snd 5D **60**
Northumberland Bldg.
NE1: Newc T 3G **69** (2E **5**)
Northumberland County Cricket Club
. . . . .1H **69**
Northumberland County Tennis Ground
. . . . .5G **57**
Northumberland Dock Rd.
NE28: W'snd 6G **61**
Northumberland Gdns.
NE2: Newc T 1A **70**
NE5: Cha P 4H **53**
Northumberland Ho.
NE23: Cra 2C **22**
Northumberland Pl. DH3: Bir . . .4G **112**
NE1: Newc T 3F **69** (3D **4**)
NE30: N Shi 1C **62**
SR8: Pet 5B **162**
Northumberland Rd.
NE1: Newc T 3F **69** (3D **4**)
NE15: Lem 3A **66**
NE40: Ryton 3C **64**
Northumberland Sq.
NE26: Whit B 6C **36**
NE30: N Shi 1C **62**
Northumberland St.
NE1: Newc T 3F **69** (2D **4**)
NE8: Gate 2E **83**
NE28: W'snd 5A **60**

Northumberland St.
NE30: N Shi 1E **63**
SR8: Pet 5F **163**
Northumberland Ter.
NE6: Newc T 3B **70**
NE28: W'snd *5D 60*
(off Northumberland Av.)
NE30: N Shi 6F **49**
Northumberland Vs.
NE28: W'snd 5C **60**
Northumberland Way
NE37: Gate, Usw, Wash . . .1A **100**
NE38: Wash 1C **114**
Northumbria Birds of Prey Cen.
. . . . .2A **44**
Northumbria Cen. 2C **100**
Northumbria Ho. NE3: Gos 1E **57**
Northumbria Lodge
NE5: Newc T 6A **56**
Northumbrian Rd. NE23: Cra 1A **22**
Northumbrian Way NE12: Kil 2B **44**
NE29: N Shi 4C **62**
Northumbria Pl. DH9: Stly 2F **123**
Northumbria Wlk.
NE5: Newc T 6D **54**
North Vw. DH1: Dur 5G **155**
DH2: Pelt 4F **125**
DH4: Hou S 1C **136**
DH5: Eas L 4E **149**
DH6: Sher 6H **157**
DH7: B'don 6E **159**
DH7: Ush M 4C **152**
DH9: Stly 6F **123**
NE6: Newc T 3B **70**
(not continuous)
NE9: Gate 2B **98**
NE12: Longb 5D **44**
NE13: Bru V 1C **42**
NE13: Din 4F **29**
NE16: Whi 4E **81**
NE22: Bed 2D **10**
NE26: Whit B 1E **49**
NE28: W'snd 5A **60**
NE29: N Shi 5B **48**
NE30: N Shi 1E **49**
NE32: Jar 3E **73**
NE34: S Shi 1H **75**
NE37: Usw 5B **100**
NE40: Ryton 4A **64**
SR2: Ryh *3F 133*
(off Stockton Rd.)
SR4: Sund 2C **116**
SR5: C'twn 4E **103**
SR6: Monk 2D **104**
SR7: Mur 3C **150**
TS27: Cas E 6B **164**
Nth. View E. NE39: Row G 3C **92**
Nth. View Ter. DH4: Hou S 3F **137**
NE10: Gate 2C **84**
Nth. View W. NE39: Row G 3B **92**
North Vs. NE23: Dud 2A **32**
NORTH WALBOTTLE 4H **53**
Nth. Walbottle Rd. NE5: Cha P . . .5G **53**
NE15: Cha P, Thro 5G **53**
(not continuous)
North Way DH2: Ous 6G **111**
Northway NE9: Gate 4B **84**
NE15: Thro 4D **52**
Nth. West Ind. Est. SR8: Pet 6A **162**
Nth. W. Radial NE2: Newc T 1D **68**
Northwood Ct. SR5: S'wck 3C **104**
Northwood Rd. SR7: S'hm 3H **141**

Norton Av. SR7: S'hm 2G 141
Norton Cl. DH2: Ches S 2A 134
Norton Rd. SR5: S'wck 2A 104
Norton Way NE15: Lem 3C 66
Norway Av. SR4: Sund 3G 117
Norwich Av. NE13: Wide O 6D 30
Norwich Cl. DH3: Gt Lum 4H 135
Norwich Rd. DH1: Dur 6D 144
Norwich Way NE23: Cra 2A 22
(not continuous)
   NE32: Jar 2F 87
Norwood Av. NE3: Gos 4E 43
   NE6: Newc T 6B 58
Norwood Ct. NE9: Spri 3C 98
   NE12: Longb 1D 58
Norwood Cres. NE39: Row G 3F 93
Norwood Gdns. NE9: Gate 3A 84
Norwood Rd. NE11: Gate 4D 82
   NE15: Lem 1B 66
Nottingham Ct. NE22: Bed 3F 9
Nottingham Pl. SR8: Pet 5B 162
Nottinghamshire Rd.
   DH1: Carr 4A 156
Numbers Gth. SR1: Sund 6E 105
Nuneaton Way NE5: Cha P 3H 53
Nunn St. DH4: Hou S 4E 129
Nuns La. NE1: Newc T 4F 69 (5C 4)
   NE8: Gate 6H 69
NUNS MOOR 6A 56
Nuns Moor Cres. NE4: Newc T . . .2A 68
Nuns Moor Rd. NE4: Newc T 2A 68
Nuns' Row DH1: Dur 4F 155
Nun St. NE1: Newc T 4F 69 (4C 4)
Nunthorpe Av. SR2: Sund 6F 119
Nunwick Gdns. NE29: N Shi 1G 61
Nunwick Way NE7: Newc T 4D 58
Nurseries, The SR6: Cle 2A 90
Nursery Cl. SR3: Sund 5A 118
Nursery Cotts. DH1: Dur 6B 154
Nursery Gdns. NE5: Newc T 1F 67
   SR8: Eas 2B 162
Nursery La. NE10: Gate 4C 84
   SR6: Cle 2A 90
(not continuous)
Nursery Rd. SR3. Sund 5A 118
Nutley Pl. NE15: Newc T 4E 67
Nye Bevan Ho. NE24: Bly 1D 18
Nye Dene SR5: C'twn 4D 102

O

Oakapple Cl. NE22: Bed 4H 9
Oak Av. DH1: Dur 6G 155
   DH4: Hou S 2H 137
   NE11: Dun 4B 82
   NE13: Din 4G 29
   NE34: S Shi 4A 76
Oak Cres. DH2: Plaw 1A 144
   SR6: Whit 2G 91
Oakdale NE22: H Bri 5D 8
Oakdale Cl. NE15: Lem 3B 66
Oakdale Ter. DH2: Pelt 4E 125
   DH3: Choo S 1C 134
Oakenshaw NE15: Lem 3C 66
Oakerside Dr. SR8: Pet 2C 164
OAKERSIDE PARK 4C 164
Oakey's Rd. DH9: Tan L 1D 122
Oakfield Av. NE16: Whi 5F 81
Oakfield Cl. NE16: Whi 5F 81
   SR3: E Her 3E 131
Oakfield Ct. SR3: E Her 3E 131

Oakfield Dr. NE12: Kil 2F 45
   NE16: Whi 5F 81
Oakfield Gdns. NE15: Newc T . . .4H 67
   NE28: W'snd 4F 59
Oakfield Grange NE13: Din 4F 29
Oakfield Nth. NE40: Ryton 4B 64
Oakfield Rd. NE3: Gos 4D 56
   NE11: Gate 5C 82
   NE16: Whi 6D 80
Oakfields NE16: Burn 6H 93
Oakfield Ter. NE3: Gos 3D 56
   NE10: Gate 2G 85
   NE12: Kil 4E 45
Oakfield Way NE23: Seg 2F 33
Oak Grn. Flats DH7: B'don 5D 158
Oak Gro. NE12: Longb 5D 44
   NE28: W'snd 6B 60
Oakham Av. NE16: Whi 5D 80
Oakham Dr. DH1: Carr 2B 156
Oakham Gdns. NE29: N Shi 3A 62
Oakhurst Dr. NE3: Ken 4C 56
Oakhurst Ter. NE12: Longb 1D 58
Oakland Rd. NE2: Newc T 5F 57
   NE25: Whit B 1H 47
Oaklands NE3: Gos 4E 57
   NE16: Swa 2F 81
   NE20: Pon 1D 38
Oaklands Av. NE3: Gos 4E 57
Oaklands Ct. NE20: Pon 1D 38
Oaklands Cres. SR5: S'wck 3H 103
Oaklands Ter. SR4: Sund 2A 118
Oaklea DH2: Ches S 4A 126
Oakleigh Gdns. SR6: Cle 1A 90
Oakley Cl. NE23: Dud 3B 32
Oakley Dr. NE23: Cra 2C 22
Oakmere Cl. DH4: Pen 3F 129
Oakridge NE16: Whi 5D 80
Oakridge Rd. DH7: Ush M 5C 152
Oak Rd. NE29: N Shi 6F 47
   SR8: Eas 1C 162
Oak Sq. NE8: Gate 2E 83
Oaks, The DH4: Pen 1F 129
   NE40: G'sde 2B 78
   SR2: Sund 2E 119
Oak St. DH4. Hou S 2C 136
   NE13: Sea B 3E 31
   NE15: Thro 5D 52
   NE32: Jar 2E 73
   NE38: Wash 3D 114
   SR1: Sund 1F 119
Oaks W., The SR2: Sund 2D 118
Oak Ter. DH2: Pelt 2E 125
   DH9: Ann P 4F 121
   DH9: Stly 6F 123
   DH9: Tan L 5H 107
   NE16: Burn 6A 94
   NE21: Bla T 2A 80
   SR7: Mur 2D 150
   SR8: Pet 1G 165
Oaktree Av. NE6: Walk 6G 59
Oaktree Gdns. NE25: Whit B 2A 48
(not continuous)
Oakwellgate NE8: Gate 5H 69
Oakwood DH6: S Hot 6B 150
   DH9: Ann P 5E 121
   NE10: Gate 6E 85
(not continuous)
   NE31: Heb 2A 72
Oakwood Av. NE9: Gate 2A 98
   NE13: Wide O 6E 31
Oakwood Cl. NE9: Spri 4F 99
Oakwood Ct. DH9: Ann P 5E 121

Oakwood Gdns. NE11: Gate 5D 82
Oakwood Pl. NE5: Newc T 6G 55
Oakwood St. SR2: Sund 2B 118
Oakwood Ter. NE28: W'snd 5H 61
Oates St. SR4: Sund 1A 118
Oatlands Rd. SR4: Sund 3G 117
Oatlands Way DH1: Dur 5C 144
Oban Av. NE28: W'snd 3D 60
(not continuous)
Oban Ct. NE6: Newc T 4C 70
Oban Gdns. NE6: Newc T 4C 70
Oban St. NE10: Gate 2C 84
   NE32: Jar 6A 74
Oban Ter. NE10: Gate 2C 84
Obelisk La. DH1: Dur 5B 154
Occupation Rd. NE34: S Shi 6H 75
Ocean Beach Pleasure Pk. 3G 63
Ocean Rd. NE33: S Shi 4E 63
   SR2: Sund 5F 119
Ocean Rd. E. SR2: Sund 5G 119
Ocean Rd. Nth. SR2: Sund 5F 119
(off Ocean Rd.)
Ocean Rd. Sth. SR2: Sund 5F 119
(off Ocean Rd.)
Ocean Vw. NE26: Whit B 6D 36
   SR2: Ryh 2F 133
   SR8: Pet 6G 163
Ochiltree Cl. NE26: Sea S 3H 25
Octavia Cl. NE22: Bed 3G 9
Octavia Ct. NE28: W'snd 3C 60
Octavian Way NE11: Gate 2E 97
OFFERTON 4A 116
Offerton Cl. SR4: Sund 1C 116
Offerton La. SR4: Pen 5G 115
   SR4: Sund 1B 116
Offerton St. SR4: Sund 1A 118
Office Pl. DH5: Hett H 2C 148
Office Row DH4: E Her 2A 130
   NE23: Dud 6C 32
   NE38: Wash 6G 113
Office St. SR8: Eas 1F 163
Ogden St. SR4: Sund 1A 118
Ogle Av. NE13: Bru V 1C 42
Ogle Dr. NE24: Bly 1A 18
Ogle Gro. NE32: Jar 6E 73
O'Hanlon Cres. NE28. W'snd 3G 59
Oil Mill Rd. NE6: Walk 2H 71
Okehampton Ct. NE9: Gate 3A 98
Okehampton Dr. DH4: Hou S 5G 129
Okehampton Sq. SR5: S'wck 2A 104
OLD BENWELL 4F 67
Old Blackett St. DH9: Ann P 4E 121
Old Brewery Cl.
   NE2: Newc T 2H 69 (1G 5)
Old Brewery, The
   DH4: Hou S 3A 138
Old Coronation St.
   NE33: S Shi 5E 63
Old Course Rd. SR6: Cle 3A 90
Old Crow Hall La. NE23: Nel V . . .2H 21
Old Customs Ho. NE29: N Shi . . .3D 62
OLD DURHAM 1F 161
Old Durham Rd. NE8: Gate 2H 83
   NE9: Gate 2H 83
Old Elvet DH1: Dur 6D 154 (3C 6)
Old Farm Ct. NE16: Sun 3F 95
Oldfield Rd. NE6: Walk 6F 71
OLD FOLD 1B 84
Old Fold Rd. NE10: Gate 1B 84
Old George Yd.
   NE1: Newc T 4F 69 (5D 4)
Old Gt. Nth. Rd. NE13: Sea B 3A 20

Old Mill La. DH3: Gt Lum 6F **135**
Old Mill Rd. SR2: Sund 2F **119**
  SR5: S'wck 2A **104**
Old Newbiggin La.
  NE5: Newc T 2D **54**
Old Pit La. DH1: Dur 6C **144**
Old Pit Ter. DH1: Dur 6C **144**
Old Rectory Cl. DH9: Tan L ...3B **108**
Old Sta. Ct. NE20: Pon 2C **38**
Oldstead Gdns. SR4: Sund 3G **117**
Oldstone Rd. NE23: E Cram 4E **23**
Old Vicarage Wlk.
  NE6: Newc T 4C **70**
Old Well La. NE21: Bla T 2H **79**
Olga Ter. NE39: Row G 4C **92**
Olive Gdns. NE9: Gate 5A **84**
Olive Pl. NE4: Newc T 2H **67**
Oliver Av. NE4: Newc T 3A **68**
Oliver Cl. NE6: Walk 6F **71**
Oliver Cres. DH3: Bir 1C **112**
Oliver Pl. DH1: Dur 2A **160**
Oliver St. DH9: Stly 5C **122**
  NE38: Wash 3C **114**
  SR7: Mur 4E **151**
  SR7: S'hm 3H **141**
Olive St. NE33: S Shi 3D **74**
  SR1: Sund 1C **118** (5F **7**)
Ollerton Dr. NE15: Thro 5B **52**
Ollerton Gdns. NE10: Gate 5C **84**
Olney Cl. NE23: Cra 2D **22**
O'Neil Dr. SR8: Pet 2E **165**
Ongar Way NE12: Longb 6B **44**
Onix Ind. Est. NE29: N Shi 1G **61**
Onslow Gdns. NE9: Gate 6H **83**
Onslow St. SR4: Sund 6G **103**
Onslow Ter. DH7: B'don 4G **159**
Open, The NE1: Newc T ...3F **69** (3C **4**)
Orange Gro. NE16: Whi 4G **81**
  NE23: Dud 2B **32**
Orchard Av. NE39: Row G 4D **92**
Orchard Cl. DH9: Stly 3C **124**
  NE12: Kil 3F **45**
  NE16: Sun 2F **95**
  NE39: Row G 5D **92**
Orchard Ct. NE40: Ryton 4C **64**
Orchard Dene NE39: Row G 4D **92**
Orchard Dr. DH1: Dur 4E **155**
Orchard Gdns. DH3: Ches S 2C **134**
  NE9: Gate 1A **98**
  NE28: W'snd 4G **59**
  SR6: Whit 3E **91**
Orchard Grn. NE5: Newc T 4H **55**
Orchard Ho. DH1: Dur 4C **6**
Orchard Leigh NE15: Lem 3C **66**
Orchard Pk. DH3: Bir 3C **112**
Orchard Pl. NE2: Newc T 6H **57**
Orchard Ri. NE15: Lem 2H **65**
Orchard Rd. NE16: Whi 4G **81**
  NE39: Row G 4D **92**
Orchards, The NE24: Cow 5H **11**
Orchard St. DH2: Pelt 2G **125**
  DH3: Bir 3C **112**
  NE1: Newc T 5F **69** (6D **4**)
  SR4: Sund 6H **103**
Orchard Ter. DH3: Ches S 2C **134**
  NE15: Lem 3A **66**
  NE15: Thro 5D **52**
Orchard, The DH1: Dur 6B **144**
  DH3: Ches S 5D **126**
  NE15: Lem 3B **66**
  NE16: Whi 4G **81**
  (not continuous)

Orchard, The NE29: N Shi 1C **62**
Orchid Cl. SR3: New S 4D **74**
Orde Cl. NE4: Newc T 2H **67**
Orde Av. NE28: W'snd 4C **60**
Ordley Cl. NE15: Lem 3C **66**
Orde St. NE4: Newc T 6E **69**
Oriole Ho. NE12: Longb 6D **44**
Orkney Dr. SR2: Ryh 1D **132**
Ormesby Rd. SR6: Monk 2D **104**
Ormiscraig NE15: Lem 3C **66**
Ormiston NE15: Lem 3C **66**
Ormonde Av. NE15: Newc T 3E **67**
Ormonde St. NE32: Jar 2F **73**
  SR4: Sund 2H **117**
Ormsby Grn. NE5: Newc T 1E **67**
Ormskirk Cl. NE15: Lem 3B **66**
Ormskirk Gro. NE23: Cra 2C **22**
Ormston St. NE23: E Har 4B **16**
Orpen Av. NE34: S Shi 6E **75**
Orpington Av. NE6: Walk 2E **71**
Orpington Rd. NE23: Cra 2C **22**
Orr Av. SR3: New S 3B **132**
Orwell Cl. NE34: S Shi 1D **88**
  SR8: Pet 3B **164**
Orwell Gdns. DH9: Stly 5C **122**
Orwell Grn. NE3: Ken 4A **56**
Osbaldeston Gdns. NE3: Ken 4D **56**
Osborne Av. NE2: Newc T 1G **69**
  NE33: S Shi 6F **63**
Osborne Bldgs. DH9: Stly 5B **122**
Osborne Cl. NE22: Bed 3C **10**
Osborne Ct. NE2: Newc T 1H **69**
Osborne Gdns. NE26: Whit B 6B **36**
  NE29: N Shi 6C **48**
Osborne Ho. NE28: W'snd 5C **60**
Osborne Pl. NE12: Longb 4F **45**
Osborne Rd. DH3: Ches S 6C **126**
  NE2: Newc T 4F **57**
  SR5: Sund 6C **102**
Osborne St. SR6: Monk 3D **104**
Osborne Ter.
  NE2: Newc T 2G **69** (1F **5**)
  NE8: Gate 2F **83**
  NE23: Cra 2A **22**
  SR8: Eas 1B **162**
Osborne Vs. DH9: Stly 1C **122**
  NE2: Newc T 1G **69**
Oslo Cl. NE29: N Shi 3F **61**
Osman Cl. SR2: Sund 2E **119**
Osman Ter. DH4: Hou S 1E **137**
Osmond Ter. DH4: Hou S 3E **129**
Osprey Dr. NE24: News 2C **18**
  NE28: W'snd 1E **61**
Osprey Ho. NE2: Newc T 6G **57**
Osprey Way NE34: S Shi 5C **74**
Oswald Av. DH1: Dur 6G **155**
Oswald Cl. DH1: Dur 6G **155**
Oswald Cotts. NE9: Gate 2C **98**
Oswald Ct. DH1: Dur ...1D **160** (5C **6**)
Oswald Rd. DH5: Hett H 6C **138**
Oswald St. DH9: Stly 6H **123**
  NE34: S Shi 6E **75**
  SR4: Sund 6A **104**
Oswald Ter. DH9: Stly 6C **122**
  NE8: Gate 2F **83**
  SR2: Sund 5F **119**
  SR8: Eas 1D **162**
Oswald Ter. Sth. SR5: C'twn ...4E **103**
Oswald Ter. W. SR5: C'twn 4E **103**

Oswald Wlk. NE3: Gos 2F **57**
Oswestry Pl. NE23: Cra 2C **22**
  (not continuous)
Oswin Av. NE12: Longb 5D **44**
Oswin Ct. NE12: Longb 4E **45**
Oswin Rd. NE12: Longb 4D **44**
Oswin Ter. NE29: N Shi 2H **61**
Otley Cl. NE23: Cra 2D **22**
Otterburn Av. NE3: Gos 3C **56**
  NE25: Well, Whit B 1F **47**
Otterburn Cl. NE12: Longb 5F **45**
Otterburn Ct. NE8: Gate 2F **83**
  NE25: Whit B 1F **47**
Otterburn Cres. DH4: Hou S ...2G **137**
Otterburn Gdns. NE9: Gate 6G **83**
  NE11: Dun 4C **82**
  NE16: Whi 4F **81**
  NE34: S Shi 3G **75**
Otterburn Gro. NE24: Bly 2H **17**
Otterburn Rd. NE29: N Shi 6B **48**
Otterburn Ter. NE2: Newc T 6G **57**
Otterburn Vs. NE2: Newc T 6G **57**
  (off Otterburn Ter.)
Otterburn Vs. Nth.
  NE2: Newc T 6G **57**
  (off Otterburn Ter.)
Otterburn Vs. Sth.
  NE2: Newc T 6G **57**
  (off Otterburn Ter.)
Ottercap Cl. NE15: Lem 3B **66**
Otterington NE38: Wash 3F **115**
Ottershaw NE15: Lem 3C **66**
Otto Ter. SR2: Sund 2B **118**
Ottovale Cres. NE21: Bla T 2G **79**
Ottringham Cl. NE15: Lem 3B **66**
Oulton Cl. NE5: Newc T 3F **55**
  NE23: Cra 2C **22**
Ousby Ct. NE3: Ken 6H **41**
Ouseburn Cl. SR2: Sund 1F **133**
Ouseburn Rd. NE1: Newc T 3A **70**
  NE6: Newc T 2A **70**
Ouse Burn Water Sports 4A **70**
Ouse Cres. DH3: Gt Lum 4H **135**
Ouselaw NE11: Kib 1F **111**
Ouse St. NE1: Newc T 4A **70**
Ouslaw La. NE11: Kib 1D **110**
OUSTON 5H **111**
Ouston Cl. NE10: Gate 4A **86**
Ouston La. DH2: Pelt 2H **125**
  (not continuous)
Ouston St. NE15: Newc T 4D **66**
Outram St. DH5: Hou S 2A **138**
Oval Pk. Vw. NE10: Gate 4D **84**
Oval, The DH2: Ches S 4B **134**
  DH2: Ous 5H **111**
  DH4: Hou S 3H **137**
  NE6: Walk 6D **70**
  NE12: Longb 1E **59**
  NE13: Wool 5D **40**
  NE22: Bed 4C **10**
  NE24: News 4H **17**
  NE37: Usw 5B **100**
  NE40: Ryton 4C **64**
  SR5: S'wck 3B **104**
  (off Burnbank)
Overdene NE15: Newc T 2D **66**
  SR7: Mur 6F **141**
Overfield Rd. NE3: Ken 2B **56**
Overhill Ter. NE8: Gate 2F **83**
Overman St. DH1: H Shin 5H **161**
Overstone Av. NE40: G'sde 1A **78**
Overton Cl. NE15: Lem 3B **66**

Overton Rd. NE29: N Shi 5A 48
Ovingham Cl. NE38: Wash 2D 114
Ovingham Gdns.
  NE13: Wide O 5D 30
Ovington Gro. NE5: Newc T 2G 67
Owen Brannigan Dr.
  NE23: Dud 4B 32
Owen Ct. NE2: Newc T 2E 69
Owen Dr. NE35: Bol C 3D 88
  NE36: W Bol 3D 88
Owengate DH1: Dur 6C 154 (3B 6)
Owen Ter. DH9: Tan L 5H 107
Owlet Cl. NE21: Bla T 2G 79
Oxberry Gdns. NE10: Gate 4C 84
Oxbridge St. SR2: Sund 5F 119
OXCLOSE 2G 113
Ox Cl. NE41: Wylam 6D 50
Oxclose Rd. NE38: Wash 3C 114
Oxclose Village Cen.
  NE38: Wash 3G 113
Oxford Av. NE23: Cra 2C 22
  NE28: W'snd 4G 59
  NE33: S Shi 1F 75
  NE37: Usw 5H 99
Oxford Cl. SR3: New S 1H 131
Oxford Cres. DH5: Hett H 1B 148
  NE31: Heb 3D 72
Oxford Pl. DH3: Bir 6C 112
Oxfordshire Dr. DH1: Carr 4A 156
Oxford Sq. SR4: Sund 6G 103
Oxford St. DH9: Ann P 4F 121
  NE1: Newc T 3G 69 (3E 5)
  NE24: Bly 6D 12
  NE26: Whit B 6C 36
  NE30: N Shi 6F 49
  NE33: S Shi 1F 75
  SR4: Sund 6G 103
  SR7: S'hm 4G 141
Oxford Ter. DH4: Hou S 3E 129
  NE8: Gate 2G 83
Oxford Way NE32: Jar 2F 87
OXHILL 3B 122
Oxhill Vs. DH9: Ann P 4H 121
Oxley Ter. DH1: Dur 6A 144
Oxnam Cres. NE2: Newc T 2D 68
Oxted Cl. SR3: Cra 2D 22
Oxtod Pl. NE6: Walk 6E 71
Oystershell La.
  NE4: Newc T 4E 69 (5A 4)
Oyston St. NE33: S Shi 5E 63
Ozanan Cl. NE23: Dud 4B 32

P

Pacific Hall Cl. SR7: S'hm 3E 141
Packham Rd. SR4: Sund 2E 117
Paddock Cl. DH4: Hou S 4D 128
  SR6: Cle 2G 89
Paddock Hill NE20: Pon 4F 27
Paddock La. SR3: New S 2B 132
Paddock, The DH4: E Her 2B 130
  DH9: Tan L 1A 122
  NE10: Gate 5F 85
  NE12: Kil 2E 45
  NE13: Wool 5D 40
  NE15: Thro 6F 53
  NE23: E Cram 4D 22
  NE24: Cow 6A 12
  NE25: Sea D 6C 24
  NE39: H Spen 1A 92
Pader Cl. NE13: Bru V 6C 30

Padgate Rd. SR4: Sund 1E 117
Padonhill SR3: New S 4G 131
Padstow Cl. SR2: Ryh 1F 133
Padstow Gdns. NE9: Gate 3H 97
Padstow Rd. NE29: N Shi 3A 62
Page Av. NE34: S Shi 2G 75
Page's Bldgs. NE35: Bol C 3A 88
Page St. NE31: Heb 2D 72
Paignton Av. NE4: Newc T 4A 68
  NE25: Whit B 1H 47
Paignton Sq. SR3: Sund 5G 117
Painter Heugh
  NE1: Newc T 5G 69 (6E 5)
Paisley Sq. SR3: Sund 5G 117
Palace Grn. DH1: Dur . . .6C 154 (4B 6)
Palace Rd. NE22: Bed 3D 10
Palace St. NE4: Newc T . . .5D 68 (6A 4)
Palatine St. NE33: S Shi 3E 63
Palatine Vw. DH1: Dur 6B 154
     (off Margery La.)
  DH6: Sher 6G 157
Palermo St. SR4: Sund 5H 103
Paley St. SR1: Sund 6C 104 (3E 7)
Palgrove Rd. SR4: Sund 2E 117
Palgrove Sq. SR4: Sund 2E 117
Palladian Chapel 4G 93
Pallinsburn Ct. NE5: Newc T 4F 55
PALLION 5H 103
Pallion Ind. Est. SR4: Sund 6F 103
Pallion New Rd. SR4: Sund 5H 103
Pallion Pk. SR4: Sund 6H 103
Pallion Quay SR4: Sund 5H 103
Pallion Retail Pk. SR4: Sund 5G 103
Pallion Rd. SR4: Sund 1H 117
Pallion Station (Metro) 5G 103
Pallion Subway SR4: Sund 5G 103
Pallion Way SR4: Sund 6F 103
Pallion W. Ind. Est.
  SR4: Sund 5F 103
Palm Av. NE4: Newc T 2A 68
  NE34: S Shi 4A 76
Palm Ct. NE12: Kil 4F 45
Palmer Cres. NE31: Heb 3D 72
Palmer Gdns. NE10: Gate 3A 86
Palmer Rd. DH9: Dip 6E 107
  SR8: Pet 2A 164
Palmersn Gth. DH1: Dur . .6D 154 (4C 6)
Palmers Grn. NE12: Kil 4F 45
Palmer's Hill Rd.
  SR6: Monk 5D 104 (1H 7)
Palmerston Av. NE6: Walk 2E 71
Palmerstone Rd. SR4: Sund 3E 117
Palmerston Rd. SR4: Sund 4C 116
Palmerston Sq. SR4: Sund 3E 117
Palmerston St. NE33: S Shi 1E 75
Palmerston Wlk. NE8: Gate 1E 83
Palmer St. DH6: S Het 6B 150
  DH9: Stly 4B 122
  NE32: Jar 2E 73
PALMERSVILLE 4F 45
Palmersville NE12: Kil 4F 45
     (not continuous)
Palmersville Station (Metro) . . .5G 45
Palm Lea DH7: B'don 5C 158
Palmstead Rd. SR4: Sund 2D 116
Palmstead Sq. SR4: Sund 2E 117
Palm Ter. DH9: Stly 6F 123
  DH9: Tan L 4A 108
Panatta Fitness Cen. 2E 83
     (within church)
Pancras Rd. SR3: Sund 5G 117
Pandon NE1: Newc T 4G 69 (5F 5)

Pandon Bank
  NE1: Newc T 4G 69 (5F 5)
Pandon Bldg. NE2: Newc T 2F 5
Pandon Ct.
  NE2: Newc T 3H 69 (2G 5)
Panfield Ter. DH4: Hou S 1C 136
Pangbourne Cl. NE15: Lem 1A 66
Pankhurst Gdns. NE10: Gate 3G 85
Pankhurst Pl. DH9: Stly 4F 123
Pann La. SR1: Sund 6D 104 (3G 7)
Panns Bank SR1: Sund . . .6D 104 (2G 7)
Pantiles, The NE37: Usw 3B 100
Parade Cl. NE6: Walk 4G 71
Parade, The DH2: Pelt 3E 125
     (not continuous)
  DH3: Ches S 2D 134
  NE6: Walk 4G 71
  NE11: Dun 1G 81
  NE28: W'snd 2B 60
  NE38: Wash 3C 114
  SR2: Sund 1F 119
PARADISE 5G 67
Paradise Cres. SR8: Eas 1D 162
Paradise La. SR8: Eas 1D 162
Paradise Row NE23: Cra 3B 22
Paradise St. SR8: Pet 6H 163
Paramount Fitness Cen. 4H 9
Park & Ride
  Callerton Parkway 4C 40
  East Boldon 4G 89
  Four Lane Ends 1C 58
  Heworth 3F 85
  Kingston Park 1G 55
  Regent Centre 1E 57
Park Av. DH9: Stly 2D 122
  NE3: Gos 1C 56
     (not continuous)
  NE3: Ken 6B 42
  NE11: Dun 4A 82
  NE21: Bla T 1H 79
     (Blaydon Bank)
  NE21: Bla T 1A 80
     (Widdrington Rd.)
  NE22: Bed 2E 11
  NE26: Whit B 6C 36
  NE27: Shir 2D 46
  NE28: W'snd 5H 59
  NE30: N Shi 6E 49
  NE34: S Shi 5H 75
  NE37: Usw 4B 100
  SR3: New S 2B 132
  SR6: Monk 2E 105
Park Chare NE38: Wash 2B 114
Park Cl. DH9: Ann P 6G 121
  NE4: Newc T 5C 68
Park Cl. NE6: Walk 6G 59
  NE8: Gate 6H 69
     (off Hopper St.)
  NE11: Gate 2F 9
Park Cres. NE27: Shir 2D 46
     (not continuous)
  NE30: N Shi 6D 48
Park Cres. E. NE30: N Shi 6E 49
Parkdale Ri. NE16: Whi 4D 80
Park Dr. NE3: Gos 4E 43
  NE12: Longb 5E 45
  NE16: Whi 4G 81
  NE24: News 3H 17
  NE61: Hep 4A 8
Parker Av. NE3: Gos 3D 56
Parker Ct. NE11: Dun 1A 82
Pk. Farm Vs. NE24: News 5A 18

Parkfield NE26: Sea S 3G **25**
  NE32: Jar 2G **87**
Park Fld. NE40: Ryton 4B **64**
Parkfield Ter. NE40: Ann P 3E **121**
Park Gdns. NE26: Whit B 6C **36**
Park Ga. SR6: Monk 2E **105**
Parkgate DH5: Hett H 2E **149**
Parkgate La. NE21: Bla T 3H **79**
Park Gro. NE27: Shir 2D **46**
  NE37: Usw 4B **100**
Parkham Cl. NE23: Cra 6B **16**
Parkhead DH9: Ann P 6E **121**
Parkhead Gdns. NE21: Bla T 3H **79**
Pk. Head Rd. NE7: Newc T 5A **58**
  NE7: Newc T 6A **58**
Parkhead Sq. NE21: Bla T 2A **80**
Parkhouse Av. SR5: C'twn 5D **102**
Pk. House Cl. DH6: Sher 5D **156**
Pk. House Gdns. DH6: Sher 5D **156**
  (not continuous)
Pk. House Rd. DH1: Dur 2A **160**
Parkhurst Rd. SR4: Sund 3D **116**
Parkin Gdns. NE10: Gate 4E **85**
Parkinson Cotts. NE40: Ryton 5E **65**
Parkland NE12: Longb 1D **58**
  NE21: Bla T 5G **65**
Parkland Av. NE21: Bla T 3H **79**
Parkland Ct. SR7: S'hm 3H **141**
Parklands NE10: Gate 3A **86**
  NE20: Pon 3B **38**
  NE39: Ham M 2A **106**
Parklands Ct. NE10: Gate 2A **86**
  TS27: Cas E 6B **164**
Parklands Dr. TS27: Cas E 6B **164**
Parklands Gro. DH6: S Het 6B **150**
Parklands Way NE10: Gate 3A **86**
Parkland Ter. SR7: S'hm 3H **141**
Park La. NE8: Gate 6H **69**
  NE21: Bla T 3H **79**
  NE27: Shir 2D **46**
  SR1: Sund 1C **118** (4F **7**)
  SR7: Mur 2B **150**
  SR8: Pet 6G **163**
Park La. Interchange
  SR1: Sund 5F **7**
Park Lane Station (Metro)
  . . . . .1D **118** (5G **7**)
Park Lea SR3: E Her 3C **130**
Parklea NE26: Sea S 3G **25**
Pk. Lea Rd. SR6: Monk 2E **105**
Parkmore Rd. SR4: Sund 4C **116**
Park Pde. NE26: Whit B 6C **36**
  SR6: Monk 3E **105**
Park Pl. DH3: Ches S 4D **126**
  DH5: Hett H 2C **148**
Park Pl. E. SR2: Sund . . .2D **118** (6H **7**)
Park Pl. W. SR2: Sund . . .2D **118** (6H **7**)
Park Ri. NE15: Lem 2A **66**
Park Rd. DH5: Hett H 1C **148**
  DH6: Sher 5D **156**
  DH9: Stly 4B **122**
  NE4: Newc T 5C **68**
  NE8: Gate 6A **70**
  NE10: Gate 6A **70**
  NE15: Thro 1F **65**
  NE22: Bed 4A **10**
  NE24: Bly 6D **12**
  NE25: Sea D 6A **24**
  NE26: Whit B 5C **36**
  NE27: Shir 2D **46**
  NE28: W'snd 5H **59**
  NE31: Heb 4C **72**

Park Rd. NE32: Jar 3E **73**
  NE39: Row G 3D **92**
  SR2: Sund 2D **118** (6G **7**)
  SR8: Pet 5F **163**
Park Rd. Central
  DH3: Ches S 6D **126**
Park Rd. Nth. DH3: Ches S 3C **126**
Park Rd. Sth. DH3: Ches S 2C **134**
Park Row NE10: Gate 3D **84**
  SR5: S'wck 4H **103**
Parkshiel NE34: S Shi 5A **76**
PARKSIDE 6A **142**
Park Side NE61: Hep 1B **8**
Parkside DH1: Dur 5B **154**
  DH9: Tan L 6A **108**
  NE11: Dun 3B **82**
  NE12: Kil 3A **44**
  NE15: Thro 6E **53**
  NE22: Bed 2E **11**
  NE28: W'snd 4B **60**
  NE30: N Shi 4F **49**
  NE31: Heb 5A **72**
  SR3: E Her 3D **130**
Parkside Av. NE7: Newc T 2B **58**
  NE21: Bla T 2A **80**
Parkside Cotts. DH9: Tan L 6A **108**
Parkside Ct. NE13: Wide O 5E **31**
Parkside Cres. NE30: N Shi 5F **49**
  SR7: S'hm 6A **142**
Parkside Rd. SR7: S'hm 5A **142**
Parkside Sth. SR3: E Her 3D **130**
Parkside Ter. NE28: W'snd 3G **59**
Parks Leisure Cen. 3B **62**
Parks, The DH3: Ches S 2E **135**
Parkstone Cl. SR4: Sund 5C **116**
Park St. SR7: S'hm 5B **142**
Park St. Sth. SR5: C'twn 4E **103**
Park Ter. NE2: Newc T 2F **69** (1C **4**)
  NE11: Dun 3B **82**
  NE12: Kil 3B **44**
  NE16: Burn 1G **107**
  NE16: Swa 2E **81**
  NE21: Bla T 2B **80**
  NE22: Bed 2D **10**
  NE26: Whit B 5C **36**
  NE28: W'snd 5H **59**
  NE30: N Shi 6E **49**
  NE37: Usw 4B **100**
  SR5: S'wck 3H **103**
  SR8: Pet 1G **165**
Park Vw. DH2: Ches S 4B **126**
  DH2: Plaw 1A **144**
  DH4: Hou S 3F **129**
  (Beatrice Ter.)
  DH4: Hou S 5H **128**
  (Church Cl.)
  DH5: Hett H 2C **148**
  DH7: B'don 3G **159**
  NE6: Walk 4G **71**
  NE10: Gate 3D **84**
  NE12: Longb 5D **44**
  NE13: Wide O 5E **31**
  NE16: Burn 1H **107**
  NE16: Swa 2D **80**
  NE21: Bla T 3A **80**
  NE23: Cra *3B* **22**
  (off Station Rd.)
  NE24: Bly 6D **12**
  NE25: Sea D 6B **24**
  (not continuous)
  NE26: Whit B 6C **36**
  NE28: W'snd 5H **59**

Park Vw. NE32: Jar 5F **73**
  SR7: S'hm 3F **141**
  SR8: Pet 6G **163**
Pk. View Cl. NE40: Ryton 4D **64**
Pk. View Ct. NE3: Ken 2A **56**
  NE12: Longb 3B **44**
  NE26: Whit B 6C **36**
Pk. View Gdns. NE40: Ryton 4D **64**
Pk. View Sports Complex 2A **56**
Park Vs. DH9: Dip 2C **120**
  NE3: Gos 5D **56**
  NE28: W'snd 5H **59**
Parkville NE6: Newc T 2A **70**
Park Wlk. SR3: New S 4A **132**
Parkway NE38: Wash 2A **114**
Parkwood Av. DH7: Ush M 4C **152**
Parliament St. NE31: Heb 2A **72**
Parmeter St. DH9: Stly 5C **122**
Parmontley St. NE15: Newc T . . .4D **66**
Parnell St. DH4: Hou S 3F **137**
Parry Dr. SR6: Whit 2E **91**
Parson's Av. NE6: Walk 4F **71**
Parson Dr. NE40: Ryton 4C **64**
Parsons Gdns. NE11: Dun 2B **82**
Parsons Ind. Est. NE37: Wash . . .6H **99**
Parsons Rd. NE37: Wash 6H **99**
  SR8: Pet 4D **162**
Parsons St. *NE24: Bly* *5C* **12**
  (off Union St.)
Partick Rd. SR4: Sund 3D **116**
Partick Sq. SR4: Sund 3E **117**
Partnership Ct. SR7: Sea 1E **141**
Partridge Cl. NE38: Wash 3F **113**
Passfield Sq. SR8: Eas 2C **162**
Passfield Way SR8: Pet 3A **164**
Pasteur Rd. DH6: S Het 6H **149**
Paston Rd. NE25: Sea D 1B **34**
Pastures, The NE24: News 3B **18**
PATH HEAD 6G **65**
Path Head Water Mill 5G **65**
Pathside NE32: Jar 1G **87**
Path, The NE9: Gate 1A **98**
Patience Av. NE13: Sea B 3E **31**
Patina Cl. NE15: Lem 1A **66**
Paton Rd. SR3: Sund 5H **117**
Paton Sq. SR3: Sund 5H **117**
Patrick Cain Ho. NE33: S Shi 1D **74**
Patrick Cres. DH6: S Het 5G **149**
Patrick Ter. NE23: Dud 4B **32**
Patterdale Cl. DH1: Carr 3C **156**
  NE36: E Bol 4E **89**
Patterdale Gdns. NE7: Newc T . . .4B **58**
Patterdale Gro. SR5: Monk 1C **104**
Patterdale Rd. NE24: Cow 5G **11**
Patterdale St. DH5: Hett H 3C **148**
Patterdale Ter. NE8: Gate 3H **83**
Patterson Ho. NE24: Bly 1C **18**
Patterson St. NE21: Bla T 5C **66**
Pattinson Gdns. NE9: Gate 4B **84**
  NE10: Gate 1C **84**
Pattinson Ind. Est.
  NE38: Wash 3E **115**
  (Barmston Rd.)
  NE38: Wash 1F **115**
  (Mandarin Way)
Pattinson Nth. Ind. Est.
  NE38: Wash 2F **115**
Pattinson Rd. NE38: Wash 4D **114**
Pattinson Sth. Ind. Est.
  NE38: Wash 4D **114**
Pauline Av. SR6: Monk 2D **104**
Pauline Gdns. NE15: Newc T 2E **67**

Paul Lea DH9: Beam 1A **124**
Pauls Grn. DH5: Hett H 5C **138**
Paul's Rd. SR1: Sund 1E **119**
Paulsway NE32: Jar 3A **74**
Pavilion M. NE2: Newc T 1H **69**
Pavilion Ter. DH5: Hett H 2C **148**
Pavilion, The NE16: Swa 2D **80**
Pavillion Ct. SR1: Sund 5H **7**
Pawston Rd.
   NE21: Bla T, H Spen 6A **78**
   NE39: H Spen 6A **78**
Paxford Cl. NE7: Longb 2A **58**
Paxton Ter. SR4: Sund 6A **104**
Peacehaven Ct. NE37: Usw 3A **100**
Peacock Cl. NE11: Gate 4D **82**
Peacock St. W. SR4: Sund 1H **117**
Pea Flatts La. DH3: Gt Lum 4A **136**
Peak Body Fitness Club 3H **83**
Peak Fitness
   Jesmond 1H **69**
   (off Jesmond Rd.)
   Whitley Bay 6C **36**
   (off Park Vw.)
Peareth Ct. *NE8: Gate* 6H **69**
   (off Hopper St.)
Peareth Edge NE9: Spri 4F **99**
Peareth Gro. SR6: Monk 2F **105**
Peareth Hall Rd. NE9: Spri 4F **99**
   NE37: Usw 3H **99**
Peareth Rd. SR6: Monk 1E **105**
Peareth Ter. DH3: Bir 3C **112**
Pear Lea DH7: B'don 5C **158**
Pearl Rd. SR3: Sund 5H **117**
Pea Rd. DH9: Stly 3B **122**
Pearson Ct. NE21: Bla T 5C **66**
Pearson Pl. NE30: N Shi 1D **62**
   NE32: Jar 1G **73**
Pearson St. DH9: Stly 1D **122**
   NE33: S Shi 3F **63**
Peart Cl. DH6: Sher 6E **157**
Peartree Gdns. NE6: Walk 6G **59**
Peartree M. SR2: Sund 3C **118**
Pear Tree Ter. DH3: Gt Lum . . .2H **135**
Peary Cl. NE5: Newc T 5D **54**
Pease Av. NE15: Newc T 3G **67**
Peasemore Rd. SR4: Sund 2D **118**
Pease Rd. SR8: Pet 5A **162**
Pebble Beach SR6: Monk 4F **91**
Pecket Cl. NE24: Bly 2G **17**
Peddars Way NE34: S Shi 4D **74**
Peebles Cl. NE29: N Shi 5G **47**
Peebles Rd. SR3: Sund 5G **117**
Peel Av. DH1: Dur 5H **155**
Peel Cen., The NE37: Wash . . .6D **100**
Peel Ct. NE13: Sea B 3D **30**
Peel Gdns. NE34: S Shi 5A **74**
Peel Ho. NE1: Newc T 5B **4**
Peel La. NE1: Newc T 5E **69** (6B **4**)
Peel Retail Pk.
   NE37: Wash 6D **100**
Peel St. NE1: Newc T 4E **69** (6B **4**)
   SR2: Sund 2E **119** (6H **7**)
Peggy's Wicket DH9: Beam 1B **124**
Pegwood Ho. *NE4: Newc T* *3D **68***
   (off Barrack Rd.)
Pegwood Rd. SR4: Sund 2E **117**
PELAW 2G **85**
Pelaw Av. DH2: Ches S 4B **126**
   DH9: Stly 1E **123**
Pelaw Bank DH3: Ches S 5C **126**
Pelaw Cres. DH2: Ches S 4B **126**
   (not continuous)

Pelaw Grange Ct.
   DH3: Ches S 1C **126**
Pelaw Grange Stadium 1C **126**
Pelaw Ind. Est. NE10: Gate 2G **85**
Pelaw Leazes La.
   DH1: Dur 5D **154** (2D **6**)
Pelaw Pl. DH2: Ches S 4C **126**
Pelaw Rd. DH2: Ches S 4C **126**
Pelaw Sq. DH2: Ches S 4B **126**
   SR4: Sund 6E **103**
Pelaw Station (Metro) 2G **85**
Pelaw Ter. DH2: Ches S 4B **126**
Pelaw Way NE10: Gate 3G **85**
Peldon Cl. NE7: Longb 2H **57**
Pelham Ct. NE3: Ken 6H **41**
PELTON 2G **125**
Peltondale Av. NE24: Cow 1G **17**
PELTON FELL 5G **125**
Pelton Fell Rd.
   DH2: Ches S, Pelt 5G **125**
Pelton Ho. Farm Est.
   DH2: Pelt 3G **125**
Pelton La. DH2: Pelt 2E **125**
   (Beamish La.)
   DH2: Pelt 2G **125**
   (Fieldside)
   DH2: Pelt 5C **124**
   (Newbridge Banks)
PELTON LANE ENDS 3E **125**
Pelton M. DH2: Pelt 3E **125**
Pelton Rd. SR4: Sund 3E **117**
Pemberton Bank DH5: Eas L . . .4D **148**
Pemberton Cl. SR5: S'wck 4B **104**
Pemberton Gdns. SR3: Sund 4B **118**
Pemberton St. DH5: Hett H 1C **148**
Pemberton Ter. Nth.
   DH9: Stly 6F **123**
Pemberton Ter. Sth.
   DH9: Stly 6F **123**
Pembridge NE38: Wash 2G **113**
Pembroke Av. DH3: Bir 6D **112**
   (not continuous)
   NE6: Walk 1F **71**
   SR3: New S 3B **132**
Pembroke Ct. NE3: Ken 6H **41**
   NE24: Bly 0D **12**
   SR5: C'town 1C **102**
Pembroke Dr. NE20: Pon 6A **26**
Pembroke Gdns. NE28: W'snd . . .3E **61**
Pembroke Pl. SR8: Pet 5B **162**
Pembroke Ter. NE33: S Shi 2E **75**
Pendeford NE38: Wash 3E **115**
Pendle Cl. NE38: Wash 4H **113**
   SR8: Pet 2B **164**
Pendle Grn. SR4: Sund 2A **118**
Pendleton Dr. NE23: Cra 6A **16**
Pendower Way NE15: Newc T . . .3G **67**
Pendragon DH3: Gt Lum 3H **135**
Penfold Cl. NE7: Newc T 3C **58**
Penhale Dr. SR2: Ryh 2F **133**
Penhill Cl. DH2: Ous 6H **111**
Penistone Rd. SR4: Sund 3C **116**
Penman Pl. NE29: N Shi 3C **62**
Penman Sq. SR4: Sund 3D **116**
Pennant Sq. SR4: Sund 1E **117**
Pennine Av. DH2: Ches S 1B **134**
   (not continuous)
Pennine Ct. DH9: Ann P 6F **121**
   SR3: New S 3H **131**
Pennine Dr. SR8: Pet 2A **164**
Pennine Gdns. DH9: Stly 4E **123**
   NE11: Gate 4C **82**

Pennine Gro. NE36: W Bol 4D **88**
Pennine Ho. NE37: Wash 3H **113**
Pennine Way NE12: Longb 1A **58**
Penn Sq. SR4: Sund 1E **117**
Penn St. NE4: Newc T 6D **68**
Pennycross Rd. SR4: Sund 3C **116**
Pennycross Sq. SR4: Sund 2C **116**
Pennyfine Cl. NE29: N Shi 5C **48**
Pennyfine Rd. NE16: Sun 2G **95**
Pennygate Sq. SR4: Sund 2C **116**
Pennygreen Sq. SR4: Sund 2C **116**
Pennymore Sq. SR4: Sund 3C **116**
PENNYWELL 3D **116**
Pennywell Bus. Cen.
   SR4: Sund 2E **117**
Pennywell Ind. Est.
   SR4: Sund 3C **116**
Pennywell Rd. SR4: Sund 3E **117**
Pennywell Shop. Pct.
   SR4: Sund 3D **116**
Penrith Av. NE30: N Shi 3C **48**
Penrith Ct. NE22: Bed 3F **9**
Penrith Gdns. NE9: Gate 1B **98**
Penrith Gro. NE9: Gate 1B **98**
Penrith Rd. NE31: Heb 5D **72**
   SR5: Monk 1C **104**
Penrose Grn. NE3: Ken 2B **56**
Penrose Rd. SR4: Sund 3D **116**
Penryn Av. SR7: Mur 2D **150**
Penryn Way DH7: B'don 5E **159**
Pensford Ct. NE3: Ken 1G **55**
PENSHAW 1F **129**
Penshaw Gdns. DH9: Stly 2F **123**
   (not continuous)
Penshaw Grn. NE5: Newc T 4H **55**
Penshaw La. DH4: Pen 1F **129**
Penshaw Monument 6G **115**
Penshaw Vw. DH3: Bir 4E **113**
   NE10: Gate 3A **86**
   NE31: Heb 5B **72**
   NE32: Jar 5F **73**
Penshaw Way DH3: Bir 3E **113**
Pensher St. NE10: Gate 2C **84**
   SR4: Sund 1B **118**
Pensher St. E. NE10: Gate 2C **84**
Pensher Vw. NE37: Usw 4D **100**
Pentland Cl. NE23: Cra 6B **16**
   NE29: N Shi 4B **48**
   NE38: Wash 4H **113**
   SR8: Pet 2A **164**
Pentland Ct. DH2: Ches S 1C **134**
Pentland Gdns. NE11: Gate 4C **82**
Pentland Gro. NE12: Longb 4B **44**
Pentlands Ter. DH9: Stly 4E **123**
Pentridge Cl. NE23: Cra 2C **22**
Penwood Rd. SR4: Sund 2E **117**
Penyghent Way NE37: Wash 1G **113**
Penzance Bungs. SR7: Mur 1D **150**
Penzance Ct. SR7: Mur 1D **150**
Penzance Pde. NE31: Heb 1E **87**
Penzance Rd. SR4: Sund 3D **116**
Peoples Theatre 6B **58**
Peplow Sq. SR4: Sund 6E **103**
Peppercorn Ct. NE1: Newc T 6F **5**
Percival St. SR4: Sund 6H **103**
Percy Av. DH9: Ann P 4E **121**
   NE26: Whit B 6B **36**
   NE30: N Shi 1E **49**
Percy Bldg. NE1: Newc T 1C **4**
Percy Cotts. NE25: Sea D 6C **24**
   (not continuous)
Percy Ct. NE29: N Shi 4H **61**

Percy Cres. NE29: N Shi 4H **61**
Percy Gdns. NE11: Dun 4C **82**
  NE12: Longb 5D **44**
  NE25: Whit B 1C **48**
  NE30: N Shi 5F **49**
Percy Gdns. Cotts.
  NE30: N Shi 5G **49**
                (off Percy Gdns.)
Percy La. DH1: Dur 6A **154**
PERCY MAIN 4H **61**
Percy Main Station (Metro) 4H **61**
Percy Pk. NE30: N Shi 5F **49**
Percy Pk. Rd. NE30: N Shi 5F **49**
Percy Rd. NE26: Whit B 6D **36**
Percy Scott St. NE34: S Shi 6E **75**
Percy Sq. DH1: Dur 2A **160**
Percy St. DH5: Hett H 1D **148**
  DH9: Stly 4B **122**
  NE1: Newc T 3F **69** (3C **4**)
  NE12: Longb 4G **45**
  NE15: Lem 3A **66**
  NE23: Cra 4C **22**
  NE24: Bly 5D **12**
  NE28: W'snd 5A **60**
  NE30: N Shi 6G **49**
                (East St.)
  NE30: N Shi 6F **49**
                (Percy Pk. Rd.)
  NE32: Jar 2G **73**
  NE33: S Shi 5F **63**
Percy St. Sth. NE24: Bly 6D **12**
Percy Ter. DH1: Dur 6A **154**
  DH4: Pen 1E **129**
  DH9: Ann P 5H **121**
  NE3: Gos 2G **57**
  NE15: Thro 2F **65**
  NE25: Whit B 6A **36**
  SR2: Sund 3E **119**
                (not continuous)
  SR6: Whit 2F **91**
Percy Ter. Sth. SR2: Sund 4E **119**
Percy Way NE15: Thro 6G **53**
Peregrine Ct. NE29: N Shi 1B **62**
Peregrine Pl. NE12: Longb 6A **44**
Perivale Rd. SR4: Sund 3D **116**
PERKINSVILLE 1H **125**
Perrycrofts SR3: New S 5A **132**
                (not continuous)
Perry St. NE9: Gate 3H **83**
Perth Av. NE32: Jar 6A **74**
  NE34: S Shi 6B **74**
Perth Cl. NE28: W'snd 3D **60**
  NE29: N Shi 5G **47**
Perth Ct. NE11: Gate 3G **97**
  SR3: Sund 6G **117**
Perth Gdns. NE28: W'snd 3D **60**
Perth Grn. NE32: Jar 6A **74**
Perth Rd. SR3: Sund 6G **117**
Perth Sq. SR3: Sund 5H **117**
Peterborough Cl. NE8: Gate 1G **83**
Peterborough Rd. DH1: Dur 6E **145**
Peterborough Way NE32: Jar 2F **87**
PETERLEE 1D **164**
Peterlee Cl. SR8: Pet 6C **162**
Peterlee Leisure Cen. 2D **164**
Peterlee Sports & Social Cen.
  . . . . .4B **162**
Peter's Bank DH9: Tan L 2G **121**
Petersfield Rd. SR4: Sund 3D **116**
Petersham Rd. SR4: Sund 1E **117**
Peter Stracey Ho. SR6: Monk . . .1D **104**
Petherton Ct. NE3: Ken 1G **55**

Peth Grn. DH5: Eas L 4D **148**
Peth La. NE40: Ryton, Thro 3D **64**
Petrel Cl. NE33: S Shi 4E **63**
Petrel Way NE24: News 3D **18**
Petteril NE38: Wash 6G **113**
Petwell Cres. SR8: Eas 1C **162**
Petwell La. SR8: Eas 1B **162**
Petworth Cl. NE33: S Shi 4F **63**
Pevensey Cl. NE29: N Shi 4B **48**
Pexton Way NE5: Newc T 1E **67**
Phalp St. DH6: S Het 6B **150**
Pheasantmoor NE37: Wash 6G **99**
PHILADELPHIA 5H **129**
Philadelphia Complex
  DH4: Hou S 4H **129**
Philadelphia La. DH4: Hou S 3F **129**
Philip Ct. NE9: Gate 6B **84**
Philiphaugh
  NE28: Walk, W'snd 1H **71**
Philip Pl. NE4: Newc T 3C **68**
Philipson St. NE6: Walk 3F **71**
Philip Sq. SR3: Sund 5G **117**
Philip St. NE4: Newc T 3C **68**
Phillips Av. NE16: Whi 3E **81**
Phoenix Chase NE29: N Shi 5F **47**
Phoenix Ct. NE29: N Shi 5G **47**
Phoenix Hot Glass Studio and Gallery
  . . . . .5C **154** (2B **6**)
Phoenix Rd. NE38: Wash 1E **113**
  SR4: Sund 1E **117**
Phoenix St. NE24: Bly 3H **17**
Phoenix Theatre, The 6D **12**
Phoenix Way DH4: Hou S 4G **137**
Phoenix Workshops
  SR8: Pet 5G **163**
Physique Health Club 5B **84**
Piccadilly SR3: E Her 1G **131**
Picherwell NE10: Gate 4D **84**
Pickard Cl. SR8: Pet 6E **163**
Pickard St. SR4: Sund 6A **104**
Pickering Cl. NE32: Jar 2E **73**
Pickering Grn. NE9: Gate 3B **98**
PICKERING NOOK 3G **107**
Pickering Rd. SR4: Sund 4C **116**
Pickering Sq. SR4: Sund 3D **116**
Pickersgill Ho. SR5: C'twn 2E **103**
Pickhurst Rd. SR4: Sund 4C **116**
Pickhurst Sq. SR4: Sund 4D **116**
PICKTREE 2E **127**
Picktree Cotts. DH3: Ches S 5D **126**
Picktree Cotts. E.
  DH3: Ches S 5D **126**
Picktree Farm Cotts.
  NE38: Ches S, Wash 2E **127**
Picktree La. DH3: Ches S 5D **126**
  DH3: Ches S, Lam P 3E **127**
  NE38: Ches S, Wash 1E **127**
Picktree Lodge DH3: Ches S 1D **126**
Picktree M. DH3: Ches S 5D **126**
Picktree Ter. DH3: Ches S 5D **126**
Pickwick Cl. DH1: Dur 2B **160**
Pier Amusement Cen. 3G **63**
Pier Pde. NE33: S Shi 3G **63**
Pier Pavilion Theatre 3G **63**
Pier Rd. NE30: N Shi 6G **49**
Pier Vw. NE6: Monk 3F **105**
Pikestone Cl. NE38: Wash 4G **113**
Pikesyde DH9: Dip 2B **120**
Pilgrim Cl. SR5: S'wck 4C **104**
Pilgrims Ct. NE2: Newc T 1G **69**
Pilgrim St. NE1: Newc T . . .4F **69** (4D **4**)
                (New Bri. St. W.)

Pilgrim St. NE1: Newc T . . .5G **69** (6F **5**)
                (Tyne Bri.)
Pilgrims Way DH1: Dur 4F **155**
Pilgrimsway NE9: Gate 4A **84**
  NE32: Jar 3A **74**
Pilton Rd. NE5: Newc T 4D **54**
Pilton Wlk. NE5: Newc T 4D **54**
Pimlico DH1: Dur 1C **160** (5A **6**)
Pimlico Ct. NE9: Gate 1H **97**
Pimlico Rd. DH5: Hett H 4D **148**
  SR4: Sund 3D **116**
Pinders Way DH6: Sher 6H **157**
Pine Av. DH1: Dur 6G **155**
  DH4: Hou S 3H **137**
  NE3: Ken 6B **42**
  NE13: Din 4G **29**
  NE16: Burn 1F **107**
  NE34: S Shi 4A **76**
Pinedale Dr. DH6: S Het 6H **149**
Pinegarth NE20: Pon 3C **38**
Pine Lea DH7: B'don 5C **158**
Pine Pk. DH7: Ush M 6D **152**
Pine Rd. NE21: Bla T 1A **80**
Pines, The NE4: Newc T 6C **68**
  NE40: G'sde 2B **78**
Pine St. DH2: Beam 2D **124**
  DH2: Pelt 4C **124**
  DH3: Bir 2C **112**
  DH3: Ches S 6C **126**
  DH9: Stly 5B **122**
  NE13: Sea B 3E **31**
  NE15: Thro 4D **52**
  NE32: Jar 3E **73**
  NE40: G'sde 2B **78**
  SR4: Sund 6H **103**
Pinesway SR3: Sund 4B **118**
Pine Ter. DH9: Ann P 4E **121**
Pinetree Cen. DH3: Bir 4C **112**
Pinetree Gdns. NE25: Whit B 2A **48**
Pinetree Way NE11: Dun 1F **81**
Pine Vw. DH9: Stly 5B **122**
Pinewood Av. NE13: Wide O 6E **31**
  NE23: Cra 6B **16**
  NE38: Wash 6A **114**
Pinewood Cl. NE3: Ken 6F **41**
  NE6: Walk 6F **59**
  NE38: Wash 4D **114**
Pinewood Gdns. NE11: Gate 6C **82**
Pinewood Rd. SR5: S'wck 3H **103**
Pinewoods NE21: Bla T 5F **79**
Pinewood Sq. SR5: S'wck 3H **103**
Pinewood Vs. DH4: Hou S 2C **136**
Pinewood Vs. NE34: S Shi 3A **76**
Pink La. NE1: Newc T 4E **69** (5B **4**)
                (not continuous)
Pinner Pl. NE6: Walk 5E **71**
Pinner Rd. SR4: Sund 2E **117**
Pintail Ct. NE34: S Shi 5C **74**
Pioneer Ter. NE22: Bed 3C **10**
Pipershaw NE37: Wash 1F **113**
Pipe Track La. NE4: Newc T 5H **67**
Pipewell Ga. NE8: Gate 6F **69**
Pitcairn Rd. SR4: Sund 2D **116**
Pit La. DH1: Dur 1B **154**
  DH7: B'don 4A **158**
  NE23: Seg 2E **33**
Pit Row SR3: New S 1H **131**
PITTINGTON 6E **147**
Pittington La. DH1: Carr 2C **156**
  DH6: Carr, H Pitt 2C **156**

Pittington Rd.
DH5: H Pitt, W Rai 5D **146**
DH6: H Pitt 5D **146**
Pitt St. NE4: Newc T 3D **68** (3A **4**)
PITY ME 6A **144**
Pity Me By-Pass DH1: Dur 2H **153**
PLAINS FARM 5H **117**
Plains Rd. SR3: Sund 5H **117**
Plaistow Sq. SR4: Sund 1E **117**
Plaistow Way NE23: Cra 6B **16**
Planesway NE10: Gate 6E **85**
Planetarium, The 1G **75**
Planet Ho. SR1: Sund 4G **7**
Planet Pl. NE12: Kil 3C **44**
Planetree Av. NE4: Newc T 1H **67**
Plane Tree Ct. SR3: New S 3G **131**
Plantagenet Av. DH3: Ches S . . .1D **134**
Plantation Av. DH6: H Pitt 4H **157**
NE16: Swa 3E **81**
Plantation Gro. NE10: Gate 1H **85**
Plantation Rd. SR4: Sund 6G **103**
Plantation Sq. SR4: Sund 6G **103**
Plantation St. NE28: W'snd 1H **71**
Plantation, The NE9: Gate 6A **84**
Plantation Vw. DH9: Stly 3B **124**
Plantation Wlk. DH6: S Het 6H **149**
PLAWSWORTH 1A **144**
Plawsworth Gdns. NE9: Gate . . .2D **98**
Pleasant Pl. DH3: Bir 2C **112**
Plenmeller Pl. NE16: Sun 2E **95**
Plessey Av. NE24: Bly 1D **18**
Plessey Ct. NE24: News 3H **17**
Plessey Cres. NE25: Whit B 1D **48**
Plessey Gdns. NE29: N Shi 2H **61**
Plessey Old Waggonway
NE24: Bly 4E **17**
Plessey Rd. NE24: Bly, News . . .3H **17**
(not continuous)
Plessey St. NE23: E Har 4B **16**
Plessey Ter. NE7: Newc T 5D **58**
Plessey Woods Country Pk. Vis. Cen.
. . . . .2D **14**
Plough Rd. SR3: New S 4H **131**
Plover Cl. NE24: News 3C **18**
NE38: Wash 4F **113**
Plover Dr. NE16: Burn 2A **108**
Plover Lodge DH3: Bir 1C **112**
Plummer Chare
NE1: Newc T 5G **69** (6F **5**)
Plummers Tower 4G **69** (4E **5**)
Plummer St. NE4: Newc T 6F **69**
Plumtree Av. SR5: C'twn 3E **103**
(not continuous)
Plunkett Rd. DH9: Dip 6E **107**
Plunkett Ter. DH2: Pelt 5F **125**
Plymouth Cl. SR7: Mur 5F **141**
Plymouth Sq. SR3: Sund 5G **117**
POINT PLEASANT 5D **60**
Point Pleasant Ind. Est.
NE28: W'snd 5D **60**
Point Pleasant Ter.
NE28: W'snd 5C **60**
Polden Cl. SR8: Pet 2A **164**
Polden Cres. NE29: N Shi 4D **40**
Polebrook Rd. SR4: Sund 1E **117**
Polemarch St. SR7: S'hm 5B **142**
Police Ho's. SR8: Pet 1C **164**
Pollard St. NE33: S Shi 4F **63**
Polmaise St. NE21: Bla T 1A **80**
Polmuir Rd. SR3: Sund 5G **117**
Polmuir Sq. SR3: Sund 5G **117**
Polpero Cl. DH3: Bir 4D **112**

Polperro Cl. SR2: Ryh 2F **133**
Polton Sq. SR4: Sund 1E **117**
Polwarth Cres. NE3: Gos 5E **43**
Polwarth Dr. NE3: Gos 4D **42**
Polwarth Pl. NE3: Gos 5E **43**
Polwarth Rd. NE3: Gos 4E **43**
Polworth Sq. SR3: Sund 5H **117**
Ponds Cotts. NE40: G'sde 2A **78**
Pond St. DH1: H Shin 5H **161**
Pontdyke NE10: Gate 1F **99**
Pontefract Rd. SR4: Sund 4D **116**
PONTELAND 5E **27**
Ponteland Cl. NE29: N Shi 6G **47**
NE38: Wash 3F **113**
Ponteland Leisure Cen. 5F **27**
Ponteland Rd. NE2: Newc T 1C **68**
NE3: Ken 1F **55**
NE4: Newc T 6B **56**
NE5: Newc T 6A **56**
NE13: Wool 2B **40**
NE15: Thro 3D **52**
Pont Haugh NE20: Pon 4F **27**
Ponthaugh NE39: Row G 2F **93**
PONTOP 3A **120**
Pontop Ct. DH9: Ann P 5F **121**
Pontop Pike La.
DH9: Ann P, Dip 4B **120**
Pontop Sq. SR4: Sund 6E **103**
Pontop St. DH5: W Rai 1G **147**
Pontopsyde DH9: Dip 2C **120**
Pontop Ter. DH9: Ann P 6E **121**
Pontop Vw. DH9: Dip 2B **120**
NE39: Row G 3D **92**
Pont Pk. NE20: Wool 1G **27**
Pont Vw. NE20: Pon 4F **27**
Pool Bri. NE10: Gate 4C **86**
Poole Cl. NE23: Cra 2C **22**
Poole Rd. SR4: Sund 1E **117**
Pooley Cl. NE5: Newc T 6F **55**
Pooley Rd. NE5: Newc T 1F **67**
Poplar Av. DH4: Hou S 3H **137**
NE6: Walk 6F **59**
NE13: Din 4G **29**
NE16: Burn 1F **107**
NE24: Bly 4B **12**
Poplar Cl. NE31: Heb 6C **72**
Poplar Ct. DH9: Ches S 6C **126**
Poplar Cres. DH3: Bir 2B **112**
NE8: Gate 2G **83**
NE11: Dun 4B **82**
Poplar Dr. DH1: Dur 4G **155**
SR6: Whit 2F **91**
Poplar Gro. DH9: Dip 1E **121**
NE22: Bed 4B **10**
NE34: S Shi 4H **75**
SR2: Ryh 1E **133**
Poplar Lea DH7: B'don 5C **158**
Poplar Pl. NE3: Gos 2E **57**
Poplar Rd. DH1: Carr 3B **156**
NE21: Bla T 2A **80**
Poplars, The DH3: Ches S 1D **134**
DH4: Pen 1F **129**
DH5: Eas L 4E **149**
NE3: Gos 1E **57**
NE4: Newc T 6C **68**
NE38: Wash 3B **114**
SR4: Sund 1C **116**
SR5: S'wck 3H **103**
Poplar St. DH2: Beam 2D **124**
DH3: Ches S 6C **126**
DH9: Stly 5B **122**
NE15: Thro 5D **52**

Poplar Ter. DH3: Ches S 5D **126**
Popplewell Gdns. NE9: Gate . . .1A **98**
Popplewell Ter. NE29: N Shi 5C **48**
Poppyfields DH2: Ches S 1A **134**
Porchester Dr. NE23: Cra 1C **22**
Porchester St. NE33: S Shi 2D **74**
Porlock Ct. NE23: Cra 6A **16**
Porlock Ho. NE32: Jar 4H **73**
Porlock Rd. NE32: Jar 4H **73**
Portadown Rd. SR4: Sund 4D **116**
Portberry St. NE33: S Shi 1D **74**
Portberry St. Ind. Est.
NE33: S Shi 6D **62**
Portberry Way NE33: S Shi 6D **62**
(not continuous)
Portchester Gro. NE35: Bol C . . .3A **88**
Portchester Rd. SR4: Sund 2E **117**
Portchester Sq. SR4: Sund 3E **117**
Porter Ter. SR7: Mur 2C **150**
Portland Av. SR7: S'hm 4G **141**
Portland Cl. DH2: Ches S 2A **134**
NE28: W'snd 2E **61**
Portland Gdns. NE9: Gate 3H **97**
NE23: Cra 2C **22**
NE30: N Shi 6C **48**
Portland M.
NE2: Newc T 2H **69** (1G **5**)
Portland Rd.
NE2: Newc T 2H **69** (1G **5**)
(not continuous)
NE15: Thro 5E **53**
SR3: Sund 5H **117**
Portland Sq. SR3: Sund 4H **117**
Portland St. NE4: Newc T 5B **68**
NE10: Gate 2G **85**
NE24: Bly 4B **12**
Portland Ter.
NE2: Newc T 2H **69** (1G **5**)
Portman M. NE2: Newc T 2H **5**
Portman Pl. NE6: Walk 6E **71**
Portman Sq. SR4: Sund 2E **117**
Portmarnock NE37: Usw 3H **99**
PORTMEADS 4D **112**
Portmeads Ri. DH3: Bir 3D **112**
Portmeads Rd. DH3: Bir 2D **112**
PORTOBELLO 4E **113**
Portobello Ind. Est. DH3: Bir 3E **113**
Portobello La. SR6: Monk 4D **104**
(not continuous)
Portobello Rd. DH3: Bir 2E **113**
Portobello Ter. DH3: Bir 4E **113**
Portobello Way DH3: Bir 3D **112**
Portree Cl. DH3: Bir 6D **112**
Portree Sq. SR3: Sund 5G **117**
Portrush Cl. NE37: Usw 3A **100**
Portrush Rd. SR4: Sund 1E **117**
Portrush Way NE7: Newc T 2C **58**
Portslade Rd. SR4: Sund 3D **116**
Portsmouth Rd. NE29: N Shi 2G **61**
SR4: Sund 2D **116**
Portsmouth Sq. SR4: Sund 2D **116**
Portugal Pl. NE28: W'snd 6H **59**
Post Office La. NE20: N Shi 5C **48**
(off Orchard Ct.)
Post Office Sq. NE24: Bly 5D **12**
(off Post Office St.)
Post Office St. NE24: Bly 5D **12**
Potterhouse La. DH1: Dur 5A **144**
Potterhouse Ter. DH1: Dur 5A **144**
Potteries, The NE33: S Shi 6G **63**
Potter Pl. DH9: Stly 4F **123**

Potters Bank DH1: Dur . . .2A **160** (6A **6**)
Potters CI. DH1: Dur 2B **160**
Potter Sq. SR3: Sund 5H **117**
Potter St. NE28: W'snd 6E **61**
  NE32: Jar 2E **73**
Pottersway NE9: Gate 4A **84**
Pottery Bank NE6: Walk 6F **71**
  SR1: Sund 5F **105**
Pottery La. NE1: Newc T 6E **69**
  SR4: Sund 1C **116**
Pottery Rd. SR5: S'wck 4A **104**
Pottery Yd. DH4: Hou S 3A **138**
Potts St. NE6: Newc T 3C **70**
Poulton CI. NE38: Wash 1H **127**
Poultry Farm DH4: Hou S 3G **129**
Powburn CI. DH2: Ches S 2A **134**
Powburn Gdns. NE4: Newc T 1A **68**
Powerleague 2D **82**
Powis Rd. SR3: Sund 5H **117**
Powis Sq. SR3: Sund 5H **117**
Powys PI. NE4: Newc T 3C **68**
Poynings CI. NE3: Ken 2G **55**
Praetorian Dr. NE28: W'snd 6H **59**
Prebend Row DH2: Pelt 3F **125**
Prebends Fld. DH1: Dur 3F **155**
Prebends' Wlk.
  DH1: Dur 1C **160** (5A **6**)
Precinct, The NE21: Bla T 6B **66**
  SR2: Sund 1B **118**
      (Chester Rd.)
  SR2: Sund 5C **118**
      (Leechmere Rd.)
Prefect PI. NE9: Gate 4A **84**
Premier Health & Fitness 1A **118**
      (off Hylton Rd.)
Premier Rd. SR3: Sund 5G **117**
Prendwick Av. NE31: Heb 6B **72**
Prendwick CI. DH2: Ches S 3A **134**
Prendwick Ct. NE31: Heb 6B **72**
Prengarth Av. SR6: Monk 2D **104**
Prensgarth Way NE34: S Shi 6B **74**
Prescot Rd. SR4: Sund 1E **117**
Press La. SR1: Sund 6D **104** (3H **7**)
Prestbury Av. NE23: Cra 6A **16**
Prestbury Rd. SR4: Sund 3C **116**
Prestdale Av. NE24: Cow 6G **11**
Presthope Rd. SR4: Sund 3C **116**
Prestmede NE10: Gate 4E **85**
PRESTON 6C **48**
Preston Av. NE30: N Shi 6C **48**
Preston Ct. *NE29: N Shi* *5C **48***
      (off Rosebery Av.)
Preston Ga. NE29: N Shi 4B **48**
PRESTON GRANGE 4B **48**
Prestonhill SR3: New S 4G **131**
Preston Nth. Rd. NE29: N Shi . . .3B **48**
Preston Pk. NE29: N Shi 6C **48**
Preston Rd. NE29: N Shi 5C **48**
  SR2: Sund 3F **119**
Preston Ter. NE27: Shir 4C **46**
  NE29: N Shi 5B **48**
Preston Towers NE29: N Shi 6C **48**
Preston Wood NE30: N Shi 4C **48**
PRESTWICK 6A **28**
Prestwick NE10: Gate 6E **85**
Prestwick Av. NE29: N Shi 6G **47**
Prestwick Carr Rd. NE13: Din . . .4E **29**
Prestwick CI. NE37: Usw 3A **100**
Prestwick Dr. NE10: Gate 4A **86**
Prestwick Gdns. NE3: Ken 3B **56**
Prestwick Ho. *NE4: Newc T* *3D **68***
      (off Barrack Rd.)

Prestwick Ind. Est. NE20: Wool . . .2A **40**
Prestwick Pit Ho's. NE20: Wool . . .1A **40**
Prestwick Rd. NE13: Din 4E **29**
  SR4: Sund 1E **117**
PRESTWICK ROAD END 1A **40**
Prestwick Ter. NE20: Wool 2A **40**
Pretoria Sq. SR3: Sund 5G **117**
Pretoria St. NE15: Newc T 4E **67**
Price St. NE31: Heb 2A **72**
Priestfield Gdns. NE16: Burn 1F **107**
Priestley Ct. NE34: S Shi 6C **74**
Priestley Gdns. NE10: Gate 3H **85**
Priestly Cres. SR4: Sund 5B **104**
Priestman Ct. SR4: Sund 1F **117**
Priestsfield CI. SR3: New S 4H **131**
Primary Gdns. SR2: Sund 2F **119**
Primate Rd. SR3: Sund 6G **117**
PRIMROSE 5G **73**
Primrose Av. NE34: S Shi 4D **74**
  SR8: Pet 6F **163**
Primrose CI. NE23: Dud 3A **32**
Primrose Cres. DH4: Hou S 6C **128**
  SR6: Monk 2D **104**
Primrose Gdns. DH2: Ous 5H **111**
  NE28: W'snd 3G **59**
Primrose Hill DH4: Hou S 1C **136**
  NE9: Gate 6A **84**
  NE32: Jar 6G **73**
Primrose Hill Ter. NE32: Jar 6G **73**
Primrose PI. NE9: Gate 6H **83**
Primrose Pct. SR6: Monk 2D **104**
Primrose St. SR4: Sund 1C **116**
Primrose Ter. DH3: Bir 3D **112**
  NE32: Jar 5F **73**
Prince Albert Ter.
  NE2: Newc T 3H **69** (3G **5**)
Prince Consort Ind. Est.
  NE31: Heb 3B **72**
Prince Consort La. NE31: Heb . . .3B **72**
      (not continuous)
Prince Consort Rd. NE8: Gate . . .1G **83**
  NE31: Heb 3A **72**
  NE32: Jar 3G **73**
Prince Consort Way
  NE29: N Shi 4C **62**
Prince Edward Ct. NE34: S Shi . . .4A **76**
Prince Edward Gro.
  NE34: S Shi 3C **76**
Prince Edward Rd. NE34: S Shi . . .4H **75**
Prince George Av. SR6: Monk . . .1D **104**
Prince George Sq. NE33: S Shi . . .4F **63**
Prince of Wales CI.
  NE34: S Shi 4G **75**
Prince Philip CI. NE15: Newc T . . .4G **67**
Prince Rd. NE28: W'snd 4H **59**
Princes Av. NE3: Gos 6D **42**
  SR6: Monk 6E **91**
Princes CI. NE3: Gos 5D **42**
Princes Gdns. NE24: Cow 5A **12**
  NE25: Whit B 6A **36**
  SR6: Monk 6E **91**
Princes Mdw. NE3: Gos 2C **56**
Princes Pk. NE11: Gate 6D **82**
      (not continuous)
Princes Rd. NE3: Gos 4D **42**
Princess Ct. NE29: N Shi 4B **62**
Princess Dr. NE8: Dun 2C **82**
Princess Gdns. DH5: Hett H 6C **138**
Princess Louise Rd.
  NE24: Bly 6B **12**
Princess Mary Ct. NE2: Newc T . .1F **69**
Princess Rd. SR7: S'hm 4A **142**

Princess Sq.
  NE1: Newc T 3G **69** (3E **5**)
Princess St. NE10: Gate 2G **85**
  NE16: Sun 3F **95**
  SR2: Sund 2C **118** (6F **7**)
Princes St. DH1: Dur 5B **154**
  DH4: Hou S 4E **129**
  DH9: Ann P 4E **121**
  NE30: N Shi 6D **48**
Prince St. SR1: Sund 6D **104** (3G **7**)
Princesway NE11: Gate 1E **97**
Princesway Central NE11: Gate . . .1E **97**
Princesway Nth. NE11: Gate 5E **83**
Princesway Sth. NE11: Gate 1E **97**
      (not continuous)
Princetown Ter. SR3: Sund 5G **117**
Princeway NE30: N Shi 5F **49**
Pringle CI. DH7: New B 2A **158**
Pringle Gro. DH7: New B 2B **158**
Pringle PI. DH7: New B 2B **158**
Prinn PI. NE16: Sun 3F **95**
Priors CI. DH1: Dur 5A **154**
Priors Grange DH6: H Pitt 2F **157**
Prior's Ho. NE30: N Shi 6G **49**
Priors Path DH1: Dur 6B **154**
Prior's Ter. NE30: N Shi 6F **49**
Priors Way NE28: W'snd 5C **60**
Priory Av. NE25: Whit B 1B **48**
Priory Cotts. NE26: Whit B 5C **36**
Priory Ct. *NE8: Gate* *6H **69***
      (off Hopper St.)
  NE10: Gate 3H **85**
  NE30: N Shi 5G **49**
  NE33: S Shi 2F **63**
Priory Grange NE24: Cow 6A **12**
Priory Grn. NE6: Newc T 3B **70**
Priory Gro. SR4: Sund 2H **117**
Priory M. NE30: N Shi 6F **49**
Priory Orchard DH1: Dur 6B **154**
Priory PI. NE6: Newc T 4C **70**
  NE13: Wide O 6C **30**
Priory Rd. DH1: Dur 2B **154**
  NE32: Jar 1G **73**
Priory Way NE5: Newc T 3D **54**
Proctor Ct. NE6: Walk 4G **71**
Proctor Sq. SR3: Sund 5H **117**
Proctor St. NE6: Walk 4G **71**
Promenade NE26: Whit B 5C **36**
  NE33: S Shi 3G **63**
      (Harbour Dr.)
  NE33: S Shi 5H **63**
      (Sth. Foreshore)
  SR6: Monk 1F **105**
Promenade Ter. NE30: N Shi 6G **49**
Promontory Ter. NE26: Whit B . . .1E **48**
Promotion CI. SR6: Monk 3E **105**
Prospect Av. NE25: Sea D 6A **24**
  NE28: W'snd 4H **59**
Prospect Av. Nth. NE28: W'snd . .3H **59**
Prospect Cotts. NE9: Spri 4F **99**
Prospect Ct. NE4: Newc T 4C **68**
Prospect Cres. DH5: Eas L 5E **149**
Prospect Gdns. NE36: W Bol 4C **88**
Prospect PI. DH7: New B 1A **158**
  NE4: Newc T 4C **68**
Prospect Row SR1: Sund 6F **105**
Prospect St. DH3: Ches S 5C **126**
Prospect Ter. DH1: Dur 1A **160**
  DH1: H Shin 3G **161**
  DH3: Ches S 5C **126**
  DH7: New B 1B **158**
  DH9: Ann P 5H **121**

Prospect Ter. NE9: Spri 3F **99**
(Springwell Rd.)
NE9: Spri 4D **98**
(Thomas St.)
NE11: Kib 1E **111**
NE16: Burn 3G **107**
NE30: N Shi 1E **63**
NE36: E Bol 4E **89**
Prospect Vw. DH4: W Rai 3D **146**
Providence Cl. DH1: Dur 1C **6**
Providence Pl. DH1: Dur 1C **6**
DH1: Dur 4H **155**
NE10: Gate 2D **84**
Providence Row
DH1: Dur 5D **154** (2C **6**)
Provident St. DH2: Pelt 3E **125**
Provident Ter. DH9: Stly 6H **123**
NE28: W'snd 5G **59**
Provost Gdns. NE15: Newc T 5H **67**
Prudhoe Chare
NE1: Newc T 3F **69** (3D **4**)
Prudhoe Ct. NE3: Ken 6A **42**
Prudhoe Gro. NE32: Jar 6E **73**
Prudhoe Pl.
NE1: Newc T 3F **69** (3C **4**)
Prudhoe St.
NE1: Newc T 3F **69** (3C **4**)
NE29: N Shi 2C **62**
SR4: Sund 6H **103**
Prudhoe Ter. NE29: N Shi 2C **62**
NE30: N Shi 5F **49**
Pudding Chare
NE1: Newc T 4F **69** (5D **4**)
Pudsey Ct. DH1: Dur 1C **154**
Puffin Cl. NE24: News 4D **18**
Pullman Ct. NE9: Gate 6G **83**
Puma Sunderland Tennis Cen.
. . . . .6A **118**
Pump La. NE6: Newc T 4B **70**
Purbeck Cl. NE29: N Shi 3B **48**
Purbeck Gdns. NE23: Cra 2C **22**
Purbeck Rd. NE12: Longb 1B **58**
Purley NE38: Wash 3E **115**
Purley Cl. NE28: W'snd 3D **60**
Purley Gdns. NE3: Ken 3B **56**
Purley Rd. SR3: Sund 5G **117**
Purley Sq. SR3: Sund 5G **117**
Putney Sq. SR4: Sund 3D **116**
Pykerley M. NE25: Whit B 1A **48**
Pykerley Rd. NE25: Whit B 6A **36**

Q

Quadrant, The NE29: N Shi 2A **62**
SR1: Sund 6F **105**
QUAKING HOUSES 6C **122**
Quality Row NE6: Newc T 4A **70**
Quality Row Rd. NE16: Swa 2E **81**
Quality St. DH1: H Shin 4H **161**
Quantock Av. DH2: Ches S 1A **134**
(not continuous)
Quantock Cl. NE29: N Shi 3A **48**
Quantock Pl. SR8: Pet 1A **164**
Quarry Bank Ct. NE4: Newc T 4D **68**
Quarry Cotts. NE13: Din 4F **29**
NE23: Dud 5C **32**
Quarry Cres. DH7: Ush M 4C **152**
Quarryfield Rd. NE8: Gate 5H **69**
Quarryheads La.
DH1: Dur 1B **160** (5A **6**)
Quarry Ho. Gdns. DH5: W Rai . . .1G **147**

Quarry Ho. La. DH1: Dur 6H **153**
DH5: W Rai 1H **147**
Quarry La. NE34: S Shi 4A **76**
(not continuous)
Quarry Rd. DH9: Stly 2D **122**
NE15: Lem 3A **66**
NE31: Heb 4C **72**
SR3: New S 2B **132**
Quarry Row NE10: Gate 2D **84**
Quarry St. SR3: New S 2A **132**
Quay Rd. NE24: Bly 5D **12**
Quaysgate NE8: Gate 5H **69**
QUAYSIDE 5G **69** (6F **5**)
Quayside NE1: Newc T 4A **70**
(High Quay)
NE1: Newc T 5G **69** (6F **5**)
(Tyne Bri.)
NE6: Newc T 5B **70**
NE24: Bly 5D **12**
Quayside Bus. Development Cen.
NE6: Newc T 4B **70**
Quayside Ct. NE24: Bly 5D **12**
NE30: N Shi 2D **62**
Quayside Ho. *NE1: Newc T* 5G **5**
(off Quayside)
Quay, The DH5: Hett H 2C **148**
Quay Vw. NE28: W'snd 5E **61**
Queen Alexandra Bri.
SR4: Sund 5A **104**
SR5: Sund 5A **104**
Queen Alexandra Rd.
NE29: N Shi 6B **48**
SR2: Sund 4C **118**
SR3: Sund 3A **118**
SR7: S'hm 5B **142**
Queen Alexandra Rd. W.
NE29: N Shi 6A **48**
Queen Anne Ct. NE6: Newc T 2C **70**
Queen Anne St. *NE6: Walk* 2C **70**
(off Shields Rd.)
Queen Elizabeth Av. NE9: Gate . . .6B **84**
Queen Elizabeth Ct.
NE34: S Shi 6B **74**
Queen Elizabeth Dr.
DH5: Eas L 5F **149**
Queen's Av. SR6: Monk 6E **91**
SR7: Mur 5F **141**
Queensberry St. SR4: Sund 6B **104**
Queensbridge NE12: Longb 6H **43**
Queensbury Dr. NE15: Cha P 4G **53**
Queensbury Ga. NE12: Longb 1A **58**
Queensbury Rd. SR7: S'hm 4G **141**
Queens Ct. NE3: Gos 3E **43**
NE4: Newc T 3D **68** (3A **4**)
NE8: Gate 2E **83**
NE15: Thro 6G **53**
Queen's Cres. NE28: W'snd 4G **59**
NE31: Heb 5B **72**
SR4: Sund 2A **118**
Queens Dr. NE16: Sun 3F **95**
NE16: Whi 6G **81**
NE26: Whit B 6C **36**
Queens Gdns. NE12: Longb 1D **58**
NE23: Dud 2B **32**
NE24: Cow 5A **12**
Queens Gro. DH1: Dur 2A **160**
Queens Hall Bldgs.
NE25: Sea D 6B **24**
(off Hayward Av.)
Queensland Av. NE34: S Shi 5B **74**
Queens La.
NE1: Newc T 5G **69** (6D **4**)

Queensmere DH3: Ches S 2C **126**
Queens Pde. DH9: Ann P 5F **121**
SR6: Monk 6F **91**
Queens Pk. DH3: Ches S 1D **134**
NE11: Gate 5E **83**
Queens Rd. NE2: Newc T 6G **57**
(not continuous)
NE5: Newc T 4E **55**
NE15: Thro 6G **53**
NE22: Bed 3D **10**
NE23: Dud 2B **32**
NE26: Sea S 3H **25**
NE26: Whit B 5B **36**
SR5: S'wck 4A **104**
Queens Sq.
NE1: Newc T 3F **69** (3D **4**)
Queens Ter. NE2: Newc T 6H **57**
NE28: W'snd 4H **59**
Queen St. DH2: Pelt 4C **124**
DH3: Bir 3B **112**
DH5: Hett H 6C **138**
NE1: Newc T 5G **69** (6F **5**)
NE8: Gate 3E **83**
NE30: N Shi 1D **62**
NE33: S Shi 4E **63**
SR1: Sund 6C **104** (2F **7**)
(Gill Rd.)
SR1: Sund 6D **104** (3G **7**)
(St Mary's Way)
SR2: Ryh 1F **133**
SR7: S'hm 4A **142**
Queen St. E. SR1: Sund 6E **105**
Queensway DH5: Hou S 4B **138**
NE3: Gos 4D **42**
NE4: Newc T 1H **67**
NE20: Pon 2D **38**
NE30: N Shi 5F **49**
NE38: Wash 3C **114**
Queensway Ct. NE11: Gate 5E **83**
Queensway Nth. NE11: Gate 4E **83**
Queensway Sth. NE11: Gate 1F **97**
Queen Victoria Rd.
NE1: Newc T 3F **69** (2C **4**)
Queen Victoria St.
NE10: Gate 2F **85**
Quentin Av. NE3: Ken 2H **55**
Que Sera DH5: Hett H 2C **148**
Quigley Ter. DH3: Bir 1B **112**
Quinn Cl. SR8: Pet 2D **164**
Quinn's Ter. DH1: Dur 1A **160**
Quin Sq. DH6: S Het 6A **150**

R

Rabbit Banks Rd. NE8: Gate 6F **69**
Raby Cl. DH4: Hou S 2E **137**
NE22: Bed 4F **9**
Raby Cres. NE6: Newc T 3C **70**
Raby Cross NE6: Newc T 4C **70**
Raby Dr. SR3: E Her 2E **131**
Raby Gdns. NE16: Burn 1E **107**
NE32: Jar 5F **73**
Raby Ga. NE6: Newc T 3C **70**
Raby Rd. DH1: Dur 6C **144**
NE38: Wash 2F **113**
Raby St. NE6: Newc T 3B **70**
(not continuous)
NE8: Gate 3H **83**
SR4: Sund 1B **118**
Raby Wlk. NE6: Newc T 3C **70**
Raby Way NE6: Newc T 3C **70**

Rachel Cl. SR2: Ryh 2C **132**
Rackley Way SR6: Whit 3F **91**
(not continuous)
Radcliffe Pl. NE5: Newc T 5H **55**
Radcliffe Rd. SR5: C'twn 3G **103**
Radcliffe St. DH3: Bir 4C **112**
Radlett Rd. SR5: C'twn 3F **103**
Radnor Gdns. NE28: W'snd 4E **61**
Radnor St. NE1: Newc T . . .3G **69** (2F **5**)
Radstock Pl. NE12: Longb 6C **44**
Rae Av. NE28: W'snd 3H **59**
Raeburn Av. NE38: Wash 3C **114**
Raeburn Gdns. NE9: Gate 4B **84**
Raeburn Rd. NE34: S Shi 1F **89**
SR5: C'twn 2E **103**
Raey Ct. DH2: Ches S 1C **134**
Raglan NE38: Wash 2G **113**
Raglan Av. SR2: Sund 4E **119**
Raglan Pl. NE16: Burn 6H **93**
Raglan Row DH4: Hou S 4G **129**
Raglan St. NE32: Jar 2G **73**
Raich Carter Sports Cen. 3F **119**
Railton Gdns. NE9: Gate 5B **84**
Railway Cl. DH6: Sher 6C **156**
Railway Cotts. DH1: Dur 6H **153**
DH2: Ches S 4A **126**
DH3: Bir 3B **112**
DH4: Hou S 3D **136**
DH4: Pen 1E **129**
NE24: Cow 5E **11**
NE24: News 5A **18**
SR4: Sund 1C **116**
Railway Gdns. DH9: Ann P 5F **121**
Railway Row SR1: Sund 1B **118**
Railway St. DH4: Hou S 1H **137**
DH5: Hett H 1C **148**
DH9: Ann P 6G **121**
NE4: Newc T 6D **68** (6B **4**)
NE11: Dun 2C **82**
(Ravensworth Vw.)
NE11: Dun 1B **82**
(St Omers Rd.)
NE29: N Shi 2C **62**
NE31: Heb 2D **72**
NE32: Jar 2E **73**
SR1: Sund 1F **119**
SR4: Sund 6H **103**
Railway Ter. DH4: E Her 3H **129**
DH4: Pen 1E **129**
DH5: Hett H 6C **138**
NE4: Newc T 6D **68**
NE24: Bly 6B **12**
NE28: W'snd 6B **60**
NE29: N Shi 2C **62**
NE38: Wash 3D **114**
SR4: Sund 1C **116**
Railway Ter. Nth.
DH4: E Her 2H **129**
Raine Gro. SR1: Sund 1E **119**
Rainford Av. SR2: Sund 4E **119**
Rainhill Cl. NE37: Usw 4D **100**
Rainhill Rd. NE37: Usw 4C **100**
Rainton Bank DH5: Hou S 5B **138**
Rainton Bri. Nth. Ind. Est.
DH4: Hou S 4G **137**
Rainton Bri. Sth. Ind. Est.
DH4: W Rai 5F **137**
Rainton Cl. NE10: Gate 5A **86**
RAINTON GATE 4D **146**
Rainton Gro. DH5: Hou S 5A **138**
Rainton Meadows Nature Reserve
. . . . .5F **137**

Rainton St. DH4: Pen 1F **129**
SR4: Sund 1A **118**
SR7: S'hm 5B **142**
Rainton Vw. DH4: W Rai 3D **146**
Rake La. NE29: N Shi 4G **47**
Raleigh Cl. NE33: S Shi 1D **74**
Raleigh Rd. SR5: C'twn 3F **103**
Raleigh Sq. SR5: C'twn 3F **103**
Ralph Av. SR2: Ryh 1E **133**
Ralph St. NE31: Heb 2D **72**
Ramilies SR2: Ryh 3D **132**
Ramillies Rd. SR5: C'twn 2E **103**
Ramillies Sq. SR5: C'twn 2E **103**
Ramparts, The NE15: Lem 1C **66**
Ramsay Sq. SR5: C'twn 2G **103**
Ramsay St. NE21: Bla T 2H **79**
NE39: H Spen 6A **78**
Ramsey Cl. DH1: Dur 5G **155**
SR8: Pet 5D **162**
Ramsey St. DH3: Ches S 1C **134**
Ramsgate Rd. SR5: C'twn 2G **103**
Ramshaw Cl. NE7: Newc T 4E **59**
Ramside Vw. DH1: Carr 2B **156**
Randolph St. NE32: Jar 2G **73**
Range Vs. SR6: Whit 2F **91**
Rangoon Rd. SR5: C'twn 2E **103**
Ranksborough St. SR7: S'hm . . .3H **141**
(not continuous)
Ranmere Rd. NE15: Newc T 4F **67**
Ranmore Cl. NE23: Cra 2B **22**
Rannoch Av. DH2: Ches S 2B **134**
Rannoch Cl. NE10: Gate 3A **86**
Rannoch Rd. SR5: C'twn 2E **103**
Ranson Cres. NE34: S Shi 4B **74**
Ranson St. SR2: Sund 3B **118**
SR4: Sund 3B **118**
Raphael Av. NE34: S Shi 6E **75**
Rapperton Ct. NE5: Newc T 4D **54**
Rathmore Gdns. NE30: N Shi 6C **48**
Ratho Ct. NE10: Gate 5E **85**
Ravel Ct. NE32: Jar 3G **73**
Ravenburn Gdns.
NE15: Newc T 3D **66**
Ravenna Rd. SR5: C'twn 2D **102**
Ravensbourne Av. NE36: E Bol . .3F **89**
Ravensburn Wlk. NE15: Thro 5C **52**
Ravenscar Cl. NE16: Whi 6C **80**
Ravenscourt Pl. *NE8: Gate* *2F **83***
(off Airey Ter.)
Ravenscourt Rd. SR5: C'twn 2E **103**
Ravensdale Cres. NE9: Gate 5A **84**
Ravensdale Gro. NE24: Cow 6G **11**
Ravenshill Rd. NE5: Newc T 6B **54**
Ravenside Rd. NE4: Newc T 1A **68**
Ravenstone NE37: Wash 6H **99**
Ravenswood Cl. NE12: Longb 5E **45**
Ravenswood Gdns. NE9: Gate . . .2H **97**
Ravenswood Rd. NE6: Newc T . . .6C **58**
SR5: C'twn 2D **102**
Ravenswood Sq. SR5: C'twn 2D **102**
Ravensworth SR2: Ryh 3C **132**
Ravensworth Av.
DH4: Hou S 2E **137**
NE9: Spri 3C **98**
Ravensworth Castle 2C **96**
Ravensworth Cl. NE28: W'snd . . .5D **60**
Ravensworth Ct. DH6: S Het 5H **149**
NE3: Ken 6H **41**
NE11: Dun 2C **82**
NE22: Bed 2D **10**
Ravensworth Cres.
NE16: Burn 5B **94**

Ravensworth Gdns. DH3: Bir 2B **112**
Ravensworth Pk. Est.
NE11: Gate 1B **96**
Ravensworth Rd. DH3: Bir 2B **112**
NE11: Dun 3C **82**
Ravensworth St. NE22: Bed 2D **10**
NE28: W'snd 5D **60**
SR4: Sund 6B **104**
Ravensworth Ter.
DH1: Dur 5D **154** (2D **6**)
NE4: Newc T 4D **68** (5A **4**)
NE11: Dun 3C **82**
NE16: Sun 3F **95**
NE22: Bed 2D **10**
NE32: Jar 6F **73**
NE33: S Shi 1E **75**
Ravensworth Vw. NE11: Dun 1C **82**
Ravensworth Vs. NE9: Gate 2C **98**
Raven Ter. DH3: Bir 2C **112**
Ravine Ter. SR6: Monk 2F **105**
(not continuous)
Rawdon Rd. SR5: C'twn 2G **103**
Rawling Rd. NE8: Gate 3F **83**
Rawlston Way NE5: Newc T 4G **55**
Rawmarsh Rd. SR5: C'twn 2E **103**
Raydale SR5: C'twn 2G **103**
Raydale Av. NE37: Usw 5H **99**
Raylees Gdns. NE11: Dun 4C **82**
Rayleigh Dr. NE13: Wide O 4D **30**
Rayleigh Gro. NE8: Gate 4F **83**
Raynham Cl. NE23: Cra 6H **21**
Raynham Ct. NE33: S Shi 6E **63**
Readhead Dr. NE33: S Shi 6G **63**
Readhead Dr. NE6: Walk 5F **71**
Readhead Rd. NE34: S Shi 1G **75**
Reading Rd. NE33: S Shi 2F **75**
SR5: C'twn 2F **103**
Reading Sq. SR5: C'twn 2E **103**
Reasby Gdns. NE40: Ryton 4B **64**
Reasby Vs. NE40: Ryton 4B **64**
Reavley Av. NE22: Bed 2E **11**
Reay Cres. NE35: Bol C 3D **88**
Reay Gdns. NE5: Newc T 4E **55**
Reay Pl. NE3: Gos 2C **56**
NE34: S Shi 4D **74**
Reay St. NE10: Gate 1H **85**
Rectory Av. NE3: Gos 3F **57**
Rectory Bank NE36: W Bol 4C **88**
Rectory Cotts. NE40: Ryton 3C **64**
Rectory Ct. NE16: Whi 4F **81**
Rectory Dr. NE3: Gos 3G **57**
Rectory Grn. NE36: W Bol 4B **88**
Rectory Gro. NE3: Gos 2F **57**
Rectory La. NE16: Whi 5F **81**
NE21: Bla T 2H **79**
Rectory Pl. NE8: Gate 2F **83**
Rectory Rd. DH5: Hett H 2C **148**
NE3: Gos 4F **57**
NE8: Gate 2F **83**
NE10: Gate 4C **84**
Rectory Rd. E. NE10: Gate 4D **84**
(not continuous)
Rectory Ter. NE3: Gos 3G **57**
NE36: W Bol 5B **88**
Red Admiral Ct. NE11: Gate 4D **82**
Red Banks DH2: Ches S 1A **134**
Red Barns
NE1: Newc T 4H **69** (4H **5**)
Redberry Way NE34: S Shi 5D **74**
Red Briar Wlk. DH1: Dur 6A **144**
Red Bungs. NE9: Spri 4E **99**
Redburn Cl. DH4: Hou S 3G **137**

Redburn Rd. DH4: Hou S 4F **137**
 DH4: W Rai 4F **137**
 NE5: Newc T 3D **54**
Redburn Row DH4: Hou S 4F **137**
Redby Cl. SR6: Monk 3D **104**
Redcar Rd. NE6: Newc T 6D **58**
 NE28: W'snd 4E **61**
 SR5: C'twn, S'wck 3F **103**
Redcar Sq. SR5: C'twn 3G **103**
Redcar Ter. NE36: W Bol 5C **88**
Redcliffe Way NE5: Newc T . . .4F **55**
Red Courts DH7: B'don 5E **159**
Redcroft Grn. NE5: Newc T 4F **55**
Redditch Sq. SR5: C'twn 2F **103**
Rede Av. NE31: Heb 3C **72**
Redemarsh NE10: Gate 5F **85**
Redesdale Av. NE3: Ken 1C **56**
 NE21: Bla T 3F **79**
Redesdale Cl. NE12: Longb 5C **44**
 NE15: Lem 2C **66**
Redesdale Gdns. NE11: Dun 4B **82**
Redesdale Gro. NE29: N Shi 1H **61**
Redesdale Pl. NE24: Cow 6H **11**
Redesdale Rd. DH2: Ches S 2A **134**
 NE29: N Shi 1G **61**
 SR5: C'twn 2E **103**
Rede St. NE11: Gate 6E **83**
 NE32: Jar 4E **73**
Redewater Gdns. NE16: Whi 5E **81**
Redewater Rd. NE4: Newc T 1A **68**
Redewood Cl. NE5: Newc T 6E **55**
Red Firs DH7: B'don 5D **158**
Redford Pl. NE23: Dud 6C **32**
Redgrave Cl. NE8: Gate 1B **84**
Red Hall Dr. NE7: Newc T 4D **58**
REDHEUGH 1E **83**
Redheugh Bri. Rd.
 NE4: Newc T 1E **83**
Redheugh Ct. NE8: Gate 3D **82**
Redheugh Rd. NE25: Well 6F **35**
Redhill SR6: Whit 3E **91**
Redhill Dr. NE16: Whi 1C **94**
Redhill Rd. SR5: C'twn 2F **103**
Redhills La. DH1: Dur 5A **154**
Red Hills Ter. DH1: Dur 6A **154**
Redhills Way DH5: Hett H 3C **148**
Redhill Vw. DH1: Dur 5D **154**
Redhill Wlk. NE23: Cra 2B **22**
Red Ho. Dr. NE25: Whit B 5G **35**
Red Ho. Farm Est.
 NE22: Bed 5F **9**
Red Ho. Rd. NE31: Heb 3D **72**
Redland Av. NE3: Ken 1H **55**
Redlands DH4: Pen 2E **129**
 NE16: Sun 5E **95**
Red Lion Bldg. NE9: Spri 4D **98**
Red Lion La. NE37: Usw 3A **100**
Redmayne Cl. NE10: Gate 3D **84**
Redmires Cl. DH2: Ous 6G **111**
Redmond Rd. SR5: C'twn 2G **103**
Redmond Sq. SR5: C'twn 2G **103**
Rednam Pl. NE5: Newc T 5F **55**
Red Ridges DH7: B'don 4E **159**
Red Rose Ter. DH3: Ches S 1D **134**
Red Row NE22: Bed 1C **10**
Red Row Ct. NE22: Bed 1C **10**
Red Row Dr. NE22: Bed 2C **10**
Redruth Gdns. NE9: Gate 3H **97**
Redruth Sq. SR5: C'twn 2F **103**
Redshank Cl. NE38: Wash 5F **113**
Redshank Dr. NE24: News 3C **18**
Redstart Ct. NE39: Row G 4D **92**

Red Wlk. NE2: Gos 4H **57**
 NE7: Newc T 4H **57**
Redwell Ct. NE34: S Shi 2C **76**
Redwell La. NE34: S Shi 2D **76**
Redwing Cl. NE38: Wash 4F **113**
Redwing Cl. NE6: Walk 2E **71**
Redwood Cl. DH5: Hett H 2B **148**
 NE12: Kil 1C **44**
Redwood Flats DH7: B'don 5D **158**
Redwood Gdns. NE11: Gate 6D **82**
Redwood Gro. SR3: New S 2B **132**
Reed Av. NE12: Kil 6C **32**
Reedham Ct. NE5: Newc T 3F **55**
Reedling Ct. SR5: C'twn 1E **103**
Reedside NE40: Ryton 4D **64**
Reedsmouth Pl. NE5: Newc T . . .1F **67**
Reed St. NE30: N Shi 1D **62**
 NE33: S Shi 1D **74**
Reedswood Cres.
 NE23: E Cram 4D **22**
Reestones Pl. NE3: Ken 2H **55**
Reeth Rd. SR5: C'twn 3F **103**
Reeth Sq. SR5: C'twn 3F **103**
Reeth Way NE15: Thro 6C **52**
Regal Bus. Cen. NE4: Newc T . . .5B **68**
Regal Rd. SR4: Sund 6A **104**
Regal Sunderland Greyhound Stadium
 . . . . .5H **89**
Regency Ct. NE2: Newc T 1H **69**
 SR7: S'hm 4B **142**
Regency Dr. NE16: Whi 5D **80**
 SR3: New S 1B **132**
Regency Gdns. NE29: N Shi 1A **62**
Regency Way NE20: Pon 6A **26**
Regent Av. NE3: Gos 2D **56**
Regent Centre Station (Metro) . .1E **57**
Regent Cen., The NE3: Gos 1E **57**
Regent Ct. NE8: Gate 1H **83**
 NE24: Bly 6B **12**
 NE31: Heb 4D **72**
 NE33: S Shi 6E **63**
Regent Dr. NE16: Whi 1D **94**
Regent Farm Ct. NE3: Gos 2E **57**
Regent Farm Rd. NE3: Gos 1C **56**
Regent Rd. NE3: Gos 2E **57**
 NE28: W'snd 4G **59**
 NE32: Jar 3G **73**
 SR2: Ryh 4G **133**
Regent Rd. Nth. NE3: Gos 2E **57**
Regents Cl. NE12: Longb 4B **44**
Regents Ct. NE28: W'snd 3E **59**
Regents Dr. NE30: N Shi 4E **49**
Regents Pk. NE28: W'snd 4E **59**
Regent St. DH5: Hett H 6C **138**
 DH9: Ann P 4F **121**
 NE8: Gate 1G **83**
 NE24: Bly 4C **12**
 NE33: S Shi 6D **62**
Regent Ter. NE8: Gate 1G **83**
 NE29: N Shi 6A **48**
 SR2: Sund 5F **119**
Reginald St. NE10: Gate 2B **84**
 NE35: Bol C 3B **88**
 (not continuous)
 SR4: Sund 6H **103**
Regina Sq. SR5: C'twn 2F **103**
Reg Vardy Arts Foundation Gallery
 . . . . .3D **118**
Reid Av. NE28: W'snd 4H **59**
Reid Pk. Cl. NE2: Newc T 5H **57**
Reid Pk. Ct. NE2: Newc T 5H **57**
Reid Pk. Rd. NE2: Newc T 5H **57**

Reid's La. NE23: Seg 2E **33**
Reigate Sq. NE23: Cra 2B **22**
Rekendyke Ind. Est.
 NE33: S Shi 1D **74**
Rekendyke La. NE33: S Shi 6D **62**
Relley Gth. DH7: B'don 4F **159**
Relly Cl. DH7: Ush M 6D **152**
Relly Path DH1: Dur 1A **160**
Relton Av. NE6: Newc T 5D **70**
Relton Cl. DH4: Hou S 4E **137**
Relton Ct. NE25: Whit B 6A **36**
Relton Pl. NE25: Whit B 6A **36**
Relton Ter. DH3: Ches S 1C **134**
 NE25: Whit B 6A **36**
Rembrandt Av. NE34: S Shi 6E **75**
Remus Av. NE15: Hed W 5F **51**
Remus Cl. NE13: Wide O 6D **30**
Renaissance Point
 NE30: N Shi 1E **63**
Rendel St. NE11: Dun 2B **82**
Rendle Rd. NE6: Walk 5H **71**
Renforth Cl. NE8: Gate 1B **84**
Renforth St. NE11: Dun 3B **82**
Renfrew Cl. NE29: N Shi 5G **47**
Renfrew Grn. NE5: Newc T 4F **55**
Renfrew Pl. DH3: Bir 5D **112**
Renfrew Rd. SR5: C'twn 2F **103**
Rennie Rd. SR5: C'twn 2D **102**
Rennie Sq. SR5: C'twn 2D **102**
Rennington NE10: Gate 6F **85**
Rennington Av. NE30: N Shi 4E **49**
Rennington Cl. NE30: N Shi 4E **49**
Rennington Pl. NE5: Newc T 5H **55**
Renny's La. DH1: Dur 5G **155**
 (not continuous)
Renny St. DH1: Dur 5E **155**
Renoir Gdns. NE34: S Shi 1F **89**
Renwick Av. NE3: Ken 1A **56**
Renwick Rd. NE24: Bly 6B **12**
Renwick St. NE6: Walk 3D **70**
Renwick Ter. NE8: Gate 3E **83**
Rescue Sta. Cotts.
 DH5: Hou S 5D **130**
Resida Cl. NE15: Lem 1A **66**
Retail World NE11: Gate 3F **97**
Retford Rd. SR5: C'twn 2F **103**
Retford Sq. SR5: C'twn 2F **103**
Retreat, The NE15: Thro 2F **65**
 SR2: Sund 1B **118**
Revell Ter. NE5: Newc T 6A **56**
Revelstoke Rd. SR5: C'twn 2D **102**
Revesby St. NE33: S Shi 3E **75**
Reynolds Av. NE12: Kil 3B **44**
 NE34: S Shi 6F **75**
 NE38: Wash 3C **114**
Reynolds Cl. DH9: Stly 3D **122**
Reynolds Ct. SR8: Pet 1H **165**
Reyrolle Cl. NE31: Heb 4B **72**
Rheims Ct. SR4: Sund 6F **103**
Rheydt Av. NE28: W'snd 5F **59**
Rhoda Ter. SR2: Sund 6F **119**
Rhodesia Rd. SR5: C'twn 2F **103**
Rhodes St. NE6: Walk 4G **71**
Rhodes Ter. DH1: Dur 1H **159**
Rhondda Rd. SR5: C'twn 2D **102**
Rhuddlan Ct. NE5: Newc T 3F **55**
Rhyl Pde. NE31: Heb 1E **87**
Rhyl Sq. SR5: C'twn 2G **103**
Ribbledale Gdns. NE7: Newc T . . .4B **58**
Ribble Rd. SR5: C'twn 3E **103**
Ribblesdale DH4: Pen 2F **129**
 NE28: W'snd 3F **59**

Ribblesdale Av. NE24: Cow 5G 11
(not continuous)
Ribble Wlk. NE32: Jar 6G 73
Richard Av. SR4: Sund 3A 118
Richard Browell Rd.
  NE15: Thro 6D 52
Richardson Av. NE34: S Shi 5B 74
(not continuous)
Richardson Rd.
  NE2: Newc T 2D 68 (1A 4)
NE28: W'snd 5A 60
Richardson Ter. NE37: Usw 5B 100
(not continuous)
SR2: Ryh 3G 133
Richard St. DH5: Hett H 2C 148
NE24: Bly 6C 12
Richmond SR2: Ryh 2C 132
Richmond Av. NE10: Gate 2A 86
NE16: Swa 2F 81
NE38: Wash 1B 114
Richmond Cl. NE22: Bed 3G 9
Richmond Ct. DH1: Dur 6D 144
NE8: Gate 2H 83
NE9: Gate 1H 97
NE32: Jar 2E 73
Richmond Dr. DH4: Hou S 2B 136
Richmond Flds. NE20: Pon 6A 26
Richmond Gdns. NE28: W'snd 4C 60
Richmond Gro. NE29: N Shi 2A 62
Richmond M. NE3: Gos 4D 56
Richmond Pk. NE28: W'snd 3E 59
Richmond Pl. DH3: Bir 5C 112
Richmond Rd. DH1: Dur 6D 144
NE34: S Shi 3E 75
Richmond St.
  SR5: Monk 5C 104 (1F 7)
Richmond Ter. NE8: Gate 2G 83
NE10: Gate 3D 84
NE15: Thro 6F 53
NE26: Whit B 4B 36
Richmond Way NE20: Pon 6A 26
NE23: Cra 6H 21
Rickaby St. SR1: Sund 5F 105
Rickgarth NE10: Gate 6F 85
(not continuous)
RICKLETON 1E 127
Rickleton Av. DH3: Ches S 4D 126
Rickleton Village Cen.
  NE38: Wash 1F 127
Rickleton Way NE38: Wash 6F 113
Riddell Av. NE15: Newc T 4G 67
Riddell Ct. DH2: Ches S 1C 134
Riddell Ter. NE3: Gos 2C 56
Riddings Rd. SR5: C'twn 2F 103
Riddings Sq. SR5: C'twn 2F 103
Ridge Ct. NE13: Bru V 1D 42
Ridgely Cl. NE20: Pon 5G 27
Ridgely Dr. NE20: Pon 5G 27
Ridge Ter. NE22: Bed 4G 9
Ridge, The NE40: Ryton 5C 64
Ridge Vs. NE22: Bed 4G 9
Ridgeway DH3: Bir 1C 112
NE4: Newc T 1A 68
NE10: Gate 4H 85
NE25: H'wll 2C 34
SR2: Ryh 3C 132
Ridgeway Cres. SR3: Sund 4B 118
Ridge Way, The NE3: Ken 3B 56
Ridgeway, The DH5: Hett H 2C 148
NE34: S Shi 6H 75
Ridgewood Cres. NE3: Gos 2H 57

Ridgewood Gdns. NE3: Gos 2G 57
Ridgewood Vs. NE3: Gos 2G 57
Riding Barns Way NE16: Sun 3E 95
Riding Hill DH3: Gt Lum 4G 135
Riding Hill Rd. DH9: Ann P 4G 121
Riding La. NE11: Beam, Kib 2C 110
Riding Lea NE21: Bla T 2G 79
Ridings, The NE25: Whit B 5G 35
Riding, The NE3: Ken 4A 56
Ridley Av. DH2: Ches S 1B 134
NE24: Bly 6D 12
NE28: W'snd 3E 61
SR2: Ryh 2F 133
Ridley Bldg. NE2: Newc T 1C 4
Ridley Cl. NE3: Ken 5B 42
Ridley Ct. NE1: Newc T 4F 69 (5D 4)
Ridley Gdns. NE16: Swa 2E 81
Ridley Gro. NE34: S Shi 2A 76
Ridley Ho. NE3: Gos 2E 57
Ridley Pl. NE1: Newc T 3F 69 (2D 4)
Ridley St. DH9: Stly 2D 122
NE8: Gate 3F 83
NE23: Cra 4C 22
NE24: Bly 5D 12
SR5: S'wck 3A 104
Ridley Ter. NE10: Gate 3E 85
NE24: Camb 1B 12
SR2: Sund 2F 119
Ridsdale Av. NE5: Newc T 6B 54
Ridsdale Cl. NE25: Sea D 6A 24
NE28: W'snd 3A 60
Ridsdale Ct. NE8: Gate 2F 83
Rievaulx NE38: Wash 4A 114
Riga Sq. SR5: C'twn 2E 103
Riggs, The DH5: Hou S 3B 138
DH7: B'don 4E 159
Rignall NE38: Wash 2E 115
Riley St. NE32: Jar 2E 73
Ringlet Cl. NE11: Gate 4D 82
Ringmore Ct. SR2: Sund 5C 118
Ringway SR5: C'twn 5B 102
Ringwood Dr. NE23: Cra 2B 22
Ringwood Grn. NE12: Longb 6C 44
Ringwood Rd. SR5: C'twn 2F 103
Ringwood Sq. SR5: C'twn 2F 103
Rink St. NE24: Bly 5D 12
Rink Way NE25: Whit B 2B 48
Ripley Av. NE29: N Shi 2A 62
(Tonbridge Av.)
NE29: N Shi 3A 62
(Waterville Rd.)
Ripley Cl. NE22: Bed 3F 9
Ripley Ct. NE9: Gate 4B 98
Ripley Dr. NE23: Cra 6H 21
Ripley Ter. NE6: Walk 3E 71
Ripon Cl. NE23: Cra 6H 21
Ripon Gdns. NE2: Newc T 1A 70
NE28: W'snd 4C 60
Ripon Rd. DH1: Dur 5D 144
Ripon Sq. NE32: Jar 2F 87
Ripon St. DH3: Ches S 2C 134
NE8: Gate 2G 83
SR6: Monk 3E 105
Ripon Ter. DH2: Plaw 2A 144
SR7: Mur 2C 150
Rise, The NE3: Ken 3A 56
NE8: Gate 2D 04
(off Duncan St.)
NE20: Pon 2B 38
NE21: Bla T 5G 65
NE26: Sea S 5H 25
Rishton Sq. SR5: C'twn 2E 103

Rising Sun Cotts. NE28: W'snd ...2H 59
Rising Sun Countryside Cen. 5A 46
Rising Sun Vs. NE28: W'snd 2H 59
Ritson Av. DH7: Ush M 4C 152
Ritson Cl. NE29: N Shi 6A 48
Ritson St. DH9: Stly 3D 122
SR6: Monk 1E 105
Ritz Bingo 5E 45
Riverbank Rd. SR5: C'twn 3F 103
Riverdale SR5: C'twn 5D 102
River Dr. NE33: S Shi 4E 63
River Gth. *SR1: Sund* 6E 105
(off High St. E.)
River La. NE40: Ryton 3C 64
Rivermead NE38: Wash 6C 114
Rivermede NE20: Pon 4F 27
Riversdale Ct. NE15: Lem 3A 66
Riversdale Rd. NE8: Gate 6F 69
Riversdale Ter. SR2: Sund 2B 118
Riversdale Way NE15: Lem 3H 65
Riverside DH3: Ches S 1E 135
NE20: Pon 5E 27
Riverside Bus. Pk.
  NE28: W'snd 6E 61
Riverside Ct. NE11: Dun 2C 82
NE21: Bla T 5B 66
NE33: S Shi 5D 62
Riverside E. Ind. Est.
  NE6: Newc T 5B 70
Riverside Pk. SR4: Sund 6D 102
Riverside Rd. SR5: S'wck 3F 103
Riverside Sth. SR4: Sund 5G 103
Riverside Sports Complex 1E 135
Riverside Studios NE4: Newc T ..6B 68
Riverside, The NE31: Heb 2A 72
Riverside Vw. NE6: Walk 6F 71
Riverside Way NE11: Dun, Swa ..6E 67
NE16: Swa 6E 67
NE39: Row G 5D 92
River St. NE33: S Shi 1C 74
River Ter. DH3: Ches S 5D 126
River Vw. NE21: Bla T 1H 79
NE22: Bed 4D 10
NE30: N Shi 1E 63
NE40: Ryton 4E 65
River Vw. Cl. NE22: Bed 4D 10
Riverview Lodge NE4: Newc T ..5H 67
Roachburn Rd. NE5: Newc T ..5C 54
Roadside Cotts. NE21: Bla T 4F 65
Robert Allen Ct. NE13: Bru V ...5C 30
Robert Owen Gdns. NE10: Gate ...4C 84
Robertson Ct. DH3: Ches S 1C 134
Robertson Rd. SR5: C'twn 3D 102
Robertson Sq. SR5: C'twn 2D 102
Robert Sq. SR7: S'hm 5C 142
Roberts St. NE15: Newc T 5E 67
Roberts Ter. NE32: Jar 4F 73
Robert St. NE24: Bly 6C 12
NE33: S Shi 6F 63
SR3: New S 2B 132
SR4: Sund 6A 104
SR7: S'hm 5C 142
Robert Ter. DH9: Stly 1D 122
NE39: H Spen 1A 92
Robert Ter. Cotts.
  NE39: H Spen 1A 92
Robert Westall Way
  NE29: N Shi 4C 62
Robert Wheatman Ct.
  SR2: Sund 5E 119
Robin Ct. DH5: W Rai 2G 147
Robin Gro. SR5: C'twn 4E 103

Robin La. DH5: W Rai 4E 147
Robinson Gdns. NE28: W'snd 4E 61
  SR6: Whit 2F 91
Robinson Ho. SR8: Pet 6G 163
Robinson St. NE6: Newc T 3C 70
  NE33: S Shi 6F 63
Robinson Ter. NE16: Burn 3G 107
  NE38: Wash 3D 114
  SR2: Sund 3F 119
Robinswood NE9: Gate 6H 83
Robsheugh Pl. NE5: Newc T 1G 67
Robson Av. SR8: Pet 6D 162
Robson Pl. SR2: Ryh 3G 133
Robson St. NE6: Newc T 3B 70
  NE9: Gate 6H 83
Robson Ter. DH1: H Shin 3F 161
  DH9: Dip 5F 107
  NE9: Spri 4D 98
  NE39: Row G 2A 92
Rochdale Rd. SR5: C'twn 2F 103
Rochdale St. DH5: Hett H 3C 148
  NE28: W'snd 6G 59
Rochdale Way SR5: C'twn 2F 103
Roche Ct. NE38: Wash 3A 114
Rochester Gdns. NE11: Dun 3C 82
Rochester Rd. DH1: Dur 6D 144
Rochester Sq. NE32: Jar 2F 87
Rochester Ter. NE6: Walk 5G 71
Rochester Ter. NE10: Gate 3E 85
Rochford Gro. NE23: Cra 6A 22
Rochford Rd. SR5: C'twn 2E 103
Rockcliffe NE26: Whit B 6E 37
           (off Promenade)
  NE33: S Shi 6H 63
Rockcliffe Av. NE26: Whit B 1F 49
Rockcliffe Gdns. NE15: Newc T . . .2D 66
Rockcliffe St. NE26: Whit B 6E 37
Rockcliffe Way NE9: Spri 3C 98
Rocket Way NE12: Longb 5F 45
Rock Gro. NE9: Gate 6H 83
Rockingham Rd. SR5: C'twn . . .2E 103
Rockingham Sq. SR5: C'twn 2E 103
Rock Lodge Gdns.
  SR6: Monk 2E 105
Rock Lodge Rd. SR6: Monk 2F 105
Rockmore Rd. NE21: Bla T 2A 80
Rock Ter. DH7: New B 1B 158
  NE2: Newc T 3H 69 (2G 5)
  NE37: Usw 5C 100
Rockville SR6: Monk 1E 105
Rock Wlk. DH3: Lam P 3H 127
Rookwood Hill Rd.
  NE40: G'sde 2A 78
Rodham Ter. DH9: Stly 1D 122
Rodin Av. NE34: S Shi 1F 89
Rodney Cl. NE30: N Shi 6F 49
  SR2: Ryh 3C 132
Rodney Ct. NE26: Whit B 4H 35
       (off Woodburn Sq.)
Rodney St. NE6: Newc T 4B 70
Rodney Way NE26: Whit B 4H 35
Rodsley Av. NE8: Gate 3G 83
Roeburn Way NE3: Ken 4B 56
Roedean Rd. SR5: C'twn 2G 103
Roeheadge NE10: Gate 5H 85
Rogan Av. NE37: Wash 1G 113
        (off Thirlmoor)
Rogerley Ter. DH9: Ann P 4E 121
Rogers Cl. SR8: Pet 1G 165
Rogerson Ter. NE5: Newc T 5C 54
Roger St. NE6: Newc T 3B 70

Rogues La. NE39: H Spen 5A 78
Rokeby Av. NE15: Lem 3B 66
Rokeby Dr. NE3: Ken 3B 56
Rokeby Sq. DH1: Dur 2A 160
Rokeby St. NE15: Lem 3B 66
  SR4: Sund 1B 118
Rokeby Ter. NE6: Newc T 6C 58
        (not continuous)
Rokeby Vw. NE9: Gate 3A 98
Rokeby Vs. NE15: Lem 3A 98
ROKER 2E 105
Roker Av. NE25: Whit B 1A 48
  SR6: Monk 5D 104
Roker Baths Rd. SR6: Monk 3D 104
Rokerby Av. NE16: Whi 5G 81
Roker Pk. Cl. SR6: Monk 3E 105
Roker Pk. Rd. SR6: Monk 3E 105
Roker Ter. SR6: Monk 3F 105
Roker Ter. SR6: Monk 2F 105
Roland Rd. NE28: W'snd 5C 60
Roland St. NE38: Wash 3C 114
Rollesby Ct. NE5: Newc T 3F 55
Rolling Mill Rd. NE32: Jar 1E 73
Romaldkirk Cl. SR4: Sund 2D 116
Roman Av. DH3: Ches S 6D 126
  NE6: Walk 2E 71
Roman Ct. NE28: W'snd 3C 60
Roman Forum NE11: Dun 1G 81
        (off Metro Cen.)
Roman Rd. DH7: B'don 6C 158
  NE32: Jar 1F 87
        (not continuous)
  NE33: S Shi 3F 63
Roman Rd. Nth. NE33: S Shi 2E 63
Roman Way, The
  NE5: Newc T 6B 54
Romford Cl. NE23: Cra 6A 22
Romford Pl. NE9: Gate 3A 84
Romford St. SR4: Sund 1H 117
Romiley Gro. NE10: Gate 4B 86
Romilly St. NE33: S Shi 5F 63
Romney Av. NE34: S Shi 6F 75
  NE38: Wash 3C 114
  SR2: Sund 4E 119
Romney Cl. DH4: Hou S 4G 129
  NE26: Whit B 1F 49
Romney Dr. DH1: Carr 2B 156
Romney Gdns. NE9: Gate 4B 84
Romney Vs. NE38: Wash 3C 114
Romsey Cl. NE23: Cra 2B 22
Romsey Dr. NE35: Bol C 3H 87
Romsey Gro. NE15: Lem 1A 66
Ronald Dr. NE15: Newc T 3E 67
Ronald Gdns. NE31: Heb 5B 72
Ronaldsay Cl. SR2: Ryh 1E 133
Ronald Sq. SR6: Monk 2D 105
Ronan M. DH4: W Rai 3E 147
Ronsdorf Ct. NE32: Jar 3F 73
Rookery Cl. NE24: Cow 6H 11
Rookery La. NE16: Whi 1C 94
Rookery, The NE16: Burn 1F 107
Rookhope NE38: Wash 1F 127
Rooksleigh NE21: Bla T 2H 79
Rookswood Gdns.
  NE30: Row Q 2E 93
Rookwood Dr. NE13: Sea B 3E 31
Rookwood Rd. NE5: Newc T 1E 67
Roosevelt Rd. DH1: Dur 4F 155
Ropery La.
  DH3: Ches S, Gt Lum 1D 134
  NE28: W'snd 5C 60
  NE31: Heb 3B 72

Ropery Rd. NE8: Gate 3D 82
  SR4: Sund 5A 104
Ropery Stairs NE30: N Shi 2D 62
Ropery, The NE6: Newc T 5D 70
Ropery Wlk. SR7: S'hm 5B 142
Rosalie Ter. SR2: Sund 3F 119
Rosalind Av. NE22: Bed 5A 10
Rosamond Pl. NE24: Bly 6D 12
Rosa St. NE33: S Shi 5F 63
Rose Av. DH4: Hou S 2D 136
  DH9: Stly 4B 122
  NE16: Whi 4F 81
  NE23: Nel V 1H 21
Rosebank Cl. SR2: Ryh 1E 133
Rosebank Hall NE28: W'snd 5C 60
Rosebay Rd. DH7: B'don 4G 159
Roseberry Ct. NE37: Usw 5C 100
Roseberry Grange
  NE12: Longb 4G 45
Roseberry St. DH9: Beam 2H 123
Roseberry Ter. NE35: Bol C 2A 88
Roseberry Vs. DH2: Pelt 4E 125
Rosebery Av. NE8: Gate 3A 84
  NE24: Bly 6B 12
  NF29: N Shi 5C 48
  NE33: S Shi 6G 63
Rosebery Ct. NE25: Whit B 6A 36
Rosebery Cres. NE2: Newc T 1A 70
Rosebery Pl. NE2: Newc T 1H 69
Rosebery St. SR5: S'wck 4D 104
Rosebud Cl. NE16: Swa 2E 81
Roseburn Dr. NE12: Longb 2A 58
Roseby Rd. SR8: Pet 6F 163
Rose Cotts. DH6: S Het 6A 150
  NE16: Burn 2E 107
Rose Ct. NE31: Heb 4B 72
  SR8: Pet 4B 164
Rose Cres. DH4: Hou S 6B 128
  SR6: Whit 1F 91
        (not continuous)
Rosedale NE22: Bed 4G 9
  NE28: W'snd 3F 59
Rosedale Av. SR6: Monk 5E 91
Rosedale Ct. NE5: Newc T 5B 54
Rosedale Cres. DH4: Hou S 1F 137
Rosedale Rd. DH1: Carr 3B 156
  NE40: Ryton 6A 64
Rosedale St. DH5: Hett H 4A 148
  SR1: Sund 1B 118
Rosedale Ter. DH4: Hou S 6A 130
  NE2: Newc T 2H 69 (1G 5)
  NE30: N Shi 6D 48
  SR6: Monk 1E 105
  SR8: Pet 6F 163
Roseden Ct. NE12: Longb 6C 44
Rosedene Vs. NE23: Cra 3D 22
Rosefinch Lodge NE9: Gate 6H 83
Rose Gdns. NE11: Kib 1E 111
  NE28: W'snd 3H 59
Rosegill NE37: Wash 1H 113
ROSEHILL 4C 60
Rosehill Bank NE28: W'snd 5C 60
Rosehill Rd. NE28: W'snd 5D 60
Rosehill Ter. NE28: W'snd 5C 60
      (off Willington Ter.)
Rosehill Way NE5: Newc T 6G 55
Roselea NE32: Jar 2G 87
Roselea Av. SR2: Ryh 2F 133
Rosemary Gdns. NE9: Spri 3D 98
Rosemary La.
  NE1: Newc T 4F 69 (5D 4)
  SR8: Eas 1B 162

Rosemary Rd. SR5: C'twn 2F 103
Rosemary Ter. NE24: Bly 1D 18
Rosemount DH1: Dur 5D 144
  DH9: Stly 2C 124
  NE5: Newc T 5D 54
  SR4: Sund 2C 116
Rosemount Av. NE10: Gate 4H 85
Rosemount Cl. NE37: Usw 3A 100
Rosemount Ct. NE36: W Bol 4D 88
Rosemount Way NE7: Newc T ..2C 58
  NE25: Whit B 6G 35
Rose Pk. NE23: Seg 2E 33
Rose St. DH4: Hou S 3H 137
  NE8: Gate 1E 83
  NE31: Heb 4B 72
  SR4: Sund 6B 104
Rose St. E. DH4: Pen 1F 129
Rose St. W. DH4: Pen 1F 129
Rose Ter. DH2: Pelt 4G 125
  NE5: Newc T 6A 56
  NE40: G'sde 2C 78
Rosetown Av. SR8: Pet 1G 165
Rose Villa La. NE16: Whi 4F 81
Rose Vs. NE4: Newc T 4B 68
Roseville St. SR4: Sund 2B 118
Rosewell Pl. NE16: Whi 6E 81
Rosewood NE12: Kil 2F 45
Rosewood Av. NE3: Gos 1F 57
Rosewood Cres. NE6: Walk 6F 59
  NE26: Sea S 5H 25
Rosewood Gdns.
  DH2: Ches S 4B 126
  NE3: Ken 3B 56
  NE9: Gate 6B 84
Rosewood Sq. SR4: Sund 5C 116
Rosewood Ter. DH3: Bir 2B 112
  NE28: W'snd 5E 61
Rosewood Wlk. DH7: Ush M ...5B 152
Roseworth Av. NE3: Gos 4E 57
Roseworth Cl. NE3: Gos 3F 57
Roseworth Cres. NE3: Gos 4F 57
Roseworth Ter. NE3: Gos 3E 57
  NE16: Whi 4F 81
Roslin Pk. NE22: Bed 4C 10
Roslin Way NE23: Cra 6A 22
Ross DH2: Ous 5A 112
Ross Av. NE11: Dun 2B 82
Rosse Cl. NE37: Wash 5H 99
Rossendale Pl. NE12: Longb ...1H 57
Ross Gth. DH5: Hou S 4A 138
Ross Gro. NE23: Nel V 2H 21
Ross Lea DH4: Hou S 5E 129
Rosslyn Av. NE3: Ken 2A 56
  NE9: Gate 5A 84
  SR2: Ryh 2F 133
Rosslyn M. SR4: Sund 1A 118
  (not continuous)
Rosslyn Pl. DH3: Bir 5D 112
Rosslyn St. SR4: Sund 1A 118
Rosslyn Ter. SR4: Sund 1A 118
Ross St. SR5: S'wck 4C 104
  SR7: S'hm 4B 142
Ross Way NE3: Ken 5B 42
  NE26: Whit B 4A 36
Rosyth Rd. SR5: C'twn 2G 103
Rosyth Sq. SR5: C'twn 2G 103
Rotary Way DH1: Dur 5B 144
  NE20: Pon 1E 39
  NE24: Bly, News 1C 18
  NE29: N Shi 4A 62
Rothay Pl. NE5: Newc T 5G 55
Rothbury SR2: Ryh 3D 132

Rothbury Av. NE3: Gos 1C 56
  NE10: Gate 2G 85
  NE24: Bly 1H 17
  NE32: Jar 5E 73
  SR8: Pet 5F 163
Rothbury Cl. DH2: Ches S 2A 134
  NE12: Kil 2C 44
Rothbury Gdns. NE11: Gate 6C 82
  NE13: Wide O 5E 31
  NE28: W'snd 4D 60
Rothbury Rd. DH1: Dur 6C 144
  SR5: C'twn 2F 103
Rothbury Ter. NE6: Newc T 1B 70
  NE29: N Shi 3G 61
Rotherfield Cl. NE23: Cra 2B 22
Rotherfield Gdns. NE9: Gate ...3A 98
Rotherfield Rd. SR5: C'twn 3E 103
Rotherfield Sq. SR5: C'twn 2E 103
Rotherham Cl. DH5: Hou S 5H 137
Rotherham Rd. SR5: C'twn 2E 103
Rothesay DH2: Ous 6H 111
Rothesay Ter. NE22: Bed 4B 10
Rothley NE38: Wash 5D 114
Rothley Av. NE5: Newc T 2G 67
  SR8: Pet 5F 163
Rothley Cl. NE3: Gos 2F 57
  NE20: Pon 4D 26
Rothley Ct. NE12: Kil 2C 44
  SR5: S'wck 1H 103
Rothley Gdns. NE30: N Shi 4D 48
Rothley Gro. NE25: Sea D 6A 24
Rothley Way NE26: Whit B 4A 36
Rothwell Rd. NE3: Gos 2E 57
  SR5: C'twn 3E 103
Rotterdam Ho. NE1: Newc T ...5H 5
Roundhill NE32: Jar 2H 87
Roundhill Av. NE5: Newc T 5G 55
Roundstone Cl. NE7: Newc T ...3D 58
Roundway, The NE12: Longb ...6B 44
Routledge's Bldgs.
  NE22: Bed 2C 10
Rowan Av. NE38: Wash 6A 114
Rowanberry Rd. NE12: Longb ..1B 58
Rowan Cl. NE22: Bed 3H 9
  SR4: Sund 2D 116
Rowan Ct. NE12: Longb 5F 45
  NE16: Burn 1H 107
  NE24: Bly 1B 18
Rowan Dr. DH1: Bras 5E 145
  DH5: Hett H 2B 148
  NE3: Ken 1A 56
  NE20: Pon 4E 27
Rowan Gro. NE23: E Cram 4D 22
Rowan Lea DH7: B'don 5D 158
Rowans, The NE9: Spri 3D 98
  (not continuous)
Rowan Tree Av. DH1: Dur 3G 155
Rowantree Rd. NE6: Walk 6G 59
Rowanwood Gdns.
  NE11: Gate 6C 82
Rowedge Wlk. NE5: Newc T ...5E 55
Rowell Cl. SR2: Ryh 3C 132
Rowes M. NE6: Newc T 5C 70
Rowland Burn Way
  NE39: Row G 3E 93
Rowlands Bldgs. NE23: Dud ...2A 32
ROWLANDS GILL 4F 93
Rowlandson Ter. NE10: Gate ...3D 84
  SR2: Sund 3E 119
Rowley Cl. DH7: New B 2A 158
Rowley Dr. DH7: Ush M 6D 152
Rowley St. NE24: Bly 6C 12

Rowntree Way NE29: N Shi 4C 62
Rowsley Rd. NE32: Jar 4G 73
Row's Ter. NE3: Gos 2G 57
Roxborough Ho.
  NE26: Whit B 6C 36
Roxburgh Cl. NE21: Bla T 3G 79
Roxburgh Pl. NE6: Newc T 2B 70
Roxburgh St. SR6: Monk 3D 104
Roxburgh Ter. NE26: Whit B 6C 36
Roxby Gdns. NE29: N Shi 2A 62
Royal Arc. NE1: Newc T ..4G 69 (5E 5)
Royal Cres. NE4: Newc T 1A 68
Royal Ind. Est. NE32: Jar 2D 72
Royal Northumberland Yacht Club
  ....2E 19
Royal Quays Outlet Shop.
  NE29: N Shi 5A 62
Royal Rd. DH9: Stly 2C 122
Royalty, The SR2: Sund 1B 118
Royalty Theatre, The 1B 118
  (off Royalty, The)
Roydon Av. SR2: Sund 4E 119
Royle St. SR2: Sund 5F 119
Royston Ter. NE6: Walk 5G 71
Ruabon Cl. NE23: Cra 6A 22
Rubens Av. NE34: S Shi 6F 75
Ruby St. DH4: Hou S 1H 137
Rudby Cl. NE3: Gos 5F 43
Rudchester Pl. NE5: Newc T ...1G 67
Ruddock Sq. NE6: Newc T 4C 70
Rudyard Av. SR2: Sund 4E 119
Rudyerd Ct. NE29: N Shi 2D 62
Rudyerd St. NE29: N Shi 2C 62
Rugby Gdns. NE9: Gate 2C 98
  NE28: W'snd 4C 60
Ruislip Pl. NE23: Cra 6H 21
Ruislip Rd. SR4: Sund 2C 116
Runcorn SR2: Ryh 2C 132
Runcorn Rd. SR5: C'twn 2E 103
Runhead Est. NE40: Ryton 5D 64
Runhead Gdns. NE40: Ryton ...4D 64
Runhead Ter. NE40: Ryton 4E 65
Runnymede DH3: Gt Lum 3G 135
  SR2: Ryh 2D 132
Runnymede Rd. NE16: Whi 5E 81
  NE20: Pon 1A 38
  SR5: C'twn 2F 103
Runnymede Way NE3: Ken 3A 56
  SR5: C'twn 2F 103
Runswick Av. NE12: Longb 1H 57
Runswick Cl. SR3: New S 2C 132
Rupert Sq. SR5: C'twn 2G 103
Rupert St. SR6: Whit 2F 91
Rupert Ter. NE15: Thro 1F 65
Rushall Pl. NE12: Longb 1B 58
Rushbury Ct. NE27: Back 6A 34
Rushcliffe SR6: Monk 2D 104
Rushey Gill DH7: B'don 5C 158
Rushford SR2: Ryh 2D 132
Rushie Av. NE15: Newc T 4G 67
Rushley Cres. NE21: Bla T 6A 66
Rushsyde Cl. NE16: Whi 6C 80
Rushton Av. SR2: Sund 4E 119
Rushyrig NE37: Wash 1G 113
Ruskin Av. DH2: Pelt 6G 125
  DH5: Eas L 5E 149
  NE11: Dun 2B 82
  NE12: Longb 4C 44
Ruskin Cl. DH9: Stly 2F 123
Ruskin Cres. NE34: S Shi 6D 74
Ruskin Dr. NE7: Newc T 5D 58
  NE35: Bol C 3C 88

Ruskin Rd. DH3: Bir 3C **112**
  NE10: Gate 4B **84**
  NE16: Swa 3E **81**
Russel Ct. NE2: Newc T 5H **57**
Russell Av. NE34: S Shi 3A **76**
Russell Ct. NE8: Gate 2E **83**
Russell Sq. NE13: Sea B 3D **30**
Russell St. NE29: N Shi 2C **62**
  NE32: Jar 2G **73**
  NE33: S Shi 4E **63**
  NE37: Usw 5A **100**
  SR1: Sund 6E **105**
Russell Ter. DH3: Bir 1B **112**
  (not continuous)
  NE1: Newc T 3H **69** (3G **5**)
  NE22: Bed 5H **9**
Russell Way NE11: Dun 1G **81**
Ruswarp Dr. SR3: New S 3B **132**
Ruth Av. NE21: Bla T 1A **80**
Rutherford Av. SR7: S'hm 3F **141**
Rutherford Hall
  NE1: Newc T 3G **69** (2E **5**)
Rutherford Ho. SR8: Eas 1D **162**
Rutherford Rd. NE37: Usw 4C **100**
  SR5: C'twn 2D **102**
Rutherford Sq. SR5: C'twn 2D **102**
Rutherford St.
  NE4: Newc T 4E **69** (5B **4**)
  NE24: Bly 6B **12**
  NE28: W'snd 4F **61**
Rutherglen Rd. SR5: C'twn 2G **103**
Rutherglen Sq. SR5: C'twn 2G **103**
Rutland Av. NE6: Walk 2G **71**
  SR3: New S 2H **131**
Rutland Pl. NE29: N Shi 1A **62**
  NE37: Usw 3B **100**
Rutland Rd. NE28: W'snd 6G **59**
  NE31: Heb 6D **72**
Rutland Sq. DH3: Bir 2C **112**
Rutland St. DH5: Hett H 1B **148**
  NE34: S Shi 3D **74**
  SR4: Sund 6H **103**
  SR7: S'hm 3H **141**
  (not continuous)
Rutland Wlk. SR8: Pet 5C **162**
Ryal Cl. NE24: Bly 6A **12**
  NE25: Sea D 6B **24**
Ryall Av. NE13: Bru V 1C **42**
Ryal Ter. NE6: Walk 4F **71**
Ryal Wlk. NE3: Ken 3H **55**
Rydal NE10: Gate 3G **85**
Rydal Av. DH5: Eas L 5E **149**
  DH9: Stly 4B **122**
  NE30: N Shi 3C **48**
Rydal Cl. NE12: Kil 2F **45**
  NE36: E Bol 3E **89**
Rydal Cres. NE21: Bla T 3H **79**
  SR8: Pet 1E **165**
Rydal Gdns. NE34: S Shi 3G **75**
Rydal Mt. SR5: C'twn 5C **102**
  SR5: Monk 2C **104**
  SR8: Eas 1D **162**
Rydal Rd. DH2: Ches S 2B **134**
  NE3: Gos 2F **57**
  NE15: Lem 1B **66**
Rydal St. NE8: Gate 2G **83**
Rydal Ter. NE13: Wide O 1D **42**
Ryde Pl. NE23: Cra 2B **22**
Ryde Ter. DH9: Ann P 5F **121**
  NE11: Dun 2C **82**
Ryde Ter. Bungs. DH9: Ann P 4F **121**
  (off Lwr. Church St.)

Rye Cl. NE15: Thro 6E **53**
Ryedale DH1: Carr 4B **156**
  NE28: W'snd 2F **59**
  SR6: Monk 4F **91**
Ryedale Ct. NE34: S Shi 5C **74**
Ryehaugh NE20: Pon 5F **27**
Rye Hill NE4: Newc T 5D **68**
Rye Hill Sports Cen. 5D **68**
Ryehill Vw. DH5: W Rai 1G **147**
Ryelands Way DH1: Dur 5C **144**
Ryemount Rd. SR2: Ryh 2D **132**
Rye Vw. SR2: Ryh 2F **133**
RYHOPE 3G **133**
Ryhope Beach Rd. SR2: Ryh . . .3G **133**
RYHOPE COLLIERY 1E **133**
Ryhope Engines Mus. 4E **133**
Ryhope Gdns. NE9: Gate 1D **98**
Ryhope Grange Ct. SR2: Sund . . .6F **119**
Ryhope Rd. SR2: Ryh, Sund 2D **118**
Ryhope St. DH5: Hou S 3B **138**
  SR2: Sund 5F **119**
Ryhope St. Nth. SR2: Ryh 2E **133**
Ryhope St. Sth. SR2: Ryh 2F **133**
Rymers Cl. SR8: Eas 2A **162**
RYTON .4C **64**
Ryton Cl. NE33: S Shi 6F **63**
Ryton Crawcrook By-Pass
  NE21: Bla T, G'side, Ryton . . .6E **65**
  NE40: G'side, Ryton 1A **78**
Ryton Cres. DH9: Stly 1E **123**
  SR7: S'hm 4G **141**
Ryton Gdns. NE28: W'snd 3D **60**
Ryton Hall Dr. NE40: Ryton 3C **64**
Ryton Ind. Est. NE21: Bla T 4F **65**
Ryton Sq. SR2: Sund 4E **119**
Ryton Ter. NE6: Walk 5F **71**
  NE27: Shir 4B **46**
RYTON VILLAGE 3C **64**
RYTON WOODSIDE 1B **78**

S

Sabin Ter. DH9: Ann P 5H **121**
Sackville Rd. NE6: Newc T 6C **58**
  SR3: Sund 4G **117**
Sacriston Av. SR3: Sund 4H **117**
Sacriston Gdns. NE9: Gate 3C **98**
Saddleback NE37: Wash 6H **99**
Saddler's La. DH1: Dur 6C **154** (3B **6**)
Saddler St. DH1: Dur 5C **154** (2B **6**)
Saffron Pl. NE6: Walk 4G **71**
Saga Ct. NE6: Walk 6F **59**
Sage Cl. NE15: Lem 1A **66**
Sage Gateshead, The 5H **69** (6G **5**)
St Agathas Cl. DH7: B'don 4E **159**
St Aidans Av. DH1: Dur 2B **154**
  NE12: Longb 4A **46**
  SR2: Sund 6F **119**
St Aidans Cl. NE29: N Shi 5H **47**
St Aidan's Ct. DH4: E Her 3A **130**
  NE30: N Shi 6E **49**
St Aidan's Cres. DH1: Dur 5A **154**
  DH9: Ann P 6F **121**
St Aidan's Rd. NE28: W'snd 6G **59**
  NE33: S Shi 3F **63**
St Aidan's Sq. NE12: Longb 4A **46**
St Aidans St. NE8: Gate 2F **83**
St Aidan's Ter. DH4: E Her 3A **130**
St Aidans Way SR8: Pet 2D **164**
St Albans Cl. DH3: Gt Lum 5H **135**
  NE25: Well 6E **35**

St Albans Cres. NE6: Newc T 5D **58**
  NE10: Gate 4C **84**
St Albans Pl. NE10: Gate 4C **84**
  NE30: N Shi 6F **49**
St Alban's St. SR2: Sund 4E **119**
St Alban's Ter. NE8: Gate 2G **83**
St Albans Vw. NE27: Shir 3C **46**
St Aldate's Ct. SR4: Sund 4C **116**
  (off Gartland Rd.)
St Aldwyn Rd. SR7: S'hm 3H **141**
St Andrew's DH4: Hou S 3F **137**
St Andrew's Av. NE37: Usw 5H **99**
St Andrews Cl. NE25: Whit B 6H **35**
St Andrews Ct.
  DH1: Dur 6D **154** (3C **6**)
  NE7: Newc T 2C **58**
  NE29: N Shi 5B **48**
  (off Walton Av.)
St Andrew's Dr. NE9: Gate 2G **97**
St Andrew's Rd. DH9: Tan L 6D **108**
St Andrew's Sq. SR7: Mur 1E **151**
St Andrew's St.
  NE1: Newc T 4E **69** (4B **4**)
  NE31: Heb 2A **72**
St Andrew's Ter. SR6: Monk 3E **105**
St Anne's Ct. NE25: Whit B 2A **48**
St Ann's Cl. NE1: Newc T . .4A **70** (4H **5**)
St Ann's St. NE1: Newc T . .4H **69** (5H **5**)
St Ann's Wharf NE1: Newc T 5H **5**
St Ann's Yd. NE1: Newc T 4A **70**
St Anselm Cres. NE29: N Shi 6G **47**
St Anselm Rd. NE29: N Shi 6G **47**
ST ANTHONY'S 6F **71**
St Anthony's Ct. NE6: Walk 3F **71**
St Anthony's Rd. NE6: Walk 4E **71**
St Anthony's Wlk. NE6: Walk 6F **71**
St Asaph Cl. NE7: Newc T 3D **58**
St Aubyns Way DH9: Stly 2F **123**
St Austell Cl. NE5: Newc T 3G **55**
St Austell Gdns. NE9: Gate 3H **97**
St Barnabas DH4: Hou S 6B **128**
St Barnabas Way SR2: Sund 2F **119**
St Bede's NE36: E Bol 4F **89**
  (not continuous)
St Bedes Cl. DH1: Dur 6A **154**
  DH5: Hett H 1C **148**
St Bede's Dr. NE8: Gate 1H **83**
St Bede's Pk.
  SR2: Sund 2D **118** (6H **7**)
St Bedes Pl. NE24: News 3H **17**
St Bedes Rd. NE24: News 3H **17**
St Bede's Ter.
  SR2: Sund 2D **118** (6H **7**)
St Bedes Wlk. NE27: Longb 4A **46**
St Bede's Way DH7: B'don 4G **159**
St Brandon's Gro. DH7: B'don . . .5C **158**
St Brelades Way DH9: Stly 2F **123**
St Buryan Cres. NE5: Newc T . . .3G **55**
St Catherine's Ct. SR5: Sund 4F **103**
St Catherine's Gro.
  NE2: Newc T 2A **70**
St Chad's Cres. SR3: E Her 2D **130**
St Chad's Rd. SR3: E Her 2D **130**
St Chad's Vs. NE36: E Bol 4F **89**
St Christopher's Rd.
  SR3: Sund 5A **118**
St Christopher Way
  NE29: N Shi 4H **61**
St Clements Ct. NE3: Ken 4A **56**
  NE12: Longb 1A **58**
  SR4: Sund 1F **117**
St Columba Ct. SR5: S'wck 3C **104**

Saint Ct. SR3: New S 4A **132**
St Cuthbert Av. DH3: Ches S . . .6D **126**
St Cuthberts Av. DH1: Dur 2A **154**
　NE34: S Shi 1A **76**
St Cuthberts Cl. DH5: Hett H . . .1C **148**
　NE27: Longb 4A **46**
St Cuthberts Ct. NE3: Gos 2C **56**
　NE8: Gate 1F **83**
　NE24: Bly 6D **12**
St Cuthbert's Dr. NE10: Gate 4F **85**
　(not continuous)
St Cuthbert's Grn. NE5: Newc T . .2G **67**
St Cuthbert's Pk. NE16: Sun 5E **95**
St Cuthbert's Pl. NE8: Gate 2F **83**
St Cuthberts Rd. DH4: E Her . . .2B **130**
　DH4: Hou S 6H **129**
　NE5: Newc T 2F **67**
　(not continuous)
　NE8: Gate 1F **83**
　(not continuous)
　NE16: Sun 4F **95**
　NE27: Kil 4A **46**
　NE28: W'snd 4B **60**
　SR8: Pet 2D **164**
St Cuthbert's Ter. SR4: Sund 6B **104**
　SR7: Mur 6F **141**
St Cuthberts Wlk.
　DH3: Ches S 6C **126**
　DH7: B'don 4G **159**
St Cuthberts Way DH6: Sher 6D **156**
　NE21: Bla T 6B **66**
　NE27: Longb 4A **46**
St David's Cl. NE26: Whit B 3A **36**
St David's Ct. NE26: Whit B 3A **36**
St David's Way NE26: Whit B 3B **36**
　NE32: Jar 2G **87**
St Edmund's Ct. NE8: Gate 2A **84**
St Edmund's Dr. NE10: Gate 4F **85**
St Edmund's Rd. NE8: Gate 2H **83**
St Edmund's Ter. DH9: Dip 2C **120**
St Elvins Pl. DH3: Gt Lum 4H **135**
St Etienne Ct. *NE10: Gate* *2D 84*
　(off Carlisle St.)
St Gabriel's Av. NE6: Newc T 6B **58**
　SR4: Sund 1H **117**
St George's Av. NE33: S Shi 1G **75**
　NE34: S Shi 1G **75**
St George's Cl. NE2: Newc T 5G **57**
St Georges Ct. NE10: Gate 4H **85**
St Georges Cres. NE25: Whit B . . .1B **48**
　NE29: N Shi 2B **62**
St George's Est. NE38: Wash . . .6A **114**
St George's Pl. NE15: Lem 4C **66**
St George's Rd. NE15: Lem 4C **66**
　NE30: N Shi 2E **49**
St George's Ter. NE2: Newc T 6G **57**
　NE15: Lem 4C **66**
　NE36: E Bol 4F **89**
　SR6: Monk 3F **105**
St George's Way
　SR2: Sund 2D **118** (6G **7**)
St Giles Cl. DH1: Dur 5F **155**
St Godric's Cl. DH1: Dur 6C **144**
St Godrics Ct. DH1: Dur 2A **6**
St Godric's Dr. DH4: W Rai 3E **147**
St Gregorys Ct. NE33: S Shi 4H **75**
St Helen's Cres. NE9: Gate 6G **83**
St Helen's Ter. NE9: Gate 6H **83**
St Heliers Way DH9: Stly 2F **123**
St Hilda Ind. Est. NE33: S Shi . . .5E **63**
St Hildas Av. NE28: W'snd 4C **60**
St Hilda's La. NE33: S Shi 4E **63**

St Hilda St. NE33: S Shi 5E **63**
St Hilds Ct. DH1: Dur 5G **155**
St Hilds La. DH1: Dur 5E **155**
St Ignatius Cl. SR2: Sund 2E **119**
St Ives Pl. SR7: Mur 1D **150**
St Ives Way NE5: Newc T 3G **55**
St James' Blvd.
　NE1: Newc T 5E **69** (6A **4**)
St James Ct. NE10: Gate 2B **84**
St James' Cres. NE15: Newc T . . .5H **67**
St James Gdns. NE15: Newc T . . .4H **67**
St James' Ga. NE1: Newc T 5E **69**
St James' Mall NE31: Heb 4B **72**
St James' Pk. 3E **69** (3B **4**)
St James Rd. NE8: Gate 1A **84**
　NE15: Newc T 4H **67**
St James Sq. NE8: Gate 6A **70**
St James Station (Metro)
　. . . . . .4E **69** (4B **4**)
St James St.
　NE1: Newc T 3E **69** (3B **4**)
　NE3: Gos 2F **57**
St James Ter. NE1: Newc T 3B **4**
　NE29: N Shi 4H **61**
St Johns SR1: Sund 5F **105**
St John's Av. NE31: Heb 4B **72**
St John's Cl. NE26: Whit B 3B **36**
St John's Ct. NE27: Back 6A **34**
St John's Cres. NE22: Bed 2D **10**
St John's Grn. NE29: N Shi 4H **61**
St John's Ho. *NE33: S Shi* *4F 63*
　(off Beach Rd.)
St John's Mall NE31: Heb 4B **72**
St John's Pl. DH3: Bir 3C **112**
　(not continuous)
　NE10: Gate 3D **84**
　NE22: Bed 2D **10**
　NE26: Whit B 3B **36**
St John's Pct. *NE31: Heb* *4B 72*
　(off St John's Mall)
St John's Rd. DH1: Dur 6A **154**
　DH6: H Pitt 1F **157**
　DH7: B'don 5F **159**
　NE4: Newc T 5A **68**
　NE22: Bed 3D **10**
St John's Sq. SR7: S'hm 4B **142**
St John's Ter. DH9: Dip 2C **120**
　NE29: N Shi 4H **61**
　NE32: Jar 2F **73**
　NE36: E Bol 4G **89**
　SR7: S'hm 2E **141**
St John St. NE1: Newc T 4F **69** (5C **4**)
　NE29: N Shi 4H **61**
　(not continuous)
St Johns Va. SR4: Sund 3C **116**
St John's Wlk. NE4: Newc T 5A **68**
　(not continuous)
　NE29: N Shi 4H **61**
　NE31: Heb 4C **72**
St John's W. NE22: Bed 2D **10**
St Josephs Cl. DH1: Dur 5G **155**
St Josephs Ct. DH3: Bir 2C **112**
　DH9: Stly 3D **122**
　NE31: Heb 6B **72**
St Joseph's Way NE32: Jar 2G **87**
St Jude's Ter. NE33: S Shi 1E **75**
St Julien Gdns. NE7: Newc T 4D **58**
　NE28: W'snd 4F **61**
St Just Pl. NE5: Newc T 3G **55**
St Keverne Sq. NE5: Newc T 3G **55**
St Kitt's Cl. NE26: Whit B 3B **36**
ST LAWRENCE 4B **70**

St Lawrence Cl. DH6: H Pitt 2G **157**
St Lawrence Rd. DH6: H Pitt 2F **157**
　NE6: Newc T 4B **70**
St Lawrence Sq. NE6: Newc T 4B **70**
St Leonards Dr. DH1: Dur 4B **154**
St Leonards Cl. SR8: Pet 2B **164**
St Leonard St. SR2: Sund 3E **119**
St Lucia Cl. NE26: Whit B 3A **36**
　SR2: Sund 2E **119**
St Lukes Cres. NE31: Heb 5B **72**
St Luke's Rd. NE29: N Shi 4H **61**
　SR4: Sund 2D **116**
St Luke's Ter. SR4: Sund 6H **103**
St Margarets Av. NE12: Longb . . .1D **58**
　SR5: C'twn 4C **102**
St Margarets Ct. DH1: Dur 6B **154**
　NE26: Whit B *1E 49*
　(off Margaret Rd.)
　SR5: C'twn 4C **102**
St Margaret's Dr. DH9: Tan L 4B **108**
St Margarets Gth. DH1: Dur 6B **154**
St Margarets M. DH1: Dur 6B **154**
St Margaret's Rd.
　NE15: Newc T 5E **67**
St Mark's Cl. NE6: Newc T 2C **70**
St Marks Cl. NE5: Newc T 3D **54**
　NE27: Shir 2C **46**
　NE29: N Shi 5H **61**
St Marks Cres. SR4: Sund 1B **118**
St Mark's Rd. SR4: Sund 1A **118**
St Mark's St. NE6: Newc T 2C **70**
　SR4: Sund 1B **118**
St Mark's Ter. SR4: Sund 1B **118**
St Mark's Way NE33: S Shi 6E **63**
St Martin's Cl. NE26: Whit B 4A **36**
St Martin's Ct. NE26: Whit B 4A **36**
St Martin's Way NE26: Whit B 4A **36**
St Mary's Av. NE26: Whit B 4B **36**
　(not continuous)
　NE34: S Shi 3H **75**
St Marys Cl. DH1: H Shin 3F **161**
　DH2: Ches S 2B **134**
　SR8: Eas 2A **162**
　(not continuous)
St Mary's Ct. NE8: Gate 6H **69**
St Mary's Dr. DH4: W Rai 3E **147**
　DH6: Sher 6D **156**
　NE24: Bly 2H **17**
St Mary's Pl.
　NE1: Newc T 3F **69** (2D **4**)
　NE15: Thro 5E **53**
St Mary's Pl. E. NE1: Newc T 2D **4**
St Mary's RC Cathedral 5E **69** (6B **4**)
St Mary's Rd. DH1: Carr 3A **156**
St Mary's Sq. NE8: Gate . . .5H **69** (6G **5**)
St Mary's Ter. NE10: Gate 3F **85**
　NE33: S Shi 2D **74**
　NE36: E Bol 4G **89**
　NE40: Ryton 4B **64**
St Mary's Vw. *NE26: Whit B* *5D 36*
　(off Brook St.)
St Mary's Way
　SR1: Sund 6C **104** (3F **7**)
St Mary's Wynd NE26: Sea S 5H **25**
St Matthew's Ter. DH4: Hou S . . .5H **129**
St Matthew's Vw. NE33: S New S . .2A **132**
St Michael DH4: Hou S 3F **137**
St Michaels Av. NE25: Sea D 3B **24**
　NE33: S Shi 6F **63**
St Michaels Av. Nth.
　NE33: S Shi 6F **63**
St Michael's Mt. NE6: Newc T 4C **70**

St Michael's Rd. NE6: Newc T 4B 70
St Michael's Way NE11: Dun 2F 81
  SR1: Sund 6C 104 (3E 7)
St Michaels Workshops
  NE6: Newc T 4B 70
    (off Albion Row)
St Monica Gro. DH1: Dur 6A 154
St Nicholas Av. NE3: Gos 3E 57
  (not continuous)
  SR3: Sund 4B 118
St Nicholas Bldg.
  NE1: Newc T 5F 69 (6D 4)
St Nicholas Cathedral 4G 69 (5E 5)
St Nicholas Chambers
  NE1: Newc T 6E 5
    (off Amen Cnr.)
St Nicholas Chyd.
  NE1: Newc T 4F 69 (5D 4)
St Nicholas Dr. DH1: Dur 3H 153
St Nicholas Pk. Nature Reserve
  . . . . .2C 56
St Nicholas Pct. NE1: Newc T 5D 4
St Nicholas Rd. NE36: W Bol 4C 88
St Nicholas Sq.
  NE1: Newc T 4F 69 (5D 4)
St Nicholas St.
  NE1: Newc T 5F 69 (6D 4)
St Nicholas Ter. SR8: Eas 1D 162
St Nicholas Vw. NE36: W Bol 4C 88
St Omers Rd. NE11: Dun 1A 82
St Oswald's Av. NE6: Walk 2E 71
St Oswald's Ct. NE10: Gate 3D 84
St Oswald's Dr. DH1: Dur 4A 160
St Oswald's Grn. NE6: Walk 2E 71
St Oswald Sq. DH1: Dur 6A 144
St Oswald's Rd. NE28: W'snd 3B 60
  NE31: Heb 2D 72
St Oswald's Ter. DH4: Hou S 3F 129
St Oswin's Av. NE30: N Shi 2E 49
St Oswin's Pl. NE30: N Shi 5F 49
St Oswin's St. NE33: S Shi 2F 75
St Patricks Cl. NE10: Gate 3D 84
St Patrick's Ter. SR2: Ryh 3F 133
St Patrick's Wlk. NE10: Gate 3D 84
St Paul's Ct. NE0: Gate 2E 83
St Pauls Dr. DH4: Pen 1C 128
St Paul's Gdns. NE25: Whit B 1C 48
St Paul's Monastery (remains of)
  . . . . .2H 73
St Pauls Pl. NE4: Newc T 4C 68
St Paul's Rd. NE32: Jar 2G 73
St Paul's Ter. DH9: Stly 2C 124
  SR2: Ryh 3F 133
ST PETER'S 5C 70
St Peters Av. NE34: S Shi 3C 75
St Peters Basin Marina
  NE6: Newc T 5C 70
St Peter's Church & Visitor Cen.
  . . . . .5E 105
St Peters Ct. NE6: Newc T 5C 70
  NE28: W'snd 5B 60
St Peter's Quayside W.
  NE6: Newc T 5C 70
St Peter's Riverside Sculpture Trail
  . . . . .5F 105
St Peter's Rd. NE6: Newc T 5C 70
  NE28: W'snd 4B 60
St Peter's Stairs NE29: N Shi 3D 62
St Peters Station (Metro)
  . . . . .5D 104 (1G 7)
St Peter's Vw.
  SR6: Monk 5D 104 (1H 7)

St Peters Way SR6: Monk 5E 105
St Peter's Wharf NE6: Newc T 5C 70
St Philips Cl. NE4: Newc T 4D 68
St Philips Way NE4: Newc T 4D 68
St Rollox St. NE31: Heb 4B 72
St Ronan's Dr. NE26: Sea S 2F 25
St Ronan's Rd. NE25: Whit B 1B 48
St Ronans Vw. NE9: Gate 3A 98
St Simon St. NE34: S Shi 5C 74
St Stephen's Cl. NE25: Sea D 6H 23
St Stephens Way NE29: N Shi 5H 61
St Stevens Cl. NE24: Pen 1C 128
St Thomas Cl. SR8: Eas 2A 162
St Thomas Cres.
  NE1: Newc T 3F 69 (2C 4)
St Thomas Sq.
  NE1: Newc T 3F 69 (2C 4)
St Thomas St.
  NE1: Newc T 3F 69 (2C 4)
  NE9: Gate 6A 84
  SR1: Sund 6D 104 (3H 7)
St Thomas St. Bus. Cen.
  NE1: Newc T 3F 69 (2C 4)
St Thomas' Ter.
  NE1: Newc T 3F 69 (2C 4)
St Vincent Ct. NE8: Gate 2A 84
St Vincent Ho. NE30: N Shi 6F 49
St Vincent's Cl. NE15: Lem 1C 66
St Vincents Pl. NE26: Whit B 3B 36
St Vincent St. NE8: Gate 2A 84
  NE33: S Shi 6G 63
  SR2: Sund 2E 119 (6H 7)
St Vincent's Way NE26: Whit B . . .3B 36
Saker Pl. NE28: W'snd 6H 59
    (off Elton St.)
Salcombe Av. NE32: Jar 4H 73
Salcombe Cl. SR7: S'hm 5G 141
Salcombe Gdns. NE9: Gate 3H 97
Salem Hill SR2: Sund 2E 119
Salem Rd. SR2: Sund 2E 119
Salem St. NE32: Jar 2G 73
  NE33: S Shi 4E 63
  SR2: Sund 2E 119
Salem St. Sth. SR2: Sund 2E 119
Salem Ter. SR2: Sund 2F 119
Salisbury Av. DH3: Ches S 1C 134
  NE20: N Chi 6B 48
Salisbury Cl. DH3: Gt Lum 5G 135
  NE23: Cra 3G 21
Salisbury Gdns. NE2: Newc T 1A 70
Salisbury Pl. NE33: S Shi 4G 63
Salisbury Rd. DH1: Dur 5E 145
Salisbury St. DH9: Stly 4B 122
  NE10: Gate 2G 85
  NE24: Bly 5B 12
  NE33: S Shi 5F 63
  SR1: Sund 1E 119 (1H 7)
  SR4: Sund 6C 102
Salisbury Way NE32: Jar 2F 87
Salkeld Gdns. NE9: Gate 3A 84
Salkeld Rd. NE9: Gate 5A 84
Sallyport Cres.
  NE1: Newc T 4G 69 (5F 5)
Sallyport Ho.
  NE1: Newc T 4G 69 (5F 5)
Salmon St. NE33: S Shi 1F 75
Saltburn Cl. DH4: Hou S 2G 137
Saltburn Gdns. NE28: W'snd 4F 61
Saltburn Rd. SR3: Sund 4G 117
Saltburn Sq. SR3: Sund 4G 117
Salterfen La. SR2: Ryh 1G 133
Salterfen Rd. SR2: Sund 1G 133

Salter La. SR3: Sund 1D 130
Salters Cl. NE3: Gos 1G 57
Salters Ct. NE3: Gos 1G 57
Salters La. DH5: Hou S 2G 139
  DH6: Eas, Has, S Het 6G 149
  (not continuous)
  NE12: Gos, Longb 1H 57
  SR7: Hett H, Mur 3G 149
Salters La. Ind. Est.
  NE12: Longb 4A 44
Salters Rd. NE3: Gos 3C 56
Saltford NE9: Gate 3A 98
SALTMEADOWS 5A 70
Saltmeadows Ind. Pk.
  NE8: Gate 6B 70
Saltmeadows Rd. NE8: Gate 5A 70
Saltwell Crematorium
  NE9: Gate 5G 83
Saltwell Pk. NE9: Gate 4G 83
Saltwell Pk. Mansion 5G 83
Saltwell Pl. NE8: Gate 3F 83
Saltwell Rd. NE8: Gate 3F 83
Saltwell Rd. Sth. NE9: Gate 6G 83
Saltwell St. NE8: Gate 3F 83
Saltwell Vw. NE8: Gate 4G 83
Sams Ct. NE23: Dud 3H 31
Samson Cl. NE12: Kil 3C 44
Sancroft Dr. DH5: Hou S 4A 138
Sandalwood NE34: S Shi 6F 75
Sandalwood Sq. SR4: Sund 5C 116
Sandbach DH3: Gt Lum 3G 135
Sanderling Cl. NE40: Ryton 5E 65
Sanderlings NE28: W'snd 6H 59
Sanderlings, The SR2: Ryh 3G 133
Sanders Gdns. DH3: Bir 2C 112
Sanders Memorial Homes
  DH2: Ches S 6C 126
Sanderson Rd. NE2: Newc T 5G 57
  NE26: Whit B 6B 36
Sanderson's Ter. NE23: Cra 6C 22
Sanderson St. NE4: Newc T 6B 68
Sandfield Rd. NE22: E Sle 1H 11
  NE30: N Shi 2D 48
Sandford Av. NE23: Cra 6B 16
Sandford M. NE13: Wide O 6C 30
Sandgate DH9: Ann P 6H 121
  NE1: Newc T 4H 69 (5G 5)
Sandgate Ho.
  NE1: Newc T 4H 69 (5G 5)
Sandgrove SR6: Cle 2A 90
Sandhill NE1: Newc T 5G 69 (6E 5)
  NE21: Bla T 2H 79
Sandhoe Gdns. NE15: Newc T 4F 67
Sandholm Cl. NE28: W'snd 2D 60
Sandhurst Av. NE30: N Shi 3D 48
Sandiacres NE32: Jar 2G 87
Sandison Ct. NE13: Bru V 5B 30
Sandlewood Wlk. DH9: Stly 2E 123
Sandmere Pl. NE15: Newc T 3E 67
Sandmere Rd. SR2: Sund 6D 118
Sandon Cl. NE27: Back 6A 34
Sandown NE25: Whit B 6H 35
Sandown Cl. NE25: Sea D 1B 34
Sandown Ct. NE28: W'snd 3F 61
Sandown Gdns. NE8: Gate 3E 83
  NE28: W'snd 3D 60
  SR3: New S 1H 131
Sandpiper Cl. NE24: News 3D 18
  NE38: Wash 5F 113
  NE40: Ryton 5D 64
Sandpiper Ct. NE30: N Shi 5F 49
Sandpiper Pl. NE12: Longb 6A 44

Sand Point Rd. SR6: Monk 4E **105**
Sandray Cl. DH3: Bir 6D **112**
Sandrigg Sq. NE34: S Shi 4G **75**
Sandringham Av. NE12: Longb . . .1C **58**
Sandringham Cl. NE25: Whit B . . .1F **47**
Sandringham Ct. NE10: Gate 3C **84**
  NE12: Longb 1A **58**
Sandringham Cres.
  SR3: E Her 3E **131**
  SR8: Pet 1H **165**
Sandringham Dr. DH9: Ann P . . .4F **121**
  NE16: Whi 4E **81**
  NE24: News 4A **18**
  NE25: Whit B 1F **47**
Sandringham Gdns.
  NE29: N Shi 6C **48**
Sandringham M. NE28: W'snd . . .3D **60**
Sandringham Rd. NE3: Gos 3G **57**
  NE5: Newc T 1C **66**
  SR6: Monk 3D **104**
Sandringham Ter. SR6: Monk . .3E **105**
Sandringham Way NE20: Pon 1C **38**
Sandsay Cl. SR2: Ryh 1D **132**
Sands Flats, The
  DH1: Dur 5D **154** (1C **6**)
Sands Ind. Est. NE16: Swa 2E **81**
Sands Rd. NE16: Swa 2E **81**
Sands, The DH1: Dur 5D **154** (1C **6**)
Sandstone Cl. NE34: S Shi 6B **74**
Sand St. DH9: Stly 2E **123**
Sandwell Dr. DH4: Pen 1D **128**
Sandwich Rd. NE29: N Shi 4B **48**
Sandwich St. NE6: Walk 6F **71**
Sandy Chare SR6: Whit 3E **91**
Sandy Cres. NE6: Walk 5E **71**
Sandyford DH2: Pelt 2F **125**
Sandyford Ho.
  NE2: Newc T 2G **69** (1F **5**)
Sandyford Pk. NE2: Newc T 1H **69**
Sandyford Pl. DH2: Pelt 2G **125**
Sandyford Rd.
  NE1: Newc T 3G **69** (2E **5**)
  NE2: Newc T 2G **69** (1E **5**)
Sandygate M. NE16: Sun 4F **95**
Sandy La. NE3: Gos 1F **43**
  NE9: Spri 4D **98**
  NE13: Bru V, Din 5G **29**
  NE13: Wide O 1E **43**
Sandy La. Ind. Area
  NE3: Gos 1G **43**
Sandypath La. NE16: Burn 6G **93**
    (not continuous)
Sanford Ct. SR2: Sund 4C **118**
Sans St. SR1: Sund 6E **105**
Sans St. Sth. SR1: Sund 1E **119**
Sargent Av. NE34: S Shi 1F **89**
Satley Gdns. NE9: Gate 3C **98**
  SR3: Sund 5B **118**
Saturn Cl. SR8: Eas 1C **162**
Saturn St. SR7: S'hm 4G **141**
Saunton Ct. DH4: Hou S 6G **129**
Saville Ct. *NE33: S Shi* *4F 63*
    (off Saville St.)
Saville Pl. NE1: Newc T 3E **5**
  SR1: Sund *1E 119*
    (off Borough Rd.)
Saville Row
  NE1: Newc T 3F **69** (3D **4**)
Saville St. NE29: N Shi 2D **62**
  NE30: N Shi 2D **62**
  NE33: S Shi 4F **63**
Saville St. W. NE29: N Shi 2C **62**

Savory Rd. NE28: W'snd 4D **60**
Saw Mill Cotts. DH9: Dip 5E **107**
Sawmills La. DH7: B'don 5C **158**
Saxilby Dr. NE3: Gos 5F **43**
Saxon Cl. SR6: Cle 2G **89**
Saxon Cres. SR3: Sund 4H **117**
Saxondale Rd. NE3: Ken 2A **56**
Saxon Dr. NE30: N Shi 4E **49**
Saxon Way NE32: Jar 1G **73**
Saxton Gro. NE7: Newc T 3A **58**
Sayer Wlk. SR8: Pet 2E **165**
Scafell DH3: Bir 6D **112**
Scafell Cl. SR8: Pet 1E **165**
Scafell Ct. DH9: Ann P 6E **121**
  SR3: New S 3H **131**
Scafell Dr. NE5: Newc T 4H **55**
Scafell Gdns. NE11: Gate 5C **82**
Scalby Cl. NE3: Gos 5F **43**
Scarborough Ct. NE6: Newc T . . .3D **70**
  NE23: Cra 4B **22**
Scarborough Pde. NE31: Heb 1E **87**
Scarborough Rd.
  NE6: Newc T, Walk 3D **70**
    (not continuous)
  SR3: New S 1H **131**
Scardale Way DH1: Carr 3C **156**
Sceptre Ct. NE4: Newc T 5C **68**
Sceptre Pl. NE4: Newc T 4C **68**
    (not continuous)
Sceptre St. NE4: Newc T 4C **68**
Schalksmuhle Rd. NE22: Bed 4H **9**
Schimel St. SR5: S'wck 3B **104**
School App. NE34: S Shi 3A **76**
School Av. DH4: W Rai 4D **146**
  NE11: Dun 3B **82**
School Cl. NE10: Gate 5D **84**
School Ct. DH6: Sher 6D **156**
Schoolhouse La. NE16: Sun 5C **94**
School La. DH1: Dur 1D **160** (5C **6**)
  DH9: Stly 4B **122**
  NE16: Whi 4G **81**
  NE39: H Spen 2A **92**
School Rd. DH5: W Rai 1G **147**
  NE22: Bed 2D **10**
School St. DH3: Bir 3C **112**
  NE8: Gate 1F **83**
  NE16: Whi 4E **81**
  NE31: Heb 2C **72**
  SR7: S'hm 6B **142**
  SR8: Eas 1E **163**
School Ter. DH4: Hou S 2C **136**
  DH9: Stly 4B **122**
School Vw. DH4: W Rai 3D **146**
  DH5: Eas L 5F **149**
Scorer's La. DH3: Gt Lum 2H **135**
Scorer St. NE29: N Shi 2B **62**
Scotby Gdns. NE9: Gate 2B **98**
Scotland Ct. NE21: Bla T 2G **79**
SCOTLAND GATE 1H **9**
Scotland Head NE21: Bla T 4G **79**
Scotland St. SR2: Ryh 3G **133**
SCOTSWOOD 4E **67**
Scotswood Bri. Works
  NE21: Bla T 6E **67**
Scotswood Rd.
  NE4: Newc T 5E **69** (6B **4**)
  NE15: Lem, Newc T 3B **66**
Scotswood Sports & Social Cen.
  . . . . .3D **66**
Scotswood Sta. App.
  NE15: Newc T 5E **67**
Scotswood Vw. NE11: Dun 6F **67**

Scott Av. NE23: Nel V 1H **21**
Scott Ct. DH3: Gt Lum 4G **135**
  NE34: S Shi 6C **74**
Scotts Bank SR5: S'wck 4A **104**
Scotts Cotts. DH1: Dur 5H **153**
Scotts Ct. NE10: Gate 5H **85**
Scott's Ter. DH5: Hett H 1C **148**
Scott St. DH4: Hou S 3H **137**
  DH9: Stly 3C **122**
  NE23: E Har 4B **16**
Scripton Gill DH7: B'don 5C **158**
Scripton Gill Rd. DH7: B'don . . .6B **158**
Scrogg Rd. NE6: Walk 2E **71**
Scruton Av. SR3: Sund 5G **117**
Sea Banks NE30: N Shi 5G **49**
SEABURN 1E **105**
Seaburn Av. NE25: Sea D 3B **24**
Seaburn Cen. 6E **91**
Seaburn Cl. SR6: Monk 1E **105**
Seaburn Ct. SR6: Monk 1E **105**
Seaburn Dr. DH4: Hou S 3G **137**
Seaburn Fun Pk. 6E **91**
Seaburn Gdns. NE9: Gate 2D **98**
  SR6: Monk 1E **105**
Seaburn Gro. NE26: Sea S 3G **25**
Seaburn Hill SR6: Monk 1E **105**
Seaburn Station (Metro) 1C **104**
Seaburn Ter. SR6: Monk 1F **105**
Seaburn Vw. NE25: Sea D 3B **24**
Seacombe Av. NE30: N Shi 2D **48**
Seacrest Av. NE30: N Shi 2D **48**
Seafield Rd. NE24: News 2C **18**
Seafields SR6: Monk 6E **91**
Seafield Ter. NE33: S Shi 4F **63**
Seafield Vw. NE30: N Shi 5F **49**
Seaforth Rd. SR3: Sund 4A **118**
Seaforth St. NE24: Bly 5C **12**
SEAHAM 4B **142**
Seaham Cl. NE34: S Shi 3B **76**
Seaham Gdns. NE9: Gate 3C **98**
Seaham Grange Ind. Est.
  SR7: Sea 1F **141**
Seaham Leisure Cen. 4H **141**
Seaham Rd. DH5: Hou S 3B **138**
  SR2: Ryh 3G **133**
Seaham Station (Rail) 3A **142**
Seaham St. SR3: New S 2A **132**
  SR7: S'hm 6C **142**
Sea La. SR6: Monk 1E **105**
  SR6: Whit 4F **91**
Sea Rd. NE33: S Shi 3G **63**
  SR6: Monk 1D **104**
Seascale Pl. NE9: Gate 1B **98**
Seaside La. SR8: Eas 1B **162**
Seaside La. Sth. SR8: Eas 1E **163**
Seatoller Ct. SR3: New S 3H **131**
SEATON
  Seaham 3D **140**
  Whitley Bay 4D **24**
Seaton Av. DH5: Hou S 3B **138**
  NE22: Bed 4B **10**
  NE23: Dud 2B **32**
  NE24: News 3A **18**
SEATON BURN 3D **30**
Seaton Cl. NE10: Gate 5H **85**
Seaton Cres. NE25: H'wll 1D **34**
  NE25: Whit B 6A **36**
  SR7: S'hm 2E **141**
Seaton Cft. NE23: Dud 3C **32**
SEATON DELAVAL 6A **24**
Seaton Delaval Hall 4E **25**
Seaton Gdns. NE9: Gate 2C **98**

Seaton Gro. SR7: Sea 3D **140**
Seaton Holme
　(Discovery/Exhibition Cen.)
　. . . . . .1A **162**
Seaton La. SR7: Sea 2D **140**
Seaton Pk. SR7: S'hm 3F **141**
Seaton Pl. NE6: Walk 6E **71**
　NE13: Wide O 6C **30**
Seaton Rd. NE27: Shir 1E **47**
　SR3: Sund 4F **117**
SEATON SLUICE 3H **25**
SEATON TERRACE 6B **24**
Seatonville Cres. NE25: Whit B . .2A **48**
Seatonville Gro. NE25: Whit B . . .2A **48**
Seatonville Rd. NE25: Whit B . . .1H **47**
Sea Vw. SR2: Ryh 3G **133**
　SR8: Eas 2B **162**
Sea Vw. Cotts TS27: Hes 6F **165**
Sea Vw. E. SR2: Sund 5F **119**
Sea Vw. Gdns. SR6: Monk 2E **105**
　SR8: Pet 5G **163**
Seaview Ind. Est. SR8: Pet 4G **163**
Sea Vw. Pk. NE23: Cra 3D **22**
　SR8: Whit 3D **90**
Sea Vw. Rd. SR2: Sund 5E **119**
Sea Vw. Rd. W. SR2: Sund 5D **118**
Sea Vw. St. SR2: Sund 5F **119**
Seaview Ter. NE33: S Shi 4G **63**
Sea Vw. Vs. NE23: Cra 3D **22**
Sea Vw. Wlk. SR7: Mur 1E **151**
Sea Way NE33: S Shi 4G **63**
Second Av. DH2: Ches S 1A **134**
　(Drum Rd.)
　DH2: Ches S 1B **134**
　(Gray Av.)
　NE6: Newc T 1C **70**
　NE11: Gate 5D **82**
　NE24: Bly 1B **18**
　NE29: N Shi 3F **61**
Second St. NE8: Gate 2F **83**
Secretan Way NE33: S Shi 5E **63**
Sedbergh Rd. NE30: N Shi 3C **48**
Sedgefield Ct. NE12: Kil 2C **44**
SEDGELETCH 1F **137**
Sedgeletch Ind. Est.
　DH4: Hou S 1E **137**
Sedgeletch Rd. DH4: Hou S 2E **137**
Sedgemoor NE12: Kil 1D **44**
Sedgemoor Av. NE15: Newc T . . .4E **67**
Sedgewick Pl. NE8: Gate 2G **83**
Sedley Rd. NE28: W'snd 6H **59**
Sedling Rd. NE38: Wash 5H **113**
Sefton Av. NE6: Newc T 6C **58**
Sefton Ct. NE23: Cra 6C **16**
Sefton Sq. SR3: Sund 4G **117**
Segedunum Cres. NE28: W'snd . .3C **60**
Segedunum Roman Fort, Baths & Mus.
　. . . . . .1A **162**
Segedunum Way NE28: W'snd . .6H **59**
SEGHILL 2F **33**
Seghill Ind. Est. NE23: Seg 1F **33**
Seine Ct. NE32: Jar 3G **73**
Selborne Av. NE9: Gate 1G **97**
Selborne Gdns. NE2: Newc T . . .1A **70**
Selbourne Cl. NE23: Cra 3G **21**
Selbourne St. NE33: S Shi 5F **63**
　SR6: Monk 4D **104**
　(not continuous)
Selbourne Ter. NE24: Camb 2B **12**
Selby Cl. NE23: Cra 6B **16**
Selby Ct. NE6: Walk 5F **71**
　NE32: Jar 2F **73**

Selby Gdns. NE6: Walk 1F **71**
　NE28: W'snd 4H **59**
Selby Sq. SR3: Sund 4G **117**
Selina Pl. SR6: Monk 4E **105**
Selkirk Cres. DH3: Bir 1C **112**
Selkirk Gro. NE23: Cra 6C **16**
Selkirk Sq. SR3: Sund 4F **117**
Selkirk St. NE32: Jar 6A **74**
Selkirk Way NE29: N Shi 5G **47**
Selsdon Av. SR4: Sund 5C **116**
Selsey Ct. NE10: Gate 5E **85**
Selwood Ct. NE34: S Shi 4H **75**
Selwyn Av. NE25: Whit B 2H **47**
Selwyn Cl. NE5: Newc T 4H **55**
Serin Ho. NE5: Newc T 4E **55**
Serlby Cl. NE37: Usw 4A **100**
Serlby Pk. DH5: Hett H 2D **148**
Seton Av. NE34: S Shi 5B **74**
Seton Wlk. NE34: S Shi 5B **74**
Setting Stones NE38: Wash 1G **127**
Settlingstone Cl. NE7: Newc T . . .4D **58**
Sevenacres DH3: Gt Lum 3H **135**
Sevenoaks Dr. SR4: Sund 4C **116**
Seventh Av. DH2: Ches S 6B **126**
　NE6: Newc T 2C **70**
　NE11: Gate 1F **97**
　NE24: Bly 1B **18**
　(not continuous)
Seventh St. SR8: Pet 6G **163**
　(not continuous)
Severn Av. NE31: Heb 6C **72**
Severn Cl. SR8: Pet 3C **164**
Severn Ct. SR3: New S 3H **131**
Severn Cres. DH9: Stly 4C **122**
Severn Dr. NE32: Jar 1G **87**
Severn Gdns. NE8: Gate 2B **84**
Severn Ho's. NE37: Wash 5E **101**
Severs Ter. NE5: Cal 1H **53**
Severus Rd. NE4: Newc T 2A **68**
Seymour Cl. NE11: Dun 2C **82**
Seymour Sq. SR3: Sund 4G **117**
Seymour St. NE11: Dun 2C **82**
　NE29: N Shi 3C **62**
　SR8: Pet 1H **165**
Seymour Ter. DH5: Eas L 4D **148**
　NE40: Ryton 4A **64**
Shadfen Pk. Rd. NE30: N Shi . . .2C **48**
Shadforth Cl. SR8: Pet 3A **164**
Shadon Way DH3: Bir 4E **113**
Shaftesbury Av. NE26: Whit B . . .4B **36**
　NE32: Jar 3H **73**
　NE34: S Shi 3H **73**
　SR2: Ryh 2E **133**
Shaftesbury Cres. NE30: N Shi . .2C **48**
　SR3: Sund 4H **117**
Shaftesbury Gro. NE6: Newc T . .2B **70**
Shaftesbury Wlk. NE8: Gate 1E **83**
Shafto Ct. NE15: Newc T 4F **67**
Shafto Cl. NE40: Ryton 6A **64**
Shaftoe Ct. NE3: Ken 6C **42**
　NE12: Kil 2D **44**
Shaftoe Rd. SR3: Sund 5F **117**
Shaftoe Sq. SR3: Sund 5F **117**
Shaftoe Way NE13: Din 4F **29**
Shafto St. NE15: Newc T 4E **67**
　NE28: W'snd 4C **60**
Shafto St. Nth. NE28: W'snd . . .4C **60**
Shafto Ter. DH9: Stly 6H **123**
　(Craghead La.)
　DH9: Stly 1D **122**
　(Newburn Rd.)
　NE37: Wash 6B **100**

Shaftsbury Dr. DH7: B'don 6C **158**
Shakespeare Av. NE31: Heb 3C **72**
　(not continuous)
Shakespeare Cl. DH9: Stly 2F **123**
　(not continuous)
Shakespeare St. DH5: Hou S . . .4A **138**
　NE1: Newc T 4F **69** (4D **4**)
　NE8: Gate 1A **84**
　NE28: W'snd 4D **60**
　NE32: Jar 1F **73**
　NE33: S Shi 6F **63**
　SR5: S'wck 3B **104**
　SR7: S'hm 4B **142**
Shakespeare Ter. DH2: Pelt 6G **125**
　SR2: Sund 2C **118** (6E **7**)
　SR8: Eas 1C **162**
Shalcombe Cl. SR3: New S 3A **132**
Shallcross SR2: Sund 3B **118**
Shalstone NE37: Usw 4D **100**
Shamrock Cl. NE15: Lem 1A **66**
Shandon Way NE3: Ken 2A **56**
SHANKHOUSE 5C **16**
Shanklin Pl. NE23: Cra 3G **21**
Shannon Cl. SR5: C'twn 4C **102**
Shannon Ct. NE3: Ken 6G **41**
Shap Cl. NE38: Wash 4B **114**
Shap Ct. SR3: New S 3H **131**
Shapers 1B **118**
　(off Chester Rd.)
Shap La. NE5: Newc T 6E **55**
Shap Rd. NE30: N Shi 3D **40**
Sharnford Cl. NE27: Back 6B **34**
Sharon Cl. NE12: Kil 3B **44**
Sharp Cres. DH1: Dur 4G **155**
　(not continuous)
Sharpendon St. NE31: Heb 2C **72**
Sharperton Dr. NE3: Gos 4C **42**
Sharpley Dr. SR7: S'hm 2E **141**
Shaw Av. NE34: S Shi 5D **74**
Shawbrow Cl. NE7: Newc T 4E **59**
Shawdon Cl. NE5: Newc T 3F **55**
Shaw Gdns. NE10: Gate 3H **85**
Shaw St. SR7: S'hm 4B **142**
Shaw Wood Cl. DH1: Dur 4A **154**
Shearlegs Rd. NE8: Gate 6A **70**
Shearwater SR6: Whit 6F **77**
Shearwater Av. NE12: Longb 6A **44**
Shearwater Cl. NE5: Newc T 3F **55**
Shearwater Way NE24: News . . .3C **18**
Sheelin Av. DH2: Ches S 2C **134**
Sheen Cl. DH4: W Rai 3E **147**
Sheen Ct. NE3: Ken 2F **55**
Sheepfolds Nth.
　SR5: Monk 5D **104** (1G **7**)
Sheepfolds Rd.
　SR5: Monk 5D **104** (1G **7**)
SHEEP HILL 1H **107**
Sheep Hill NE16: Burn 1H **107**
Shefton Mus. of Greek Art &
　Archaeology, The 2F **69** (1C **4**)
Sheldon Ct. NE12: Longb 4C **44**
Sheldon Gro. NE3: Ken 4C **56**
　NE23: Cra 6B **16**
Sheldon Rd. NE34: S Shi 6H **63**
Sheldon St. NE32: Jar 2F **73**
Shelford Gdns. NE15: Lem 2C **66**
Shellbark DH4: Hou S 3D **128**
Shelley Av. DH5: Eas L 5F **149**
　NE9: Spri 4F **99**
　NE34: S Shi 4B **76**
　NE35: Bol C 3C **88**
Shelley Cl. DH9: Stly 3E **123**
Shelley Ct. DH2: Pelt 6H **125**

Shelley Cres. NE24: Bly 2A 18
Shelley Dr. NE8: Gate 1A 84
Shelley Gdns. DH2: Pelt 6G 125
Shelley Rd. NE15: Thro 2F 65
Shelley Sq. SR8: Eas 2C 162
Shelley St. SR7: S'hm 4B 142
Shepherd Cl. NE23: Dud 5C 32
Shepherd's Quay NE29: N Shi 3D 62
Shepherd St. SR4: Sund 6A 104
Shepherds Way NE36: W Bol 4C 88
Shepherd Way NE38: Wash 5C 114
Sheppard Ter. SR5: C'twn 4D 102
Sheppey Ct. SR3: New S 3A 132
Shepton Cotts. NE16: Sun 2G 95
Sheraton NE10: Gate 6G 85
Sheraton St. NE2: Newc T 1D 68
Sherborne DH3: Gt Lum 3H 135
Sherborne Av. NE29: N Shi 5H 47
SHERBURN 6D 156
Sherburn Grange Nth.
  NE32: Jar 4E 73
Sherburn Grange Sth.
  NE32: Jar 4E 73
Sherburn Grn. NE39: Row G 2F 93
Sherburn Gro. DH4: Hou S 2G 137
SHERBURN HILL 6G 157
Sherburn Pk. Dr. NE39: Row G . .2E 93
Sherburn Rd. DH1: Dur 5F 155
Sherburn Rd. Est. DH1: Dur 6G 155
Sherburn Rd. Flats DH1: Dur . . .5F 155
  (off Sherburn Rd.)
Sherburn Sports Cen. 5D 156
Sherburn Ter. NE9: Gate 3C 98
Sherburn Way NE10: Gate 5A 86
Sherfield Dr. NE7: Newc T 5D 58
Sheridan Dr. DH9: Stly 3E 123
Sheridan Grn. NE38: Wash 6G 113
Sheridan Rd. NE34: S Shi 6C 74
Sheridan St. SR4: Sund 6H 103
SHERIFF HILL 6A 84
Sheriff Mt. Nth. NE9: Gate 4A 84
Sheriff Mt. Sth. NE9: Gate 4A 84
Sheriffs Cl. NE10: Gate 3B 84
Sheriffs Hall Vs. NE9: Gate 5A 84
Sheriff's Highway NE9: Gate 5A 84
Sheriff's Moor Av. DH5: Eas L . . .5E 149
Sheringham Av. NE29: N Shi 6H 47
Sheringham Cl. SR3: New S . . .5A 132
Sheringham Dr. NE23: Cra 3G 21
Sheringham Gdns.
  NE15: Thro 5B 52
Sheringham Ho. NE38: Wash . . .3E 114
Sherringham Av. NE3: Ken 2A 56
Sherwood NE27: Shir 3F 47
Sherwood Cl. NE27: Shir 3F 47
  NE38: Wash 2B 114
Sherwood Ct. SR3: New S 3A 132
Sherwood Pl. NE3: Gos 3E 43
Sherwood Vw. NE28: W'snd 3G 59
Shetland Cl. SR3: New S 3A 132
Shibdon Bank NE21: Bla T 2A 80
Shibdon Bus. Pk. NE21: Bla T . . .6C 66
Shibdon Ct. NE21: Bla T 6A 66
  (off Shibdon Rd.)
Shibdon Cres. NE21: Bla T 1B 80
Shibdon Pk. Vw. NE21: Bla T 1B 80
Shibdon Rd. NE21: Bla T 6A 66
Shibdon Way NE21: Bla T 1D 80
Shield Av. NE16: Swa 2F 81
Shieldclose NE37: Wash 1G 113
Shield Ct. NE2: Newc T 2H 69 (1G 5)
SHIELDFIELD 3H 69 (3G 5)
Shieldfield Ho.
  NE2: Newc T 3H 69 (2G 5)
Shieldfield Ind. Est.
  NE2: Newc T 3H 69 (3H 5)
Shieldfield La.
  NE2: Newc T 3H 69 (3H 5)
Shield Gro. NE3: Gos 1F 57
SHIELD ROW 1E 123
Shield Row DH9: Stly 2D 122
Shield Row Gdns. DH9: Stly 1D 122
Shieldrow La. DH9: Ann P 6G 121
Shields La. NE6: Newc T 3C 70
Shields Pl. DH5: Hou S 2A 138
Shields Rd.
  DH3: Ches S, Gt Lum 4D 126
  NE6: Newc T 3B 70
  NE6: Walk 2C 70
  NE10: Gate 2G 85
    (Cartmel Pk.)
  NE10: Gate 3F 85
    (St Mary's Ter.)
  NE22: H Bri 2D 14
  NE25: Whit B 2B 48
  SR6: Cle, S Shi 6H 75
  SR6: Monk, S'wck 5B 90
Shields Rd. By-Pass
  NE6: Newc T 3B 70
Shields Rd. W. NE6: Newc T 3A 70
Shield St. NE2: Newc T . . .3H 69 (3G 5)
Shiel Gdns. NE23: Cra 3G 21
Shillaw Pl. NE23: Dud 5B 32
Shilmore Rd. NE3: Ken 2B 56
Shilton Cl. NE34: S Shi 4A 76
SHINCLIFFE 3G 161
Shincliffe Av. SR5: C'twn 3E 103
Shincliffe Gdns. NE9: Gate 2C 98
Shincliffe La.
  DH1: H Shin, Sher 2H 161
SHINEY ROW 4E 129
Shinwell Ter. SR7: Mur 2B 150
Shipby SR3: New S 2H 131
SHIPCOTE 3G 83
Shipcote La. NE8: Gate 3H 83
Shipcote Ter. NE8: Gate 3H 83
Shipley Art Gallery 3H 83
Shipley Av. NE4: Newc T 3A 68
  SR6: Monk 1E 105
Shipley Ct. NE8: Gate 2H 83
Shipley Pl. NE6: Newc T 3B 70
Shipley Ri. NE6: Newc T 3C 70
Shipley Rd. NE30: N Shi 6E 49
Shipley St. NE15: Lem 3A 66
Shipley Wlk. NE6: Newc T 3B 70
Shipton Cl. NE35: Bol C 2A 88
Shire Chase DH1: Dur 5D 144
SHIREMOOR 2D 46
Shiremoor By-Pass
  NE27: Back 2A 46
Shiremoor Station (Metro) 2D 46
Shirlaw Cl. NE5: Newc T 3D 54
Shirley Gdns. SR3: Sund 4B 118
Shirwood Av. NE16: Whi 6E 81
Shop Row DH4: Hou S 4G 129
Shop Spouts NE21: Bla T 6A 66
Shoreham Ct. NE3: Ken 6G 41
Shoreham Sq. SR3: Sund 4G 117
Shorestone Av. NE30: N Shi 2D 48
Shore St. SR6: Monk 4D 104
Shoreswood Dr. SR3: New S 2B 132
Short Gro. SR7: Mur 2A 150
Shortridge St. NE33: S Shi 4F 63
Shortridge Ter. NE2: Newc T 6H 57
Short Row DH4: Hou S 5C 128
  NE5: Cal 1H 53
Shot Factory La. NE4: Newc T 6E 69
Shotley Av. SR5: S'wck 2B 104
Shotley Gdns. NE9: Gate 4A 84
SHOTTON 6A 14
Shotton Av. NE24: Bly 1C 18
Shotton Bank SR8: Pet 5A 164
SHOTTON EDGE 3A 20
Shotton La. NE23: Cra, Nel V 5D 14
  NE61: Sea B 6A 14
  SR8: Pet 2A 164
Shotton Rd. SR8: Pet 6F 163
Shotton St. NE23: E Har 4B 16
Shotton Way NE10: Gate 5C 86
Shrewsbury Cl. NE7: Newc T 3D 58
  SR8: Pet 2B 164
Shrewsbury Cres. SR3: Sund . . .4G 117
Shrewsbury Dr. NE27: Back 6A 34
Shrewsbury St. NE11: Dun 3B 82
  SR7: S'hm 6B 142
Shrewsbury Ter. NE33: S Shi 2E 75
Shrigley Cl. NE38: Wash 1H 127
Shrigley Gdns. NE3: Ken 2B 56
Shropshire Dr. DH1: Carr 5A 156
Shummard Cl. DH4: Hou S 4D 128
Shunner Cl. NE37: Wash 1G 113
Sibthorpe St. NE29: N Shi 2D 62
Side NE1: Newc T 5G 69 (6E 5)
  (not continuous)
Side Cliff Rd. SR6: Monk 2D 104
Side Gallery 6E 5
Sidegate DH1: Dur 5C 154 (1A 6)
Side La. NE61: Hep 1A 8
Sidgate NE1: Newc T 3D 4
  (off Eldon Sq.)
Sidings, The DH1: Dur 5E 155
Sidlaw Av. DH2: Ches S 1A 134
  NE29: N Shi 4B 48
Sidmouth Cl. DH4: Hou S 5G 129
  SR7: Mur 5F 141
Sidmouth Rd. NE9: Gate 2H 97
  NE29: N Shi 1G 61
Sidney Cl. DH9: Stly 3F 123
Sidney Gro. NE4: Newc T 3C 68
  NE8: Gate 2F 83
Sidney St. NE24: Bly 6B 12
  NE29: N Shi 2C 62
  NE35: Bol C 3B 88
Sidney Ter. DH9: Tan L 1B 122
Silkeys La. NE29: N Shi 2B 62
Silkstun Ct. SR3: New S 2A 132
SILKSWORTH 3G 131
Silksworth Cl. SR3: New S 1H 131
Silksworth Gdns. NE9: Gate 3C 98
Silksworth Hall Dr.
  SR3: New S 3H 131
Silksworth La. SR3: E Her 2E 131
  (not continuous)
  SR3: New S 2G 131
Silksworth Rd. SR3: E Her 2E 131
  SR3: New S 2G 131
Silksworth Row
  SR1: Sund 6C 104 (3E 7)
  (not continuous)
Silksworth Ski Slope 6H 117
Silksworth Sports Complex 6H 117
Silksworth Ter. SR3: New S 2A 132
Silksworth Way SR3: New S 3G 131
Silkwood Cl. NE23: Cra 6B 16
Silloth Av. NE5: Newc T 1E 67
Silloth Dr. NE37: Usw 3A 100

Silloth Pl. NE30: N Shi 3D 48
Silloth Rd. SR3: Sund 5F 117
Silverbirch Ind. Est. NE12: Kil 1B 44
Silverbriar SR5: Sund 4H 103
Silver Ct. NE9: Gate 3A 84
Silver Courts DH7: B'don 5D 158
Silverdale SR3: New S 5A 132
Silverdale Av. NE10: Gate 3B 86
Silverdale Dr. NE21: Bla T 2F 79
Silverdale Rd. NE23: Cra 6B 16
Silverdale Ter. NE8: Gate 3H 83
Silverdale Way NE16: Whi 6D 80
    NE34: S Shi 6B 74
Silver Fox Way
    NE27: N Shi, Shir 5C 46
Silverhill Dr. NE5: Newc T 2E 67
Silverlink Bus. Pk.
    NE27: N Shi 5E 47
    NE28: W'snd 6D 46
Silverlink Nth., The NE27: Shir . . .4C 46
Silverlink, The NE28: W'snd 6E 47
Silver Lonnen NE5: Newc T 2E 67
Silvermere Dr. NE40: Ryton 5D 64
Silverstone NE12: Kil 2E 45
Silverstone Way NE37: Usw 5C 100
Silver St. DH1: Dur 6C 154 (3A 6)
    NE30: N Shi 6F 49
    SR1: Sund 5F 105
Silvertop Gdns. NE40: G'sde 2A 78
Silvertop Ter. NE40: G'sde 2A 78
Silverwood Gdns. NE11: Gate . . .6D 82
Simonburn NE38: Wash 3F 110
Simonburn Av. NE4: Newc T 1A 68
    NE29: N Shi 1G 61
Simon Pl. NE13: Wide O 6C 30
SIMONSIDE 4C 74
Simonside NE26: Sea S 5H 25
    NE34: S Shi 4C 74
Simonside Av. NE28: W'snd 3D 60
Simonside Cl. NE26: Sea S 5H 25
Simonside E. Ind. Est.
    NE32: Jar 4A 74
Simonside Hall NE34: S Shi 4B 74
Simonside Ind. Est. NE32: Jar . . .4H 73
Simonside Pl. NE9: Gate 2C 98
Simonside Rd. NE21: Bla T 2A 80
    SR3, Sund 4F 117
Simonside Ter. NE6: Newc T 1B 70
Simonside Vw. NE16: Whi 4E 81
    NE20: Pon 4D 26
    NE32: Jar 5G 73
Simonside Wlk. NE11: Gate 6C 82
Simonside Way NE12: Kil 1F 45
Simpson Cl. NE35: Bol C 3A 88
    (not continuous)
Simpsons Memorial Homes
    NE40: Ryton 5A 64
Simpson St. DH9: Stly 2D 122
    NE24: Bly 5C 12
    NE29: N Shi 2A 62
    NE30: N Shi 1E 49
    NE40: Ryton 5E 65
    SR4: Sund 5B 104
Simpson Ter.
    NE2: Newc T 3H 69 (3G 5)
    NE15: Thro 6H 53
Sinclair Ct. NE13: Bru V 5C 30
Sinclair Dr. DH3: Ches S 1D 126
Sinclair Gdns. NE25: Sea D 6B 24
Sinderby Cl. NE3: Gos 5F 43
Sir Godfrey Thomson Ct.
    NE10: Gate 3C 84

Sitwell Rd. DH9: Stly 3E 123
Sixth Av. DH2: Ches S 6B 126
    NE6: Newc T 2C 70
    NE11: Gate 1E 97
    NE24: Bly 2B 18
Sixth St. SR8: Pet 6G 163
Skaylock Dr. NE38: Wash 4G 113
Skegness Pde. NE31: Heb 1E 87
Skelder Av. NE12: Longb 1B 58
Skelton Ct. NE3: Ken 5A 42
Skerne Cl. SR8: Pet 3C 164
Skiddaw Cl. SR8: Pet 1E 165
Skiddaw Dr. DH9: Ann P 6F 121
Skiddaw Dr. SR6: Monk 6C 90
Skiddaw Pl. NE9: Gate 1B 98
Skinnerburn Rd. NE4: Newc T 1D 82
Skipper Cl. NE11: Gate 4D 82
Skippers Mdw. DH7: Ush M 6D 152
    (not continuous)
Skipsea Vw. SR2: Ryh 2D 132
    (not continuous)
Skipsey Ct. NE29: N Shi 4H 61
Skipton Cl. NE22: Bed 3F 9
    NE23: Cra 6C 16
Skipton Grn. NE9: Gate 3B 98
Skirlaw Cl. NE38: Wash 3B 114
Ski Vw. SR3: New S 2H 131
Skye Ct. SR3: New S 3A 132
Skye Gro. NE32: Jar 1A 88
Slaidburn Rd. DH9: Stly 2D 122
Slake Rd. NE32: Jar 1H 73
Slake Ter. NE34: S Shi 2D 74
Slaley NE38: Wash 6C 114
Slaley Cl. NE10: Gate 4A 86
Slaley Ct. NE22: Bed 4A 10
    SR3: New S 3A 132
Slater's Row DH3: Gt Lum 4G 135
    (not continuous)
Slatyford La. NE5: Newc T 1E 67
Sledmere Cl. SR8: Pet 5D 162
Sleekburn Av. NE22: Bed 2D 10
Slockburn Ho. NE22: Bed 2D 10
Sleetburn La. DH7: B'don 3F 159
Slingley Cl. SR7: S'hm 2E 141
Slingsby Gdns. NE7: Newc T 4D 58
Slipway, The NE10: Gate 1G 85
Sloane Ct. NE2: Newc T 2G 69 (1E 5)
Smailes La. NE39: Row G 3C 92
Smailes St. DH9: Stly 4C 122
SMALLBURN 2D 26
Smeaton Ct. NE28: W'snd 6F 61
Smeaton St. NE28: W'snd 6E 61
Smillie Cl. SR8: Pet 6D 162
Smillie Rd. SR8: Pet 4E 163
Smithburn Rd. NE10: Gate 4D 84
Smith Cl. DH6: Sher 6D 156
Smithfield DH1: Dur 5B 144
Smith Gro. SR2: Ryh 3E 133
Smith's Ter. DH5: Eas L 4D 148
Smith St. NE33: S Shi 1D 74
    SR2: Ryh 3F 133
Smith St. Sth. SR2: Ryh 3F 133
Smithyford NE9: Gate 4A 98
Smithy La. NE9: Gate, Kib 4G 97
    NE11: Kib 4G 97
Smithy Sq. NE23: Cra 3B 22
Smithy St. NE33: S Shi 4E 63
Smuggler's Cove 2F 49
Smyrna Pl. SR1: Sund 1E 119
Sniperley Gro. DH1: Dur 2H 153
Snipes Dene NE39: Row G 2E 93
Snowdon Ct. DH9: Ann P 6E 121

Snowdon Gdns. NE11: Gate 5C 82
Snowdon Gro. NE36: W Bol 4D 88
Snowdon Pl. SR8: Pet 2A 164
Snowdon Ter. SR2: Ryh 2F 133
Snowdrop Av. SR8: Pet 6F 163
Snowdrop Cl. NE21: Bla T 1G 79
Soane Gdns. NE34: S Shi 6F 75
Softley Pl. NE15: Newc T 2D 66
Solar Ho. SR1: Sund 4G 7
Solingen Est. NE24: Bly 2D 18
Solway Av. NE30: N Shi 3C 48
Solway Rd. NE31: Heb 6D 72
Solway Sq. SR3: Sund 4G 117
Solway St. NE6: Newc T 5C 70
Somerford NE9: Spri 3F 99
Somersby Dr. NE3: Ken 2A 56
Somerset Cotts. SR3: New S 6A 118
Somerset Gdns. NE28: W'snd . . .4G 59
Somerset Gro. NE29: N Shi 5H 47
Somerset Pl. NE4: Newc T 5D 68
Somerset Rd. NE31: Heb 6D 72
    SR3: Sund 4F 117
Somerset Sq. SR3: Sund 4F 117
Somerset St. SR3: New S 1A 132
Somerset Ter. NE36: E Bol 4F 89
Somerton NE3: Ken 1G 55
Somervyl Av. NE12: Longb 1H 57
Somervyl Ct. NE12: Longb 6H 43
Sophia SR7: S'hm 4B 142
Sophia St. SR7: S'hm 4D 142
Sophy St. SR5: S'wck 3C 104
Sorley St. SR4: Sund 1A 118
Sorrel Gdns. NE34: S Shi 6G 75
Sorrell Cl. NE4: Newc T 2H 67
Soulby Ct. NE3: Ken 5H 41
Sourmilk Hill La.
    NE9: Gate 5A 84
Souter Point Lighthouse 4F 77
Souter Rd. NE3: Gos 2C 56
Souter Vw. SR6: Whit 1F 91
South App. DH2: Ches S 6B 126
South Av. NE16: Whi 6F 81
    NE34: S Shi 4H 75
    NE37: Usw 5A 100
    NE40: Ryton 4C 64
South Railey DH1: Dur . . .1C 160 (5B 6)
South Bend NE3: Gos 4D 42
SOUTH BENTS 5F 91
Sth. Bents Av. SR6: Monk 5E 91
SOUTH BENWELL 5A 68
Sth. Benwell Rd.
    NE15: Newc T 5G 67
SOUTH BOLDON 4D 88
Southburn Cl. DH4: Hou S 3G 137
South Burns DH3: Ches S 5C 126
Sth. Burn Ter. DH4: Hou S 3G 129
South Cliff SR6: Monk 3F 105
Southcliff NE26: Whit B 1E 49
South Cl. DH5: Eas L 5F 149
    NE34: S Shi 4H 75
    NE40: Ryton 5C 64
    SR2: Ryh 3F 133
    (off Stockton Rd.)
Sth. Coronation St. SR7: Mur 3D 150
    (off George St.)
Southcote NE16: Whi 6E 81
Sth. Cramlington Ind. Est.
    NE23: Dud 1H 31
South Cres. DH1: Dur 4B 154
    DH4: Hou S 2D 136
    NE35: Bol C 3B 88
    NE38: Wash 1H 127

South Cres. SR7: S'hm 4C 142
SR8: Pet 4E 163
South Cft. NE12: Longb 6E 45
Southcroft NE38: Wash 6B 114
Sth. Cross St. NE3: Gos 2E 57
South Dene NE34: S Shi 4D 74
Southdowns DH2: Ches S 1C 134
South Dr. NE13: Sea B 3A 20
NE13: Wool 5E 41
NE31: Heb 5A 72
SR6: Cle 2H 89
Sth. Durham Ct. SR1: Sund 1E 119
Sth. East Vw. SR8: Pet 6H 163
Sth. Eldon St. NE33: S Shi 2D 74
South End DH6: H Pitt 2G 157
SR6: Cle 3G 89
Southend Av. NE24: Bly 1A 18
Southend Pde. NE31: Heb 1E 87
Southend Rd. NE9: Gate 1A 98
SR3: Sund 5G 117
Southend Ter. NE9: Gate 5B 84
Southern Prom.
NE26: Whit B 6E 37
Southern Rd. NE6: Walk 5F 71
Southern Way NE40: Ryton 5C 64
Southernwood NE9: Gate 4A 98
Southey St. NE33: S Shi 1E 75
(not continuous)
Southfield DH2: Pelt 2G 125
Southfield Gdns. NE16: Whi ...4G 81
Southfield Grn. NE16: Whi 5G 81
Southfield La.
NE17: Ham C, Ham M 5A 106
Southfield Rd. NE12: Longb 1C 58
NE16: Whi 5G 81
NE34: S Shi 1H 75
Southfields DH9: Stly 5C 122
NE23: Dud 4A 32
Southfields Ho. NE6: Newc T 3B 70
(off Heaton Rd.)
Southfield Ter. NE6: Walk 5G 71
NE16: Whi 5G 81
Southfield Way DH1: Dur 3A 154
Sth. Foreshore NE33: S Shi 5H 63
Southfork NE15: Lem 1A 66
Sth. Frederick St. NE33: S Shi ...2D 74
South Front NE2: Newc T 1G 69
Southgate NE12: Kil 3C 44
Southgate Ct. NE12: Longb 1H 57
SOUTH GOSFORTH 3G 57
South Gosforth Station (Metro)
................3G 57
South Gro. NE40: Ryton 5D 64
Sth. Harbour NE24: Bly 1E 19
SOUTH HETTON 6A 150
Sth. Hetton Ind. Est.
DH6: S Het 6A 150
Sth. Hetton Rd.
DH5: Eas L, S Het 5F 149
Sth. Hill Cres. SR2: Sund 2B 118
Sth. Hill Rd. NE8: Gate 2E 83
SOUTH HYLTON 1C 116
South Hylton Station (Metro) ...1D 116
Southill Rd. NE34: S Shi 3A 76
Southlands NE7: Newc T 5A 58
NE9: Spri 3C 98
(not continuous)
NE30: N Shi 5D 48
NE32: Jar 2H 87
SR2: Ryh 3F 133
South La. NE36: E Bol 4E 89
South Lea NE21: Bla T 2A 80

Sth. Leam Farm NE10: Gate 1G 99
South Leigh DH9: Tan L 6B 108
Southleigh NE26: Whit B 6D 36
Sth. Lodge Wood NE61: Hep 1A 8
Sth. Market St. DH5: Hett H 1D 148
Southmayne Rd. SR4: Sund 3F 117
Southmead Av. NE5: Newc T 6F 55
Sth. Mdws. DH9: Dip 1D 120
SOUTH MOOR 5B 122
Sth. Moor Rd. DH9: Stly 5C 122
Southmoor Rd. NE6: Walk 2F 71
Sth. Nelson Ind. Est.
NE23: Nel V 1G 21
Sth. Nelson Rd. NE23: Nel V 1G 21
SOUTH NEWSHAM 4B 18
South Newsham Nature Reserve
................4A 18
Sth. Newsham Rd.
NE24: News 4A 18
South Pde. NE10: Gate 1H 85
NE26: Whit B 6D 36
NE29: N Shi 5A 62
SOUTH PELAW 4B 126
Southport Pde. NE31: Heb 6E 73
Sth. Preston Gro. NE29: N Shi ...2C 62
Sth. Preston Ter. NE29: N Shi ...2C 62
(off Albion Rd. W.)
South Prom. NE33: S Shi 4H 63
Sth. Railway St. SR7: S'hm 4B 142
South Ridge NE3: Gos 5D 42
Sth. Riggs NE22: Bed 5H 9
South Rd. DH1: Dur 4B 160 (6B 6)
South Row NE8: Gate 5A 70
South Sherburn NE39: Row G 4D 92
SOUTH SHIELDS 4E 63
South Shields Bowls Cen. 6H 63
South Shields Station (Metro) ...4E 63
Sth. Shore Rd. NE8: Gate 6B 70
(Baltic Bus. Cen.)
NE8: Gate 5H 69 (6G 5)
(Hillgate, not continuous)
South Side SR8: Eas 2B 162
SOUTH STANLEY 5C 122
South St. DH1: Dur 6C 154 (4A 6)
DH2: Ches S 5B 126
DH4: Hou S 3E 137
(Blumer St.)
DH4: Hou S 6H 129
(Houghton Rd.)
DH4: W Rai 3E 147
DH5: W Rai 1G 147
DH6: Sher 6E 157
NE1: Newc T 5F 69 (6C 4)
NE3: Gos 2C 56
NE8: Gate 2H 83
(not continuous)
NE27: Shir 1D 46
NE31: Heb 2D 72
NE39: H Spen 1A 92
SR1: Sund 6C 104 (3F 7)
(not continuous)
Southstreet Banks
DH1: Dur 1C 160 (4A 6)
South Ter. DH1: Dur 2A 154
NE28: W'snd 5C 60
NE61: Hep 1A 8
SR5: S'wck 4B 104
SR7: Mur 3D 150
(off E. Coronation St.)
SR7: S'hm 4C 142
SR8: Pet 6F 163
South Thorn DH9: Stly 2D 122

Sth. Tyneside Crematorium
NE34: S Shi 6C 74
South Vw. DH1: Dur 5F 155
DH2: Beam 2C 124
DH2: Pelt 4E 125
(Newfield)
DH2: Pelt 2G 125
(Pelton)
DH2: Plaw 2A 144
DH3: Bir 3D 112
DH4: Hou S 3F 129
DH5: Eas L 5F 149
DH6: Sher 6H 157
DH7: B'don 6E 159
DH7: Ush M 4D 152
(Sth. View Ter.)
DH7: Ush M 5B 152
(Whitehouse La.)
DH9: Ann P 6G 121
DH9: Stly 6F 123
DH9: Tan L 5H 107
NE5: Newc T 1C 66
NE9: Spri 4F 99
NE13: Bru V 1C 42
NE13: Din 4E 29
NE22: E Sle 1F 11
NE23: Dud 2B 32
NE24: News 3A 18
NE32: Jar 3E 73
NE38: Wash 6C 114
NE39: H Spen 2A 92
NE40: Ryton 5A 64
SR4: Sund 2C 116
SR6: Monk 2D 104
SR6: Whit 6F 77
SR7: Mur 6F 141
SR7: Mur 2D 150
(off E. Coronation St.)
TS27: Cas E 6B 164
Sth. View E. NE39: Row G 3C 92
Sth. View Gdns. DH9: Ann P ...6G 121
Sth. View Pl. NE23: Cra 3B 22
Sth. View Rd. SR4: Sund 2C 116
Sth. View Ter. DH4: Hou S 3F 137
DH7: Ush M 4D 152
NE10: Gate 3D 84
NE16: Swa 3F 81
NE16: Whi 5F 81
Sth. View W. NE6: Newc T 3A 70
NE39: Row G 3B 92
Southward NE26: Sea S 4H 25
Southward Cl. NE26: Sea S 4H 25
Southward Way NE25: H'wll 2C 34
Southway NE9: Gate 5B 84
NE15: Lem 2C 66
SR8: Pet 2C 164
SOUTH WELLFIELD 1F 47
Sth. West Ind. Est. SR8: Pet ...1A 164
SOUTHWICK 3B 104
Southwick Goods Yd.
SR5: S'wck 4A 104
Southwick Ind. Est.
SR5: S'wck 3H 103
Southwick Rd. SR5: S'wck 3B 104
(not continuous)
Southwold Gdns. SR3: New S ...1H 131
(not continuous)
Southwold Pl. NE23: Cra 3G 21
3th. Woodbine St. NE33: S Shi ...5F 63
Southwood Cres.
NE39: Row G 3F 93
Southwood Gdns. NE3: Ken 3A 56

Sovereign Ct. NE2: Newc T 1H 69
NE4: Newc T 4C 68
Sovereign Ho. NE30: N Shi 6F 49
Sovereign Pl. NE4: Newc T 5C 68
Spalding Cl. NE7: Newc T 3C 58
Spanish City Bldgs.
NE26: Whit B 5C 36
Sparkwell Cl. DH4: Hou S 5H 129
Spartylea NE38: Wash 6D 114
Spa Well Cl. NE21: Bla T 3H 79
Spa Well Dr. SR5: C'twn 3E 103
Spa Well Rd. NE21: Bla T 5B 80
Speculation Pl. NE37: Usw 5B 100
Speedwell NE9: Gate 6C 84
Spelter Works Rd. SR2: Sund ..5F 119
Spen Burn NE39: H Spen 2A 92
Spencer Cl. DH9: Stly 3F 123
Spencer Ct. NE24: Cow 4H 11
Spencer Gro. NE16: Whi 3F 81
Spencer Ind. Est. DH3: Bir 3B 112
Spencer Rd. NE24: Cow 4H 11
Spencers Bank NE16: Swa 2E 81
Spencer St. NE6: Newc T 1C 70
NE29: N Shi 2C 62
NE31: Heb 2D 72
NE32: Jar 1F 73
Spencer Ter. NE15: Thro 6H 53
Spence Ter. NE29: N Shi 2B 62
Spenfield Rd. NE5: Newc T 4H 55
Spen La. NE39: H Spen 4A 78
(Rogues La.)
NE39: H Spen, Row G 1A 92
(Ashtree La.)
NE40: G'sde, H Spen 4A 78
Spen Rd. NE39: H Spen 6A 78
Spenser Wlk. NE34: S Shi 6C 74
Spen St. DH9: Stly 4C 122
Spinneyside Gdns. NE11: Dun ..4B 82
Spinney Ter. NE6: Walk 3F 71
Spinney, The NE7: Newc T 5B 58
NE12: Kil 3E 45
NE23: Dud 3C 32
NE38: Wash 5B 114
SR8: Eas 1A 162
Spire Hollin SR8: Pet 1C 164
Spire Rd. NE37: Wash 1D 114
Spires La. NE6: Newc T 3C 70
Spital Ter. NE3: Gos 2E 67
SPITAL TONGUES 2D 68
Split Crow Rd. NE8: Gate 3A 84
NE10: Gate 3A 84
Spohr Ter. NE33: S Shi 4F 63
Spoors Cotts. NE16: Whi 5E 81
Spoor St. NE11: Dun 2B 82
Sport Northumbria Cen.
...................3G 69 (2F 5)
Spout La. NE37: Usw 5B 100
NE37: Wash 6B 100
NE38: Wash 1B 114
Springbank Rd. NE2: Newc T ...2A 70
SR3: Sund 4F 117
Springbank Sq. SR3: Sund 4F 117
Spring Cl. DH9: Ann P 6G 121
Springfeld NE10: Gate 1F 99
Springfell DH3: Bir 4D 112
(not continuous)
Springfield NE20: N Shi 1C 62
Springfield Av. NE9: Spri 4C 98
Springfield Cres. SR7: S'hm ...5A 142
Springfield Gdns.
DH3: Ches S 4C 126
NE28: W'snd 3F 59

Springfield Gro. NE25: Whit B ...2A 48
Springfield Pk. DH1: Dur 4A 154
NE12: Longb 5D 44
Springfield Pl. NE9: Gate 5A 84
Springfield Rd. DH4: Hou S ...6H 129
NE5: Newc T 6G 55
NE21: Bla T 1A 80
Springfield Ter. DH2: Pelt 4G 125
NE10: Gate 4C 84
SR8: Eas 2F 163
Spring Gdn. Cl. SR1: Sund 6E 105
Spring Gdn. La.
NE4: Newc T 3D 68 (3A 4)
Spring Gdns. NE29: N Shi 2B 62
Spring Gdns. Ct. NE29: N Shi ..1C 62
Springhill Gdns. NE15: Newc T ..3H 67
Spring Pk. NE22: Bed 5A 10
Springs Health Club 5H 83
Springs, The DH3: Birt 4D 112
(not continuous)
Spring St. NE4: Newc T ...3D 68 (3A 4)
Springsyde Cl. NE16: Whi 6C 80
Spring Ter. NE29: N Shi 1C 62
Spring Ville NE22: E Sle 1F 11
SPRINGWELL
Gateshead 4F 99
Washington 4F 117
Springwell Av. DH1: Dur 4A 154
NE6: Walk 5E 71
NE9: Gate 2C 98
NE32: Jar 3G 73
Springwell Bldgs. SR8: Pet 6G 163
Springwell Cl. NE21: Bla T 2B 80
SPRINGWELL ESTATE 1E 99
Springwell La. NE9: Spri 2E 99
Springwell Rd. DH1: Dur 4A 154
NE9: Gate 2C 98
NE9: Spri 3F 99
NE32: Jar 4F 73
SR3: Sund 3F 117
SR4: Sund 4E 99
Springwell Ter. DH5: Hett H ...2C 148
NE9: Gate 2E 99
Springwood NE31: Heb 2A 72
Square Ho's. NE10: Gate 4B 84
Square, The NE16: Whi 4F 81
NE20: Wool 0A 28
Squires Bldg.
NE1: Newc T 2G 69 (1E 5)
Squires Gdns. NE10: Gate 4D 84
Stable La. NE3: Ken 5B 42
Stables, The DH4: E Her 2B 130
SR7: Sea 1A 140
Stack Gth. DH7: B'don 4E 159
Stadium Ind. Pk. NE10: Gate ...6B 70
Stadium of Light 5C 104 (1F 9)
Stadium of Light Station (Metro)
...................4D 104
Stadium Rd. NE10: Gate 6B 70
Stadium Vs. NE28: W'snd 5A 60
Stadium Way SR5: Monk 4C 104
Stadon Way DH4: Hou S 5G 129
Stafford Gro. SR2: Ryh 3E 133
SR5: S'wck 3B 104
Stafford La. SR6: Whit 3F 91
Stafford Pl. SR8: Pet 6B 162
Staffordshire Dr. DH1: Carr 4B 156
Stafford St. DH5: Hett H 1B 148
SR1: Sund 5F 105
Stafford Vs. NE9: Spri 4F 99
Stagshaw NE12: Kil 6C 32
Staindrop NE10: Gate 6G 85

Staindrop Rd. DH1: Dur 1D 154
Staindrop Ter. DH9: Ann P 5F 121
Staines Rd. NE6: Newc T, Walk ..5D 70
Stainmore Dr. DH3: Gt Lum ...4H 135
Stainton Dr. NE10: Gate 3D 84
Stainton Gdns. NE9: Gate 3C 98
Stainton Gro. SR6: Monk 6C 90
Stainton Way SR8: Pet 1C 164
Staithes Av. NE12: Longb 1C 58
Staithes Ho. NE38: Wash 4E 115
Staithes Rd. NE11: Dun 1C 82
NE38: Wash 4E 115
Staithes St. NE6: Walk 3H 71
Staith La. NE21: Bla T 5G 65
Stakeford Rd. NE22: Bed 2C 10
Stalks Rd. NE13: Wide O 5D 30
Stamford NE12: Kil 1D 44
Stamford Av. NE25: Sea D 1C 34
SR3: Sund 4H 117
Stamfordham Av. NE29: N Shi ...2H 61
Stamfordham Cl. NE8: W'snd ...5G 59
Stamfordham M. NE5: Newc T ...6H 55
Stamfordham Rd.
NE5: Cal, Cha P, Newc T 6E 39
NE15: Cal, Hed W, Pon, Thro
...................5A 38
Stamp Exchange NE1: Newc T ..6D 4
Stampley Cl. NE21: Bla T 3G 79
Stamps La. SR1: Sund 6F 105
Standerton Ter. DH9: Stly 6F 123
Standish St. DH9: Stly 4B 122
Stanelaw Way DH9: Tan L 6D 108
Staneway NE10: Gate 6E 85
Stanfield Bus. Cen.
SR2: Sund 2F 119
Stanfield Ct. NE7: Newc T 4E 59
Stanfield Gdns. NE10: Gate 3A 86
Stang Wlk. NE12: Longb 6C 44
Stanhope NE38: Wash 2F 113
Stanhope Chase SR8: Pet 4D 164
Stanhope Cl. DH1: Dur 6D 144
DH4: Hou S 4H 137
DH7: B'don 5E 159
Stanhope Gdns. DH9: Ann P ...5F 121
Stanhope Pde. NE33: S Shi 1F 75
Stanhope Rd. NE32: Jar 4H 73
NE33: S Shi 3D 74
SR6: Monk 1E 105
Stanhope St.
NE4: Newc T 3C 68 (3A 4)
NE33: S Shi 4F 63
Stanhope Way NE4: Newc T 3D 68
Stank La. DH1: Dur 4A 144
STANLEY 3C 122
Stanleyburn Ct. DH9: Ann P ...5H 121
Stanleyburn Vw. DH9: Ann P ...5H 121
Stanley By-Pass DH9: Stly 4B 122
Stanley Cl. DH6: Sher 6D 156
Stanley Ct. DH9: Stly 3E 123
Stanley Cres. NE26: Whit B 1D 48
(off Alma Pl.)
Stanley Gdns. NE9: Gate 3C 98
NE23: Seg 2F 33
Stanley Gro. NE7: Newc T 4A 58
NE22: Bed 4B 10
Stanley Indoor Bowling Cen. ...3C 122
Stanley St. DH5: Hou S 2A 138
NE4: Newc T 5B 68
NE8: Bly 5D 12
NE28: W'snd 4D 60
NE29: N Shi 2C 62
NE32: Jar 2G 73

Stanley St. NE34: S Shi 4D 74
SR5: C'twn 4D 102
SR7: S'hm 3H 141
Stanley St. W. NE29: N Shi 2C 62
Stanley Ter. DH3: Ches S 1D 134
DH4: Pen 3F 129
Stanmore Rd. NE6: Newc T 6C 58
Stannington Av. NE6: Newc T ...2B 70
Stannington Gdns. SR2: Sund ..5C 118
Stannington Gro. NE6: Newc T ..2B 70
SR2: Sund 4C 118
Stannington Pl. NE6: Newc T ...2C 70
NE20: Pon 3E 27
Stannington Rd. NE29: N Shi ...2G 61
Stannington Sta. Rd. NE61: Hep ..5A 8
Stannington St. NE24: Bly 6D 12
Stansfield St. SR6: Monk 4E 105
Stanstead Cl. SR5: C'twn 5C 102
Stanton Av. NE24: Bly 2H 17
NE34: S Shi 2G 75
Stanton Cl. NE10: Gate 4B 86
Stanton Gro. NE30: N Shi 4C 48
Stanton Rd. NE27: Shir 2C 46
NE30: N Shi 4B 48
Stanton St. NE4: Newc T 3C 68
Stanway Dr. NE7: Newc T 4A 58
Stanwick St. NE30: N Shi 5F 49
Stapeley Ct. NE3: Ken 2H 55
Stapeley Vw. NE3: Ken 2H 55
Stapleford Cl. NE5: Newc T 6F 55
Staple Rd. NE32: Jar 2G 73
Stapylton Dr. SR2: Sund 3B 118
Starbeck Av.
  NE2: Newc T 2H 69 (1H 5)
Starbeck M.
  NE2: Newc T 2H 69 (1G 5)
Stardale Av. NE24: Cow 1G 17
STARGATE 5D 64
Stargate Gdns. NE9: Gate 3C 98
Stargate Ind. Est. NE40: Ryton ..6D 64
Stargate La. NE21: Bla T, G'sde ..6C 65
NE40: Ryton 4E 65
Starlight Cres. NE25: Sea D ...6A 24
Starling Wlk. NE16: Sun 3G 95
Startforth Cl. DH3: Gt Lum ...4H 135
Stately Pk. DH5: Hett H 2D 148
Station App. DH1: Dur ...5B 154 (2A 6)
NE11: Gate 1F 97
NE12: Longb 1D 58
NE33: S Shi 4E 63
  (off Queen St.)
NE33: S Shi 4E 63
NE36: E Bol 3G 89
Station Av. DH5: Hett H 2C 148
DH7: B'don 5E 159
Station Av. Nth. DH4: Hou S ...2D 136
Station Av. Sth. DH4: Hou S ...2D 136
Station Bank DH1: Dur ...5C 154 (2A 6)
NE40: Ryton 3C 64
Station Cotts. DH9: Beam 1A 124
NE3: Ken 1B 56
NE12: Longb 1D 58
NE20: Pon 5E 27
NE23: Seg 2G 33
NE34: S Shi 3D 74
NE39: Ham M 1C 106
SR8: Pet 1H 165
Station Cres. SR7: S'hm 3H 141
Station Est. E. SR7: Mur 2A 150
Station Est. Nth. SR7: Mur 2A 150
  (not continuous)
Station Est. Sth. SR7: Mur 2A 150

Station Fld. Rd. DH9: Tan L ...6D 108
Station Ho's. DH2: Pelt 4G 125
Station La. DH1: Dur 5E 155
DH2: Bir 3B 112
DH2: Pelt 2F 125
DH3: Bir 3B 112
Station M. NE30: N Shi 6F 49
Station Rd. DH3: Ches S 6C 126
DH4: Hou S 2H 137
DH4: Leam, W Rai 3C 146
DH4: Pen 6C 114
DH5: Hett H 2C 148
DH6: H Pitt 1E 157
DH7: B'don 5E 159
DH7: Ush M 6B 152
DH9: Ann P 6F 121
DH9: Beam 1A 124
DH9: Stly 2D 122
NE3: Gos 2G 57
NE6: Walk 5G 71
NE9: Gate 6G 83
NE10: Gate 1H 85
  (Reay St.)
NE10: Gate 1H 85
  (South Pde.)
NE12: Kil 6B 32
NE12: Longb 5D 44
NE13: Wool 1F 55
NE15: Hed W 5H 51
NE15: Thro 2F 65
NE22: Bed 3C 10
NE23: Cra 2H 21
NE23: Dud 3H 31
NE23: Seg 2F 33
NE24: News 3A 18
NE25: Sea D 5G 23
NE26: Whit B 1D 48
NE27: Back 1A 46
NE28: W'snd 6E 61
  (Armstrong Rd.)
NE28: W'snd 4G 59
  (Queen's Cres.)
NE29: N Shi 3H 61
NE30: N Shi 2E 49
NE31: Heb 3B 72
NE33: S Shi 5E 63
NE35: Bol C 1A 88
NE36: E Bol 4F 89
NE38: Wash 2C 114
NE39: Row G 4E 93
SR2: Ryh 3G 133
SR6: Monk 1C 104
SR7: Mur 2A 150
SR7: S'hm 3F 141
SR8: Eas 1F 163
TS27: Hes 6G 165
Station Rd. Nth. DH5: Hett H ...2C 148
NE12: Longb 5D 44
NE28: W'snd 1F 59
SR7: Mur 2A 150
Station Rd. Sth. SR7: Mur 2A 150
Station Sq. NE26: Whit B 1D 48
Station St. NE22: Bed 2D 10
NE24: Bly 5C 12
NE32: Jar 2F 73
SR1: Sund 6D 104 (3G 7)
Station Ter. DH4: Hou S 2D 136
NE30: N Shi 6F 49
NE36: E Bol 4G 89
NE37: Usw 5C 100
Station Vw. DH2: Ches S 6C 126
DH5: Hett H 2C 148

Station Vs. DH9: Stly 1D 122
Staveley Rd. SR6: Monk 6C 90
SR8: Pet 1E 165
Stavordale St. SR7: S'hm 5B 142
  (not continuous)
Stavordale St. W. SR7: S'hm ..6B 142
Stavordale Ter. NE9: Gate 4A 84
Staward Av. NE25: Sea D 1B 34
Staward Ter. NE6: Walk 5F 71
Staynebrigg NE10: Gate 5F 85
Steadings, The DH1: Dur 2A 160
NE40: G'sde 2A 78
Steadlands Sq. NE22: Bed 4C 10
Stead La. NE22: Bed 4B 10
Stead St. NE28: W'snd 4E 61
Stedham Cl. NE37: Usw 3C 100
Steep Hill SR3: E Her 2E 131
STELLA 5G 65
Stella Bank NE21: Bla T 4F 65
Stella Cotts. NE21: Bla T 5G 65
Stella Gill Ind. Est. DH2: Pelt ..4H 125
Stella Hall Dr. NE21: Bla T 5G 65
Stella La. NE21: Bla T 5F 65
Stella Rd. NE21: Bla T 4G 65
Stephen Ct. NE32: Jar 3G 73
Stephenson Bldg. NE2: Newc T ...1C 4
  (off Stoddart St.)
NE2: Newc T 2H 5
Stephenson Cl. DH5: Hett H ...1C 148
Stephenson Ct. NE30: N Shi ...2D 62
  (off Stephenson St.)
Stephenson Ho. NE12: Kil 3C 44
Stephenson Ind. Est. NE12: Kil ..3C 44
NE37: Usw 3C 100
Stephenson Railway Mus. 6E 47
Stephenson Rd. NE7: Newc T ...6B 58
NE37: Usw 3B 100
SR8: Pet 4C 162
Stephenson's La.
  NE1: Newc T 5F 69 (6D 4)
Stephenson Sq. SR8: Eas 2C 162
Stephenson St. NE8: Gate 3F 83
NE28: W'snd 6E 61
NE30: N Shi 6F 49
  (Percy St.)
NE30: N Shi 1D 62
  (Suez St., not continuous)
SR7: Mur 2C 150
Stephenson Ter. NE10: Gate ...4D 84
NE15: Thro 6H 53
  (Blucher Colliery Rd.)
NE15: Thro 5C 52
  (Hexham Rd.)
Stephenson Trail, The
  NE12: Kil 4F 45
Stephenson Way NE21: Bla T ...3H 79
NE22: Bed 1A 10
Stephens Rd. SR7: Mur 2B 150
Stephen St. NE6: Newc T 3A 70
NE23: E Har 4B 16
NE24: Bly 5C 12
Stepney Bank
  NE1: Newc T 3A 70 (3H 5)
Stepney La.
  NE1: Newc T 4H 69 (4G 5)
Stepney Rd.
  NE2: Newc T 3H 69 (2H 5)
Sterling St. SR4: Sund 1A 118
Stevens Cl. NE5: Newc T 5B 54
Stevenson Rd. DH9: Stly 3E 123
Stevenson St. DH4: Hou S 3H 137
NE33: S Shi 6F 63

Steward Cres. NE34: S Shi 2B 76
Stewart Av. SR2: Ryh 3E 133
Stewart Dr. NE36: W Bol 4D 88
Stewartsfield NE39: Row G 3D 92
Stewart St. SR3: New S 2A 132
  SR4: Sund 2B 118
  SR7: S'hm 5C 142
  SR8: Eas 1D 162
Stewart St. E. SR7: S'hm 5C 142
Stileford NE10: Gate 4G 85
Stillington Cl. SR2: Ryh 4F 133
Stirling Av. NE32: Jar 5A 74
  NE39: Row G 4E 93
Stirling Cl. NE38: Wash 3E 115
Stirling Cotts. NE10: Gate 4C 84
Stirling Ct. NE11: Gate 3G 97
Stirling Dr. NE22: Bed 3C 10
  NE29: N Shi 5G 47
Stirling La. NE39: Row G 4E 93
Stobart St. SR5: Monk ...5C 104 (1F 7)
Stobb Ho. Vw. DH7: B'don 4E 158
Stock Bri. NE1: Newc T ...4G 69 (5F 5)
Stockdale Gdns. NE6: Walk 5G 71
  (off Rochester St.)
Stockfold NE38: Wash 5C 114
Stockholm Cl. NE29: N Shi 2F 61
Stockley Av. SR5: C'twn 3E 103
Stockley Ct. DH7: Ush M 6E 153
Stockley Rd. NE38: Wash 1D 114
Stocksfield Av. NE5: Newc T ...2G 67
Stocksfield Gdns. NE9: Gate 3A 98
Stockton Av. SR8: Pet 5F 163
Stockton Rd. DH1: Dur ...1D 160 (6C 6)
  NE29: N Shi 4B 62
  SR1: Sund 1C 118 (5F 7)
  SR2: Ryh 5F 133
  SR2: Sund 1C 118 (6G 7)
  SR7: Mur, S'hm, Sea 6F 133
  SR8: Eas 3A 162
  TS27: Cas E 6B 164
Stockton Rd. E. SR7: Eas 5H 151
Stockton Rd. W. SR7: Eas 5H 151
Stockton St. SR7: S'hm 3H 141
Stockton Ter. SR2: Sund 5F 119
Stockwell Grn. NE6: Walk 1F 71
Stoddart Ho.
  NE2: Newc T 3H 69 (2G 5)
Stoddart St.
  NE2: Newc T 3H 69 (2H 5)
  NE34: S Shi 3D 74
Stoker Av. NE34: S Shi 5B 74
Stoker Ter. NE39: H Spen 2A 92
Stokesley Gro. NE7: Newc T 4A 58
Stone Cellar Rd. NE37: Usw 3H 99
Stonechat Cl. NE38: Wash .....,4F 113
Stonechat Ml. NE21: Bla T 4G 65
Stonechat Pl. NE12: Longb 6A 44
Stonecroft Gdns. NE7: Newc T ..4D 58
Stonecrop NE9: Gate 6C 84
Stonefold Cl. NE5: Newc T 4D 54
Stonehaugh Way NE20: Pon 3B 38
Stonehills NE10: Gate 2H 85
Stoneleigh NE61: Hep 1A 8
Stoneleigh Av. NE12: Longb 1H 57
Stoneleigh Cl. DH4: Hou S 2G 137
Stoneleigh Pl. NE12: Longb 1A 58
Stone Row DH2: Pelt 4C 124
Stonesdale DH4: Pen 1C 128
Stone St. NE10: Gate 5C 84
Stonethwaite NE29: N Shi 4H 61
Stoney Bank NE28: W'snd 5C 60
Stoneycroft E. NE12: Kil 3E 45

Stoneycroft W. NE12: Kil 3E 45
STONEYGATE 5C 130
Stoneygate Cl. NE10: Gate 2E 85
Stoney Ga. Gdns. NE10: Gate ...2E 85
Stoneygate La. NE10: Gate 3E 85
Stoneyhurst Av. NE15: Newc T ..4F 67
Stoneyhurst Rd. NE3: Gos 3G 57
Stoneyhurst Rd. W. NE3: Gos ...3F 57
Stoney La. DH9: Beam 2C 124
  NE9: Spri 4F 99
  SR5: S'wck 4A 104
Stoneylea Rd. NE5: Newc T 1B 66
Stonycroft NE37: Wash 6A 100
STONY HEAP 6B 120
Stonyheap La. DH8: Con 6B 120
  DH9: Ann P 6B 120
Store Bldgs. NE35: Bol C 3A 88
Store St. NE15: Lem 3A 66
  NE21: Bla T 2H 79
Store Ter. DH5: Eas L 4D 148
Storey Cl. NE21: Bla T 5C 66
Storey I a. NE21: Bla T 5G 65
Storey St. NE23: Cra 4C 22
Stormont Grn. NE3: Ken 4B 56
Stormont St. NE29: N Shi 2C 62
Stotfold Cl. SR7: S'hm 3E 141
Stothard St. NE32: Jar 2G 73
Stotts Rd. NE6: Walk 1G 71
Stowell Sq.
  NE1: Newc T 4E 69 (5B 4)
Stowell St. NE1: Newc T ,..4F 69 (5B 4)
Stowell Ter. NE10: Gate 3E 85
Straker St. NE32: Jar 3H 73
Straker Ter. NE34: S Shi 4D 74
Strand, The SR3: E Her 1G 131
Strangford Av. DH2: Ches S ...2B 134
Strangford Rd. SR7: S'hm 4H 141
Strangways St. SR7: S'hm 5B 142
Stranton Ter. SR6: Monk 3D 104
Stratfield St. SR4: Sund 6G 103
Stratford Av. SR2: Sund 4E 119
  NE23: Cra 2G 21
Stratford Gdns. NE9: Gate 5H 83
Stratford Gro. NE6: Newc T 2A 70
Stratford Gro. Ter.
  NE6: Newc T 2A 70
Stratford Gro. W.
  NE6: Newc T 2A 70 (1H 5)
Stratford Rd. NE6: Newc T 2A 70
  (not continuous)
  NE38: Wash 4E 115
Stratford Vs. NE6: Newc T 2A 70
Strathearn Way NE3: Ken 1R 56
Strathmore DH3: Gt Lum 3G 135
Strathmore Av. NE39: Row G ...4E 93
Strathmore Cl. DH9: Stly 2F 123
Strathmore Cres. NE4: Newc T ..4A 68
  NE16: Burn 5B 94
Strathmore Rd. NE3: Gos 6E 43
  NE9: Gate 4B 84
  NE39: Row G 4D 92
  SR3: Sund 5G 117
Strathmore Sq. SR3: Sund 5G 117
Stratton Cl. SR2: Ryh ,...,...1G 133
Stratus Cl. SR3: New S 3A 132
Strawberry Gdns. NE28: W'snd ..3G 59
Strawberry La. DH1: H Shin ...5G 161
  (not continuous)
Strawberry Pl.
  NE1: Newc T 4E 69 (4B 4)

Strawberry Ter. NE13: Bru V ...1B 42
  NE23: Dud 6C 32
STREET GATE 2G 95
Streetgate Pk. NE16: Sun 2G 95
Street Ho's. NE20: Pon 1H 39
Stretford Ct. NE9: Gate 3A 98
Stretton Cl. DH4: Hou S 4E 137
Stretton Way NE27: Back 6A 34
Stridingedge NE37: Wash 1G 113
  (not continuous)
Stronsay Cl. SR2: Ryh 1E 133
Strothers Rd. NE39: H Spen 6A 78
Struan Ter. NE36: E Bol 4G 89
Struddars Farm Ct.
  NE21: Bla T 1D 80
Stuart Ct. NE3: Ken 1F 55
Stuart Gdns. NE15: Thro 5C 52
Stuart Ter. NE10: Gate 2D 84
Stubbs Av. NE16: Whi 3E 81
Studdon Wlk. NE3: Ken 2H 55
Studland Cl. NE29: N Shi 4B 48
Studley Gdns. NE9: Gate 6H 83
  NE25: Whit B 1C 48
Studley Ter. NE4: Newc T 2C 68
Studley Vs. NE12: Longb 6E 45
Sturdee Gdns. NE2: Gos 4G 57
Styan Av. NE26: Whit B 6D 36
Styford Gdns. NE15: Lem 2C 66
SUCCESS 5F 129
Success Rd. DH4: Hou S 5F 129
Sudbury Way NE23: Cra 2G 21
Suddick St. SR5: S'wck 4B 104
Suez Rd. NE30: N Shi 1D 62
Suffolk Gdns. NE28: W'snd 3C 60
  NE34: S Shi 2C 76
Suffolk Pl. DH3: Bir 6D 112
  NE8: Gate 5A 70
Suffolk Rd. NE31: Heb 6D 72
Suffolk St. DH5: Hett H 1B 148
  NE32: Jar 3F 73
  SR2: Sund 2E 119
Suffolk Wlk. SR8: Pet 5C 162
Suffolk Way DH1: Dur 5D 144
Sugley Cl. NE15: Lem 1C 66
Sugley Dr. NE15: Lem 3B 66
Sugley St. NE15: Lem 3B 66
  (not continuous)
Sugley Vs. NE15: Lem 3D 66
SULGRAVE 4C 100
Sulgrave Ind. Est. NE37: Usw ..4D 100
Sulgrave Rd. NE37: Usw 4D 100
Sullivan Wlk. NE31: Heb 4C 72
Summerfield DH9: Stly 3C 124
Summerfield Rd. NE9: Gate 4H 83
Summerhill NE4: Newc T 5C 68
  NE21: Bla T 6G 65
  NE32: Jar 2H 87
  SR1: Sund 1B 118
  SR3: E Her 2D 130
Summerhill Av. NE3: Gos 4F 43
Summerhill Gro.
  NE4: Newc T 4D 68 (5A 4)
Summerhill Rd. NE34: S Shi 2A 76
Summerhill St. NE4: Newc T ...4D 68
Summerhill Ter.
  NE4: Newc T 5E 69 (6A 4)
Summerhouse Farm
  DH5: W Rai 6H 137
Summerson St. DH5: Hett H ...1D 148
Summerson Way NE22: Bed 3D 10
Summers St. NE24: Bly 5C 12
Summer St. NE10: Gate 2D 84

Summerville DH1: Dur 6B **154**
Sunbury Av. NE2: Newc T 5G **57**
SUNDERLAND 1D **118** (4G **7**)
Sunderland AFC (Stadium of Light)
. . . . .5C **104** (1F **7**)
Sunderland Av. SR8: Pet 5F **163**
Sunderland Bowl & Ballroom
. . . . .4D **104**
Sunderland By-Pass
NE36: W Bol 5H **87**
SR3: E Her 1C **130**
SR4: Sund 1B **116**
SR5: Wash 2A **102**
SR7: Sea 1C **140**
Sunderland Crematorium
SR4: Sund 2G **117**
Sunderland Ent. Pk.
SR5: Sund 5E **103**
(Colima Av.)
SR5: Sund 4G **103**
(Wearfield)
Sunderland Highway NE9: Bir . . .1E **113**
NE37: Wash 1E **113**
SR5: Wash 1E **115**
Sunderland Marine Activities Cen.
. . . . .3F **105**
Sunderland Minster 4F **7**
Sunderland Mus. & Art Gallery
. . . . .1D **118** (4H **7**)
Sunderland Retail Pk.
SR6: Monk 4D **104**
Sunderland Rd. DH1: Dur 5F **155**
DH4: Hou S 6A **130**
NE8: Gate 1H **83**
NE10: Gate 6C **84**
(Green La.)
NE10: Gate 4H **85**
(Lingey La.)
NE33: S Shi 1G **75**
NE34: S Shi 1G **75**
NE36: E Bol, S'wck 4F **89**
SR5: S'wck 4F **89**
(East Boldon)
SR5: S'wck 3A **104**
(Southwick)
SR6: Cle, Whit 2B **90**
SR6: S Shi 4H **75**
SR7: Eas 6H **151**
SR8: Eas . . . . .6H **151** & 1B **162**
SR8: Pet 3F **163**
Sunderland Rd. Vs. NE10: Gate . . .3F **85**
Sunderland Station (Rail & Metro)
. . . . .1D **118** (4G **7**)
Sunderland St. DH4: Hou S 3A **138**
DH5: Hou S 2A **138**
NE1: Newc T 4E **69** (5A **4**)
(not continuous)
SR1: Sund 6E **105** (2H **7**)
Sunderland Technology Pk.
SR1: Sund 5E **7**
Sunderland Wall 5H **103**
Sunderland Yacht Club 4F **105**
Sundew Rd. NE9: Gate 1C **98**
NE10: Gate 6C **84**
Sundridge Dr. NE10: Gate 4A **86**
Sun Hill DH5: Hett H 2B **148**
Sunhill NE16: Sun 3F **95**
Sunholme Dr. NE28: W'snd 2G **59**
Sunlea Av. NE30: N Shi 2E **49**
Sunley Ho. NE3: Gos 2E **57**
Sunnidale NE16: Whi 6C **80**
Sunnilaws NE34: S Shi 6A **76**

Sunningdale NE25: Whit B 6G **35**
NE33: S Shi 6G **63**
Sunningdale Av. NE6: Walk 2G **71**
NE28: W'snd 5A **60**
Sunningdale Cl. NE10: Gate 4D **84**
Sunningdale Dr. NE37: Usw 3A **100**
Sunningdale Rd. SR3: Sund . . .4F **117**
Sunnirise NE34: S Shi 5A **76**
SUNNISIDE
Houghton-le-Spring 1G **137**
Newcastle upon Tyne 3F **95**
Sunniside NE29: N Shi 2H **61**
SR4: Sund 1C **116**
Sunniside Ct. NE16: Sun 2F **95**
Sunniside Dr. NE34: S Shi 5A **76**
Sunniside Gdns. NE9: Gate 3C **98**
NE15: Newc T 3F **67**
Sunniside Ladies Fitness Cen. *3H **7***
(off W. Sunniside)
Sunniside La. NE34: S Shi 1A **90**
SR6: Cle 2B **90**
Sunniside Rd. NE16: Sun, Whi . . .6F **81**
Sunniside Ter. SR6: Cle 1A **90**
Sunnybank Av. NE15: Newc T 4H **67**
Sunny Blunts SR8: Pet 3C **164**
Sunnybrow SR3: New S 1H **131**
Sunnycrest Av. NE6: Walk 3F **71**
Sunnygill Ter. NE40: G'sde 1A **78**
Sunnyside NE23: Cra 2A **22**
Sunny Ter. DH9: Dip 2C **120**
DH9: Stly 2C **122**
Sunnyway NE5: Newc T 5G **55**
Sunrise Ent. Pk. SR5: C'twn 5C **102**
Sunrise La. DH4: Hou S 2H **137**
Sun St. NE16: Sun 3F **95**
Sun Vw. Ter. SR6: Cle 2G **89**
Surrey Av. SR3: New S 3A **132**
Surrey Pl. DH4: Hou S 3G **129**
NE4: Newc T 4C **68**
Surrey Rd. NE29: N Shi 1H **61**
NE31: Heb 6D **72**
Surrey St. DH4: Hou S 3G **129**
DH5: Hett H 1B **148**
NE32: Jar 3E **73**
Surrey Ter. DH3: Bir 6C **112**
Surtees Dr. DH1: Dur 5A **154**
Surtees Rd. SR8: Pet 1D **164**
Surtees St. SR2: Sund 2F **119**
Surtees Ter. DH9: Stly 6H **123**
Sussex Ct. SR1: Sund 6E **105**
Sussex Gdns. NE28: W'snd 4C **60**
Sussex Pl. NE37: Usw 4B **100**
Sussex St. NE24: Bly 5D **12**
NE32: Jar 3E **73**
SR3: New S 1A **132**
Sutherland Av. NE4: Newc T 2A **68**
Sutherland Bldg. NE1: Newc T 2E **5**
Sutherland Ct. NE34: S Shi 1F **89**
Sutherland Grange
DH4: E Her 3H **129**
Sutherland Pl. DH1: Dur 6G **155**
Sutherland St. NE8: Gate 2H **83**
SR6: Monk 3D **104**
SR7: S'hm 3H **141**
Sutton Cl. DH4: Pen 3F **129**
Sutton Ct. NE28: W'snd 2F **59**
Sutton Dwellings NE4: Newc T . . .3D **68**
Sutton Est. NE4: Newc T 5A **68**
Sutton Est., The NE4: Newc T . . .3D **68**
Sutton St. DH1: Dur 6B **154**
NE6: Walk 1E **71**
Sutton Way NE34: S Shi 4B **76**

Swainby Cl. NE3: Gos 5F **43**
Swale Cres. DH3: Gt Lum 4H **135**
Swaledale NE28: W'snd 2F **59**
SR6: Monk 4F **91**
Swaledale Av. NE24: Cow 6G **11**
Swaledale Cl. DH5: Hett H 4A **148**
Swaledale Ct. NE24: Cow 6G **11**
Swaledale Cres. DH4: Pen 1E **129**
Swaledale Gdns. NE7: Newc T . . .4B **58**
SR4: Sund 2H **117**
Swallow Ct. NE12: Kil 1B **44**
Swallow Pond Nature Reserve
. . . . .6A **46**
Swallows, The NE28: W'snd 6C **46**
Swallow St. SR7: S'hm 3H **141**
(not continuous)
Swallow Tail Ct. NE34: S Shi 5D **74**
Swallow Tail Dr. NE11: Gate 4D **82**
SWALWELL 2E **81**
Swalwell Bank NE16: Swa 2E **81**
Swalwell Vis. Cen. 3D **80**
Swan Av. NE28: W'snd 4B **60**
Swan Cl. NE8: Dun 2C **82**
Swan Dr. NE11: Dun 2C **82**
Swan Ind. Est. NE38: Wash 4D **114**
Swan Rd. NE6: Walk 5H **71**
NE38: Wash 4D **114**
SR8: Pet 2A **164**
Swan St. DH9: Ann P 4E **121**
NE8: Gate 6H **69**
SR5: S'wck 4C **104**
Swanton Cl. NE5: Newc T 3F **55**
Swanway NE9: Gate 4B **84**
Swards Rd. NE10: Gate 4E **85**
Swarland Av. NE7: Newc T 2B **58**
Swarland Rd. NE25: Sea D 1B **34**
Swarth Cl. NE37: Wash 1G **113**
Sweetbriar Way NE24: News 3A **18**
Sweethope Av. NE24: Cow 5B **12**
Swiftdale Cl. NE22: Bed 4H **9**
Swiften Dr. SR4: Sund 3C **116**
Swinbourne Gdns.
NE26: Whit B 5B **36**
Swinbourne Ter. NE32: Jar 6F **73**
Swinburne Pl. DH3: Bir 4C **112**
NE4: Newc T 4E **69** (5A **4**)
NE8: Gate 6G **69**
Swinburne St. NE8: Gate 6G **69**
NE32: Jar 3A **74**
Swinburne Ter. DH9: Dip 2B **120**
Swinburn Rd. NE25: Sea D 1B **34**
Swindale Cl. NE21: Bla T 3A **80**
Swindale Dr. NE12: Kil 2C **44**
Swindon Rd. SR3: Sund 4F **117**
Swindon Sq. SR3: Sund 4G **117**
Swindon St. NE31: Heb 3B **72**
Swindon Ter. NE6: Newc T 6B **58**
Swinhoe Gdns. NE13: Wide O . . .4D **30**
Swinhope NE38: Wash 1G **127**
Swinley Gdns. NE15: Newc T 3D **66**
Swinside Dr. DH1: Carr 3A **156**
Swirle, The
NE1: Newc T 4H **69** (5H **5**)
Swirral Edge NE37: Wash 6A **100**
Swiss Cotts. NE38: Wash 6A **114**
Swordfish, The NE4: Newc T 6B **68**
Swyntoft NE10: Gate 4H **85**
Sycamore DH2: Ches S 4A **126**
Sycamore Av. NE13: Din 4G **29**
NE20: Pon 1D **38**
NE24: Bly 4B **12**
NE25: Whit B 1B **48**

Sycamore Av. NE34: S Shi 5H 75
  NE38: Wash 6H 113
Sycamore Cl. NE2: Newc T 5H 57
Sycamore Cotts. SR4: Sund 3E 117
Sycamore Ct. NE39: H Spen 6A 78
Sycamore Dr. SR5: S'wck 2B 104
  TS27: Hes 6F 165
Sycamore Gro. NE9: Spri 4F 99
  NE10: Gate 3E 85
Sycamore Pk. DH7: B'don 4D 158
Sycamore Pl. NE12: Kil 1C 44
Sycamore Rd. DH2: Plaw 2A 144
  NE21: Bla T 1A 80
  SR6: Whit 2F 91
Sycamore Sq. SR8: Eas 2C 162
Sycamores, The
  NE4: Newc T 6C 68
  NE16: Burn 2A 108
  SR2: Sund 4E 119
Sycamore St. NE15: Thro 4D 52
  NE28: W'snd 6A 60
Sycamore Ter. DH9: Ann P 5H 121
Sydenham Ter. NE33: S Shi 4F 63
  SR4: Sund 2A 118
Sydney Ct. NE8: Gate 6G 69
Sydney Gdns. NE34: S Shi 6B 74
Sydney Gro. NE28: W'snd 2G 59
Sydney St. DH2: Beam 2C 124
  DH4: Hou S 1C 136
Syke Rd. NE16: Burn 1F 107
Sylverton Gdns. NE33: S Shi . . .6H 63
Sylvia Ter. DH9: Stly 1D 122
Symington Gdns.
  SR3: New S 1H 131
Syon St. NE30: N Shi 5F 49
Syron NE16: Whi 5D 80
Syston Cl. DH4: Hou S 4F 137

T

Taberna Cl. NE15: Hed W 5G 51
Todcaster Rd. SR3: Sund 6E 117
Tadema Rd. NE33: S Shi 5H 63
Toibot Cl. NE38: Wash 3B 114
Talbot Cotts. DH3: Bir 3C 112
Talbot Grn. NE5: Newc T 1D 66
Talbot Pl. SR7: S'hm 4B 142
Talbot Rd. NE34: S Shi 3F 75
  SR6: Monk 2E 105
Talbot Ter. DH3: Bir 3C 112
Talgarth NE38: Wash 2F 115
Talisman Cl. DH6: Sher 6D 156
Talisman Vw. NE9: Gate 3A 98
Talloy Cl NE38: Wash 2A 114
Tamar Cl. NE29: N Shi 5G 47
  SR8: Pet 2C 164
Tamar Ct. SR3: New S 3H 131
Tamarisk Way NE9: Gate 6C 84
Tamar St. DH5: Eas L 5E 149
Tamerton Dr. DH3: Bir 5D 112
Tamerton St. SR4: Sund 1H 117
Tamworth Rd. NE4: Newc T 3C 68
Tamworth Sq. SR3: Sund 6E 117
Tanbark DH4: Hou S 3D 128
TANFIELD 4B 108
Tanfield Comprehensive School
  Sports Cen. 1B 122
Tanfield Gdns. NE34: S Shi 3B 76
TANFIELD LEA 1B 122
Tanfield Lea Nth. Ind. Est.
  DH9: Tan L 6B 108

Tanfield Lea Sth. Ind. Est.
  DH9: Tan L 6C 108
Tanfield Pl. NE9: Gate 3C 98
Tanfield Railway 5F 95
Tanfield Rd. NE9: Gate 3C 98
  NE15: Newc T 3E 67
  SR3: Sund 5F 117
Tanfield St. SR4: Sund 6G 103
Tangmere Cl. NE23: Cra 2C 22
TAN HILLS 1A 144
Tankerville Pl. NE2: Newc T 6G 57
Tankerville Ter. NE2: Newc T . . .1G 69
Tanmeads DH2: Plaw 1A 144
Tanners Bank NE30: N Shi 1E 63
Tanners Ct. NE1: Newc T 5B 4
                (off Friars St.)
Tantallon DH3: Bir 5D 112
               (not continuous)
Tantallon Ct. DH4: Hou S 2B 136
TANTOBIE 5H 107
Tantobie Rd. NE15: Newc T 3E 67
Tarlton Cres. NE10: Gate 3C 84
Tarn Cl. SR8: Pet 1E 165
Tarn Dr. SR2: Sund 1F 133
Tarragon Way NE34: S Shi 6G 75
Tarrington Cl. NE28: W'snd 2D 60
Tarset Pl. NE3: Ken 1C 56
Tarset Rd. NE25: Well 6F 35
Tarset St. NE1: Newc T 4A 70
Tasmania Rd. NE34: S Shi 6B 74
Tasman Rd. SR3: Sund 1E 131
Tate St. NE24: Bly 1J 23
Tatham St. SR1: Sund 1E 119 (4H 7)
Tatham St. Bk.
  SR1: Sund 1E 119 (4H 7)
Tattershall SR2: Sund 3B 118
Taunton Av. NE29: N Shi 4H 47
  NE32: Jar 4A 74
Taunton Cl. NE28: W'snd 2D 60
Taunton Pl. NE23: Cra 1B 22
Taunton Rd. SR3: Sund 6F 117
Taunton Sq. SR3: Sund 5F 117
Tavistock Ct. DH4: Hou S 6G 129
Tavistock Pl. NE32: Jar 4A 74
  SR1: Sund 1D 118 (4H 7)
Tavistock Rd. NE2: Newc T 5G 57
Tavistock Sq. SR3: New S 1A 132
Tavistock Wlk. NE23: Cra 1B 22
Taylor Av. DH7: Ush M 4D 152
  NE13: Wide O 5E 31
  NE39: Row G 4F 93
Taylor Gdns. NE10: Gate 2G 85
  NE26: Sea S 3H 25
  SR2: Sund 3L 119
Taylor's Bldgs. NE22: Bed 3D 10
Taylor St. DH9: Ann P 4E 121
  NE24: Cow 5G 11
  NE33: S Shi 1D 74
Taylor Ter. NE27: Shir 4B 46
  NE34: S Shi 5B 74
Taynton Gro. NE23: Seg 1F 33
Tay Rd. SR3: Sund 5E 117
Tay St. DH5: Eas L 5F 149
Teal Av. NE24: News 3D 18
Teal Cl. NE7: Longb 2C 58
  NE38: Wash 4F 113
TEAMS 3E 83
Team St. NE8: Dun, Gate 2C 82
Team Va. Vs. NE11: Gate 5D 82
TEAM VALLEY 2F 97
Team Valley Bus. Cen.
  NE11: Gate 5F 83

Team Valley Trad. Est.
  NE11: Gate 2F 97
              (Seventh Av.)
  NE11: Gate 5E 83
               (Third Av.)
Teasdale Ho. NE5: Newc T 2E 55
Teasdale St. SR2: Sund 2F 119
Teasdale Ter. DH1: Dur 5H 155
Tebay Dr. NE5: Newc T 1D 66
Tedco Bus. Cen. NE32: Jar 1D 72
Tedco Bus. Works
  NE33: S Shi 5E 63
Teddington Cl. NE3: Ken 6F 41
Teddington Rd. SR3: Sund 5E 117
Teddington Sq. SR3: Sund 5E 117
Tedham Rd. NE15: Lem 2A 66
Tees Cl. SR8: Pet 3C 164
Tees Ct. NE34: S Shi 3E 75
  SR3: New S 3H 131
Tees Cres. DH9: Stly 4D 122
Teesdale Av. DH4: Pen 1E 129
Teesdale Gdns. NE7: Newc T 4B 58
Teesdale Gro. NE12: Longb 5D 44
Teesdale Pl. NE24: Cow 5F 11
Teesdale Ter. DH9: Ann P 5G 121
Tees Rd. NE31: Heb 6C 72
Tees St. DH5: Eas L 5F 149
  SR7: S'hm 3B 142
  SR8: Pet 6C 163
Tees Ter. NE37: Usw 5B 100
Teign Cl. SR8: Pet 2C 164
Teikyo University of Japan in Durham
  .2C 160
Teindland Cl. NE4: Newc T 5A 68
Tel-el-Kebir Rd. SR2: Sund 3E 119
Telewest Arena Newcastle 6E 69
Telford Cl. DH1: H Shin 5H 161
  NE27: Back 6A 34
Telford Ct. NE28: W'snd 5G 61
Telford Rd. SR3: Sund 5F 117
Telford St. NE8: Gate 4F 83
  NE28: W'snd 5G 61
Temperance Ter. DH7: Ush M . . .5B 152
Tempest Rd. SR7: S'hm 4A 142
Tempest St. NE21: Bla T 5G 65
  SR3: New S 2A 132
Temple Av. NE24: Cow 5A 12
Temple Grn. NE8: Gate 3E 83
  NE34: S Shi 4G 75
Temple Park Leisure Cen. 5G 75
Temple Pk. Rd. NE33: S Shi 3E 75
  NE34: S Shi 3E 75
Temple St. NE1: Newc T . . .5E 69 (6B 4)
  NE10: Gate 2D 84
  NE33: S Shi 2D 74
Temple St. W. NE33: S Shi 2D 74
Temple Town NE33: S Shi 1D 74
Tenbury Cres. NE12: Longb 6C 44
  NE29: N Shi 4A 48
Tenby Rd. SR3: Sund 1E 131
Tenby Sq. NE23: Cra 1C 22
Ten Flds. DH5: Hett H 2B 148
Tennant St. NE31: Heb 4B 72
  NE34: S Shi 5C 74
Tennyson Av. NE31: Heb 3D 72
  NE35: Bol C 3D 88
Tennyson Cl. NE8: Gate 1A 84
Tennyson Cres. NE16: Swa 3E 81
Tennyson Gdns. DH9: Dip 2C 120
Tennyson Grn. NE3: Ken 4A 56
Tennyson Rd. DH2: Pelt 6G 125
  SR8: Eas 1D 162

Tennyson St. NE33: S Shi 5F **63**
SR5: S'wck 3A **104**
Tennyson Ter. NE29: N Shi 3C **62**
Tenter Gth. NE15: Thro 5C **52**
Tenter Ter. DH1: Dur 5C **154** (2A **6**)
Tenth Av. DH2: Ches S 6B **126**
NE6: Newc T 1C **70**
NE11: Gate 3F **97**
NE24: Bly 2B **18**
Tenth Av. W. NE11: Gate 3E **97**
Tenth St. SR8: Pet 6G **163**
Tern Cl. NE31: Heb 3D **18**
Terrace Pl. NE1: Newc T . . .3E **69** (3B **4**)
Terrace, The DH7: B'don 5F **159**
NE35: Bol C 2A **88**
NE36: E Bol 4F **89**
SR4: Sund 1C **116**
Terrier Cl. NE22: Bed 4C **10**
Territorial La.
DH1: Dur 6D **154** (3D **6**)
Tesla St. DH4: Hou S 5H **129**
Tetford Pl. NE12: Longb 6C **44**
Teviot NE38: Wash 6G **113**
Teviotdale Gdns. NE7: Newc T . . .4B **58**
Teviot St. DH5: Eas L 5E **149**
NE8: Gate 3A **84**
Teviot Way NE32: Jar 4E **73**
Tewkesbury NE12: Kil 1D **44**
Tewkesbury Rd. NE15: Lem 1A **66**
Thackeray Rd. SR3: Sund 5F **117**
Thackeray St. DH4: Hou S 3H **137**
Thames Av. NE32: Jar 6G **73**
Thames Cres. DH4: Hou S 3E **137**
DH9: Stly 5D **122**
Thames Gdns. NE28: W'snd 6H **59**
(not continuous)
Thames Rd. NE31: Heb 5D **72**
SR3: Sund 1E **131**
SR8: Pet 2C **164**
Thames St. DH5: Eas L 5E **149**
NE8: Gate 3A **84**
Thanet Rd. SR3: Sund 6F **117**
Tharsis Rd. NE31: Heb 4B **72**
Thatcher Cl. NE16: Whi 1E **95**
Theatre Pl. NE29: N Shi 2C **62**
Theatre Royal 4F **69** (4D **4**)
Thelma St. SR4: Sund 1B **118**
Theme Rd. SR3: Sund 1E **131**
Theresa Russell Ho.
NE6: Newc T 3C **70**
Theresa St. NE21: Bla T 6A **66**
(not continuous)
SR7: S'hm 6C **142**
(off Queen Alexandra Rd.)
Thetford NE38: Wash 3B **114**
Third Av. DH2: Ches S 6B **126**
(Bullion La.)
DH2: Ches S 2B **126**
(Drum Rd.)
NE6: Newc T 2C **70**
NE11: Gate 5E **83**
NE24: Bly 1B **18**
NE29: N Shi 2F **61**
Third St. DH9: Stly 6B **122**
NE28: W'snd 6B **60**
SR8: Pet 6G **163**
Thirkeld Pl. DH4: Pen 2E **129**
Thirlaway Ter. NE16: Sun 3G **95**
Thirlington Cl. NE5: Newc T 4F **55**
Thirlmere Cl. DH3: Bir 5E **113**
NE10: Gate 3G **85**
SR6: Cle 2A **90**

Thirlmere Av. DH2: Ches S 2B **134**
DH5: Eas L 5E **149**
NE30: N Shi 3C **48**
Thirlmere Cl. NE12: Kil 2F **45**
Thirlmere Ct. NE31: Heb 4D **72**
Thirlmere Cres. DH4: Hou S . . .3F **129**
NE21: Bla T 3H **79**
Thirlmere Rd. SR8: Pet 6E **163**
Thirlmere Way NE5: Newc T . . .6F **55**
NE24: Cow 4G **11**
Thirlmoor NE37: Wash 1G **113**
Thirlwell Gro. NE32: Jar 6E **73**
Thirlwell Rd. NE8: Gate 6A **70**
Thirsk Rd. SR3: Sund 5F **117**
Thirston Dr. NE23: Cra 3C **22**
Thirston Pl. NE29: N Shi 6H **47**
Thirston Way NE3: Ken 2H **55**
Thirteenth St. SR8: Pet 6F **163**
Thistle Av. NE40: Ryton 5A **64**
Thistle Ct. NE31: Heb 4B **72**
Thistlecroft DH5: Hou S 4A **138**
Thistledale SR2: Sund 2F **119**
Thistledon Av. NE16: Whi 5D **80**
Thistle Rd. DH7: B'don 5H **159**
SR3: Sund 6E **117**
Thistley Cl. NE6: Walk 1E **71**
Thistley Grn. NE10: Gate 2H **85**
Thomas Bell Ho. NE34: S Shi 5C **74**
Thomas Bewick Sq.
NE1: Newc T 5F **69** (6C **4**)
Thomas Dr. NE31: Heb 3B **72**
Thomas Ferguson Ct.
NE30: N Shi 1E **63**
Thomas Hawksley Pk.
SR3: Sund 4A **118**
Thomas Holiday Homes
NE22: Bed 2D **10**
(off Burnside)
Thomas Horsley Ho.
NE15: Newc T 4F **67**
Thomas St. DH3: Ches S 1C **134**
DH5: Hett H 6D **138**
(not continuous)
DH9: Ann P 5G **121**
DH9: Stly 6G **123**
(not continuous)
NE5: Newc T 5D **54**
NE9: Spri 4D **98**
NE16: Whi 4E **81**
NE33: S Shi 4E **63**
NE37: Usw 5D **100**
SR2: Ryh 3F **133**
SR8: Eas 1E **163**
Thomas St. Nth. SR6: Monk . . .5D **104**
Thomas St. Sth. SR2: Ryh 3F **133**
SR5: Sund 4A **104**
Thomas Taylor Cotts.
NE27: Back 6A **34**
Thompson Av. NE12: Kil 1C **44**
Thompson Cres. SR5: C'twn 4D **102**
Thompson Gdns. NE28: W'snd . . .5H **59**
Thompson Pl. NE10: Gate 3D **84**
Thompson Rd. SR5: S'wck 3B **104**
Thompson's Bldgs.
DH4: Hou S 4G **129**
Thompson St. NE22: Bed 2D **10**
NE24: Bly 4B **12**
SR8: Pet 6G **163**
Thompson Ter. SR2: Ryh 3G **133**
Thorburn St. SR6: Monk 1D **104**
Thoresby Ho. NE6: Walk 6E **71**
(off McCutcheon Ct.)

Thornbank Cl. SR3: New S 5A **132**
Thornbridge NE38: Wash 2E **115**
Thornbury Av. NE23: Seg 1G **33**
Thornbury Cl. NE3: Ken 2F **55**
NE35: Bol C 2A **88**
Thornbury Dr. NE25: Whit B 5G **35**
Thornbury St. SR4: Sund 6A **104**
Thorncliffe Pl. NE29: N Shi 2A **62**
Thorn Cl. NE13: Wide O 6C **30**
Thorndale Pl. NE24: Cow 5G **11**
Thorndale Rd. DH1: Carr 3B **156**
NE15: Newc T 4D **66**
SR3: Sund 6E **117**
Thorne Av. NE10: Gate 3H **85**
Thornebrake NE10: Gate 4G **85**
Thorne Rd. SR3: Sund 6E **117**
Thornes Cl. SR8: Pet 1F **165**
Thorne Sq. SR3: Sund 6E **117**
Thorne Ter. NE6: Walk 2E **71**
Thorneyburn Av. NE25: Well 6F **35**
Thorneyburn Cl. DH4: Hou S . . .1G **137**
Thorneyburn Way
NE24: Cow 5H **11**
THORNEY CLOSE 6F **117**
Thorney Cl. Rd. SR3: Sund 6F **117**
Thorneyfield Dr. NE12: Kil 3B **44**
Thorneyford Pl. NE20: Pon 4E **27**
Thorneyholme Ter. DH9: Stly 3D **122**
NE21: Bla T 6A **66**
Thornfield Gro. SR2: Sund 5E **119**
Thornfield Pl. NE39: Row G 2E **93**
Thornfield Rd. NE3: Gos 3D **56**
Thorngill NE37: Wash 1A **114**
Thornhaugh Av. NE16: Whi 6D **80**
Thornhill Cl. NE11: Gate 3C **82**
NE25: Sea D 1B **34**
Thornhill Cres.
SR2: Sund 1C **118** (5F **7**)
Thornhill Gdns. NE16: Burn 2F **107**
SR2: Sund 3C **118**
Thornhill Pk. NE20: Pon 4E **27**
SR2: Sund 2C **118**
Thornhill Reach SR7: S'hm 3H **141**
Thornhill Rd. NE12: Longb 1D **58**
NE20: Pon 4E **27**
Thornhill St. DH4: Hou S 3H **137**
Thornhill Ter.
SR2: Sund 2C **118** (6E **7**)
Thornholme Av. NE34: S Shi 3B **76**
Thornholme Rd.
SR2: Sund 3B **118** (6E **7**)
Thornhope Cl. NE38: Wash 1D **114**
Thornlea NE61: Hep 1A **8**
Thornlea Gdns. NE9: Gate 5H **83**
Thornleigh Gdns. SR6: Cle 1A **90**
Thornleigh Rd. NE2: Newc T 6G **57**
Thornley Av. NE10: Gate 5H **85**
NE23: Cra 3C **22**
Thornley Cl. DH7: Ush M 6D **152**
NE16: Whi 1E **95**
Thornley La.
NE21: Bla T, Row G 5G **79**
NE39: Row G 5G **79**
Thornley Rd. NE5: Newc T 1D **66**
Thornley Vw. NE39: Row G 3F **93**
Thornley Wood Country Pk. 5H **79**
Thornley Wood Country Pk. Vis. Cen.
. . . . .6H **79**
Thornton Av. NE33: S Shi 2D **74**
Thornton Cl. DH4: Pen 2F **129**
Thornton Cotts. NE40: Ryton 3C **64**
(off Northumberland Rd.)

Thornton Ct. NE1: Newc T 6B **4**
  NE38: Wash 2A **114**
Thornton Cres. NE21: Bla T 6A **66**
Thornton Lea DH2: Pelt 2F **125**
Thorntons Cl. DH2: Pelt 2F **125**
Thornton St.
  NE1: Newc T 5E **69** (6B **4**)
Thornton Ter. NE12: Longb 4G **45**
Thorntree Av. NE13: Sea B . . .2D **30**
Thorntree Cl. NE25: Whit B 1F **47**
Thorntree Cotts. NE13: Sea B . . .2D **30**
Thorntree Ct. NE12: Longb 5F **45**
Thorntree Dr. NE15: Newc T 3E **67**
  NE22: Bed 3H **9**
  NE25: Whit B 1F **47**
Thorntree Gill SR8: Pet 2G **165**
Thorntree M. SR1: Sund 1E **119**
  (off Up. Union St.)
  SR3: Sund 5E **117**
Thorntree Ter. DH9: Stly 2F **123**
Thorntree Wlk. NE32: Jar 1H **87**
Thorntree Way NE24: Cow 6F **11**
Thornwood Gdns. NE11: Gate . . .5D **82**
Thornyford Ho. NE4: Newc T 3D **68**
  (off Barrack Rd.)
Thornygarth NE10: Gate 4E **85**
Thoroton St. NE24: Bly 5C **12**
Thorp Cl. NE24: Bly 2H **17**
Thorp Cotts. NE40: Ryton 4A **64**
Thorp Dr. NE40: Ryton 4D **64**
Thorpe Cl. NE4: Newc T 3C **68**
Thorpe Cres. SR8: Pet 4F **163**
Thorpeness Rd. SR3: Sund 6E **117**
Thorpe Rd. SR8: Eas, Pet 2B **162**
Thorpe St. NE4: Newc T 3C **68**
  SR8: Eas 1E **163**
  SR8: Pet 6G **163**
Threap Gdns. NE28: W'snd 3C **60**
Three Mile Ct. NE3: Gos 5E **43**
Three Rivers Ct. NE36: W Bol . . .4C **88**
  (not continuous)
Threlkeld Gro. SR6: Monk 6C **90**
Thrift St. NE29: N Shi 3C **62**
Thristley Gdns. SR2: Sund 4C **118**
THROCKLEY 5D **52**
Throckley Ind. Est. NE15: Thro . . .4D **52**
Throckley Pond Nature Reserve
  . . . . .1B **64**
Throckley Way NE34: S Shi 3D **74**
Thropton Av. NE7: Newc T 2B **58**
  NE24: Bly 2A **18**
Thropton Cl. DH1: H Shin 4H **161**
  DH2: Ches S 2A **134**
  NE10: Gate 5A **86**
Thropton Ct. NE24: Bly 6A **12**
Thropton Cres. NE3: Gos 1D **56**
Thropton Pl. NE29: N Shi 6H **47**
Thropton Ter. NE7: Newc T 5B **58**
Thrunton Ct. DH5: Hou S 3B **138**
Thrush Cross Pl. DH1: Dur 4H **155**
Thrush Gro. SR5: C'twn 4E **103**
Thurleston DH4: Hou S 5G **129**
Thurlow Way DH5: Hou S 4H **137**
Thursby DH3: Bir 5E **113**
  (not continuous)
Thursby Av. NE30: N Shi 3D **48**
Thursby Gdns. NE9: Gate 2B **98**
Thurso Cl. SR3: Sund 6D **116**
Tiberius Ct. NE28: W'snd 6H **59**
Tiger Stairs NE29: N Shi 2D **62**
  (off Bedford St.)
Tilbeck Sq. SR3: New S 4B **132**

Tilbury Cl. DH4: Hou S 4G **129**
Tilbury Gdns. SR3: Sund 1E **131**
Tilbury Gro. NE30: N Shi 2C **48**
Tilbury Rd. SR3: Sund 1E **131**
Tileshed La. NE36: E Bol 2E **89**
Till Av. NE21: Bla T 1H **79**
Tilley Rd. NE38: Wash 2F **113**
Tillmouth Av.
  NE25: H'wll, Sea D 1B **34**
Tillmouth Gdns. NE4: Newc T . . .3G **67**
Tillmouth Pk. Rd. NE15: Thro . . .6D **52**
Till St. NE6: Newc T 5C **70**
Tilson Way NE3: Ken 1B **56**
Timber Beach Nature Reserve
  . . . . .4F **103**
Timber Beach Rd. SR5: Sund . . .4F **103**
Timber Rd. SR8: Pet 4G **163**
Times Sq. NE1: Newc T 5E **69** (6B **4**)
Timlin Gdns. NE28: W'snd 4F **61**
Timothy Duff Ct. NE30: N Shi . . .6G **49**
  (off Front St.)
Tindal Cl. NE4: Newc T 4D **68**
Tindale Av. DH1: Dur 2A **154**
  NE23: Cra 3C **22**
Tindale Dr. NE16: Whi 5E **81**
Tindal St. NE4: Newc T 4D **68**
Tinklers La. DH1: Dur 5D **154** (2D **6**)
Tinkler Ter. DH3: Gt Lum 2H **135**
Tinn St. NE8: Gate 2F **83**
Tintagel DH3: Gt Lum 3H **135**
Tintagel Cl. NE23: Cra 1B **22**
  SR3: Sund 6D **116**
Tintagel Dr. SR7: S'hm 3A **142**
Tintern NE38: Wash 4A **114**
Tintern Cl. DH4: Hou S 1G **137**
Tintern Cres. NE6: Newc T 2B **70**
  NE29: N Shi 5H **47**
Tintern St. SR4: Sund 1B **118**
Tiree Cl. DH7: B'don 4E **159**
Tiree Cl. SR3: New S 3A **132**
Tirril Pl. NE5: Newc T 6E **55**
Titan Ho. NE6: Walk 3G **71**
Titan Rd. NE6: Walk 3G **71**
Titchfield Rd. NE38: Wash 3A **114**
Titian Av. NE34: S Shi 1E **89**
Titlington Gro. NE31: Heb 6B **72**
Tiverton Av. NE4: Newc T 4A **68**
  NE29: N Shi 4G **47**
Tiverton Cl. DH4: Hou S 5H **129**
  NE28: W'snd 2D **60**
Tiverton Gdns. NE9: Gate 2H **97**
Tiverton Pl. NE23: Cra 1B **22**
Tiverton Sq. SR3: Sund 6E **117**
Tivoli Bldgs. DH4: Hou S 3G **129**
Toberty Gdns. NE10: Gate 3H **85**
Todd's Nook NE4: Newc T 4D **68**
Toft Cres. SR7: Mur 1C **150**
Togstone Pl. NE5: Newc T 6G **55**
Toll Bar Rd. SR2: Sund 6D **118**
Toll Bri. Rd. NE21: Bla T 6D **66**
Tollerton Dr. SR5: C'twn 5B **102**
Tollgate Bungs. DH9: Ann P 4E **121**
Tollgate Flds. DH4: W Rain 4D **146**
Tollgate Rd. NE39: Ham M 2A **106**
Tollgate Ter. DH9: Ann P 4E **121**
Toll Ho. Rd. DH1: Dur 5H **153**
Tolls Cl. NE25: Whit B 6G **35**
Toll Sq. NE30: N Shi 1E **63**
Tomlinson Ct. SR6: Monk 6C **90**
Tom Urwin Ho. SR3: New S 2A **132**
  (off Silksworth Ter.)

Tonbridge Av. NE29: N Shi 2A **62**
Toner Av. NE31: Heb 6B **72**
Topaz St. SR7: S'hm 4G **141**
Topcliff SR6: Monk 5E **105**
Topcliffe Grn. NE9: Gate 3B **98**
Top Gear Indoor Karting 5A **156**
Toppings St. NE35: Bol C 2A **88**
Torcross Way NE23: Cra 1B **22**
Tor Mere Cl. NE37: Wash 1G **113**
Toronto Rd. SR3: Sund 5F **117**
Toronto Sq. SR3: Sund 5F **117**
Torquay Gdns. NE9: Gate 2H **97**
Torquay Pde. NE31: Heb 6E **73**
Torquay Rd. SR3: Sund 5F **117**
Torrens Rd. SR3: Sund 5F **117**
Torrington Cl. DH4: Hou S 5G **129**
Torver Cl. NE13: Wide O 6D **30**
  SR8: Pet 1E **165**
Torver Cres. SR6: Monk 6C **90**
Torver Pl. NE9: Gate 1B **98**
Torver Way NE30: N Shi 3B **48**
Tosson Cl. NE22: Bed 4B **10**
Tosson Pl. NE29: N Shi 2H **61**
Tosson Ter. NE6: Newc T 6C **58**
Totnes Cl. SR3: Sund 6D **116**
Totnes Dr. NE23: Cra 1B **22**
Tourist Info. Cen.
  Durham 5C **154** (2B **6**)
  Gateshead 3H **83**
  Jarrow 2H **73**
  Newcastle International Airport
  . . . . .2B **40**
  Newcastle Station . . .5F **69** (6C **4**)
  Newcastle upon Tyne
  . . . . .4F **69** (4D **4**)
  Royal Quays Outlet Shopping
  . . . . .5A **62**
  South Shields 4E **63**
  (Fowler St.)
  South Shields 4H **63**
  (Sea Rd.)
  Sunderland 1D **118** (4G **7**)
  Whitley Bay 5C **36**
Toward Rd. SR1: Sund . .1D **118** (4H **7**)
  SR2: Sund 2E **119** (6H **7**)
Tower Ct. DH5: Eas L 4E **149**
  NE11: Dun 2C **82**
Tower Gdns. NE40: Ryton 4C **64**
Tower Ho. NE1: Newc T 4H **69** (5G **5**)
Tower Pl. SR2: Sund 2E **119**
Tower Rd. NE37: Wash 6C **100**
Towers Av. NE2: Newc T 4G **57**
Towers Cl. NE22: Bed 5A **10**
Towers Pl. NE34: S Shi 4A **74**
Towers, The SR4: Sund 1D **116**
Tower St. NE1: Newc T 4G **69** (4F **5**)
  SR2: Sund 2F **119**
  SR8: Eas 1F **163**
Tower St. W. SR2: Sund 3E **119**
Tower Vw. NE15: Newc T 3G **67**
TOWN CENTRE 2A **114**
Town Cen. NE23: Cra 3A **22**
Towne Ga. NE15: Hed W 5G **51**
Towneley Ct. DH9: Stly 4C **122**
Towneley Flds. NE39: Row G 3F **93**
Towneley St. DH9: Stly 3C **122**
Townend Ct. NE34: S Shi 4E **75**
TOWN END FARM 1C **102**
Townfield Gdns. NE15: Thro 1F **65**
Towngate Bus. Cen.
  DH7: B'don 4G **159**
Townley Cotts. NE40: Ryton 5A **64**

Townley Rd. NE39: Row G 3D 92
TOWN MOOR 1D 68
Townsend Rd. SR3: Sund 1E 131
Townsend Sq. SR3: Sund 1E 131
Town Sq. NE28: W'snd 5H 59
Townsville Av. NE25: Whit B 2H 47
Towton NE12: Kil 1D 44
Toynbee NE38: Wash 2E 115
Tracey Av. NE36: W Bol 3D 88
Trafalgar Ho. NE30: N Shi 6F 49
Trafalgar Rd. NE37: Usw 4C 100
Trafalgar Sq. SR1: Sund 6F 105
Trafalgar St.
　　NE1: Newc T 4G 69 (4F 5)
Trafford NE9: Gate 3A 98
Trafford Rd. SR5: S'wck 4A 104
Trafford Wlk. NE5: Newc T 4C 54
Trajan Av. NE33: S Shi 3F 63
Trajan St. NE33: S Shi 3F 63
Trajan Wlk. NE15: Hed W 5F 51
Transbritannia Ct.
　　NE21: Bla T 5C 66
Tranwell Cl. NE3: Ken 5B 42
Tranwell Dr. NE25: Sea D 1C 34
Travers St. DH4: Hou S 3G 129
Treasury Mus. & Monks Dormitory
　　..............6C 154 (4B 6)
Treby St. SR4: Sund 6A 104
　　(not continuous)
Tredegar Cl. NE5: Newc T 3F 55
Treecone Cl. SR3: New S 4A 132
Tree Cl. SR3: New S 3H 131
Treen Cres. SR7: Mur 2D 150
Tree Top M. NE28: W'snd 2B 60
Trefoil Rd. DH9: Tan L 1B 122
Tregoney Av. SR7: Mur 1D 150
Treherne Rd. NE2: Gos 4F 57
Trent Av. NE31: Heb 6C 72
Trent Cres. DH3: Gt Lum 3H 135
Trent Dr. NE32: Jar 1G 87
Trent Gdns. NE8: Gate 3B 84
Trentham Av. NE7: Newc T 2B 58
Trenton Av. NE38: Wash 1B 114
Trent Rd. SR3: Sund 6E 117
Trent St. DH5: Eas L 5E 149
Trevarren Dr. SR2: Ryh 2F 133
Trevelyan Av. NE22: Bed 4B 10
　　NE24: Bly 1A 18
Trevelyan Cl. SR3: Sund 6D 116
Trevelyan Dr. NE5: Newc T 2E 55
Trevelyan Pl. SR8: Pet 2B 164
Trevethick St. NE8: Gate 3F 83
Trevone Pl. NE23: Seg 1G 33
Trevone Sq. SR7: Mur 2D 150
Trevor Gro. SR6: Cle 3A 90
Trevor Ter. NE30: N Shi 6C 48
Trewhitt Rd. NE6: Newc T 1C 70
Trewitt Rd. NE26: Whit B 1D 48
Tribune Pl. NE9: Gate 5B 84
Trident Rd. SR3: New S 2A 132
Trimdon Gro. NE9: Gate 2D 98
Trimdon St. SR4: Sund 6B 104
Trimdon St. W. SR4: Sund 5B 104
Trinity Bldg. NE1: Newc T 2E 5
Trinity Bldgs. NE30: N Shi 2E 63
Trinity Chare
　　NE1: Newc T 5G 69 (6F 5)
Trinity Cl. NE29: N Shi 3C 62
Trinity Ct. NE8: Gate 6H 69
　　NE29: N Shi 2C 62
　　(not continuous)
Trinity Courtyard NE6: Newc T 5D 70

Trinity Gro. NE23: Seg 1G 33
Trinity Maritime Cen. 5F 5
Trinity Pk. DH4: Hou S 4F 129
Trinity Pl. NE29: N Shi 3C 62
Trinity Sq. NE8: Gate 6H 69
　　(not continuous)
　　SR1: Sund 6E 105
Trinity St. NE29: N Shi 3C 62
　　SR5: S'wck 3H 103
Trinity Ter. NE29: N Shi 3C 62
Trinity Wlk. NE33: S Shi 6D 62
Trojan Av. NE6: Walk 2E 71
Tromso Cl. NE29: N Shi 2G 61
Trool Ct. SR3: New S 4A 132
Troon Cl. NE37: Usw 3A 100
Trotter Gro. NE22: Bed 4C 10
Trotter Ter. SR2: Ryh 3F 133
Troutbeck Av. NE6: Walk 4F 71
Troutbeck Gdns. NE9: Gate 2A 98
Troutbeck Rd. SR6: Monk 6C 90
Troutbeck Way NE34: S Shi 6C 74
　　SR8: Pet 6E 163
Troutdale Pl. NE12: Longb 1H 57
Trout's La. DH1: Dur 1F 153
Troves Cl. NE4: Newc T 5A 68
Trowbridge Way NE3: Ken 2B 56
Trowsdale St. DH9: Ann P 4E 121
Truro Av. SR7: Mur 1D 150
Truro Gro. NE29: N Shi 5H 47
Truro Rd. SR3: Sund 6F 117
Truro Way NE32: Jar 3G 87
Tuart St. DH3: Ches S 6C 126
Tudor Av. NE29: N Shi 1A 62
Tudor Ct. NE20: Pon 1C 38
Tudor Dr. DH9: Tan L 4B 108
Tudor Grange SR8: Eas 2A 162
Tudor Gro. SR3: Sund 4H 117
Tudor Rd. DH3: Ches S 4D 126
　　NE33: S Shi 5D 62
Tudor Wlk. NE3: Ken 2G 55
　　(Brunton La.)
　　NE3: Ken 6G 41
　　(Hersham Cl.)
　　NE3: Ken 1G 55
　　(Petherton Ct.)
Tudor Way NE3: Ken 1F 55
Tudor Wynd NE6: Newc T 5D 58
Tulip Cl. NE21: Bla T 1H 79
Tulip Ct. DH4: Pen 1F 129
Tulip St. NE10: Gate 2C 84
Tummel Ct. SR3: New S 3A 132
Tumulus Av. NE6: Walk 1G 71
Tunbridge Rd. SR3: Sund 5F 117
Tundry Way NE21: Bla T 5D 66
Tunis Rd. SR3: Sund 5F 117
TUNSTALL 2B 132
Tunstall Av. NE6: Walk 4C 118
Tunstall Av. NE6: Walk 3D 70
　　(not continuous)
Tunstall Bank SR2: Ryh 2C 132
　　SR3: New S 2C 132
Tunstall Hill Cl. SR2: Sund 5C 118
TUNSTALL HILLS 5B 118
Tunstall Hope Rd.
　　SR3: New S 6C 118
Tunstall Pk. SR2: Sund 3C 118
Tunstall Rd. SR2: Sund ...1C 118 (6F 7)
　　SR3: Sund 5B 118
Tunstall Ter. SR2: Ryh 2D 132
　　SR2: Sund 1C 118 (5F 7)
　　SR3: New S 2A 132

Tunstall Ter. W.
　　SR2: Sund 1C 118 (5E 7)
Tunstall Va. SR2: Sund 3C 118
Tunstall Vw. SR3: New S 1B 132
Tunstall Village Grn.
　　SR3: New S 2C 132
Tunstall Village Rd.
　　SR3: New S 2B 132
Tunstall Vs. SR3: New S 2B 132
Turbinia Gdns. NE7: Newc T ...5C 58
Turfside NE10: Gate 4G 85
　　(not continuous)
　　NE32: Jar 2H 87
Turnberry DH2: Ous 5H 111
　　NE25: Whit B 6G 35
　　NE33: S Shi 6G 63
Turnberry Cl. NE37: Usw 3A 100
Turnberry Ct. NE10: Gate 4H 85
Turnberry Way NE3: Gos 2G 57
　　NE23: Cra 3C 22
Turnbull Cl. DH1: Dur 5G 155
Turnbull Cres. SR7: Mur 2C 150
Turnbull St. SR1: Sund 5F 105
Turner Av. NE34: S Shi 6F 75
Turner Cl. NE40: Ryton 5D 64
Turner Cres. NE3: Gos 2C 56
Turner St. NE27: Shir 4C 46
Turnham Rd. SR3: Sund 6E 117
Turn Pk. DH3: Ches S 6C 126
Turnstile M. SR6: Monk 3E 105
Turnstone Dr. NE38: Wash 4F 113
Turret Rd. NE15: Newc T 1D 66
Tuscan Cl. DH7: New B 2A 158
Tuscan Rd. SR3: Sund 6E 117
Tuthill Stairs
　　NE1: Newc T 5F 69 (6D 4)
Tweed Cl. DH2: Ous 1H 125
　　SR2: Sund 1F 133
　　SR8: Pet 2C 164
Tweed Dr. NE61: Hep 4A 8
Tweed Gro. NE15: Lem 2A 66
Tweedmouth Ct. NE3: Gos 3G 57
Tweed St. DH5: Eas L 5E 149
　　NE4: Newc T 4B 68
　　NE8: Gate 2A 84
　　NE31: Heb 3B 72
　　NE32: Jar 4E 73
　　NE38: Wash 3D 114
Tweed Ter. DH9: Stly 4D 122
Tweedy's Bldgs. NE40: Ryton ...4B 64
Tweedy St. NE24: Cow 5G 11
Tweedy Ter. NE6: Walk 4F 71
Twelfth Av. DH2: Ches S 5B 126
　　NE24: Bly 1B 18
Twelfth St. SR8: Pet 6F 163
Twentieth Av. NE24: Bly 2A 18
Twentyfifth Av. NE24: Bly 2B 18
Twentysecond Av. NE24: Bly 2A 18
Twentysixth Av. NE24: Bly 2A 18
Twentythird Av. NE24: Bly 2A 18
Twickenham Ct. NE23: Seg 1F 33
Twickenham Rd. SR3: Sund ...5E 117
Twizell Av. NE21: Bla T 1H 79
Twizell La. DH9: Stly 4B 124
Twizell Pl. NE20: Pon 4E 27
Twizell St. NE24: Bly 1D 18
Two Ball Lonnen
　　NE4: Newc T 2G 67
Twyford Cl. NE23: Cra 1B 22
Tyldesley Sq. SR3: Sund 6E 117
Tyndal Gdns. NE11: Dun 2B 82
Tyne App. NE32: Jar 1E 73

Tynebank NE21: Bla T 1H 79
Tyne Bri. NE1: Newc T . . .5G 69 (6E 5)
NE8: Gate 5G 69 (6F 5)
Tyne Bri. Twr. NE8: Gate 5G 69
(off Church St.)
Tynedale Av. NE26: Whit B 5B 36
NE28: W'snd 3H 59
Tynedale Ct. NE28: W'snd 3E 61
Tynedale Cres. DH4: Pen 2F 129
Tynedale Dr. NE24: Cow 5F 11
Tynedale Ho. NE15: Newc T 4F 67
Tynedale Rd. NE34: S Shi 1G 75
SR3: Sund 6E 117
Tynedale St. DH5: Hett H 4A 148
Tynedale Ter. DH9: Ann P 5G 121
NE12: Longb 1D 58
TYNE DOCK 2D 74
Tyne Dock Station (Metro) 3D 74
Tyne Gdns. NE37: Usw 4B 100
NE40: Ryton 5E 65
Tynegate Pct. NE8: Gate 1H 83
Tyne Ho. SR3: New S 3H 131
Tynell Wlk. NE3: Ken 2F 55
Tyne Main Rd. NE10: Gate 6C 70
TYNEMOUTH 6F 49
Tynemouth Castle 6G 49
Tynemouth Cl. NE6: Newc T 3B 70
Tynemouth Ct. NE6: Newc T 2C 70
(off Elvet Cl.)
NE29: N Shi 1B 62
Tynemouth Crematorium
NE29: N Shi 6B 48
Tynemouth Pl. NE30: N Shi 6F 49
Tynemouth Pool 5B 48
Tynemouth Priory (remains of)
. . . . .6G 49
Tynemouth Priory Theatre 5F 49
Tynemouth Rd. NE6: Newc T 2B 70
(not continuous)
NE28: W'snd 5D 60
NE30: N Shi 1D 62
NE32: Jar 1F 87
Tynemouth Sq. SR3: Sund 6F 117
Tynemouth Squash Rackets Club
. . . . .6H 47
Tynemouth Station (Metro) 6F 49
Tynemouth Ter. NE30: N Shi 6F 49
Tynemouth Volunteer Life Brigade Mus.
. . . . .6G 49
Tynemouth Way NE6: Newc T . . .2C 70
Tynepoint Ind. Est. NE32: Jar . . .4A 74
Tyne Rd. DH9: Stly 4C 122
Tyne Rd. E. DH9: Stly 4D 122
NE8: Gate 1E 83
Tyneside Cinema 4F 69 (4D 4)
Tyneside Retail Pk.
NE28: W'snd 1E 61
Tyneside Rd. NE4: Newc T 6D 68
Tyneside Works NE32: Jar 1F 73
Tyne St. DH5: Eas L 5E 149
NE1: Newc T 4A 70
NE10: Gate 1E 85
NE21: Bla T 5A 66
(Blaydon)
NE21: Bla T 2H 79
(Winlaton)
NE30: N Shi 2D 62
NE31: Heb 2B 72
NE32: Jar 1F 73
SR7: S'hm 4B 142
Tyne Ter. NE34: S Shi 4E 75
SR8: Eas 1D 162

Tyne Tunnel NE32: Jar, W'snd 1G 73
Tyne Tunnel Trad. Est.
NE29: N Shi 3F 61
(Narvik Way)
NE29: N Shi 2F 61
(Tromso Cl.)
Tynevale Av. NE21: Bla T 2A 80
Tynevale Ter. NE8: Gate 2E 83
NE15: Lem 3A 66
(not continuous)
Tyne Vw. NE15: Lem 3A 66
NE16: Whi 3G 81
NE21: Bla T 2A 80
NE31: Heb 3A 72
Tyne Vw. Gdns. NE10: Gate 2F 85
Tyneview Pk. NE12: Newc T 2D 58
Tyne Vw. Pl. NE8: Gate 2E 83
Tyne Vw. Ter. NE28: W'snd 6G 61
Tyne Wlk. NE15: Thro 6D 52
Tynewold Cl. NE8: Gate 2E 83
Tyzack Cres. SR6: Monk 3D 104

U

UCI Cinema
Derwenthaugh 1H 81
UCI Silverlink Cinema 1E 61
Uldale Ct. NE3: Ken 6H 41
Ullerdale Cl. DH1: Carr 3C 156
Ullswater Av. DH5: Eas L 5F 149
NE32: Jar . . . . .GH 73
Ullswater Cl. NE24: Cow 5E 11
Ullswater Cres. NE21: Bla T 3H 79
Ullswater Dr. NE12: Kil 2F 45
Ullswater Gdns. NE34: S Shi 2F 75
Ullswater Gro. SR5: Monk 1C 104
Ullswater Rd. DH2: Ches S 2B 134
Ullswater Ter. DH6: S Het 5G 149
Ullswater Way NE5: Newc T 6F 55
Ulverstone Ter. NE6: Walk 2E 71
Ulverston Gdns. NE9: Gate 1B 98
Underhill Rd. NE9: Gate 5A 84
Underhill Rd. SR6: Cle 3H 89
Underhill Ter. NE9: Spri 4G 99
Underwood NE10: Gate 5G 85
Underwood Gro. NE23: Cra 6A 16
Unicorn Ho. NE30: N Shi 1D 62
Union Alley NE33: S Shi 4E 63
Union Ct. DH3: Ches S 1C 134
Union Hall Rd. NE15: Lem 3A 66
Union La. DH2: Ches S 4B 134
SR1: Sund 6E 105
Union Pl. DH1: Dur 6C 6
Union Quay NE30: N Shi 2E 63
Union Rd. NE6: Newc T 3C 70
NE6: Walk 3C 70
NE30: N Shi 1E 63
Union Stairs NE30: N Shi 2D 62
Union St. DH5: Hett H 1C 148
NE2: Newc T 3H 69 (3H 5)
(not continuous)
NE24: Bly 5C 12
NE28: W'snd 1H 71
NE30: N Shi 2D 62
NE32: Jar 1F 73
NE33: S Shi 3D 74
SR1: Sund 6D 104 (3G 7)
SR4: Sund 1C 116
SR7: S'hm 5B 142
Unity Ter. DH9: Ann P 5H 121
DH9: Dip 2E 121

Unity Ter. DH9: Tan L 5H 107
NE24: Camb 1B 12
University Gallery 3G 69 (2E 5)
University of Durham
Botanic Gardens 3C 160
Graham Sports Cen., The
. . . . .2F 161
Hatfield College 6D 154 (4C 6)
Palace Green 6C 154 (3B 6)
St Chad's College . . .1C 160 (5B 6)
St John's College . . .1C 160 (5B 6)
Trevelyan College 2C 160
University of Newcastle upon Tyne
Botanical Grounds 1C 68
Queen Victoria Road
. . . . .2F 69 (1C 4)
University of Northumbria at Newcastle
City Campus 2G 69 (1E 5)
Coach Lane Campus 3C 58
University of Sunderland
City Campus 1C 118 (4E 7)
University Station (Metro)
. . . . .1C 118 (5E 7)
Uplands NE25: Whit B 6H 35
Uplands, The DH3: Bir 2D 112
NE3: Ken 3B 56
Uplands Way NE9: Spri 3F 99
Up. Camden St. NE30: N Shi 1C 62
Up. Chare SR8: Pet 1D 164
Up. Crone St. NE27: Shir 1D 46
Up. Elsdon St. NE29: N Shi 3C 62
Up. Nile St. SR1: Sund 1E 119
Up. Norfolk St. NE30: N Shi 1D 62
Up. Pearson St. NE30: N Shi 1D 62
Up. Penman St. NE29: N Shi 3C 62
Up. Queen St. NE30: N Shi 1D 62
Up. Sans St. SR1: Sund 6E 105
Up. Yoden Way SR8: Pet 1D 164
Upton St. NE8: Gate 2D 82
Urban Gdns. NE37: Wash 6B 100
Urfa Ter. NE33: S Shi 3F 63
URPETH 5G 111
Urpeth Ter. DH2: Beam 2C 124
NE6: Newc T 4C 70
(off St Peter's Rd.)
Urpoth Vs. DH9: Dean 2B 124
Urswick Ct. NE3: Ken 2F 55
Urwin St. DH5: Hett H 2D 148
USHAW MOOR 5C 152
Ushaw Rd. NE31: Heb 3D 72
Ushaw Ter. DH7: Ush M 5B 152
Ushaw Vs. DH7: Ush M 5B 152
(not continuous)
Usher Av. DH6: Sher 5D 156
Usher St. SR5: S'wck 4B 104
Usk Av. NE32: Jar 6G 73
Uswater Sta. Rd. NE37: Usw 5C 100
(not continuous)
USWORTH 4A 100
Usworth Hall NE37: Usw 3C 100
Uxbridge Ter. NE10: Gate 2D 84

V

Valebrooke SR2: Sund 2C 118
(off Tunstall Rd.)
Valebrooke Av. SR2: Sund 2C 118
Valebrooke Gdns. SR2: Sund 2C 118
Valehead NE25: Whit B 6H 35
Vale Ho. NE2: Newc T 1A 70
Valentia Av. NE6: Walk 2E 71

Valeria Cl. NE28: W'snd 1B **60**
Valerian Av. NE15: Hed W 5H **51**
Valeshead Ho. NE28: W'snd 5H **59**
Valeside DH1: Dur 5B **154**
  NE15: Thro 5C **52**
          (not continuous)
Vale St. DH5: Eas L 5D **148**
  SR4: Sund 2B **118**
Vale St. E. SR4: Sund 2B **118**
Valley Ct. SR2: Sund 2E **119**
Valley Cres. NE21: Bla T 1G **79**
Valley Dr. NE9: Gate 4H **83**
  NE11: Dun 4B **82**
  NE16: Swa 3E **81**
Valley Forge NE38: Wash 1B **114**
Valley Gdns. NE9: Gate 4A **84**
  NE25: Whit B 6H **35**
  NE28: W'snd 4B **60**
          (not continuous)
Valley La. NE34: S Shi 3C **76**
Valley Rd. DH2: Pelt 5G **125**
  NE25: H'wll 1D **34**
Valley Shop. Village
  NE11: Gate 6E **83**
Valley Vw. DH3: Bir 1B **112**
  DH5: Hett H 4H **147**
  DH7: Ush M 6D **152**
  DH9: Ann P 4F **121**
  DH9: Stly 5C **122**
  NE2: Newc T 6H **57**
  NE15: Lem 2H **65**
  NE16: Burn 6F **93**
  NE32: Jar 5F **73**
  NE38: Wash 6C **114**
  NE39: Row G 3C **92**
Vallum Ct. NE4: Newc T 4D **68**
Vallum Pl. NE9: Gate 5B **84**
Vallum Rd. NE6: Walk 3E **71**
  NE15: Thro 5D **52**
Vallum Way NE4: Newc T 4D **68**
Vanburgh Ct. NE25: Sea D 1B **34**
Vance Bus. Pk. NE11: Gate 3D **82**
Vance Ct. NE21: Bla T 5C **66**
Vancouver Dr. NE7: Newc T 5D **58**
Vane St. SR3: New S 2A **132**
          (not continuous)
Vane Ter. SR2: Sund 2F **119**
  SR7: S'hm 3B **142**
Vane Vs. DH1: Dur 6H **155**
Vanguard Ct. SR3: New S 3H **131**
          (not continuous)
Vanmildert Cl. SR8: Pet 3B **164**
Vardy Ter. DH4: E Her 3A **130**
Vauxhall Rd. NE6: Walk 1G **71**
Vedra St. SR5: S'wck 4B **104**
Velville Ct. NE3: Ken 1F **55**
Ventnor Av. NE4: Newc T 4B **68**
Ventnor Cres. NE9: Gate 6G **83**
Ventnor Gdns. NE9: Gate 5G **83**
  NE26: Whit B 5C **36**
Verdun Av. NE31: Heb 3C **72**
Vermont NE37: Usw, Wash 5B **100**
Verne Rd. NE29: N Shi 2G **61**
Vernon Cl. NE33: S Shi 1D **74**
Vernon Dr. NE25: Whit B 1A **48**
Vernon St. NE37: Usw 5B **100**
Veryan Gdns. SR3: Sund 4B **118**
Vespasian Av. NE33: S Shi 3F **63**
Vespasian St. NE33: S Shi 3F **63**
Viador DH3: Ches S 5C **126**

Viaduct St. NE28: W'snd 5C **60**
Vicarage Av. NE34: S Shi 3G **75**
Vicarage Cl. DH2: Pelt 2G **125**
  SR3: New S 2H **131**
Vicarage Ct. NE10: Gate 3F **85**
Vicarage Flats DH7: B'don 5D **158**
Vicarage Gdns. NE22: Bed 5A **10**
Vicarage La. SR4: Sund 1C **116**
Vicarage Rd. SR3: New S 2A **132**
Vicarage St. NE29: N Shi 2C **62**
Vicarage Ter. NE22: Bed 5A **10**
  SR7: Mur 3C **150**
Vicarsholme Cl. SR3: New S 4G **131**
Vicars La. NE7: Longb 2A **58**
Viceroy St. SR7: S'hm 4B **142**
Victoria Av. DH7: B'don 5E **159**
  NE10: Gate 3C **84**
  NE12: Longb 6D **44**
  NE26: Whit B 6D **36**
  NE28: W'snd 5H **59**
  SR2: Sund 5E **119**
  SR4: Sund 1D **116**
Victoria Av. W. SR2: Sund 5E **119**
Victoria Bldgs. SR1: Sund 4E **7**
Victoria Cotts. DH1: Dur 1A **154**
Victoria Ct. DH7: Ush M 5C **152**
  NE8: Gate 2E **83**
  NE12: Longb 4C **44**
  NE25: Sea D 6B **24**
  NE30: N Shi 2E **49**
  NE31: Heb 4B **72**
  SR2: Sund 5E **7**
Victoria Cres. NE29: N Shi 2B **62**
  NE30: N Shi 2E **49**
          (Beverley Ter.)
  NE30: N Shi 1E **49**
          (Eskdale Ter.)
Victoria Ho. NE4: Newc T 6D **68**
  NE8: Gate 2E **83**
Victoria Ind. Est. NE31: Heb 6A **72**
Victoria M. NE2: Newc T 1A **70**
  NE24: Bly 6B **12**
  NE26: Whit B 6D **36**
Victoria Parkway NE7: Newc T . . .4E **59**
Victoria Pl. DH3: Ches S 1C **134**
  NE25: Whit B 1A **48**
  NE37: Usw 5B **100**
  SR1: Sund 1E **119** (5H **7**)
  SR4: Sund 1B **118**
Victoria Rd. NE8: Gate 3E **83**
  NE33: S Shi 6E **63**
  NE37: Usw 5B **100**
Victoria Rd. E. NE31: Heb 4C **72**
Victoria Rd. W. NE31: Heb 1A **86**
Victoria Sq.
  NE2: Newc T 2G **69** (1E **5**)
  NE10: Gate 3D **84**
Victoria St. DH5: Hett H 1C **148**
  NE4: Newc T 5D **68**
  NE11: Dun 2C **82**
  NE29: N Shi 3C **62**
  NE31: Heb 2A **72**
  SR7: S'hm 4A **142**
Victoria Ter. DH1: Dur 5B **154**
  DH2: Beam 2C **124**
  DH2: Pelt 3E **125**
          (Parade, The)
  DH2: Pelt 4G **125**
          (Wesley Ter.)
  DH4: Pen 2G **129**
  DH9: Ann P 5F **121**
  NE9: Gate 2C **98**

Victoria Ter. NE9: Spri 4F **99**
  NE10: Gate 3D **84**
  NE15: Thro 5D **52**
  NE22: Bed 4B **10**
          (not continuous)
  NE26: Whit B 6D **36**
  NE32: Jar 3E **73**
  NE36: E Bol 4E **89**
  NE39: Row G 4C **92**
  SR7: Mur 3D **150**
Victoria Ter. Bk. NE15: Thro 5D **52**
Victoria Ter. Sth. SR5: S'wck 4D **104**
          (off Warwick St.)
Victoria Vs. NE22: Bed 4B **10**
Victor St. DH3: Ches S 6C **126**
  SR6: Monk 4E **105**
       (off Brandling St. Sth.)
Victor Ter. DH7: Ush M 4D **152**
Victory Cotts. NE23: Dud 2A **32**
Victory Ho. NE30: N Shi 6F **49**
Victory St. SR4: Sund 5G **103**
Victory St. E. DH5: Hett H 1D **148**
Victory St. W. DH5: Hett H 1D **148**
Victory Way SR3: E Her 4E **131**
Viewforth Dr. SR5: S'wck 2C **104**
Viewforth Grn. NE5: Newc T 6G **55**
Viewforth Rd. SR2: Ryh 4F **133**
Viewforth Ter. SR5: S'wck 2B **104**
          (not continuous)
Viewforth Vs. DH1: Dur 5H **153**
View La. DH9: Stly 2D **122**
View Tops DH9: Beam 1B **124**
VIGO 5E **113**
Vigodale DH3: Bir 6E **113**
Vigo La. DH3: Bir, Ches S 1C **126**
  DH3: Ches S 6E **113**
  NE38: Wash 1F **127**
Vigour Gym 6G **69**
Viking Ind. Est. NE32: Jar 1D **72**
Viking Pct. NE32: Jar 2F **73**
Viking Shop. Cen., The
  NE32: Jar 2F **73**
Villa Cl. SR4: Sund 1H **117**
Village Ct. NE26: Whit B 6B **36**
Village E. NE40: Ryton 3C **64**
Village Farm NE15: Thro 6G **53**
Village Hgts. NE8: Gate 1F **83**
Village La. NE38: Wash 1A **114**
Village Pl. NE6: Newc T 4C **70**
Village Rd. NE23: Cra 3C **22**
VILLAGE, THE 6D **164**
Village, The SR2: Ryh 3G **133**
Village W. NE40: Ryton 3C **64**
Villa Pl. NE8: Gate 2G **83**
Villas, The DH9: Ann P 6E **121**
  NE13: Wide O 6E **31**
  SR2: Ryh 4F **133**
  SR5: C'twn 4E **103**
Villa Vw. NE9: Gate 5A **84**
Villette Brooke St.
  SR2: Sund 3E **119**
Villette Path SR2: Sund 3E **119**
Villette Rd. SR2: Sund 3E **119**
Villettes, The DH4: Hou S 6H **129**
Villiers Pl. DH3: Ches S 5C **126**
Villiers St. SR1: Sund . . .6E **105** (3H **7**)
Villiers St. Sth. SR1: Sund 1E **119**
Vimy Av. NE31: Heb 3C **72**
Vincent St. SR7: S'hm 5B **142**
  SR8: Eas 1E **163**
Vincent Ter. DH9: Ann P 6G **121**
Vine Cl. NE8: Gate 1E **83**

Vine La. NE1: Newc T 3F 69 (2D 4)
Vine La. E. NE1: Newc T . .3G 69 (2E 5)
Vine Pl. DH4: Hou S 3A 138
SR1: Sund 1C 118 (5F 7)
Vine St. NE28: W'snd 6A 60
NE33: S Shi 3D 74
Viola Cres. DH2: Ous 5H 111
Viola St. NE37: Usw 5B 100
Viola Ter. NE16: Whi 4F 81
Violet Cl. NE4: Newc T 5H 67
Violet St. DH4: Hou S 3H 137
SR4: Sund 6B 104
(Deptford Rd.)
SR4: Sund 1C 116
(Primrose St.)
Violet Ter. DH4: Hou S 6B 128
Viscount Rd. SR3: New S 2A 132
Vivian Cres. DH2: Ches S 1C 134
Vivian Sq. SR6: Monk 2D 104
Voltage Ter. DH4: Hou S 5H 129
Vue Cinemas 3G 69 (3F 5)
Vulcan Pl. NE22: Bed 5A 10
SR6: Monk 4D 104
Vulcan Ter. NE12: Longb 4E 45

W

Waddington St. DH1: Dur 5B 154
Wadham Cl. SR8: Pet 2B 164
Wadham Ct. SR2: Ryh 2E 133
Wadham Ter. NE34: S Shi 4D 74
Wadsley Sq. SR2: Sund 4E 119
Wagon Way NE20: W'snd 5B 60
Wagonway Ind. Est. NE31: Heb . .1C 72
Wagonway Rd. NE31: Heb 2B 72
Wagtail Cl. NE21: Bla T 3A 80
Wagtail La. DH9: Stly 6G 123
Wakefield Av. NE34: S Shi 4B 76
Wakenshaw Rd. DH1: Dur 4F 155
WALBOTTLE 6F 53
Walbottle Hall Gdns.
NE15: Thro 6C 53
Walbottle Rd. NE15: Thro 6F 53
Walden Cl. DH2: Ous 5F 111
Waldo St. NE29: N Shi 2D 62
Waldridge Cl. NE37: Wash 1G 113
Waldridge Gdns. NE9: Gate 2D 98
Waldridge La. DH2: Ches S, Plaw
. . . . .6H 125 & 4A 134
Waldridge Rd. DH2: Ches S . . .1A 134
Waldron Sq. SR2: Sund 4E 119
WALKER 4G 71
Walkerburn NE23: Cra 6B 22
Walker Ct. NE16: Whi 4E 81
(off Fellside Rd.)
Walkerdene Ho. NE0: Walk 1H 71
WALKERGATE 1E 71
Walkergate DH1: Dur 2B 6
Walker Ga. Ind. Est.
NE6: Walk 3H 71
Walkergate Station (Metro) 1E 71
Walker Gro. NE6: Walk 1F 71
Walker Pk. Cl. NE6: Walk 5G 71
Walker Pk. Gdns. NE6: Walk 5G 71
Walker Pl. NE30: N Shi 1E 71
WALKER RIVERSIDE 5H 71
Walker Riverside Ind. Pk.
NE6: Walk 4H 71
Walker Rd. NE6: Newc T 4B 70
NE6: Walk 5D 70
Walker Swimming Pool 4G 71

Walker Ter. NE8: Gate 1G 83
Walker Vw. NE10: Gate 3D 84
WALKERVILLE 6G 59
Wallace Av. NE16: Whi 3G 81
Wallace Gdns. NE9: Gate 2E 99
Wallace St. DH4: Hou S 3H 137
NE2: Newc T 2D 68
NE11: Dun 2C 82
SR5: S'wck 4C 104
Wallace Ter. NE25: Sea D 6C 24
(off Astley Rd.)
NE40: Ryton 4C 64
Wallaw Cinema 6C 12
Wall Cl. NE3: Gos 2C 56
Waller Ter. DH5: Hou S 4A 138
(not continuous)
Wallflower Av. SR8: Pet 6F 163
Wallinfen NE10: Gate 4E 85
Wallingford Av. SR2: Sund 5E 119
NE30: N Shi 4C 48
Wallington Cl. NE22: Bed 3C 10
Wallington Ct. NE3: Ken 6H 41
NE12: Kil 2C 44
NE25: Sea D 6B 24
NE30: N Shi 4D 48
Wallington Dr. NE15: Lem 1C 66
Wallington Gro. NE33: S Shi 4F 63
Wallis St. DH4: Pen 1F 129
NE10: Gate 3D 84
NE33: S Shi 4E 63
Wallridge Dr. NE25: H'wll 1C 34
WALLSEND 6H 59
Wallsend Rd. NE29: N Shi 4G 61
(not continuous)
Wallsend Sports Cen. 5F 59
Wallsend Station (Metro) 6A 60
Wall St. NE3: Gos 2C 56
Wall Ter. NE6: Walk 2E 71
Walmer Ter. NE9: Spri 4D 98
Walnut Gdns. NE8: Gate 3E 83
Walnut Pl. NF3: Ken 4B 56
Walpole Cl. SR7: S'hm 5F 141
Walpole Ct. SR4: Sund 1H 117
Walpole St. NE6: Walk 1E 71
NE33: S Shi 6D 62
Walsham Cl. NE24: Bly 2H 17
Walsh Av. NE31: Heb 2C 72
Walsingham NE38: Wash 4A 114
Walter Dr. NE13: Bru V 5C 30
NE32: Jar 1F 73
Walter Ter. DH5: Eas L 4D 148
NE4: Newc T 3C 68
Walter Thomas St.
SR5: S'wck 3H 103
Waltham NE38: Wash 3B 114
Waltham Cl. NE28: W'snd 4F 59
Waltham Pl. NE5: Newc T 5F 55
Walton Av. NE24: Cow 5A 12
NE29: N Shi 6B 48
SR7: S'hm 5F 141
Walton Cl. DH9: Stly 4E 123
Walton La. SR1: Sund 6E 105
Walton Pk. NE29: N Shi 5B 48
Walton Rd. NE5: Newc T 6E 55
NE38: Wash 1E 115
Walton's Bldgs. DH7: Ush M 5B 152
Walton's Ter. DH7: New B 1B 158
Walwick Av. NE29: N Shi 1H 61
Walwick Rd. NE25: Well 6F 35
Walworth Av. NE34: S Shi 3C 76
Walworth Gro. NE32: Jar 6F 73

Walworth Way
SR1: Sund 6C 104 (3F 7)
Wandsworth Rd. NE6: Newc T 2B 70
Wanless Ter. DH1: Dur . . .5D 154 (1C 6)
Wanley St. NE24: Bly 5C 12
Wanny Rd. NE22: Bed 4B 10
Wansbeck NE38: Wash 6G 113
Wansbeck Av. DH9: Stly 4D 122
NE24: News 1C 18
NE30: N Shi 2E 49
Wansbeck Cl. DH2: Ous 2H 125
NE16: Sun 2E 95
Wansbeck Ct. SR3: New S 3H 131
SR8: Pet 3C 164
Wansbeck Gro. NE25: Sea D 3B 24
Wansbeck Rd. NE23: Dud 3H 31
NE32: Jar 4E 73
Wansbeck Rd. Nth. NE3: Gos 1C 56
Wansbeck Rd. Sth. NE3: Gos . . .1C 56
Wansbeck Road Station (Metro)
. . . . .1C 56
Wansbeck St. NE23: Dud 3H 31
Wansdown NE10: Gate 6F 85
Wansfell Av. NE5: Newc T 4H 55
Wansford Av. NE5: Newc T 6F 55
Wansford Way NE16: Whi 1D 94
Wantage Av. NE29: N Shi 3H 61
Wantage Rd. DH1: Carr 2B 156
Wantage St. NE33: S Shi 2F 75
Wapping Rd. NE24: Bly 3D 12
Wapping St. NE33: S Shi 3D 62
Warbeck Cl. NE3: Ken 1F 55
Warburton Cres. NE9: Gate 3A 84
Warcop Ct. NE3: Ken 6A 42
Ward Cl. SR2: Sund 2E 119
Warden Gro. DH5: Hou S 4B 138
WARDEN LAW 2F 139
Wardenlaw NE10: Gate 6F 85
Warden Law La. SR3: New S 3G 131
Wardill Gdns. NE9: Gate 4B 84
Wardle Av. NE33: S Shi 6G 63
Wardle Dr. NE23: Dud 3B 32
Wardle Gdns. NE10: Gate 4E 85
Wardles Ter. DH1: Dur 3A 6
Wardle St. DH9: Stly 6C 122
NE3: Gos 2G 57
WARDLEY 3A 86
Wardley Ct. NE10: Gate 3B 86
Wardley Dr. NE10: Gate 3B 86
Wardley Grn. NE10: Gate, Heb . . .1A 86
Wardley La. NE10: Gate 3B 86
(not continuous)
Wardroper Ho. NE6: Walk 5G 71
Ward St. SR2: Sund 2E 119
Warenford Cl. NE23: Cra 5C 22
Warenford Pl. NE5: Newc T 2G 67
Warenmill Cl. NE15: Lem 2H 65
Warennes St. SR4: Sund 6G 103
Warenton Pl. NE29: N Shi 4F 47
Waring Av. NE26: Sea S 2F 25
Waring Ter. SR7: Mur 5F 141
Wark Av. NE27: Shir 1D 46
NE29: N Shi 1G 61
Wark Ct. NE3: Gos 3G 57
Wark Cres. NE32: Jar 1F 87
Warkdale Av. NE24: Cow 6G 11
Wark St. DH3: Ches S 2C 134
Warkworth Av. NE24: News 2C 18
NE26: Whit B 6C 36
NE28: W'snd 3A 60
NE34: S Shi 2B 76
SR8: Pet 5F 163

Warkworth Cl. NE38: Wash 3H 113
Warkworth Cres. NE3: Gos 1D 56
NE15: Thro 2F *65*
(off Newburn Rd.)
SR7: S'hm 4E 141
Warkworth Dr. DH2: Ches S . . .2A 134
NE13: Wide O 4E 31
Warkworth Gdns. NE10: Gate . . .3C 84
Warkworth Rd. DH1: Dur 6C 144
Warkworth St. NE15: Lem 3A 66
Warkworth Ter. NE30: N Shi 5F 49
(not continuous)
NE32: Jar 6F 73
Warkworth Woods
NE3: Gos, Wide O 3D 42
Warnbrook Av. *SR7: Mur* *3D 150*
(off E. Coronation St.)
Warnham Av. SR2: Sund 5E 119
Warnhead Rd. NE22: Bed 4B 10
Warren Av. NE6: Walk 1G 71
Warren Cl. DH4: Hou S 5G 129
Warrenmor NE10: Gate 4G 85
Warren Sq. SR1: Sund 5F 105
SR8: Pet 1G 165
Warren St. SR8: Pet 6G 163
Warrens Wlk. NE21: Bla T 2G 79
Warrington Rd. NE3: Ken 1A 56
NE4: Newc T 5C 68
Warton Ter. NE6: Newc T 1C 70
Warwick Av. NE16: Whi 6E 81
Warwick Cl. NE16: Whi 6E 81
NE23: Seg 2E 33
Warwick Ct. DH1: Dur 2A 160
NE3: Ken 6H 41
NE8: Gate 1H 83
Warwick Dr. DH5: Hou S 5A 138
NE16: Whi 6F 81
NE37: Usw 3B 100
SR3: E Her 2E 131
Warwick Gro. NE22: Bed 4F 9
Warwick Hall Wlk.
NE7: Newc T 4D 58
Warwick Pl. SR8: Pet 6B 162
Warwick Rd. NE5: Newc T 1C 66
NE28: W'snd 6H 59
NE31: Heb 6D 72
NE33: S Shi 1F 75
NE34: S Shi 2F 75
Warwickshire Dr. DH1: Carr . . .5A 156
Warwick St.
NE2: Newc T 2H **69** (1H **5**)
NE6: Newc T 2H 69
NE8: Gate 1H 83
NE24: Bly 3A 18
SR5: S'wck 4D 104
Warwick Ter. SR3: New S 1A 132
Warwick Ter. Nth. *SR3: New S* . . .*1A 132*
(off Warwick Ter.)
Warwick Ter. W. SR3: New S 1A 132
Wasdale Cl. NE23: Cra 6C 22
SR8: Pet 1E 165
Wasdale Ct. SR6: Monk 6C 90
Wasdale Cres. NE21: Bla T 3H 79
Wasdale Rd. NE5: Newc T 1F 67
WASHINGTON 2C 114
Washington Arts Cen. 5B 114
Washington 'F' Pit Mus. 6A 100
Washington Gdns. NE9: Gate 2C **98**
Washington Highway
DH4: Pen 1A 128
NE37: Wash 5G 99
NE38: Wash 4A 114

Washington Leisure Cen. 3A 114
Washington Old Hall 1C 114
Washington Rd. NE36: W Bol . . .1A 102
NE37: Wash, W Bol 5E 101
SR5: C'twn 2B 102
SR5: W Bol 3H 101
SR5: Wash 3H 101
Washington Sq. SR8: Eas 2B 162
WASHINGTON STAITHES 4E 115
Washington St. SR4: Sund 1H 117
Washington Ter. NE30: N Shi 6E 49
WASHINGTON VILLAGE 1B 114
Washington Wildfowl & Wetlands Trust
. . . . .2G 115
Washingwell La. NE16: Whi 4G 81
Washingwell Pk. NE16: Whi 5G 81
Waskerley Cl. NE16: Sun 2E 95
Waskerley Gdns. NE9: Gate 2D 98
Waskerley Rd. NE38: Wash 2D 114
Watch Ho. Cl. NE29: N Shi 4C 62
Watcombe Cl. NE37: Usw 3D 100
Water Activities Cen. 2F 63
Waterbeach Pl. NE5: Newc T . . .5F 55
Waterbeck Cl. NE23: Cra 6C 22
Waterbury Cl. SR5: S'wck 2H 103
Waterbury Rd. NE3: Gos 4D 42
Waterfield Rd. NE22: E Sle 1H 11
Waterford Cl. DH5: W Rai 1H 147
NE26: Sea S 3H 25
Waterford Cres. NE26: Whit B . . .1D 48
Waterford Pk. NE13: Bru V 5B 30
Watergate NE1: Newc T . . .5G **69** (6E **5**)
Watergate Bank NE11: Gate 1A 96
WATERGATE ESTATE 5G 81
Waterloo Ct. NE37: Usw 5C 100
Waterloo Pl. NE29: N Shi 1C 62
SR1: Sund 1D **118** (4G **7**)
Waterloo Rd. NE24: Bly 6B 12
NE25: Well 6E 35
NE37: Usw 4C 100
(Manor Rd.)
NE37: Usw 3D 100
(Rutherford Rd.)
Waterloo Sq. NE33: S Shi 4E 63
Waterloo St.
NE1: Newc T 5E **69** (6B **4**)
NE21: Bla T 2G 79
Waterloo Va. NE33: S Shi 4E 63
Waterloo Wlk. *NE37: Usw* *5C 100*
(off Waterloo Ct.)
Waterlow Cl. SR5: S'wck 1H 103
Watermark, The
NE11: Dun, Swa 6F 67
Watermill NE40: Ryton 4C 64
Watermill La. NE10: Gate 3E 85
Watermill Pk. NE10: Gate 4D 84
Water Row NE15: Thro 2E 65
Waterside Dr. NE11: Dun 1A 82
Waterside Pk. NE31: Heb 3A 72
Water St. NE4: Newc T 6D 68
Waterview Pk. NE38: Wash 2G 115
Waterville Pl. NE29: N Shi 2C 62
Waterville Rd. NE29: N Shi 3H 61
Waterville Ter. NE29: N Shi 2C 62
Waterworks Rd.
SR1: Sund 1B **118** (4E **7**)
SR2: Ryh 4E 133
Waterworks, The SR2: Ryh 4E 133
Watford Cl. SR5: S'wck 1H 103
Watkin Cres. SR7: Mur 2C 150
Watling Av. SR7: S'hm 5E 141
Watling Pl. NE9: Gate 5B 84

Watson Av. NE23: Dud 3H 31
NE34: S Shi 4B 76
Watson Cl. SR7: Mur 5F 141
Watson Gdns. NE28: W'snd 4E 61
Watson Pl. NE34: S Shi 4B 76
Watson St. DH9: Stly 1D 122
NE8: Gate 2E 83
NE16: Burn 1H 107
NE32: Jar 1G 73
NE39: H Spen 6A 78
Watson Ter. NE35: Bol C 4B 88
Watts Moses Ho. *SR1: Sund* . . .*6F 105*
(off High St. E.)
Watt's Slope NE26: Whit B 5C 36
Watts St. SR7: Mur 2C 150
Watt St. NE8: Gate 4F 83
Wave Health & Fitness Cen. . . .1D 104
(off Sea Rd.)
Wavendon Cres. SR4: Sund 3F 117
Waveney Gdns. DH9: Stly 5C 122
Waveney Rd. SR8: Pet 3B 164
Waverdale Av. NE6: Walk 2G 71
Waverdale Way NE33: S Shi 3D 74
Waverley Av. NE22: Bed 4C 10
(Roslin Pk.)
NE22: Bed 3C 10
(Waverley Dr.)
NE25: Whit B 1B 48
Waverley Cl. NE21: Bla T 3F 79
Waverley Cr. NE22: Bed 3C 10
Waverley Cres. NE15: Lem 2B 66
Waverley Dr. NE22: Bed 3C 10
(not continuous)
Waverley Lodge NE2: Newc T 1G 5
Waverley Rd. NE4: Newc T 5D 68
NE9: Gate, Spri 3A 98
Waverley Ter. DH9: Dip 6E 107
SR4: Sund 6G 103
Waverton Cl. NE23: Cra 6B 22
Wawn St. NE33: S Shi 1F 75
Wayfarer Rd. SR5: S'wck 4A 104
Waygood Gallery 4F **69** (5D **4**)
Wayland Sq. SR2: Sund 6E 119
Wayman St. SR5: S'wck 4C 104
Wayside NE15: Newc T 4F 67
NE34: S Shi 3B 76
SR2: Sund 3B 118
Wayside Ct. DH7: Ush M 4D 152
Wealcroft NE10: Gate 1F 99
Wealcroft Ct. NE10: Gate 6F 85
WEAR 5H 113
Wear Ct. NE34: S Shi 4E 75
Wear Cres. DH3: Gt Lum 4H 135
Weardale Av. NE6: Walk 2G 71
NE12: Longb 5C 44
NE24: Cow 5F 11
NE28: W'snd 3H 59
NE37: Usw 5A 100
SR6: Monk 5E 91
Weardale Cres. DH4: Pen 2F 129
Weardale Ho. NE37: Wash 3H 113
Weardale St. DH5: Hett H 4A 148
Weardale Ter. DH3: Ches S 1D 134
DH9: Ann P 5G 121
Weardale Way DH3: Gt Lum 5G 135
Wearfield SR5: Sund 4G 103
Wearhead Dr. SR4: Sund 3B 118
Wear Ind. Est. NE38: Wash 5H 113
Wear Lodge DH3: Ches S 2C 126
Wearmouth Av. SR5: Monk 3D 104
Wearmouth Dr. SR5: Monk 3C 104
Wearmouth St. SR6: Monk 4D 104

Wear Rd. DH9: Stly 3D **122**
NE31: Heb 5C **72**
Wearside Dr. DH1: Dur . . .5D **154** (1C **6**)
Wear St. DH3: Ches S 1D **134**
DH4: Hou S 4E **137**
DH5: Hett H 2C **148**
NE32: Jar 2F **73**
SR1: Sund 1F **119**
SR4: Sund 6C **102**
SR5: Sund 4A **104**
SR7: S'hm 4B **142**
Wear Ter. NE38: Wash 3D **114**
SR8: Eas 1D **162**
Wear Vw. DH1: Dur . . .5D **154** (1D **6**)
SR4: Sund 6D **102**
Weathercock La. NE9: Gate 6H **83**
Weatherside NE21: Bla T 2H **79**
Webb Av. SR7: Mur 1C **150**
SR7: S'hm 4E **141**
Webb Gdns. NE10: Gate 3G **85**
Webb Sq. SR8: Pet 4E **163**
Wedder Law NE23: Cra 6B **22**
Wedgewood Cotts. NE15: Lem . . .3B **66**
Wedgewood Rd. SR7; S'hm 5F **141**
Wedmore Rd. NE5: Newc T 5B **54**
Weetman St. NE33. S Shi 6D **62**
Weetslade Cres. NE23: Dud 4A **32**
Weetslade Ind. Est.
NE23: Gos 6H **31**
Weetslade Rd. NE23: Dud 3H **31**
Weetslade Ter. NE23: Dud 6B **32**
Weetwood Rd. NE23: Cra 5C **22**
Weidner Rd. NE15: Newc T 3H **67**
Welbeck Grn. NE6: Walk 4E **71**
Welbeck Rd.
NE6. Newc T, Walk 4C **70**
Welbury Way NE23: Cra 6B **22**
Welby Dr. DH7: Ush M 5B **152**
Weldon Av. SR2: Sund 5E **119**
Weldon Cres. NE7: Newc T 5B **58**
Weldon Pl. NE29: N Shi 5H **47**
Weldon Rd. NE12: Longb 1B **58**
NE23: E Cram 4D **22**
Weldon Ter. DH3: Ches S 1D **134**
Weldon Way NE3: Gos 1D **56**
Welfare Cl. SR8: Eas 1E **163**
Welfare Cres. DH6: S Het 6B **150**
Welfare Rd. DH5: Hett H 1B **148**
(not continuous)
Welford Av. NE3: Gos 2C **56**
Welland Cl. SR8: Pet 3C **164**
Wellands Cl. SR6: Whit 2E **91**
Wellands Ct. SR6: Whit 2E **91**
Wellands Dr. SR6: Whit 2E **91**
Wellands La. SR6: Whit 2E **91**
Well Bank Rd. NE37: Usw 4H **99**
Wellburn Pk. NE2: Newc T 6A **58**
Wellburn Rd. NE37: Usw 4H **99**
Well Cl. Wlk. NE16: Whi 5E **81**
Wellesley Cl. NE33: S Shi 3E **63**
Wellesley St. NE32: Jar 4F **73**
Wellesley Ter. NE4: Newc T 4C **68**
WELLFIELD 6F **35**
Wellfield Cl. NE15: Thro 6C **52**
Wellfield La. NE5: Newc T 5E **55**
Wellfield M. SR2: Ryh 4E **133**
Wellfield Rd. NE4: Newc T 4H **67**
(not continuous)
NE39: Row G 4C **92**
SR7: Mur 2B **150**
Wellfield Ter. NE10: Gate 2H **85**
(off Shields Rd.)

Wellfield Ter. NE10: Gate 4C **84**
SR2: Ryh 4E **133**
Wellgarth Rd. NE37: Usw 4H **99**
Wellhope NE38: Wash 1F **127**
Wellington Av. NE25: Well 6E **35**
Wellington Ct. NE10: Gate 3C **84**
NE37: Usw 5C **100**
Wellington Dr. NE33: S Shi 3E **63**
Wellington La. SR4: Sund 5B **104**
Wellington Rd. NE11: Dun 2H **81**
(not continuous)
Wellington Row DH4: Hou S 4G **129**
Wellington St. DH6: H Pitt 2F **157**
NE4: Newc T 3E **69** (3A **4**)
NE8: Gate 5G **69**
NE10: Gate 3C **84**
NE15: Lem 3B **66**
NE24: Bly 6D **12**
(not continuous)
NE31: Heb 4B **72**
Wellington St. E. NE24: Bly 5D **12**
Wellington St. W. NE29: N Shi . . .2C **62**
Wellington Wlk. NE37: Usw 5C **100**
(off Wellington Ct.)
Well La. NE27: Shir 3F **47**
(not continuous)
Wellmere Rd. SR2: Sund 6F **119**
Well Ridge Cl. NE25: Whit B 5G **35**
Well Ridge Pk. NE25: Whit B 4G **35**
Wells Cl. NE7: Newc T 3D **58**
Wells Cres. SR7: S'hm 4F **141**
Wells Gdns. NE9: Gate 3H **97**
Wells Gro. NE34: S Shi 2A **76**
Wellshede NE10: Gate 4H **85**
Wells St. NE35: Bol C 2A **88**
Well St. SR4: Sund 6H **103**
Wellway NE32: Jar 1F **87**
Welsh Ter. DH9: Ann P 6G **121**
Welwyn Av. NE22: Bed 2D **10**
Welwyn Cl. NE28: W'snd 3F **59**
SR5: C'twn 5C **102**
Wembley Av. NE25: Whit B 1A **48**
Wembley Cl. SR5: S'wck 2H **103**
Wembley Rd. SR5: S'wck 2H **103**
Wendover Cl. SR5: S'wck 1G **103**
Wendover Way SR5: S'wck 1G **103**
Wenham Sq. SR2: Sund 3B **118**
Wenlock Dr. NE29: N Shi 5A **48**
Wenlock Lodge NE34: S Shi 4C **74**
Wenlock Pl. NE34: S Shi 5C **74**
Wenlock Rd. NE34: S Shi 4B **74**
Wensley Cl. DH2: Ous 6G **111**
NE5: Newc T 3G **55**
Wensleydale NE28: W'snd 2F **59**
Wensleydale Av. DH4: Pen 2E **129**
NE37: Usw 5A **100**
Wensleydale Dr. NE12: Longb . . .5D **44**
Wensleydale Ter. NE24: Bly 1D **18**
Wensley Ho. SR3: New S 4H **131**
Wentworth NE33: S Shi 6G **63**
Wentworth Cl. NE10: Gate 4D **84**
Wentworth Ct. NE20: Pon 1C **38**
Wentworth Dr. NE37: Usw 3A **100**
Wentworth Gdns. NE25: Whit B . . .1G **47**
Wentworth Grange NE3: Goo 3F **57**
Wentworth Ter. SR4: Sund 6B **104**
Werhale Grn. NE10: Gate 3D **84**
Wesley Cl. DH9: Stly 2E **123**
Wesley Ct. DH9: Ann P 4F **121**
NE10: Gate 2C **84**
NE21: Bla T 6B **66**

Wesley Dr. NE12: Kil 4H **45**
Wesley Sq.
NE1: Newc T 5H **69** (6G **5**)
Wesley St.
NE2: Newc T 3H **69** (2G **5**)
NE9: Gate 6H **83**
NE33: S Shi 4E **63**
Wesley Ter. DH2: Pelt 4G **125**
DH3: Ches S 6C **126**
DH6: Sher 6G **157**
DH9: Ann P 5F **121**
DH9: Dip 6D **106**
Wesley Way NE12: Kil 4H **45**
NE15: Thro 5D **52**
SR7: S'hm 4F **141**
Wessex Cl. SR5: S'wck 1H **103**
Wessington Ind. Est.
SR5: C'twn 4E **103**
Wessington Ter. NE37: Wash 6B **100**
Wessington Way SR5: Sund 6B **102**
Westacre Gdns. NE5: Newc T 2G **67**
West Acres NE13: Din 4F **29**
W. Acres Av. NE16: Whi 6F **81**
Westacres Cres. NE15: Newc T . . .3G **67**
WEST ALLOTMENT 4C **46**
W. Allotment By-Pass
NE27: Shir 3B **46**
West Av. DH2: Ches S 4A **134**
NE3: Gos 3F **57**
NE5: Newc T 5D **54**
NE12: Longb 1D **58**
(Thornhill Rd.)
NE12: Longb 4F **45**
(Young Rd.)
NE25: Whit B 6A **36**
NE29: N Shi 2H **61**
NE34: S Shi 3G **75**
NE38: Wash 6H **113**
NE39: Row G 4D **92**
SR6: Whit 2E **91**
SR7: Mur 3C **150**
West Bailey NE12: Kil 1B **44**
WEST BOLDON 4C **88**
Westbourne Av. NE3: Gos 6E **43**
NE6: Walk 1F **71**
NE8: Gate 3G **83**
Westbourne Cotts.
DH4: Hou S 3E **129**
Westbourne Dr. DH4: Hou S 3E **129**
Westbourne Gdns. NE6: Walk . . .3G **71**
Westbourne Rd. SR1: Sund 1B **118**
Westbourne Ter. DH4: Hou S 4F **129**
NE25: Sea D 6C **24**
W. Bridge St. DH4: Pen 1C **128**
NE24: Camb 2B **12**
Westbrooke Ho. SR2: Sund 3D **118**
W. Brunton Farm Cotts.
NE13: Bru V 3H **41**
Westburn Ter. NE28: W'snd 3F **59**
Westburn Ter. SR6: Monk 3E **105**
Westbury Av. NE6: Walk 1G **71**
Westbury Cl. NE12: Longb 2A **58**
Westbury Rd. NE29: N Shi 5B **48**
Westbury St. SR4: Sund 6B **104**
WEST CHIRTON 2H **61**
W. Chirton Ind. Est.
NE29: N Shi 1G **61**
W. Chirton (Middle) Trad. Est.
NE29: N Shi 6F **47**
W. Chirton Nth. Ind. Est.
NE29: N Shi 6E **47**

Westcliff Cl. SR8: Eas 2A **162**
Westcliffe Rd. SR6: Monk 1F **105**
Westcliffe Way NE34: S Shi 6B **74**
W. Clifton NE12: Kil 1C **44**
West Copperas NE15: Lem 2C **66**
  (not continuous)
W. Coronation St. SR7: Mur 2D **150**
Westcott Av. NE33: S Shi 6G **63**
Westcott Dr. DH1: Dur 2A **154**
Westcott Rd. NE34: S Shi 4E **75**
  SR8: Pet 6D **162**
Westcott Ter. DH4: Pen 1G **129**
West Ct. DH1: Dur 2C **160**
  NE3: Gos 2C **56**
  NE24: Bly 1A **18**
West Cres. NE10: Gate 3A **86**
  SR8: Eas 1C **162**
Westcroft Pk. SR6: Whit 2E **91**
Westcroft Rd. NE12: Longb 6E **45**
W. Dene Dr. NE30: N Shi 5C **48**
W. Denton Cl. NE15: Lem 1B **66**
W. Denton Retail Pk.
  NE5: Newc T 5E **55**
W. Denton Rd. NE15: Lem 1B **66**
W. Denton Way NE5: Newc T 5B **54**
West Dr. DH2: Ches S 1A **134**
  NE24: News 3A **18**
  SR6: Cle 2G **89**
W. Ellen St. SR7: Mur 3D **150**
West End NE26: Sea S 5H **25**
Wester Ct. SR3: New S 4H **131**
Westerdale DH4: Pen 1C **128**
  NE28: W'snd 3F **59**
Westerdale Pl. NE6: Walk 3H **71**
Westerham Cl. SR5: S'wck 1H **103**
WESTERHOPE 5D **54**
Westerhope Gdns.
  NE5: Newc T 6H **55**
Westerhope Rd. NE38: Wash . . .2D **114**
Westerhope Small Bus. Pk.
  NE5: Newc T 3C **54**
Westerkirk NE23: Cra 6C **22**
Western App. NE33: S Shi 2D **74**
Western App. Ind. Est.
  NE33: S Shi *6E* **63**
  (off Western App.)
Western Av. NE4: Newc T 4A **68**
  NE5: Newc T 6B **54**
  NE11: Gate 1E **97**
  NE25: Sea D 6H **23**
Western Ct. *NE26: Whit B* *3B* **36**
  (off Western Way.)
Western Dr. NE4: Newc T 4B **68**
Western Highway DH3: Wash . .5E **113**
  NE38: Wash 5E **113**
WESTERN HILL 4A **154**
Western Hill SR2: Ryh 2E **133**
  SR2: Sund 1B **118**
Westernmoor NE37: Wash 1F **113**
Western Rd. NE28: W'snd 5D **60**
  NE32: Jar 2E **73**
Western Ter. NE23: Dud 3H **31**
  NE36: E Bol, W Bol 4C **88**
  NE37: Wash 6B **100**
Western Ter. Nth. SR7: Mur . . .2D **150**
Western Ter. Sth. SR7: Mur . . .2D **150**
Western Vw. NF9: Spri 4C **98**
Western Way NE20: Pon 1A **38**
  NE21: Bla T 1C **80**
  NE26: Whit B 3B **36**
  NE40: Ryton 5C **64**
W. Farm Av. NE12: Longb 1H **57**

W. Farm Ct. DH7: Ush M 1E **159**
  NE12: Kil 3E **45**
  NE23: Cra 2B **22**
W. Farm Rd. NE6: Walk 2E **71**
  NE28: W'snd 4C **60**
  SR6: Cle 3B **90**
W. Farm Wynd NE12: Longb 2H **57**
Westfield NE3: Gos 5D **56**
  NE10: Gate 5E **85**
  NE23: Dud 3H **31**
  NE32: Jar 2G **87**
Westfield Av. NE3: Gos 4E **57**
  NE13: Bru V 5C **30**
  NE25: Whit B 1H **47**
Westfield Ct. NE28: W'snd 1H **71**
  NE32: Jar 3F **73**
  SR4: Sund 3G **117**
Westfield Cres. NE9: Spri 4F **99**
Westfield Dr. NE3: Gos 4E **57**
Westfield Gro. NE3: Gos 4D **56**
  SR4: Sund 3G **117**
Westfield La. NE40: Ryton 3B **64**
Westfield Pk. NE3: Gos 4E **57**
  NE28: W'snd 5G **59**
Westfield Rd. NE8: Gate 3G **83**
  NE15: Newc T 4G **67**
Westfields DH9: Stly 4B **122**
Westfield Ter. NE8: Gate 3G **83**
  NE9: Spri *4E* **99**
  (off Windsor Rd.)
Westgarth NE5: Newc T 3C **54**
Westgarth Ter. NE37: Usw 5C **100**
Westgate Av. SR3: New S 1A **132**
Westgate Cen. for Sport 3H **67**
Westgate Cl. NE25: Whit B 5G **35**
Westgate Gro. *NE4: Newc T* *4D* **68**
  (off Westgate Rd.)
Westgate Gro. SR3: New S 1A **132**
Westgate Hill Ter.
  NE4: Newc T 4E **69** (5A **4**)
Westgate Rd.
  NE1: Newc T 4E **69** (5B **4**)
  NE4: Newc T 3B **68**
W. George Potts St.
  NE33: S Shi 6E **63**
West Grange SR5: S'wck 2C **104**
West Gro. SR4: Sund 2D **116**
  SR7: S'hm 4F **141**
W. Hartford Bus. Cen.
  NE23: E Har 4H **15**
WEST HARTON 4E **75**
Westheath Av. SR2: Sund 6D **118**
WEST HERRINGTON 2B **130**
W. High Horse Cl.
  NE39: Row G 1G **93**
West Hill SR4: Sund 3G **117**
Westhills DH9: Tan L 5G **107**
W. Holborn NE33: S Shi 6D **62**
Westholme Gdns.
  NE15: Newc T 3H **67**
Westholme Ter. *SR2: Sund* *5F* **119**
  (off Ryhope Rd.)
WEST HOLYWELL 5B **34**
Westhope Cl. NE34: S Shi 2A **76**
Westhope Rd. NE34: S Shi 2A **76**
WEST JESMOND 5G **57**
W. Jesmond Av. NE2: Newc T . . .5G **57**
West Jesmond Station (Metro)
  . . . . .5G **57**
WEST KYO 4F **121**
Westlands NE5: Cha P 6A **54**
  NE7: Newc T 5A **58**

Westlands NE26: Sea S 3F **25**
  NE30: N Shi 4D **48**
  NE32: Jar 2H **87**
Westlands, The SR4: Sund 2H **117**
West La. DH3: Ches S 1C **134**
  DH6: S Het 6B **150**
  NE12: Kil 4D **44**
  NE16: Burn 4A **94**
  NE21: Bla T 3G **79**
  SR7: Eas 6F **151**
West Lawn SR2: Sund 3D **118**
W. Lawrence St. SR1: Sund 1E **119**
WESTLEA 4F **141**
West Lea DH4: E Her 3H **129**
  NE21: Bla T 3A **80**
Westlea NE22: Bed 5F **9**
Westlea Rd. DH4: Hou S 6G **129**
  SR7: S'hm 4F **141**
West Leigh DH9: Tan L 1B **122**
Westley Av. NE26: Whit B 2A **36**
Westley Cl. NE26: Whit B 2A **36**
Westline Ind. Est. DH2: Bir 5B **112**
Westlings DH5: Hett H 2C **148**
Westloch Rd. NE23: Cra 6B **22**
Westmacott St. NE15: Thro 1E **65**
West Mdws. NE5: Cha P 3B **54**
West Mdws. Dr. SR6: Cle 4A **90**
West Mdws. Rd. SR6: Cle 3B **90**
Westminster Av. NE29: N Shi . . .5F **47**
  (not continuous)
Westminster Cl. NE26: Whit B . . .1E **49**
Westminster Cres. NE31: Heb . .1C **86**
Westminster Dr. NE11: Dun 5B **82**
Westminster St. NE8: Gate 3F **83**
  SR2: Sund 5F **119**
Westminster Way NE7: Newc T . . .3D **58**
W. Moffett St. NE33: S Shi 6F **63**
WEST MONKSEATON 1H **47**
West Monkseaton Station (Metro)
  . . . . .1H **47**
WEST MOOR 4B **44**
W. Moor Ct. NE12: Longb 4B **44**
W. Moor Dr. SR6: Cle 4A **90**
Westmoor Dr. NE12: Longb 4B **44**
Westmoor Rd. SR4: Sund 6F **103**
Westmorland Av. NE22: Bed 4G **9**
  NE28: W'snd 5F **61**
  NE37: Usw 4B **100**
Westmorland Ct. NE31: Heb 4B **72**
Westmorland Gdns. NE9: Gate . .6H **83**
Westmorland La.
  NE1: Newc T 5E **69** (6B **4**)
Westmorland Retail Pk.
  NE23: Cra 3H **21**
Westmorland Ri. SR8: Pet 5B **162**
Westmorland Rd.
  NE1: Newc T 5E **69** (6B **4**)
  NE4: Newc T 5B **68**
  NE29: N Shi 6F **47**
  NE34: S Shi 2C **76**
Westmorland St. NE28: W'snd . . .5A **60**
Westmorland Wlk.
  NE4: Newc T 6B **68**
Westmorland Way NE23: Cra . . .3H **21**
West Mt. NE12: Kil 2C **44**
  SR4: Sund 2G **117**
WESTOE 6G **63**
Westoe Av. NE33: S Shi 6G **63**
Westoe Dr. NE33: S Shi 6G **63**
Westoe Fitness Cen. 1F **75**
Westoe Rd. NE33: S Shi 5F **63**
Westoe Village NE33: S Shi 1G **75**

Weston Av. NE16: Whi 6D **80**
Weston Vw. SR8: Pet 6C **162**
W. Ousterley Rd. DH9: Stly 5D **122**
Westover Gdns. NE9: Gate 4H **83**
West Pde. NE4: Newc T 5D **68**
NE31: Heb 4B **72**
West Pk. *NE11: Dun* *2B 82*
(off Meadow La.)
SR3: E Her 3D **130**
W. Park Gdns. NE21: Bla T 2A **80**
W. Park Rd. NE8: Gate 4G **83**
NE33: S Shi 1E **75**
SR6: Cle 2A **90**
W. Park Vw. NE23: Dud 3H **31**
W. Pastures NE36: W Bol 1G **101**
WEST PELTON 3C **124**
W. Percy Rd. NE29: N Shi 3A **62**
W. Percy St. NE29: N Shi 2C **62**
Westport Cl. SR5: S'wck 1H **103**
W. Quay Rd. SR5: Sund 4H **103**
WEST RAINTON 3D **146**
Westray DH2: Ches S 2A **134**
Westray Cl. SR2: Ryh 1D **132**
West Riggs NE22: Bed 5H **9**
West Rig, The NE3: Ken 3A **56**
West Rd. DH9: Ann P 6F **121**
DH9: Tan L 6G **107**
NE5: Newc T 1D **66**
NE15: Newc T 1D **66**
NE20: Pon 5D **26**
NE22: Bed 3D **10**
West Rd. Crematorium
NE5: Newc T 2F **67**
West Row DH3: Bir 4E **113**
W. Salisbury St. NE24: Bly 5B **12**
W. Shield Row Vs. DH9: Stly ...1C **122**
W. Spencer Ter. NE15: Thro ...6H **63**
W. Stainton St. NE33: S Shi 6E **63**
(not continuous)
W. Stevenson St. NE33: S Shi ...4C **63**
West St. DH2: Pelt 4C **124**
DH3: Bir 3C **112**
DH9: Tan L 1B **122**
NE8: Gate 6G **69**
NE16: Whi 4E **81**
NE27: Shir 4B **46**
NE28: W'end 4G **59**
NE31: Heb 2D **72**
SR1: Sund 6C **104** (3F 7)
SR3: New S 1A **132**
SR7: S'hm 4B **142**
W. Sunniside
SR1: Sund 6D **104** (3H 7)
Westsyde NE20: Pon 2A **38**
West Ter. DH1: Dur 5B **154**
NE26: Sea S 3H **25**
W. Thorns Wlk. NE16: Whi 5E **81**
West Thorp NE5: Newc T 2D **54**
West Va. NE15: Thro 5B **52**
West Vallum NE15: Newc T 2D **66**
West Vw. DH1: Dur 5E **155**
DH3: Ches S 5C **126**
DH4: Hou S 5F **129**
(Bournmoor)
DH4: Hou S 5F **129**
(Success)
DH4: Pen 1F **129**
DH6: Sher 6G **157**
DH7: B'don 6E **159**
DH9: Stly 6C **122**
NC4: Newc T 5B **68**
NE9: Gate 1C **98**

West Vw. NE9: Spri 4E **99**
NE11: Kib 1F **111**
NE12: Longb 5D **44**
NE13: Wide O 4D **30**
NE15: Lem 3A **66**
NE16: Burn 1G **107**
NE21: Bla T 6A **66**
NE22: Bed 2C **10**
NE23: Cra 4C **22**
NE23: Dud 3A **32**
NE23: Seg 2F **33**
NE25: Well 6E **35**
NE35: Bol C 2H **87**
NE37: Usw 5B **100**
SR2: Ryh *3E 133*
(off Blackhills Rd.)
SR5: C'twn 4D **102**
SR6: Monk 2D **104**
SR7: Mur 3C **150**
(Church St.)
SR7: Mur 6F **141**
(Overdene)
SR8: Eas 2B **162**
SR8: Pet 6G **163**
W. View Bldgs. NE30: N Shi 2E **49**
W. View Gdns. DH9: Stly 2C **122**
W. View Ter. NE11: Dun 1A **82**
Westview Ter. DH9: Ann P 6E **121**
West Vs. DH9: Stly 3B **124**
West Wlk. DH3: Lam P 3G **127**
West Walls
NE1: Newc T 4E **69** (5B 4)
W. Walpole St. NE33: S Shi 6D **62**
Westward Ct. NE5: Newc T 4C **54**
Westward Grn. NE25: Whit B ...1G **47**
Westward Pl. NE38: Wash 6H **113**
West Way NE11: Dun 3C **82**
NE33: S Shi 2D **74**
Westway NE15: Thro 4D **52**
NE21: Bla T 1H **79**
SR8: Pet 2C **164**
Westway Ind. Pk. NE15: Thro ...4D **52**
W. Wear St.
SR1: Sund 6D **104** (2H 7)
Westwell Ct. NE3: Newc T 3H **57**
Westwood Av. NE6: Newc T 6B **58**
Westwood Cl. NE16: Burn 6H **93**
Westwood Gdns. NE3: Ken 3A **56**
NE9: Gate 2D **98**
NE38: Wash 2C **114**
Westwood Rd. NE3: Gos 4E **43**
Westwood St. SR4: Sund 1H **117**
Westwood Ter. DH3: Ches S ...1C **134**
Westwood Vw. DH3: Ches S ...2C **134**
Westwood Wlk. NE8: Gate 1F **83**
West Wynd NE12: Kil 2C **44**
Wetheral Gdns. NE6: Walk 2A **98**
Wetheral Ter. NE6: Walk 5F **71**
Wetherburn Av. SR7: Mur 2B **150**
Wetherby Gro. NE8: Gate 4F **83**
Wetherby Rd. SR2: Sund 6G **119**
Wet 'n' Wild Water Pk. 5B **62**
Wettondale Av. NE24: Cow 6G **11**
Weybourne Sq. SR2: Sund 5E **119**
Weyhill Av. NE29: N Shi 3H **61**
Weymouth Dr. DH4: Hou S 4D **128**
SR7: Mur, S'hm 5F **141**
Weymouth Gdns. NE9: Gate ...3H **97**
Weymouth Ho. NE4: Newc T ...1C **82**
Weymouth Rd. NE29: N Shi 2G **61**
SR3: New S 4G **131**
Whaggs La. NE16: Whi 5F **81**

Whalton Av. NE3: Ken 1C **56**
Whalton Cl. DH6: Sher 6E **157**
NE10: Gate 4A **86**
Whalton Ct. NE3: Ken 1C **56**
NE34: S Shi 3G **75**
Wharfedale DH4: Pen 1E **129**
Wharfedale Av. NE37: Usw 5H **99**
Wharfedale Dr. NE33: S Shi 2E **75**
Wharfedale Gdns. NE24: Cow ...5G **11**
Wharfedale Grn. NE9: Gate 4B **98**
Wharfedale Pl. NE6: Walk 3H **71**
Wharmlands Gro.
NE15: Newc T 2D **66**
Wharmlands Rd.
NE15: Newc T 2D **66**
Wharncliffe St. SR1: Sund 1B **118**
Wharrier St. NE6: Walk 5F **71**
Wharton Cl. DH5: W Rai 1H **147**
Wharton St. NE24: Bly 2H **17**
NE33: S Shi 5F **63**
Wheatall Dr. SR6: Whit 6F **77**
Wheatall Way SR6: Whit 1F **91**
Wheatear Cl. NE38: Wash 4F **113**
Wheatfield Gro. NE12: Longb ...6B **44**
Wheatfield Rd. NE5: Newc T ...4D **54**
Wheatfields NE25: Sea D 5H **23**
Wheatlands Way DH1: Dur 5C **144**
Wheatley Gdns. NE36: W Bol ...4C **88**
Wheatleywell La. DH2: Plaw ...1A **144**
DH3: Ches S, Plaw 1A **144**
Wheatridge NE25: Sea D 5H **23**
Wheatridge Row NE25: Sea D ...5H **23**
Wheatsheaf Ct. SR6: Monk 4F **105**
Wheldon Ter. DH2: Pelt 2G **125**
Wheler St. DH4: Hou S 2H **137**
Whernside Cl. NE37: Wash 1G **113**
Whernside Ct. SR3: New S 3H **131**
Whernside Pl. NE23: Cra 6B **22**
Whernside Wlk. NE40: Ryton ...5D **64**
WHICKHAM 4F **81**
Whickham Bank NE16: Swa 4E **81**
Whickham Cl. DH4: Hou S 3G **137**
Whickham Gdns.
NE6: Newc T 4C **70**
Whickham Glebe Sports Club ...4F **81**
Whickham Highway
NE11: Dun, Gate 4A **82**
NE16: Whi 4H **81**
Whickham Ind. Est.
NE16: Swa 3D **80**
Whickham Lodge NE16: Whi ...4G **81**
Whickham Lodge Ri.
NE16: Whi 4G **81**
Whickham Pk. NE16: Whi 4G **81**
(Dockendale M.)
NE16: Whi 4G **81**
(Heron Way)
Whickham Rd. NE31: Heb 4B **72**
Whickham St. SR6: Monk 4E **105**
SR8: Eas 1D **162**
Whickham St. E. SR6: Monk ...4E **105**
Whickham Thorns Outdoor
Activity Cen. 3H **81**
Whickham Vw. NE9: Gate 6A **84**
NE15: Newc T 2E **67**
Whickhope NE38: Wash 5C **114**
Whinbank NE20: Pon 3D **38**
Whinbrooke NE10: Gate 5G **85**
Whinbush Pl. NE15: Newc T 4E **67**
Whinfell NE37: Wash 6H **99**
Whinfell Cl. NE23: Cra 6C **22**

Whinfell Ct. SR3: New S 3H **131**
Whinfell Rd. NE20: Pon 2D **38**
Whinfield Ind. Est.
  NE39: Row G 4C **92**
Whinfield Ter. NE39: Row G 3D **92**
Whinfield Way NE39: Row G 4C **92**
Whinlatter Gdns. NE9: Gate 1A **98**
Whinlaw NE9: Gate 1C **98**
Whinmoor Pl. NE5: Newc T 6A **56**
Whinney Cl. NE21: Bla T 3G **79**
Whinneyfield Rd. NE6: Walk 2F **71**
Whinney Hill DH1: Dur ...1D **160** (5D **6**)
Whinshaw NE10: Gate 4F **85**
Whinside DH9: Stly 2B **122**
Whinstone M. NE12: Longb 1D **58**
Whinway NE37: Wash 6H **99**
Whistler Gdns. NE34: S Shi 6F **75**
Whitbeck Ct. NE5: Newc T 6E **55**
Whitbeck Rd. NE5: Newc T 1D **66**
Whitbourne Cl. NE37: Usw 3C **100**
Whitbrey Ho. NE6: Walk 6E **71**
  (off Oval, The)
WHITBURN 3F **91**
Whitburn Bents Rd.
  SR6: Monk, Whit 5F **91**
WHITBURN COLLIERY 1F **91**
Whitburn Gdns. NE9: Gate 2D **98**
Whitburn Pl. NE23: Cra 6B **22**
Whitburn Rd. NE36: E Bol 3G **89**
  SR6: Cle 3G **89**
  SR6: Monk 6F **91**
Whitburn Rd. E. SR6: Cle 2B **90**
Whitburn St. SR6: Monk 5D **104**
Whitburn Ter. NE36: E Bol 4F **89**
  SR6: Monk 1D **104**
Whitby Av. SR6: Monk 5F **91**
Whitby Cl. NE8: Gate 2H **83**
Whitby Cres. NE12: Longb 1C **58**
Whitby Dr. NE38: Wash 4B **114**
Whitby Gdns. NE28: W'snd 3C **60**
Whitby St. NE30: N Shi 1D **62**
Whitchester Ho. NE4: Newc T 3D **68**
  (off Barrack Rd.)
Whitchurch Cl. NE35: Bol C 2A **88**
  SR5: S'wck 1H **103**
Whitchurch Rd. SR5: S'wck 1H **103**
Whitdale Av. NE24: Cow 1G **17**
Whitebark SR3: New S 5G **131**
Whitebeam Pl. NE4: Newc T 6D **68**
Whitebridge Cl. NE3: Gos 5F **43**
Whitebridge Ct. NE3: Gos 6E **43**
Whitebridge Pk. NE3: Gos 5F **43**
Whitebridge Parkway
  NE3: Gos 5F **43**
Whitebridge Wlk. NE3: Gos 5F **43**
White Cedars DH7: B'don 6C **158**
Whitecliff Cl. NE29: N Shi 5B **48**
White Cotts. NE32: Jar 5E **73**
White Cres. TS27: Hes 6G **165**
Whitecroft Rd. NE12: Kil 3B **44**
Whitecross Way
  NE1: Newc T 4F **69** (4C **4**)
Whitefield Cres. DH4: Pen 2E **129**
Whitefield Gdns. NE40: G'sde ...3A **78**
Whitefield Gro. NE10: Gate 3D **84**
Whitefield Ter. NE6: Newc T 6D **58**
Whiteford Pl. NE23: Seg 1G **33**
Whitefriars Pl. NE1: Newc T 5F **69**
  (off Hanover Sq.)
Whitegate Cl. NE11: Dun 1B **82**
White Gates Dr. DH5: Eas L 3D **148**
Whitegates Rd. DH6: Sher 4D **156**

Whitehall Rd. NE8: Gate 3F **83**
  NE15: Thro 6F **53**
Whitehall St. NE33: S Shi 3E **75**
Whitehall Ter. SR4: Sund 1H **117**
White Hart Yd.
  NE1: Newc T 4F **69** (5D **4**)
Whitehead St. NE33: S Shi 3D **74**
  (Hudson St., not continuous)
  NE33: S Shi 2D **74**
  (Western App.)
WHITEHILL 6G **125**
Whitehill NE10: Gate 6F **85**
Whitehill Cres. DH2: Pelt 5G **125**
  (not continuous)
Whitehill Dr. NE10: Gate 5C **84**
White Hill Rd. DH5: Eas L 5E **149**
Whitehill Rd. NE23: Cra 6A **16**
WHITEHILLS 6F **85**
Whitehill Hall Gdns.
  DH2: Ches S 5A **126**
Whitehill Way DH2: Ches S 6H **125**
White Horse Vw. NE34: S Shi 3C **76**
Whitehouse Av. DH7: Ush M ...5B **152**
Whitehouse Ct. DH7: Ush M ...4C **152**
  (not continuous)
  SR8: Eas 2B **162**
  SR8: Pet 5B **162**
Whitehouse Cres. NE9: Gate 1E **99**
Whitehouse Ent. Cen.
  NE15: Newc T 5G **67**
Whitehouse Ind. Est.
  NE15: Newc T 5G **67**
Whitehouse La. DH7: Ush M ...5B **152**
  NE9: Gate 1C **98**
  (Bramblelaw)
  NE9: Gate 1D **98**
  (Harebell Rd.)
  NE29: N Shi 5H **47**
  (Whitehouse Av., not continuous)
Whitehouse M. NE28: W'snd 5A **60**
Whitehouse Rd.
  NE15: Newc T 5F **67**
White Ho. Rd. SR2: Sund 1E **119**
  (not continuous)
White Ho. Way NE10: Gate 6E **85**
Whitehouse Way SR8: Pet 1A **164**
White Ladies Cl. NE38: Wash ...1B **114**
Whitelaw Pl. NE23: Cra 5C **22**
Whitelea Cl. SR8: Pet 2F **165**
WHITELEAS 1F **89**
Whiteleas Way NE34: S Shi 5E **75**
WHITE-LE-HEAD 6G **107**
White-le-Head Gdns.
  DH9: Tan L 5G **107**
Whiteley Cl. NE40: G'sde 2A **78**
Whiteley Rd. NE21: Bla T 5C **66**
Whitemere Cl. SR2: Sund 6E **119**
White Mere Gdns. NE10: Gate ...3A **86**
Whiteoak Av. DH1: Dur 4H **155**
White Oaks NE10: Gate 6E **85**
White Rocks Gro. SR6: Whit 6F **77**
White Rose Way NE10: Gate 6C **86**
Whites Gdns. NE31: Heb 3B **72**
WHITESMOCKS 4H **153**
Whitesmocks DH1: Dur 3A **154**
Whitesmocks Av. DH1: Dur 4H **153**
White St. NE6: Walk 4H **71**
Whitethorn Cres. NE5: Newc T ..5H **55**
Whitethroat Cl. NE38: Wash ...4F **113**
Whitewell Cl. NE40: Ryton 4C **64**
Whitewell La. NE40: Ryton 4C **64**

Whitewell Rd. NE21: Bla T 1A **80**
Whitewell Ter. NE40: Ryton 3C **64**
Whitfield Dr. NE12: Longb 1C **58**
Whitfield Rd. NE12: Longb 5D **44**
  NE15: Newc T 4D **66**
  NE25: Sea D 6B **24**
Whitfield Vs. NE33: S Shi 3D **74**
Whitgrave Rd. NE5: Newc T 4H **55**
Whithorn Ct. NE24: Cow 6A **12**
Whitlees Ct. NE3: Ken 6A **42**
WHITLEY BAY 6D **36**
Whitley Bay Crematorium
  NE26: Whit B 2A **36**
Whitley Bay Holiday Pk.
  NE26: Whit B 1A **36**
Whitley Bay Ice Rink 2B **48**
Whitley Bay Leisure Pool 4B **36**
Whitley Bay Playhouse 5C **36**
Whitley Bay Station (Metro) ...1D **48**
Whitley Ct. NE9: Gate 2D **98**
Whitley Pl. NE25: H'wll 1C **34**
Whitley Rd. NE12: Kil, Longb ...6G **45**
  NE12: W'snd, Longb, Newc T
  ....1D **58**
  NE25: Well 6E **35**
  NE26: Whit B 6D **36**
  NE27: Kil, Longb 4H **45**
WHITLEY SANDS 4A **36**
Whitley Ter. NE22: Bed 2D **10**
  NE25: H'wll 1C **34**
Whitmore Rd. NE21: Bla T 6A **66**
Whitsun Av. NE22: Bed 4A **10**
Whitsun Gdns. NE22: Bed 4A **10**
Whitsun Gro. NE22: Bed 4A **10**
Whitticks, The NE36: E Bol 4D **88**
Whittingham Cl. NE30: N Shi ...3E **49**
Whittingham Ct. NE8: Gate 2F **83**
  (off Second St.)
Whittingham Rd. NE5: Newc T ...3D **54**
  NE30: N Shi 3E **49**
Whittingham Rd. Bungs.
  NE5: Newc T 3E **55**
Whittington Gro. NE5: Newc T ..2G **67**
Whittleburn NE10: Gate 6F **85**
Whitton Av. NE24: Bly 2H **17**
Whitton Gdns. NE29: N Shi 6H **47**
Whitton Pl. NE7: Newc T 3B **58**
  NE25: Sea D 6B **24**
Whittonstall NE38: Wash 6D **114**
Whitton Way NE3: Gos 1D **56**
Whitwell Acres DH1: H Shin ...4H **161**
Whitworth Cl. NE6: Walk 4G **71**
  NE8: Gate 4F **83**
Whitworth Pl. NE6: Walk 4G **71**
Whitworth Rd. NE37: Wash 6F **99**
  SR8: Pet 1A **164**
WHORLTON 3C **54**
Whorlton Grange
  NE5: Newc T 3C **54**
Whorlton Grange Cotts.
  NE5: Newc T 3C **54**
Whorlton La.
  NE5: Newc T, Wool 6H **39**
Whorlton Pl. NE5: Newc T 4C **54**
Whorlton Ter. NE5: Cha P 3H **53**
Whyndyke NE10: Gate 6F **85**
Whytrigg Cl. NE25: Sea D 5H **23**
Wickham Av. NE11: Dun 3B **82**
Widdrington Av. NE34: S Shi ...1B **76**
Widdrington Gdns.
  NE13: Wide O 5E **31**
Widdrington Rd. NE21: Bla T ...1A **80**

Widdrington Ter. NE21: Bla T 5G **65**
  NE29: N Shi 2C **62**
  (not continuous)
WIDE OPEN 5E **31**
Widnes Pl. NE12: Longb 6C **44**
Wigeon Cl. NE38: Wash 5G **113**
Wigham Chare NE2: Newc T 2G **5**
Wigham Ter. DH4: Pen 2F **129**
  NE16: Burn 3G **107**
Wigmore Av. NE6: Walk 5E **71**
Wilber Ct. SR4: Sund 6H **103**
Wilberforce St. NE28: W'snd 1H **71**
  NE32: Jar 2G **73**
Wilberforce Wlk. NE8: Gate 1F **83**
Wilber St. SR4: Sund 1H **117**
Wilbury Pl. NE5: Newc T 5G **55**
Wildbriar NE38: Wash 5B **114**
Wilden Cl. SR3: Sund 5A **118**
Wilden Rd. NE38: Wash 3D **114**
Wildshaw Cl. NE23: Cra 6C **22**
Wilfred St. DH3: Bir 4C **112**
  DH3: Ches S 1C **134**
  NE6: Newc T 3A **70**
  NE35: Bol C 4B **88**
  SR4: Sund 6G **103**
Wilkes Cl. NE5: Newc T 5D **54**
Wilkinson Av. NE31: Heb 6B **72**
Wilkinson Ct. NE32: Jar 2F **73**
Wilkinson Rd. SR8: Pet 4E **163**
Wilkinson St. NE34: S Shi 4D **74**
Wilkinson Ter. SR2: Ryh 3E **133**
Wilkwood Cl. NE23: Cra 5C **22**
Willans Bldgs. DH1: Dur 5F **155**
Willerby Ct. NE9: Gate 4B **98**
Willerby Dr. NE3: Gos 5F **43**
Willerby Gro. SR8: Pet 6B **162**
William Allan Homes
  NE22: Bed 4F **9**
William Armstrong Dr.
  NE4: Newc T 6A **68**
William Cl. NE12: Longb 5G **45**
William Doxford Cen.
  SR3: New S 3H **131**
William Johnson St.
  SR7: Mur 3D **150**
William Leech Bldg.
  NE2: Newc T 1B **4**
William Morris Av.
  NE39: Row G 3D **92**
William Pl. DH1: Dur 5F **155**
William Roberts Ct. NE12: Kil 4D **44**
Williams Cl. DH9: Stly 3E **123**
Williamson Ter.
  SR6: Monk 5D **104** (1H **7**)
Williams Pk. NE12: Longb 1C **58**
Williams Rd. SR7: Mur 2C **150**
William's Ter. SR2: Ryh 3E **133**
William St. DH2: Pelt 4E **125**
  DH3: Ches S 5C **126**
  DH9: Ann P 6G **121**
  DH9: Stly 6G **123**
  (Edward St.)
  DH9: Stly 5B **122**
  (Grasmere Ter.)
  NE3: Gos 2G **57**
  NE10: Gate 2D **84**
  NE16: Whi 4E **81**
  NE24: Bly 6C **12**
  NE29: N Shi 2C **62**
  NE31: Heb 2B **72**
  (not continuous)
  NE33: S Shi 4E **63**

William St. SR1: Sund . . .6D **104** (2H **7**)
  SR4: Sund 1C **116**
William St. W. NE29: N Shi 2C **62**
  NE31: Heb 3B **72**
William Ter. DH4: Hou S 6H **129**
  NE31: Heb 3B **72**
William Whiteley Homes
  NE40: G'sde 2A **78**
  (off Whiteley Cl.)
WILLINGTON 3D **60**
WILLINGTON QUAY 6E **61**
WILLINGTON SQUARE 2D **60**
Willington Ter. NE28: W'snd 4C **60**
Willis St. DH5: Hett H 6C **138**
Willmore St. SR4: Sund 1A **118**
Willoughby Dr. NE26: Whit B 4A **36**
Willoughby Rd. NE29: N Shi 1H **61**
Willoughby Way NE26: Whit B . . .4A **36**
Willow Av. NE4: Newc T 1H **67**
  NE11: Dun 3B **82**
  NE24: Bly 4B **12**
Willowbank Gdns. NE2: Gos 4G **57**
Willow Bank Rd. SR2: Sund 4C **118**
Willow Cl. DH7: B'don 5D **158**
  NE16: Whi 5F **81**
Willow Ct. NE29: N Shi 6B **48**
  NE40: Rylon 3D **64**
Willow Cres. NE24: News 3A **18**
Willowdene NE12: Kil 4E **45**
  NE23: Dud 4H **31**
Willowfield Av. NE3: Ken 1B **56**
Willow Gdns. NE12: Kil 1C **44**
Willow Grange NE32: Jar 2E **73**
Willow Grn. SR2: Sund 3C **118**
Willow Gro. NE10: Gate 3D **84**
  NE28: W'snd 5B **60**
  NE34: S Shi 4H **75**
  SR8: Pet 1H **165**
Willow Lodge NE29: N Shi 6C **48**
Willow Pl. NE20: Pon 1E **39**
Willow Rd. DH4: Hou S 3G **137**
  NE21: Bla T 1B **80**
Willows Bus. Cen., The
  NE21: Bla T 4F **65**
Willows Cl. NE13: Wide O 6C **30**
  NE38: Wash 3D **114**
Willows, The DH1: Carr 2R **156**
  NE4: Newc T 6C **68**
  NE15: Thro 6D **52**
  NE31: Heb 5C **72**
  NE32: Jar 2G **87**
  NE38: Wash 3D **114**
Willow Tree Av. DH1: H Shin 3G **151**
Willowtree Av. DH1: Dur 3G **155**
Willowvale DH2: Ches S 4A **126**
Willow Vw. NE16: Burn 1G **107**
Willow Way NE20: Pon 3D **38**
Wills Bldg. NE7: Newc T 5E **59**
Wills M. NE7: Newc T 5E **59**
Wills Oval NE7: Newc T 5E **59**
Wilmington Cl. NE3: Ken 1F **55**
Wilson Av. DH3: Bir 2C **112**
  NE22: E Sle 1H **11**
Wilson Cres. DH1: Dur 4G **155**
Wilson Dr. NE36: W Bol 3D **88**
Wilson Gdns. NE3: Ken 4D **56**
Wilson Pl. SR8: Pet 5D **162**
Wilson's Ct.
  NE1: Newc T 4F **69** (5D **4**)
Wilson's La. NE9: Gate 6H **83**
Wilson St. NE11: Dun 3B **82**
  NE28: W'snd 5H **59**

Wilson St. NE33: S Shi 6E **63**
  SR4: Sund 1H **117**
Wilson St. Nth.
  SR5: Monk 5C **104** (1F **7**)
Wilson Ter. NE12: Longb 5D **44**
  SR3: New S 1A **132**
Wilsway NE15: Thro 5C **52**
Wilton Av. NE6: Walk 4E **71**
Wilton Cl. NE23: Cra 6C **22**
  NE25: Whit B 6G **35**
Wilton Dr. NE25: Whit B 1F **47**
Wilton Gdns. Nth. NE35: Bol C . . .2A **88**
Wilton Gdns. Sth. NE35: Bol C . . .2A **88**
Wilton Manse NE25: Whit B 1F **47**
Wilton Sq. SR2: Sund 6E **119**
Wiltshire Cl. DH1: Carr 4A **156**
  SR5: S'wck 1G **103**
Wiltshire Dr. NE28: W'snd 3F **59**
Wiltshire Gdns. NE28: W'snd 4F **59**
Wiltshire Pl. NE37: Usw 3B **100**
Wiltshire Rd. SR5: S'wck 2G **103**
Wimbledon Cl. SR5: S'wck 2H **103**
Wimborne Cl. NE35: Bol C 3A **88**
Wimbourne Av. SR4: Sund 3G **117**
Wimbourne Grn. NE5: Newc T 4D **54**
Wimbourne Quay NE24: Bly 4C **12**
Wimpole Cl. NE37: Usw 3C **100**
Wimslow Cl. NE28: W'snd 4F **59**
Winalot Av. SR2: Sund 5E **119**
Wincanton Pl. NE29: N Shi 3A **62**
Winchcombe Pl. NE7: Newc T 4A **58**
Winchester Av. NE24: Bly 4C **12**
Winchester Cl. DH3: Gt Lum 4G **135**
Winchester Ct. NE32: Jar 2F **87**
Winchester Dr. DH7: B'don 6C **158**
  SR8: Pet 2A **164**
Winchester Rd. DH1: Dur 6E **145**
Winchester St. NE33: S Shi 4F **63**
Winchester Ter. NE4: Newc T 4D **68**
Winchester Way NE22: Bed 3H **9**
Wincomblee NE6: Walk 4G **71**
Wincomblee Rd. NE6: Walk 6G **71**
Wincomblee Workshops
  NE6: Walk 4H **71**
  (off White St.)
Windburgh Dr. NE23: Cra 6B **22**
Windermere DH3: Bir 5D **112**
  SR6: Cle 2A **90**
Windermere Av. DH2: Ches S 2C **134**
  DH5: Eas L 5E **149**
  NE10: Gate 3F **85**
Windermere Cl. NE23: Cra 6B **22**
Windermere Cres.
  DH4: Hou S 3F **129**
  NE21: Bla T 3H **79**
  NE31: Heb 4D **72**
  NE32: Jar 6H **73**
  NE34: S Shi 3G **75**
Windermere Dr. NE12: Kil 2C **44**
Windermere Gdns. NE16: Whi 4G **81**
Windermere Rd. DH6: S Het 5B **150**
  NE5: Newc T 1F **67**
  SR7: S'hm 4E **141**
Windermere St. NE8: Gate 2G **83**
  SR2: Sund 5F **119**
Windermere St. W. NE8: Gate 2G **83**
Windermere Ter. DH9: Stly 5B **122**
  NE29: N Shi 1B **62**
Windhill Rd. NE6: Walk 6F **71**
Winding, The NE13: Din 4F **29**
Windlass Ct. NE34: S Shi 4E **75**

Windlass La. NE37: Wash 6A **100**
Windmill Ct. NE2: Newc T 1E **69**
Windmill Gro. NE24: Cow 5G **11**
Windmill Hill DH1: Dur 2B **160**
  NE33: S Shi 6D **62**
Windmill Ind. Est. NE23: Nel V ..5E **15**
Windmill Sq. SR5: Monk 1C **104**
Windmill Way NE8: Gate 1F **83**
  NE31: Heb 1C **72**
Winds La. SR7: Mur 3A **150**
Winds Lonnen Est.
  SR7: Mur 2A **150**
Windsor Av. NE3: Gos 3G **57**
  NE8: Gate 3G **83**
  NE26: Whit B 1E **49**
Windsor Cl. NE16: Whi 1E **95**
  NE28: W'snd 3E **61**
Windsor Cnr. SR8: Pet 1H **165**
Windsor Cotts. NE28: W'snd ...3E **61**
Windsor Ct. NE3: Gos 3G **57**
  NE3: Ken 6A **42**
  NE10: Gate 3C **84**
  NE22: Bed 5H **9**
  NE23: Cra 6A **16**
  NE39: Row G 3F **93**
  SR8: Eas 2A **162**
Windsor Cres. DH5: Hou S ...3B **138**
  NE5: Newc T 4E **55**
  NE26: Whit B 1E **49**
  NE31: Heb 3D **72**
Windsor Dr. DH5: Hou S 5A **138**
  DH6: S Het 5H **149**
  DH9: Ann P 4F **121**
  NE24: News 4B **18**
  NE28: W'snd 4D **60**
  SR3: New S 2A **132**
  SR6: Cle 2H **89**
Windsor Gdns. NE10: Gate 3B **84**
  NE22: Bed 5H **9**
  NE26: Whit B 5B **36**
  NE29: N Shi 6C **48**
  NE34: S Shi 2G **75**
Windsor Gdns. W.
  NE26: Whit B 5B **36**
Windsor Pk. NE28: W'snd 4F **59**
Windsor Pl.
  NE2: Newc T 2G **69** (1E **5**)
  NE20: Pon 1B **38**
  NE27: Kil 4A **46**
Windsor Rd. DH3: Bir 1B **112**
  (not continuous)
  NE9: Spri 4E **99**
  NE25: Whit B 6A **36**
  SR7: S'hm 4F **141**
Windsor St. NE6: Newc T 3B **70**
  NE28: W'snd 5H **59**
Windsor Ter. DH3: Gt Lum ...4H **135**
  DH9: Ann P 5H **121**
  DH9: Dip 2B **120**
  NE2: Newc T 2F **69** (1E **5**)
  NE3: Gos 3G **57**
  NE9: Spri 4F **99**
  NE26: Whit B 1E **49**
  NE40: Ryton 5A **64**
  NE62: Sco G 1H **9**
  SR2: Sund 5F **119**
  SR3: E Her 3E **131**
  SR7: Mur 2D **150**
  SR8: Pet 1H **165**
Windsor Wlk. NE3: Ken 6H **41**
Windsor Way NE3: Ken 6G **41**
Windt St. NE13: Bru V 6C **30**

Windyhill Carr NE16: Whi 6D **80**
WINDY NOOK 5C **84**
Windy Nook Rd. NE9: Gate 5B **84**
  NE10: Gate 5B **84**
Windy Ridge NE10: Gate 4C **84**
Windy Ridge Vs. NE10: Gate ...4C **84**
Wingate Cl. DH4: Hou S 3H **137**
  NE15: Lem 3C **66**
Wingate Gdns. NE9: Gate 2D **98**
Wingrove NE39: Row G 4D **92**
Wingrove Av. NE4: Newc T 3B **68**
  SR6: Monk 2E **105**
Wingrove Gdns. NE4: Newc T ..3B **68**
Wingrove Ho. NE5: Newc T 6A **56**
  NE33: S Shi 3E **75**
Wingrove Rd. NE4: Newc T 3B **68**
Wingrove Rd. Nth.
  NE5: Newc T 6A **56**
  (not continuous)
Wingrove Ter. NE9: Spri 4F **99**
  NE10: Gate 2H **85**
Winifred Gdns. NE28: W'snd ...6A **60**
Winifred St. SR6: Monk 1E **105**
Winifred Ter. SR1: Sund 1E **119**
WINLATON 2H **79**
WINLATON MILL 5A **80**
Winsford Av. NE29: N Shi 4B **48**
Winshields NE23: Cra 5C **22**
Winshields Wlk. NE15: Thro ...6C **52**
Winship Cl. NE34: S Shi 6E **75**
Winship Gdns. *NE6: Newc T* *3D **70***
  (off Grace St.)
Winship St. NE24: Bly 3A **18**
Winship Ter. NE6: Newc T 3C **70**
Winskell Rd. NE34: S Shi 5B **74**
Winslade Cl. SR3: New S 1B **132**
Winslow Cl. NE6: Walk 3G **71**
  NE35: Bol C 1B **88**
  SR5: S'wck 1H **103**
Winslow Cres. SR7: S'hm 4E **141**
Winslow Gdns. NE9: Gate 6G **83**
Winslow Pl. NE6: Walk 3G **71**
Winson Grn. DH4: Pen 1D **128**
Winster NE38: Wash 6G **113**
Winster Pl. NE23: Cra 6B **22**
Winston Cl. NE9: Spri 4F **99**
Winston Cres. SR4: Sund 3G **117**
Winter Gardens 5H **7**
Winters Bank DH4: Hou S 3F **137**
Winton Cl. NE23: Seg 1G **33**
Winton Ct. NE21: Bla T 3A **80**
Winton Way NE3: Ken 2B **56**
Wirralshir NE10: Gate 5G **85**
Wiseton Ct. NE7: Longb 2H **57**
Wishart Ho. NE4: Newc T 5A **68**
Wishart Ter. NE39: H Spen 1A **92**
Wishaw Cl. NE23: Cra 5C **22**
Wishaw Ri. NE15: Lem 2C **66**
Witham Grn. NE32: Jar 1G **87**
Witham Rd. NE31: Heb 6D **72**
Witherington Cl. NE7: Newc T ...4E **59**
Withernsea Gro. SR2: Ryh 2D **132**
WITHERWACK 1G **103**
Witney Cl. SR5: S'wck 1G **103**
Witney Way NE35: Bol C 4A **88**
Witton Av. NE34: S Shi 3A **76**
Witton Ct. NE3: Ken 1A **56**
  NE38: Wash 3H **113**
  SR3: Sund 5B **118**
Witton Gdns. NE9: Gate 3D **98**
  NE32: Jar 6F **73**
Witton Gth. SR8: Pet 4C **164**

Witton Gro. DH1: Dur 2H **153**
  DH4: Hou S 4G **137**
Witton Rd. NE27: Shir 2D **46**
  NE31: Heb 1D **72**
Wittonstone Ho. *NE4: Newc T* ...*3D **68***
  (off Barrack Rd.)
Witty Av. NE31: Heb 4D **72**
Woburn NE38: Wash 3B **114**
Woburn Cl. NE23: Cra 6A **16**
  NE28: W'snd 4F **59**
Woburn Dr. NE22: Bed 3C **10**
  SR3: New S 3A **132**
Woburn Way NE5: Newc T 5E **55**
Wolmer Rd. NE24: Bly 2D **18**
Wolseley Cl. NE8: Gate 2E **83**
Wolseley Gdns. NE2: Newc T ...1A **70**
Wolsey Cl. NE34: S Shi 3E **75**
Wolsey Rd. SR7: S'hm 5E **141**
Wolsingham Ct. NE23: Nel V ...2H **21**
Wolsingham Dr. DH1: Dur 1D **154**
Wolsingham Gdns. NE9: Gate ...2D **98**
Wolsingham Rd. NE3: Gos 3D **56**
Wolsingham Ter. DH9: Ann P ...5F **121**
Wolsington St. NE4: Newc T ...6C **68**
Wolsington Wlk. NE4: Newc T ...6B **68**
Wolsley Rd. NE24: Bly 6C **12**
Wolveleigh Ter. NE3: Gos 2F **57**
Wolviston Gdns. NE9: Gate 2D **98**
Woodbine Av. NE3: Gos 3E **57**
  NE28: W'snd 5H **59**
  SR8: Pet 5F **163**
Woodbine Cl. NE4: Newc T 5B **68**
Woodbine Cotts.
  DH2: Ches S 5A **126**
Woodbine Pl. NE8: Gate 2G **83**
Woodbine Rd. DH1: Dur 6A **144**
  NE3: Gos 3E **57**
Woodbine St. NE8: Gate 2G **83**
  NE33: S Shi 4F **63**
  (Anderson St.)
  NE33: S Shi 4F **63**
  (Ocean Rd.)
  SR1: Sund 1F **119**
Woodbine Ter. DH3: Bir 3D **112**
  DH7: New B 1A **158**
  DH9: Ann P 5H **121**
  NE8: Gate 3B **84**
  (Balmoral Dr.)
  NE8: Gate 2G **83**
  (Bewick Rd.)
  NE10: Gate 2G **85**
  NE24: Bly 6D **12**
  SR4: Sund 5H **103**
Woodbrook Av. NE5: Newc T ...1E **67**
Woodburn DH9: Tan L 1A **122**
  NE10: Gate 6E **85**
Woodburn Av. NE4: Newc T 6A **56**
Woodburn Cl. DH4: Hou S 1C **136**
  NE21: Bla T 3G **79**
Woodburn Dr. DH4: Hou S 2G **137**
  NE26: Whit B 4A **36**
Woodburn Gdns. NE11: Dun ...4C **82**
Woodburn Sq. NE26: Whit B ...4H **35**
Woodburn St. NE15: Lem 2A **66**
Woodburn Way NE26: Whit B ...4A **36**
Woodchurch Cl. NE7: Newc T ...3D **58**
Woodcock Rd. SR3: New S 4A **132**
Woodcroft Cl. NE23: Dud 2B **32**
Woodend NE20: Pon 3D **38**
Woodend Way NE13: Ken 5G **41**
Wood Fld. SR8: Pet 1C **164**

Woodfields NE20: Pon 5F 27
Woodford NE9: Gate 3H 97
Woodford Cl. SR5: S'wck 1H 103
Woodgate Gdns. NE10: Gate 2H 85
Woodgate La. NE10: Gate 1H 85
Wood Grn. NE10: Gate 2A 86
Wood Gro. NE15: Newc T 2D 66
Woodhall Cl. DH2: Ous 5G 111
Woodhall Ct. NE25: Sea D 6A 24
Woodhall Spa DH4: Hou S 5E 129
Woodhead Rd. NE6: Walk 1E 71
Woodhill Rd. NE23: Cra 5C 22
Woodhorn Gdns. NE13: Wide O . .5D 30
Woodhouse Ct. NE34: S Shi 2C 76
Woodhouses La. NE16: Swa 4E 81
  NE16: Whi 6C 80
Woodhurst Gro. SR4: Sund 5C 116
Woodkirk Cl. NE23: Seg 1G 33
Woodland Av. SR8: Pet 1G 165
Woodland Cl. DH7: Ush M 4C 152
  NE25: Well 6E 35
Woodland Cres. NE15: Newc T . .5G 67
Woodland Dr. SR4: Sund 3G 117
Woodland Grange
  DH4: Hou S 2D 136
Woodland M. NE2: Newc T 5H 67
Woodland Ri. SR3: New S 3G 131
Woodland Rd. DH7: Ush M 4C 152
Woodlands DH3: Ches S 5C 126
  NE3: Gos 4E 57
  NE15: Thro 5C 52
  NE20: Pon 2D 38
  NE29: N Shi 6C 48
  NE38: Wash 1E 127
  SR7: S'hm 2G 141
Woodlands Av. NE3: Gos 4E 57
Woodlands Cl. NE39: H Spen . . .2A 92
Woodlands Ct. NE11: Kib 1F 111
  NE15: Thro 5C 52
Woodlands Dr. SR6: Cle 3A 90
Woodlands Grange NE12: Kil 4E 45
Woodlands Pk. NE13: Wide O . . .6E 31
Woodlands Pk. Dr. NE21: Bla T . .1B 80
Woodlands Pk. Vs.
  NE13: Wide O 1E 43
Woodlands Rd. NE15: Lem 2B 66
  NE39: Row G 3D 92
  SR6: Cle 3H 89
Woodlands Ter. DH9: Dip 2C 120
  NE10: Gate 3C 84
  NE12: Longb 4E 45
  NE33: S Shi 3F 63
Woodlands, The NE11: Kib 1F 111
  NE38: Wash 3C 114
Woodlands Vw. SR6: Cle 3A 90
Woodland Ter. DH4: Pen 1E 129
  DH7: Ush M 4C 152
  NE37: Usw 5C 100
Woodland Vw. DH4: W Rai 4D 146
Wood La. NE22: Bed 4B 10
Wood Lea DH5: Hou S 4C 138
Woodlea NE12: Longb 4D 44
Woodlea Cl. DH5: Hett H 1C 148
Woodlea Ct. NE29: N Shi 4A 62
Woodlea Cres. NE29: N Shi 4A 62
Woodlea Gdns. NE3: Gos 1G 57
Woodlea Rd. NE30: Row G 3B 92
Woodlea Sq. NE29: N Shi 4A 62
Woodleigh Rd. NE25: Whit B 6H 35
Woodleigh Vw. NE3: Ken 4A 56
Woodmansey Cl. SR8: Pet 6B 162
Woodman St. NE28: W'snd 4F 61

Woodmans Way NE16: Whi 1C 94
Woodpack Av. NE16: Whi 5D 80
WOOD SIDE 4C 146
Woodside DH9: Beam 1B 124
  DH9: Stly 2D 122
              (off Quarry Rd.)
  NE20: Pon 2C 38
  NE22: Bed 4C 10
  NE24: Bly 1D 18
  SR2: Sund 2C 118
  SR3: E Her 3E 131
Woodside Av. DH7: Ush M 4C 152
  NE6: Walk 2H 71
  NE15: Thro 6E 53
  NE25: Sea D 1B 34
Woodside Cl. NE40: Ryton 4B 64
Woodside Cres. NE12: Longb . . .5E 45
Woodside Gdns. DH9: Stly 5G 123
  NE11: Dun 4B 82
Woodside Gro. DH9: Tan L 5A 108
  SR3: E Her 3E 131
Woodside La. DH4: Leam 4C 146
  NE40: G'sde 2A 78
  NE40: Ryton 5B 64
Woodside Rd. NE40: Ryton 4B 64
Woodside Ter. SR3: E Her 3E 131
Woodside Wlk. NE39: Row G . . .4C 92
Woodside Way NE33: S Shi 2D 74
  NE40: Ryton 4C 64
Woods Ter. NE8: Gate 2A 84
  SR7: Mur 2D 150
Woods Ter. E. SR7: Mur 2D 150
              (off Wood's Ter.)
Woods Ter. Nth. SR7: Mur 2D 150
              (off Wood's Ter.)
Woodstock Av. SR2: Sund 5E 119
              (not continuous)
Woodstock Rd. NE9: Gate 3A 98
  NE15: Newc T 4D 66
Woodstone Ter. DH4: Hou S 2B 136
WOODSTONE VILLAGE 2C 136
Woodstone Village Ind. Est.
  DH4: Hou S 1B 136
Wood St. DH2: Pelt 2G 125
  NE11: Dun 3B 82
  NE16: Burn 1G 107
  SR4: Sund 6A 104
Wood Ter. NE10: Gate 1H 85
  NE32: Jar 5E 73
  NE33: S Shi 1F 75
  NE37: Usw 5B 100
  NE39: Row G 3A 92
Woodthorne Rd. NE2: Gos 4G 57
Woodvale NE20: Pon 3C 38
Woodvale Dr. NE31: Heb 5A 72
Woodvale Gdns. NE10: Gate 5C 84
  NE15: Lem 2C 66
Woodvale Rd. NE12: Kil 1B 44
  NE21: Bla T 1B 80
Wood Vw. DH1: H Shin 3F 161
Woodville Ct. SR4: Sund 3G 117
Woodville Cres. SR4: Sund 3G 117
Woodville Rd. NE15: Lem 1B 66
Woodwynd NE10: Gate 5F 85
              (Monkton)
  NE10: Gate 6F 85
              (Wealcroft)
Wooler Av. NE29: N Shi 3H 61
Wooler Cres. NE8: Gate 3D 82
Wooler Grn. NE15: Lem 2H 65
Wooler Sq. NE13: Wide O 5E 31
  SR2: Sund 4E 119

Woolerton Dr. NE10: Gate 5B 84
  NE15: Lem 2C 66
Wooler Wlk. NE32: Jar 5E 73
Wooley Dr. DH7: Ush M 6E 153
Wooley St. NE28: W'snd 6H 59
Woolmer Ct. NE7: Newc T 4E 59
WOOLSINGTON 5D 40
Woolsington By-Pass
  NE3: Ken 2F 55
  NE13: Wool 2A 40
  NE20: Wool 2A 40
Woolsington Ct. NE22: Bed 4H 9
Woolsington Gdns.
  NE13: Wool 5D 40
Woolsington Pk. Sth.
  NE13: Wool 5D 40
Woolsington Rd. NE29: N Shi . . .6G 47
Woolwich Cl. SR5: S'wck 1H 103
Woolwich Rd. SR5: S'wck 1H 103
Wooperton Gdns.
  NE5: Newc T 2G 67
Worcester Cl. DH3: Gt Lum 5G 135
Worcester Grn. NE8: Gate 1G 83
Worcester Rd. DH1: Dur 6D 144
Worcester St.
  SR2: Sund 2C 118 (6F 7)
Worcester Ter.
  SR2: Sund 2C 118 (6F 7)
Worcester Way NE13: Wide O . . .6D 30
Wordsworth Av. DH2: Pelt 6C 125
  DH5: Eas L 5F 149
  NE16: Whi 3F 81
  NE24: Bly 2A 18
  NE31: Heb 3C 72
  SR7: S'hm 4E 141
Wordsworth Av. E.
  DH5: Hou S 4A 138
Wordsworth Av. W.
  DH5: Hou S 4A 138
Wordsworth Cres. NE9: Spri 4C 99
Wordsworth Gdns. DH9: Dip 1D 120
Wordsworth Rd. SR8: Eas 1C 162
Wordsworth St. NE8: Gate 1A 84
Worley Av. NE9: Gate 1H 97
Worley Cl. NE4: Newc T 4C 68
Worley M. NE9: Gate 1H 97
Worley St. NE4: Newc T 4D 68
Worley Ter. DH9: Tan L 6G 107
  NE9: Gate 6H 83
Worm Hill Ter. NE38: Wash 6C 114
Worsdell St. NE24: Bly 4C 12
Worsley Cl. NE28: W'snd 4F 59
Worswick St.
  NE1: Newc T 4G 69 (4E 5)
Worthing Cl. NE28: W'snd 4F 59
Worthington Ct. NE2: Newc T . . .1H 69
Wouldhave Ct. NE33: S Shi 4F 63
Wouldhave St. NE33: S Shi 4G 63
Wraith Ter. SR2: Ryh 3E 133
  SR8: Pet 5F 163
Wranghams Entry NE1: Newc T . .5G 5
Wraysbury Ct. NE3: Ken 6H 41
Wreay Wlk. NE23: Cra 6C 22
Wreigh St. NE31: Heb 3B 72
Wreken Gdns. NE10: Gate 3A 86
WREKENTON 2C 98
Wrekenton Row NE9: Gate 3C 98
Wren Cl. NE38: Wash 4G 113
Wren Gro. SR5: C'twn 4E 103
Wretham Pl.
  NE2: Newc T 3H 69 (2G 5)
Wright Dr. NE23: Dud 4A 32

Wrightson St. NE23: E Har 4B 16
Wright St. NE24: Bly 5B 12
Wright Ter. DH4: Hou S 4E 129
Wroxham Ct. NE5: Newc T 3F 55
   SR2: Sund 5E 119
Wroxton NE38: Wash 4A 114
Wuppertal Ct. NE32: Jar 3F 73
Wychcroft Way NE5: Newc T 5G 55
Wych Elm Cres. NE7: Newc T . .4C 58
Wycliffe Av. NE3: Ken 4B 56
Wycliffe Rd. SR4: Sund 3H 117
   SR7: S'hm 4E 141
Wye Av. NE32: Jar 6G 73
Wye Rd. NE31: Heb 6C 72
Wylam Av. NE25: H'wll 1D 34
Wylam Cl. NE34: S Shi 4G 75
   NE37: Usw 4C 100
Wylam Gdns. NE28: W'snd 3D 60
Wylam Gro. SR1: Sund 1E 119
Wylam Rd. DH9: Stly 2D 122
   NE29: N Shi 4B 62
Wylam St. NE32: Jar 2F 73
Wylam Ter. DH9: Stly 1D 122
Wylam Vw. NE21: Bla T 1H 79
Wylam Wharf SR1: Sund 6E 105
Wynbury Rd. NE9: Gate 6A 84
Wyncote Ct. NE7: Newc T 5B 58
Wynde, The NE20: Pon 1D 38
   NE34: S Shi 4E 75
Wyndfall Way NE3: Ken 4C 56
Wyndham Av. NE3: Ken 4B 56
Wyndham Way NE29: N Shi 5F 47
Wynding, The NE22: Bed 4G 9
   NE23: Dud 3A 32
Wyndley Cl. NE16: Whi 6D 80
Wyndley Ho. NE3: Ken 5B 56
Wyndley Pl. NE3: Ken 4B 56
Wyndrow Pl. NE3: Ken 4C 56
   (not continuous)
Wyndsail Pl. NE3: Ken 4C 56
Wynd, The DH2: Pelt 2G 125
   NE3: Ken 3C 56
   NE12: Longb 4E 45
   NE15: Thro 6D 52
   NE30: N Shi 5C 48
Wyndtop Pl. NE3: Ken 4C 56
Wyndward Pl. NE3: Ken 4C 56
Wyndways Dr. DH9: Dip 6E 107

Wynn Gdns. NE10: Gate 2F 85
Wynyard DH2: Ches S 6A 126
Wynyard Dr. NE22: Bed 2C 10
Wynyard Gdns. NE9: Gate 3C 98
Wynyard Gro. DH1: Dur 5F 155
Wynyard Sq. SR2: Sund 5E 119
Wynyard St. DH4: Hou S 3E 137
   NE11: Dun 3B 82
   SR3: New S 2A 132
   SR7: S'hm 6B 142
Wythburn Pl. NE9: Gate 1B 98
Wyvern Sq. SR2: Sund 5E 119

X

XS Superbowl 6F 45

Y

Yardley Cl. SR3: New S 4B 132
Yardley Gro. NE23: Cra 1A 22
Yarmouth Cl. SR7: S'hm 5G 141
Yarmouth Dr. NE23: Cra 1A 22
Yatesbury Av. NE5: Newc T 5F 55
Yeadon Ct. NE3: Ken 6G 41
Yeavering Cl. NE3: Gos 3D 56
Yellow Leas Farm
   NE36: E Bol 4E 89
Yelverton Ct. NE23: Cra 1A 22
Yelverton Cres. NE6: Walk 6F 71
Yeoman St. NE29: N Shi 2D 62
Yeovil Cl. NE23: Cra 1A 22
Yetlington Dr. NE3: Gos 3C 56
Yewbank Av. DH1: Dur 4H 155
Yewburn Way NE12: Longb 1C 58
Yewcroft Av. NE15: Newc T 3D 66
Yewdale Gdns. NE9: Gate 1A 98
Yewtree Av. SR5: S'wck 3H 103
Yewtree Dr. NE22: Bed 3H 9
Yewtree Gdns. NE6: Walk 6G 59
Yewtrees NE10: Gate 6E 85
Yewvale Rd. NE5: Newc T 6H 55
Yoden Av. SR8: Pet 5F 163

Yoden Cres. SR8: Pet 5F 163
Yoden Rd. SR8: Pet 6D 162
Yoden Way SR8: Pet 1D 164
   (not continuous)
York Av. NE32: Jar 5F 73
   SR8: Pet 6F 163
York Cl. NE23: Cra 1A 22
York Ct. DH3: Ches S 1D 134
   NE28: W'snd 6G 59
York Cres. DH1: Dur 5D 144
   DH5: Hett H 1B 148
Yorkdale Pl. NE6: Walk 3G 71
York Dr. NE28: W'snd 6H 59
York Gro. NE22: Bed 3F 9
York Rd. DH3: Bir 6C 112
   NE26: Whit B 6D 36
   SR8: Pet 5C 162
Yorkshire Dr. DH1: Carr 4B 156
York St. DH3: Bir 6C 112
   DH5: Hett H 4A 148
   DH9: Ann P 4F 121
   NE4: Newc T 4D 68
   NE10: Gate 2G 85
   NE24: Bly 5C 12
   NE32: Jar 3E 73
   SR1: Sund 6D 104 (3G 7)
   SR3: New S 1A 132
York Ter. DH3: Ches S 1D 134
   NE10: Gate 3D 84
   NE29: N Shi 2C 62
York Way NE34: S Shi 4A 76
Yorkwood NE31: Heb 2A 72
Youll's Pas. SR1: Sund 5F 105
Younghall Cl. NE40: G'sde 2A 78
Young Rd. NE12: Longb 4F 45
Young St. DH1: Dur 5F 155

Z

Zetland Dr. NE25: Whit B 3B 48
Zetland Sq. SR6: Monk 4E 105
Zetland St. SR6: Monk 4E 105
Zion St. SR1: Sund 6E 105
Zion Ter. NE21: Bla T 2H 79
   SR5: Monk 2C 104

HOSPITALS and HOSPICES
covered by this atlas.

N.B. Where Hospitals and Hospices are not named on the map, the reference
given is for the road in which they are situated.

BENSHAM HOSPITAL 4F **83**
Fontwell Drive
GATESHEAD
NE8 4YL
Tel: 0191 4820000

BLYTH COMMUNITY HOSPITAL 5B **12**
Thoroton Street
BLYTH
NE24 1DX
Tel: 01670 396400

CHERRY KNOWLE HOSPITAL 5E **133**
Stockton Road
Ryhope
SUNDERLAND
SR2 0NB
Tel: 0191 5656256

CHESTER-LE-STREET COMMUNITY HOSPITAL 1C **134**
Front Street
CHESTER LE STREET
DH3 3AT

COUNTY HOSPITAL (DURHAM) 5B **154**
North Road
DURHAM
DH1 4ST
Tel: 0191 3336262

DRYDEN ROAD DAY HOSPITAL 4A **84**
134 Dryden Road
GATESHEAD
NE9 5RY
Tel: 0191 4036600

DUNSTON HILL HOSPITAL 4H **81**
Whickham Highway
GATESHEAD
NE11 9QT
Tel: 0191 4820000

EARLS HOUSE HOSPITAL 1G **153**
Lanchester Road
DURHAM
DH1 5RD
Tel: 0191 3336262

FLEMING NUFFIELD UNIT, THE 1G **69**
Burdon Terrace
NEWCASTLE UPON TYNE
NE2 3AE
Tel: 0191 2196400

FREEMAN HOSPITAL 3A **58**
Freeman Road
High Heaton
NEWCASTLE UPON TYNE
NE7 7DN
Tel: 0191 2843111

HUNTERS MOOR HOSPITAL 1D **68**
Hunter's Road
NEWCASTLE UPON TYNE
NE2 4NR
Tel: 0191 2195661

MARIE CURIE HOSPICE CENTRE 5B **68**
Marie Curie Drive
NEWCASTLE UPON TYNE
NE4 6SS
Tel: 0191 2191000

MONKWEARMOUTH HOSPITAL 3C **104**
Newcastle Road
SUNDERLAND
SR5 1NB
Tel: 0191 5656256

NEWCASTLE GENERAL HOSPITAL 3D **68**
Westgate Road
NEWCASTLE UPON TYNE
NE4 6BE
Tel: 0191 2738811

NEWCASTLE NUFFIELD HOSPITAL, THE 1G **69**
Clayton Road
NEWCASTLE UPON TYNE
NE2 1JP
Tel: 0191 2816131

NEWCASTLE UPON TYNE DENTAL HOSPITAL
.............................2E **69** (1A **4**)
Richardson Road
NEWCASTLE UPON TYNE
NE2 4AZ
Tel: 0191 2325131

NORTH TYNESIDE GENERAL HOSPITAL 4A **48**
Rake Lane
NORTH SHIELDS
NE29 8NH
Tel: 0191 2596660

PALMER COMMUNITY HOSPITAL 2F **73**
Wear Street
JARROW
NE32 3UX
Tel: 0191 4516000

PETERLEE COMMUNITY HOSPITAL 2D **164**
O'Neil Drive
PETERLEE
SR8 5TZ
Tel: 0191 5863474

PRIMROSE HILL HOSPITAL 5G **73**
Primrose Terrace
JARROW
NE32 5HA
Tel: 0191 4516375

Hospitals & Hospices

PRIORY DAY HOSPITAL 1B **62**
Hawkeys Lane
NORTH SHIELDS
NE29 0SF
Tel: 0191 2196629

QUEEN ELIZABETH HOSPITAL 6B **84**
Queen Elizabeth Avenue
GATESHEAD
NE9 6SX
Tel: 0191 4820000

ROYAL VICTORIA INFIRMARY 2E **69** (1B **4**)
Queen Victoria Road
NEWCASTLE UPON TYNE
NE1 4LP
Tel: 0191 2325131

RYHOPE GENERAL HOSPITAL 4F **133**
Stockton Road
Ryhope
SUNDERLAND
SR2 0LY
Tel: 0191 5656256

ST BENEDICT'S HOSPICE 3C **104**
Monkwearmouth Hospital
Newcastle Road
SUNDERLAND
SR5 1NB
Tel: 0191 5699191

ST CLARE'S HOSPICE 5G **73**
Primrose Hill Hospital
Primrose Terrace
JARROW
NE32 5HA
Tel: 0191 4516378

ST CUTHBERT'S HOSPICE 2A **160**
Park House Road
DURHAM
DH1 3QF
Tel: 0191 3861170

ST NICHOLAS HOSPITAL 2C **56**
Jubilee Road
Gosforth
NEWCASTLE UPON TYNE
NE3 3XT
Tel: 0191 2130151

ST OSWALD'S HOSPICE 2E **57**
Regent Avenue
NEWCASTLE UPON TYNE
NE3 1EE
Tel: 0191 2850063

SIR G.B. HUNTER MEMORIAL HOSPITAL 5A **60**
The Green
WALLSEND
NE28 7PB
Tel: 0191 2205953

SOUTH MOOR HOSPITAL 5E **123**
Middles Road
STANLEY
DH9 6AD
Tel: 0191 3336262

SOUTH TYNESIDE DISTRICT HOSPITAL 4F **75**
Harton Lane
SOUTH SHIELDS
NE34 0PL
Tel: 0191 4548888

SUNDERLAND EYE INFIRMARY 4D **118**
Queen Alexandra Road
SUNDERLAND
SR2 9HP
Tel: 0191 5656256

SUNDERLAND ROYAL HOSPITAL 1A **118**
Kayll Road
SUNDERLAND
SR4 7TP
Tel: 0191 5656256

UNIVERSITY HOSPITAL OF NORTH DURHAM 3A **154**
Southfield Way
DURHAM
DH1 5TW
Tel: 0191 3332333

WALKERGATE HOSPITAL 1E **71**
Benfield Road
NEWCASTLE UPON TYNE
NE6 4QD
Tel: 0191 2194300

WASHINGTON BUPA HOSPITAL 1E **127**
Picktree Lane
WASHINGTON
NE38 9JZ
Tel: 0191 4151272

Printed and bound in the United Kingdom by Polestar Wheatons Ltd.